D0861497

In Conversation with God
Meditations for each day of the year

Volume Three
Ordinary Time: Weeks 1 – 12

Francis Fernandez

In Conversation
with God
Meditations for each day of the year

Volume Three
Ordinary Time: Weeks 1 – 12

SCEPTER
London – New York

This edition of *In Conversation with God – Volume 3* is published:
in England by Scepter (U.K.) Ltd., 21 Hinton Avenue, Hounslow
  TW4 6AP; e-mail: scepter@pobox.com;
in the United States by Scepter Publishers Inc.; 800-322-8773; e-
  mail: info@scepterpublishers.org; www.scepterpublishers.org

This is a translation of *Hablar con Dios – Vol III*, first published in
1987 by Ediciones Palabra, Madrid, and in 1990 by Scepter.

With ecclesiastical approval

British Library Cataloguing in Publication Data

Fernandez-Carvajal, Francis
In Conversation with God — Volume 3
Ordinary Time: Weeks 1 – 12.
1. Christian life — Daily Readings
I Title   II Hablar con Dios *English*
242'.2

ISBN Volume 7   978-0-906138-36-6
ISBN Volume 6   978-0-906138-25-0
ISBN Volume 5   978-0-906138-24-3
ISBN Volume 4   978-0-906138-23-6
ISBN Volume 3   978-0-906138-22-9
ISBN Volume 2   978-0-906138-21-2
ISBN Volume 1   978-0-906138-20-5
ISBN Complete set 978-0-906138-19-9

Cover design & typeset in England by KIP Intermedia, and printed in
China.

Contents

FIRST WEEK: MONDAY
1. The Calling of the First Disciples   27
1.1 Our Lord calls them in the midst of their work.
1.2 The sanctification of work. Christ's example.
1.3 Work and prayer.

FIRST WEEK: TUESDAY
2. Children of God   33
2.1 Divine filiation gives meaning to our day.
2.2 Some of the consequences. Fraternity.
2.3 Co-heirs with Christ. Joy: a foretaste of the glory we
    must not allow discouragement to take away from us.

FIRST WEEK: WEDNESDAY
3. Prayer and Apostolate   39
3.1 A man's heart is made to love God. God wants and
    searches for a personal encounter with each one of us.
3.2 We should not waste any opportunity for doing
    apostolate. Strengthening our apostolic hope.
3.3 Prayer and apostolate.

FIRST WEEK: THURSDAY
4. Sacramental Communion   45
4.1 Jesus Christ waits for us each day
4.2 The real presence of Christ in the Tabernacle. How
    we behave in consequence.
4.3 Our Lord heals and purifies us in Holy Communion
    and he gives us the graces we need.

FIRST WEEK: FRIDAY
5. Human Virtues and Apostolate   52
5.1 The curing of the paralytic in Capharnaum.
5.2 Prudence and 'false prudence'.
5.3 Being effective instruments of grace.

FIRST WEEK: SATURDAY
6. Getting on with all the people around us.   58
6.1 Christ shows us how to relate to other people.
6.2 The human virtue of affability.
6.3 Other virtues are needed for our everyday lives.

SECOND SUNDAY: YEAR A
7. The Lamb of God   65
7.1 The figure and reality of this title with which John the
     Baptist designates Jesus.
7.2 The hope of being forgiven. Examination of
     conscience, contrition and purpose of amendment.
7.3 Frequent Confession.

SECOND SUNDAY: YEAR B
8. Purity and the Christian Life   72
8.1 Holy purity, a condition for loving God.
8.2 If we are to live this virtue we need good formation.
8.3 The means to conquer.

SECOND SUNDAY: YEAR C
9. The First Miracle of Jesus   78
9.1 The miracle at Cana. Our Lady is called *Virgin most
     powerful*.
9.2 The turning of water into wine. Our work too can
     become a means to grace. Finishing our work well.
9.3 The generosity of Jesus. He always gives us more
     than we ask him for.

SECOND WEEK: MONDAY
10. The Holiness of the Church 84
10.1 The Church is holy and produces fruits of holiness.
10.2 The holiness of the Church. Sinful members of the
   Church.
10.3 Being good sons and daughters of the Church.

SECOND WEEK: TUESDAY
11. Dignity of the Person 90
11.1 The greatness and dignity of the human person.
11.2 Principles of the social doctrine of the Church.
11.3 A just society.

SECOND WEEK: WEDNESDAY
12. Practising the Faith in Ordinary Things 97
12.1 Faith is to be practised and should give shape and
   value to the little happenings of each day.
12.2 Faith and supernatural outlook.
12.3 Faith and the human virtues.

SECOND WEEK: THURSDAY
13. Giving Good Doctrine 103
13.1 A pressing need for this apostolate.
13.2 Formation in the truths of faith.
13.3 Prayer and mortification accompanies all apostolate.

SECOND WEEK: FRIDAY
14. A Vocation to Holiness 109
14.1 The vocation of the *twelve*. It is God who calls, and
   who gives the grace to persevere.
14.2 In fulfilling his vocation, man gives glory to God
   and discovers the true greatness of his life.
14.3 Our faithfulness to the personal call that we have
   received from God.

SECOND WEEK: SATURDAY
15. Cheerfulness   **116**
15.1 It is based on divine filiation.
15.2 The cross and cheerfulness. Causes of sadness.
15.3 The apostolate of cheerfulness.

THIRD SUNDAY: YEAR A
16. Light in Darkness   **123**
16.1 Jesus brings light to a world submerged in darkness.
     Faith illumines our whole life.
16.2 As Christians we are *the light of the world*.
     Professional competence.
16.3 Doctrinal formation and interior life are necessary to
     sanctify earthly realities.

THIRD SUNDAY: YEAR B
17. Detachment to follow Christ.   **129**
17.1 The disciples follow Christ, *leaving all things* to do so.
17.2 Some details of Christian poverty and detachment.
17.3 Almsgiving and detachment from material goods.

THIRD SUNDAY: YEAR C
18. Doctrinal Formation   **136**
18.1 The Reading of the Gospel.
18.2 A Christian's formation continues throughout his
     life. The need for good formation.
18.3 Spiritual reading.

THIRD WEEK: MONDAY
19. Justice in our Speech and in our Judgements   **142**
19.1 Sins of the tongue. If one cannot praise, say nothing.
19.2 We should not be hasty in our judgements.
19.3 Respect for privacy.

THIRD WEEK: TUESDAY
20. The Will of God   148
20.1 Our Lady and fulfilment of God's Will.
20.2 Signs of God's will. The fulfilment of our duties.
20.3 Prayer as a means of discovering God's will.

THIRD WEEK: WEDNESDAY
21. Sowing and Reaping   155
21.1 The Parable of the Sower. We are fellow-labourers
     with Christ. Giving doctrine.
21.2 Optimism in the apostolate. Patience and constancy.
21.3 The harvest is always greater than the seed.

THIRD WEEK: THURSDAY
22. Growth in Interior Life   162
22.1 Interior life is destined to grow.
22.2 Faithfulness in little things and to a spirit of sacrifice.
22.3 Contrition and interior growth.

THIRD WEEK: FRIDAY
23. Fidelity to Grace   169
23.1 God's grace always bears fruit.
23.2 The effectiveness of our correspondence.
23.3 Avoiding the discouragement that arises when
     defects do not disappear.

THIRD WEEK: SATURDAY
24. Fraternal Correction   175
24.1 The duty of making fraternal correction.
24.2 Fraternal correction was practised frequently by the
     first Christians. False excuses for not making it.
24.3 Virtues that have to be practised when making a
     correction. The way we should receive it.

10   Contents

FOURTH SUNDAY: YEAR A
25. The Way of the Beatitudes   182
25.1 The Beatitudes; a way of sanctity and happiness.
25.2 Our happiness comes from God.
25.3 We will not lose our joy if we seek for God in everything.

FOURTH SUNDAY: YEAR B
26. The Slavery of Sin   189
26.1 Christ came to free us from the devil and from sin.
26.2 The malice of sin.
26.3 The liberating character of Confession.

FOURTH SUNDAY: YEAR C
27. The Virtue of Charity   196
27.1 The essence of charity.
27.2 The qualities of this virtue.
27.3 Charity lasts eternally. Here on earth it is a foretaste
     and beginning of heaven.

FOURTH WEEK: MONDAY
28. Detachment and the Christian Life   203
28.1 Christ's presence in our lives may sometimes mean
     giving up some earthly goods.
28.2 Earthly things must bring us closer to Christ.
28.3 Detachment: some details.

FOURTH WEEK: TUESDAY
29. Spiritual Communions   209
29.1 The faith of a sick woman. Our meeting with Christ
     is in the Holy Eucharist.
29.2 Spiritual communions. Our desire to receive Christ.
29.3 Sacramental Communion.

Contents

FOURTH WEEK: WEDNESDAY
30. Doing our Work well 216
30.1 Jesus' life in Nazareth: the sanctification of work.
30.2 Jesus and the world of work.
30.3 The redemptive meaning of work.

FOURTH WEEK: THURSDAY
31. The Sick: God's Favoured Children 222
31.1 We should imitate Christ in his love for the sick.
31.2 The Anointing of the Sick.
31.3 The co-redeeming value of pain and sickness.

FOURTH WEEK: FRIDAY
32. Fortitude in Ordinary Life 229
32.1 The example of the martyrs. Our testimony as
  ordinary Christians. The virtue of fortitude.
32.2 We need fortitude if we are to follow Christ.
32.3 Heroism in the simple and normal life of a
  Christian. Giving good example.

FOURTH WEEK: SATURDAY
33. The Need to sanctify our Rest 236
33.1 Contemplation of Jesus' Sacred Humanity.
33.2 Our tiredness is not useless. Learning to sanctify it.
33.3 We have a duty to rest. Resting in order to serve
  God and other people better.

FIFTH SUNDAY: YEAR A
34. The Light of our Good Example 243
34.1 As Christians we must be *salt* and *light* in the world.
  Our good example has to precede us.
34.2 Good example in family life, at work, etc.
34.3 Our good example of charity and temperance. Salt
  that loses its savour is useless.

FIFTH SUNDAY: YEAR B
35. Spreading the Truth   **250**
35.1 The urgency and responsibility of taking Christ's
     doctrine to all environments.
35.2 Apostolate and proselytism stem from our
     conviction that we possess the truth.
35.3 Fidelity to the teaching we have to transmit.

FIFTH SUNDAY: YEAR C
36. Faith and Obedience in the Apostolate   **256**
36.1 Faith and obedience are essential in the apostolate.
36.2 Our Lord calls all of us to follow him closely and to
     be apostles in the middle of the world.
36.3 The Apostles' readiness to follow Our Lord.

FIFTH WEEK: MONDAY
37. Living in Society   **263**
37.1 The social dimension of man.
37.2 Charity and human fellowship.
37.3 Our contribution to the common good.

FIFTH WEEK: TUESDAY
38. The Fourth Commandment   **270**
38.1 God's blessing on those who keep this
     commandment. The promise of a long life.
38.2 Love for our parents is shown with deeds.
38.3 Love for one's children. Some of the duties of
     parents.

FIFTH WEEK: WEDNESDAY
39. The Dignity of Work   **277**
39.1 The divine command to work is a blessing.
39.2 Professional prestige. Laziness, the enemy of work.
39.3 The virtues involved in doing our work well.

FIFTH WEEK: THURSDAY
40. Humility and Perseverance in Prayer   **283**
40.1 The curing of the daughter of the Canaanite woman.
   Conditions for true prayer.
40.2 Filial confidence and perseverance in our petitions.
40.3 We should ask for supernatural graces.

FIFTH WEEK: FRIDAY
41. *He did all things well*   **289**
41.1 Jesus, our Exemplar and Model, carried out his
   work at Nazareth with human perfection.
41.2 Hard work, professional competence.
41.3 Finishing off our work well. The little details that
   make any job *professional*.

FIFTH WEEK: SATURDAY
42. Mother of Mercy   **295**
42.1 Mary shares to an eminent degree in the divine
   mercy.
42.2 Health of the sick, Refuge of sinners.
42.3 Comfort of the afflicted, Help of Christians.

SIXTH SUNDAY: YEAR A
43. Steadfast in the Faith   **301**
43.1 The Deposit of Faith. The Church keeps it faithfully
   with the help of the Holy Spirit.
43.2 Avoid whatever undermines the virtue of faith.
43.3 Prudence in reading.

SIXTH SUNDAY: YEAR B
44. The Leprosy of Sin   **307**
44.1 Our Lord has come to cure our deep-rooted ills.
44.2 Leprosy, an image of sin.
44.3 Apostolate of Confession.

SIXTH SUNDAY: YEAR C
45. Personal Humility and Trust in God   **313**
45.1 Only the humble can truly trust in God.
45.2 The great obstacle is pride. Signs of pride.
45.3 Practising the virtue of humility.

SIXTH WEEK: MONDAY
46. The Sacrifice of Abel   **319**
46.1 The best of our life is for God: our love, our time,
     our worldly goods ...
46.2 Generosity with regard to the objects used in
     worship.
46.3 Love for Jesus in the Tabernacle.

SIXTH WEEK: TUESDAY
47. The Redemptive Mission Of The Church   **325**
47.1 Where salvation is to be found – in the Church.
47.2 Prayer for the Church.
47.3 By Baptism we are made into instruments of
     salvation in our own environments.

SIXTH WEEK: WEDNESDAY
48. With Clear Sight   **331**
48.1 Guarding the Sight.
48.2 In the midst of the world without being worldly.
48.3 A Christian does not go to places or shows which
     are incompatible with his state as a disciple of Christ.

SIXTH WEEK: THURSDAY
49. The Mass: Centre of the Christian Life   **338**
49.1 Participation of the faithful in the sacrifice of the
     Mass.
49.2 The *priestly soul* of the Christian and the Mass.
49.3 To live the Mass throughout the day. Preparation.

SIXTH WEEK: FRIDAY
50. Humility   344
50.1 Relying on God.
50.2 Pride and selfishness.
50.3 How to grow in humility.

SIXTH WEEK: SATURDAY
51. Resolutions from the Prayer   351
51.1 Jesus speaks to us in prayer.
51.2 We should not get discouraged.
51.3 Specific, well-thought-out resolutions.

SEVENTH SUNDAY: YEAR A
52. Treat Everyone Well   358
52.1 We must live charity at all times and in all
     circumstances.
52.2 Charity towards all: including those who do not like
     us. Our prayer for them.
52.3 Charity gives friendship a deep Christian sense.

SEVENTH SUNDAY: YEAR B
53. Helping to do Good   363
53.1 Helping the spiritual and material good of others.
53.2 Not being mere spectators of social life. Initiative.
53.3 Protecting and fostering whatever is good. Spirit of
     cooperation. Noticing what is positive.

SEVENTH SUNDAY: YEAR C
54. Magnanimity   369
54.1 The disposition to undertake great things for God
     and mankind always accompanies a holy life.
54.2 Magnanimity shows itself many ways: the capacity
     to pardon offences promptly, to forget resentments ...
54.3 It is a fruit of interior life.

SEVENTH WEEK: MONDAY
55. Ask for more Faith   376
55.1 Faith is a gift of God.
55.2 Good dispositions in order to believe.
55.3 Faith and Prayer. Pray with more Faith.

SEVENTH WEEK: TUESDAY
56. The Lord, King of Kings   382
56.1 The Psalm of royalty and triumph of Christ.
56.2 The rejection of God in the world.
56.3 Divine filiation.

SEVENTH WEEK: WEDNESDAY
57. Unity and Variety in the Church's apostolate   389
57.1 A narrow-minded and exclusive attitude toward
     apostolate is not Christian.
57.2 We need to bring the Church's teaching to all.
57.3 The unity of the Church does not mean uniformity.

SEVENTH WEEK: THURSDAY
58. Getting to Heaven   395
58.1 The thing that matters in life is getting to heaven.
58.2 Hell exists. We must practice a holy fear of God.
58.3 We are instruments in the salvation of many people.

SEVENTH WEEK: FRIDAY
59. Defending the Family   402
59.1 Jesus returns the dignity of matrimony to its original
     purity. Unity and indissolubility of marriage.
59.2 Education on the nature of marriage. Example of
     spouses. Sanctity of the family.
59.3 Christian matrimony.

SEVENTH WEEK: SATURDAY
60. With the Simplicity of Children   408

60.1 Spiritual childhood and simplicity.
60.2 Manifestations of piety and Christian naturalness.
60.3 In order to be simple.

EIGHTH SUNDAY: YEAR A
61. Today's Task   **415**
61.1 Live the present to the full, without anxiety. Divine
     filiation. Trust and abandonment in God.
61.2 Fruitless worry.
61.3 Seeing God in our work. Mortify the imagination, to
     live in the present: *hic et nunc.*

EIGHTH SUNDAY: YEAR B
62. God's Love for men   **421**
62.1 God loves us with an infinite love, without our
     meriting it in any way.
62.2 The great evil of indifference to God's love.
62.3 God loves us with a personal, individual love: He
     has showered blessings upon us.

EIGHTH SUNDAY: YEAR C
63. Triumph over Death   **427**
63.1 Death, the consequence of sin.
63.2 The Christian meaning of death.
63.3 Fruits of meditating on our last end.

EIGHTH WEEK: MONDAY
64. The Rich Young Man   **434**
64.1 God calls everyone.
64.2 The response to vocation.
64.3 Poverty and detachment in daily life.

EIGHTH WEEK: TUESDAY
65. Generosity and Detachment   **440**
65.1 Practical detachment from material goods.

65.2 Jesus rewards with unlimited generosity.
65.3 It is always worth while following Christ.

EIGHTH WEEK: WEDNESDAY
66. Learning to Serve   **447**
66.1 The example of Christ. *To serve is to rule*.
66.2 Different services we can render the Church.
66.3 Serve with joy and be competent in your profession.

EIGHTH WEEK: THURSDAY
67. The Faith of Bartimaeus   **454**
67.1 Bartimaeus' prayer overcomes all obstacles.
67.2 Faith and detachment in order to follow Jesus.
67.3 Following Christ on the way.

EIGHTH WEEK: FRIDAY
68. Love means Deeds: Apostolate   **460**
68.1 An opportunity to produce fruits of holiness.
68.2 *Love means deeds, not sweet words*.
68.3 An apostolate which is cheerful and enterprising.

EIGHTH WEEK: SATURDAY
69. The Right and the Duty to do Apostolate   **466**
69.1 The right and duty of every Christian.
69.2 Rejecting excuses.
69.3 Jesus sends us now, as he sent his disciples.

NINTH SUNDAY: YEAR A
70. Built upon Rock   **472**
70.1 Holiness means carrying out the will of God.
70.2 We want what God wants.
70.3 Doing and loving God's will in all aspects of life.

NINTH SUNDAY: YEAR B
71. Sundays and Holydays of Obligation   **478**

71.1 Christian feast days.
71.2 *The Lord's Day*.
71.3 The nature of Holydays of Obligation and Sundays.

NINTH SUNDAY: YEAR C
72. Devotion to the Saints   **485**
72.1 They are our intercessors before God.
72.2 Cult of the saints. The *dies natalis*.
72.3 Veneration and regard for *relics*. *Images*.

NINTH WEEK: MONDAY
73. The Cornerstone.   **491**
73.1 Jesus Christ is the corner stone.
73.2 Faith gives us light to recognise the true reality of
     things and of events.
73.3 The Christian has his own scale of values.

NINTH WEEK: TUESDAY
74. Being Exemplary Citizens   **498**
74.1 The Christian in public life. The exemplary
     fulfilment of our duties.
74.2 Unity of life.
74.3 Our union with God.

NINTH WEEK: WEDNESDAY
75. We will rise again with our own bodies   **505**
75.1 A truth of faith expressly taught by Jesus.
75.2 Qualities and endowments of glorified bodies.
75.3 Unity between the body and the soul.

NINTH WEEK: THURSDAY
76. The First Commandment   **512**
76.1 We should adore the *one God*. Modern idolatry
76.2 Reasons for loving God.
76.3 The first commandment embraces all aspects of life.

NINTH WEEK: FRIDAY
77. The Guardian Angel   **518**
77.1 The continuous presence of our Guardian Angel.
77.2 Devotion. Help in our daily life and in apostolate.
77.3 Asking his help for the interior life.

NINTH WEEK: SATURDAY
78. The Value of Little Things   **524**
78.1 The alms of the *poor widow*.
78.2 Love gives value to things of little importance.
78.3 Holiness is *a cloth woven of little details*.

TENTH SUNDAY: YEAR A
79. The Virtue of Hope   **530**
79.1 The virtue of the wayfarer. Its foundation.
79.2 Hope in spite of setbacks, obstacles and pain.
79.3 Frequently calling to mind hope of becoming saints.

TENTH SUNDAY: YEAR B
80. The Roots of Evil   **536**
80.1 Human nature in its original state of justice and holiness.
80.2 The fellowship of all men in Adam.
80.3 Directing all human realities to God once again.

TENTH SUNDAY: YEAR C
81. Our Response to Sorrow and Need   **543**
81.1 The raising of the son of the widow of Nain.
81.2 Imitating Our Lord. Love with deeds.
81.3 In order to love we need to understand.

TENTH WEEK: MONDAY
82. The Divine Mercy   **549**
82.1 God's mercy is infinite, eternal and universal.
82.2 Mercy presupposes justice.
82.3 Some effects of mercy.

TENTH WEEK: TUESDAY
83. Salt that has lost its Savour 555
83.1 Lukewarmness.
83.2 True piety, feelings, spiritual aridity.
83.3 We have to be *the salt of the earth*.

TENTH WEEK: WEDNESDAY
84. Actual Graces 562
84.1 We need grace in order to do good.
84.2 Actual graces.
84.3 Our correspondence.

TENTH WEEK: THURSDAY
85. Reasons for Penance 568
85.1 Removing obstacles. Renouncing one's own ego.
85.2 The Church's invitation to penance. Penance and
     prayer. Friday, a day of penance.
85.3 Some practices of penance.

TENTH WEEK: FRIDAY
86. Purity of Heart 574
86.1 The ninth commandment and purity of soul.
86.2 Guarding one's heart and fidelity according to one's
     vocation and state in life.
86.3 Guarding our eyes, affections and internal senses.

TENTH WEEK: SATURDAY
87. Keeping one's word 580
87.1 Jesus praises those who keep their word.
87.2 Love for the truth always and in every circumstance.
87.3 Loyalty and fidelity to commitments.

ELEVENTH SUNDAY: YEAR A
88. The most effective way 586
88.1 Urgency in the apostolate.

88.2 Prayer is the most effective and necessary means.
88.3 Asking God for vocations.

ELEVENTH SUNDAY: YEAR B
89. The Mustard Seed   591
89.1 God makes use of little things to act in the world.
89.2 The difficulties we encounter in apostolate ought
      not to discourage us.
89.3 God is our strength. The need to overcome false
      human respect.

ELEVENTH SUNDAY: YEAR C
90. Contrition for Sin   597
90.1 Contrition makes us forget ourselves and make our
      way to God.
90.2 We cannot ignore our faults and failings.
90.3 Humility and repentance. Confession. Sincerity.

ELEVENTH WEEK: MONDAY
91. Life of Grace   603
91.1 A new life. Dignity of the Christian.
91.2 Sanctifying grace giving a share in divine nature.
91.3 Grace leads to identification with Christ: docility,
      life of prayer, love for the Cross.

ELEVENTH WEEK: TUESDAY
92. Holiness in the World   610
92.1 The Universal call to holiness.
92.2 Becoming saints wherever we find ourselves.
92.3 All circumstances are good to help us grow in
      holiness and carry out a fruitful apostolate.

ELEVENTH WEEK: WEDNESDAY
93. Mental Prayer   616
93.1 Necessity and fruits of such prayer.

93.2 The preparatory prayer.
93.3 The help of the Communion of Saints.

ELEVENTH WEEK: THURSDAY
94. Vocal Prayers   623
94.1 The need for such prayer.
94.2 Vocal Prayers.
94.3 Attention while praying.

ELEVENTH WEEK: FRIDAY
95. Where is your heart?   629
95.1 The family, *the first appropriate environment in
     which to sow the seed of the Gospel.*
95.2 Careful attention towards those God has placed in
     our charge.
95.3 Devoting the necessary time, which comes before
     other interests. Family prayers.

ELEVENTH WEEK: SATURDAY
96. Everything works out well   636
96.1 Loving the will of God.
96.2 Abandonment in God and responsibility.
96.3 *Omnia in bonum* – for those who love, everything
     works out in the best possible way.

TWELFTH SUNDAY: YEAR A
97. *Do not be afraid*   642
97.1 Courage in ordinary life.
97.2 Our strength is based on an awareness of our divine
     filiation.
97.3 Courage and trust in God in the great trials and in
     the little things of ordinary life.

TWELFTH SUNDAY: YEAR B
98. Calmness in the Face of Difficulties   647

98.1 The storm on the lake. God will never abandon us to face difficulties alone.
98.2 In the midst of the world we must be ready to face up to misunderstandings.
98.3 Our attitude towards difficulties.

TWELFTH SUNDAY: YEAR C
99. The Love and Fear of God   **653**
99.1 Love of God and submission to his infinite holiness.
99.2 The importance of filial fear for the uprooting of sin.
99.3 Confession and the holy fear of God.

TWELFTH WEEK: MONDAY
100. The Speck in our brother's eye   **659**
100.1 Pride leads us to exaggerate our neighbour's faults.
100.2 Accepting people with their defects.
100.3 Positive criticism.

TWELFTH WEEK: TUESDAY
101. The Narrow Path   **665**
101.1 Temperance and mortification.
101.2 Need for mortification, struggle against comfort-seeking.
101.3 Some examples of temperance and mortification.

TWELFTH WEEK: WEDNESDAY
102. You will know them by their Fruits   **671**
102.1 Good fruit is produced by a sound tree.
102.2 Intimacy with God and Christian works.
102.3 The bitter fruit of laicism.

TWELFTH WEEK: THURSDAY
103. The Fruits of the Mass   **677**
103.1 The Eucharistic sacrifice and the ordinary life of the Christian.

103.2 Taking part in the Mass conscious of what we are
    doing, with devotion and full collaboration.
103.3 Preparation for Mass. Apostolate and the
    Eucharistic Sacrifice.

TWELFTH WEEK: FRIDAY
104. The Virtue of Faithfulness   **683**
104.1 Faithfulness – a virtue required by love, faith and
    vocation.
104.2 The foundations of faithfulness.
104.3 Love and fidelity in little things.

TWELFTH WEEK: SATURDAY
105. Mary, Co-redemptrix With Christ   **689**
105.1 Mary present in the sacrifice of the Cross.
105.2 Co-redemptrix with Christ.
105.3 Mary and the Mass.

Index to quotations from the Fathers and Popes   **695**

Subject Index   **709**

Scheduled Use of this Volume in *Ordinary Time*

From the Epiphany to Ash Wednesday				
Year	Cycle	1st Week begins on Monday	Shrove Tuesday	Ends in Week
2020	A	13 Jan	25 Feb	7
2021	B	11 Jan	16 Feb	6
2022	C	10 Jan	1 Mar	8
2023	A	9 Jan	21 Feb	7
2024	B	8 Jan	13 Feb	6
2025	C	13 Jan	4 Mar	8
2026	A	12 Jan	17 Feb	6
2027	B	11 Jan	9 Feb	5
2028	C	10 Jan	29 Feb	8
2029	A	8 Jan	13 Feb	6
2030	B	14 Jan	5 Mar	8

After Eastertide				
Year	Cycle	Begins in Week	From Monday	To Saturday in Week 12
2020	A	9	1 June	27 June
2021	B	8	24 May	26 June
2022	C	10	6 June	25 June
2023	A	8	29 May	1 July
2024	B	7	20 May	29 June
2025	C	10	9 June	28 June
2026	A	8	25 May	27 June
2027	B	7	17 May	26 June
2028	C	9	5 June	1 July
2029	A	7	21 May	30 June
2030	B	10	10 June	29 June

FIRST WEEK: MONDAY

1. THE CALLING OF THE FIRST DISCIPLES

1.1 Our Lord calls them in the midst of their work. He calls us too, so that we can sanctify our occupations and make him known through them.

After his baptism, with which He begins his public life, Jesus seeks out those people whom he will ask to be sharers in his saving mission. He finds them at their daily work. They are men who are tough and adaptable, used to a simple way of life and hard work. *And passing along by the Sea of Galilee*, we read in the Gospel of today's Mass, *He saw Simon and Andrew the brother of Simon casting a net into the sea; for they were fishermen. And Jesus said to them, 'Follow me and I will make you become fishers of men!'* [1]

The apostles responded generously to God's call. Those four disciples, Peter, Andrew, James and John, already know Our Lord,[2] but this is the precise moment, when, responding to God's call, they decide to throw in their lot with him completely, without any conditions, any calculations, any reservations at all. Many today follow him just like this in the middle of the world, with a total dedication, in apostolic celibacy. From now on, Christ will be the centre of their lives, and He will exert an indescribable and growing attraction on their souls. Jesus Christ seeks them out in the midst of the business of their daily lives, in the same way as He did the Magi (as we contemplated only recently) through what was most

---

[1] Mark 1:14-20
[2] John 1:35-42

familiar to them – the shining of a star. It was the same
when the angel called the shepherds to Bethlehem, as they
were carrying out their duty of watching over the sheep,
and led them to go and adore the Child-God and be with
Mary and Joseph that night.

It is in the midst of our work, of our ordinary
occupations, that Jesus invites us to follow him, so as to
make him the centre of our very existence and serve him in
the task of evangelising the world. *God draws us from the
shadows of our ignorance, our stumbling and groping
through history, and, no matter what our occupation in the
world, He calls us with a strong voice, as He once called
Peter and Andrew: 'Follow me and I will make you fishers
of men.'* [3]

He chooses us where we are, and leaves us – the
majority of Christians, lay people – just where we were: in
our family, in our own job, in the cultural or sports
association that we belong to ... so that in the very
environment in which we are found we should love him
and make him known through family ties, through
relationships at work and among friends. From the moment
that we decide to make Christ the centre of our lives,
everything we do is affected by that decision. We must ask
ourselves whether we are consistent with what it means to
turn our work into a vehicle for growing in friendship with
Jesus Christ, through developing our human and
supernatural virtues in it.

1.2 The sanctification of work. Christ's example.

God calls us, having put us in our own environment
and our own profession. But he wants our work to be
different from now on: *You are writing to me in the
kitchen, by the stove. It is early afternoon. It is cold. By*

---

[3] St. J. Escrivá, *Christ is passing by*, 45

your side, your younger sister – the last one to discover the divine folly of living her Christian vocation to the full – is peeling potatoes. To all appearances – you think – her work is the same as before. And yet, what a difference there is! It is true: before, she only peeled potatoes – now she is sanctifying herself peeling potatoes.[4]

In order to sanctify ourselves through our housework, or surrounded by the clips and swabs of the operating theatre (or in the hospital ward with that habitual smile for the patient!), in the office, the lecture room, driving a tractor or leading mules, cleaning up a mess or preparing vegetables ... our work has to be like that of the Christ we have contemplated in Joseph's workshop just a few days ago and, like that of the Apostles. Today, in the Gospel of the Mass, we see them fishing. We must fix all our attention on the Son of God made Man as he works, and ask ourselves very often, what would Jesus do in my place? How would he do my work? The Gospel tells us that *He has done all things well*,[5] with human perfection without the least carelessness. All of this means working with a spirit of service towards our neighbours, with order, serenity and intensity of concentration. He would have had orders ready on time. He would have lovingly put the finishing touches to his craftsmanship, thinking of the pleasure of the customers when they would receive his simple but perfect work. He would have been tired ... Jesus also carried out his work with full supernatural effectiveness, because at the same time, through the work, He was carrying out the redemption of mankind, united to his Father by love and for love, united to men also through love for them.[6] What we do out of love becomes a serious

---

[4] *ibid, Furrow*, 498
[5] Mark 7:37
[6] cf J. L. Illanes, *On the Theology of Work*

commitment for us, and is charged with meaning.

No Christian can ever think that although his work is apparently of little importance – as some might imply with their contemptuous or supercilious attitude to it – he can do it in any old way. God sees the work, and it has an importance that we cannot even suspect. *You asked what you could offer the Lord. I don't have to think twice about the answer; offer the same things as before, but do them better, finishing them off with a loving touch that will lead you to think more about him and less about yourself.*[7]

1.3 Work and prayer.

For a Christian who lives thinking of God, work has got to be prayer – for it would be a great pity if *she only peels potatoes*, instead of sanctifying herself as she peels them well. Prayer is a way of being with Our Lord throughout the day, and a great opportunity for practising virtues, without which the Christian could not reach the sanctity to which he has been called. At the same time it is an effective means of apostolate.

Prayer is talking to God. It is raising our heart and our soul to him in order to praise him, to thank him, to offer him reparation, and to ask him for more help. It can involve our thoughts, our words or our affections. Our prayer can be either mental or vocal, but it can also be expressed in actions capable of communicating to God how much we want to love him and how much we need him. So we can see that prayer is also *any work that is well-finished and carried out with supernatural outlook.*[8] That is to say, we have to collaborate consciously with God in the perfecting of created things, and endeavour to impregnate them with love of Christ, so as to complete his

---

[7] St. J. Escrivá, *Furrow*, 495
[8] cf R. Gomez Perez, *Faith and Life*

redemptive work, which was carried out not only on Calvary, but also in the workshop at Nazareth.

The Christian who is united to Christ through grace converts his good works into prayer. This is why the devotion of *the morning offering* is so important. Each morning when we get up we tell Our Lord in a few words that our whole day is for him. It is very important for our interior life that we renew it several times during the day, and especially during the Holy Mass. But the value of this prayer which is the work of a Christian will depend on the love we put into carrying it out, on our rectitude of intention, on the way we practise charity, on the effort we make to finish it off properly. The more aware we are of our intention to convert our work into an instrument of redemption, the better we will do it materially, and the greater the help we will be giving to the whole Church. The nature of some types of work that demand great concentration makes it difficult to turn one's mind in the course of it frequently to God, but if we get used to talking to him, making an effort to find him, he will be like *an appropriate background music* for everything we do. If we work in this way, work and interior life will not interrupt each other, *just as the beating of the heart does not interrupt our attention to our activities whatever they may be.*[9] Rather must work and prayer complement each other, in the same way that voices mingle with instruments to form a harmony. Work not only does not disturb the life of prayer, but becomes a channel for it. Then what we ask for in that beautiful prayer[10] becomes a reality: *'Actiones nostras, quaesumus, Domine, aspirando praeveni et adiuvando prosequere: ut cuncta nostra oratio et operatio a te semper incipiat, et per te coepta finiatur':* May the

---

[9] St. J. Escrivá, *Letter*, 15 September 1948
[10] *Enchiridion Indulgentiarum*, 1

whole of our day, our prayer and our work take their strength from you and always begin with you, O Lord, and may all that we have begun through you reach a happy conclusion.[11]

If Jesus Christ, whom we have made the centre of our existence is to be at the heart of everything we undertake, it will become more and more natural for us to make use of the breaks that occur in every job to turn that *background music* into real song. When we change activities; when we are sitting in the car at a red traffic light; when we finish our session of studying a certain subject; while we are awaiting a telephone call; as we put the things back in their place ... there will arise that ejaculatory prayer, that opportunity for a glance at an image of Our Lady or at the Crucifix, a wordless petition to our guardian angel, which will give us inner strength and help us to go on with our task.

As love is very resourceful, very good at inventing, we will find we are able to make use of *human stratagems*, reminders which help us never to forget that we have to go to God through what is human. *Place on your desk, in your room, in your wallet, a picture of Our Lady, and glance at it when you begin your work, while you are doing it, and when you finish it. She will obtain, I can assure you, the strength for you to turn your task into a loving dialogue with God.*[12]

---

[11] cf S. Canals, *Jesus as Friend*
[12] St. J. Escrivá, *Furrow*, 531

FIRST WEEK: TUESDAY

2. CHILDREN OF GOD

2.1 Awareness of our divine filiation gives meaning to our day.

'I have been set by him as a king on Sion, his holy mountain, to tell of his decrees. The Lord said to me: You are my son, today I have begotten you' (Ps 2:6-7). The kindness of God our Father has given us his Son to be our king ... 'You are my son': the words are addressed to Christ – and to you and me if we decide to become other Christs, Christ himself.[1] That is exactly what we are trying to do; to imitate Christ, to identify ourselves with him. We want to be good children of God in the midst of our work and our normal daily activities, despite our weaknesses. Last Sunday we contemplated Jesus as he came to John, just like one more person, to be baptised in the Jordan. The Holy Spirit descended upon him, and the voice of the Father could be heard saying *Thou art my beloved son.*[2] From all eternity Jesus Christ is the Only Son of God: Eternally begotten of the Father ... begotten, not made, of one being with the Father. Through him all things were made, we confess in the Creed during Mass. In him and through him – true God and true Man – we have been made children of God and heirs to Heaven.

Throughout the New Testament, divine filiation occupies a central position in the preaching of the Good News of Christianity. It is presented as a reality that gives expression to God's love for men. *See what love the Father has given us, that we should be called children of God; and*

---

[1] St. J. Escrivá, *Christ is passing by*, 185
[2] cf Mark 1:9-12

so we are.[3] Jesus Christ himself constantly revealed this truth to his disciples. He showed it to them in a direct way, by teaching them to talk to God as their Father.[4] He explained sanctity to them in terms of a son imitating his father.[5] He also developed this truth of divine filiation for them through numerous parables in which God is represented as the father. A particularly moving picture of our Father God is drawn for us in the parable of the prodigal son.

In his infinite goodness, God created man and elevated him to the supernatural order, so that, with sanctifying grace, we could enter into the intimacy of the Blessed Trinity, without destroying or distorting that nature proper to us as creatures. He did this through the ineffable gift of divine filiation.[6] He makes us his children. Our divine filiation is not merely a title; it is a real elevation, an effective transformation of our inmost being. That is why *God sent his Son, born of woman ... so that we might receive adoption as sons. And because you are sons, God has sent the Spirit of his Son into our hearts, crying Abba! Father! So through God you are no longer a slave but a Son, and if a son then an heir.*[7]

Our Lord gained for us the most precious Gift, the Holy Spirit, who makes us cry out 'Abba Father!', who identifies us with Christ and makes us children of God. 'You are my Son'. Not a stranger, not a well-treated servant, not a friend – that would be a lot already. A son! He gives us free access to treat him as sons do, with a son's piety – and I would even say with the boldness and

---

[3] John 3:1
[4] cf Matt 6:9
[5] cf Matt 5:48
[6] cf F. Ocariz, *Awareness of our Divine Filiation*, Pamplona, 1985
[7] Gal 4:5-7

daring of a son whose Father cannot deny him anything.[8]

The Lord said to me *'You are my son, today I have begotten you'.* These words of Psalm II, which refer principally to Christ, are spoken also to each one of us. They can truly 'make our day' and give meaning to our whole life, if we once resolve – in spite of our weaknesses and our frailty – to follow Jesus Christ, to try to imitate him, to identify ourselves with him in our own particular circumstances. In our ascetical struggle we will at times try to consider more deeply the consequences of our divine filiation. And at times this will become the object of our 'particular examination of conscience'.

2.2 Some of the consequences. Fraternity. Our attitude towards difficulties. Trust in prayer.

When we are living as good children of God, we see everything that happens, including the minor occurrences of any ordinary day, in the light of faith, and we become accustomed to thinking and acting constantly in accordance with Christ's will.[9] In the first place we try to see as brothers all the people we meet, because we are all children of the same Father. Our appreciation and respect for others will generate within us the same desire that resides in the heart of Christ – the desire for their sanctification. Above all, fraternal love will move us to wish that those people should come ever closer to Christ and should be more fully children of our Father God. We will make our own the concern of Christ for the apostolate, his zeal for his Father's glory and the salvation of all mankind.[10] The manifestations of fraternity rooted in spiritual childhood will be countless throughout any one of our days. Prayer

---

[8] St. J. Escrivá, *op cit*, 185
[9] cf M. Eguibar, *Why do the Gentiles Rage?*, Madrid, 1986
[10] B. Perquin, *Abba, Father*, London 1965

for others will remind us. Little opportunities of helping in
material things will have their obvious motivation. And
understanding for the defects of others will be more readily
achieved if we see in them the faults of our brothers and
sisters.

Spiritual childhood is not just one more aspect of our
lives. It determines our whole supernatural character and
shows us how to deal with every situation. It is not a
particular virtue that has its own acts, but the permanent
condition of our being, suffusing and permeating all the
virtues.[11] Whatever our circumstances or the situations that
affect us, we are children of God, and this firm conviction
fills the whole of our life and our entire way of behaving.
*We are children of God all day long, even though we do set
aside special moments for considering the fact so that we
can fill ourselves with awareness of our divine filiation,
which is the essence of true piety.*[12]

If we frequently consider this truth – I am a child of
God – if we go deeper into its meaning, our day will be
filled with peace, serenity and joy. We will make a
resolution to rely on God our Father, on whom everything
depends when difficulties and disappointments arise, and
when sometimes we seem to be fighting an uphill battle.[13]
It will be easier for us to return to our Father's house, like
the prodigal son, if we should ever leave it through our
faults and sins. We will not lose sight of the truth that our
Father is waiting to embrace us and to give us back our
dignity as his children, if ever we lose it. He is waiting to
fill us with good things at a splendid banquet, even though
we may have behaved badly a thousand times and more.
Our prayer, just like these moments we are dedicating

---

[11] cf F. Ocariz, *op cit*
[12] *Conversations with Monsignor Escrivá*, 102
[13] cf J. Lucas, *We are Children of God*, Madrid, 1973

exclusively to God, will really be the conversation of a son with his father. The son knows that his father understands him, that He listens to him and that he gives him the whole of his attention in a way that nobody else has ever done. It is a conversation with God that is full of trust, that moves us frequently to a prayer of petition because we are small and needy children; it is a conversation with God that has our life as its theme. *Everything that is on our mind and in our heart; our joys, sorrows, hopes, disappointments, successes, failures; even the most trivial happenings of our day. We will discover that our heavenly Father is interested in everything about us.*[14]

2.3 Co-heirs with Christ. Joy: a foretaste of the glory we must not allow discouragement to take away from us.

A son is also an heir; he has a certain 'right' to his father's goods. We are *heirs of God and fellow-heirs with Christ.*[15] Psalm II, the psalm that speaks of the royalty of Christ and divine filiation, and with which we began these moments of prayer, continues with these words: *Ask of me and I will make the nations your heritage, and the ends of the earth your patrimony.*[16]

We get a foretaste in this life of the inheritance we have been promised. It is the *gaudium cum pace,* joy with peace, the profound happiness of knowing that we are children of God. This does not depend on our own merits, on our health or on how successful we are; neither does it consist in the absence of difficulties. Born from our union with God, it is founded on the consideration that He loves us, He is always ready to welcome us and to forgive us. He

---

[14] St. J. Escrivá, *Friends of God*, 245
[15] Rom 8:17
[16] Ps 2:8

has prepared for us a Heaven by his side, for all eternity. We lose this happiness when we fail to see God's will for us, which is ever-wise and loving, in the frustrations and setbacks each day brings with it.

Our Father does not want us to lose this deep-rooted happiness. He wants to see us happy always, just as fathers on earth want to see their children happy.

With this serene and joyful attitude to life, the *gaudium cum pace*,[17] the Christian does a great deal of good. This does not mean, however, that he will not sometimes meet with difficulties in his life. True happiness is a marvellous means of apostolate. *The Christian is a sower of joy, a communicator of gladness; this is why he achieves great things. Joy is one of the most irresistible powers in the world; it brings about calm; it soothes away anger, it wins people over. He who is cheerful is a natural apostle. A cheerful countenance attracts men to God, showing them what the presence of God produces within the soul. This is why the Holy Spirit gives us the advice, 'Do not be downcast or look troubled, for the joy of the Lord is your strength' (Neh 8:10).*[18]

---

[17] *Roman Missal*, *Preparation for Mass*
[18] M. V. Bernadot, *The Eucharist and the Trinity*, Madrid

3. PRAYER AND APOSTOLATE

3.1 A man's heart is made to love God. God wants and searches for a personal encounter with each one of us.

One day, after he had spent the previous evening curing the sick, talking and giving his attention to the crowds of people who approached him, Jesus got up, *and in the morning, a great while before day, left Simon's house, went out to a lonely place, and there He prayed.* Simon and those who had been with him followed him. They found him and said to him, *Everyone is searching for you.* This is related by Saint Mark in the Gospel of today's Mass.[1]

Everyone is searching for you. Now too, in our own day, the crowds are *hungry* for God. Those words of Saint Augustine at the beginning of his Confessions still hold good today; *You have made us, Lord, for yourself, and our hearts are restless until they rest in you.*[2] The human heart is made to seek and to love God. And God facilitates this encounter, for he too seeks out each one of us through countless graces and a Fatherly care which is filled with consideration and love. Whenever we look at somebody within visual range of us, or read about somebody in a newspaper or hear someone on the radio or on television, we can always think, without fear of being wrong: *Christ is calling this person. He has effective graces prepared for him.* Just think, there are so many men and women on earth, and the Master does not fail to call every single one of them. *He calls them to a Christian life, to life eternal.*[3]

---

[1] Mark 1:29-39
[2] St Augustine, *Confessions*, 1, 1, 1
[3] St. J. Escrivá, *The Forge*, 13

This is the foundation of our apostolic hope. In one way or another, Christ continues to seek out each one of us. Our mission (which is God's task for us) is to facilitate these encounters with grace.

Commenting on this passage of the Gospel, Saint Augustine writes, *The human race lies grievously ill, not of a bodily sickness, but because of its sins. It lies like a great sick man throughout the whole of the world, from East to West. In order to cure this dying man, the omnipotent Doctor came down. He humbled himself so as to take on mortal flesh.*[4] Only a few weeks have gone by since we were contemplating Jesus in the cave at Bethlehem, poor and defenceless, having taken on our human nature so as to be very close to us men and to save us. Later we meditated on his hidden life in Nazareth, working away just like any other man, so as to teach us to look for him in our ordinary lives, so as to make himself accessible to everyone, and, through his Sacred Humanity, enable us to reach the Blessed Trinity. Like Saint Peter, we too go to meet him in our prayer – in our personal dialogue with him – and say to him, Everyone is searching for you... Help, Lord, to make it easier for our relatives, our friends, our colleagues, and every single person who crosses our path, to find you. You, Lord, are the one they need. Teach us to make you known through the example we give of a cheerful life, through moving hearts by our words.

3.2 We should not waste any opportunity for doing apostolate. Strengthening our apostolic hope.

A church in a little German village which was virtually destroyed during the Second World War, had a very old crucifix, to which the local people had great devotion. When they came to rebuilding the church, the villagers

---

[4] St Augustine, *Sermon 87*, 13

found among the ruins this magnificent carving of the crucified Christ without its arms. They could not decide what to do. Some were in favour of putting the same crucifix back, restored, with new arms. Others thought it would be better to have a replica of the original crucifix made. Finally, after much deliberation, they decided to put the carving, which had always stood in front of the altarpiece, back just as it had been found, but with the inscription, *You are my arms* ... It can be seen today above the altar.[5]

We are God's arms in the world, because He has willed to need men. God sends us out so that He may come closer to this ailing world which so often just cannot find the physician who could restore it to health. We will talk to many people about God with the certain hope that God knows each one of them, and that it is only in him that they will find salvation and the words of eternal life. This is why we must not (either through laziness, love of comfort, weariness or human respect) waste a single opportunity; it might be one of the normal happenings of each day, a comment, perhaps, about a news item, a small service, maybe, that we do for somebody or that somebody does for us. The special events too can present their opportunities, such as the illness or the death of a relative. *Those who travel abroad for international activities, on business or on holiday, should keep in mind that, no matter where they may be, they are the travelling messengers of Christ and should bear themselves really as such.*[6] Pope John Paul I, in his first message to the faithful, exhorted them to study all the ways, all the means, of announcing *in season and out of season*[7] salvation to all peoples. *If the sons of the*

---

[5] cf F. Fernandez, *Lukewarmness - The Devil in Disguise*
[6] Second Vatican Council, *Apostolicam actuositatem*, 7
[7] 2 Tim 4:2

Church, said the Roman Pontiff, *were to be untiring missionaries of the Gospel, there would be a new flowering of holiness and of renewal in this world which thirsts for love and for truth.*[8]

Let us maintain a firm hope in the apostolate, even though the times may seem unpromising. The ways of grace are, indeed, inscrutable. But God has wanted to count on us to save souls. What a pity, if through the omissions of Christians, many men never come close to God. This is why we must feel a personal responsibility for not letting any friend, acquaintance or neighbour to whom we have ever spoken be able to say to God, *hominem non habeo,*[9] there was nobody to speak to me about You, or to teach me the way. Sometimes it is our friendship that will be the beginning of the way that leads to Christ; a well-timed comment, a book to reaffirm our friends' faith, some sound advice, a word of encouragement ... and always the richness and example of upright conduct.

Christianity possesses the great gift of being able to remedy and cure completely the one deep wound of human nature, and its success owes more to this than to whole encyclopaedias of scientific knowledge and a whole library of controversies; because of this, Christianity will last for as long as human nature lasts.[10] Let us ask ourselves today, How many people have I helped to live in a Christian way this Christmas which has just passed? We should pray for those friends of ours whom we are encouraging to go to Confession or to some means that will improve their formation and their knowledge of God's doctrine.

---

[8] John Paul I, *Address*, 27 August 1978
[9] John 5:7
[10] St J. H. Newman, *The Religious Sense*

3.3 Prayer and apostolate.

God wants us to be his instruments for making his redemptive work present in the midst of secular tasks, in ordinary life. But how can we be good instruments of God if we do not ourselves really cherish our life of piety, if we do not really have a personal relationship with Christ in prayer? *Can a blind man lead a blind man? Will they not both fall into a pit?*[11] The apostolate is the fruit of love for Christ. It is He who is the Light with which we are to give light, the Truth that we must teach, the Life that we have to communicate. And this will only be possible if we are men and women who are united to God through prayer. It is moving to see how, in the midst of so much apostolic activity, Our Lord gets up early in the morning, *a great while before day,* to talk to his Father God, and to entrust the new day to him, a day that will be full of attention to particular souls.

We must imitate him. It is in prayer, in talking to Jesus, that we learn to understand, to remain cheerful, to welcome and to appreciate the people God places in our path. Without prayer, the Christian would be like a plant without roots. Such a plant quickly dries up, and cannot bear any fruit. Throughout our day we can and we must speak very frequently to God. He is not far away. He is close to us, beside us. He always hears us, but more especially at those times – such as this – that we dedicate expressly to speaking to him, without remaining anonymous, in person-to-person contact with him. According to the measure in which we make ourselves open to God's demands, our day will become *supernaturally* effective and we will find it easier not to interrupt our dialogue with Jesus. It can truly be said that our apostolic life is worth

---

[11] Luke 6:39

what our prayer is worth.[12]

Prayer is always fruitful. It is capable of sustaining our whole life. It is from prayer that we will obtain the strength to face up to difficulties with the assurance and equanimity of the children of God. We will obtain that perseverance – constancy in our friendship – that all apostolate needs. This is why our friendship with Christ has to grow deeper and more sincere each day. This is why we must seriously make up our minds to avoid any deliberate sin, to keep our hearts for God alone, to try to get rid of the those useless thoughts which often leave the way open for faults and sins. We need frequently to rectify our intention, directing our whole being and all our works to God.

It may sometimes happen that we have to struggle against discouragement, which can make us think that we are not improving in our personal prayer. If this should happen, it is then easy for the devil to tempt us to give up prayer. We must never give it up, even if we are tired and cannot give it all our attention, even though we don't experience any affections at all, even though (without our wanting it) we find we are very distracted. Our prayer is the mainstay of our life and the irreplaceable condition for doing any apostolate.

We should turn, at the end of this time of prayer, to the powerful intercession of Saint Joseph, magnificent teacher of the interior life. We ask him, who lived beside Jesus for so many years, to teach us to love him and to talk to him trustingly all the days of our life – even on those days when we are so busy we find it more difficult to dedicate our usual time of prayer to him... Our Mother, Mary, will intercede with the Holy Patriarch for us.

---

[12] cf St. J. Escrivá, *The Way*, 108

FIRST WEEK: THURSDAY

4. SACRAMENTAL COMMUNION

4.1 Jesus Christ waits for us each day

A leper came up to Jesus.[1] He knelt down and said to him: *If you will, you can make me clean.* And Our Lord, who always wants what is good for us, took pity on him, touched him, and said: *'I will; be clean.' And immediately the leprosy left him and he was made clean. That man kneels down, prostrating himself on the ground, which is a sign of humility, the virtue by which each one may become ashamed of the stains in his life. But shame must not prevent confession: the leper showed his sores and asked for a cure. Moreover, his prayer is full of piety – that is, he acknowledged that the power to cure him lay in Our Lord's hands.*[2]

Jesus Christ himself waits for us each day in the Blessed Eucharist. There he is *really, truly and substantially present,* with his Body, Blood, Soul and Divinity. There he is to be found with all the splendour of his glory, for *Christ being raised from the dead will never die again.*[3] The Body and Soul remain inseparably united for ever to the Person of the Word. The whole mystery of the Incarnation of the Son of God is contained in the Sacred Host, together with the profound richness of his most Sacred Humanity and the infinite grandeur of his Divinity, both of them veiled and hidden. In the Blessed Eucharist we find Our Lord himself, who said to the leper: *'I will; be clean.'* This is the very same Lord whom the angels and

---

[1] Mark 1:40-45
[2] St Bede, *Commentary on St Mark's Gospel*
[3] Rom 6:9

saints contemplate and praise for all eternity.

Whenever we go to the Tabernacle, we find him there. Perhaps we have often repeated in his presence the hymn in which Saint Thomas Aquinas expressed the faith and piety of the Church, and which so many Christians have turned into their own personal prayer:

> *O Godhead hid, devoutly I adore thee,*
> *Who truly art within the forms before me;*
> *To thee my heart I bow with bended knee,*
> *As failing quite in contemplating Thee.*
>
> *Sight, touch and taste in Thee are each deceived;*
> *The ear alone most safely is believed.*
> *I believe all the Son of God has spoken:*
> *Than Truth's own word there is no truer token.*
>
> *God only on the Cross lay hid from view,*
> *But here too lies hid at once the manhood too:*
> *And I, in both professing my belief,*
> *Make the same prayer as the repentant thief.*
>
> *Thy wounds, as Thomas saw, I do not see;*
> *Yet Thee confess my Lord and God to be.*
> *Make me believe Thee ever more and more,*
> *In Thee my hope, in Thee my love to store.*[4]

This marvellous presence of Jesus among us should give us new life each day. When we receive him, when we visit him, we can say in the strictest sense: *Today I have been with God.* He makes us like the Apostles and like his disciples, like the holy women who accompanied Our Lord throughout Judaea and Galilee. *Non alius sed aliter; He is not other, but He is in another way,* the theologians like to say.[5] He is

---

[4] Hymn, *Adoro te devote*, St Thomas Aquinas
[5] cf M. M. Philipon, *Our Transformation into Christ*

here with us, in every city and town. With how much faith do we pay him a visit? With how much love do we receive him? How do we prepare ourselves in body and soul to receive Holy Communion?

4.2 The real presence of Christ in the Tabernacle. How we behave in consequence.

The leper's body was cleansed when it felt the touch of Christ's hand. We can be divinised through our contact with Jesus in Holy Communion. Even the angels are amazed at such a great Mystery. The Soul of Christ is in the Sacred Host. In it all his human faculties preserve the same properties as in Heaven. Nothing escapes the loving and lovable gaze of Christ: not material creation, nor the glory of the blessed in Heaven, nor the activity of the angels. He knows the past, the present and the future. *His eucharistic life is a life of love. The fervour of an infinite charity rises ceaselessly from the Heart of Christ. The whole intimate life of the priestly soul of the Incarnate Word – adoration, petition, thanksgiving, expiation – is inspired by this love which knows no limits.*[6] The Blessed Trinity finds immense and unending glory in Jesus Christ present in the Tabernacle.

Saint Thomas Aquinas teaches[7] that the Body of Christ is present in the Blessed Eucharist just as it is in himself, as is also the Soul of Christ, together with his intellect and will. Only those relations are excluded that refer to quantity, for Christ is not present in the Sacred Host in the way of a quantity localised in space.[8] He is there with his glorious Body in a real, though mysterious and ineffable way.

---

[6] *ibid*
[7] cf St Thomas, *Summa Theologiae*, III, q76, a5 ad 5
[8] cf *ibid*, III, q81, a4

The Second Person of the Blessed Trinity is there, in the Tabernacle that we visit each day, the Tabernacle which is perhaps very near to our home, or very close to the office where we work. Perhaps it is in the chaplaincy of the University, or in an oratory or a chapel at a hospital or at an airport. He is there with the sovereign power of his uncreated Divinity. He, the only Son of God, before whom the Thrones and Dominations tremble, by whom all things were made, equal in power and wisdom and mercy to the other Persons of the Blessed Trinity, remains perpetually with us, like one of us, without ever ceasing to be God. Truly is He there: *Among you stands one whom you do not know.*[9] As we go about, fully involved in our normal business, our customary work, our daily concerns, do we frequently consider that our merciful and omnipotent God is really living along there, very near us, next door to our home? Our great failure, the greatest mistake of our lives, would be if they could say of us at some stage those words with which the Holy Spirit inspired the pen of Saint John: *He came to his own home, and his own people received him not.*[10] Because, we might add, they were busy about their own affairs, their work, preoccupied with things that without him don't have the slightest importance. But today we make a firm resolution to stay awake and remain lovingly vigilant. We will rejoice when we see the walls of a church, and during the day we will make many spiritual communions, and many acts of faith and love. We will tell him of our desire to make up for those who pass him by without a word or as much as a glance.

---

[9] John 1:26
[10] John 1:11

4.3 Our Lord heals and purifies us in Holy Communion and he gives us the graces we need.

> *O Thou, memorial of Our Lord's own dying!*
> *O living bread, to mortals life supplying!*
> *Make Thou my soul henceforth on Thee to live;*
> *Ever a taste of heavenly sweetness give.*
>
> *O loving Pelican! O Jesu Lord!*
> *Unclean I am but cleanse me in Thy Blood;*
> *Of which a single drop, for sinners spilt,*
> *Can purge the entire world from all its guilt.*
>
> *Jesu! whom for the present veiled I see,*
> *What I so thirst for, oh, vouchsafe to me:*
> *That I may see Thy countenance unfolding,*
> *And may be blest Thy glory in beholding. Amen.*[11]

In the Blessed Eucharist Our Lord gives to each one who receives him the very same life of grace that he brought into the world through his Incarnation.[12] If we had more faith, the same miracles would be performed in us as we come into contact with his Sacred Humanity; in each Communion he would cleanse the innermost part of our souls from human weaknesses and imperfections. *Make me believe Thee ever more and more* ... the Eucharistic hymn invites us to exclaim and to beg interiorly. If we approach him with faith, we will hear the same words that he spoke to the leper: *'I will: be clean.'* At other times we will see how he stands up confronting the waves, as on Lake Tiberias, in order to calm the storm. And in our souls too there will be a great calm; our souls will be filled with peace ... *O loving Pelican! O Jesu Lord!* In Holy Communion, Our Lord does not offer us only spiritual

---

[11] Hymn, *Adoro te devote*
[12] cf St Thomas, *op cit*, I, q3, a79

nourishment, but gives himself to us as Food. The Ancients thought that when the chicks of a pelican died, the pelican opened his breast and with his blood fed his dead young, in this way bringing them back to life ... Christ with his own Blood gives us eternal life. When we receive Holy Communion with the right dispositions, it rouses in our soul fervent acts of love, transforms us, and identifies us with Christ. The Master comes to each one of his disciples with his love, which is at one and the same time effective, creative and redemptive. He presents himself to us as the Saviour of our lives, offering us his friendship. This Sacrament is the food of all intimacy with Christ, for which there is no substitute.

Through contact with Christ, the soul is purified, and we find in this meeting the energy we need to practise charity in the thousands of small incidents that occur each day. It enables us to give good example in the way we carry out our own duties, to live holy purity, to carry out with courage and a spirit of sacrifice the apostolate that He himself has entrusted to us ... In the Blessed Eucharist we find the cure for our daily faults, so as to get rid of that lax attitude and lack of correspondence, which do not indeed kill the soul, but which weaken it and let it drift into luke-warmness. A fervent Communion leads us effectively towards God even in the face of our own indisputable frailty and cowardice. It is there that we find each day the strength we need, the food that our souls cannot do without. Human existence has its realisation, its pledge of eternal life in Christ. *Christ is the bread of life. As ordinary bread stands and sensibly answers to earthly hunger, so Christ is the extraordinary bread proportioned to the spiritual hunger of man, which in the desperation of its need is out of all proportion. It is capable, indeed anxious, to open itself out to infinite aspirations ... Christ is the bread of life. Christ is necessary for all men, for all communities.*[13] We could not live without him.

Jesus waits for us in the Blessed Eucharist so as to restore our strength: *Come to me, all who labour and are heavy laden, and I will give you rest.*[14] Basically, it is those sicknesses that have no cure apart from Christ that weigh heavily on us and exhaust us. *Come to me all* ... Jesus does not exclude anybody. *I will not cast out* ...[15] him who comes to me. Jesus will remain with us, as long as the time of the Church Militant shall last, as the source of all the graces of which we will possibly be in need.

With Saint Thomas Aquinas we can say to Jesus, as we go to receive him, present in the Blessed Eucharist: *I come to the Sacrament of your Only Begotten Son, our Lord Jesus Christ, as one sick to the physician of life, as one unclean to the fountain of mercy, as one blind to the light of eternal brightness, as one poor and needy to the Lord of heaven and earth. I ask, therefore, for the abundance of your immense generosity, that you may graciously cure my sickness, wash away my defilement, give light to my blindness, enrich my poverty, and clothe my nakedness, so that I may receive the Bread of angels, the King of kings and Lord of lords, with such reverence and humility, such contrition and devotion, such purity and faith, such purpose and intention as are conducive to the salvation of my soul.*[16]

Our Mother, the Blessed Virgin, always encourages us to talk to Jesus in the Blessed Sacrament. *Come closer to the Lord. Closer! Until he becomes your Friend, your Guide, in whom you can trust.*[17]

---

[13] St Paul VI, *Homily*, 8 August 1976
[14] Matt 11:28
[15] cf John 6:37
[16] *Roman Missal, Preparation for Mass*
[17] St. J. Escrivá, *Furrow*, 680

5. HUMAN VIRTUES AND APOSTOLATE

5.1 The curing of the paralytic in Capharnaum. Operative faith, without human respect. Optimism.

The Gospel of today's Mass[1] shows Jesus teaching the crowds who have come from many towns of Galilee and Judaea. *And many were gathered together, so that there was no longer room for them, not even about the door; and He was preaching the word to them. And they came, bringing to him a paralytic carried by four men.* Although they made a bold effort, they were unable to reach Jesus, but they did not slacken in their determination to come close to the Master with their friend, who was lying on a stretcher-bed. Then, when other people would have given up because of all the difficulties they were meeting with, these men remained undaunted and climbed up on to the roof. They removed pieces from the roof above the place where Our Lord was, and when they had made a hole in it, they let down the bed with the paralytic on it. Jesus was amazed at the faith and audacity of these men. It was because of them and the humility of the paralytic, who allowed himself to be helped, that a great miracle took place: the forgiveness of the sick man's sins and the cure of his paralysis.

In some way, the paralytic represents every man who is prevented by his sins or his ignorance from reaching God. Commenting on this passage, Saint Ambrose exclaims, *How great is the Lord, who through the merits of some, forgives others!*[2] The friends who take the man,

---

[1] Mark 2:1-12
[2] St Ambrose, *Commentary on St Luke's Gospel*

incapacitated by his illness, to Our Lord are a vivid example of apostolate. As Christians we are instruments of God's so that he may work real miracles on our friends, who if they are left alone, seem unable for so many reasons to reach Christ, who is waiting for them.

If we are to carry out the task of apostolate, we must be moved by a concern to help men to find Jesus. In order to do this, we need, among other things, a series of *supernatural virtues*, just as we find in the behaviour of the friends of that sick man of Capharnaum. They are men who have great faith in the Master, whom they have already met on other occasions; perhaps it was Jesus himself who told them to take the sick man to him. It is a faith with deeds, because they use the ordinary and extraordinary means that the case calls for. They are men full of hope and optimism, convinced that Jesus is the very person their friend really needs.

The Gospel narrative also points out to us many *human virtues*, which are essential for apostolic work. In the first place, *the men concerned are men who have got rid of any human respect*; they do not mind at all what others – and there were a lot of people around – think about their action, which could easily have been judged as extreme, inopportune, eccentrically different from what others did who had gone to listen to the Master. Only one thing matters to them: to reach Jesus with their friend whatever the cost. This is only possible when we have great rectitude of intention, when all that matters is God's approval, and we are not interested in the opinions of other people. Do we behave like this? Are we sometimes more concerned about what other people will say than we are about what God thinks? Are we reluctant to seem different from other people, when precisely what God and the people who see our actions need, is that we should stand out by doing what we have to do? When necessary, do we

know how to show our faith and our love for Jesus Christ
in public?

5.2 Prudence and 'false prudence.'

In accomplishing their task, these four friends
practised the virtue of *prudence* which leads us to seek the
best way of reaching any good end. They placed to one
side that 'false prudence' that Saint Paul calls *prudence of
the flesh*.[3] This so easily turns into cowardice, and leads us
to seek only what is useful to bodily well-being, as though
this were the principal or only end of life. 'False prudence'
is the same as deceit, hypocrisy, cunning, selfish and self-
interested calculation, whose main concern is material
advantage. This is why that false virtue is really an
amalgam of fear, cowardice, pride and laziness ... If those
men had allowed themselves to be led by the *prudence of
the flesh*, their friend would not have reached Jesus, and
they would not have felt the immense joy they saw shining
in Jesus' eyes as He cured the sick man. They would have
remained outside the door of that house crowded with
people, and from there they would not even have heard
Jesus.

Those men lived the virtue of prudence fully, the
virtue that tells us in each case what we should do *even
though it may be difficult*, or what we should not do. It is
the virtue that shows us the means that lead to the end we
are seeking, which tells us *how* and *when* we should act.
Those friends knew exactly what their end was – to reach
Our Lord – and they looked for the means of achieving it.
Go up to the terrace of the house. Make a big enough hole
and lower the paralytic down on his pallet, until he lies at
the feet of Jesus. They did not worry about the falsely
'prudent' words of other people who advised them to wait

---

[3] cf Rom 8:6-8

for another and more suitable occasion.

Those men from Capharnaum were real friends to that poor fellow who could not reach the Master by himself. It is *proper for the friend to do good to his friends, particularly to those who are in greatest need.*[4] There is no need greater than our need for God. So, the first sign of appreciation for our friends is that of bringing them closer and closer to Christ, the source of all good. We cannot be satisfied with their simply not doing evil, still less with their behaving badly. We must get them to aspire to the sanctity to which we have been called, *all of us*, and for which God will give them the necessary grace. There is no greater favour than that of helping them along their path towards God. We will not find any greater good to give them. This is why we should endeavour to have many friends and foster true friendships. *The true friend cannot have two different faces for his friend. If it is to be loyal and sincere, friendship demands sacrifice, uprightness, and an exchange of favours and of noble and licit acts of service. A friend is strong and true to the extent that, in accordance with supernatural prudence, he thinks generously about others, and undergoes personal sacrifice on their behalf. We expect a friend to correspond to the climate of trust which true friendship establishes; we expect the recognition of ourselves as we are, and when necessary the friend will go without hesitation and in forthright fashion to our defence.*[5]

From the beginning *friendship* has been the natural channel through which many people have found faith in Jesus Christ, and found even their vocation to a life of more complete dedication. It is a natural and simple way which eliminates many obstacles and difficulties. Our Lord

---

[4] St Thomas, *Commentary on the Nicomachean Ethics*
[5] St. J. Escrivá, *Letter*, 11 March 1940

often counts on this means of making himself known. The first disciples to meet Our Lord went off to communicate the Good News to those they loved, before they told anybody else. Andrew brought Peter, his brother. Philip brought his friend Nathanael. John certainly set his brother James on the path to Our Lord.[6] Do we do this? Do we want as soon as possible to communicate to those we care for most the greatest good we have ever found? Do we talk about God to our friends, our relatives, our fellow students or our workmates? Is our friendship a channel for others to come closer to Christ?

5.3 Other virtues. Being effective instruments of grace.

In his apostolic task, the Christian has to practise other human virtues if he is to be a good instrument of God in his mission of rechristianising the world: *fortitude*, when we meet with the obstacles that present themselves in one way or another in every apostolic task; *constancy and patience*, because, like a seed, a soul sometimes takes time before it bears fruit, and because we cannot achieve in a matter of days what God has perhaps foreseen, should take months or even years; *audacity*, so that we introduce deeper subjects into our conversations, which may never arise if we do not bring them up at the right moment, and also that we propose higher ideals for our friends who cannot even conjecture at them for themselves; *truthfulness and authenticity*, without which friendship cannot exist. Our world needs men and women who are all of a piece, who are exemplary in their work, men and women without complexes, who are sober, serene, profoundly human, firm, understanding but intransigent in matters concerning Christ's doctrine, courteous, just, loyal, cheerful, optimistic, generous, hard-working, simple, courageous ...

---

[6] cf John 1:41 *et seq*

In this way they will be good collaborators with God's grace, for *the Holy Spirit uses man as an instrument.*[7] Then their works take on a divine effectiveness, like a tool which of itself is incapable of producing anything, but in the hands of a good craftsman can produce a masterpiece.

Imagine the joy of those men in the Gospel account as they go back with their friend cured in body and soul! Their encounter with Christ would have strengthened their friendship still more, which is what happens in all true apostolate. We should not forget that there is no sickness that cannot be cured by Christ. We can never consider the people we meet each day as fellow-students, colleagues or workmates, relatives or next-door neighbours as beyond recovery. Many of them have been, it seems, prevented from coming closer to Jesus Christ. It is up to us, with the help of grace, to lead them to him. Great love for Christ will be what moves us to an operative faith, without human respect, without our allowing ourselves to be stopped by the normal difficulties we will come up against. When we find ourselves, today, close to the Tabernacle, let us make sure we talk to the Master about those friends of ours whom we want to take to him so that he can cure them.

---

[7] St Thomas, *Summa Theologiae*, II-II, 177, 1

6. GETTING ON WITH ALL THE PEOPLE AROUND US.

6.1 A Christian cannot be closed in on himself, without any concern for what is happening around him. Jesus Christ shows us how to relate to other people.

After he had responded to Our Lord's call, Matthew gave a banquet at which Jesus, his disciples and some other people were present. Amongst the latter there were *many tax collectors and sinners* who were all friends of Matthew. The Pharisees were surprised to see Jesus sit at table with this kind of person, so they said to his disciples: *why does he eat with tax-collectors and sinners?*[1]

Jesus enjoys being with these people who are so different from each other. He feels at ease with every one of them, because he has come to save everyone. *Those who are well have no need of a physician, but those who are sick.* As all of us are sinners we can all feel we are at the very least unwell. Jesus does not separate himself from us. In this scene we can contemplate how Our Lord never avoids social relationships; rather does he look out for them. Jesus gets on with people of all types and characters; with a convicted thief; with innocent and simple children; with cultured and powerful men such as Nicodemus and Joseph of Arimathaea; with beggars, lepers, whole families ... This interest clearly shows the concern Jesus has to save everyone, regardless of status or walk of life.

Our Lord had friends, like those in Bethany, who invited him, or to whose home sometimes he invited

---
[1] Mark 2:13-17

himself. Lazarus is *our friend*.[2] Jesus has friends in Jerusalem who lend him a room in which to celebrate the Passover with his disciples. He also knows a man *who will lend him a colt for his solemn entry into Jerusalem*, and knows him so well that the disciples can take it without more ado.[3]

Jesus showed great regard for the family, in which the most important thing is to learn to get on with other people and to practise all the virtues this demands. The family is the first and most important place for social relationships to be developed. We are shown as much by those years of hidden life in Nazareth. Rather than many other little events that he could have recorded for us, the Evangelist tells us that Jesus was subject to his parents.[4] It was to be one of the things that Mary would never forget about those years. In order to give a picture of the love of God the Father for men, Our Lord talks about the love of a father for his son, *who does not give him a stone if he asks for bread, or a serpent if he asks him for a fish*.[5] He brings the son of the widow of Naim back to life,[6] because He has compassion on her loneliness – *the young man was an only son* – and on her sorrow. In the midst of his sufferings on the Cross He himself is solicitous for his Mother, entrusting her to John.[7] This is how the Apostle understood it: *and from that hour the disciple took her to his own home*.[8]

Jesus gives us such a clear example because we have to learn to get on with everyone, no matter what their defects, their ideas or peculiarities. We must learn from

---

[2] John 11:11
[3] cf Mark 11:3
[4] cf Luke 2:51
[5] cf Matt 9:7
[6] cf Luke 7:11
[7] cf John 19:26-27
[8] John 19:26-27

him to be the kind of people who are open to others, with a capacity for making friends, always ready to understand and forgive. A Christian, if he really does follow Christ, cannot be shut in on himself without any concern for what is going on around him.

6.2 The human virtue of affability.

A major part of our life consists of brief encounters with people we see in the lift, in the bus queue, in the doctor's waiting room, caught up in the traffic of a huge city, or in the one and only chemist's shop in the little village where we live ... Although these moments are sporadic and sometimes fleeting and unrepeated, they occur many times a day, and are beyond counting in the course of a lifetime. They are important for a Christian as they are opportunities that God gives us of praying for those we meet and of showing them our esteem, as children of the same Father should do. Usually we do this through our good manners and courtesy, which easily become channels of the supernatural virtue of Charity. People are very different one from another, but they all expect something of a Christian – *what Christ would have done in our place*.

We also come into contact with unique and very dissimilar people within our family circle, at work and among the neighbours ... All of them have very different characters, and human and cultural backgrounds. We need to make an effort to learn the art of living together. Saint Thomas points to the importance of the particular virtue this art requires, a virtue which *maintains a man in a becoming order towards other men as regards their mutual relations with one another, in point of both deeds and words.*[9] This particular virtue *which contains many others,*

---

[9] St Thomas, *Summa Theologiae*, II-II, 114, 1

is *affability*, which leads us to make life more pleasant for the people we see every day.

This virtue, which should be, as it were, the framework of human relationships, is probably scarcely noticed, but when it is lacking it is greatly missed. Relationships become tense, and there are many faults against charity. Sometimes relationships become strained or even break down completely. Affability and the other virtues related to it make everyday life pleasant: within the family, at work, in traffic, with neighbours ... Of their very nature they are virtues directly opposed to selfishness, signs of annoyance, fiery temper, bad manners, disorder and lack of consideration for the tastes, concerns or interests of others. Saint Francis de Sales wrote, *It is necessary to have a good stock of these virtues close to hand, for they have to be used almost continually.*[10]

A Christian will be able to turn the multiple details of the human virtue of *affability* into demonstrations of the virtue of charity if he is motivated in them by love of God. Then charity turns affability itself into a stronger virtue, richer in content, and gives it a much broader horizon. We must also practise it when a firm and unwavering attitude is called for: *You have to learn to disagree charitably with others – whenever the need arises – without becoming unpleasant.*[11]

By means of faith and charity, a Christian learns to see his brother men as sons of God, who always deserve the greatest respect and signs of attention and consideration.[12] Because of this we must take heed of the thousands of opportunities that each day brings with it.

---

[10] St Francis de Sales, *Introduction to the Devout Life*, III, 1
[11] St. J. Escrivá, *Furrow*, 429
[12] cf F. Fernandez, *Anthology of Texts*, *see* Affability

6.3 Other virtues, too, are needed for our everyday lives with other people: think of gratitude, warmth, friendship, cheerfulness, optimism, mutual respect ...

All the Gospels tell us about the respect with which Jesus treated everybody: the healthy, the sick, rich and poor, children, elderly folk, beggars, sinners ... Our Lord has a big heart, which is both divine and human. He does not dwell on the defects and deficiencies of the people who come to him or of those He seeks out. It is vital that we, his followers, should want to imitate him, although at times we may find it difficult.

There are many virtues that make it easier to live with other people, and that even make it possible to do so at all; take *kindness* and *forgiveness*, for example, which lead us to judge people and the way they behave in a favourable light, without dwelling on their defects and errors; take *gratitude*, which is that appreciation of a good received, with the desire of acting in some corresponding way. Often we will only be able to say *thank you* or something similar by way of expressing gratitude; it is not difficult to be grateful and it does a great deal of good. If we are attentive to the people around us we will be aware of the surprisingly big number of people who do different little acts of service for us.

Affection and *friendship* are of enormous help in our daily dealings with people. How wonderful it would be if we could consider as *friends* all those we work or study with, our parents, our children, the people we live with or meet! Consider them as *friends* – not only as colleagues or fellow workers. This would show that we had really made an effort to live those many human virtues that make the growth of friendship possible: lack of self-interest; understanding; a spirit of co-operation; optimism; loyalty. Friendship can be particularly close within our own family; between brothers and sisters, with our children, with our parents. Friendship can overcome the most disparate differences of age when it is inspired by the example of Jesus Christ, perfect God and perfect Man, who practised the human virtues fully, in their every aspect.

In our daily relationships with people, *cheerfulness*, which we show by smiling at the right moment or by being pleasant to those we encounter, opens the door for many souls who are on the point of closing themselves to any sort of dialogue or understanding. Cheerfulness encourages people and helps them in their work, and assists in overcoming the numerous reverses that life sometimes brings. A person who habitually lets himself succumb to gloominess and pessimism and does not struggle to overcome it straightaway, will be a dead weight, something of a morbid liability for others. Cheerfulness enriches other people, because it is the expression of an interior richness that is not improvised, stemming as it does from the deep conviction that we are, and recognise that we are, children of God. Many people have found God through the joy and the peace emanating from Christians they come in contact with.

Mutual respect is another indispensable virtue in our relationships with others. It moves us to consider other people as unrepeatable images of God. In his personal relationship with God, a Christian learns to venerate *the image of God that is found in each and every man.*[13] We also have to see the image of God in those who, for whatever reason, we find less lovable, less likeable, less amusing. Being with others also teaches us to have respect for things, because they belong to God and are at the service of men. Respect is a necessary condition if we are to help other people improve, because if ever we try to lord it over others, our advice, our attempts to correct, and our

---

[13] St. J. Escrivá, *Friends of God*, 230

suggestions, become ineffective.

Jesus' example inclines us to live in a way that is pleasantly open towards other people; it leads us to *understand* them, to regard them always with an initial sympathy which will be a growing one. It tends to make us accept optimistically the whole gamut of virtues and defects that exist in the life of each of us. It is a gaze that reaches deep down into somebody's heart and there finds that hidden goodness that exists in everyone. A person who feels understood easily opens his heart and lets himself be helped. Anyone who lives the virtue of charity can easily understand people, because he makes it a rule not to judge others' inmost intentions, which are known only to God.

Closely allied to understanding is the capacity to *forgive* readily. We would be poor Christians if, at the slightest upset, our charity were to grow cold and we were to distance ourselves from members of our family, or from people at work. A Christian should examine himself to see how he reacts to the annoyances that being with other people always produces. Today, Saturday, let us finish our prayer by making a resolution, in honour of Our Lady, to do our best to live these details of true charity towards our neighbour.

SECOND SUNDAY: YEAR A

7. THE LAMB OF GOD

7.1 The figure and reality of this title with which John the Baptist designates Jesus at the beginning of his public life.

We have contemplated Jesus born in Bethlehem and adored by the Shepherds and the Magi, *but this Sunday's Gospel leads us, once again, to the banks of the River Jordan, where thirty years after that birth, John the Baptist is preparing men for his coming. And when the Baptist sees Jesus coming towards him he says 'Behold, the Lamb of God, who takes away the sin of the world' (John 1:29) ... We have got used to the words 'Lamb of God', but nevertheless they are still wonderful, mysterious words; powerful words.*[1] What overtones these words would have had for their hearers, who knew the meaning of the paschal lamb, its blood shed on the night the Jews were freed from slavery in Egypt! Furthermore, all the Israelites were familiar with the words of Isaiah, who had compared the sufferings of the Servant of Yahweh, the Messiah, with the sacrifice of a lamb.[2] The Paschal Lamb which was sacrificed in the Temple each year recalled both their liberation and the covenant that God had made with his people. All of this was a promise and a prefiguring of the true Lamb, Christ, the Victim in the sacrifice of Calvary on behalf of all mankind. *He is the true Lamb who has taken away the sins of the world; by dying he has destroyed our death, and by rising restored our life.*[3] For his part, Saint

---

[1] St John Paul II, *Homily*, 18 January 1981
[2] cf Is 53:7
[3] *Roman Missal, Preface of Easter I*

Paul would say to the first Christians at Corinth that Christ, *our paschal lamb has been sacrificed*[4] and he invites them to a new life; a holy life.

This expression, Lamb of God, has been widely meditated and commented on by theologians and spiritual writers. It is a title ... *rich in theological content. It is one of those resources of human language that attempts to express a plurivalent and divine reality. But it would be nearer the truth to say that it is one of those expressions coined by God, in order to reveal something very important about himself.*[5]

Behold, the Lamb of God, who takes away the sin of the world announces Saint John the Baptist: and *sin of the world* means all types of sin: original sin, which through Adam, also passed to his descendents, and the personal sins of men and women throughout the ages. Our hope of salvation is in Jesus. He is himself a strong call to hope, because Christ has come to forgive and to cure the wounds of sin. Each day, before they administer Holy Communion to the faithful, the priests pronounce these words of John as they show Jesus to the people. *This is the Lamb of God* ... The prophecy of Isaiah was fulfilled on Calvary, and again comes to pass in each and every Mass, as we recall today in the prayer over the offerings *for whenever the memorial of this sacrifice is celebrated, the work of our redemption is accomplished.*[6] The Church wants us to thank Our Lord for giving himself up to death for our salvation, and for having wanted to be the food of our souls.[7]

From very early times, Christian art has represented

---

[4] 1 Cor 5:7
[5] A. Garcia Moreno, *Christ, Son of God and Redeemer of Man*, Pamplona 1982
[6] *Prayer over the Offerings*
[7] cf *The Navarre Bible*, note to John 1:29

Jesus Christ, God and Man, as the Paschal Lamb. Borrowing sometimes from *The Book of Life*, iconography seeks to recall what our faith teaches us; it is He who takes away the sin of the world. It is He who was sacrificed and who possesses all the power and the glory. Before him the twenty-four elders bow down in adoration – according to the Vision of the Apocalypse[8] – He presides over the great marriage supper; he receives the Bride; he purifies the blessed with his blood ... and he is the only one who can open the book of the seven seals; the Beginning and the End, the Alpha and the Omega, the Redeemer filled with gentleness and the all-powerful Judge who is to come to recompense each one according to his works.[9]

Jesus has come to bring forgiveness. He is the Redeemer, the Reconciler. He does not forgive just once, neither does he forgive mankind in the abstract, or as a whole. He forgives each one of us as often as, repentant, we draw close to him ... He forgives us and He gives us a new birth; He opens the gates of grace to us once again so that we can – filled with hope – continue on our way.[10] Let us thank God for the many times he has forgiven us. Let us ask that we may never fail to approach that source of divine mercy, which is Confession.

7.2 The hope of being forgiven. Examination of conscience, contrition and purpose of amendment.

Behold, the Lamb of God, who takes away the sin of the world! Jesus became the spotless Lamb,[11] who offered himself up with absolute docility and meekness to make reparation for the sins of men, for their crimes and their

---

[8] cf Rev 19
[9] A. Garcia Moreno, *loc cit*
[10] G. Redondo, *Reason for Hope*, Pamplona 1977
[11] cf St John Paul II, *loc cit*

betrayals. This is why we find the title he is given so expressive, *for*, comments Fray Luis de León, *Lamb, referring to Christ, means three things: meekness of condition, purity and innocence of life, and satisfaction of sacrifice and offering.*[12]

Christ's insistence on reaching out constantly to sinners is quite remarkable. *The Son of Man has come to save what was lost.*[13] He *has freed us from our sins by his blood.*[14] Most of his contemporaries knew him precisely for his merciful attitude: the Scribes and the Pharisees murmured amongst themselves and said: he is *a friend of tax-collectors and sinners and he eats with them.*[15] They were amazed because He forgave the woman taken in adultery with the simple words, *Go, and do not sin again.*[16] He gives us the same lesson in the parable of the tax-collector and the Pharisee, *God be merciful to me a sinner!*[17] and in the parable of the prodigal son ... The story of his teachings and of his merciful encounters with sinners is unending, *wonderfully continuing*. Can we ever lose hope of being forgiven when it is Christ who forgives? Can we ever lose hope of receiving the graces we need to be saints when it is Christ who can give them to us? The assurance fills us with peace and joy.

Through the sacrament of Penance we obtain as well the graces we need to fight against or overcome those defects which are perhaps deeply rooted in our character and which are often the cause of our discouragement and despondency. So as to find out today whether we receive all the graces that Our Lord has prepared for us in this

---

[12] Fray Luis de Granada, *The Names of Christ*, Madrid 1957
[13] Matt 18:11
[14] Rev 1:5
[15] Matt 11:19
[16] John 8:11
[17] Luke 18:13

sacrament, we must examine ourselves on three counts: *examination of conscience*, our *sorrow for sins*, and our *purpose of amendment. We could say that they are, respectively: acts of faith – the supernatural knowledge of our conduct, according to our obligations; of love – which gives thanks for goods received and weeps over its own lack of correspondence; and of hope, which returns to the struggle with ever-renewed willingness so long as God grants us time to sanctify ourselves. And as the greatest of these three virtues is love, so sorrow – compunction, contrition – is the most important part of the examination of conscience; if our examination does not end in sorrow, this is perhaps an indication that we are dominated by blindness, or that our examination is not motivated by the love of God. On the other hand, when our faults lead us to that sorrow ... there immediately comes forth a determined and effective resolution.*[18]

Lord, teach me to repent; show me the way of love! Make my weaknesses lead me to love you more and more! May your grace move me to contrition whenever I stumble!

7.3 Frequent Confession. The road that leads to refinement of soul and to sanctity.

Jesus Christ comes to call us to holiness and constantly gives us the graces we need for our sanctification. He constantly gives us 'the power to become children of God' as today's liturgy proclaims in the Alleluia verse. This, the sanctification of men ... is the gift of the Lamb of God.[19] This holiness comes about through a constant purification of our innermost soul, which is an essential condition for loving God more and more each

---

[18] Bl. A. del Portillo, *Letter*, 8 December 1976, 16
[19] St John Paul II, *loc cit*

day. That is why a love for frequent Confession is a clear sign of interior sensitivity, of love of God. Despising frequent Confession, or being indifferent to it, when we easily excuse ourselves or delay it – indicate a lack of refinement in our souls and perhaps even lukewarmness, coarseness and lack of responsiveness to the motions the Holy Spirit arouses in our hearts.

We need to travel light and to jettison anything that impedes us, the weight of our faults. Every contrite Confession helps us to look to the future and to walk cheerfully and full of hope along the path that still stretches ahead. Each time we receive this sacrament we hear, like Lazarus, those words of Christ: *Unbind him and let him go...,*[20] because our faults, weaknesses, venial sins ... bind and entangle the Christian, and prevent him from following his way with a light step. *Just as the dead man came forth still bound up, so he who goes to Confession is still guilty. So that he should be freed of his sins Our Lord has said to the minister 'Unbind him and let him go...'*[21] The sacrament of Penance breaks all the bonds that the devil tries to fasten us with so that we cannot go quickly towards Christ.

The frequent Confession of our sins is closely related to holiness, to love of God, for it is there that God refines us and teaches us to be humble. And, as we are weak, it is only frequent Confession that will enable us to remain in a permanent state of integrity and love. It becomes the best remedy against any assault of lukewarmness, of comfortable well-being, of lack of love in our interior life.

One of the principal reasons for esteeming frequent Confession highly is that, when practised as it should be, it is an infallible safeguard against tepidity. Perhaps it is this

---

[20] John 11:44

[21] St Augustine, *Commentary on St John's Gospel*, 29, 24

conviction that makes the Church recommend so strongly ... frequent or weekly Confession.[22] This is why we should make a real effort to receive it punctually and with ever better dispositions.

Christ, the spotless Lamb, has come to cleanse us of our sins; not only of our serious sins, but of those deficiencies in purity of intention and of love that occur in our ordinary life. We should examine today how much love we put into receiving the sacrament of Penance and whether we go to receive it as frequently as Our Lord asks us to.

---

[22] B. Baur, *Frequent Confession*, pg. 121

SECOND SUNDAY: YEAR B

8. PURITY AND THE CHRISTIAN LIFE

8.1 Holy purity, an indispensable condition for loving God and for the apostolate.

Now that the feasts of Christmastide are over, during which we considered mainly the mysteries of Our Lord's hidden life, we can let the liturgy help us contemplate the years of Christ's public life. From the very beginning of his mission we see Christ seeking out his disciples and calling them to his service; this is what Yahweh did in earlier times, as we are reminded by the *First Reading*, which tells us of the calling of Samuel.[1] The Gospel speaks of that apparently chance meeting of Our Lord with those first three disciples (Peter, James and John), who were later on to become the foundation of his Church.[2]

Following Christ, now as well as then, means giving him our heart, our whole being, our life itself. We can well understand that to follow Christ we need to live holy purity and purify our hearts. Saint Paul tells us in the *Second Reading*: *Keep away from fornication... Your body, you know, is the temple of the Holy Spirit, who is in you since you received him from God. You are not your own property: you have been bought and paid for. That is why you should use your body for the glory of God.* [3] No one has ever taught about the dignity of the body in the way that the Church does. *Purity is the glory of the human body before God. It is the glory of God in the human body.*[4]

---

[1] cf *First Reading of the Mass*: 1 Sam 3:3-10; 19
[2] cf John 1:35-42
[3] cf 1 Cor 6:13-15; 17-20
[4] St John Paul II, *General Audience*, 18 March 1981

If we are to follow Christ, chastity, outside or within matrimony, according to each one's state, is absolutely necessary. It demands our personal struggle and effort, together with God's grace. The wounds of original sin *in our intellect, our will, our passions and affections* did not disappear with the guilt of it when we were baptised. On the contrary those wounds introduced a principle of disorder into our nature; our soul tends to rebel against God in very different ways, and protests against its subjection to the body. Our personal sins stir up the dross left by original sin and open up the wounds which it produced in our souls.

Holy purity, which is part of the virtue of temperance, inclines us readily and joyfully to moderate our use of the generative faculty, according to the light of reason, helped by faith.[5] The opposite is *licentiousness*, which destroys men's dignity, weakens the will towards good, and dulls the understanding in its yearning to know and love God and many noble human things. Impurity often brings with it the heavy burden of selfishness, and places the victim in situations where violence and cruelty are common. If we do not apply the remedy, it makes us lose any sense of the things of God or of anything transcendental. An impure heart cannot see Christ as he passes by and calls to us; it is blinded to all that really matters.

Acts of renunciation *with prohibitions directed at looking, doing, desiring and imagining*, although necessary, are not everything with regard to chastity. The essence of chastity is love. It fosters delicacy and tenderness towards God, and respect for people whom it perceives as children of God. Impurity destroys love, even on a human plane, whilst chastity *keeps love young in any state in life.*[6]

---

[5] cf St Thomas, *Summa Theologiae*, II-II, 151, 2, 1
[6] St. J. Escrivá, *Christ is passing by*, 25

Purity is an indispensable requirement if we are to love at all. Chastity is neither the first nor the most important of the virtues, and a Christian's life cannot be reduced to it alone. Nevertheless, without it there is no charity, and since charity is the first virtue and the one on which all the others are founded, the one in which they find their perfection, the vital importance of purity is clear.[7]

The first Christians, who are told by Saint Paul to glorify God in their bodies, were surrounded by a climate of corruption, and many of them came from that environment. *Do not be deceived*, the Apostle says, *neither the immoral, nor idolaters, nor adulterers ... will inherit the kingdom of God. And such were some of you...*[8] Saint Paul taught these people that they had to struggle to live this virtue which was held in low esteem, and often despised in that culture. Each one of them had to be a living example of the faith in Christ that they carried in their hearts and of the spiritual riches that they bore within them.

8.2 If we are to live this virtue we need good formation. Different spheres in which chastity grows.

We must be firmly convinced that holy purity can be lived always, despite the strength of contrary pressures, so long as we use the means that God gives us to win through, and so long as we avoid dangerous occasions.

If we are to live this virtue it is absolutely necessary that we have good formation. We must talk about these matters in spiritual direction with finesse and supernatural sensitivity, but clearly and without any ambiguity. In this way we will learn to clarify or correct wrong ideas we may have. Sometimes problems, which have been wrongly

---

[7] cf J. L. Soria, *Loving and living chastity*, Madrid 1976
[8] cf 1 Cor 6:9-10

qualified as scruples, arise because we have not spoken in depth about them: they are invariably solved when we speak about the objective facts in spiritual direction and in Confession.

A Christian who really wants to follow Christ has to unite purity of soul to purity of body: he must order his affections so that God may occupy the centre of his soul at every moment. So the struggle to live this virtue and to grow in it has to be extended to the sphere of the affections, to the *custody of the heart*, and to all those matters that even indirectly can make it easier or more difficult: for example, mortification of the sight and of the imagination, the inclination to comfort, to reminisce...

In order to fight effectively so as to acquire and perfect this virtue, we must, first of all, be deeply convinced of its value, of its absolute necessity and of the countless fruits that it produces in the interior life and in the apostolate. We have to ask God for this grace, *for not all men can receive this precept*.[9] Another fundamental condition for the effectiveness of this struggle is humility: anyone who is truly conscious of his own weakness resolutely avoids dangerous occasions; he is sincere and contrite in acknowledging occasions where he has imprudently or even recklessly lowered his guard; he asks for the help he needs; and gratefully recognises the true worth of his body and of his soul.

Perhaps, depending on the epoch or the circumstances, the Christian needs to fight more strenuously in one area, and at other times in a very different one; *sensitivity*, which may be heightened because we have failed to avoid more or less remote voluntary causes; *reading matter*, for example, which although not obviously impure may leave a climate of sensuality in our soul; a lack of care in

---

[9] Matt 19:11

guarding our sight...

Other areas related to this virtue of holy purity, and which we need to guard carefully are; the internal senses *imagination and memory*, which although they may not have rested directly on thoughts against the ninth Commandment, are frequently occasions for temptation. It shows very little generosity towards God if we do not avoid them; *custody of the heart*, which is made for loving, and in which we must preserve a clean love in accord with our own vocation, and in which God must always occupy the first place. We cannot go around with our heart in our hands, as though we were offering goods for sale.[10] Related to the guarding of the heart is vanity, that tendency to attract attention to ourselves and to be the centre of things. There are, too, certain likes and preferences that are sometimes less well-ordered than they ought to be.

8.3 The means to conquer.

If we are to follow Christ with a clean heart and be an apostle in the midst of the circumstances it has fallen to each of us to live in, we need to practise a series of human and supernatural virtues. These must be founded on the grace which will never fail us if we do all that we are able to, and if we humbly ask for it.

Amongst the virtues that help us to live holy purity is that of *industriousness*; of constant, intense work. Often problems of purity are problems connected with idleness or laziness. We also need *courage* and *fortitude* if we are to avoid temptation, without falling into the ingenuous delusion of thinking that a particular thing does no harm; or of foolishly underestimating its danger with false pretexts of age or experience. We need complete *sincerity* which leads us to tell the whole truth clearly and to be

---

[10] cf St. J. Escrivá, *The Way*, 146

forewarned against *the devil that ties the tongue*,[11] who tries to deceive us, taking all substance away from sin or temptation, or magnifying it to make us fall into the temptation of *being ashamed to speak*. Sincerity is absolutely necessary if we are to win through, for without it the soul is bereft of an indispensable help.

No means would be sufficient if we did not talk to Our Lord in *prayer* and in *the Blessed Eucharist*. There we always find the help we need, the strength that turns our frailty into firmness, the love that fills our heart, created as it was for eternity and always unsatisfied with everything this world has to offer. In the *sacrament of Penance* we purify our conscience, receive the specific graces of the sacrament to win in some particular battle, perhaps a skirmish in which we had been previously overcome, and also the strength that true spiritual direction always gives.

If we want to understand love for Jesus Christ as it was understood by the Apostles, the first Christians and the saints of all times, we have to live this virtue of holy purity; if not, we remain earthbound and unable to understand anything.

We turn to Mary, *Mater Pulchrae Dilectionis*,[12] Mother of Fair Love, because she creates within the soul of a Christian the refinement and filial tenderness which enable this virtue to grow. She will grant us the strong virtue of purity if we turn lovingly and trustingly to her.

---

[11] cf *ibid*, 236
[12] Sir 24:24

9. THE FIRST MIRACLE OF JESUS

9.1 The miracle at Cana. Our Lady is called V*irgin most powerful.*

A wedding takes place in Cana. This town is only a short distance from Nazareth, where the Virgin Mary lives. As a friend or relation, she is present at this modest celebration and Jesus has been invited as well, with his first disciples.

It was customary for the women who knew the family to help in the preparation of all that was needed. The wedding feast began and, either through lack of foresight or because there turned out to be an unexpectedly large number of guests, the wine ran out. Our Lady, who is helping, realises that the wine is running sort. Jesus is there, her Son and her God; the Messiah has just begun his public preaching and ministry. She, better than anyone else, knows this. The Gospel of today's Mass presents to us this simple and loving dialogue which takes place between the Mother and the Son.[1] *The Mother of Jesus said to him, 'They have no wine'.* Without asking for anything, she points to a need. *They have no wine.* She teaches us to pray.

Jesus answered her: 'O woman, what have you to do with me? My hour has not yet come.'

It looks as if Jesus is going to refuse Mary what she asks: *'My hour has not yet come,'* he says to her. But Mary, who knows the heart of her Son very well, behaves as though He had acceded to her petition immediately: *'Do whatever he tells you,* she says to the servants.

---

[1] cf John 2:2-12

Mary is a mother who is more attentive to all our needs than any mother on earth ever has been or ever will be. The miracle takes place because Our Lady has interceded; it happens only because of her petition.

Why do Mary's prayers have such efficacy before God? The prayers of saints are the prayers of servants, whereas those of Mary are the prayers of a Mother, whence they receive their efficacy and authoritative character. As Jesus' love for his mother is limitless she cannot ask for anything without being heard ... Nobody asked the Blessed Virgin to intercede with her Son on the distressed couple's behalf. Above all, Mary's heart, which never fails to have pity on the unfortunate ... impelled her to take upon herself the task of intercessor and beg her Son for the miracle, even though nobody had asked her to ... If Our Lady acted thus without being asked, how would it have been if they 'had' asked?[2] What will we not receive if we persist in turning to her time and again?

Virgin most powerful. This is the name Christian piety has given to our Mother Mary, because her Son is God and cannot refuse her anything.[3] She is always aware of our spiritual and material needs; she desires, even more than we do, that we should not cease imploring her intervention before God on our behalf. There we are, so needy and yet so slow to ask! We show so little trust, so little patience when what we ask for seems a long time in coming!

Oughtn't we to turn more frequently to Our Lady? Shouldn't we put more trust into our petitions, knowing that she will always obtain for us all that we need most? If she obtained from her Son wine that was not absolutely necessary, will she not find a solution for all those urgent

---

[2] St Alphonsus Liguori, *Abbreviated Sermons, 48: On Trust in the Mother of God*
[3] cf St John Paul II, *Homily*, Pompeii, 21 October 1979, 4-6

needs that we have? *I want, Lord, to abandon the care of all my affairs into your generous hands. Our Mother, your Mother – will have let you hear those words, now as in Cana: 'They have none!' I believe in you. I hope in you. I love you, Jesus. I want nothing for myself: it's for them.*[4]

9.2 The turning of water into wine. Our work too can be turned into grace. Finishing our work well.

Saint John calls Our Lady *Mother of God* twice. The next occasion will be on Calvary.[5] Between the two events – Cana and Calvary – there are several analogies. One occurrence is placed at the beginning and the other at the end of Jesus' public life, as though to indicate that all of Our Lord's work is accompanied by Mary's presence. Both episodes highlight Mary's concern for men; in Cana she intercedes when the timing of her intervention might well have seemed inopportune: *My hour has not yet come.*[6] On Calvary she offers the redeeming death of her Son, and accepts the mission that Jesus confers on her of being the Mother of all believers.[7]

At Cana in Galilee there is shown only one concrete aspect of human need, apparently a tiny one and of little importance: 'They have no wine'. But it has a symbolic value: this coming to the aid of human needs means, at the same time, bringing those needs within the radius of Christ's Messianic mission and salvific power. Thus there is a mediation. Mary places herself between her Son and mankind in the reality of their wants, needs and sufferings. In her position as mother, she puts herself 'in the middle', that is to say, she acts as a mediatrix not as an outsider.

---

[4] St. J. Escrivá, *The Forge*, 807
[5] cf John 19:25
[6] cf John 2:4
[7] cf Second Vatican Council, *Lumen gentium*, 58

She knows that in this way she can point out to her Son the needs of mankind, and in fact, she 'has the right' to do so.[8]

His mother said to the servants, 'Do whatever he tells you'. The servants obeyed readily and efficiently: they filled *six stone jars standing there for the Jewish rites of purification* as Our Lord told them to. Saint John points out that *they filled them up to the brim*.

'Now draw some out,' Our Lord says to them, *and take it to the steward of the feast*. This wine is better than any other wine that men have ever drunk.

Our lives, like the water, were flat and without the ferment of purpose until Jesus came to us. He transforms our work, our sorrows and our joys; even death is different beside Christ. Our Lord only wants us to carry out our duties *usque ad summum* right up to the top, to the brim; finishing them off so well so that he can work a miracle. If all the people who work in universities, in hospitals, in the home, in finance and in factories ... were to do their work with human perfection and a Christian spirit, we will get up tomorrow morning to a completely different world. Our Lord will turn our efforts and our work, which would otherwise remain supernaturally sterile, into the most exquisite of wines. Then the world will be a wedding feast, a more worthy dwelling place for mankind in which the presence of Jesus and Mary will imprint a special delight.

'Fill the jars with water,' Our Lord says to us. We must not let routine, impatience or laziness cause us to only half-fulfil our daily duties. What we have to offer is very little; but Our Lord wants us to place it at his disposal. Jesus could just as well have performed the miracle with empty jars, but he wanted men to cooperate, with their own effort, and with all the means they had. He worked the prodigy at his mother's request.

---

[8] St John Paul II, *Redemptoris Mater*, 25 March 1987, 20

Imagine the joy of those obedient and efficient servants when they saw the water turned into wine! They, like the master's disciples, whose faith in Jesus was confirmed, are silent witnesses of the miracle. Imagine our joy, when, through God's mercy, we contemplate in Heaven all our deeds turned into glory!

9.3 The generosity of Jesus. He always gives us more than we ask him for.

Jesus does not refuse us anything. In particular does he grant us what we ask for through his Mother. She takes it upon herself to unravel our prayers if they are somewhat tangled up, just as mothers do. He always grants us more, much more, than we ask for, as he did at that wedding feast at Cana in Galilee. An ordinary wine would have been enough, even one inferior to what had already been served, and very probably a much smaller quantity would have been sufficient

Saint John is particularly interested in emphasising that it was a matter of *six stone jars ... each holding twenty or thirty gallons*. He wants to show how abundant the gift was, just as he would when he tells us about the miracle of the multiplication of the loaves.[9] Indeed one of the signs of the Messiah's coming was to be this very abundance.

Commentators calculate that Our Lord turned into wine a quantity somewhere between 100 and 160 gallons, depending on the capacity of those great Jewish jars.[10] And it was the best wine! In the same way, in our lives, God gives us more and better than we deserve.

We find here the concurrence of two fundamental images which had been used to describe the true Messiah: the wedding feast and the marriage ceremony. *You shall be*

---

[9] John 6:12-13
[10] *The Navarre Bible*, note to John 2:6

a crown of beauty in the hand of the Lord, and a royal diadem in the hand of your God, Isaiah tells us in an extremely beautiful image presented in the *First Reading* of the Mass. *You shall no more be termed 'Forsaken', and your land shall no more be termed 'Desolate': but you shall be called 'My delight is in her', and your land 'Married': for the Lord delights in you and your land shall be married. For as a young man marries a virgin, so shall your sons marry you, and as the bridegroom rejoices over the bride, so shall your God rejoice over you.*[11] It is the joy and intimacy that God wants to have with all of us.

Those first disciples, one of whom was Saint John, were amazed. The miracle helped them to take a step forward in their newly-found faith. Jesus confirms them in their faith, as he does all those who follow him.

Do whatever he tells you. These are Our Lady's last words in the Gospel. There could have been no better words, no more profitable advice.

---

[11] Is 62:3-5

10. THE HOLINESS OF THE CHURCH

10.1 The Church is holy and produces fruits of holiness.

In a great number of different ways the Old Testament announces and prefigures everything that is to take place in the New Testament. The New Testament is the fulness and fulfilment of the Old Testament. Christ shows the contrast between the spirit He brings and that of the Judaism of his time. This new spirit will not be like a patch added on to something old; rather it will be a complete and definitive new beginning which replaces the provisional and imperfect realities of the ancient Revelation. Like new wine, the newness of Christ's message, its fulness, does not fit into the mould of the Old Law. *No one puts new wine into old wineskins ...*[1]

His listeners well understand the figures and images Our Lord uses to speak about the Kingdom of Heaven. Nobody must fall into the error of mending an old garment with a piece of new cloth, because the new cloth will shrink as soon as it is washed, tearing the old worn garment even more, so that both together will be spoilt.

The Church is the new garment, without any rent or tear in it; she is the new vessel prepared to receive the spirit of Christ. She will generously carry the message and saving strength of her Lord to the ends of the earth, for so long as men shall exist on it.

With the Ascension, one stage in Revelation is closed, and with Pentecost, the new age, the time of the Church, commences.[2] The Church is the Mystical Body of Christ,

---

[1] Mark 2:22
[2] cf Second Vatican Council, *Lumen gentium*, 4

which continues the sanctifying action of Jesus, principally through the sacraments. She obtains abundant graces for us by interceding with Christ and also through the sacraments and the external rites that she has instituted: blessings, holy water ... The Church's doctrine enlightens our minds, brings us to know Our Lord, and enables us to converse intimately with him and to love him. This is why the Church, our Mother, has never admitted differences in matters of doctrine by teaching a partial or deformed truth; she has always remained vigilant so as to keep the faith in all its purity, and it is this faith she has taught throughout the world. Thanks to her unfailing faithfulness, with the help of the Holy Spirit, we are able to know the doctrine taught by Jesus Christ without any change or variation of the sense in which he taught it. From the day of Pentecost up to the present day we continue to hear Christ's voice.

Every sound tree bears good fruit,[3] and the Church produces fruits of sanctity.[4] From the first Christians, who called each other *saints* up to our own day, saints of all ages, races and social condition have shone out. Holiness is not generally conspicuous in ways that attract attention; it does not make a lot of noise; it is supernatural; but it is immediately recognisable, because charity, which is the essence of holiness, has external manifestations: in the way it lives all the virtues, in the way it does the work it has to do, in its apostolic endeavour. *See how they love one another,* it was said of the first Christians.[5] The inhabitants of Jerusalem had great admiration and respect for them, because they perceived the action of the Holy Spirit in them.[6]

Today in our prayer and throughout the day we can

---

[3] Matt 7:17
[4] cf *Catechism of the Council of Trent*, I, 10, 15
[5] Tertullian, *Apologetics*, 39:7
[6] cf Acts 2:33

thank God for all the many good things we have received through our Mother, the Church. They are gifts we can never repay. What would our life be like without those means of sanctification which is what the sacraments are? How could we know the Word of Jesus, *words of eternal life!* and his teachings, if they had not been guarded for us so faithfully?

10.2 The holiness of the Church. Sinful members of the Church.

From the very moment of its foundation, God has had in his Church *a people of his own who are zealous for good deeds.*[7] It can be affirmed that *The Church of God, without ever ceasing to offer spiritual sustenance to men, engenders and forms new generations of holy men and women for Christ.*[8] Holiness in her Head, Christ, is echoed in the holiness of many of her members, holiness that comes from the exemplary exercise of human and supernatural virtues. Sanctity is heroic *in those who are of flesh, but do not live according to the flesh. They live on earth but their homeland is Heaven ... They love others and others persecute them ... They are calumniated and they bless. They suffer detraction and they honour their detractors ... Their attitude ... is a manifestation of God's power.*[9] We could never count the number of the faithful who have lived their faith heroically; they are all in Heaven, although the Church has only canonised a few of them. Neither could we count here on earth the mothers, who, full of faith, bring up their families generously and without thinking of themselves; the workers engaged in all types of honest occupation who sanctify their work; the students who carry

---

[7] Titus 2:14
[8] Pius XI, Encyclical, *Quas primas*, 11 December 1925, 4
[9] *Epistle to Diognetus*, 5, 6, 16:7, 9

out an effective apostolate and know how to go cheerfully against the current of opinion; and the many sick people who with joy and peace offer up their lives at home or in hospital for their brothers and sisters in the Faith.

No one puts new wine into old wineskins: the divine potency of Christ's teaching, of the life that he dispensed to us when he brought us the Church, has to be contained within the soul of each of us, a receptacle that should be worthy but which is defective, can fail and let us down. If we have faith and love, we can understand that the Church is holy whilst her members have defects, are sinners. In her, *good and bad are gathered together. She is made up of a diversity of children, because she brings them all forth in the faith. She does this although, through their own fault, she does not manage to lead all of them to the freedom of grace by a renewal of their lives.*[10] The Church herself is made up of men and women who have already reached their eternal destiny – the saints in heaven; of others who are being cleansed whilst waiting for their definitive reward – the holy souls in Purgatory; and by those who, here on earth, have to struggle against their defects and evil inclinations in order to be faithful to Christ. It is not reasonable, going against both faith and justice, to judge the Church by the behaviour of some of her members who do not know how to respond to God's call. This is a serious and unjust deformation which pays scant attention to Christ's sacrifice, *as Christ loved the Church and gave himself up for her, that He might sanctify her, having cleansed her by the washing of water with the Word, that He might present the Church to himself in splendour, without spot or wrinkle or any such thing, that she might be holy and without blemish.*[11] Don't let us forget Our

---

[10] St Gregory the Great, *Homily*, 38:7
[11] Eph 5:25-27

Lady, St Joseph and the countless martyrs and saints; let us always keep before our eyes the holiness of her doctrine, of her worship ... of the sacraments, and of the moral teaching of the Church. Let us frequently consider the Christian virtues and the works of mercy that adorn and always will adorn the lives of so many Christians. This will move us always to behave as good children of the Church, to love her more and more, and to pray for those brothers and sisters of ours who are in greatest need.

10.3 Being good sons and daughters of the Church.

The Church does not cease to be holy because of the faults of her children, which are always strictly personal, even though these faults may have a great influence on the rest of their brothers and sisters. That is why a good son of the Church will not allow people to insult his Mother, or blame her for defects she does not have. He will not let people criticise her or treat her badly.

Still, even during those times in which her true face has been covered over by the infidelity of many who should have been faithful, and when only lives of very indifferent piety seem to be common, at those very times, perhaps hidden from people's gaze, holy and heroic souls exist. Even in the epochs most obscured by materialism, sensuality, and a desire for physical well-being, there are faithful men and women who, in the midst of their everyday affairs are God's joy in the world.

The Church is a Mother: her mission is that of *bringing forth children, and educating and directing them; guiding with motherly care the lives of individuals and of whole peoples*.[12] She – holy, and mother of all of us[13] – provides us with the means to reach sanctity. Nobody can

---

[12] St John XXIII, Encyclical, *Mater et magistra*, Introduction
[13] St Cyril of Jerusalem, *Catechesis*, 18, 26

become a good child of God without lovingly and piously living these means of sanctification, because *he cannot have God for his Father who does not have the Church for his Mother.*[14] Thus we cannot imagine anyone having great love for God without having great love for the Church.

As our love for God springs from the love He has for us, *in this is love, not that we love God but that he loves us.*[15] Our love for the Church must flow from our gratitude for the means He offers us to reach sanctity. We owe him love for the priesthood, for all the Sacraments, and, very especially, for the Blessed Eucharist, for the liturgy, for the treasure of the Faith that she has faithfully safeguarded down the centuries ... We look at her with eyes of love and faith. We see she is holy, pure, without spot, unwrinkled.

If, by the will of Jesus Christ, the Church is our Mother, a good mother, we must have the attitude of good children. We must not allow her to be treated as though she were a human society, forgetting the profound mystery enclosed within her. Let us never tolerate criticism against priests or bishops ... And if ever we see errors and defects in those who perhaps should give better example, may we know how to make excuses for them and bring other positive aspects of those people to the fore ... and, when appropriate, help them with fraternal correction if we can. *Love is repaid with love.* Love should be expressed in deeds, that should be noticed by the people who frequently come into contact with us.

We will finish our prayer invoking Mary, *Mater Ecclesiae*, Mother of the Church, so that she can teach us to love the Church more and more each day.

---

[14] St Cyprian, *On the Unity of the Catholic Church*, 6
[15] 1 John 4:10

11. DIGNITY OF THE PERSON

11.1 The greatness and dignity of the human person.

Jesus was going through a cornfield. The disciples plucked some of the ripe ears and rubbed the chaff off the grains between their hands so as to eat them. It was a Sabbath day. The Pharisees wanted the Master to rebuke his disciples, for – according to their reasoning – it was not licit to do even that amount of work on the Sabbath. Jesus came to the defence of his disciples and of the Sabbath rest itself. He does this by turning to Sacred Scripture: *Have you never read what David did, when he was in need and was hungry, he and those who were with him: how he entered into the house of God, when Abiathar was High Priest, and ate the bread of the Presence, which it is not lawful for any but the priests to eat, and also gave to those who were with him.* And he said to them, *The Sabbath was made for man, not man for the Sabbath.* Then he went on to present them with a still deeper reason: *The Son of Man is Lord even of the Sabbath.*[1] Everything is ordered in the direction of work for Christ and the individual: even the Sabbath rest.

The bread of the Presence consisted of twelve loaves which were placed each week on the table of the sanctuary, by way of paying homage to the twelve tribes of Israel.[2] The loaves that were removed from the altar were reserved for the priests who performed the ceremony.

Abiathar's conduct was an anticipation of the doctrine that Christ teaches in this gospel passage. Already in the

---

[1] Mark 2:23-28
[2] cf Lev 24:5-9

Old Testament, God had established an order in the precepts of the Law in such a way that lesser precepts should give way to those of a higher order. This explains how a ceremonial precept, as was this of the loaves, should give way to a precept of natural law.[3] The precept of the Sabbath had to yield precedence to the basic needs of subsistence.

The Second Vatican Council is inspired by this passage to emphasise the value of the person above that of economic and social development.[4] After God comes man; any such consideration intervening would introduce real disorder in human affairs, as unfortunately we see happening frequently.

The most sacred Humanity of Christ casts a light that enlightens the being and the life of each of us, because it is only in Christ that we can recognise the totally immeasurable value of a man. *'When you wonder about the mystery of yourselves,'* St John Paul II said to a gathering of young people, *look at Christ, who is the one who gives meaning to our lives*.[5] It is He alone; no other being can give meaning to our existence, and this is why we cannot give a definition of man taking as our starting point inferior created realities, and still less man's labour, his production, the material result of his efforts. The greatness of the human person derives from the spiritual reality of his soul, his divine filiation, his eternal destiny, all of which he has received from God. This places him above the whole of created nature. The dignity and immense respect that he merits are granted to him at the moment of his conception, and are the foundation of the right to the inviolability of life and our veneration for motherhood.

---

[3] cf *The Navarre Bible*, EUNSA, Pamplona 1983 *in loc*
[4] cf Second Vatican Council, *Gaudium et spes*, 26
[5] St John Paul II, *Homily*, New York, 3 October 1979

The most important title bestowed on human dignity is that of being the only reality of visible creation that God has loved for itself, creating it in his own image and likeness and raising it to the order of grace. Furthermore, man assumed a new value after the Son of God, through his Incarnation, took on our nature and gave his life for all men: *propter nos homines et propter nostram salutem descendit de coelis. Et incarnatus est.* This is why we are interested in all the souls around us: there isn't a single soul that remains outside Christ's love. We should not withhold our respect and consideration from a single person. We should look around us, at the people we see and speak to each day, and consider in God's presence whether in fact this is the case, whether we do show that appreciation and have genuine veneration for others.

11.2 Dignity of the person through work. Principles of the social doctrine of the Church.

The dignity of the human being – a creature made in God's image – is the only criterion by which to judge the real progress of society, of work, of science ... and not the reverse.[6] Man's dignity is expressed by the whole of his personal and social activity: particularly in the field of work. It is in the area of work that God's creature man at once realized and accomplished the command of his Creator, who brought him out of nothing and put him into a world without sin *ut operaretur*, so that he should work,[7] and in this way give glory to him. This is why the Church defends the dignity of the person who works, and who is deprived of this dignity when he is esteemed only for what he produces, when work is considered merely as merchandise, and more value is given to *the work than to*

---

[6] cf *ibid, Address,* 15 June 1982, 7
[7] Gen 2:15

the workman, to the object more than to the subject who accomplished it,[8] as St John Paul II says expressively, when work is used as an element for gain, esteeming the worker only by what he produces.

It is not a matter of external gesture towards them or of a way of treating workers, because even with cordial relationships it is possible to proceed against other people's dignity if they are subordinated to merely utilitarian ends, such as mechanisation, in order to raise productivity or to keep peace within the firm; we have to venerate God's image in every individual person.

We would be far from having a Christian outlook if our sight were fixed on the ground. The most reliable indicators of justice in social relations are neither the volume of wealth created nor the manner of its distribution ... we need to examine *whether the structure, the functioning, the environment of an economic system, are such that they curtail the human dignity of all those who expend their own energy in it.*[9] We have to keep ever in mind that the supreme criterion in the use of material goods must be *that of facilitating and promoting the spiritual perfection of human beings, in both the natural and the supernatural order,*[10] beginning, as is logical, with those who produce the goods.

This is why the intimate connection between work and ownership demands, for its own perfection, that the person who carries out the work can consider in some way that *he is putting his labour into something which is to some extent and in a very real sense his own.*[11]

The dignity of work is given expression in the *just*

---

[8] St John Paul II, *Address*, 24 November 1979
[9] St John XXIII, Encyclical, *Mater et magistra*, 15 May 1961, 83
[10] *ibid*, 246
[11] St John Paul II, *Laborem exercens*, 15

wage, the basis of all social justice, even where it is a matter of a free contract, for although the stipulated salary may be in accordance with the letter of the law, this does not legitimise any recompense that may be agreed on. If the contractor, the head of a Company, the builder, the owner, the mistress of the house ... wants to take advantage of a situation where there is a surplus of labour, for example, so as to pay salaries incommensurate with the workers' dignity as a human being, it would be an offence against the men or women concerned (as well as being against their Creator) because they have an inalienable natural right to sufficient means for the support of themselves and of their families, which takes precedence over the right of free contract.[12] Another *logical consequence is that we all have a duty to do our work well ... We cannot neglect our duty or be satisfied with working in a half-hearted manner.*[13] Laziness and work badly done similarly offend against social justice.

11.3 A just society.

We need to bear in mind that the principal aim of economic development *does not consist merely in the increased volume of goods produced, any more than it consists in profit, or in the enhancement of the employer's prestige; it is directed to the service of man, of man, that is, in his totality, taking into account his material needs and the requirements of his intellectual, moral, spiritual and religious life.*[14] This does not deny a sphere of legitimate autonomy to economics, an autonomy that is proper to the temporal order, which will lead men to study the causes of economic problems, suggest technical and political

---

[12] cf St Paul VI, *Populorum progressio,* 24 March 1967, 59

[13] St John Paul II, *Address,* 7 November 1982

[14] Second Vatican Council, *loc cit,* 64

solutions, etc. But these solutions must always be subject to a higher criterion, of a moral order, for they are not absolutely independent and autonomous; and we must not trust purely technologically-provided solutions when we come up against problems that have their root cause in some moral disorder.

There is a long way to go before we reach a just society in which the dignity of the person, a child of God, is fully acknowledged and respected. This is a task that belongs to us as Christians, together with all men of good will, because *We do not live justice if we do not wish to see it fulfilled in the lives of others. In the same way, it is wrong to shut oneself up in comfortable religiosity, forgetting the needs of other people. The man who wishes to be just in God's eyes also tries to establish the reign of justice among men.*[15] We must live respect towards every individual, with all its consequences, in the most varied spheres, defending life, for example, as soon as it is conceived, because there is a child of God with the right to life. God has given something that nobody can take away. Equally a matter of grave obligation is defending the weak and the elderly, for we must be merciful, with a mercy that the world seems to be losing. As employees or workers we will exercise this virtue by working well and having professional expertise, or as entrepreneurs, being thoroughly familiar with the social doctrine of the Church so as to put it into practice.

We have to acknowledge that same dignity of the person in our normal relationships in life, considering the people we deal with – in spite of their possible defects – as children of God, avoiding any type of malicious gossip and anything that could be to their detriment. *Get into the habit of praying to the Guardian Angel of each person you are*

---

[15] St. J. Escrivá, *Christ is passing by*, 52

*concerned about. His Angel will help him to be good and
faithful and cheerful.*[16] Then it will be much easier for us to
get on with them, and our relationship will grow in
affection, in peace and mutual respect.

The Son of Man is lord even of the Sabbath. All of us
must subject everything to the good of Christ – the highest
Good – and of the human person, for whose salvation
Christ immolated himself on Calvary. No earthly good –
not even the Sabbath – is greater than man.

---

[16] *ibid, The Forge*, 1012

SECOND WEEK: WEDNESDAY

12. PRACTISING THE FAITH IN ORDINARY THINGS

12.1 Faith is to be practised and should give shape and value to the little happenings of each day.

Jesus went into a synagogue and there saw a man *who had a withered hand*. It was paralysed. St Mark tells us that all the onlookers waited to see if He would heal him on the Sabbath.[1] Our Lord does not act in secret or conceal what He does; quite the contrary. He asked the man to stand up in the midst of those who were present so that everybody could take a good look at him. He then said to the onlookers *Is it lawful on the Sabbath to do good or to do harm, to save life or to kill? But they were silent.* Then Jesus, angered by their hypocrisy, looked at them wrathfully, although at the same time He was *grieved at their hardness of heart.* The anger in Jesus' look, caused by the hardness of their hearts, was obvious to everyone. He spoke to the man. *'Stretch out your hand.'* He stretched it out, and his hand was restored.

That handicapped man, standing out in front of everyone, is filled with trust in Jesus. His faith manifests itself in obeying Our Lord and in carrying out what, from long experience, he knows he has been unable to do up till then; to stretch out his hand. His trust in Our Lord, as he disregards his chronic condition, makes the miracle possible. *All things are possible to Jesus.* Faith enables us to reach targets we had always thought beyond us; to solve intractable problems, perhaps of a personal nature, or perhaps connected with some apostolic task, that we had

---

[1] Mark 3:1-6

always thought to be insoluble; it enables us to get rid of firmly-rooted defects in our own character.

This man's life was to take a whole new direction after the small effort Christ required of him; this is what he asks of us too in the most normal matters of our daily life. Today we must consider *how a Christian, in his ordinary daily life, in the simplest details, can put faith, hope and charity into practice. There lies the essence of the conduct of a man who relies on divine help.*[2] We need Our Lord's help if we are to get rid of our incapability.

Faith is something we have *to practise*. It should shape all our decisions, big or small. At the same time it will usually show in the way we undertake our ordinary daily duties. It is not enough for us to give assent to the great truths of the Creed, to have good formation. We need, besides this, *to live our faith*, to put it into practice. It should give birth to a *life of faith*, which should be both the fruit and the manifestation of what we believe. God asks us to serve him with the whole of our life, with deeds, with all the strength of our body and soul. Faith is something that is related to life, to normal everyday life. With it, human existence itself appears as an unfolding of the Faith, as we live in accordance with our beliefs,[3] and with what we know is God's will for each one of us. Do we live a *life of faith*? Does our faith have a truly significant bearing on our behaviour, on the decisions we make ...? Does it?

12.2 Faith and supernatural outlook.

The practice of the virtue of faith in our daily lives adds up to what is commonly known as *supernatural outlook*. This consists in a way of seeing things, even the most ordinary, apparently quite commonplace things, in

---

[2] St. J. Escrivá, *Christ is passing by*, 169
[3] cf P. Rodriguez, *Faith and Life of Faith*, Pamplona 1974, p.172

relation to God's plan for each person as regards his own salvation and the salvation of many others. It leads us to accustom ourselves to *undertake our daily activities as though we were constantly glancing at God to see whether what we are doing is really his Will, whether ours is the way He wants us to do things. It leads us to get used to discovering God in people, to recognise him behind what the world calls chance or coincidence, in fact, to see his mark everywhere.*[4]

Christian life, holiness, *is not a kind of protective garment* that shields the Christian against, or prevents him from knowing all that is properly human. So it follows that the supernatural virtues should influence the human virtues and make of the Christian a man who is honest, exemplary at work and with his family, filled with a sense of honour and justice. A man who stands out before other men by his style of conduct in which loyalty, truthfulness, resilience and joy shine forth ... *whatever is true, whatever is honourable, whatever is just, whatever is pure, whatever is lovely, whatever is gracious, if there is any excellence, if there is anything worthy of praise – think about these things,*[5] Saint Paul reminded the first Christians at Caesarea Philippi.

The Christian's life of faith leads him, therefore, to be a man who has human virtues, because he practises his faith in his ordinary activities. He will not only feel moved to make an act of faith as he sees the walls of a church in the distance, but he will turn to God to ask him for light and help when confronted with a problem at work or at home. He will know how to attune his thinking when he has to accept a setback, when faced with pain or sickness, when offering up some joy, when he continues, for love, the work that he was

---

[4] F. Suarez, *On being a Priest*
[5] Phil 4:8

about to abandon through tiredness. In the apostolate he will ask for the light of grace for those people he wants to take to the sacrament of Penance. He will have a truly supernatural outlook when there are no fruits to be seen because work is just starting on that soul and *The ploughshare that breaks up the earth and opens up the furrow sees neither the seed nor the harvest ...*[6] Faith has to be practised constantly, and hope, and charity ... Faced with problems and obstacles, perhaps already of long standing, Our Lord bids us *stretch out your hand* ... Faith is not a virtue to be practised just occasionally, during pious practices, but rather during sport, at the office, in the middle of traffic. Much less should faith be reserved, as some Christians seem to think, for a Sunday at the time of fulfilling the Sunday precept.

Today let us examine how often we put into practice the Christian ideal that gives shape to all we do, increases its value, *and gives a new meaning to all that is human*. It can transform literally everything we do into something supernaturally fruitful. Let us examine too how we live *supernatural outlook* in all our daily activities.

12.3 Faith and the human virtues.

Christian faith leads us to a complete amendment of our lives. It demands that we continually rectify our conduct, and constantly make an effort towards improvement in our way of being and behaving. Among other consequences, faith will lead us to imitate Jesus Christ, who was *perfect God and perfect man*.[7] It will lead us to be well-balanced men and women, without complexes or undue concern about what others will think of us. It will make us truthful, honest, just in our judgements and in our business dealings; in our conversations ... The human

---

[6] St. J. Escrivá, *Furrow*, 215
[7] *Athanasian Creed*

virtues are proper to man as man; they are precisely what makes a man manly, a woman womanly and this is why Jesus Christ, perfect man, lived them fully. Even his enemies were surprised at the sheer human strengths he had, of his strong manliness. *Teacher*, they said on one occasion, *we know that you are true and teach the way of God truthfully, and care for no man.*[8]

The first thing to attract our attention when we study the human features of Jesus is his manly clear-sightedness in action, his impressive loyalty, his unwavering sincerity; in a word, the heroic character of his personality. This was, in the first place, what attracted his disciples.[9] He gave us the example of a whole series of intertwined human qualities, which any Christian should live.

He considers the perfection of the human virtues so important that he admonishes his disciples: *If I have told you earthly things and you do not believe, how will you believe if I tell you heavenly things?*[10] If we do not have human resilience when confronted with a difficulty, or with heat, or cold, or a slight illness, on what will the cardinal virtue of fortitude be founded? How can a person who is continually grumbling and complaining acquire the virtue of fortitude and live it? How can a student, say, who keeps postponing getting down to study become responsible and prudent? How can someone live charity if he has little or no regard for human warmth, affability or the details of good manners? Although God's grace can completely transform someone, we find examples of this in Scripture and in the life of the Church, it is most usual for God to count on the contribution afforded by the human virtues.

Christian life is expressed through human action, which

---

[8] Matt 22:16
[9] K. Adam, *Jesus Christ*
[10] John 3:5

it dignifies and raises to the supernatural level. On the other hand, what is human in a person sustains and makes possible the supernatural virtues. Perhaps during the course of our lives we have met *so many people who call themselves Christian because they have been baptised and have received other sacraments, but then prove to be disloyal and deceitful, insincere and proud and ... in consequence fail to achieve anything. They are like shooting stars, lighting up the sky for an instant and then falling away to nothing.*[11] The human foundations failed them and they could not remain upright. The practice of faith, hope, charity and of the moral virtues will enable the Christian to be that living example the world expects of him. God looks for mothers who have the strength to bear Christian witness through their motherhood and their joy, mothers who know how to make friends with their children. He looks for honest businessmen; for doctors who do not neglect their professional formation, but learn to put aside some hours for study; who attend their patients with understanding, just as they would like to be treated themselves if they were in the same circumstances – efficiently and pleasantly. At the same time doctors should take an interest in their fellow professionals. God looks for similar commitment from farmworkers, craftsmen, factory workers, men on building sites ... God wants accomplished men and women who can express the great ideal they have discovered precisely through the ordinariness of their everyday lives.

In Saint Joseph we find a magnificent model of *'vir justus' – the just man*,[12] who lived by faith in all the circumstances of his life. Let us ask him to help us to be as Christ wants each one of us to be in our own environment and our own circumstances.

---

[11] St. J. Escrivá, *Friends of God*, 75
[12] Matt 1:19

13. GIVING GOOD DOCTRINE

13.1 A pressing need for this apostolate.

On numerous occasions the Gospels tell us that the crowds pressed in upon Our Lord so that He might cure them.[1] We read in the Gospel of today's Mass[2] that Jesus was followed by *a great multitude from Galilee; also from Judaea and Jerusalem and Idumea and from beyond the Jordan and from about Tyre and Sidon.* The crowd is so great that Our Lord tells his disciples to get a boat ready *lest they should crush him; for he had healed many, so that all who had diseases pressed upon him to touch him.* These people turn to Christ in their need. He attends to them because He has a compassionate and merciful heart. During the three years of his public life he has healed many people, he has freed those possessed by the devil, he has raised the dead ... But He did not heal all the sick people in the world, nor did He eliminate all the sufferings of this life, for *pain is not an absolute evil*, as sin is, and it can have an incomparable redemptive value, if we unite it to the sufferings of Christ.

Jesus performed miracles which, in specific cases, cured pain and suffering; but above all, his miracles were a sign and a proof of his divine mission, of universal and eternal redemption. As Christians we continue Christ's mission in time. *Go therefore and make disciples of all nations, baptising them ... and teaching them to observe all that I have commanded you; and lo, I am with you always,*

---

[1] cf Luke 6:19; 8:45 etc
[2] Mark 3:7-12

to the close of the age.[3] Before his Ascension into Heaven
He left us the treasure of his doctrine, the only doctrine that
saves, and the richness of the sacraments, so that we should
receive them in our search for supernatural life.

The masses of men are just as much in need today as
they were then. Now, too, we see them as *sheep without
shepherds*. They are confused and lost and do not know
which way to direct their lives. In spite of all the progress
made over these twenty centuries, mankind still has to
endure physical and moral suffering, but more than
anything else it suffers from a great ignorance of Christ's
doctrine, which the Magisterium of the Church has
preserved for us without error. Our Lord's words are still
the words of eternal life. They teach us to flee from sin, to
sanctify our ordinary life, our joys, our failures and
sicknesses ... and they open to us the way to salvation. This
is the great need the world has. And the crowds – we have
experienced it so often! – *want desperately to hear God's
message even though outwardly they may not show it.
Some perhaps have forgotten Christ's teachings. Others,
through no fault of their own, have never known them, and
think that religion is something extraneous. Of this we can
be sure, that in every man's life there comes a time, sooner
or later, when his soul feels frustrated and exhausted. He
has had enough of the usual explanations. The lies of the
false prophets no longer satisfy him. Even though they may
not admit it at the time, such people are longing to slake
their thirst for the truth with the teachings of Our Lord.*[4]
We have this treasure of doctrine in our hands. We are
meant to give it away *in season and out of season*,[5]
whether the time seems opportune or not, by every means

---

[3] Matt 28:19-20
[4] St. J. Escrivá, *Friends of God*, 260
[5] cf 2 Tim 4:2

at our disposal. This is the one really urgent task we have as Christians.

13.2 Formation in the truths of faith. Studying and teaching the Catechism. Handing on the truths that we receive.

If we are to give Christ's doctrine to others we have to have absorbed it into our understanding and hold it in our hearts. We have to meditate on it and love it. All Christians, each one according to the gifts he has received – talents, education, circumstances ... whatever they may be – need to use the means to acquire this doctrine. Sometimes this formation will begin by our learning *the Catechism* thoroughly. That book, *faithful to the essential truths contained in Revelation, and brought up to date regarding teaching methods, is capable of educating each new generation of Christians robustly in the faith,*[6] says St John Paul II.

The life of faith of an ordinary Christian often leads to a constant process of acquiring and transmitting the faith. *Tradidi quod accepi ... For I received from the Lord what I also delivered to you,*[7] Saint Paul said to the Christians at Corinth. The faith of the Church is a living faith, because it is constantly being received and handed on. From Christ to the Apostles; from the Apostles to their successors; and so, to our days. The Faith continues to resound, ever identical with itself, in the living Magisterium of the Church.[8] The doctrine of the Faith is *received and handed down* by the mother of a family, by a student, a business man, a secretary. What effective spokesmen and women Our Lord

---

[6] St John Paul II, Apostolic Exhortation, *Catechesis tradendae*, 16 October 1979
[7] cf 1 Cor 11:23
[8] cf P. Rodriguez, *Faith and Life of Faith*

would have if we Christians all decided (each one in his own place) to proclaim Christ's saving doctrine, as our brothers and sisters in the faith have done! *Go and teach* ... Christ himself says to every last one of us. We are talking about that spontaneous spreading of doctrine, perhaps carried out in an informal way but extraordinarily effective, as the first Christians did. Family with family, workers with their colleagues; neighbours with neighbours; parents with other parents at a particular school; in neighbourhoods; in market-places; in the streets of towns and cities, in technical colleges, in universities, in civic life. All locations become channels for a discreet and pleasant catechesis which penetrates deep into the customs of society, into men's lives and cultures. *Believe me, the apostolate of giving doctrine usually has to be, as it were, capillary, spreading from one to another, from each believer to his immediate companion.*

The children of God care about every soul there is, because every soul is important.[9] How moved God must be by those mothers who, often, with very little time at their disposal, patiently explain the truths of the catechism to their children ... and perhaps to the children of their neighbours and friends! Or by the student who treks across the city to explain those same truths – even though he is studying for an examination and needs to do well at it.

Now, when the doctrine of the Church is attacked in so many quarters and by such a variety of methods, we need, as Christians, to make up our minds to use every possible means to acquire a deep knowledge of the doctrine of Jesus Christ. We need to understand the implications these teachings have for contemporary society and for individuals. Loving God with deeds will often mean dedicating as much time as is required to this formation;

---

[9] St. J. Escrivá, *Furrow*, 943

study, the care we take over spiritual reading, paying close attention to the talks of formation we receive. We should make good use of the days we do not have to go to work, which give us more time for these activities. Loving God with deeds will mean knowing how to appreciate those truths which have their origin in Christ himself. We should think of them as a treasure that we have to love and meditate on frequently. Nobody gives what he does not have: to give doctrine we need to have it first.

13.3 Prayer and mortification must accompany all apostolate. We can overcome all obstacles with God's help.

As Christians we cannot remain unresponsive to so much ignorance and so many errors about Christ, his Church ... the most fundamental truths, for God has constituted us 'the salt of the earth' (Matt 5:13) and 'the light of the world' (Matt 5:14). Every Christian has to share in the task of Christian formation. He has to feel the urgency of evangelising, since 'that gives me no grounds for boasting. For necessity is laid upon me' (1 Cor 9:16).[10] Nobody can opt out of this urgent task. *The task of a Christian is to drown evil in an abundance of good. It is not a question of negative campaigns, or of being 'anti' anything. On the contrary, we should live positively, full of optimism, with youthfulness, joy and peace. We should be understanding with everybody, with the followers of Christ and with those who abandon him, or with those who have never known him at all. Understanding does not mean holding back, or remaining indifferent, but being active.*[11] We need to have initiative, to want everyone to see the lovable face of Christ.

---

[10] St John Paul II, *Address*, Granada, 15 November 1982
[11] St. J. Escrivá, *Furrow*, 864

As we become aware of this task of spreading the doctrine of Jesus Christ, we have to start by asking God to increase our faith: *fac me tibi semper magis credere*. Make me believe you ever more and more, we beg in the *Adoro te devote*, that Eucharistic hymn of Saint Thomas Aquinas. In this way we will be able to say, also in the words of the hymn:

I believe all the Son of God has spoken:
Than Truth's own word there is no truer token.

As our faith grows stronger we will prepare ourselves to be instruments in the hands of God, who grants light to minds dimmed by ignorance and error. Only God's grace can move the will to assent to the truths of faith. That is why, when we want to attract somebody to the Christian Faith, we have to accompany that apostolate with humble and constant prayer; and with that prayer, penance – mortification, perhaps in little details connected with our work, our family life ... but supernatural and specific.

When the environment is difficult and we come up against barriers or apparently insurmountable obstacles, we will be filled with optimism if we remember that God's grace can move even the hardest of hearts, that the greater the difficulties we encounter, the greater the supernatural help we will receive.

Lord, teach us to make you known! Today, too, the crowds have lost their way and need you. They are so often ignorant without the light to know which way to turn, which way to go. Holy Mary, help us not to waste a single opportunity of making your Son Jesus Christ known. Guide us so that we can make many other people long to carry out this noble task of spreading the truth!

SECOND WEEK: FRIDAY

14. A VOCATION TO HOLINESS

14.1 The vocation of the 'twelve'. It is God who calls, and who gives the grace to persevere.

After spending the whole night in prayer,[1] Jesus chose the twelve apostles to accompany him, and later to continue his mission on earth. The Evangelists recorded their names and today we recall them in the Gospel at Mass.[2] They have already been following the Master, with other disciples, along the roads of Palestine for several months, prepared to give themselves without limit. Now they become the object of a very special love.

By making this choice, Our Lord lays the foundations of his Church. These twelve men are like the twelve Patriarchs of the new People of God, his Church. This new People is not to be born according to the flesh, as the people of Israel had been, but to be born of the Spirit. How is it that these men came to enjoy such great favour in the sight of God? Why precisely was it these men and not others? It is no use wondering why they were chosen. It is simply that Our Lord called them, and it is as a result of this completely free selection by Christ, *He called to him those whom he desired*, that the honour and essence of their vocation comes into being. *You did not choose me*, He would say to them later, *but I chose you.*[3] The choice is always God's. The Apostles had not been noted for their wisdom, their influence, their importance ... they were very ordinary, normal men who responded with faith and

---

[1] cf Luke 6:12
[2] Mark 3:13-19
[3] John 15:16

generosity to Jesus' call.

Christ chooses his own, and this call is the only claim to a distinctive title they will receive. Saint Paul, for example, in order to emphasise by what authority he teaches and admonishes the faithful, often begins his *Letters* in this way: *This is by Paul, an apostle – not from men nor through men, but through Jesus Christ and God the Father*;[4] he wants to make it clear that he has been called and chosen to preach God's Gospel.[5] Saint Paul constantly reflects on this reality: he was chosen by God.

Jesus calls in a manner both imperious and gentle, just as Yahweh called and sent out his prophets: Moses, Samuel, Isaiah ... Those who were called never deserved in any way the vocation for which they were chosen, either because of their good behaviour or their personal qualities. Saint Paul was to say explicitly of those who were called: *He called us with a holy calling, not in virtue of our works but in virtue of his own purpose*.[6] In fact, God usually calls to his service and for his work people with virtues and qualities which are manifestly inadequate to the task they are to accomplish with God's help. *For consider your call, brethren: not many of you were wise according to worldly standards*.[7] Our Lord calls us also to continue his redemptive work in the world. We should not be surprised or discouraged by our weaknesses, or the lack of proportion between our abilities and the task God gives us to do. He always provides the increment; He asks only for our good will and the little help our hands are able to give him.

---

[4] Gal 1:1
[5] 2 Tim 1:9
[6] *ibid*
[7] 1 Cor 1:26

14.2 In fulfilling his vocation, man gives glory to God and discovers the true greatness of his life. Christ has called all of us to follow him, to imitate him and to bring other people to know him.

He called to him those whom He desired. A vocation is always, and above anything else, a choice on God's part, whatever the circumstances prevailing at the moment when we accepted that choice. This is why once a vocation has been received it should never be laid open to human scrutiny, assessment or approval. Human reasoning, which is frequently poor and short-sighted, is invariably incapable of fully understanding it. God always gives, along with a vocation, the grace we need to persevere in it, because, as Saint Thomas teaches, God prepares those He has chosen for a mission, and disposes them so that they are able to carry out what they were chosen to do.[8] In the fulfilment of this mission, man discovers the real greatness of his life, *because the divine call, and in the final instance, the revelation that God makes as to the mystery of a man's being, is a word that discloses the meaning and at the same time, the substance of a man's life. It is in hearing and accepting God's word that a man comes to understand himself, and thus his whole being acquires coherence ... Hence my most integral manliness, the most perfect honesty and coherence within my own being, come about through my commitment to God who calls.*[9] Fidelity to our vocation is fidelity to God, to the mission he entrusts us with and for which we have been created; it is our specific and personal way of giving glory to God.

A new life at the side of Christ started that day for *the twelve*. One of them, Judas, was not faithful, in spite of having been expressly chosen. The others, as the years

---

[8] cf St Thomas, *Summa Theologiae*, III, 27, 4

[9] P. Rodriguez, *Vocation, Work, Contemplation*, Pamplona, 1986

passed, would remember the moment they were chosen as the most important and transcendental moment of their lives. God wanted to use these men, even though none of them, from the human point of view, had the qualities required for a task with such far-reaching consequences. Nevertheless, they obeyed; they were docile; they received the grace they needed, and God looked after them in a very special way. Because of this they were to carry the message with which God had entrusted them *to the ends of the earth*.

In our day, too, Our Lord calls his apostles *to be with him* – in reception of the sacraments and a life of prayer, in intimate and profound conversation with him, in personal holiness – and he sends them out to preach *to do apostolate in all environments*. And, although the Master calls some individuals in a special way, the Christian life of every member of the faithful, however ordinary it may be, brings with it a unique vocation, an invitation to follow Christ into a new life to which He holds the key: *If any man would come after me ...*[10] The first Christians always considered their situation in life to be the condition and the fruit of a divine vocation. Those who had been baptised in Rome or Corinth would be *called to be saints*.[11]

In one way or another Christ has called all of us to follow him closely, to imitate him and to make him known to others. We are called, all of us, to follow him closely, to imitate him and to make him known to others. We are called to make the work of Redemption present in the world, *until He comes again. All Christians, no matter in what state or walk of life, are called to the fulness of a life in Christ, and to the perfection of love; by this holiness a more human manner of life is fostered also in earthly*

---

[10] Matt 16:24
[11] cf Rom 1:1-7; 2 Cor 1:1

society.[12]

This fulness of Christian life demands heroism in living all the virtues, and will be particularly noticeable in circumstances where the 'life-style', or the ambitions that many have proposed to themselves in life, are far from the Christian ideal. Our Lord wants us to be *holy*, in the strict sense of the word. Our holiness has to be cheerful and attractive, and it will draw others to an encounter with Christ. He gives us the necessary strength and help. These means that God gives all of us, so that we should follow him and be faithful to him, and which we would be rash to ignore or pay little heed to, are especially necessary when God calls us to an apostolic celibacy in the midst of secular tasks.

May we know how to tell Jesus often that he can count on us, on our good will and our determination to follow him, wherever we are, without setting any limits or conditions to our service.

14.3 Our faithfulness to the personal call that we have received from God.

The discovery of our personal vocation is the most important moment in our whole existence. Our happiness and the happiness of many others depends on our faithful response to this call. God creates us, He prepares us and He calls us according to a divine plan. *If there are so many Christians who today live aimlessly with little depth, and hemmed in on all sides by narrow horizons, it is due, above all, to their lack of any clear idea of why they, personally, exist ... What elevates a man and truly gives him a personality of his own is the consciousness of his vocation, the consciousness of his own specific task in the universe.*[13]

---

[12] Second Vatican Council, *Lumen gentium*, 40
[13] F. Suarez, *Mary of Nazareth*

Our first decision to follow Christ lays the foundation for many other responses throughout life. Fidelity is built up day by day, generally in things that might seem to have little transcendence – little relevance to a divine mission – such as the ordinary minor actions and duties of each day, as we repeatedly reject anything in them that we now see could damage the very essence of our life.

It is not sufficient merely to keep our vocation intact. It is necessary to renew it constantly and reaffirm it: when it seems easy, and at other times when everything seems frustratingly difficult, when the attacks of the devil, the world or the flesh make themselves felt and strike with all their power. We will always be given all the help we need in order to be faithful. The greater the difficulties, the more the grace. If we keep up a well-planned ascetical struggle – with a very specific *particular examination of conscience*, love grows and becomes stronger as time passes, and our self-surrender, far from turning into mere routine, becomes more conscious, more mature. *It is not a matter of growing in quantity, like a stack of hay; but in quality, as when heat becomes more intense, or as when science, without coming to new conclusions, becomes more penetrating, deeper, more unified, more certain. In the same way, charity inclines us to love God above all things, and our neighbour as ourselves, in a way which is more perfect, pure and intimate, so that we may give glory to God in time and in eternity.*[14] This is the growth that God asks of us.

If we make an effort to grow in holiness, in love for Christ and for all men for Christ's sake, we will ensure our faithfulness, and at the same time experience joy and increased charity; our life will be full of meaning.

Saint Paul used a comparison taken from the athletic games in the stadium to explain that the ascetical struggle

---

[14] R. Garrigou-Lagrange, *The Mother of the Saviour*

of a Christian has to be cheerful, and virtually a supernatural 'Olympic contest'. As the apostle considers that he has not yet reached perfection, he struggles to obtain the promised reward: *One thing I do, forgetting what lies behind and straining forward to do what lies ahead. I press on toward the goal for the prize of the upward call of God in Christ Jesus.*[15] From the moment that Christ entered his life as he was on his way to Damascus, he dedicated himself with all his strength to seek him, to love him and serve him. The Apostles did just the same from the day that Jesus passed by and called them. Their defects did not instantly disappear, but day by day they followed the Master with a friendship which grew steadily; and they were faithful. This is what we have to do. We must correspond each day with the graces we receive; we must be faithful every day. This is how we will reach the goal, where Christ is waiting for us.

---

[15] cf Phil 3:13-14

SECOND WEEK: SATURDAY

15. CHEERFULNESS

15.1 It is based on divine filiation.

When the world first issued from the Creator's hands, everything overflowed with goodness, which reached its culmination with the creation of man.[1] But evil came into the world with sin, and rooted itself like a weed in human nature. True joy, which is always united to goodness, came to earth fully on the day that Our Lady gave her consent, and the Son of God took flesh in her womb. A profound joy already reigned within her, because she had been conceived without original sin, and her union with God the Father, God the Son and God the Holy Spirit was complete. At her loving response to God's plans she became the cause of new happiness in the world. This is because Jesus Christ came to us through her. Christ the *full joy* of the Father, of the angels and of men, in whom God is well pleased.[2] Mary's mission, then and now, is to give Jesus, her Son, to us. This is why we call Our Lady *Cause of our Joy*.

A few weeks ago we contemplated the announcement made by the angel to the shepherds. *Be not afraid, for behold I bring you good news of a great joy which will come to all the people: ... this day in the city of David ...*[3] True joy, the joy that lasts in spite of all contradiction and pain, is the joy of those who encounter God in all sorts of different circumstances and then find it in them to follow him; it is the abundant joy of the old man, Simeon, as he

---

[1] cf Prov 8:30-31
[2] cf Matt 3:17
[3] Luke 2:10

holds the child Jesus in his arms.[4] It is the immense joy – *gaudio magno valde*[5] – of the Magi when they discover the new star that will lead them to Jesus, Mary and Joseph. It is the joy of all those people, who without expecting it, come face to face one day with Jesus. *Why did you not bring him?* the chief priests and the Pharisees asked the officers, who possibly were themselves arrested or lost their jobs for having disobeyed orders. *No man ever spoke like this man,*[6] they said. It is the happiness of Peter on Mount Tabor, *Master, it is well that we are here.*[7] It is the same spirit of joy that the downhearted disciples know again when they recognise Jesus ...[8] It is the tremendous joy the Apostles experience each time they see the risen Christ ...[9] In the midst of all this joy there is the joy of Mary: *My soul magnifies the Lord, and my spirit rejoices in God my saviour.*[10] She possesses Jesus fully and her joy is the greatest any human heart can contain.

Joy is the immediate consequence of a certain fulness of life. For the individual this fulness consists above all in knowledge and love.[11] Through his infinite mercy, God has made us his children in Jesus Christ, and sharers in his nature, which is exactly that – fulness of life: infinite knowledge, immense love. We cannot reach any greater joy than that which is based on being children of God through grace, a joy capable of being retained, and of persisting in spite of illness and failure: *Your hearts will rejoice*, Our Lord promised at the Last Supper, *and no one*

---

[4] cf Luke 2:29-30
[5] cf Matt 2:10
[6] John 7:46
[7] Mark 9:5
[8] cf Luke 24:13-35
[9] cf John 16:22
[10] Luke 1:46-47
[11] cf St Thomas, *Summa Theologiae*, II-II, 28, 4 *et seq*

will take your joy from you.[12] The closer we are to God, the
greater our share in his love and in his life. The more we
grow in divine filiation, the greater and more appreciable
will our joy be. Is the way I usually behave a cheerful one?
Is it positive and optimistic? Do I easily lose my
cheerfulness when setbacks and disappointments occur?
Do I often give in to gloomy thoughts?

15.2 The cross and cheerfulness. Causes of sadness. Remedies.

How different this true gladness is from a happiness
dependent on material well-being, on health (how fragile it
is!), on our moods (which change so easily!), on
temporarily not having any difficulties or lacking in the
things we need. We are children of God and nothing should
trouble us, not even death itself.

Saint Paul reminded the first Christians at Philippi of
the grounds they had for rejoicing: *Rejoice in the Lord
always*, he said. *Again I will say, rejoice.*[13] And straightaway he gave them the reason: *The Lord is at hand.* In the
midst of that difficult environment in which they are living,
always harsh and often violently aggressive, the Apostle
suggests to them the best remedy: *Rejoice!* This command
is still more admirable when we consider that when he
wrote this *Letter* he was shut up in prison. On another
occasion, in extraordinarily difficult circumstances, he was
to write, *I am filled with consolation. With all our
afflictions, I am overjoyed.*[14] If our joy is authentic, the
circumstances that surround us are never immutable or
conclusive, because our joy is founded on faithfulness to
God in carrying out our duty, and in embracing the Cross.

---

[12] John 16:22
[13] Phil 4:4
[14] 2 Cor 7:4

How is it possible to be cheerful when we are bowed down by sickness, when we see the threat of injustice or suffer its cruelty? Won't that cheerfulness be a deceptive illusion or an irresponsible means of escapism? No! It is Christ who gives us the answer – only Christ! Only in him do we find the true meaning of our own life and the key to human history. Only in him – in his doctrine, in his redeeming Cross whose salvific strength makes itself present in the sacraments of the Church – will you always find the vigour to make the world a better place, a happier place, a place more worthy of man who is God's image.

Christ on the Cross: this is the only authentic key. On the Cross, He accepts suffering in order to make us happy; and He teaches us that, united to him, we too can give a salvific value to our suffering, which is then turned into joy. It is the profound joy of offering sacrifice for the good of others and the joy of doing penance for our personal sins and the sins of the world. *In the light of Christ's Cross, therefore, there is no room for a fear of pain, because we understand that love is shown through pain: the truth of love, of our love for God and for all men.*[15]

In the Old Testament, God had already spoken through Nehemiah: *Do not be grieved,* said the prophet, *for the joy of the Lord is your strength.*[16] It is true. Joy is one of the most powerful allies we have to help us achieve victory.[17] It is an excellent remedy, a specific for all evils. We can only lose this great good by separating ourselves from God *by sin, by lukewarmness, by unwillingness to get to know God, by the selfishness of thinking about ourselves* or when we do not accept the Cross, which comes to us in so many

---

[15] Bl. A. del Portillo, *Homily during the Mass for participants in the Jubilee of Youth,* 12 March 1984
[16] Neh 8:10
[17] cf 1 Mac 3:2 *et seq*

different ways: as pain, sickness, failure, setbacks, compelled changes of plan, humiliations ... Gloominess does great harm to us and to those around us. It is a harmful plant that we must uproot as soon as it appears. *Delight your soul and comfort your heart; remove sorrow far from you, for sorrow has destroyed many, and there is no profit in it.*[18]

Whenever circumstances tend to be a cause of worry we can regain our joy if we know how to open our hearts: speak, give vent to what is oppressing the soul. Having recourse to prayer, or going with a contrite heart to Confession are the most effective ways of recovering our joy, especially if we have lost it through sin or through culpable carelessness in our relationship with God. The remedy lies in forgetting ourselves, and making sure we are not excessively concerned about our own affairs. In a word: humility. Humility is essential if we are to open ourselves to God as good children; this it is that forms the basis of all true joy. If we pray trustingly, which means that we talk confidently to God, we will learn to accept a particular disappointment which is perhaps the cause of our sadness. We will decide to open our soul in spiritual direction – to say what worries us – or to be generous in giving God what he asks of us and perhaps (through lack of clear vision) what we are finding it difficult to give Him.

15.3 The apostolate of cheerfulness.

The apostolate God asks of us is that of transmitting to others the joy of being close to him, and we find that this itself consists in a superabundance of supernatural and human joy. When this happiness *spills over into other men, it gives birth to hope, to optimism, to impulses to be generous in our daily toil, and spreads its welcome*

---

[18] Sir 30:23

contagion to the whole of society.

My children, said St John Paul II, *only if you have within you this divine grace, which is joy and peace, will you be able to construct something of value for men.*[19]

The family is a particularly important sphere in which we need to sow and spread great joy. The outstanding characteristic of our homes has to be the habitual smile (even though we may be tired or worried), together with optimistic warm-hearted behaviour which in its effect is like the 'pebble dropped into the lake',[20] which produces a widening, expanding circle, and then another still wider: we end up creating a pleasant atmosphere in which it is easy and natural for people to live in harmony with others, and in which, in an habitual way, a fruitful apostolate can be carried out with our children, our parents, our brothers, and sisters ... On the other hand, if our outlook on life is gloomy and pessimistic, our attitude cantankerous and intolerant, it separates us from people and from God, constantly creates new tensions and inevitably leads to a lack of charity. Saint Thomas, quoting Aristotle, says that *'no one can put up with the gloomy and disagreeable man all day long.' Thus a person is bound, by a certain natural debt in decency to get along amicably with others.*[21] The effort to rise above our introspective silences, our fatigue and our personal worries will always be a kind of mortification that is very pleasing to God.

We have to spread this cheerful, optimistic, smiling outlook, founded on our divine filiation, to our work, to our friends and our neighbours; we should extend it to those we may only briefly come across in the whole course of our life. We must pass it on to the customer we may never

---

[19] St John Paul II, *Address*, 10 April 1979
[20] cf St. J. Escrivá, *The Way*, 831
[21] St Thomas, *op cit*, II-II, 114, 2, 2

see again; to the patient, who once cured, will not want to
see the hospital any more; to that fellow who stops us in
the street to ask the way ... They will all take away from us
– their fleeting contact with us – a friendly smile and a
prayer to their Guardian Angel ... It is through a Christian's
cheerfulness that many will discover the path that leads to
God, which perhaps they might never have found in any
other way.

*Let us imagine the joyful gaze of Jesus, the same
ineffable look that would shine smiling from the eyes of his
Mother, who is unable to contain her joy: 'Magnificat
anima mea dominum!' Her soul glorifies the Lord, from
the moment she first carried him within her, till now and
forever.*

*O Mother, may ours, like yours, be the joy of being
always with him and having him close to us.[22] Today,
beside her, we make a sincere resolution: to make the way
lovable for others, and easy, since life brings enough
bitterness without our adding to it.[23]*

[22] St. J. Escrivá, *Furrow*, 95
[23] *ibid*, 63

THIRD SUNDAY: YEAR A

16. LIGHT IN DARKNESS

16.1 Jesus brings light to a world submerged in darkness. Faith illumines our whole life.

Dominus illuminatio mea et salus mea: quem timebo? The Lord is my light and my salvation, whom shall I fear?[1] These words of the *Responsorial Psalm* are a confession of faith and a manifestation of our certainty – faith in Our Lord, who is the Light of our lives, and certainty because it is in Christ that we find the strength we need to stick to our path each day. In the Creed which we say during Mass we refer to the Son of God as *Light from light.*

Mankind walked in darkness until Jesus was born in Bethlehem and a light shone on earth. Over these past weeks we have considered how Christ's brightness shone on Mary and Joseph, on the shepherds and the Magi. Then He, that *bright morning star*[2] hides himself for years in the little town of Nazareth and lives the normal life of his fellow countrymen. In fact He still continues to give light to men's lives, for in the years at Nazareth he has shown us, through his hidden life, that ordinary life can and should be sanctified. Now, after he has left Nazareth and has been baptised in the Jordan, he goes to Capharnaum to begin his public life.[3]

In today's Gospel, Saint Matthew reminds us of the prophecy of Isaiah which said that the Messiah would give light to the whole world. *The people who sat in darkness have seen a great light and for whose who sat in the region*

---

[1] Ps 26:1
[2] Rev 22:16
[3] cf St John Paul II, *Homily*, 25 January 1981

and shadow of death light has dawned.[4] Like a newly-risen sun, Jesus brings the radiance of truth to the world, and a supernatural clarity to minds which no longer want to remain in a state of darkness, ignorance and error.

Saint Matthew also tells us that once Christ had begun his public life, the first men to receive the powerful influence of this light were those disciples whom he called *as he walked by the Sea of Galilee.* The first were Simon and Andrew, who were fishermen: Jesus called them and *immediately they left their nets and followed him*; and then came two more brothers, James and John, who also left everything immediately and followed Jesus. *These men experienced the fascination of the hidden light that emanated from him, and they followed him without delay so that their path through life might shine with his brightness. But that light of Jesus shines out for everyone.*[5] He dispels our darkness and gives meaning to our lives; to our daily work, to our weariness, to our sorrows and our joys ...

The Gospels tell us how for many individuals, for whole crowds, the life of Jesus is like a story told to them of an unexpected meeting; we too sometimes find ourselves in the dark but know that the light can scarcely wait to break through.[6] We hear in the *First Reading* of the Mass that today, too, the prophecy of Isaiah is being fulfilled. *The people who walked in darkness have seen a great light; those who dwelt in a land of deep darkness, on them has light shined... Thou hast increased their joy; they rejoice before thee as with joy at the harvest, as men rejoice when they divide the spoil.*[7] It is the joy that comes

---

[4] Matt 4:16; cf Is 9:1-4
[5] St John Paul II, *ibidem*
[6] cf A. G. Dorronsoro, *Notes on the Virtue of Hope*, Madrid, 1974
[7] Is 9:2-3

from faith and which gives light to all our activities: it is the marvel of Jesus, who gives meaning to everything that happens to us and to everything we do.

16.2 As Christians we are *the light of the world*. Professional competence.

Jesus Christ, *the light of the world*,[8] first called some simple men from Galilee. He infused new light into their lives, won them over to his cause and asked them for an unconditional commitment. Those fishermen from Galilee emerged from the half-light of a flat, visionless existence and followed the Master, as others were to do after them. Since then, men and women have not ceased to follow him throughout the centuries. They have followed him to the point of giving their lives for him. We too follow him.

Our Lord is calling us now to come after him, and to enlighten men's lives and their now noble activities with the light of faith. We are well aware that faith in Jesus Christ, our Master and Lord, is the remedy for the many evils that afflict mankind. Without Christ men walk in darkness, so that they stumble and fall. The faith that we must communicate to others conveys light to the intelligence, a light incomparable; *outside the faith is darkness – natural darkness in the face of supernatural truth, and infranatural darkness, which is a consequence of sin.*[9]

Our words will take root in the hearts of our friends who have already seen the way we are doing things: starting our work on time; using our time well whilst studying or working; showing fortitude so as not to lose our serenity when hedged in by difficulties; helping our colleagues, as we often do, in little ways; practising the

---

[8] John 8:12
[9] St. J. Escrivá, *Letter*, 19 March 1967

human virtues proper to a Christian – optimism, warmth, resilience, loyalty to our firm and to our friends; never giving way to negative criticism or malicious gossip. A Christian will not be consistent with his faith if he does not endeavour to be competent at his work; still less will he be consistent with it if he acts in any way contrary to justice in his relationships with others at work and in his attitude towards individuals or society.

So that we can take the light of faith into our own environment, we need to know the authentic teaching of the Church and to have good formation as regards matters of topical importance, which affect people according to their particular profession. We need this formation if we are to create a social order which is just, and which fosters the dignity and rightful freedoms of the human person. Putting Christ's doctrine into practice has specific consequences in the lives of those who desire to be good Christians. It can well happen that the generosity and justice we try to bring to our work will be at variance in a more or less open fashion with the way our colleagues do things, or simply with the selfishness and general atmosphere of comfort-seeking prevalent at a given moment. Our Lord asks each of his disciples to show fortitude and courage in being really faithful to the truth, because in this way He will help many to reconsider their particular behaviour and the meaning they give to their lives. It is good to recall Saint Paul's warning to the Christians at Corinth: *We preach Christ crucified, a stumbling block to the Jews and folly to the Gentiles.*[10] Christ's message will always clash with the views of a society that has grown sick through a surfeit of materialism and whose attitude to life is one of conformity and of comfortable well-being.

Viriliter age. Be strong and let your heart take

---

[10] 1 Cor 1:23

courage.[11] We can ask ourselves today whether people notice the consistency of our lives and the good example we give through our work, or through our study if we are students. This good example should be the result of the courage that is given us by the Holy Spirit. We can ask ourselves whether we are known for the way we practise the human and supernatural virtues each day, and for the way we have been fulfilling the corporal and spiritual works of mercy.

16.3 Doctrinal formation and interior life are necessary to sanctify earthly realities.

Our Lord calls each one of us to be *the light of the world,*[12] and that light must not be kept hidden. *We are lamps which have been lit with the light of truth.*[13] Our knowledge of Christ's doctrine should be appropriate to our level of education, to our age, to the level of our responsibility for young people, the environment and the society in which we live. We must therefore strive to acquire a deep knowledge of this doctrine if we are to teach it to other people, and if it is to be the guiding light of our own lives. We should have a very precise knowledge of the duties of justice that affect our particular work, and of the demands made by charity, which go even beyond the demands of justice. We should be constantly aware of the good that we have the opportunity of doing, and actually be doing it; we should be equally aware of the evil that could result from a particular way of behaving, as well as avoiding it. We have to admit that on occasion we need to ask for advice so that we can afterwards act with the personal responsibility of a good Christian who is at the

---

[11] Ps 26:14
[12] Matt 5:14
[13] St Augustine, *Commentary on St John's Gospel*, 23, 3

same time a good citizen. We have to behave in a faithful and responsible way towards our family, towards our work and our study.

Our Lord has deposited the treasure of his Faith in his Church. We should shape our course by her Magisterium, just as ships shape their course by the lighthouse, looking towards it in order to find light and guidance for the many problems that have a bearing on salvation and on the very dignity of the human person. As Christians who live within the general framework of society we have to sanctify ourselves *in and through* our work. We need to have a very good grasp of the principles of professional ethics and apply them to our work, even though we may find our criteria demanding and difficult when we have to put them into practice.

You need interior life and doctrinal formation. Be demanding on yourself! As a Christian man or woman, you have to be the salt of the earth and the light of the world, for you are obliged to give good example with holy shamelessness. The charity of Christ should urge you on. Feeling and knowing yourself to be another Christ from the moment you told him that you would follow him, you must not separate yourself from your equals – your relatives, friends and colleagues – any more than you would separate salt from the food it is seasoning. Your interior life and your formation include the piety and the principles a child of God must have in order to give flavour to everything by his active presence there. Ask the Lord that you may always be that good seasoning in the lives of others.[14]

We turn too to Our Lady. We ask her for the fortitude and simplicity to live like the first Christians in the middle of the world without being worldly, and to be the light of Christ within our profession and environment.

---

[14] St. J. Escrivá, *The Forge*, 450

17. DETACHMENT TO FOLLOW CHRIST.

17.1 The disciples follow Christ *leaving all things* to do so.

Today's Gospel tells us how Christ called four of his disciples: they were Peter, Andrew, James and John.[1] These four were fishermen and they were at their work casting their nets, or mending them, at the moment when Jesus passed by and called them. These Apostles had already met Our Lord[2] and had felt profoundly attracted to him and to his doctrine. The call they now received was final: *Follow me and I will make you into fishers of men.* Jesus sought them out at their work and he drew on their occupation, as fishermen to choose a simile by which to tell them what their new mission in life was to be.

Those fishermen *immediately* left everything in order to follow the Master. We know too that Saint Matthew – *relictis omnibus* – left everything, *and got up and followed him.* We see each one of the Apostles doing the same when Christ seeks him out in his own particular circumstances.

If we are to follow Christ, our soul has to be free from any attachments: from love of self in the first place; from an excessive concern for our health or for the future... from riches and material goods. When the heart is set upon and filled with concern for earthly goods, there is no room in it for God. God will ask of some people an absolute renunciation, so that they can be completely at his disposal. He asked this of the Apostles; He asked it of the rich young

---

[1] Mark 1:14-20
[2] John 1:35-42

man,[3] as He has done of so many men and women throughout the centuries. These people have found in him their treasure and their riches. Christ demands of everyone who really wants to follow him *an effective detachment* from self and from everything he possesses. If this detachment is real, it will manifest itself in many aspects of ordinary life, for since the created world is good, the heart tends to attach itself in a disordered fashion to people and to things. This is why the Christian needs to be constantly on the watch, and to examine himself frequently, so as not to allow creatures or created things to stand in the way of his union with God, but rather to let them become a means of loving and serving him. *Hence, let them all see to it that they guide their affections rightly*, admonishes the Second Vatican Council; *otherwise, they will be thwarted in the search for perfect charity by the way they use earthly possessions, and by a fondness for riches which goes against the gospel spirit of poverty. The Apostle has sounded the warning: 'let those who make use of this world not get bogged down in it, for the structure of this world is passing away'* (cf 1 Cor 7:31).[4] These words of Saint Paul to the Christians at Corinth, taken from the Second Reading of today's Mass, are an invitation to us to place our heart in what is eternal, in God.

The renunciation God asks of us has to be effective and specific. As Jesus was to say later, it is impossible *to serve God and mammon.*[5] If we are able to give up our life for Christ, with how much greater reason should we give up transient goods, which, after all, last only a short time and are of little value.

---

[3] Mark 10:21
[4] Second Vatican Council, *Lumen gentium*, 42
[5] Luke 16:13

17.2 Some details of Christian poverty and detachment.

Christian detachment has nothing to do with disdain for material goods, if they are acquired and used in accordance with God's will. Rather it has to do with making that counsel of Our Lord's a reality in our own lives: *Seek first his kingdom and righteousness, and all these things shall be yours as well.*[6] We will discover that the more we struggle to detach ourselves completely from things, the greater will be our capacity to love others and to appreciate the goodness and beauty of creation.

If we allow our heart to become lukewarm, and share our love of God with a love of things; if we seek comfort and self-satisfaction, we will soon find that we have dislodged Christ from our heart, and that we have been taken prisoner by material things which will then be nothing but a source of harm to us. We must not forget that as a result of original sin we are all powerfully influenced by a yearning for an easy, comfortable life. We all dream of having power, and we all worry in greater or less degree about our future. As well as these tendencies, which exist in every heart, there is an urge to make a headlong rush, which seems to be spreading more and more in the society in which we live, to possess and enjoy material goods as though they were the most important thing in life. We can observe everywhere an obvious tendency, not to a legitimate standard of comfort, but to downright luxury, to not depriving ourselves of any pleasure at all. It is a serious pressure to which we are all subject nowadays, and which we cannot afford to ignore or forget about, if we really want to be free of those chains in order to follow Christ and to be living examples of the virtue of temperance, in the midst of that society that we must bring to God. Sheer abundance and the possession of material goods will never

---

[6] Matt 6:33

bring happiness to the world; the human heart will find the fulness for which it was created only in its God and Lord. If we do not act with the fortitude we need to live this detachment, we will find that *The heart is left sad and unsatisfied. It starts following paths which lead to everlasting unhappiness and ends up, even in this world, a slave, the victim of the very same goods which had perhaps been acquired at the cost of great effort and countless renunciations.*[7]

Christian poverty and detachment have nothing in common with squalor and slovenliness, with neglect and bad manners. Jesus dressed well. His cloak, probably woven by his Mother, had dice thrown for it because *it was without seam, woven from top to bottom;*[8] and it had a fringe.[9] We can see how in Simon's house He notices the lack of ordinary good manners, and how he upbraids Simon for not having offered him water to wash his feet, for not greeting him with the kiss of peace, and for not having anointed his head with oil... [10] The house where the Holy Family lived would have been modest, clean, simple, tidy, cheerful, with everything in good repair. It was a place where one would have liked to be. There would often probably be some flowers there or a tastefully-placed memento or decoration.

The poverty of a Christian who has to sanctify himself in the middle of the world is closely related to the work by which he lives and supports his family. For a student, poverty is implicit in serious study and in the good use of his time. The student should realise that by receiving this opportunity to continue his education, he contracts a debt

---

[7] St. J. Escrivá, *Friends of God*, 118
[8] John 19:23
[9] Matt 9:20; 14:36
[10] Luke 7:36-50

towards society and his family; he should be aware that he has a duty to prepare himself competently to be useful. A mother's poverty is intimately linked to the care of the home, to order and cleanliness. She should make sure that things last. Her poverty will consist in prudent saving, which will lead her to be thrifty and to avoid any personal whims; it will make her consider the quality of the goods she buys and this will often mean going round several shops to compare prices. As for her children, they will be grateful for having been brought up with a certain austerity, which is appreciated by the senses and does not need long explanations when they have seen it evidenced and exemplified in their parents' lives. This is equally valid when the family is well-to-do. Parents bequeath to their children a splendid inheritance when they show them that work is the best and most reliable capital; they leave them a fortune when they show them the value of things, when they teach them to spend money wisely and at the same time to keep in mind the needs of the many people who suffer on earth; the most munificent legacy is to teach them to be generous.

17.3 Almsgiving and detachment from material goods.

Effective detachment from things demands sacrifice. Any detachment which is not hard is not real. Christian life is such that it calls for a radical change in attitude towards earthly goods. We must acquire them and use them not as an end in themselves, but as a means of serving God, the family and society. The objective of a Christian is not *to accumulate more and more* but *to love Christ more and more* through his work and his family, as well as through material goods. The generous concern for the needs of others shown by the first Christians,[11] and which Saint Paul

---

[11] cf Acts 2:44-47

taught the faithful of the communities he had founded, will always be an example that will continue to remain in force. A Christian will never be able to rest indifferent to the spiritual or material needs of other people, and he will do all he can to alleviate their needs and find solutions to their problems. Sometimes it will be by contributing financially, at others by giving his time to good works, knowing that the rendering of this service is not confined to supplying the wants of the saints (his other brothers and sisters in the faith), but also overflows in all directions in many acts of thanksgiving to God.[12]

Generosity in giving alms to people in need, or as contributions to good works, has always been a manifestation, although not the only one, of real detachment from material goods and of the spirit of evangelical poverty. Almsgiving consists not merely in giving what we find superfluous, but more particularly in making personal sacrifices, in voluntarily undergoing some genuine privation. This particular offering, made, say, by sacrificing that very thing we perhaps thought we could not do without is very pleasing to God. Almsgiving proceeds from a merciful heart and *is more useful for the one who practises it than for the one who receives it, for the man who makes a practice of almsgiving draws out a spiritual profit from his acts, whilst those who receive his alms receive only a temporal benefit.*[13]

In the same way as he invited the Apostles to follow him, Our Lord has invited each one of us, wherever we find ourselves, to follow him. If we are to respond to that call of his we must be punctilious in determining whether we too have *left all things,* even though in fact we have to

---

[12] 2 Cor 9:12
[13] St Thomas, *Commentary on the Second Epistle to the Corinthians,* 8, 10

go on making use of them. We should examine ourselves to see whether we are generous with what we have and use. Are we detached from our precious time? From our health? Do our friends know us as people who habitually live sobriety? Are we generous in almsgiving? Do we avoid incurring expenses which are only a matter of frivolity, vanity or comfort-seeking? Do we look after the things we use; our books, our tools, our clothes? We should ask ourselves, in a word, whether our desire to follow Christ is accompanied by the necessary detachment from things; is our detachment real? Does it find expression in specific deeds? Jesus passes close by us too. Let us make sure we are not giving up the chance of a deeper union with Christ for the sake of a few trifles – for what Saint Paul calls *rubbish*[14] – for nothing but junk.

---

[14] Phil 3:8

THIRD SUNDAY: YEAR C

18. DOCTRINAL FORMATION

18.1 The 'Reading of the Gospel'.

The first Reading of today's Mass[1] makes claim on our emotion as it narrates the return of the Chosen People to Israel after so many years of exile in Babylon. Once they reach Jewish soil, the priest Ezra, explains to the people the content of the Law that they had forgotten during the years spent in *a foreign land.* He read from the sacred book *from early morning until midday.* His audience stood and followed the teaching attentively and *all the people wept.* Their response is a lament compounded with joy as they hear God's Law once more, and with grief also because their previous neglect of the law had brought about their exile.

When we gather together to take part in the Holy Mass we stand, in an attitude of watchfulness, to hear the Good News that the Gospel always brings us. We have to listen to it with a disposition which is at once attentive, humble and grateful because we know that God is speaking to each one of us in particular. *We should hear the Gospel* writes St Augustine, *as if Our Lord were present and speaking to us. We must not say 'happy were those who could see him', for many of those who saw him crucified him; and many of those who have not seen him have believed in him. The very words that came from Our Lord's lips were written down and kept and preserved for us.*[2]

We can only love someone we know. In order to get to know Christ many Christians dedicate some minutes each

---

[1] Neh 8:2-6; 8-10
[2] St Augustine, *Commentary on St John's Gospel,* 30

day to reading and meditating on the Gospels. This practice leads us by the hand, as it were, to the knowledge and contemplation of Jesus Christ. It teaches us to see him as the Apostles saw him, to observe his reactions, to watch the way he behaved and listen to his words which were always filled with wisdom and authority. The Gospels show him to us on some occasions moved with compassion at the plight of people in misery. At other times they show him full of understanding for sinners, or firm with the Pharisees who are presenting a false image of their religion. He is full of patience with those disciples who so often do not grasp the meaning of his words.

It would be very difficult to love Jesus Christ, to get to know him really well, if we did not frequently hear the Word of God, if we did not attentively read part of the Gospel each day. That reading – perhaps lasting only a few minutes – nourishes and increases our piety.

At the end of each Reading of Sacred Scripture the priest says, *This is the Gospel of the Lord*, and the faithful reply, *Praise to you, Lord Jesus Christ*. How is it we praise him? Our Lord is not satisfied with our bare words; *Show me*, he says. He wants to be praised with deeds. We cannot run the risk of forgetting God's law, of allowing the teaching of the Church to remain in us as little more than truths which are diffuse and inoperative, or of which we have a merely superficial knowledge. To us this would mean an exile far more devastating than that of Babylon. God's greatest enemy in the world is ignorance, *the cause, and, as it were, the root of all the evils that poison entire nations and perturb many souls*. [3]

We know well that the one great evil that afflicts so many Christians is the lack of doctrinal formation. What is graver still is that many people are turned astray by error, a

---

[3] St John XXIII, Encyclical, *Ad Petri cathedram*, 29 June 1959

sickness even more serious than ignorance. What a pity if we, because we lack the necessary doctrine, cannot show Christ to them and give them the light they need in order to understand his teaching!

18.2 A Christian's formation continues throughout his life. The need for good formation.

In today's Mass we read the beginning of the Gospel according to Saint Luke,[4] who tells us he has resolved to write down the life of Christ so that we may know the truth of the teachings we have received. Each of us, according to the unique circumstances of his life, has the obligation to know Christ's doctrine in depth. This obligation lasts for as long as our path here on earth shall continue. *The growth of the Faith and of the Christian life, even more in the adverse context within which we are living, needs from us a positive effort and the continuous exercise of our personal liberty. This effort begins when we have come to see our faith as the most important thing in our lives. From this consideration is born an interest in knowing and practising all that is contained in our faith in God. This leads us to want to follow Christ throughout the complex and changing context of the reality of daily life.*[5] We must never allow ourselves to think we have had sufficient formation. We must never be satisfied with the amount of knowledge about Jesus Christ and his teaching that we have so far acquired. Love always seeks to know the beloved better. In professional life, doctors, say, or architects or lawyers, though they may be good at their profession never think they have finished studying once they have qualified: they go on learning – always. And so it is with the Christian. We can apply Saint Augustine's

---

[4] Luke 1:1-14; 4:14-21
[5] Spanish Episcopal Conference, *Witnesses to the living God*, 28 June 1985

maxim to doctrinal formation: *Did you say, 'enough'? You have perished.*[6]

The quality of the instrument – for that is what we all are, instruments in God's hands – can improve, it can develop new possibilities. Each day we can love a little more and give better example. But we will not achieve this if our understanding is not continually nourished by sound doctrine. *I cannot say how often I have been told that some old Irishman saying his rosary is holier than I am, with all my study. I daresay he is. For his own sake, I hope he is. But if the only evidence is that he knows less theology than I, then it is evidence that would convince neither him nor me. It would not convince him, because all those rosary-loving, tabernacle-loving old Irishmen I have ever known ... were avid for more knowledge of the faith. It does not convince me, because while it is obvious that an ignorant man can be virtuous, it is equally obvious that ignorance is not a virtue; men have been martyred who could not have stated a doctrine of the Church correctly, and martyrdom is the supreme proof of love: yet with more knowledge of God they would have loved him more still.*[7]

The so-called *plain man's faith* ('I believe it all, even though I don't know what it is') is not sufficient for a Christian in the world who is confronted each day by confusion and a lack of light regarding Christ's doctrine – the only doctrine that saves – and is daily encountering ethical problems, both new and old, at work, in his family life, and in the environment in which he lives.

A Christian needs to have the answers which enable him to counter the attacks of the enemies of the Faith, and to know how to present them in an attractive way, (nothing being gained by over-reaction, heated argument or bad

---

[6] St Augustine, *Sermon 169*, 18
[7] F. J. Sheed, *Theology for Beginners*, Sheed and Ward, London

humour), with clarity (without watering down important issues) and with precision (without sounding hesitantly uncertain.)

The *plain man's faith* can perhaps save the old Irishman in question, but in other Christians ignorance of the content of the faith generally means a lack of faith, it means negligence, a lack of love. *Ignorance is often the daughter of laziness,*[8] Saint John Chrysostom used to repeat. It is most important in the struggle against a widespread lack of faith to have, as near as possible, a precise and complete knowledge of Catholic theology. This is why *any child well instructed in the Catechism is, without realizing it, a true missionary.*[9] If we study the Catechism which is a true compendium of the Faith, and undertake the reading we are advised to do in spiritual direction, we will be able to combat the ignorance and error rife in so many places, and among so many people, and which can lay the way open to many false doctrines and teachers of error.

18.3 Spiritual reading.

It takes time and persistence to acquire good formation. Continuity helps us to understand and to incorporate, to make our own, the doctrine that is presented to our understanding. If we are to achieve this, we have first of all to ensure that the right channels are open for sound doctrine to be transmitted and received. We have to pay sufficient attention to our own formation, convinced of the transcendental importance of what we are about. We must make sure we undertake our *spiritual reading* in accordance with a well-directed plan. In this way

---

[8] St John Chrysostom, *Catena Aurea*, III, p 78
[9] St J. H. Newman, *Sermon on the inauguration of St. Bernard's Seminary*, 3 October 1873

knowledge builds up gradually in our soul.

It has been said that in order to cure a sick person it is enough to be a good doctor; it is not necessary for the physician to contract the same disease. Nobody should be *so ingenuous as to think that if he wants to have theological formation he needs to try all types of potions, even though they may be poisonous. This is a matter of common sense, not only of supernatural sense, and the experience of each one can corroborate it with many examples.*[10] For this reason asking for advice about reading is an important part of the virtue of prudence, very especially if it is a question of theological or philosophical books, which can radically affect our formation and even our faith itself. How important it is to be right about books! It is still more important to consult our spiritual director about books specifically destined to aid the formation of our soul.

If we are constant; if we are diligent in the matter of using the means by which we receive good doctrine (spiritual reading, study circles, classes of formation, spiritual direction ...), we will find, almost without realizing it, that we have been amassing a great interior richness that little by little we will be able to incorporate into our lives. We will find as well that, to other people, we are like the labourer who approaches the ploughed field with a basket full of seed, for what we receive is something useful not only for our own souls but also for transmitting to others. Seed is wasted when it does not eventually bear fruit, and the world is an immense ploughed furrow in which Christ wants us to sow his doctrine.

---

[10] cf P. Rodriguez, *Faith and Life of Faith*

THIRD WEEK: MONDAY

19. JUSTICE IN OUR SPEECH AND IN OUR JUDGEMENTS

19.1 'Sins of the tongue.' If you can't praise, say nothing.

Those who were simple at heart were amazed at Our Lord's miracles and at his preaching. Others did not want to believe in Christ's divinity, even though they saw with their own eyes the most marvellous things happening. Here is an instance. Our Lord had just cast out a devil, Saint Mark tells us in the Gospel of today's Mass.[1] While the people were absolutely astonished at what He had done,[2] *the Scribes who came down from Jerusalem said, 'He is possessed by Beelzebub, and by the prince of demons he casts out the demons.'* When people are not well-disposed they are apt to interpret God's works as the works of the devil. Everything can be confused in the absence of rectitude of conscience! At the height of their blindness the enemies of Jesus even say of him that *He has an unclean spirit.*[3] They say this of him who is holiness itself!

For love of God and of his neighbour, for love of justice, in a world where so much abuse is the result of idle words, a Christian must be *just* in what he says. *A man has a right to a good name, to respect, esteem, and the honour that he has merited. The more we know a man, the more we discover his personality, his character, his intelligence and his heart. At the same time we become more aware ... of the criterion by which we can 'measure him' and what it*

---

[1] Mark 3:22-30
[2] cf Luke 11:14
[3] Mark 3:30

means to be just towards him.[4] Often an unbridled tongue, *thoughtlessness in action and speech*, is a clear proof of *scatter-brained ideas; superficiality.*[5] It is a manifestation of a lack of interior depth and presence of God. How many injustices can be committed by pronouncing irresponsible judgements on the behaviour of people who live, work and come into contact with us! The Apostle Saint James wrote that the tongue can become an *unrighteous world.*[6]

Every person has a right to his good name so long as he has not proved by acting unworthily in a public and notorious manner that he does not deserve it. Calumny, slander, malicious gossip ... constitute seriously unjust assaults against our neighbour; *a good name is to be chosen rather than great riches,*[7] for by losing it, a man becomes incapable of doing much of the good that he could otherwise have achieved.[8] The most frequent cause of defamation, of negative criticism and slander, is envy, which cannot tolerate the good qualities of others, the prestige or success of persons or of institutions.

People are also guilty of slander when they co-operate in its propagation by the printed word, or by means of any of the mass media. They can do this by echoing and giving publicity to words that have been spoken privately; or else they can bring about similar results through their silence, as, for example, when they fail to come to the defence of an injured party. Silence often adds up to giving approval to what has been said. Defamation is possible through half-hearted 'praising' if the good done is unjustly diminished. On other occasions, commenting on unfounded rumours is a real injustice against the good name of another. When

---

[4] St John Paul II, *Address*, 8 November 1978
[5] cf St. J. Escrivá, *The Way*, 17
[6] James 3:6
[7] Prov 22:1
[8] cf St Thomas, *Summa Theologiae*, II-II, q73, a2

defamation is spread through magazines, newspapers, the radio, television etc. its diffusion is vastly increased. Hence its gravity. Not only do individuals have a right to their honour and good name, but so also do institutions. Any defamation of the latter has the same gravity as similar defamation committed against individuals, and sometimes this gravity is increased because of the consequences that public loss of reputation may have on the discredited institutions.[9]

We can ask ourselves today in our prayer whether, in the environment in which we live (family, work, friends ...), we are known as people who never speak badly of anyone, and whether we really live at all times in accordance with that wise piece of advice, *If you can't praise, say nothing.*[10]

19.2 We should not be hasty in our judgements. Our love for truth will lead us to seek the truth. We will contribute to truthfulness in the media by using the means at our disposal.

We must ask Our Lord to teach us to say the right thing and not use empty words: to speak at the right moment and with due moderation; to know how to say what is necessary and to respond with the most opportune reply; *not to converse with torrents of words and not to allow the words that spring to mind to fall like hail, through speaking impetuously.*[11] This is unfortunately something that occurs frequently in many a situation.

We will give good example in this aspect of charity and justice if, with the help of grace, we maintain an interior awareness or climate of presence of God through-

[9] F. Fernandez Carvajal, *Anthology of Texts* see: Defamation
[10] St. J. Escrivá, *op cit*, 443
[11] St Gregory of Nyssa, *Homily: On the poor who are to be loved*

out the day, avoiding or promptly averting negative judgements. Justice and charity are virtues that we must live, first of all, in our hearts, for *out of the abundance of the heart the mouth speaks.*[12] There, within ourselves, is where we need habitually to sustain an atmosphere of understanding for others, avoiding narrow-mindedness and meanness, for *many persons, even those who think themselves Christians, act in this same way. Their first impulse is to think badly of someone or something. They don't need any proof; they take it for granted. And they don't keep it to themselves; they air their snap judgements to the winds.*[13]

Our love for justice has to lead us never to jump to conclusions or form hasty judgements about people or events, based on merely superficial information. We need to uphold a sound critical spirit towards information which may be tendentious or quite simply incomplete. Very often objective facts are wrapped up in personal opinions. We must realise that when it is a question of news about the Faith, the Church, the Pope, the Bishops, etc., its import can be radically distorted if it is reported by people who are without faith or have a sectarian bias.

Our love for the truth should put us on our guard against the dangers of a comfortable conformity. It should lead us to be discerning, to flee from partial simplifications, to leave sectarian channels of information to one side, to reject the ominous 'people say ...', to look for the truth always and to contribute positively to giving people the right information. We should send letters to the press in order to clarify ideas. We can direct our attention to some partial or sectarian piece of information so as to put the topic into proper perspective in the circle of people we come in contact with each day. We can put such things

---

[12] Matt 12:34
[13] St. J. Escrivá, *Christ is passing by*, 67

right in a correct and positive way. Of course we should
never contribute – even with a single penny – to the
support of any newspaper, magazine or bulletin that
offends in this way. If all Christians were to act like this,
we would soon change the situation of confusion which in
many countries causes or permits the dignity of human
beings to be abused.

Let us begin by being just in our own judgements and
in what we say. We should do all we can to see this virtue
lived around us, without allowing calumny, slander or
defamation to creep in for any reason. A clear
manifestation that we are indeed just, and that we love
truth is for us to be prepared to rectify our opinion –
publicly if need be – if we realise that, in spite of our good
intentions, we have made a mistake, or have since acquired
new facts which oblige us to revise an earlier opinion.

19.3 Respect for privacy.

It is a fact that anyone whose sight is distorted sees
objects as though they were deformed. The eyes of the soul
can be similarly affected. Anyone who has this kind of
spiritual myopia will see twisted and obscure intentions
where there are only desires to serve God, or else will see
in others defects which in fact are really his own. Saint
Augustine had advice on this point: *Try to acquire the
virtues which you believe lacking in your brothers,* he said.
*Then you will no longer see their defects, because you will
no longer have them yourselves.*[14] Let us fervently ask Our
Lord to let us see always, and in the first place, what is
good – which is a lot – in the people around us. In this way
we will find it easy to forgive their mistakes and help them
more effectively to overcome them.

To live justice in speech and judgements also means to

---

[14] St Augustine, *Commentary on Psalm 30*

respect another's privacy. We need to protect it from the curious gaze of outsiders, and not divulge in public what should remain within the domain of the family or the small circle of friendship. It is a basic right that we frequently see infringed or denied. *It would be no trouble at all to point out present-day cases of an aggressive curiosity which pries morbidly into the private lives of others. A minimum of justice demands that, even when actual wrong-doing is suspected, an investigation of this sort be carried out with caution and moderation, lest mere possibility be converted into certainty. And it is clear that an unhealthy eagerness to perform post-mortems on actions that are not illicit but positively good should be ranked under the heading of perversion.*

Faced with traders in suspicion who prey on the private lives of others, we must defend the dignity of every person, his right to peace. All honest men, Christians or not, agree on the need for this defence, for a common value is at stake: the legitimate right to be oneself, to avoid ostentation, to keep within the family its joys, sorrows and difficulties.[15]

'Sancta Maria, Sedes Sapientiae' – Holy Mary, Seat of Wisdom'. Invoke Our Mother often in this way, so that she may fill her children, in their study, work and social relations, with the Truth that Christ has brought to us.[16]

---

[15] St. J. Escrivá, *Christ is passing by*, 69
[16] *idem, Furrow*, 607

THIRD WEEK: TUESDAY

20. THE WILL OF GOD

20.1 Our Lady and fulfilment of God's Will. Christ's 'new family'.

In today's Gospel, Saint Mark tells us[1] that the mother of Jesus came with some relatives asking for him, whilst He was speaking to a great number of people. Perhaps because of the crowd, which must have filled the house to overflowing, she remained outside and sent a message in to her Son. Then Jesus replied, *'Who are my mother and my brethren?' And looking round on those who sat about him, He said, 'Here are my mother and my brethren! Whoever does the will of God is my brother, and sister, and mother.'* This is Christ's new family, with ties that are stronger than ties of blood, and to which Mary belongs in a most eminent way, because nobody ever carried out God's will with greater love and perfection than she did.

Our Lady is united to Jesus by a double bond. First of all because, when she accepted the Angel's message, she united herself intimately to God's will in a way we can scarcely comprehend. At the same time she acquired a spiritual motherhood over the Son whom she conceived so that she was bound still more closely to that family which Jesus has now proclaimed in the presence of his disciples. Saint Augustine has pointed out that *Maternity according to the flesh would have been of little avail to Mary, if she had not first conceived Christ, in a still more fortunate way, in her heart, and only afterwards in her body.*[2] Mary becomes the mother of Jesus when she conceives him in

---

[1] Mark 3:31-35
[2] St Augustine, *On Holy Virginity*, 3

her womb, is his mother when she looks after him, feeds and protects him, just as every mother does with her child. But Jesus came to establish the great family of the children of God and *Benignly included in it Mary herself, for she did the will of the Father ... and when He spoke of this heavenly parentage to his disciples, He showed that the Virgin Mary was united to him through a new family lineage.*[3] Mary is the mother of Jesus according to the flesh, and she is also the *first* amongst all those who hear the Word of God and keep it in its completeness.[4]

We have the immense joy of *being able to belong*, with ties stronger than those of blood, *to Christ's family*, depending on the extent to which we carry out God's will. So the disciple of Christ should say, as did his Master, *My food is to do the will of him who sent me ...*[5] even when in order to do so he has to sacrifice (to put in their rightful place), the natural sentiments of a family. In his turn, Saint Thomas explains this declaration of Jesus, in which He places the link forged by grace above that of family ties, saying that, having both a temporal and an eternal generation, He places the eternal above the temporal. Every member of the faithful who does the Will of God is a brother of Christ, because he becomes like him who always did the Will of the Father.[6]

In our prayer today we can examine ourselves on whether we always have a desire to do what God wants of us, in big things as in small; in what we like and in what we dislike. We can ask our Mother Mary to teach us to love this holy Will in everything that happens, even in what we find hard to understand or to interpret adequately.

---

[3] *idem, Epistle 243*, 9-10
[4] cf St John Paul II, *Redemptoris Mater*, 25 March 1987, 20-21
[5] John 4:34
[6] cf St Thomas, *Commentary on St Matthew's Gospel*, 14, 49-50

In this way we already belong to Christ's family.

20.2 Signs of God's will. The fulfilment of our duties.

This is one of the consequences of the Christian vocation: *belonging to God's own family*, being united to him by strong ties that come from carrying out his Will in everything. The holiness we must aspire to consists in identifying our will with Christ's. *This is the key to open the door and enter the Kingdom of Heaven: 'qui facit voluntatem Patris mei qui in caelis est, ipse intrabit in regnum coelorum' – he who does the will of my Father ... 'he' shall enter!*[7]

In sharp contrast to the attitude of people who sometimes look at the fulfilment of the Master's redeeming task with sad resignation, Christ ardently loves the Will of his Father God, and makes this clear on many occasions.[8] If we want to imitate Christ, this has to be our attitude; we have to love whatever God wants, which, whether we understand it or not, is always the way that leads to Heaven, and therefore is perfectly consonant with the purpose of our lives. Saint Catherine of Siena puts these consoling words on Our Lord's lips: *My Will only wants your good, and all that I give or allow, I allow or give so that you may achieve your end, for which I created you.*[9] He wants us only what is good for us.

God makes his Will known to us through the Commandments, which are the expression of all our obligations and a practical norm so that our conduct may be directed towards God. The more faithfully we keep them, the more we will love what He wants. God also shows himself to us through the indications, counsels and

---

[7] St. J. Escrivá, *The Way*, 754
[8] cf Luke 22:42; John 6:38
[9] St Catherine of Siena, *Dialogue*, 2, 6

Commandments of Mother Church, *which help us to keep the Commandments of the Law of God,*[10] and through the advice we receive in spiritual direction. Our obligations of state determine what God wants of us, depending on the particular circumstances of our life. We will never love God, we will never sanctify ourselves, if we do not faithfully fulfil, for example, these obligations: attention and care for the family; eagerness to improve in our study or our work. The obligations of our state that fill each day enable the Christian to see clearly at each moment what God wants of him personally. Discerning and loving God's Will in those duties will give us the strength we need to carry them out with perfection. We will find scope in them for exercising the human as well as the supernatural virtues.

God's Will is also shown to us through those events that He in his omniscience permits, and which are always directed towards a greater good, if we remain more trustingly and more lovingly close to God our Father. There is a hidden providence behind each happening. Everything – even the things we don't understand, the very turn of events our will starts off by resisting – is ordered and directed towards the good of all. *Omnia in bonum.* In this life we will never fully understand the mysterious and baffling events that God allows to happen.

Getting used to making acts of identification with God's Will in the important as in the less important circumstances of each day will produce abundant fruits in our soul. *Jesus, whatever you 'want', I love!*[11] And I only want to love what you want me to love.

---

[10] *Catechism of St Pius X*, 472
[11] St. J. Escrivá, *op cit*, 773

20.3 Prayer as a means of discovering God's will for us.

Whoever does the will of my Father in Heaven is my brother and sister and mother. A Christian's only desire should be to fulfil the Will of God. When faced with everyday occurrences, he should frequently ask himself: *What does God want of me in this matter, in this situation, or in my relationship with that person? What would be the more pleasing to God?* ... Then he should go and do it. If we pray about our daily activity, about the way we conduct ourselves in family life, the way we behave towards our friends and our colleagues, we will be given plenty of light by which to find ways of fulfilling the divine Will. Our personal prayer will often move us to act in a particular way, to change, to modify our life or our behaviour so as to live more in accordance with what God wants. In other matters God will illuminate our minds as to what his Will is through personal spiritual direction.

When we see that God wants something of us, we should do it promptly and cheerfully. Many people rebel when what God wants does not coincide with their own inclination. Others accept his will with more or less reluctant resignation merely submitting to the divine plans because they can see no alternative. Others simply conform, but without any motivation of love. Nevertheless Our Lord wants us to love the divine Will with holy abandonment, with complete trust in God our Father. At the same time we should not fail to use the means that each case calls for. *What do you want me to do?* How few people are there who have become so disposed to complete obedience that they have renounced their own will to the point where the desires of their heart no longer prompt them to action![12]

In order to have these close links – closer than the ties

---

[12] cf St Bernard, *Sermon on the Conversion of St Paul*

of blood – which Christ tells us about in the Gospel, we have to try, each day, to surrender ourselves, to abandon ourselves without any reservations, and even without understanding why God allows this or that to happen. We have to be unconditionally docile to his actions, manifested to us as they are through the internal and external trials with which He wants to purify our souls. Just as we willingly accept the countless joys of family life, of our work and our rest, so too we must willingly accept the difficulties, setbacks and disappointments that life brings with it. Temptations we can expect, and maybe such tribulations as dryness in our life of piety so long as these are not the result of lukewarmness or of a lack of love, good can be brought from them. *We must accept this action on the part of God, and those things allowed by his providence, without any reservations, without curiosity, worry or mistrust, because we know that God always wants our good. We must accept them gratefully, trusting in his nearness to us and in the help of his grace. May our only reply to this action of God in us always be: Let it be done as thou wilt; thy Will be done.*[13] This must be our attitude towards pain and sickness, towards failure, towards an inexplicable disaster which may at the time seem irreparable. Then, straightaway, we must ask God our Father for strength, and use all the human means we possibly and reasonably can. We must ask that those setbacks may be overcome, if it be his Will. We must ask for the grace to draw the greatest human and supernatural fruits from what at first we can only see as insurmountable misfortune.

Everything that happens each day in the little universe of our work and our family, in the circle of our friends and acquaintances, can and must help us to find God's

---

[13] B. Baur, *In Silence with God*

providence. Fulfilment of the divine will and the knowledge that it is being done is a source of serenity and gratitude. We will often end up giving thanks for what had initially seemed to us a disaster whose catastrophic effect we could do nothing to alleviate.

The Blessed Virgin Mary, Teacher of unlimited self-giving. Do you remember? It was in praise of her that Jesus Christ said: 'Whoever fulfils the Will of my Father, he – she – is my mother! ...'[14]

---

[14] St. J. Escrivá, *Furrow*, 33

THIRD WEEK: WEDNESDAY

21. SOWING AND REAPING

21.1 The Parable of the Sower. We are fellow-labourers with Christ. Giving doctrine. The dispositions that souls have can change.

A sower went out to sow,[1] Our Lord tells us in today's Gospel. The field, the path, the thorns, the rocky ground – all receive some of the seed. The sower scatters the seed which falls broadcast all around him. Our Lord wanted to explain, through this parable, that God copiously pours out his grace on everyone. The labourer does not look for different qualities in the soil beneath his feet, but freely casts his seed in a natural and indiscriminate way. In the same way, God does not make any distinction between rich and poor, the learned and the ignorant, the fervent and the lukewarm, the man who is cowardly and the man of courage.[2] God sows his seed in everyone: he gives each single one the help he or she needs for salvation.

At work, in the office or in the pharmacy, in the surgery, the studio, the shop, in the hospital ward ... out in the fields, at the theatre ... everywhere, just where we happen to be, we can make God's message known. It is God himself who scatters the seed in souls and who, in due time, causes growth. *We are simply day-labourers, for it is God who does the sowing.*[3] We are fellow-workers in his field: Jesus *goes about his task by means of us Christians. Christ presses the grain in his wounded hands, soaks it in his blood, cleans it, purifies it, and throws it into the*

---

[1] Mark 4:1-20
[2] cf St John Chrysostom, *Homilies on St Matthew's Gospel*, 44, 3
[3] St Augustine, *Sermon 73*, 3

furrows, into the world[4] with infinite generosity.

Now it is our turn to prepare the earth and to plant seed in it in God's name. We should not let any opportunity for making our God known pass us by: journeys, leisure, work, sickness, chance meetings ..., all can be an opportunity to sow in somebody the seed that later will come to fruition. God sends us out to sow generously. It is not our job to make the seed grow; that part belongs to God.[5] The fact that the seed germinates and bears the desired fruit depends on God alone. We must always remember *that men are only instruments which God makes use of for the salvation of souls. We have to make sure those instruments are in a good state of repair so that God can use them.*[6] The person who knows he is an instrument has a great responsibility, to be in good condition.

The sower's seed fell everywhere; in the field, on the path, among thorns, on rocky ground. *What reason could he have for sowing seed among thorns or on stones or on the much-trampled path? If it had to be a matter of seed and of good earth, he would have no reason, because it is not possible for stone to become productive soil, or that the path should cease to be a path, or that the thorns should stop being what they are. With souls it is otherwise. It is possible for stone here to be transformed into rich loam, and for the path no longer to be trodden on or to remain an open thoroughfare to all those who pass by, and for all of these to become instead a fertile field. It is possible for the thorns to disappear and for seed to bear fruit on that ground.*[7]

---

[4] St. J. Escrivá, *Christ is passing by*, 157
[5] cf 1 Cor 3
[6] St Pius X, Encyclical, *Haerent animo*, 9
[7] St John Chrysostom, *op cit*, 44

There is no ground which is too hard or that has previously been too poorly cultivated for God. If we are humble and patient, our prayer and our mortification can obtain from God the grace that is needed to transform the interior dispositions of the souls we want to bring closer to him.

21.2 Optimism in the apostolate. God often permits us not to see the fruits. Patience and constancy. 'Souls, like good wine, improve with time.'

Work with souls is always effective. God, often in an unsuspected way, makes our efforts bear fruit. *My people shall not labour in vain,*[8] He has promised us.

The apostolic mission is sometimes to sow without being able to see any fruits. At other times it is reaping what others have sown with their words, or with their pain offered up from a hospital bed, or with their hidden and monotonous work which has remained unnoticed by human eyes. Whichever is the case, God wants *sower and reaper to rejoice together.*[9] The apostolate is a task which both gives joy and demands sacrifice as we go about our sowing and reaping.

The apostolic task is also *work that is patient and constant.* Just as the farm-labourer knows how to wait and wait until the first shoots appear above the ground, and wait still longer till harvest time, so must we know how to persevere in bringing souls to God. The Gospel and our own experience teach us that grace usually takes time to bear fruit in souls. We know too about the resistance many hearts put up against grace, as our own heart may have done at some time. We will then help others by having more patience (which is closely related to the virtue of

---

[8] Is 65:23
[9] cf John 4:36

fortitude) and a constancy that will not readily turn into discouragement. We should not try to gather the crop before it is ripe. *It is this very patience that moves us to be understanding with others, for we are convinced that souls, like good wine, improve with time.*[10]

Waiting patiently should not be confused with negligence or with plain abandonment. It is quite the opposite. It moves us to employ the most appropriate means for the particular situation that the person we want to help is in at a given moment – an abundance of the light of doctrine, more prayer and cheerfulness, a spirit of sacrifice, a deepening of our friendship.

It may sometimes seem that the seed has fallen on rocky ground or among thorns, and that the fruit we are hoping for is taking a long time to make its appearance. At these moments, when we see that the green blade does not come up when we want it to, we have to reject any trace of pessimism. *You are often mistaken when you say, 'I brought my children up wrongly', or 'I did not know how to do good to those around me.' What happens is that you have not achieved the result you were hoping for, that you do not yet see the fruit you would have wished for, because the harvest is not yet ripe. What does matter is that you have sown the seed, that you have given God to souls. When God wants, those souls will return to him. You may not be there to see it, but there will be others who will gather in what you have sown.*[11] What matters is that Christ, on whose behalf we have made so much effort, will be beside us.

Going on working when we do not see any results from our labours is a good sign of faith and rectitude of intention. It is a clear indication that we are really carrying

---

[10] St. J. Escrivá, *Friends of God*, 78
[11] G. Chevrot, *The Well of Life*

out our task only for God's glory. *An indispensable requirement for the apostolate is faith, which is often shown by constancy in speaking about God, even though the fruits are slow to appear.*

If we persevere and carry on in the firm conviction that the Lord wills it, signs of a Christian revolution will appear around you everywhere. Some will follow the call, others will begin to take their interior life seriously, and others – the weakest – will at least have been forewarned.[12]

21.3 The harvest is always greater than the seed which has to be forfeited. Many of our friends are waiting for us to speak to them about Christ.

We are told too, that other seed fell into good soil and brought forth grain, growing up and increasing and yielding thirtyfold and sixtyfold and a hundredfold.

Although some of the seed was lost because it fell on poor soil, the rest yielded an impressive harvest. The fertility of the good soil compensated abundantly for the seed that failed to bear the fruit it should have borne. We must never forget the fundamental optimism that the Christian message brings with it: the apostolate always yields fruit out of all proportion to the means that have been used. If we are faithful, God will grant us to see, in the next life, all the good produced by our prayer, by the hours of work we offered up for other people, the hopeful conversations we had with our friends, the hours of sickness endured in a spirit of sacrifice, the result of that encounter we never heard any more about, and the fruits of everything that seemed to us to have come to nothing. We will see the people to whom were applied those decades of the Holy Rosary we prayed on the way from College or from the office ... Nothing failed to bear fruit: some bore a

---

[12] St. J. Escrivá, *Furrow*, 207

hundredfold, some sixtyfold, some thirtyfold. The only mistake the sower could make would be not to sow his seed for fear of its falling on soil where it might not bear fruit. He would be mistaken if he ceased to speak about Christ lest he might be lacking in the ability to sow the seed well, or because somebody might misinterpret his words or seem to be not very interested ...

In the apostolate we should be aware that God knows some people will respond to our call, and that others won't. When, in his infinite wisdom, He made man free, the Creator took the risk of man's misusing his freedom. He accepted that some men would simply not want to bear fruit. *Each soul is master of its own destiny, for good or ill. I have always been impressed by this awesome capacity which you and I have, which all of us have, a capacity which indeed reveals the nobility of our state.*[13]

God delights in those who *correspond willingly* with his grace. How much glory is given to God by a soul who freely decides to accept his grace instead of rejecting it! How pleasing to God is the one who, with God's help, is determined to give fruits of holiness instead of remaining in a state of lukewarmness. Let us think how pleasing to him the saints are; how much glory Our Lady gave to him during her time on earth. This has to be the basis of our optimism in the apostolate.

God could have created us without any freedom, so that we would give glory to him in the same way that the animals and plants do when they glorify him by their existence. They move according to the laws necessary to their nature, to their instincts, subjected to the servitude of internal or external stimuli. We could have been made like even more-perfect animals, but without any freedom. However, God *wanted to create us free* so that, out of love,

---

[13] *idem, Friends of God*, 33

we might want and choose to acknowledge our dependence on him. He wanted us to be able to echo freely the Blessed Virgin's free assent: *Behold, I am the handmaid of the Lord.*[14] Making ourselves slaves of God for love makes up, to God, for all the offences that others may do him through using their freedom badly.

Let us experience the joy of sowing, *each according to his opportunity, ability, charism and ministry (cf 1 Cor 3:10); all who sow and reap (cf John 4:37) plant and water, should be one (cf 1 Cor 3:8), so that 'working together for the same end in a free and orderly manner' they might devote their powers to the building up of the Church.*[15]

---

[14] Luke 1:38
[15] Second Vatican Council, *Ad gentes*, 28

THIRD WEEK: THURSDAY

22. GROWTH IN INTERIOR LIFE

22.1 Interior life is destined to grow. We should correspond with all the grace we receive.

Jesus sometimes asks the Apostles to listen attentively to his doctrine. At other times He calls them together so that He can be alone with them and explain a parable to them once again, or show them what lesson they should draw from something that has happened. He wants them to realise that they are being given a treasure which is meant for the whole Church and of which later they will have to give an account. *Take heed* ..., He says to them on one occasion. And He gives them this lesson: *To him who has, more will be given; and from him who has not, even what he has will be taken away.*[1] Saint John Chrysostom comments: *To him who is diligent and fervent will be given all the things that depend on God; but to him who has no love or fervour and who does not do what depends on him, what belongs to God will not be given him. For 'even what he thinks he has will be taken away' (Luke 8:18), says the Lord, not because God takes it away from him, but because he is incapable of receiving fresh graces.*[2]

To him who has, more will be given ... This is a basic teaching for the interior life of every Christian. To him who corresponds with grace, more grace will be given, so that he will have still more grace. But he who fails to make the inspirations, motions and help of the Holy Spirit bear fruit will become even poorer. Those men who traded with the talents entrusted to them received a greater fortune or

---

[1] Mark 4:24-25
[2] St John Chrysostom, *Homilies on St Matthew's Gospel*, 45, 1

reward, but the man who hid his talent in the ground lost it.[3] Interior life, like love, is destined to grow: *If you say 'enough' you are already dead.*[4] The interior life always demands progress, correspondence, being ready to receive new graces. If you don't go forward, you go backwards.

God has promised that we will always have access to all the help we need. At every moment we will be able to say with the Psalmist: *The Lord takes thought for me.*[5] The difficulties, temptations, internal or external obstacles we come up against cause us to grow; the greater the difficulty, the more grace we receive. If He permits us to experience great temptations or setbacks, the Lord will give us still greater help to overcome them. Then all those things that seem to retard our struggle for holiness, or even make succeeding in it seem impossible, will become the cause of spiritual progress and of our effectiveness in the apostolate. It is only a lack of love, nothing less than lukewarmness, that causes the soul's life to fall sick or die. Only a bad will, a lack of generosity towards God, can delay or prevent our union with him. *The vessel of faith carried to the fountain is filled according to its capacity.*[6] Jesus Christ is an inexhaustible source of help, of love and of understanding. With what capacity, with what longing do we approach him? Lord, we say to him in our prayer, make us thirst for you more and more. Make me thirst for you even more intensely than the man dying in the desert thirsts for water!

22.2 Faithfulness in little things and to a spirit of sacrifice.

There are various reasons that cause us to make scant

---

[3] cf Matt 25:14-30
[4] St Augustine, *Sermon 51*, 3
[5] Ps 39:18
[6] St Augustine, *Commentary on St John's Gospel*, 17

progress in the interior life, and even to lose ground and give way to discouragement. However, these reasons can be reduced to just a few: carelessness, negligence in little things connected with service to God and friendship with him; drawing back from the sacrifices He asks of us.[7] All we have to offer to God each day are little acts of faith and love. Petitions. Acts of thanksgiving during Holy Mass. Visits to the Blessed Sacrament and being aware that we are going to meet Jesus Christ himself who is waiting for us... Our customary prayers throughout the day. Overcoming our shortcomings at work, answering people pleasantly, asking for things politely ... Many little things done with love and for love comprise our treasure for this or that day, which we will carry with us into eternity. Our interior life is normally nourished by little things carried out with love and attention. To claim anything else would be to mistake our way, to find nothing or very little to offer to God. *It is good for us to remember,* St Josemaría Escrivá points out, *the story of that character imagined by a French author, who set out to hunt lions in the corridors of his home, and naturally did not find any. Our life is quite ordinary; trying to serve God in big things would be like trying to hunt lions in the corridor. Just like the huntsman in the story, we would end up empty-handed,*[8] with nothing to offer. We have the ordinary everyday things.

Just as drops of water added to one another give life to the thirsty earth, so do our little deeds: a *glance* at an image of Our Lady, a word of encouragement for a friend, a reverent genuflection before the tabernacle, rejecting a distraction during our prayer, overcoming our laziness ... all create good habits, virtues which enable the life of our soul to flourish. If we are faithful to these little acts, if we

---

[7] cf R. Garrigou-Lagrange, *The Three Ages of the Interior Life*

[8] St. J. Escrivá, *Letter*, 24 March 1930

frequently renew our desire to please God, when something bigger arises for us to offer him such as an illness which is hard to bear or some failure at work, then, too, we will be able to gather fruit from what God has wanted or permitted. Then the words of Christ will be fulfilled: *He who is faithful in very little is faithful also in much.*[9]

Another thing that causes us to regress in the life of the soul is *refusing to accept the sacrifices that God asks of us.*[10] Such sacrifices provide an opportunity for us to go against our own selfishness – always a sign of love. They show our determination to seek Christ throughout the day instead of seeking ourselves.

Love for God *is acquired through spiritual toil,*[11] through the effort and interest that is born, with the help of grace, in the depths of our soul. There can be no love, either human or divine, without this willing sacrifice. *Love grows within us, and develops in the midst of our setbacks and the resistance each of us puts up to that love on the inside, and also grows and develops in the face of resistance from 'the outside', that is, despite the many external forces that are foreign and even hostile to it.*[12] As Our Lord has promised us that the help of his grace will never fail us, it all depends on our correspondence with it, on our determination, on our willing to start time and again without getting discouraged. The more faithful we are to grace, the more help He gives us, the easier we will find it to follow the way. We will also find that more is being demanded of us: an even greater *finesse* in our soul. Love always calls for more love.

---

[9] cf Luke 16:10
[10] R. Garrigou-Lagrange, *loc cit*
[11] St John Paul II, *Homily*, 3 February 1980
[12] *ibidem*

22.3 Contrition and interior growth.

This interior life of ours is given a special chance to grow when we are confronted with adverse situations. For the soul, there is no obstacle greater than that which is created by our own wretchedness, and as a result of our carelessness and lack of love. But in those circumstances the Holy Spirit teaches us and moves us to react in a supernatural way, with an act of contrition. *God, be merciful to me a sinner!*[13] Saint Francis de Sales teaches that we should feel ourselves strengthened by the silent saying of such ejaculatory prayers, filled with love and sorrow and desires for a deep reconciliation, so that through them we may come to trust in his merciful Heart.[14] Acts of contrition are an effective means of spiritual progress.

To ask for forgiveness is to love. It is to contemplate Christ with growing dispositions of understanding and mercy. And as we are sinners,[15] our way will be filled with acts of sorrow, of love, that fill our soul with hope and renew our longing to set off again on the way to sanctity. We need to return to Christ time and again, without becoming discouraged or over-worried, although there may be many times when we have not responded well to Love. God's mercy is infinite, and it encourages us to start again with a new determination, with renewed hope. We must be like the prodigal son, who, instead of remaining far away in a foreign land, filled with shame and living in misery, *Came to his senses and said: '... I will arise and go to my father.'*[16] Human life is in some way a constant returning to our Father's house. We return to our Father's house by

---

[13] Luke 18:13
[14] cf St Francis de Sales, *Treatise on the Love of God* 2, 20
[15] cf 1 John 1:8-9
[16] Luke 15:17-18

means of that sacrament of pardon ...

God is waiting for us like the father in the parable, with open arms, even though we don't deserve it. It doesn't matter how great our debt is. Just like the prodigal son, all we have to do is open our heart, to be homesick for our Father's house, to wonder at and rejoice in the gift which God makes us of being able to call ourselves his children, of really being his children, even though our response to him has been so poor.[17] God never abandons us. He always welcomes us, comforts us and moves us to start again with more love, with more humility.

Our weaknesses help us to seek for divine mercy, and to be humble. Growth in the virtue of humility means we are able to take many steps forward in the interior life. All the virtues benefit from our being more humble. If at times we find we fail to correspond with all the graces we have received, if we have not been as faithful to God as he was expecting us to be, we must turn trustingly to him with a contrite heart: *Create in me a clean heart, O God, and put a new and right spirit within me.*[18]

We should often think of those things which although they are small, separate us from God. Then we will be moved to sorrow and contrition, and be brought closer to him. In this way our interior life emerges enriched, not only by our contending with exterior obstacles, but also by the recognition of our weaknesses, our mistakes and our sins. If we find it more difficult to begin again we will have recourse to Mary, who makes easy the way that leads to her Son. We should ask her to help us today to make many acts of contrition. Perhaps we shall find it helpful to repeat the prayer of the tax collector, *God, be merciful to me a sinner!* or the prayer of King David, *'Cor contritum et*

---

[17] St. J. Escrivá, *Christ is passing by*, 64
[18] Ps 50:12

humiliatum, Deus, non despicies.' A humble and contrite heart, O God, thou wilt not despise.[19] It will be particularly helpful to say some ejaculatory prayers as we see the walls of a church in the distance, knowing that Jesus Christ is there in person, in the Blessed Sacrament, the fountain of all mercy.

Our Lady, who is Mother of Grace, of Mercy, of Forgiveness, will always enkindle in us the hope of attaining the ambitious target of becoming saints. Let us place the fruits of these moments of personal prayer in her hands, with the conviction that if we correspond with grace, still more grace will be given us.

---

[19] Ps 50:19

23. FIDELITY TO GRACE

23.1 God's grace always bears fruit if we do not place obstacles in its way.

The Gospel of today's Mass[1] brings to us a little parable that only Saint Mark has recorded. In it Our Lord tells us how a seed grows when it is planted in the ground. Once it has been sown it grows independently of whether the owner of the field is asleep or keeps watch over it, or whether he knows what causes growth. The seed of grace which is sown in our souls is just like this. If we do not place any obstacles in its way, if we allow it to grow, it will not fail to bear fruit. It does not depend on the person who does the sowing or the reaping: *God gives the growth.*[2]

It gives us great confidence in carrying out apostolate to consider frequently that *the teaching, the message which we have to communicate, has in its own right an infinite effectiveness which comes not from us, but from Christ.*[3] In our own interior life, it can fill us with hope to know that God's grace, (so long as we do not put obstacles in its way), brings about a deep transformation in our souls whether we ourselves sleep or remain on watch. It constantly causes us to make resolutions to be faithful, to give ourselves more fully and to correspond more fervently with God's grace. Perhaps it is acting on us now as we pray.

God constantly offers us his grace to help us to be faithful by fulfilling the little duty of each moment. He lets us know his Will so that we can become saints by fulfilling

---

[1] Mark 4:26-32
[2] cf 1 Cor 3:5-9
[3] St. J. Escrivá, *Christ is passing by*, 159

it faithfully. On our part we must accept this help from
God and co-operate with generosity and docility. In our
soul as in our body something similar happens: our lungs
need to take in oxygen constantly so as to renew our blood.
Anyone who does not breathe dies of suffocation; anyone
who does not accept with docility the grace that God
constantly gives us ends by dying of spiritual suffocation.[4]

Receiving grace with docility means being determined
to fulfil all that the Holy Spirit suggests to us in the depths
of our heart. It means fulfilling our duties perfectly; first of
all, in all those things that relate to our commitment
towards God. We have to make up our minds to acquire a
specific virtue, to bear with supernatural graciousness and
simplicity some setback or other, however long it lasts, and
however difficult we may find it. God moves us interiorly
and often reminds us of the advice we have received in
spiritual direction. The more faithful we are to such grace,
the better disposed we will be to receive further grace, the
easier we will find it to do good deeds and the happier we
will be, because happiness is always related to the way we
correspond with grace.

23.2 The effectiveness of our correspondence with grace.

We must be docile to the inspirations of the Holy
Spirit if we are to preserve our life of grace and be
supernaturally effective. As Our Lord tells us in the parable
on which we have been meditating, the seed sown in our
hearts has sufficient strength to germinate, to grow and to
bear fruit. First, however, we have to enable it to reach our
heart. We have to make room for it within us, to accept it
and not put it to one side, for *the opportunities God gives
us do not wait. They come and they go. The word of life*

---

[4] cf. R. Garrigou-Lagrange, *The Three Ages of the Interior Life*, Vol.1

does not tarry; if we do not catch hold of it, the devil will bear it away. The devil is not lazy; rather does he always have his eyes open, and be ever ready to spring, and to snatch away the gift that you do not use.[5] We need to live a series of little things. The little mortification of tidying up after our work. Going to Confession on the day we have fixed. Examining our conscience in sufficient depth so that we can be aware of where we are failing and of what God wants us to fight on the next day. Living the *heroic minute* in the morning. Changing the conversation or at least keeping silent when someone is being criticised in his absence ... Resistance to grace produces the same effect in the soul as *hail beating on a tree in blossom which gave hopes of bearing much fruit; the blossom is spoilt and the fruit does not ripen.*[6] Our interior life wanes and dies.

We cannot keep count of all the times the Holy Spirit grants us the grace to avoid deliberate venial sin and all those faults which, without properly being sins, are displeasing to God. The saints are the people who have responded with the greatest sensitivity to that supernatural help. Neither can we keep count of all the graces we receive to help us sanctify the actions of our ordinary life, carrying them out with determination, with perfection and with purity of intention, for supernatural reasons as well as for noble human ones. If we are faithful from morning to night to the help we receive, we will find we have filled each day with acts of love of God and neighbour, at both the pleasant moments and at those times when perhaps we felt tired and had less strength and enthusiasm. All these actions help to make us effective. One grace leads to another, *For to him who has, will more be given,*[7] we read

---

[5] St J. H. Newman, *Sermon for Sexagesima Sunday: Calls of Grace*
[6] R. Garrigou-Lagrange, *loc cit*
[7] Mark 4:25

in yesterday's Gospel. The soul is strengthened in goodness to the extent that it practises goodness; it depends on the distance it tries to cover. Each day is a great gift that God gives us. He wants us to fill it with love by corresponding cheerfully with his grace, and by not being surprised at any difficulties or setbacks. He wants us to count on his help to overcome such obstacles and use them so that they will urge us on to holiness and apostolate. Everything is very different when we do it with love and for Love.

23.3 Avoiding the discouragement that arises when our defects do not disappear and we fail to acquire virtues. We must constantly start again.

A man scatters the seed on the ground when he forms a good resolution in his heart ... and the seed germinates and grows without his realising it, even though he cannot be expected to be aware of its growth. Once virtue is conceived it journeys towards perfection, and the ground bears fruit of itself because, with the help of grace, a man's soul rises up spontaneously to do good. But the earth produces first the blade, then the stalk and finally the ear of grain.[8] Interior life needs time; it grows and ripens like wheat in a field.

Faithfulness to the impulses God wants us to have is also shown by our avoiding discouragement at our failures and the impatience that comes when we still find it hard, perhaps, to finish our prayer with depth, to root out a defect or to think of God often during our work. The farmer is patient. He does not dig up the seed or abandon the field because he has not found the fruit he expected within a certain time. Farmers know well that they must work and wait. They hope to have periods of warmth and sunshine.

---

[8] St Gregory the Great, *Homilies on Ezekiel*, 2, 3

They know that the seed is coming to maturity *he knows not how* and that harvest time will come. *Grace, like nature, normally acts gradually. We cannot, properly speaking, move ahead of grace. But in all that does depend on us we have to prepare the way and co-operate when God grants grace to us.*

Souls have to be encouraged to aim very high; they have to be impelled towards Christ's ideal. Lead them to the highest goals, which should not be scaled down or made less lofty in any way. But remember that sanctity is not primarily worked out with one's own hands. Grace normally takes its time, and is not normally inclined to act with violence or irresistible force.

Encourage your holy impatience, but do not lose your patience ...[9] Just as the farmer, with the wisdom of centuries, does not lose his patience, we must learn to *aim very high* in sanctity and apostolate, waiting for the right moment, without ever losing heart. We will frequently have to start again with our unmodified ambitious resolution.

We need to be able to wait and to struggle with patient perseverance, with the conviction that overcoming a defect or acquiring a virtue does not normally depend on sporadic and violent effort, but on humble constancy in the struggle, the constancy of trying time and time again, counting on God's mercy. We cannot, because of impatience, cease to be faithful to the grace we receive. That impatience, generally, has its roots in pride. *We have to be patient with everyone,* says Saint Francis, *but first of all with ourselves.*[10]

Nothing is beyond remedy for the person who hopes in the Lord; nothing is totally lost. We always have the

---

[9] St. J. Escrivá, *Furrow*, 668
[10] St Francis de Sales, *Letters*, fragment 139

possibility of being forgiven, and of beginning again; humility, sincerity, repentance ... Then we begin again. We have to correspond with God, who is determined that we shall overcome all obstacles. We experience deep joy each time we begin again, and during our time on earth we will have to do that many times, because we will always have faults, deficiencies, weaknesses, sins. We must be humble and patient. God allows for our failures, but He also expects many little victories from us throughout our lives, victories that we carry off each time we are faithful to an inspiration, to a motion of the Holy Spirit.

24. FRATERNAL CORRECTION

24.1 The duty of making fraternal correction. Its supernatural effectiveness.

Already in the Old Testament, Sacred Scripture shows us how God frequently makes use of men of fortitude and courage to point out to others that they are straying from the way that leads to God. The *Book of Samuel* tells us how the Prophet Nathan was sent by God to King David,[1] to speak to him about the grave sins he had committed. In spite of his terrible offences being so obvious, (adultery with the wife of a faithful servant, and procuring the latter's death) and the fact that the king knew the Law very well, *he perceived it not, his lust keeping in subjection all his reasoning powers, and like smoke filling his soul. Therefore he stood in need of enlightenment from the prophet and of words calling to his mind what he had done.*[2] For weeks David lived with his conscience stupefied by sin.

In order to make him realise the gravity of his fault, Nathan tells him a parable. *There were two men in a certain city, the one rich and the other poor. The rich man had very many flocks and herds; but the poor man had nothing but one little ewe lamb, which he had bought. And he brought it up, and it grew up with him and with his children; it used to eat of his morsel, and drink from his cup, and lie in his bosom, and it was like a daughter to him. Now there came a traveller to the rich man and he was unwilling to take one of his own flock or herd to*

---

[1] cf Sam 12:1-17
[2] St John Chrysostom, *Homilies on St Matthew's Gospel*, 60, 1

*prepare for the wayfarer who had come to him, but he took
the poor man's lamb, and prepared it for the man who had
come to him. Then David's anger was greatly kindled
against the man; and he said to Nathan, 'As the Lord lives,
the man who has done this deserves to die.'*

Nathan said to David, 'You are the man.' David recalled to mind his sins; he repented and expressed his
sorrow in a Psalm which the Church holds up to us as a
model of contrition. It begins, *'Have mercy on me, O God,
according to thy steadfast love; according to thy abundant
mercy blot out my transgressions ...'*[3] David did penance
and was grateful to God. All of this was thanks to the kind
of warning we are thinking about, filled with fortitude and
made at the right moment, as was the one given to the king
by Nathan.

One of the greatest benefits we can bestow on the
people we love most, and indeed on everybody, is the
sometimes heroic help of giving *fraternal correction*. In
everyday life we realise that our relatives, friends or
acquaintances – just like ourselves – can form bad habits
which are not worthy of a good Christian and which
separate them from God. They may be habitual faults such
as: failing to put effort into their work, leaving work poorly
finished, lack of punctuality, ways of speaking that verge
on the spreading of scandal or defamation, rudeness,
impatience ... They could be faults against justice in
relationships at work, giving bad example by not living
sobriety or temperance (ostentatious spending, for example,
gluttony or drunkenness), or maintaining relationships that
are a risk to matrimonial fidelity or to chastity. It is easy to
understand that when fraternal correction, filled with
charity and understanding, is given to the person concerned
in private and at the right moment, it can avert many evils

---

[3] Ps 50

– a scandal perhaps, or harm caused to the family with the likelihood of its being afterwards difficult to put right ... Or it might simply be a stimulus to somebody to correct some defect and come closer to God.

This spiritual help flows from charity, and is one of the principal manifestations of the great virtue. Sometimes, also, justice demands it, when we have a special obligation to help the person who needs correcting. We should often ask ourselves how much we really love and help the people closest to us. *Why don't you make up your mind to make that fraternal correction? Receiving such a correction hurts, because it is hard to humble oneself, at least to begin with. But making a fraternal correction is always hard. Everyone knows this.*

Making fraternal corrections is the best way you can help, after prayer and good example.[4] Do we practise it frequently? Is our love for others a love with deeds?

24.2 Fraternal correction was practised frequently by the first Christians. False excuses for not making it. The help we give.

Fraternal correction has the savour of the Gospel: the first Christians practised it frequently, just as Our Lord had established it, *Go and tell him his fault, between you and him alone,*[5] and it occupied a very important position in their lives.[6] They were very much aware of its effectiveness. Saint Paul writes to the faithful at Thessalonica: *If anyone refuses to obey what we say in this letter ... Do not look on him as an enemy, but warn him as a brother.*[7] In the *Epistle to the Galatians* the Apostle says that this

---

[4] St. J. Escrivá, *The Forge*, 641
[5] cf Matt 18:15
[6] cf *Teaching of the Apostles*, 15, 13
[7] 2 Thess 3:14-15

correction has to be made *in a spirit of gentleness*.[8] In the same way, Saint James the Apostle encourages the first Christians, reminding them of the reward that God will give them: *If anyone among you wanders from the truth and someone brings him back, let him know that whoever brings back a sinner from the error of his way will save his soul from death and (this) will cover a multitude of sins*.[9] It is no small reward. We cannot excuse ourselves and repeat once again the words of Cain, *Am I my brother's keeper?*[10]

Amongst the excuses that can lodge themselves in our mind so that we do not make or so that we put off making, fraternal correction, is the fear of offending the person we have to warn. It seems paradoxical that a doctor should not fail to tell a patient that if he wants to be cured he must undergo a painful operation, and that we Christians should be reluctant to tell people around us that the health of their soul – of how much greater value this is than bodily health – is at risk! *Unfortunately many people through a desire not to be unkind or to avoid telling someone that these are his last days, his last hours, on earth, avoid telling him how mortally sick he is, for example, and by so doing do him really grievous harm. But there are very many more people who see their friends in error or know they are in a state of sin, or are about to make a mistake or do something wrong and don't open their mouths or lift a finger to prevent this happening. Can we really call people who act in such a way our friends? Of course not. And yet they act like that because they do not want to displease us.*[11]

When we practise fraternal correction we really fulfil what we are told in Holy Scripture: *A brother helped by his*

---

[8] Gal 6:1
[9] James 5:19-20
[10] Gen 4:9
[11] S. Canals, *Jesus as Friend*, p.95

brother is like a walled city.[12] There is nothing more
powerful than charity well lived. As a result of this sign of
Christian love, not only individuals, but society itself
improves. At the same time we avoid negative criticism
and gossip, which take away the soul's peace and cause
relationships between people to be clouded over.
Friendship, if it is true friendship, becomes deeper and
more authentic when we make such sincere corrections.
Our friendship with Christ also grows when we help a
friend, a member of the family, a colleague, perhaps,
through a fraternal correction. It is an effective remedy and
should be made in a way that is attractive but at the same
time clear and courageous.

24.3 Virtues that have to be practised when making a correction. The way we should receive it.

Whenever we make a fraternal correction we have to
practise a series of virtues, without which it would not be
an act of true charity. *That is why when you have to correct,
you should do so with charity, at the opportune moment,
without humiliating. And you must be ready yourself to learn
and to improve in the very faults you are correcting.*[13] This
is how Jesus would practise it if he were in our place, with
the same delicacy and with the same fortitude.

Sometimes a certain animosity and lack of interior
peace leads us to see in others defects which are really our
own. *We must correct, then, out of love. We must not have
a desire to hurt, but have the affectionate intention of
getting our friend him to mend his ways ... Why do you
correct him? God forbid that you should do it out of self
love, for then you would do nothing for him. If it is love*

---

[12] Prov 18:19
[13] St. J. Escrivá, *The Forge*, 455

that moves you, you do well.[14]

Humility teaches us, perhaps more than any other
virtue, to find the right words and to know how not to
cause offence. It reminds us that we ourselves often need
precisely the same kind of help. *Prudence* leads us to give
the warning promptly and at the most opportune moment.
We need this virtue if we are to be aware of our friend's
character and correctly assess the circumstances he is in,
like good doctors, who do not have only one cure.[15] Skilful
physicians do not give the same prescription to all their
patients.

If it seems that the person concerned does not react to
a correction we have made, we need to help him or her still
further with our example, with more prayer and
mortification and with greater understanding.

On our part we have to receive correction with
humility and silence, without making self-justifying
excuses. We should see God's hand in that good friend,
who is being a good friend to you indeed at that moment.
We should be truly grateful that somebody is actually so
interested in us. It should make us happy to think that we
are not alone in making the path straight so that it leads us
to God. *Once you have joyfully acknowledged your
brother's warning, impose on yourself the duty of following
his advice. You should do this not only for the benefit that
correcting oneself brings with it, but also to let him see
that his concern has not been in vain and that you
appreciate his kindness towards you. A proud man, even
though he does in fact correct himself, does not want it to
be known that he has taken the advice he has received. He
prefers people to think that he would scorn such advice.
The man who is truly humble considers it a point of honour*

---

[14] St Augustine, *loc cit*
[15] St John Chrysostom, *op cit*

to submit to others for love of God, and observes the wise advice he receives as though it came from God himself. He does this whoever the instrument may be whom God has chosen.[16]

As we finish our prayer, let us turn to Our Lady, *'Mater boni consilii', Mother of Good Counsel*, and ask her to help us to live, whenever necessary, this sign of fraternal charity, of true friendship, of sincere appreciation for the people with whom we come into most frequent contact.

---

[16] J. Pecci, (Pope Leo XIII), *The Practice of Humility*, 41

FOURTH SUNDAY: YEAR A

25. THE WAY OF THE BEATITUDES

25.1 The beatitudes; a way of sanctity and happiness.

A huge crowd of people from many different places has gathered around Our Lord. They are hoping to hear from him his saving doctrine which will give meaning to their lives. *Seeing the crowds, He went up on the mountain, and when He sat down his disciples came to him. And He opened his mouth and taught them.*[1]

It is an opportunity Our Lord uses to give an in-depth picture of the true disciple. Blessed are the poor in spirit, for theirs is the kingdom of heaven. Blessed are the meek, for they shall inherit the earth. Blessed are those who mourn ...

It is not difficult for us to imagine the impression Our Lord's words must have made on his hearers. Many of them would have been disconcerted and some of them even disappointed. Jesus had just expressed in precise terms the new spirit He had come to bring on earth. It was in the most real sense a revolutionary spirit, a spirit which involved a complete change from the usual and generally accepted human values, such as those of the Pharisees who saw earthly happiness as God's blessing and reward, and who looked on unhappiness and misfortune as God's punishment.[2] In general, *ancient man, even among the People of Israel, had sought as his chief good wealth, pleasure and power, and being held in high regard by others. He considered all these things as the acme of well-being, the fount of all happiness. Jesus here proposes a*

---

[1] Matt 5:1-2
[2] cf *The Navarre Bible*, note to Matt 5:2

totally different way. He exalts and blesses poverty, meekness, mercy, purity and humility.[3]

As we meditate again in our prayer on these words of Our Lord, we see that even in our day people tend to be disconcerted by this admittedly startling contrast. They see on the one hand the tribulation that the way of the Beatitudes must necessarily bring with it, and on the other hand the genuine happiness that Jesus promises. *The essential idea that Jesus wanted to impress on his listeners was this: only serving God brings happiness to man. In the midst of poverty, of pain and a sense of having been forsaken, the true servant of God can say with Saint Paul My joy overflows in the midst of all my tribulations.* And on the other hand a man can be desperately unhappy even though he lives surrounded by opulence and possesses all earthly goods.[4] There is a reason too for those exclamations of Our Lord's appearing immediately after the Beatitudes in Saint Luke's Gospel: *Woe to you that are rich, for you have received your consolation. Woe to you who are full now ... Woe to you, when all men speak well of you, for so their fathers did to the false prophets.*[5]

The people who listened to Our Lord well understood that those *Beatitudes* were not intended to establish different categories of people, that they did not promise salvation to particular groups of society, but that they unequivocally laid down the religious dispositions and moral conduct that Jesus demands of all those who want to follow him. *That is to say, the poor in spirit, the meek, those who mourn ... do not point to headings that differentiate people from each other, but ... are like different aspects of the demands for sanctity directed to*

---

[3] Fray Justo Perez de Urbel, *Life of Christ*
[4] *ibidem*
[5] Luke 6:24-26

everyone who wants to be Christ's disciple.[6]

The *Beatitudes*, taken as a whole, point to the same ideal – sanctity. Today, as we listen again to our Lord's words calling for such far-reaching reform, let us revive our desire for holiness as the axis around which our whole life revolves. Because *Our Lord Jesus Christ preached the good news to all without distinction. One cooking pot and only one kind of food: 'My food is to do the will of him who sent me, and to accomplish his work' (John 4:34). He calls each and every one to holiness. He asks each and every one – young and old, single and married, healthy and sick, learned and unlearned, no matter where they work or where they are – to love him.*[7] Whatever the circumstances of our life, we must know that we are invited to live the Christian life in all its fulness. We cannot make excuses, we cannot say to Our Lord: 'Wait until I have solved this problem!' or 'Give me until I have recovered from this illness!' or 'Hold on until I am no longer suffering calumny or persecution, then I will really begin to seek holiness!' We would be sadly mistaken not to make best use of these *difficult* circumstances to unite ourselves more closely to God.

25.2 Our happiness comes from God.

We do not displease God by trying to find ways of overcoming pain, illness, poverty, injustice ... but the *Beatitudes* teach us that the real success of our lives is to love and fulfil God's Will for us. They show us, as well, the only path that can lead us to live with the fulness of dignity which is due to our condition as human beings. In an age when so many things lead to personal debasement and degradation, the *Beatitudes* are an invitation to an

---

[6] *The Navarre Bible*, note to Matt 5:2
[7] St. J. Escrivá, *Friends of God*, 294

upright and worthy life.[8] On the other hand, trying at all costs to throw off the weight of pain and of tribulation, as though they were absolute evils, or to seek human success as an end in itself, are ways that God cannot bless, and which do not lead to happiness.

Blessed means happy, fortunate, and in each one of the Beatitudes Jesus begins by promising happiness and pointing out the ways of achieving it. Why should Our Lord start by speaking of happiness? Because there is in all men an irresistible longing to be happy: its achievement is the end that all their actions propose to them; but they often seek happiness where it is not to be found, where they will only find wretchedness.[9]

Our Lord points here to the ways that can lead to limitless and endless happiness in eternal life, and also to happiness in this life, if we live worthily as is appropriate to our condition as human beings. These ways are very different from those all too frequently chosen by men.

Seek the Lord, all you humble of the land, who do his commands ... For I will leave in the midst of you a people humble and lowly. They shall seek refuge in the name of the Lord,[10] we read in the First Reading of today's Mass.

Poverty of spirit, a hunger for justice, for mercy, for cleanness of heart, and bearing rejection for the sake of the Gospel – all are manifestations of the same attitude of soul: abandonment in God. And this is the attitude that impels us to trust God in an absolute and unconditional way. It is the attitude of the person who is not going to be satisfied with the benefits and consolations afforded by the things of this world. Such a person has placed his ultimate hope beyond these goods, which can seem poor and small contents for a

---

[8] cf J. Orlandis, *The Eight Beatitudes*
[9] R. Garrigou-Lagrange, *The Three Ages of the Interior Life*, vol I
[10] Zeph 2:3; 3:12-13

capacity as great as that of the human heart.

Blessed are the poor in spirit ... And in the *Magnificat* pronounced by Our Lady we hear *He has filled the hungry with good things, and the rich he has sent empty away.*[11] How many men become hollow men filled with emptiness because they make do with what they already have and grasp at more of the same! Our Lord invites us not to be satisfied with the happiness that mere transitory goods can give us, and encourages us to long for those good things which He has prepared for us.

25.3 We will not lose our joy if we seek for God in everything.

Jesus says to those who follow him (He said so whilst He was on earth and He says it now), that it will be no obstacle to happiness that men *revile you and persecute you and utter all kinds of evil against you falsely on my account. Rejoice and be glad,* He tells us, *for your reward is great in Heaven.*[12] Just as nothing on earth can give us the happiness that every man seeks, so, if we are united to God nothing can rob us of it. Our happiness and our fulfilment come from God. *Oh you who feel the weight of the Cross bear more heavily on you! You who are poor and forsaken, you who mourn, who are persecuted for the cause of justice, you who pass silently by, who suffer pain unknown to others, take heart. You are the best loved in God's kingdom, the kingdom of hope, of goodness and of life. You are brothers of the suffering Christ, and together with him, if you wish, you can save the world.*[13]

We should ask God to transform our souls, to carry out

---

[11] Luke 1:53

[12] Matt 5:11-12

[13] Second Vatican Council, *Message to humanity. To the poor, the sick, to all those who suffer,* 6

in us a radical change regarding our criteria as to happiness and misfortune. We are necessarily happy if we are open to God's ways in our lives, and if we accept the good news of the Gospel.

We should ask for this even in a situation where other people seem to be amassing all the goods that can be acquired in this short life. Saint Basil says we should not consider the rich man fortunate solely because of his riches, the powerful man because of his authority and dignity, the strong man because of his bodily health or the learned man because of his great eloquence. All these things can be instruments of virtue for those who use them rightly, but in themselves they do not hold the secret of happiness.[14] We know that very often these same goods can become the cause of misfortune or disaster for the person who possesses them, and for other people, if wealth or power or physique or intellect are not ordered according to God's Will. Without God the heart will always feel dissatisfied and unhappy.

When in our search for happiness we men attempt to follow other ways, other than those willed by God, those marked out by the Master, we will find at the end of our journey only loneliness and sadness. The experience of all those who have chosen not to listen to God when He has spoken to them in their hearts has always been the same. They have learnt the bitter truth that apart from God there is no firm and lasting happiness. Far from God we can only gather Dead Sea fruit, bitter in one way or another, and end up like the prodigal son, far from his father's house, *eating the husks and feeding the swine.*[15]

Those who seek Christ, who ask for and foster a desire for holiness, are fortunate in their quest. All the good

---

[14] cf St Basil, *Homily on envy* in *How to read pagan literature*
[15] cf Luke 15:11 *et seq*

things that constitute true felicity are present in Christ.

'Laetetur cor quaerentium Dominum.' Let the hearts that seek Yahweh rejoice. There you have light, to help you discover the reasons for your gloominess.[16]

When joy is lacking, may it not be because at that moment we are not really looking for Our Lord in our work, in the people around us, in the vicissitudes of our day. May it not be that we are not yet detached from everything? *Let the hearts that seek Yahweh rejoice!*

---

[16] St. J. Escrivá, *The Way*, 666

FOURTH SUNDAY: YEAR B

26. THE SLAVERY OF SIN

26.1 Christ came to free us from the devil and from sin.

The Gospel for this Sunday's Mass[1] tells us about the cure of a man possessed by the devil. The name Belial or Beelzebub which we find in Scripture means *unclean spirit*.[2] This victory over the unclean spirit is yet another proof of the coming of the Messiah, who arrives at length to free men from their most dreaded slavery: their slavery to the devil and to sin.

This tormented man from Capharnaum cried out, What have you to do with us, Jesus of Nazareth? Have you come to destroy us? I know who you are, the Holy One of God. And Jesus strictly commanded him, Be silent and come out of him! ... And they were all amazed.

St John Paul II teaches that it is possible, in certain cases, that the evil spirit manages to exercise his influence not only on material things, but also on *a man's body*, which is why we can speak of *possession by the devil*.[3] It is not always easy to discern how much of the preternatural there is in these cases. The Church does not favour or submit easily to a tendency to attribute many happenings to the direct intervention of the devil. But in principle we cannot deny that in his determination to cause harm and to lead us to evil, Satan can resort to these extremes in order to assert his superiority.[4] Diabolical possession generally appears in the Gospels accompanied by pathological signs

---

[1] Mark 1:21-28
[2] cf St John Paul II, *General Audience*, 13 August 1986
[3] cf Mark 5:2-9
[4] cf St John Paul II, *loc cit*

like epilepsy, dumbness, deafness ... The possessed frequently lose their dominion over themselves, their movements and their words. On some occasions they are *possessed*, behaving as instruments of the devil. Thus the miracles that Our Lord performed are a sign of the coming of God's kingdom and the casting out of the devil from every end of that kingdom. *Now shall the ruler of this world be cast out.*[5] When the seventy-two disciples return, filled with joy at the results of their apostolic mission, they say to Jesus, *Lord, even the demons are subject to us in your name!* And the Master answers them, *I saw Satan fall like lightning from heaven.*[6] From the time Christ comes, the devil has to fight a rearguard action even though he has great power and *his presence becomes stronger in proportion as man and society separate themselves from God.*[7] Through mortal sin many men become subject to the slavery of the devil.[8] They separate themselves from the kingdom of God only to enter the kingdom of darkness, of evil. In one degree or another they become instruments of evil in the world and are subjected to the worst of tyrannies. *Truly, truly, I say to you, everyone who commits sin is a slave to sin.*[9] The devil's dominion can take on other forms of more nearly normal and less striking appearance.

We have to remain on the watch, so as to discern and reject the wiles of the tempter, who does not relax in his determination to harm us. He knows that as a result of original sin we have remained prone to evil, vulnerable to our passions and open to the assaults of concupiscence and

---

[5] John 12:31
[6] Luke 10:17-18
[7] St John Paul II, *loc cit*
[8] cf Council of Trent, *Session* XIV, chapter 1
[9] John 8:34

of the devil: *we were sold like slaves to sin.*[10] *The whole life of men, both individual and social, shows itself to be a struggle, and a dramatic one, between good and evil, between light and darkness. Man finds that he is unable of himself to overcome the assaults of evil successfully, so that everyone feels as though he were bound in chains.*[11] We must then give its full meaning to the last of the petitions that Christ taught us in the Our Father: *deliver us from evil.* We must keep concupiscence at a distance and, with God's help, fight against the baneful influence of the devil (who always lies in wait) – an influence which inclines us to sin.

In this specific historic event that the Gospel tells us of, we should all, with the light of faith, see in that possessed man every sinner who wants to be converted to God, every sinner who wants to free himself from Satan and from sin. Jesus has not come to free us *from dominating nations, but from the devil; not from the captivity of the body, but from the malice of the soul.*[12]

Deliver us, Lord, from Evil, from the Evil One; lead us not into temptation. Grant in your infinite mercy that we should not give in to the infidelity to which the one who has been unfaithful from the beginning endeavours to seduce us.[13]

26.2 The malice of sin.

The experience of offence against God is a reality. It is easy for the Christian to discover that deep vestigial imprint of evil in his nature and to see a world enslaved by sin.[14] The Church teaches that there are sins which are

---

[10] cf Rom 8:14
[11] Second Vatican Council, *Gaudium et spes*, 13
[12] St Augustine, *Sermon 48*
[13] St John Paul II, *loc cit*
[14] cf Second Vatican Council, *loc cit*, 2

mortal by nature, sins that cause spiritual death, the loss of supernatural life, whilst others are *venial*. Although the latter do not radically oppose God, they are an obstacle to the practice of the supernatural virtues and dispose the soul to fall into grave sin.

Saint Paul reminds us that we were ransomed at a great price.[15] He firmly exhorts us not to fall back into slavery; we have to be sincere with ourselves, so as to avoid relapsing into sin and at the same time kindle in our souls an eagerness for holiness. *If we are to banish this evil ... we must first try to ensure that our dispositions, both habitual and actual, are those of a definite aversion from sin. Sincerely, in a manly way, we must develop, both in our heart and in our mind, a lively horror of mortal sin. We must also cultivate a deep-seated hatred of deliberate venial sin, those negligences which, while they do not deprive us of God's grace, do serve to obstruct the channels through which his grace comes to us.*[16]

Mortal sin is the greatest misfortune that can befall a Christian. When he is moved by love, everything can be used for the glory of God and the service of his brother men, and earthly realities themselves are sanctified – homes, work, sport politics ... By contrast, when a Christian allows himself to be led astray by the devil, his sin brings into the world a principle of radical disorder which separates him from his Creator and is, at bottom, the cause of all the horrors that afflict mankind. Let us ask God for that purity of conscience which will lead us to abominate any offence against his sovereign goodness and never to make such an offence appear acceptable. We have to make our own that lament of the prophet Jeremiah, which has in it such a strong sense of atonement: *Be*

---

[15] cf 1 Cor 7:23
[16] St. J. Escrivá, *Friends of God*, 243

appalled, O heavens, at this; be shocked, be utterly desolate, says the Lord, for my people have committed two evils – they have forsaken me, the fountain of living waters, and hewed out cisterns for themselves, broken cisterns, that can hold no water.[17] It is here that the evil of sin resides: in that men *although they knew God ... did not honour him as God or give thanks to him, but ... became futile in their thinking and their senseless minds were darkened ... and they worshipped and served the creature rather than the Creator.*[18]

Sin, even a single sin, exercises, sometimes in a hidden way and sometimes in a visible and palpable way, a mysterious and pernicious influence on families, friends, the Church and on the whole of mankind. If a branch withers, the whole living plant is weakened; if a branch becomes sterile, the vine does not produce the fruit expected of it; and what is more, other branches can then wither and die.

Today, let us renew our firm resolution to keep away from everything (shows, unsuitable books, environments that are out of harmony with the presence of a man or woman who wants to follow Christ) which may be an occasion of offending God. Let us truly love the sacrament of Penance and teach others to love it by instructing them about this sacrament. Let us meditate frequently on Our Lord's Passion so that we can understand better the malice of sin. Let us ask Our Lord to make that well-known saying *I'd rather die than commit a sin*, into an abiding resolve for the rest of our lives.

---

[17] Jer 2:12-13
[18] Rom 1:21-25

26.3 The liberating character of Confession. We should struggle to avoid venial sins.

We can never go deep enough into the reality of sin, the *mysterium iniquitatis*. But if we catch as much as a glimpse of the malice of *any* offence against God, we will never conduct our struggle against evil at the boundary between *grave* and *slight* sin, for the greatest sin consists in *underestimating the importance of fighting skirmishes. The refusal to fight the little battles can, little by little, leave one soft, vulnerable and indifferent, insensitive to the accents of God's voice.*[19] *Venial sins* are able to have this lamentable effect on souls that do not stoutly fight to avoid them, and they constitute an excellent ally of the devil, who is determined to exploit weakness cause harm. Although they do not kill the life of grace, they debilitate it. They make it difficult to practise virtue and to hear the suggestions of the Holy Spirit. If we do not react energetically, they inevitably dispose us towards grave faults and sins. *How sad you make me feel when you are not sorry for your venial sins! For until you are, you will not begin to live a real interior life.*[20] Let us ask God to purify us with his light, his love and his fire, so that the greatness of our vocation should never be lost sight of; so that we should never become trapped in that spiritual mediocrity which a half-hearted struggle against venial sins surely leads to.

If he wants to fight against venial sins, the Christian has to assign to them their true importance. They are the cause of spiritual mediocrity and lukewarmness. They make the way of interior life really difficult. The saints have always recommended confession which is frequent, sincere and contrite, as an effective means against those

---

[19] St. J. Escrivá, *Christ is passing by*, 77
[20] *idem*, *The Way*, 330

faults and sins, and a sure way of making progress. Saint Francis de Sales advised, *Have always a true sorrow for the sins you confess, however small they may be, with a firm purpose of amendment for the future. Many who confess their venial sins by custom, and as it were by way of routine, without thinking of ridding themselves of them, remain burdened with them all their lives.*[21] *O that today you would listen to his voice! Harden not your hearts as at Meribah,*[22] we are exhorted in the *Responsorial Psalm* of the Mass. Let us ask the Holy Spirit to help us to have a heart which is ever cleaner and stronger, capable of throwing off any oppressive bonds and of opening itself to God in the way that He expects of every Christian.

---

[21] St Francis de Sales, *Introduction to the Devout Life*, II, 19
[22] *Responsorial Psalm*, Ps 94:1-2; 6-7; 8-9.

FOURTH SUNDAY: YEAR C

27. THE VIRTUE OF CHARITY

27.1 The essence of charity.

The *Second Reading* of the Mass reminds us of the so-called *hymn of charity*, one of the most beautiful of Saint Paul's *Letters*.[1] Through the Apostle, the Holy Spirit speaks to us today about a relationship between us and our fellow-men of a kind that is completely unknown in the pagan world since it has an entirely new foundation. This is love for Christ. *As you did it to one of the least of these my brethren, you did it to me.*[2] With the help of grace, a Christian discovers God in his neighbour: he knows that we are all children of the same Father and brothers of Jesus Christ. The supernatural virtue of charity brings us closer to our neighbour in a very meaningful way; it is not mere humanitarianism. *Our love is not to be confused with sentimentality or mere good fellowship, nor with that somewhat questionable zeal to help others in order to convince ourselves of our superiority. Rather, it means living in peace with our neighbour, venerating the image of God that is found in each and every man, and doing all we can to get all others in their turn to contemplate that image, so that they too may learn how to turn to Christ.*[3]

Our Lord gave a new and incomparably deeper meaning to love for our neighbour. He established it as the *New Commandment* and as the sign by which Christians will be known.[4] Divine love, *as I have loved you*, is the

---

[1] 1 Cor 12:31-13:13
[2] Matt 25:40
[3] St. J. Escrivá, *Friends of God*, 230
[4] cf John 13:34

measure of the love we must have for other people; it is, therefore, a supernatural love which God himself places in our hearts. At the same time it is a deeply human love, which is enriched and strengthened by grace.

Charity is not the same as natural sociability, the consciousness of that fraternity that comes from ties of blood, or a feeling of compassion for the victims of misfortune ... Nevertheless, the theological virtue of charity does not exclude legitimate earthly loves; rather does it raise and supernaturalise them. It purifies them and makes them deeper and more stable. The charity of a Christian usually finds itself expressed in virtues needed for living in harmony with others; in good manners and courtesy, for example, which are then elevated to a higher and definitive order.

Without charity life lacks its prime and essential ingredient ... The most sublime eloquence, and all the good works imaginable would be like the fading reverberation of a booming gong or the clash of cymbals which lasts scarcely a few moments and then fades away into nothing. Without charity, the Apostle says, even the most sought-after gifts are of little value. *If I have not love, I am nothing.* Many doctors and scribes knew more about God, much more, than the majority of those who accompanied Jesus, about whom it is said that they *do not know the law*,[5] but all their knowledge was fruitless. They did not understand what was most important – the presence of the Messiah in their midst, and his message of understanding, of respect and of love.

Lack of charity dulls the intelligence so that it cannot know God and fails to understand the dignity of man. Love sharpens and focuses all our powers. Only charity – love of God and of our neighbour for God's sake – prepares and

---

[5] John 7:49

disposes us to understand God and all that refers to him, so far as is possible for a finite creature. *He who does not love does not know God*, Saint John teaches, *for God is love.*[6] The virtue of hope also becomes sterile without charity, *for it is impossible to attain what one does not love.*[7] All our works are in vain without charity, even the most skilfully or energetically executed ones and those that demand sacrifice. *If I give away all I have, and if I deliver my body to be burned, but have not love, I gain nothing.* There is no substitute for charity.

Today, in our prayer, we could ask ourselves how we live this virtue each day. Do we perform little acts of service for the people around us? Do we try to be pleasant? Do we say we are sorry when we hurt people? Do we spread peace and joy around us? Do we help others on their way towards God, or are we, on the contrary, indifferent to them? Do we practise the works of mercy by visiting the poor and the sick, so as to live Christian solidarity with those who suffer? Do we care for the needs of the elderly and are we concerned about people who find themselves on the margin of society? In a word is our normal relationship with God shown in deeds of understanding and in service to the people who are in daily contact with us?

27.2 The qualities of this virtue.

Saint Paul tells us which are the qualities that adorn charity. First he tells us that *charity is patient* with others. In order to do good we have to know how to bear evil, renouncing in advance any signs of annoyance, bad temper or sharpness of manner.

Patience denotes great fortitude. Charity will often demand patience if we are to bear with serenity the

---

[6] 1 John 4:8
[7] St Augustine, *Treatise on faith, hope and charity*, 117

possible defects, the hostility, the suspicion and the bad humour of people we have to deal with. This virtue will lead us to give to such trifles the importance they really have, and not blow them up out of proportion; it will incline us to wait for the appropriate moment if we need to correct them. Charity will help us to give the answer that will often enable our words to reach the hearts of those who are difficult to get on with so that they can improve. Patience is a great virtue which helps us to live in harmony with others. Through it we imitate God, who is so long-suffering with our many errors and always *slow to anger*.[8] We imitate Jesus, who, although He was well aware of the malice of the Pharisees, *lowered himself to be like them in order to win them over, just like good doctors who prescribe the best remedies for those who have the more serious illnesses*.[9]

Love is kind – that is to say, it is disposed to do good to everyone. Kindness can only find room for itself in a large and generous heart. What is best in ourselves must be for others.

Love is not jealous ... Whilst jealousy is saddened by another's good, charity rejoices in that same good. Many sins against charity flow from jealousy – scandal, for example, defamation, pleasure in another's mishaps and chagrin at his good fortune. Often it is jealousy that causes friendships to collapse and fraternal ties to be broken. It is like a cancer that gnaws away at the harmony and peace among men. Saint Thomas calls it *the mother of hatred*.

Charity is not arrogant or rude ... Many of the temptations against charity can be summarised as attitudes of pride towards our neighbour. We can only serve others and concern ourselves about them to the extent that we

---

[8] cf Psalm 145:8
[9] St Cyril, *Catena Aurea*, vol VI, p. 46

forget about ourselves. Without humility no other virtue can exist, and in particular there can be no love. In many cases, faults against charity have been preceded by faults involving vanity and pride, selfishness and a desire to outdo other people. The pride that prevents us from living charity can manifest itself in many other ways ... *The proud person's horizon is terribly limited: it stops at himself. He can see no further than himself, his own qualities, his virtues, his talent. His is a godless horizon. Even other people have no place on this cramped stage: there is no room for them.*[10] *Love is not ambitious*; it does not insist on getting its own way. Charity does not ask anything for itself. It knows that it loves Jesus in others, and that is sufficient for it. Not only is it not *ambitious* with an overriding desire for gain, but it does not even *insist on its own way*; it seeks Christ. *Love does not rejoice at wrong*; it does not compile lists of personal grievances. *It endures all things* ... We should not only ask God to help us find excuses for the speck that may appear in our neighbour's eye, but we should be sorry about the beam in our own eye, about the many times we have been unfaithful to our God. *Love bears all things, believes all things, hopes all things*. All things without exception.

There is much we can give: faith, joy, a little word of praise, of affection ... We should never expect anything in return. We should not be upset if people do not reciprocate. *Love does not insist on having its own way*, on those things that, from a human point of view, we might think are owed to us. If we do not seek anything for ourselves we will discover that we have found Jesus.

---

[10] S. Canals, *Jesus as Friend*, p. 52

27.3 Charity lasts eternally. Here on earth it is a foretaste and beginning of heaven.

Love never ends; as for prophecies, they will pass away; as for tongues, they will cease; as for knowledge, it will pass away ... so faith, hope, love abide, these three; but the greatest of these is love.[11]

These three theological virtues are the most important virtues in the Christian life because they have God as their object and their end. Faith and hope do not remain in Heaven: faith there gives way to the beatific vision, hope to the possession of God. Charity, on the other hand, remains eternally. Here on earth it is already the beginning of Heaven, and eternal life will consist of an uninterrupted act of charity.[12]

Make love your aim,[13] Saint Paul exhorts us. It is Christ's greatest gift and his principal commandment. It will be the mark by which men will know that we are disciples of Christ.[14] It is a virtue which, for better or worse, we put to the test at every moment. At any time we can relieve necessity, say something pleasant, avoid gossip, give a word of encouragement, let somebody pass before us, intercede with God for someone in special need, give good advice, smile, help to create a more agreeable atmosphere amongst members of our family or at work, forgive someone, form a more favourable judgement, etc. We can do good or fail to do good; we can even do positive harm to others, and that not only through omission. Charity urges us constantly to show our love by performing works of service, by prayer and also by penance.

When we grow in charity, all our virtues are enriched

---

[11] 1 Cor 13:8-13
[12] cf St Thomas, *Summa Theologiae*, I-II, 114, a4
[13] 1 Cor 14:1
[14] cf John 13:35

and strengthened. None of them is a true virtue unless it is permeated with charity. *You have as much virtue as you have love, no more.*[15]

If we have frequent recourse to Our Lady, she will teach us how to love and how to treat other people, for she is *the Teacher of charity. So great is Mary's love for all mankind that she, too, fulfilled Christ's words when He affirmed: 'Greater love has no man than this, that he should lay down his life for his friends' (John 15:13).*[16] *Mary our Mother also gave herself up for us.*

---

[15] F. de Osuna, *A Spiritual Alphabet*, 16, 4
[16] St. J. Escrivá, *op cit*, 287

28. DETACHMENT AND THE CHRISTIAN LIFE

28.1 Christ's presence in our lives may sometimes mean giving up some earthly goods. Jesus is of far more worth.

Saint Mark tells us in the Gospel of today's Mass[1] that Jesus came to the region of the Gerasenes, a country of the Gentiles, on the other side of the Lake of Genesareth. There, as soon as He had disembarked, a man possessed by the devil ran up to him, and throwing himself down in front of him, cried out: *What have you to do with me, Jesus, Son of the Most High God? I adjure you by God, do not torment me.* For Jesus had said to him: *Come out of the man, you unclean spirit.* Jesus asked him his name and he replied: *'My name is Legion; for we are many.'* And he *begged him eagerly not to send them out of the country.* A great herd of swine was feeding nearby ...

The arrival of the Messiah brings with it the destruction of Satan's kingdom. This is why the devil demonstrates his resistance so vociferously and even violently in many passages of the Gospel. As in his other miracles, Jesus stresses his redemptive power when He casts out these devils. Our Lord always introduces himself into people's lives by freeing them from the evils that oppress them. *He went about doing good and healing all that were oppressed by the devil,*[2] Saint Peter was to say in his speech before Cornelius and his family, in which he was recalling this and the many other times that Our Lord had cast out evil spirits.

On this occasion the devils speak through this man's lips, and complain that Jesus has come to destroy their

---

[1] Mark 5:1-20
[2] Acts 10:38

kingdom on earth. They ask him to let them remain in that place. This is why they want to enter into the swine. Perhaps, too, they thought it would be a way of getting their revenge on these people and of harming them, as well as being at the same time an opportunity to turn them against Jesus? Our Lord agreed to all that the devils asked him. Then the whole herd rushed down the bank towards the sea, and perished in its waters. The swineherds fled and spread the news in the city and throughout the countryside. Everyone went to see what had happened.

Saint Mark makes the point that about two thousand pigs were drowned. It must have meant a very considerable loss to those Gentiles. Perhaps it can be considered as the ransom demanded of this people in order to free one of their number from the power of the devil ... *They lost some pigs but they recovered a man.* And this possessed man, this man who was *rebellious and divided against himself, held under the wretched domination of a host of unclean spirits, is he not perhaps a figure of men not uncommon in our own time? In any case, perhaps the heavy material price paid for that man's freedom, (the complete destruction of a valuable herd of two thousand pigs drowned in the sea of Galilee), can give some faint indication of the high price needed to ransom the whole of contemporary pagan man. It was a cost that could be measured in the case of the Gerasenes by the amount of wealth they had lost. Now it is a ransom whose price is the lived poverty of the one who generously seeks to redeem him. The real poverty of Christians is perhaps the price God has fixed as the ransom that can liberate the men of our time. It is indeed a price worth paying ...; a single man is worth immeasurably more than two thousand pigs.*[3] He is worth more than all the riches and marvels of the created world. However, in the eyes of the owners of the

---

[3] J. Orlandis, *The Christian in the World*

herd, temporal harm seemed to carry more weight than the freeing of the possessed man. As for the devils, when they perceived the exchange of a man for some pigs, they chose the side of the latter, the pigs. And when the people there saw what had happened they begged Jesus *to depart from their neighbourhood.* And Our Lord did so immediately.

The presence of Jesus in our lives can sometimes mean letting slip a good business opportunity, because it has perhaps been not completely above-board, or because we have not found ourselves able to compete using the same illicit methods as our colleagues ... or simply because He has wanted us to win his heart through our poverty. Our Lord will always ask us, if we are to stay close to him, for an effective detachment from material things, for real Christian poverty, which clearly points to the primacy of spiritual things over material things, and of our ultimate end – our own salvation and that of others – over the ephemeral temporal ends of human well-being.

28.2 Earthly things must simply be the means that bring us closer to Christ.

They begged Jesus *to depart from their neighbourhood.* May we never fall into the dreadful aberration of telling Jesus to depart from our lives, even if declaring ourselves to be Christians in some particular circumstances causes us to forfeit public office or lose us our job, or leads to our material disadvantage in some way. Just the opposite must be our course. We have to say to Our Lord very often, using the words that the priest says to himself in the Holy Mass just before Communion: *fac me tuis semper inhaerere mandatis, et a te numquam separari permittas. Keep me faithful to your teaching and never let me be parted from you.* It is far better to be with Christ and have nothing, than to have all the treasures the world contains and to be without him. *The Church knows well that God alone, whom it serves, can satisfy the deepest cravings of the human heart, for the world and what it has to offer can never fully content it.*[4]

All earthly things are simply means to bring us to God. If they do not serve that purpose they are worse than useless. Jesus is of more worth than the most lucrative and important business transaction; more than life itself. *If you drive Jesus away from you and lose him, to whom will you go? Who will you seek for your friend? Without a friend, you cannot live happily; if Jesus were not your very special friend, you would indeed be sad and desolate.*[5] You would have lost a great deal in this life and absolutely everything in the next.

Today there have been added to imprisonment, to incarceration in concentration camps or forced-labour compounds and exile from one's native land, other penalties which are less conspicuously striking but more subtle. The sentence is no longer one of death where one sheds one's 'blood' but of a sort of 'civil' death. Not only is there now segregation in a jail or a penal colony, but the permanent restriction of personal freedom by means of repressive laws or social discrimination ...[6] Would we be capable, if necessary, of surrendering our honour or of sacrificing our fortune in exchange for remaining with God?

Following Jesus is not compatible with just everything else. We have to make a choice, and give up every single thing that is an obstacle to our being with him. For this reason we must have deeply rooted in our soul a clear disposition of horror for sin, asking Our Lord and his Mother to take away from us anything that might separate us from him. *Mother, free us, your children – each one of us – from any stain, from anything that separates us from*

---

[4] Second Vatican Council, *Gaudium et spes*, 41
[5] Thomas á Kempis, *Imitation of Christ*, II, 8, 3
[6] St John Paul II, *Prayer of petition*, Lourdes, 14 August 1983

God, even though we may have to suffer, even though it may cost us our life.[7] Of what use would the whole world be to us if we were to lose Jesus?

28.3 Detachment: some details.

And among the people who dwelt in that region some were foolish, Saint John Chrysostom comments. *This can be seen very clearly from the way this whole episode ends. For when they should have fallen down in adoration and wonder at his power, they send a message to him begging him to depart from their neighbourhood.*[8] Jesus went to visit them and they were unable to understand who was there, in spite of the wonders He had worked. Not recognising Jesus was this people's greatest folly.

Our Lord passes close to us every day of our lives. If our heart is bent on acquiring and accumulating material things we will not recognise him; and there are many ways, some of them very indirect and subtle, of asking him to leave our neighbourhood, to quit our lives. *No man can serve two masters; for either he will hate the one and love the other, or he will be devoted to the one and despise the other. You cannot serve God and mammon.*[9]

Our own experience tells us of the danger we run in concentrating on earthly goods. We know how easily they lead to symptoms of a disordered desire for more and greater such goods, self-satisfaction, comfort, luxury, giving in to our whims, spending money unnecessarily, etc ... and we see, too, what is happening around us: *Many people, especially in economically advanced areas, seem to be dominated by material considerations: almost all of their personal and social lives are permeated with what*

---

[7] Bl A. del Portillo, *Letter*, 31 May 1987, 5
[8] St John Chrysostom, *Homilies on St Matthew's Gospel*, 28, 3
[9] Matt 6:24

can only be described as a kind of economic mentality.[10]
They think that their happiness lies in material goods and
they succumb entirely to vivid longings to attain them.

We have to be detached from all our belongings. Thus
we will be able to use everything on earth in the way that
accords best with the Will of God. Our heart will be for him
only and for the good things of God that never fail.
Detachment makes of life a delightful way of austerity and
effectiveness. A Christian should frequently ask himself a
series of questions: does he remain ever-vigilant so as not to
fall into a spirit of comfort, into a sort of self-satisfaction,
which is in no way compatible with being a disciple of
Christ? Does he try not to create superfluous needs? Do the
things of earth bring him closer to or take him further away
from God? We always can and should be abstemious in our
personal needs, tightening up on superfluous expenditure,
not giving in to mere whims, overcoming the tendency to
create false needs and being generous in almsgiving ...

Today, too, we can consider in our prayer whether we
are prepared to cast away from us anything that prevents us
from coming close to Christ, just as Bartimaeus did, that
blind man who begged for alms just outside Jericho.[11]

We should not allow to happen to us what happened to
the Gerasenes – *all the city came out to meet Jesus; and
when they saw him, they begged him to leave their
neighbourhood.*[12] On the contrary, we must say to him, in
the words of that prayer of Saint Benedict for use after Holy
Communion: *Be thou ever ... my heritage of wealth, my very
own. Let my heart and soul be set on thee for ever.*[13] Lord, to
whom would I go without you?

---

[10] Second Vatican Council, *loc cit*, 63
[11] cf Mark 10:50
[12] Matt 8:34
[13] *Roman Missal, Act of Thanksgiving after Mass*

FOURTH WEEK: TUESDAY

29. SPIRITUAL COMMUNIONS

29.1 The faith of a sick woman: *If I touch even his garment, I shall be made well.* **Our meeting with Christ is in the Holy Eucharist.**

Hear my prayer, O Lord; let my cry come to thee! Do not hide thy face from me in the day of my distress! Incline thine ear to me; answer me speedily in the day when I call.[1]

The Gospel of today's Mass[2] tells us of the miracle Jesus worked on that occasion when he crossed once again to *the other side of the lake*, probably to Capharnaum. Saint Luke tells us that crowds awaited him.[3] They were happy to have Jesus with them again: He immediately went towards the town, followed by his disciples and the crowd that always surrounded him.

Amongst all these people who pressed upon Christ, a somewhat hesitant woman comes close to him, then holds back: *If I touch even his garment, I shall be made well.* She had suffered from her illness for twelve years, and she had used up all her human resources. She *had suffered much at the hands of many physicians, and had spent all she had.* But that day she understood that Jesus was the only person who could cure her: she knew that she could be healed not only from an illness that made her unclean before the law, but that He could cure her whole life. She stretched out her hand and managed to touch the hem of Christ's cloak. At that moment Jesus stood still, and she instinctively felt that

---

[1] Ps 101:1
[2] Mark 5:21-43
[3] cf Luke 8:41-56

she had been cured.

Who touched my garments? asked Jesus, addressing the crowd about him. *I perceive that power has gone out from me.*[4] At that very moment the woman saw that those eyes which could pierce the depths of men's hearts had rested on her, and immediately *in fear and trembling* but filled with joy, she *fell down before him.*

We too need to have contact with Christ each day, because we are full of weakness and infirmity. It is when we receive him in sacramental Communion that this encounter with Jesus, hidden in the sacramental species, takes place. We receive such a store of good things in each Communion that Our Lord can look on us and say to us *I perceive that power has gone out from me.* We receive a torrent of grace that inundates us with joy, gives us the firmness we need to carry on, and causes the very angels to be amazed.

When we approach Christ we know that we are faced with an ineffable mystery, and that however fervent our Communions we are not worthy to receive him as He deserves. The Holy Eucharist is the hidden stream from which the soul receives indescribable benefits which last beyond our existence on this earth ... Jesus comes to remedy our need. He responds promptly to our cry for help.

As our friendship with Christ grows, we long for the moment of Communion to arrive so that we can unite ourselves intimately with him. We seek him with the same diligence as this sick woman, with all the means at our disposal – both the human and supernatural means, such as turning to our Guardian Angel. If sometimes, because of a journey, examinations, work etc., it is more difficult for us to receive him, we should make a greater effort, stir up

---

[4] cf Luke 8:46

more inventiveness, more love. We will seek him then with the same determination as Mary Magdalen when she went to the tomb at daybreak on the third day, without worrying about the soldiers who were guarding it, or the great stone that stood in her way ...

Saint Catherine of Siena uses an example to explain the importance of our desire to receive Holy Communion. Let us suppose, she says, that several people each have a candle of different weight and size. The first person carries a candle weighing one ounce; the second, two ounces; the third, three ounces; yet another person carries a candle weighing a pound. Each person lights his candle. It is only to be expected that the one who has the candle weighing one ounce has less ability to give light than the person with the candle weighing a whole pound. The same thing happens to people going to receive Holy Communion. Each one carries a candle, that is to say, the *holy desires*, greater or lesser, with which he receives this sacrament.[5] These holy desires, in whatever degree they are present, which are a necessary condition for a fervent Communion, are manifested in the first place by our determination to abhor all deliberate venial sin and any conscious lack of love for God.

29.2 Spiritual communions. Our desire to receive Christ

We can reduce all the conditions for receiving sacramental Communion fruitfully to just one – that is *hunger for the Holy Eucharist*.[6] Nothing should be allowed to take the place of this hunger and thirst for Christ.

This intense desire to receive Communion – a sure sign of faith and love – will lead us to make many *spiritual communions*; we can make them before receiving him

---

[5] St Catherine of Siena, *Dialogue*
[6] cf R. Garrigou-Lagrange, *The Three Ages of the Interior Life*, vol. I

sacramentally and throughout our day, whether we are outside, or in at our work or whatever we are engaged in. *A spiritual communion consists of an ardent desire to receive Jesus in the Holy Sacrament, and a loving embrace as though we had already received him.*[7] In some way it prolongs the fruits of our previous eucharistic Communion, and prepares us for the next. It helps us to make reparation for the times when perhaps we did not prepare ourselves with the refinement and love that Our Lord asks of us, for all those who receive Communion with grave sins and for those who, in one way or another, have failed to recollect or have forgotten that Christ has remained behind in this Holy Sacrament.

A spiritual communion can be made without anyone noticing us, without our having to fast, and it can be made at any time. It consists of an act of love. It is enough to say with all our heart: ... 'I believe, my Jesus, that you are in the Blessed Sacrament: I love you and I very much want to receive you, for you to come into my heart: I embrace you; do not leave me.[8] Or we can say that other spiritual communion that many Christians will have learned while they were preparing to receive Jesus into their heart for the first time. *I wish Lord to receive you with the purity, humility and devotion with which your most holy Mother received you, with the spirit and the fervour of the saints.*[9]

In particular we should make spiritual communions during the time leading up to Holy Mass and Communion, when we go to bed at night, when we wake up in the morning and as we get ready to begin the day. If we make an effort in this way, and if we ask our Guardian Angel for help, the Eucharist will come to preside over our existence

---

[7] St Alphonsus Liguori, *Visits to the Blessed Sacrament*
[8] *Ibidem*
[9] cf A. Vázquez de Prada, *The Founder of Opus Dei*

and will be the *centre and peak*[10] to which all our actions are directed.

Let us turn to our Guardian Angel today and ask him to remind us frequently of the presence of Christ close to us in the tabernacles of the city or the town where we live or which we happen to be passing through. Let us ask him to obtain for us abundant grace so that day by day our desires to receive Jesus may increase, and that particularly during those moments when Christ remains sacramentally in our heart our love may grow ever greater.

29.3 Sacramental Communion. Preparation and thanksgiving

On our part, we must make the effort to approach Christ with the faith of that Galilean woman, with her humility, with a desire as great as hers to be healed of the evils that beset us. *Who are we, to be so close to him? As with that poor woman in the crowd, He has given us an opportunity. And not just a chance to touch his outer garment a little, to feel for a moment the fringe, the hem of his cloak. We actually have Christ himself. He gives himself to us totally, with his Body, his Blood, his Soul and his Divinity. We consume him each day. We speak to him intimately as one does to a brother, a father, as one speaks to Love itself.*[11]

It is a reality as real as our very existence, just as the world and the people we meet each day as we move around are a reality. The glorious Body of Christ, together with his soul and his divinity are *really, truly and substantially* contained beneath the sacramental species. It is the same Christ who was born of Mary, who remained with his disciples for forty days after the Resurrection, and who

---

[10] cf Second Vatican Council, *Ad gentes*, 9
[11] St. J. Escrivá, *Friends of God*, 199

since his Ascension into Heaven watches over our earthly sojourn.

Holy Communion is not a reward for virtue, but rather nourishment provided for those who are weak and in need; for each of us, that is. Mother Church exhorts us to receive Communion frequently, if possible each day, and insists at the same time that we should endeavour to avoid routine in its reception, tepidity, and anything approaching a lack of love. She encourages us to purify our souls from venial sins through acts of contrition and frequent Confession. Above all, she teaches that we should never receive Holy Communion if we have at all incurred the stain of mortal sin, without having first gone to receive the sacrament of reconciliation.[12] Concerning slight faults, Our Lord asks us to do what we can in the way of repentance and the desire to avoid them. As well as preparing our soul fittingly with acts of faith and hope and love, we need to prepare our body too: we should not have taken any food for an hour beforehand, and we should go with an appropriate reverence, properly dressed, etc. It will be with the naturalness of a Christian who wants to show due respect to the One most worthy of it, and will be a consequence of the faith of someone who knows what Banquet it is he has been invited to. *Our whole exterior bearing must give, to those who see us, the clear impression that we are preparing for something great.*[13]

Our love for Jesus present in the Blessed Eucharist will be noticed in the way we give thanks after Communion; love is inventive and finds its own way of expressing gratitude. This happens even when the soul feels completely dry. Dryness is not lukewarmness, but love bereft of feeling. It impels us to make more effort and

---

[12] cf 1 Cor 11:27-28; St Paul VI, *Eucharisticum Mysterium*, 37
[13] St Jean Vianney, (The Curé d'Ars), *Sermon on Holy Communion*

to ask the help of our intercessors in Heaven, such as our own Guardian Angel, who will do us a great service on this occasion as on so many others.

Even our distractions should help us to be more fervent when we thank God for the imcomparable good of his having come to us. At these moments when we have God himself within us, everything should help us to awaken the best possible dispositions within our minds and hearts, in spite of all our limitations.

Our Lady will help us to prepare our souls *with the purity, humility and devotion* with which she received him after the announcement made by the Angel.

FOURTH WEEK: WEDNESDAY

30. DOING OUR WORK WELL

30.1 Jesus' life in Nazareth: the sanctification of work.

After some time Jesus returned to his home town of Nazareth, with his disciples.[1] There his mother would have greeted him with great joy. Perhaps it was the first time those first followers of the Master had seen the place where Jesus had spent his early years. In Mary's house they would be given the opportunity of recovering their strength. We can see Our Lady being particularly attentive to them and serving them as nobody else had ever done.

In Nazareth everybody knows Jesus. They know him by his occupation and by the family He belongs to; He is the same as anyone else; He is the carpenter, Mary's son. As happens to so many people in this life, Our Lord followed the occupation of the man who was his father here on earth. This is why they also call him *the carpenter's son.*[2] He had taken up Joseph's trade, Joseph having already died, perhaps some years previously. Anyway, his family, watching as it did over the greatest of treasures, the Word of God made man, was simply one more family in the neighbourhood, but one that was loved and appreciated by everybody. *The Word made Flesh willed to share in human fellowship. He was present at the wedding feast at Cana, visited the home of Zacchaeus, sat down to dine with publicans and sinners. In revealing the Father's love and man's sublime calling He made use of the most ordinary events and details of everyday social life, and illustrated his words with expressions and imagery*

---

[1] Mark 6:1-6
[2] cf Matt 13:55

drawn from everyday living. He sanctified those human ties, above all the family ties that are the normal basis of social structures everywhere. He willingly observed the laws of his country and chose to lead the life of an ordinary craftsman of his time and place.[3]

Jesus must have remained at his mother's house for several days, and have visited other relatives and acquaintances ... *And on the sabbath He began to teach in the synagogue.* The people in Nazareth were amazed. A man who made furniture and farm implements, who had often repaired such items for them when they broke down, was speaking to them with astounding authority and far greater wisdom than they had ever heard. They could only recognise in him what was human, could see no more than they had observed for thirty years – the most complete normality. It was hard for them to discover the Messiah behind such 'normality' as this ...

Our Lady's occupation similarly was that of any other housewife of her place and her day. She spoke in the particular manner proper to Galilean women, and dressed in the same way as the women of that region did.

Joseph's workshop, which Jesus had inherited, would be exactly like others to be found in those days in Palestine. Perhaps it would have been the only one in Nazareth. It would have smelt cleanly of sawn and planed wood. Joseph would certainly have charged the usual rates for his work. Perhaps he made it easier for people who may have had financial worries, but being *a just man* he charged what was fair. The tasks carried out in that little workshop were those proper to that trade. They did a little of everything. Their work might involve constructing a beam, making a simple cupboard, mending a crooked table, planing down a door which would not close ... They would

---

[3] Second Vatican Council, *Gaudium et spes*, 32

hardly have made wooden crosses there, as depicted in some pious paintings. Who would have placed such an order with them? They did not import timber from heaven, but had it supplied from the neighbouring forests ...

The inhabitants of Nazareth *took offence at him*. But Our Lady certainly did not; she looked on him with immense love and admiration. She understood him well.

Meditation on this passage of the Gospel, which indirectly reflects Jesus' early life in Nazareth, helps us to examine whether our ordinary life, filled as a rule with ordinary work and normality, is a way of sanctity, as was the life of the Holy Family. It will be such a way, if we try to live it with human perfection and honesty, as well as with faith and a supernatural outlook. We must not forget that by remaining where we are and doing our work here on earth we are gaining heaven for ourselves and at the same time helping the Church and the whole of mankind.

30.2 Jesus and the world of work.

Our Lord showed that He was familiar with the world of work. In his preaching He frequently used images, parables and comparisons taken from the occupations, trades and professions engaged in and lived by himself and his fellow country men.

Those who hear him understand the language He uses very well. Jesus did his work in Nazareth with human perfection, which means finishing it off thoroughly, and carrying it out with professional competence. This is why, when He returns to his home town, He is identified by his trade, as *the carpenter*. Today He teaches us the superlative value of ordinary life, of work and of the tasks we have to carry out each day.[4]

If our dispositions are really sincere, God will always

---

[4] cf J. L. Illanes, *On the Theology of Work*

grant us the supernatural light to imitate Our Lord's example. We will seek not only to accomplish our work well, but through it willingly and lovingly to practise an abundant self-denial and sacrifice. Our personal examination of conscience before God and our conversation with him will often turn to those tasks that occupy so much of our time. We have to have the courage to consider this matter deeply. We have to do our work conscientiously, making our time *fruitful* without giving way to laziness. We must sustain our desire to improve our professional preparedness each day, to look after the details of our daily tasks, to embrace with love the cross and the weariness that each day's toil brings with it.

Work, any honest work done conscientiously, makes us sharers in Creation and co-redeemers with Christ. *This truth*, St John Paul II taught, *by which man through work participates in the work of God himself, his Creator, has been particularly brought to the fore by Jesus Christ, by that very Jesus before whom many of his first hearers in Nazareth were astonished and said: Where did this man get all this? How did He come by such wisdom? ... Is not this the carpenter? (Mark 6:2-5)*[5]

The years Jesus spent in Nazareth are an open book where we learn to sanctify each day's occupation. Even enforced absence from work, as through illness, for example ... is a situation willed or permitted by God in order that we may practise the supernatural and human virtues.[6] *Whatever you do, in word or deed, do everything in the name of the Lord Jesus, giving thanks to God the Father through him.*[7]

---

[5] St John Paul II, *Laborem exercens*, 14 September 1981
[6] cf St Paul VI, *Address to the Association of Catholic Jurists*, 15 December 1963
[7] Col 3:17

30.3 The redemptive meaning of work. We should ask Saint Joseph to teach us to work competently and to co-redeem through our work.

The astonishment of Jesus' neighbours in Nazareth – *is not this the carpenter's son?* – is a revealing detail that throws a great deal of light on his life. It reveals to us that the greater part of the Redeemer's life was taken up by work, like the lives of all men. And the task He carried out day after day was an instrument of redemption, like all of Christ's actions. Although it was simple human labour (specifically that proper to a carpenter who in a small town would have to do many other related jobs) it could be, and was, converted into actions which were of redemptive value since they were performed by the Second Person of the Blessed Trinity made man.

Through Baptism, a Christian has to be another Christ. He has to turn all his honest human work into a work of co-redemption. Even though in men's estimation it may be lowly and unimportant, our work, if it is united to Christ, acquires a value beyond compare.

The very tiredness that any kind of work brings with it and which is a consequence of original sin, takes on a new meaning. What seemed a punishment is redeemed by Christ and turned into a mortification which is very pleasing to God, which serves to purify us of our own sins and to share in the co-redemption of the whole of mankind with Our Lord. We find here the root of the profound difference between human work done well by a pagan and that done by a Christian, which, as well as being properly finished off like any other, is offered in union with Christ.

Union with God, which we seek in our daily work, will strengthen our resolution to do everything *only* for the glory of God and the good of souls. The prestige which we are properly able to enjoy will attract the best workers to our side and we will have abundant help from Heaven to start many other people along the way of an intense Christian life. If we act in this way, the sanctification of our work and our endeavour to carry out apostolate in our daily work will run parallel in our lives. This will be a clear indication that we are really working with rectitude of intention.

Saint Joseph taught Jesus his trade. He did this gradually, as that Child whom God himself had entrusted to him grew up. One day he would have explained to him how a plane was used; another day a saw; then different kinds of chisel ... Jesus would soon have learned to distinguish the different sorts of timber and which types of wood should be used for each job. He would have learned to mix the strong adhesives for making firm joints, how to fit tongue, groove and dovetail, to adjust a joint by driving in a wedge ... Jesus would naturally have followed Joseph's instructions as to how to look after his equipment, have learned from him to sweep up the wood-shavings and sawdust at the end of the day, and to leave his tools tidily in their proper place ...

Let us turn today to Saint Joseph and ask him to teach us to work well and to love our occupation, whatever it may be. Joseph is the outstanding Teacher of how to work well, because he taught his trade to the Son of God. We will learn from him if we seek his patronage whilst we are working. If we love our daily work, we will do it well, with professional competence; then it will become part of the whole task of redemption as we offer it to God.

FOURTH WEEK: THURSDAY

31 THE SICK: GOD'S FAVOURED CHILDREN

31.1 We should imitate Christ in his love and consideration for the sick.

The Gospel of today's Mass[1] tells us how *the Twelve* were sent out through all the towns and villages of Palestine. They preached the need to repent in order to enter the Kingdom of God. *They cast out many demons, and anointed with oil many that were sick, and healed them.*

Oil was often used for healing wounds,[2] and Our Lord ordained that it should be *the matter* of the sacrament of the Anointing of the Sick. In these few words of Saint Mark's Gospel, the Church has seen the first suggestion of this sacrament,[3] which was instituted by Our Lord and later promulgated and recommended to the faithful by the Apostle Saint James.[4] It is yet another proof of the concern of Christ and his Church for those Christians who are most in need.

Our Lord always showed enormous compassion towards the sick. He revealed himself to the disciples who had been sent to him by John the Baptist by drawing their attention to what they had seen and heard: *the blind receive their sight and the lame walk; lepers are cleansed and the deaf hear; the dead are raised up, and the poor have the*

---

[1] Mark 6:7-13
[2] cf Is 1:6: Luke 10:34
[3] cf Council of Trent, *Session XIV, Doctrina de sacramento extremae unctionis*
[4] cf James 5:14 *et seq*

Good News preached to them.[5] In the parable of the wedding feast, the servants received this order: *Go out to the streets ... and bring in the poor and maimed and blind and lame ...*[6] There are many passages in which we see Jesus moved to compassion at the sight of pain and sickness, and observe that He healed many as an outward sign of the spiritual healing that He worked in souls.

Our Lord wants his disciples to imitate him by showing effective compassion towards those who suffer illness and any kind of pain. *The Church encompasses with her love all those who are afflicted by human misery, and she recognises in those who are poor and who suffer, the image of her poor and suffering founder. She does all in her power to relieve their need and in their persons she strives to serve Christ.*[7] In the sick we see Christ himself, who says to us: *as you did it to one of the least of these my brethren, you did it to me.*[8] *He who loves his neighbour must do as much good for his body as for his soul*, writes Saint Augustine. *This does not consist only in calling in the doctor, but also in caring for his neighbour's welfare – his food, his drink, his clothing, his lodging, and protecting his body from anything that might be harmful to him ... They are merciful who put consideration and humanity into providing what is necessary for resisting any type of evil and alleviating pain.*[9]

Among the ways we can show our concern for the sick are: keeping them company and visiting them as often as is opportune; trying to take away from them any anxiety they may have about their illness; making it easy for them to rest and to carry out all the doctor's indications; making

---

[5] cf Matt 11:5
[6] cf Luke 14:21
[7] cf Second Vatican Council, *Lumen gentium*, 8
[8] cf Matt 25:40
[9] St Augustine, *On the customs of the Catholic Church*, 1, 28, 56

the time we spend with them pleasant for them, so as not to let them feel lonely; helping them to offer up their pain to God and to sanctify it; making sure they receive the sacraments. We must not forget that they are *the Church's treasure*, that they are very powerful in the eyes of God and that Our Lord looks on them with a special love.

31.2 The Anointing of the Sick.

We should be concerned not only about the physical health of those who are sick, but also about the health of their souls. We should endeavour to help them with all the human means at our disposal, and especially by making them see that, if they unite it to Christ's sufferings, their suffering becomes a good of incalculable worth – an effective help, in fact, for the whole Church. It serves as purification from their past faults, and is a God-given opportunity for them to make great progress in their personal sanctity, because Christ sometimes blesses with the Cross.

The sacrament of the Anointing of the Sick is one of the means by which the Church cares for her sick children. This sacrament was instituted to help men to reach Heaven, but it cannot be administered to those who are healthy, or to anyone who does not have a serious illness, even though he may be in danger of death, because it was instituted as a type of spiritual medicine, and medicines are not given to those who are well, but to those who are sick.[10] The Church does not want us to wait for the final moments before receiving it. We should receive this sacrament when we first start to show signs of being in danger of death through sickness or old age.[11] However, it can be repeated if the sick person recovers after the Anointing, or if, during

---

[10] cf *Catechism of the Council of Trent*, II, 6, 9
[11] Second Vatican Council, *Sacrosanctum Concilium*, 73

the same illness, the danger or gravity of the illness increases.[12] It can also be administered to a person about to undergo a surgical operation, as long as the reason for the operation is a serious illness.[13]

This sacrament is a great gift from Jesus Christ, and it brings many benefits with it. Therefore we should want to receive it, and ask for it if we become seriously ill. As it is such a great good, our faith will lead us to make sure that people connected with us through family relationships or bonds of friendship, as well as all those whom we can reach with our apostolate, have the joy of receiving it. This is a duty of charity and, very often, of justice.

The greatest benefit this sacrament bestows is that of freeing a Christian from the languor and infirmity that he has contracted with his sins.[14] In this way his soul is strengthened and given back the youth and vigour that his faults and weaknesses may have caused him to lose.

St Paul VI, quoting from a document of the Council of Trent, explained and summarised the effects of this sacrament; it bestows on us *the grace of the Holy Spirit, whose anointing wipes away sins and the traces of sin, if any remain to be taken away. It also alleviates the debility and strengthens the soul of the sick person, awakening in it a great trust in divine mercy. Sustained in this way, the sick person can easily bear the trials and sufferings of the sickness, resist the temptations of the devil 'who always lies in wait' (Gen 3:15) and sometimes recover his bodily health, if this is good for the health of his soul.*[15] This sacrament infuses great peace and joy into the soul of a sick person who is conscious. It moves him to unite

---

[12] cf *Ritual of the Anointing of the Sick, Praenotanda*, 8
[13] cf *ibid*, 10
[14] *Catechism of the Council of Trent*, II, 6, 14
[15] St Paul VI, *Sacram Unctionem infirmorum*, 30 November 1972

himself to Christ on the Cross, co-redeeming with him, and *prolongs the concern that Our Lord himself showed for the physical and spiritual health of the sick as the Gospels testify. He wanted his disciples likewise to show this same concern.*[16]

Let us discover in our prayer today whether we are able to see our suffering Christ in each sick person; whether we care for the sick with affection and respect; whether we are considerate towards them and help them in those little ways which they appreciate so much. Above all, let us consider in the Lord's presence whether we help them in the best way to unite themselves more closely to him, and to co-redeem with him.

31.3 The co-redeeming value of pain and sickness. Learning to sanctify illness.

When Our Lord gives us a taste of his Cross through suffering and sickness, we should see ourselves as his favoured children. He may send us physical pain or other equally real types of suffering: humiliations, failures, insults, misunderstandings from within our own family ... We must not forget at such times that Christ's redemptive work continues through us. However unimportant we may consider ourselves, we actually can become co-redeemers with him. Then it is that pain, which had seemed useless and harmful, turns into joy and becomes a treasure. Then we will be able to say with Saint Paul: *Now I rejoice in my sufferings for your sake, and in my flesh complete what is lacking in Christ's afflictions for the sake of his body, that is, the Church.*[17] The Apostle reminds us of what the Master taught us: that we should follow in his footsteps,[18]

---

[16] *Ritual of the Anointing of the Sick, Praenotanda*, 5
[17] Col 1:24
[18] cf 1 Peter 2:21

that we should take up our cross[19] and continue the work of making Christ's teaching known to all men.

St John Paul II affirmed that *pain is not only of use to others, but it fulfils a service for which there is no substitute. In the Body of Christ ... suffering, permeated by the spirit of Christ's sacrifice, is an irreplaceable mediator and the source of those goods which are indispensable for the salvation of the world. Suffering, more than anything else, makes present in the history of mankind the power of the Redemption.*[20]

In order to benefit from this wealth of grace that reaches us in one way or another, we need *a long-term preparation, by practising daily a holy detachment from self, so that we are prepared to bear sickness or misfortune gracefully if Our Lord permits them. Begin now to make use of everyday opportunities such as foregoing cheerfully something you may have to do without, putting up uncomplainingly with small recurring pains, practising little voluntary mortifications and putting into practice the Christian virtues.*[21]

Pain, which has separated many people from God because they have not looked on it with the eyes of faith, must unite us more closely to him. We must show people who are sick the redeeming value of their sickness. Then they will bear with peace their sickness and the annoying things our Lord permits, and will come to love them, because they will have learned that even pain comes from a Father who wants only what is good for his children.

We turn to Mary, our Mother, *she who standing valiantly beside the Cross of her Son on Calvary (cf John*

---

[19] cf Matt 10:38

[20] St John Paul II, Apostolic Letter, *Salvifici doloris*, 27, 11 February 1984

[21] St. J. Escrivá, *Friends of God*, 124

19:25), shared in his passion, and always knows how to win over new souls so that they unite their own suffering to Christ's sacrifice in an 'offertory' which, transcending time and space, encompasses the whole of mankind and saves it.[22] Let us ask that our pain and sorrows (which are inevitable in this life) may help us to unite ourselves ever more to her Son, and that we may look on them when they come to us as a blessing for ourselves and the whole Church.

---

[22] St John Paul II, *Homily*, 11 November 1980

FOURTH WEEK: FRIDAY

32. FORTITUDE IN ORDINARY LIFE

32.1 The example of the martyrs. The testimony we give as ordinary Christians. The virtue of fortitude.

The Gospel of today's Mass tells us of the martyrdom of John the Baptist,[1] who was faithful to the mission he had received from God to the point of giving his life. If he had kept silent, or if he had remained on the fringe of events at the difficult moments, he would not have died with his throat cut in Herod's dungeon. But John was not like *a reed blowing in the wind.* Up to the very end he remained consistent with his vocation and true to the principles that gave meaning to his existence.

The blood John shed, together with that of the martyrs of all times, was to be united to the redeeming Blood of Christ so as to give us an example of love and steadfastness in the faith, an example of courage and of effectiveness. Martyrdom is the greatest expression of the virtue of fortitude and the supreme testimony of the truth that a person confesses to the extent of giving his life for it. The martyr's example *reminds us that we must bear witness to the faith ... a witness which is personal, definite and, if such an event should occur, given at great cost and demanding exceptional courage. It reminds us finally that the martyr for Christ is not a hero far removed from us, but one of us; he is ours.*[2] His example teaches us that, if necessary, every Christian should be prepared to give up his life as a witness to his faith.

The martyrs are not only a matchless example from the past. Our own day is also a time for martyrs. Ours also has

---

[1] Mark 6:14-29
[2] St Paul VI, *Address*, 3 November 1965

been a time of persecution even to the shedding of blood. *The persecutions for the faith in our day are often similar to those that the martyrology of the Church has already recorded in centuries past. They merely assume different types of discrimination against believers, and the whole community of the Church ...*

Today there are hundreds and hundreds of thousands of witnesses to the faith. They are often unknown to or forgotten by their contemporaries, or by 'public opinion', which finds its attention is taken up by other more engrossing events and personalities. Often only God knows them. They undergo daily privations in the most diverse regions of each of the continents.

We are speaking of believers obliged to meet clandestinely because their religious community is no longer authorised. We are speaking of bishops, priests and religious who are forbidden to exercise the holy ministry in their churches, or at public meetings ...

We are speaking of generous youths, who are prevented from entering a seminary or a place of religious formation in order to follow their own vocation there. We are speaking of parents who are denied the possibility of ensuring that their children receive an education inspired by their own faith.

We are speaking of men and women, manual workers and intellectuals, of people drawn from all the professions, who, by the simple fact of professing their faith run the risk of seeing themselves deprived of a brilliant future career in keeping and commensurate with their studies.[3]

However, God does not ask the majority of Christians to shed their blood in testimony of the faith they profess. But he does ask of everyone an heroic steadfastness in proclaiming the truth through his life and words in environments which may be difficult and hostile to the teachings of Christ. He asks

---

[3] St John Paul II, *Prayer of petition*, Lourdes, 14 August 1983

them to live fully the Christian virtues in the middle of the world, in whatever circumstances life has placed them. This is the path that the majority of Christians will have to tread – Christians who have to sanctify themselves through living heroism in the duties and circumstances of each day. Today's Christian needs the virtue of fortitude in a special way. This virtue, as well as being humanly so attractive, is indispensable given the materialistic mentality of so many people today; it is a mentality that prizes comfort and has a horror of anything that smacks of mortification, renunciation or sacrifice. So every act of virtue contains within it an act of courage, of fortitude; without it we cannot remain faithful to God.

Saint Thomas teaches[4] that this virtue is manifested in two types of acts: *to do good* without wavering at the prospect of the difficulties and dangers it may entail, and *to resist evils and difficulties* in such a way that they do not lead us into despondency. In the first case courage and audacity find their true radius of action; in the second case patience and perseverance are called for. Each day presents us with many opportunities for practising these virtues. Overcoming our moods is one of them. Avoiding useless complaints is another. So too is persevering in our work when we feel tired. Smiling when we find it difficult to do so, correcting people when necessary, starting each job at the right time – none of these is easy. Being constant in the apostolate with our relatives and friends ... even this requires a kind of bravery as well as determination.

32.2 We need fortitude if we are to follow Christ, to be faithful in little things, to live an effective detachment from earthly goods, and to be patient.

If we make following Jesus Christ closely the aim of our life, we will need fortitude if we are to make any

---

[4] St Thomas, *Summa Theologiae*, II-II, 123, 6

progress. We know that following Christ never was an easy task. The imitation of Christ is a serious business. It means a task filled with joy, great joy, but a task which also demands sacrifice. After the initial decision comes the decision of each day, of each moment. The Christian has to be strong, both to set out on the way of sanctity and to continue along every step of that way at each stage. We have to be strong in order to persevere without flagging in spite of all the obstacles, both internal and external, which will certainly present themselves.

We need fortitude *to be faithful* in the little things of each day which, when all is said and done, is what brings us close to the Lord or separates us from him. We show this fidelity, this firm stance in the way we tackle our work, in our family life, when we are confronted with pain or sickness or with the possible discouragement which would take away our peace if we were not determined to struggle to overcome it. Our struggle must always rest on the consideration that God is our Father and on the consideration that He stays close to each one of his children.

We need the virtue of fortitude if we are to avoid straying from the path and if we are to put aside the tinsel attractions of earth, without allowing our hearts to become attached to them. This is an age in which many people consider the acquisition of worldly goods to be the aim and object of their lives; they forget that God created their hearts in such away that only He can satisfy their longing for happiness. Many Christians seem to have forgotten that Christ is truly the *hidden treasure*, the *pearl of great value*[5] for whose possession it is worth while to refuse to fill our hearts with superficially attractive things that are trifles of only relative worth. For *he who knows the riches of Christ our Lord despises all things: for such a person property,*

---

[5] cf Matt 13:44-46

wealth and honours are as dung. There is nothing that can be compared with the supreme treasure, or that can be placed alongside it.[6] In order to be effectively detached from the things we use, and not turn them into ends in themselves, we need to be strong.

The virtue of fortitude leads us to be *patient* when unpleasant things happen and we are given bad news. It leads us to be patient in dealing with the obstacles that each day brings with it. We will know how to wait for the right moment to give a fraternal correction. It is not proper to a Christian who lives in the presence of his Father God to display bitterness, bad temper or gloominess when he is made to wait unduly, or when unforeseen circumstances cause him to change his plans at the last moment, or when he is confronted with the little (or big) failures that every normal life will include. Patience also helps us to be understanding with other people, when it seems they do not improve or that they are simply not interested in mending their ways. It leads us always to treat them with charity, with human appreciation and with supernatural outlook. Anyone in charge of the formation of others (parents, teachers, superiors), has a particular need for patience, because *governing often consists in knowing how, with patience and affection, to 'draw good' out of people.*[7] This advice can help all of us to examine ourselves in our personal prayer today. *Each day you must behave towards those around you with genuine understanding, with great affection, together, of course, with all the energy this will call for. Otherwise understanding and affection become complicity and selfishness.*[8] Charity is never weakness, and fortitude should never assume an aspect that is peevish, harsh or ill-humoured.

---

[6] *Catechism of the Council of Trent*, IV, 11, 15
[7] St. J. Escrivá, *Furrow*, 405
[8] *ibid*, 803

32.3 Heroism in the simple and normal life of a Christian. Giving good example.

Compared with the numbers of the faithful who make up the Church, there are few indeed of whom God requires a testimony to their faith by shedding their blood, by giving their life in martyrdom (*martyr* means witness). But He does ask us all to give our lives to him in gradual steps, little by little, with hidden heroism *in the faithful fulfilment of our duty* at work, within the family, in our struggle to be always consistent with our Christian faith. He asks us to give the kind of example that stimulates others and wins them over. Because of this it is not enough for us to live Christ's doctrine interiorly. Any faith that lacked external manifestations would be false. Christians must never give others to understand, because of their passivity, through their not wanting to commit themselves, that they do not hold their faith to be the most important thing in their lives, or that they do not consider the Church's teaching a vital element in their modes of behaviour. *The Lord needs strong and courageous souls who refuse to come to terms with mediocrity, but who will be able to enter all kinds of environments with a sure step.*[9] There may sometimes be grave reasons for so doing when charity demands that we strengthen waverers by the testimony of our faith. We are asked for a determined confession of faith, like that of John the Baptist, without any inhibiting complexes; it is this steadfastness that will attract them and give them new life.

God's honour is paramount above all human considerations. We cannot remain passive when people want to put God into parenthesis in public life or when sectarianism strives to relegate him to a corner of men's consciences. We cannot keep silent with so many around us waiting for a testimony from us that will be consistent with the faith we

---

[9] *ibid*, 416

profess. Such testimony will sometimes consist of giving good example through our professional work, through our charity and understanding for everyone. It will be given by the joy that enables people to discover in us the peace that is born of our relationship with God ... At other times it will consist in keeping silent in the face of an unjust accusation, or in our quiet but forthright defence of the Roman Pontiff or of the hierarchy of the Church, or it will consist in our refuting doctrine which is erroneous or confused. We should do this always with serenity, without becoming heated or going to extremes that do no good and are not proper to a Christian. At the same time we must always remain firm.

John's fortitude and his coherent life are an example we can imitate. It we follow his example in the ordinary simple happenings of each day, many of our friends will come to see what motivates us, and will be moved by that serene testimony, just as many were converted as they contemplated the martyrdom – the testimony of faith – of the first Christians.

FOURTH WEEK: SATURDAY

33. THE NEED TO SANCTIFY OUR REST

33.1 Jesus is tired. Contemplation of his sacred Humanity.

The apostles returned to Jesus and told him all they had done and taught. And he said to them, 'Come away by yourselves to a lonely place and rest a while.'[1] These are words taken from the Gospel of today's Mass, which show us Jesus' concern for his friends. After their intense apostolic mission the apostles feel a natural tiredness and lack of strength. Our Lord realises this immediately and shows solicitude for them: *And they went away in the boat to a lonely place by themselves.*

On other occasions it is Jesus who is really *wearied with his journey;*[2] He sits down beside a well because he cannot take another step. He is experiencing something as consonant with human nature as fatigue. He had experienced it at his work during the thirty years of his hidden life, just as we do each day at our own work. He was often exhausted at the end of the day. The evangelists tell us how during a storm on the lake Our Lord fell asleep in the stern of the boat: He had spent the whole day preaching.[3] He was so tired that he did not wake up in spite of the waves. Our Lord didn't pretend He was asleep in order to put his disciples to the test; He was really physically worn out.

At these times of real bodily weariness, Jesus is also redeeming mankind; and his weakness should help us to

---

[1] Mark 6:30-31
[2] cf John 4:6
[3] cf Mark 4:38

bear our own weakness and to co-redeem with him. How consoling it is to see our Lord exhausted! How close Jesus is to us at these times!

As we carry out our duties, as we generously go about our professional work, as we unstintingly use up so much of our energy in apostolic initiatives and undertakings of service to others, it is natural that fatigue appears as an almost inseparable companion. Far from complaining about this inescapable reality, a reality that is common to all of us, we have to learn to rest close to God and to exercise ourselves constantly in that way of thinking. *O Jesus! I rest in you,*[4] we can often say inwardly as we seek our support in him.

No one understands our tiredness better than Our Lord, because He himself was constantly in situations similar to our own. We must learn to recover our strength close to him. *Come to me,* he says to us, *all you who labour and are heavy laden, and I will give you rest.*[5] We make our burden lighter when we unite our tiredness to that of Christ, offering it up for the redemption of souls. We will find it helps us if we live charity in a purposefully pleasant way towards those around us, even if at those particular times we find it a little more difficult to do so. And we must never forget that the use of leisure also is an activity that we must sanctify. Those periods of diversion should not be isolated inertial gaps in our lives, or be seen as the chance to allow ourselves some purely selfish compensation for our exertions. Love does not take holidays.

33.2 Our tiredness is not useless. Learning to sanctify it.

Jesus also makes use of the periods when he is recuperating his energies in order to influence souls. As he

---

[4] St. J. Escrivá, *The Way*, 732
[5] Matt 11:28

was resting by Jacob's well, a woman came up to fill her jar with water. This was precisely the opportunity Our Lord seized upon to move that Samaritan woman to a radical change in her life.[6]

We too know that even our moments of weariness should not be useless. *Only after our death will we know how many sinners we have helped to save by offering up our tiredness. Only then will we understand that our forced inactivity and our sufferings can be of more use to our neighbour than our most effective deeds of service.*[7] We should never fail to offer up those times when exhaustion or illness make us feel useless. Even such circumstances should not stop us helping other people.

Tiredness teaches us to be humble and to live charity better. We discover at times like these that we cannot do everything, and that we need other people. Allowing ourselves to be helped is a wonderful way of learning humility. At the same time, since all of us become more or less tired we are able to understand better Saint Paul's advice to, *Bear one another's burdens.*[8] We understand that any help we can give to those we see overworked is always a great sign of charity.

Weariness helps us to live detachment from the many things we would like to do and which we do not manage to achieve because of the limitations of our strength. It also helps us to grow in the virtue of fortitude and in the corresponding human virtue of resilience, because it is a fact that we will not always find ourselves at the peak of our strength or be in the very best of health when we have to work, or study or see a difficult undertaking through to the end, etc. No small part of these virtues consists in our

---

[6] cf John 4:8 *et seq*
[7] G. Chevrot, *The Well of Life*
[8] Gal 6:2

getting used to going on working when we are tired, or when we perhaps do not feel physically as well as we would like to in order to get on with those tasks. If we carry them out for God, He blesses them in a special way.

The Christian considers life to be an immensely beneficial gift, which does not really belong to him and which he has to look after and be responsible for. We have to live the years that God wants, and go on to complete the task that He has entrusted us with. As a consequence, for God's sake and for the sake of other people, we must observe the norms of prudence in caring for our own health and that of the people who in any way depend on us. Among these norms is the one *that leisure be properly employed to refresh the spirit and strengthen the health of mind and body.*[9]

Subjecting oneself to a timetable, dedicating sufficient time to sleep, going occasionally for a walk or a simple outing, are means which we should use. In short, we should put order into our activity. Behaving in any other way, so long as we are not prevented by some pressing obligation, might reveal a certain thoughtlessness and laziness. This would be all the more harmful, as an attitude like this could lead us to a voluntary occasion of harming our interior life, of slipping into activism, of being more liable to lose our serenity etc. Anyone who is even moderately ordered in the organisation of his day will habitually find a way of prudently relaxing in the midst of the most demanding and self-sacrificing of activities.

33.3 We have a duty to rest. Resting in order to serve God and other people better.

We should learn to rest. If we can avoid becoming totally exhausted we should not fail to do so. God wants us

---

[9] Second Vatican Council, *Gaudium et spes*, 61

to look after our health, and to know how to recover our strength. It is part of the fifth commandment. We need to rest in order to be fit, to restore lost energy, and so that our work may be all the more effective. Above all, we need it so as to serve God and other people better.

Remember that God loves his creatures to distraction. How can a donkey work if it is not fed or given enough rest, or if its spirit is broken by too many beatings? Well, your body is like a little donkey, and it was a donkey that was God's chosen throne in Jerusalem, and this little donkey carries you along the divine pathways of this earth of ours. But it has to be controlled so that it does not stray away from God's paths. And it has to be encouraged so that it can trot along with all the briskness and cheerfulness that you would expect from a poor beast of burden.[10]

When we are tired out it is more difficult to do things well, to do them the way God wants us to do them. There may be at such times more liability to faults against charity, faults at least of omission. Saint Jerome says in an amusing way, *Experience shows me that when a donkey is tired it sits down at every corner.*

It has been said that *to rest is not to do nothing: it is to relax in activities which demand less effort.*[11] Leisure provides an opportunity for interior enrichment. It often presents an occasion for doing more apostolate, for fostering a friendship, etc. We should not confuse *rest* with *laziness.*

Mother Church has always taken an interest in the physical well-being of her children. Commenting on the passage of the Gospel that tells us how Jesus stayed and rested in the house of Martha and Mary, St John Paul II pointed out that rest means leaving one's everyday

---

[10] St. J. Escrivá, *Friends of God*, 137
[11] *idem*, *The Way*, 357

occupation, detaching oneself from the normal toil of the day, the week and the year. It is important that we do not *wander round aimlessly*; our *time off* must not just be an empty time. Sometimes, the Pontiff said, it will be good to go and enjoy nature – the mountains, the sea, the forest ... And of course it should always be desirable for one's leisure time to be filled with something different, a new content that nevertheless still leads to an encounter with God. We should open up the inward eyes of the soul to his presence in the world and incline our inward ear to this Word of truth.[12]

We are well aware that many nowadays dedicate their leisure to pastimes and activities which do not facilitate, and even on occasions obstruct, that encounter with Christ. Far from letting ourselves be influenced by what is considered fashionable, we should be attentive to this consideration: the same norm should guide our leisure as guides our work. Through it we should be able to show our love for God and for our neighbour. We will know how to choose a suitable place for our holidays; how best to plan a journey; how most profitably to arrange a weekend activity away from work. We should avoid thinking of nobody but ourselves and should seek union with Our Lord. Any time is good for thinking about other people, for looking after them, for helping them and for taking an interest in their hobbies. Any time is a good time for showing our love. Love does not allow any blank gaps. Jesus rested out of obedience to the law of Moses. He rested as a result of the demands made on him by family and friends, or because of weariness ... like anybody else. He never rested because He was tired of serving others. He never isolated himself, never made himself unavailable to people, as if to say, *Now it's my turn!* We should never act from selfish motives, not

---

[12] cf St John Paul II, *Angelus*, 20 July 1980

even when we stop *to get our breath back*. At those moments, too, we shall make sure we are close to God: our leisure time is not a pagan time, to be kept distinct and separated from our interior life.

In the Gospel of today's Mass Our Lord leaves us with a very special sign of his love: we should be concerned about the weariness and the health of those who live close to us. We see how, when He sat down exhausted beside the well of Sichar, Our Lord gave us a powerful example: He did not let slip the opportunity of doing apostolate, of converting the Samaritan woman. He did all this even though *Jews have no dealings with Samaritans*. When there is love, not even exhaustion can be an excuse for not doing apostolate.

FIFTH SUNDAY: YEAR A

34. THE LIGHT OF OUR GOOD EXAMPLE

34.1 As Christians we must be 'salt' and 'light' in the world. Our good example has to precede us.

In the Gospel of this Sunday's Mass,[1] Our Lord tells us about our responsibility to the world. *You are the salt of the earth ... You are the light of the world.* And he says it to each one of us, to every one of us who wants to follow him.

Salt gives flavour to food, makes it pleasant, preserves it from going bad. It was a symbol of divine wisdom. In the Old Testament it was prescribed that everything offered to God should be seasoned with salt,[2] signifying that the one who was offering willed that his sacrifice be pleasing to God. The creation of *light* was God's first operation in calling the universe into being.[3] Here is a symbol of the Lord himself, of Heaven and of Life. Darkness, on the other hand, symbolises disorder, death, hell and evil.

Christ's disciples, his followers throughout the centuries, are *the salt of the earth*: they give a deeper meaning to all human values. They avoid corruption, they bring wisdom to men by their words. They are also *the light of the world* which shows men the way in the midst of darkness. When they live in accordance with their faith, with their *irreproachable and upright* conduct, *they shine like bright lights in the world*.[4] Their light shines out in the midst of their work, their everyday activities, their ordinary

---

[1] Matt 5:13-16
[2] cf Lev 2:13
[3] Gen 1:1-5
[4] cf Phil 2:15

lives. On the other hand, how noticeable it is when Christians do not play their part in the family, in society, in the public life of nations! When Christians do not take Christ's doctrine to the places where they live and work, human values themselves become savourless, losing whatever transcendence they had and very often becoming corrupt.

When we look around us it is not difficult to see the results of men ceasing to be the *salt* and the *light* of Christ. *Civic life is scarred by the consequences of secularised ideologies, which range from the denial of God or the drastic limitation of religious freedom to the overriding importance of economic panaceas. These depend for their success on bizarre interpretations of human values such as work and production. They stretch from materialism and hedonism, which attack the values of large close-knit families, to false ethical theories concerned with attitudes to newly conceived life. Such erroneous 'moral' guidance has been steering generations of young people towards a nihilism that cripples the will and leaves it unable to face up to crucial problems like those of the new poor, of emigrants, of ethnic and religious minorities and so on. Society seems helpless to determine the right use of the means of communication, whilst it puts arms into the hands of terrorists.*[5] Many modern evils stem from *the defection of the baptised and of believers, fallen away or seduced in great numbers from the profound truths of their faith and the doctrinal and moral vigour of their traditional Christian view of life, a view which had guaranteed a right balance to individuals and to communities alike.*[6] We have reached this situation – in which it is necessary to evangelise Europe

---

[5] St John Paul II, *Address*, 9 November 1982
[6] *ibid*

and the world once again[7] – as a result of the accumulated omissions of so many Christians who have not been the salt and light that Our Lord asked them to be.

Christ left us his teaching and his living presence so that men could discover a meaning for their existence and find the true happiness and the salvation they were created for. *A city set on a hill cannot be hidden. Nor do men light a lamp and put it under a bushel, but on a stand, so that it gives light to all in the house.* Our Lord goes on to say in the Gospel, *Let your light so shine before men, that they may see your good works and give glory to your Father who is in Heaven.* For this we need first of all to give the example of an upright life, with a clean behaviour, and the very visible practice of the human and Christian virtues in our ordinary everyday living. The world must have light; good example has to lead the way

34.2 Good example in family life, at work, etc.

In view of this tide of materialism and sensuality that threatens to overwhelm man, Our Lord *wants another wave to issue forth from our souls – a wave that's clean and powerful, as the Lord's right hand – to overcome with its purity all the rottenness of materialism and undo the corruption that has flooded the world. It is for this, and more, that the children of God have come.*[8] It is to bring Christ to so many people whose lives are mingled with our own, so that God may not be a stranger to society.

We will really transform the world – beginning with that little corner of it in which we live and work and where our dreams are awakened – if we start to teach with the testimony of our own lives; if we are exemplary, competent and honest at our work; if, in family life, we

---

[7] *idem, Address,* 11 October 1985
[8] St. J. Escrivá, *The Forge,* 23

dedicate to our children and to our parents as much time as they need; if people see us cheerful, even in times of difficulty and suffering; if we are outgoing and warm towards others. *They will have greater faith in our deeds than in any other form of speech,*[9] and they will feel drawn to the life that our actions point out to them. Our example prepares the soil in which our words will later come to fruition. Without doing anything unusual or out of the ordinary, Christians can show what it really means to follow Christ in their daily lives, as the first Christians did. Saint Paul encouraged the faithful at Ephesus: *I beg you to lead a life worthy of the vocation to which you have been called.*[10]

We should be known as men and women who are loyal, straightforward, truthful, cheerful, hardworking and optimistic. We have to behave the way people do who carry out their duties properly and who know how to comport themselves at every moment as children of God, without letting themselves be swept along by the current of whatever is in vogue. The life of a Christian will then be a sign by which people will recognise the spirit of Christ. We must therefore often ask ourselves in our personal prayer whether our workmates, our family and our friends are likely to be moved to give glory to God when they observe our conduct, because they can discern in it the light of Christ. It will be a good sign if there is light in us and not darkness, love of God and not lukewarmness. *He needs you*, St John Paul II said. *In some way you lend him your face, your heart, your whole person, when you are convinced, dedicated to the good of others, faithful servants of the Gospel. Then it will be Jesus himself who attracts people. But if you were to be weak and evil-*

---

[9] St John Chrysostom, *Homilies on St Matthew's Gospel*, 15, 9
[10] Eph 4:1

minded, you would obscure his true identity and would give no honour to him at all.[11] We should never lose sight of this reality: other people have to see Christ in our straightforward and serene everyday behaviour. They have to see him in us when we work and when we rest, whether we receive good news or bad. They have to hear him when we speak or when we remain silent. And for all this we need to follow the Master very closely.

34.3 Our good example of charity and temperance. Salt that loses its savour is useless.

In the *First Reading*,[12] the Prophet Isaiah lists a series of works of mercy which give a Christian the possibility of showing the charity he bears in his heart, and all of which consist in loving others as God loves us.[13] We should share our bread and our shelter with others. We should clothe the naked. We should banish all threats and curses. *Then*, sings the *Responsorial Psalm*, *your light will come forth like the dawn ... your light will shine in the darkness, your darkness will become as midday.*[14] If we live charity with those around us in all the different sorts of circumstances we find ourselves in, we will be giving a testimony that will attract many people to faith in Christ, for He himself said: *By this will all men know that you are my disciples.*[15] The same ordinary norms of fellowship which many people look upon as something conventional and external and which they practise only because they facilitate social relationships, must, for Christians, also be the fruit of charity – of their union with God, which fills those actions with supernatural content – an external manifestation of

---

[11] St John Paul II, *Homily*, 29 May 1983
[12] Is 58:7-10
[13] cf John 15:12
[14] cf Psalm 3:4-5
[15] cf John 13:35

their genuine appreciation and interest. Saint Thérèse of Lisieux writes, *Now I conjecture that true charity consists in bearing all the defects of our neighbours; in not being surprised at their weaknesses; in being edified by their slightest virtues: but I have learned especially that charity should not remain shut up inside our hearts, for men 'do not light a lamp and put it under a bushel, but on a stand and it gives light to all in the house.' It seems to me that this lamp represents charity which should enlighten and brighten not only those people I love most, but all those others who happen to be in the house.*[16] The family is extended, taking in all those who have a part in our work. And such charity will often be shown through our normal good manners and courtesy.

Another important aspect in which we have to be the *salt* and *light* Our Lord speaks about embraces *temperance* and *sobriety*. Our modern age is *characterised by a search for material well-being at any price, and by the corresponding forgetfulness – it would be better to say fear, true terror – of anything that can cause suffering. Seen from this point of view, words such as God, sin, cross, mortification, eternal life ... are incomprehensible for a great number of people, who do not understand their meaning and what they connote.*[17] This is why there is a particularly pressing need to give a generous testimony of temperance and sobriety; these show the self-control of the children of God, who use earthly goods *according to their needs and duties, with the moderation of the person using them, and not of the one who attaches too much value to them and sees himself dragged down by them.*[18]

We can ask Our Lady today to help us, through our

---

[16] St Thérèse of Lisieux, *Autobiography of a Soul*, IX, 24
[17] Bl A. del Portillo, *Letter*, 25 December 1985, 4
[18] St Augustine, *On the customs of the Catholic Church*, 1, 21

lives and our words, to be the *salt* that prevents the corruption of individuals and of society, and the *light* which not only illuminates but also gives warmth. May we always be ablaze with love, not burnt out. May our conduct clearly reflect the lovable face of Jesus Christ. With the confidence that his Blessed Mother inspires in us, let us ask from the depths of our heart: Lord our God, who made of so many saints a lamp which gives both light and heat to all men, grant us to walk with this brightness of spirit as *children of light.*[19]

---

[19] cf *Collect, Mass for St Bernard, Abbot,* 20 August

FIFTH SUNDAY: YEAR B

35. SPREADING THE TRUTH

35.1 The urgency and responsibility of taking Christ's doctrine to all environments.

As on so many occasions, Jesus rose early in the morning and went outside the city to pray. The apostles found him there and said to him, *Everyone is searching for you.* And Our Lord answered them, *Let us go on to the next towns, that I may preach there also, for that is why I came out.*[1]

Christ's mission is that of spreading the Gospel, of taking the Good News to the very ends of the earth, through the Apostles[2] and Christians of all times. This is the mission of the Church, which thus carries out Our Lord's command: *Go into all the world and preach the gospel to the whole of creation.*[3] The *Acts of the Apostles* give many details of that first evangelisation. On the day of Pentecost itself, Saint Peter preaches the divinity of Jesus Christ, his redeeming Death, and his glorious Resurrection.[4] Saint Paul, quoting the Prophet Isaiah, exclaims enthusiastically, *How beautiful are the feet of those who preach the good news!*[5] The *Second Reading* of the Mass tells us of the joyful responsibility of announcing the truth that saves: *If I preach the gospel, that gives me no ground for boasting. For necessity is laid upon me. Woe to me if I do not preach the gospel!*[6]

Using the words of Saint Peter, the Church has often

---

[1] Mark 1:29-39
[2] Mark 3:14
[3] cf Matt 18:19-20
[4] cf Acts 2:38
[5] Rom 10:15; Is 52:7
[6] 1 Cor 9:16

reminded the faithful that God calls them to make use of every opportunity to spread Christ's doctrine everywhere.[7]

Saint John Chrysostom anticipated all the possible excuses for not carrying out this most gratifying obligation. *There is*, he wrote, *nothing colder than a Christian who is unconcerned about the salvation of others ... Do not say 'I am unable to help them', for if you are truly a Christian it is impossible for you to make such an admission. The properties of natural things cannot be denied them: the same thing happens with this affirmation, for it is in the nature of a Christian to act in this way ... It is easier for the sun to fail to give its light or its heat than for a Christian to cease to give light and warmth; it would be easier for light to be darkness. Do not say that the thing is impossible; what is impossible is the opposite ... If we order our conduct aright, everything else will follow as a natural consequence. The light of Christians cannot be hidden; a light that shines so brightly cannot be concealed.*[8]

Let us ask ourselves whether, in our own environment, in the place where we live and work, we are being true transmitters of the faith; whether we bring our friends to receive the sacraments more frequently. Let us examine ourselves as to whether we feel the urgency of the apostolate as one of the demands of our vocation; whether we feel the same responsibility as those first Christians did, because the need today is no less great ... *For necessity is laid upon me. Woe to me if I do not preach the gospel!*

35.2 Apostolate and proselytism stem from our conviction that we possess the truth – the only truth that can save.

The apostolate and the proselytism that we carry out,

---

[7] cf Second Vatican Council, *Apostolicam actuositatem*, 6
[8] St John Chrysostom, *Homilies on the Acts of the Apostles*, 20

and that attract people to the Faith or to a greater
dedication to God, stem from the conviction that we
possess Truth and Love. We possess the truth that saves
and the only love that can assuage the anxieties of the
heart, which ever remains unsatisfied. When this certainty
is lost, we can see no point in spreading the Faith. Then,
even if we were in a Christian environment, we might start
doubting whether we could exert any influence. We might
despair of non-Christians ever giving their support to a just
law, a law that happens to be in accord with God's will.
We would also fail to see any sense in taking Christ's
teaching to other lands where the Faith has not yet become
firmly rooted. In any case, the apostolic mission would
become merely *social action* favouring the material
advancement of those countries. We would be forgetting
the most valuable treasure we can possibly give them –
faith in Jesus Christ and the life of grace ... We would be
Christians whose faith had grown weak, and we would
have forgotten, perhaps, that truth is all of a piece; we
would have failed to remember that it makes men and
nations more human, that it opens up the way to Heaven.

It is important that the Faith should lead us to propose
social works, but *the world cannot be satisfied simply with
social reformers. It needs saints. Holiness is not the
privilege of a few; it is a gift offered to all ... If we doubt
this it means we do not fully understand Christ's
intentions.*[9] It means that we are leaving out the essential
part of his message.

Faith is truth, and gives light to our reason and
preserves it from error. It heals the wounds of original sin
and allays the propensity to stray from the way which that
primal catastrophe bestowed upon us. It is from this that
the certainty of the Christian comes, not only in what refers

---

[9] St John Paul II, *Address to Catholic Educators*, 12 November 1987

strictly to the Faith, but to all those matters connected with it – the origin of the world and of life, the unquestionable dignity of the human person, the importance of the family ... Faith is the light which enlightens a man's path. This leads us, St Paul VI teaches, to have *a dogmatic attitude, certainly, which means it is not founded on our own knowledge, but on the Word of God ... This attitude of ours does not fill us with pride because we are the fortunate and exclusive possessors of the truth, but it makes us strong and gives us the courage to defend it. It makes us love to spread it. Saint Augustine reminds us of this: 'sine superbia de veritate praesumite' – without conceit be proud of the truth.*[10]

It is an immense gift to have received the true faith, but at the same time it is a huge responsibility. The apostolic zeal of the Christian who is aware of the treasure he has received is not fanaticism. It is love for truth; a manifestation of living faith; consistency between one's thoughts and one's life. *Proselytism* in the noble and true sense of the word does not in any way mean attracting people through deceit or violence, but is the effort of an apostle to make Christ known, along with his call to all men. It is to want souls to recognise the richness that God has revealed, and for them to be saved. It is to want them to receive the vocation to a full dedication to God, if this is God's will. This proselytism is one of the noblest tasks that God has entrusted to us.

35.3 Fidelity to the teaching we have to transmit.

In this endeavour of ours to spread the Faith, whilst we treat everybody with respect and consideration, it is useless to transmit mere half-truths for fear that the fulness of truth and the demands of an authentic Christian life may clash

---

[10] St Paul VI, *Address*, 4 August 1965

with ways of thinking currently in fashion, and with the easy-going attitude of so many people. There can be no half-measures where truth is concerned, and love which is prepared to make sacrifices cannot admit of settling for less or be the object of compromise. The condition for all apostolate is *fidelity to doctrine*, even though in some cases it may be difficult to fulfil this condition and even call for behaviour which is heroic or at least filled with fortitude. We cannot omit themes such as generosity when it comes to having a large family, or the demands of social justice, or a full dedication to God when He calls someone to follow him ... We cannot expect to please everybody by diluting the claims of the gospel so as to satisfy conventional wisdom ... *We speak*, Saint Paul wrote to the Thessalonians, *not to please men, but to please God*.[11] Claiming to make the Gospel easy, keeping quiet about (or watering down) the mysteries we are to believe and the norms of conduct by which we are to live, is not the way to go about obeying Christ's command. No one has preached, or ever will preach the Gospel with greater credibility, energy or attractiveness than Jesus, and even then there were those who did not follow him faithfully. Neither can we forget that today, as always, we preach *Christ crucified, a stumbling block to Jews and folly to Gentiles, but to those who are called, both Jews and Greeks, Christ the power of God*.[12] Nevertheless, we must always make an effort to adapt ourselves to the capacity and circumstances of the person we want to take to Christ, just as He taught us throughout the Gospels that He made accessible to everyone.

Fidelity to Christ leads us to transmit faithfully and effectively what we have received. Today, just as in the

---

[11] 1 Thess 2:3-4
[12] 1 Cor 1:23-24

days of the first Christians, when the evangelisation of Europe and of the whole world was beginning, we must announce to our friends and acquaintances, to our colleagues ... the Good News of divine mercy, the joy of following Christ very closely in the midst of our daily occupations. That announcement brings with it the need to change one's life, to do penance, to renounce self, to be detached from material things, to be chaste, to seek God's forgiveness with humility, to correspond with what He has wanted from each of us from all eternity.

Our concern that many should follow Christ should encourage us to live charity better with everyone, to find more ways of bringing them as soon as possible to God who is waiting for them. *For the love of Christ urges us on* (2 Cor 5:14). This was the moving force of Saint Paul's untiring apostolic activity, and it will be what moves us also. Love for God will lead us to feel the urgency of the apostolate, and not to waste any opportunity that arises. Moreover, in many circumstances we will be the ones to provoke those opportunities which would never occur otherwise. *Everyone is searching for you* ... The world hungers and thirsts for God. So, as well as charity, hope. Our friends and acquaintances, including those who are furthest away, also need and want God, although often they do not show this. More importantly still, *God is searching for them*.

Let us ask Our Lady to give us the same concern for the apostolate and proselytism as the Apostles and the first Christians had.

FIFTH SUNDAY: YEAR C

36. FAITH AND OBEDIENCE IN THE APOSTOLATE

36.1 Faith and obedience are essential in the apostolate.

Saint Luke tells us[1] that Jesus was standing by the Lake of Gennesareth, where so many miracles took place and so much grace was poured out by the Son of God. The people were crowding around him to such an extent that they did not leave him enough room to preach. So he got into one of the boats and asked the men to row out a little so that he could speak to the crowd who remained on the shore.

The boat that Our Lord preached from belonged to Peter, who had already met Jesus and had accompanied him on some of his journeys. Christ purposely goes into his boat. He enters progressively into Peter's life and prepares him for his decisive dedication as an Apostle. God does this with every vocation, with every soul He wants to enter deeply into. Often the grace that leads us to make a definitive decision is backed by a long preliminary history, an in-depth preparation on God's part. This preparation is so discreet and affectionate that, sometimes, we are unaware of its consisting of anything other than quite natural events, of what seem at the time to be quite normal happenings.[2]

Jesus has finished his preaching. Perhaps Peter is feeling rather pleased with himself for having been the one to lend his boat to the Master. In any case we can think about it in these terms. Then, when Jesus has finished

---

[1] Luke 5:1-11
[2] cf F. Fernandez, *St Luke's Gospel*, Madrid 1981

speaking to the crowd, he tells Peter to man the oars and put out into the deep water.

It had not been a good day. Jesus had come across them as they were washing their nets after a whole night's toiling away to no effect. They must have been feeling tired, because it was tough physical work. The nets (measuring some four to five hundred yards) were formed by a system that comprised a sort of mesh curtain, which in turn was made up of three smaller nets: they had to be lowered right to the bottom of the lake and it took at least four men to handle each net.

Peter told Our Lord that they had been working all night and had caught nothing. *The fisherman's reply seemed reasonable enough. The night hours were their normal time for fishing, and this time the attempted catch had yielded nothing. What was the point of fishing by day? But Peter has faith: 'Nevertheless, at thy word I will let down the net' (Luke 5:5). He decides to act on Christ's suggestion.*[3] Although they are tired, and although it is not a man of the sea who gives the order, and although the fishermen are well aware that the time is all wrong for fishing; although they know perfectly well there are no fish around, they put all hands to lowering the nets. Now, purely out of faith, purely out of trust in the Master, they simply dismiss from their minds those considerations that normally would tell them whether fishing was advisable or not. What sets them to work again is Peter's faith in his Master. Simon simply obeys and trusts.

In the apostolate, faith and obedience are indispensable. Of what use are our efforts, our human resources, our wakeful vigils or even our mortifications, if they are separated from any supernatural sense ...? Without obedience, everything is useless in God's eyes. It would be

---

[3] St. J. Escrivá, *Friends of God*, 261

no use starting to work if we did not intend to count on Our
Lord. Even the most worthwhile of our works would be
fruitless if while doing it we did not have the desire to
carry out God's will. *God does not need our work, but He
does need our obedience,*[4] Saint John Chrysostom
succinctly teaches.

36.2 Our Lord calls all of us to follow him closely and to be apostles in the middle of the world. Apostolic effectiveness depends on our union with Christ.

Peter completed the task Our Lord had committed to
him. *They enclosed a great shoal of fish; and their nets
were bursting.* If we are guided purely by faith, the task we
undertake will bear fruit in abundance. Peter had seldom, if
ever, fished as on that occasion, when every human
indicator pointed to the futility of the task.

This miracle contains a profound lesson. It is only
when we acknowledge our own uselessness and put our
trust in Our Lord, (at the same time using all the human
means at our disposal,) that the apostolate is effective and
the fruits abundant, because for his followers, the
*fruitfulness of the apostolate depends on their living union
with Christ.*[5]

In that shoal of fish Christ contemplates a still more
copious catch throughout the centuries. Each of his
disciples will become a new fisherman who will gather
souls into God's kingdom. *In this new task of fishing, all
the power and effectiveness of God will also be at hand:
the apostles are instruments for the working of great
wonders, in spite of their personal shortcomings.*[6]

Peter is amazed at the miracle. In a single instant he

---

[4] St John Chrysostom, *Homilies on St Matthew's Gospel*, 56
[5] Second Vatican Council, *Apostolicam actuositatem*, 4
[6] St. J. Escrivá, *loc cit*

sees everything with great clarity: Christ's omnipotence and wisdom; his own calling and his unworthiness. He throws himself down at the feet of Jesus as soon as they come to land. *Depart from me,* he says, *for I am a sinful man.* He acknowledges the loftiness of Christ's great dignity, his own wretchedness and his obvious lack of ability to carry out the mission of which he already has a presentiment. But at the same time he asks the Lord to stay with him forever. If his defects and his personal unworthiness do not disqualify him for his mission or separate him from it, he knows that with Christ there is nothing he cannot do. Then Our Lord takes away his fear and reveals to him in all its clarity the new meaning of his life: *Do not be afraid; henceforth you will be catching men.* Jesus draws on Peter's occupation, in the pursuance of which He had sought him out, to make known to him his mission as an Apostle. *The awareness of God's holiness and of our condition as sinners does not separate men from God, but rather brings men closer to him. Moreover, once a man has been converted, he declares his faith openly and becomes an apostle. He feels that God's intentions are now within his reach, and they become lovable to him. His life then takes on its deepest meaning and value.*[7]

Our Lord calls all of us to be apostles in the middle of the world, whether we are sitting by a computer, or following the plough, in the great city or in a little village, with five talents or with three or with one. Jesus does not want his followers to be second-rate. He calls all of us, so that with holiness of life and by giving good human example we may be instruments of his in a world that seems to turn its back on him. *All the faithful, whatever their condition or state – though each in his own way – are called by the Lord to that perfection of sanctity by which*

---

[7] St John Paul II, *Homily*, 6 February 1983

our heavenly Father himself is perfect.[8] *By means of their special vocation it belongs to the laity to seek the kingdom of God by engaging in temporal affairs and directing them according to God's will.*[9] Our Lord calls those who are Christians, and leaves the majority of them in some job or professional occupation, so that that is where they find him, fulfilling their particular task with human perfection, and at the same time with supernatural outlook. Offering their work to God, they live charity with everyone, not spurning the little mortifications that arise and constantly seeking presence of God ...

36.3 The Apostles' readiness to follow Our Lord. He calls us too. He will give us all the help we need so that we may be good instruments.

God's call – and He calls each one of us – is first of all an initiative that He himself takes, but it demands human reciprocation: *You did not choose me, but I chose you.*[10] And perhaps we discover that we are not worthy to be so close to Christ, or that we lack the dispositions to be instruments of grace. It is the situation of each man who finds, in the depths of his soul, a strong and imperative call from God. Thus the prophet Isaiah – as we are told in the *First Reading* of today's Mass[11] – when he feels the closeness of God's majesty, exclaims: *Woe is me! I am lost; for I am a man of unclean lips, and I dwell in the midst of a people of unclean lips; for my eyes have seen the King, the Lord of hosts!* But God knows our littleness, and just as He purified Isaiah and so many of the men and women He has called to his service, He will cleanse our

---

[8] Second Vatican Council, *Lumen gentium*, 11
[9] *ibid*, 31
[10] John 15:16
[11] Is 6:1-8

lips and our hearts. *Then flew one of the seraphim to me, having in his hand a burning coal ... And he touched my mouth, and said: 'Behold, this has touched your lips; your guilt is taken away, and your sin forgiven.'* The Lord forgives us in Confession, and we purify ourselves mainly through penance.

The Gospel continues: *And when they had brought their boats to land, they left everything and followed him.* After they had contemplated Christ they did not have to puzzle over things any more. Generally the resolute decisions that transform a person's whole life are not the result of lengthy conjecture. From that time on, Peter's life was to have a wonderful objective, *to love Christ and to be a fisher of men.* Everything else in his life was to be *an instrument and means towards this end. The same is true of us. If we struggle daily to become saints, each of us in his own situation in the world and through his own job or profession, in our ordinary lives, then I assure you that God will make us into instruments that can work miracles, and, if necessary, miracles of the most extraordinary kind.*[12]

Our Lord speaks to each one of us too, so that we may feel the urgency of following him closely in the midst of our own occupations, and of carrying out a daring apostolate in our own environment. At the same time we must have faith in Jesus' word, *'Duc in altum'.* Put out into deep water! Throw aside the pessimism that makes a coward of you. *'Et laxate retia vestra in capturam.'* And pay out your nets for a catch.

Don't you see that you, like Peter, can say: 'In nomine tuo, laxabo rete.' Jesus, if you say so, I will search for souls?[13]

---

[12] St. J. Escrivá, *op cit,* 262
[13] *idem, The Way,* 792

As we contemplate the figure of Peter we too will want to say to Jesus: *Depart from me, for I am a sinful man, O Lord.* And at the same time we will beg him not to let us ever leave him, and to help us to plunge right in, *into deep water* – into friendship with him, into holiness, into carrying out a sincere apostolate. We will ask him to rid us of human respect, and to fill us with faith, because in our personal prayer we know how to listen to the voice of Our Lord, who urges us to take souls to him.

Then, though you won't see why, because you're very aware of your own wretchedness, you will find that people come to you. Then you can talk to them quite simply and naturally – on your way home from work for instance, or in a family gathering, on a bus, walking down the street, anywhere. You will chat about the sort of longings that everyone feels deep down in his soul, even though some people may not want to pay attention to them; they will come to understand them better when they begin to look for God in earnest.

Ask Mary, 'Regina Apostolorum', to help you make up your mind to share the desires of 'sowing and fishing' that fill the Heart of her Son. I can assure you that if you begin, you will see the boat filled, just like the fishermen from Galilee. And you will find Christ on the shore, waiting for you. Because the catch belongs to him.[14]

---

[14] *idem, Friends of God, 273*

FIFTH WEEK: MONDAY

37. LIVING IN SOCIETY

37.1 The social dimension of man.

The first page of Holy Scripture gives us a description, both simple and grandiose, of the creation of the world; *And God saw that it was good* – that is everything that came from his hands.[1] Finally, to crown all that He had done, He created man, and made him in his own image and likeness.[2] Scripture itself teaches us that He enriched him with supernatural gifts and privileges, and destined him to a happiness which would be ineffable and eternal. Scripture also reveals to us that all other men are descended from Adam and Eve. Although they separated themselves from their Creator, God did not cease to look on them as his children, and destined them once more to share his friendship.[3] God willed that the human creature should share in the conservation and propagation of the human race, that he should people the earth and subject it to himself. *Have dominion over the fish of the sea and over the birds of the air, and over every living thing that moves upon the earth.*[4]

God also willed that relationships between men should not be limited to an occasional and fleeting expression of concern for their neighbours, but that they should constitute stronger and lasting bonds, which would become the very pillars on which life in society would rest. Men would look to others for help in providing all that the

---

[1] cf *First Reading*, Year I, Gen 1:1 *et seq*
[2] cf Gen 1:27
[3] cf Gen 12
[4] Gen 1:28

necessities and the dignity of life would require and demand. For divine Providence ordered human nature in such a way that men should be born inclined to associate with others of their kind and to unite themselves with other people both in the society of the home and in civic society. And such associations would provide them with the necessities of life.[5] The Second Vatican Council reminds us that *by his innermost nature man is a social being, and if he does not enter into relations with others he can neither live as a human being nor develop his gifts.*[6] *Society is a natural means that man can and should use in order to reach his end.*[7] It is the ordinary sphere in which God wants us to sanctify ourselves and to serve him.

Living in society makes it easier for us to obtain the material and spiritual means that we need in order to develop our human and supernatural life. Living with others gives rise to many advantages and benefits, but also to obligations whatever the environment we happen to inhabit: think of your place within the family, in civil society, in your neighbourhood, at work ... These obligations are invested with a moral character because of the relationship of man to God his ultimate end. Observing these obligations, or failing to keep them brings us closer to or separates us further from God. They are matter for our examination of conscience.

God calls us to live with others, to simply make what contribution we can – small or large – to the good of all. In our prayer today, let us examine whether we live open to other people, but especially to those that God has placed closest to us. We should consider whether we generally make ourselves available; whether we give good example

---

[5] cf Leo XIII, *Immortale Dei*, 1 November 1885
[6] Second Vatican Council, *Gaudium et spes*, 12
[7] Pius XI, *Divini Redemptoris*, 19 March 1937

in the way we fulfil our family and social duties; whether we frequently ask God for light to know what we have to do whenever an opportunity arises, and to carry our task through to the end, courageously, with a spirit of sacrifice. We should often ask ourselves: What can I do for other people? What words can I say to console and help others? *Life is passing. We are constantly coming across people from the most varied walks in life. What a lot remains to be done ... How many words still have to be spoken ... Certainly we have to start by doing (cf Acts 1:1); but then, too, we have to speak: each ear, each heart, each mind has its own moment, its friendly voice that can call it out of its slough of despondency, and encourage it to rise out of its present state of unhappiness.*

If we love God, we cannot fail to feel the reproach of the days that pass, of the people (often so close to us) who pass by, ungreeted, unhailed ... without our being able to do whatever it was that was needed, without our even knowing how to say what we should have said.[8] We should often ask Jesus, who sees us and who hears us, never to let us turn our back in indifference on those who, by whatever chance, are encountered around us: through kinship or friendship, through working for the same firm, through coming from the same town ...

37.2 Charity and human fellowship. Consequences in the life of a Christian.

This solidarity and mutual dependence of ours on others, which proceeds from God's will, was endorsed and strengthened by Jesus Christ when He took on our human nature at the moment of his Incarnation, and when He redeemed the whole human race on the Cross. This is the new claim to unity: we have been made children of God

---

[8] C. López Pardo, *On Life and Death*, Madrid 1973

and brothers of all men. Thus we have to take an interest in everyone who crosses our path each day. *Perhaps it is a son of God who is unaware of his grandeur, and who possibly is rebelling against his Father. But in all of them, even in the most deformed, the most rebellious or distant from anything divine, there is a spark of God's greatness ... If we know how to look, we shall find that we are surrounded by kings whom we have to help to discover their roots, and the obligations of their dignity.*[9]

Moreover, on the night before his Passion, Our Lord left us a *New Commandment* that of rising above grievances, resentments, grudges ... anything that causes separation, even if this demands heroism. *This is my commandment, that you love one another as I have loved you.*[10] That is to say, without any limits, and without any excuses that permit ignoring people or being indifferent. Thus our life is full of powerful reasons for living in society, which, as our actions cause it to become more Christian, in turn becomes more human. We, men, are not like grains of sand, loose and separate and unconnected to each other, but, on the contrary, as human beings we are mutually related by natural bonds and, as Christians, by supernatural ties as well.[11]

An important part of morality concerns the duties that refer to the common good of all men – the good of the country in which we live, of the firm for which we work, of the neighbourhood of which we form part, of the family that is the object of all our care, whatever our position within it may be. It is not Christian, or even human, to consider those duties only insofar as they are useful or disadvantageous to us personally. God awaits us in the

---

[9] *ibid*
[10] John 15:12
[11] cf Pius XII, *Summi pontificatus*, 20 October 1939

efforts we make, each according to our possibilities, to improve society and the individuals who comprise it.

The apostolic and fraternal dimension is, by divine Will, so essential to man that he cannot imagine any orientation towards God which lacks the bonds that unite each person to the ones he lives with or has dealings with. We do not please God if, in any way, we separate ourselves from the people around us, if we fail to practise civic and social virtues. *We must learn to recognize Christ when He comes out to meet us in our brothers, the people around us. No human life is ever isolated. It is bound up with other lives. No man or woman is a single verse; we all make up one divine poem which God writes with the co-operation of our freedom.*[12]

Let us examine today in our personal prayer how we are contributing to the common good of all. Do we give good example in everything related to our social and civic duties (obeying the traffic laws, paying just taxes, taking part in associations, exercising our right to vote ...)? Do we remember always that we need other people, and that other people need us? Do we feel partly responsible for the moral behaviour of others? Do we try unhesitatingly to rise above anything that can cause division, or that at least does not help to establish or maintain harmony?

37.3 Our contribution to the common good.

The development of any society comes about through the contribution made by its members, each one of whom brings to it what is his – those gifts that he received from God and which he has added to by his own intellect, by the help given to him by society and by God's grace. We were endowed with such benefits and gifts so that we might develop our own personality and reach our ultimate end;

---

[12] St. J. Escrivá, *Christ is passing by*, 111

but they were also given to us so that we might serve our neighbour. Moreover, we would never be able to achieve our personal end if we did not contribute to the good of everyone else.[13]

As the development of society is by no means marginal to God's plans, the personal co-operation of each individual in the common good takes on the character of an unavoidable moral obligation. *Life in society is not something accessory to man himself: through his dealings with others, through mutual service and through fraternal dialogue man develops all his talents, and becomes able to rise to his destiny.*[14] Some obligations are of strict justice in their various forms: others are demanded by charity, which goes further than giving to each one what is strictly his due. Both types of obligation are fulfilled each time we contribute to the good of all, so that the society in which we live should be more human and more Christian, by, for instance, *fostering and helping public and private organisations devoted to bettering the conditions of life.*[15] These can comprise, works of charity and of formation, programmes of culture, publications giving sound doctrine, etc. For *there is a kind of person who boasts of grand and noble philanthropic sentiments, and who lives in practice as if he could not care less about the needs of society. There are many in various countries who make light of social laws and directives.*[16] When they do so, they turn their backs on their brother men and on God.

Let us think in God's presence about the people around us. Do I contribute as far as I can to fostering the common good by giving my time to institutions and to

---

[13] cf Leo XIII, *Rerum novarum*, 15 September 1881
[14] Second Vatican Council, *Gaudium et spes*, 25
[15] *ibid*, 30
[16] *ibid*

works that are carried on for the good of society, by co-operating financially, by supporting initiatives directed at helping others, especially the people in most need? Do I faithfully carry out the obligations that stem from living as a member of society: as far as noise, cleanliness etc. are concerned? Do I cultivate the virtues that make life pleasant for others – affability, gratitude, optimism, punctuality, order ... within my family? Am I generally moved by a desire to serve others, even though it may be in very small things? *May you acquire the custom of concerning yourself every day about others, and give yourself to the task so much that you forget you even exist.*[17] If we could do this we would find a large part of the happiness that can be found on this earth and we would have helped others to be happier – people who happen to be children of God and our brothers.

FIFTH WEEK: TUESDAY

38. THE FOURTH COMMANDMENT

38.1 God's blessing on those who keep this commandment. The promise of a long life.

In the Gospel of today's Mass,[1] Our Lord makes clear the true meaning and extent of the fourth commandment of the Decalogue. His explanation is quite different from the erroneous interpretations produced by the casuistry of the Scribes and Pharisees. God himself, through the lips of Moses, had said: *Honour your father and your mother. And he who speaks evil of father or mother, let him surely die.*

Keeping this commandment is so pleasing to God that he adorned it with the promise of countless blessings. *Whoever honours his father atones for sins, and when he prays he will be heard. Whoever glorifies his mother is like one who lays up treasure. Whoever glorifies his father will have long life.*[2] This promise of a long life for the person who loves and honours his parents is repeated time and again. *Honour your father and your mother, that your days may be long in the land which the Lord your God gives you.*[3] Explaining this passage, Saint Thomas teaches that life is long when it is full, and this fulness is not measured in terms of time, but by deeds. A full life is lived when the life concerned is filled with virtues and effectiveness; then it is that a life has been a long one, even though the body die young.[4] Our Lord also promises 'good name' (in spite of calumny), wealth, and many descendants. About the

---

[1] Mark 7:1-13
[2] Sir 3:4-5, 7
[3] Ex 20:12
[4] cf St Thomas, *On the double precept of charity*, 1245

descendants, Saint Thomas goes on to say that there are not only children according to the flesh but that there are a number of reasons that give rise to other modes of spiritual fatherhood which demand a corresponding respect and reverence.[5]

In spite of the clarity with which this commandment is explained in these and in many other passages of the Old Testament, the doctors and priests of the temple had distorted its meaning and the way it should be fulfilled.[6] They taught that if anyone said to his father or to his mother *What you would have gained from me is Corban* (that is, given to God),[7] his parents could not expect to receive any part of those goods, even though they might be in great need, for they had been declared *given to God*, and such giving away would be a sacrilege. This custom was often a mere legal device, so that they could continue to enjoy the benefits of their property whilst being released from the natural obligation of helping their parents in their necessity.[8] Our Lord, as we have said, the Messiah and Legislator, explains the true extent and meaning of the fourth commandment. He corrects the very seriously erroneous teaching about this matter which was prevalent in his day.

The divine positive Law's fourth commandment, which also happens to be a precept of the natural law, obliges *all* men, *but especially those who want to be good Christians*, to give their help and affection to their parents even though this may demand sacrifice on their part. They can do this each day in a thousand little ways, and the fulfilment of the commandment becomes particularly

---

[5] cf *ibid* 1247
[6] cf *The Navarre Bible*, note to Matt 15:5-6
[7] Mark 7:11
[8] cf B. Orchard and others, *Verbum Dei*, vol III

important when their parents are elderly or their circumstances render them more in need of help.[9] When we have true love for God we realise that He never asks for things that contradict each other. We can find the right way of showing our love for our parents even when our first duty is to obligations of a family, social or religious nature. There is great scope here for living up to our filial responsibilities. Children should frequently examine themselves in their personal prayer on how they fulfil these responsibilities in God's presence. Already in this life, God repays with happiness those who lovingly carry out these duties towards their parents, even though such duties may sometimes weigh heavily on them. St Josemaría Escrivá used to call this commandment *the most sweet commandment of the decalogue*, because it is one of the obligations God has committed to us that is most acceptable and pleasing to him.

38.2 Love for our parents is shown with deeds. The meaning of 'honouring our parents.

The sense of our divine filiation gives us one of the strongest reasons for lovingly fulfilling the fourth commandment. God is the only being who can be considered Father in all the fulness of fatherhood – He, *from whom every family in heaven and on earth takes its name.*[10] When our parents engendered us, they shared in that fatherhood of God which extends to the whole of creation. In our earthly father and mother we can see a reflection of the Creator, and when we love them and honour them as we should, we are at the same time loving and honouring God as what He is – our Father.

During the liturgical season of Christmas we

---

[9] Second Vatican Council, *Gaudium et spes*, 48
[10] Eph 3:15

contemplated the Holy Family – Jesus, Mary and Joseph – as the model and prototype of love and spirit of service for all families. Jesus left us the example we must follow, and taught us how to fulfil the *sweet precept* of the fourth commandment precisely in the way that God wills. Above all, Jesus reaffirmed *that love for God has some absolute rights to which all human love must be subordinated. He who loves father or mother more than me is not worthy of me; and he who loves son or daughter more than me is not worthy of me.*[11] So we can see that any disordered attachment to one's own family which becomes an obstacle to carrying out God's Will is contrary to his Will, and consequently is not true love at all. *But Jesus said to him: 'Leave the dead to bury their own dead; but as for you, go and proclaim the kingdom of God.'*[12]

Jesus left us a perfect example of complete surrender to the Will of his heavenly Father: *Did you not know that I must be in my father's house?*[13] He was to say to Mary and Joseph when they found him in Jerusalem. At the same time He is the perfect model of how we should keep this commandment and the perfect model of the affection we should have for family ties: He, true God as well as true man, lived subject to the authority of his parents.[14] He learned his trade from Joseph,[15] and in doing so helped him to provide for the family. It was at his mother's bidding that He worked the first of his miracles.[16] He chose three of his disciples from among his relatives.[17] Before He died for us on the Cross He entrusted his most Blessed Mother to

---

[11] Matt 10:37; cf also Luke 9:60; 14:2
[12] Luke 9:60
[13] Luke 2:49
[14] Luke 2:51
[15] cf Mark 6:3
[16] cf John 2:1-11
[17] cf Mark 3:17-18; 6:3

Saint John's care.[18] He worked countless miracles moved by the tears or the words of a mother[19] or of a father.[20] The prayers of parents for their children have a special priority about them when they reach God.

Again we honour our parents when we relieve their needs and wants, supplying them with necessary food and clothing according to those words of Christ, when He reproved the impiety of the Pharisees ... This duty becomes still more imperative when our parents are visited by severe illness. We should see to it that they do not neglect confession and the other sacraments which every Christian should receive ...

Finally, we honour our parents even after their death by attending their funeral ceremonies, procuring for them suitable obsequies and burial, having due suffrages and anniversary Masses offered for them, and faithfully executing their last wills.[21] The Catechism of the Council of Trent expresses and summarises the fourth commandment in this way.

If, sadly, our parents are far from the Faith, God will give us the grace to do apostolate with them, an apostolate which is full of reverence and respect. Generally we will do this by generously offering prayer and mortification for them, and by giving an example of filial behaviour which is cheerful, exemplary and filled with affection. We will also endeavour to find opportunities to put them in contact with people who can speak to them about God with greater authority, because children cannot set themselves up as the teachers of their parents.

---

[18] cf John 19:26-27
[19] cf Luke 7:11-17; Matt 15:22-28
[20] cf Matt 9:18-26; 17:14-20
[21] *Catechism of the Council of Trent*, III, 5, 10-12

38.3 Love for one's children. Some of the duties of parents.

The first duty of parents is to love their children with real love. This means love which comes from within, and is generous, ordered, and independent of the physical, intellectual or moral qualities of the children. Such a love will enable parents to love their children with all their defects. They must love their children because they are theirs, but also because they are children of God. From this arises the fundamental duty of parents to love and respect God's Will for their sons and daughters, particularly when they receive a vocation to give themselves completely to him. Good parents should often ask God for such a vocation, and wish it for their children, because *giving up one's children to the service of God is not a sacrifice: it is an honour and a joy.*[22] This love must be an operative love, effectively shown through deeds. True love will be seen in the effort parents make to bring up their children to be hard-working, austere, educated in the full sense of the word – and, above all, good Christians. They should help to form the beginnings of the human virtues in them: resilience, sobriety in the use of material things, a sense of responsibility, generosity, industriousness, when it comes to a question of spending money – an awareness of the needs suffered by many people throughout the world.

True love will lead parents to be concerned about the school to which they send their children, and will cause them to take a real interest in the quality of the education they receive. They should be particularly watchful about what they are taught in religious education, because their very salvation may depend on it. Love for their children will move them to look for suitable places in which to spend their holidays and their leisure time. Often this will

---

[22] St. J. Escrivá, *Furrow*, 22

involve sacrificing other tastes and interests they may have. Whenever possible they will avoid those environments which would make it impossible or at least very difficult to practise a true Christian life. Parents must not forget that they are the administrators of an immense treasure that belongs to God. As Christians they are not just one more family they will teach this to their children when the moment comes, but they form a family in which Christ is present, and this gives them certain completely new characteristics. This living reality will encourage parents to give good example all the time, in family life, professional duties, sobriety, order ... When they do so, their children will find in them the way that leads to God. *In every mother's face we can glimpse a reflection of Mary's sweetness, intuition and generosity. If you honour your mother, you will also honour her, who being Christ's mother, is likewise the Mother of each one of us.*[23]

Let us finish our prayer by placing our family under the protection of the Most Blessed Virgin and of the Guardian Angels.

---

[23] St John Paul II, *Address*, 10 January 1979

FIFTH WEEK: WEDNESDAY

39. THE DIGNITY OF WORK

39.1 The divine command to work is a blessing.

After God had created the earth and enriched it with all manner of good things, He *took the man and put him in the garden of Eden to till it and keep it.*[1] That is to say, to work in it. God, who had made man *in his own image and likeness,*[2] wanted him also to share in his creative activity. He wanted him to transform matter, to discover the treasures within it and to mould beauty into the works of his hands. Work was not in any way a punishment, but, on the contrary, *dignity of life and a duty imposed by the Creator, for man was created 'ut operaretur', that he might work. Work is a means by which man shares in the task of creation, and therefore, whatever it may consist of, it is not only something that dignifies man, but is an instrument by which he attains human – earthly – perfection, as well as supernatural perfection.*[3]

The divine command to work was already in existence before our first parents sinned. Original sin, however, was the cause of work's becoming something hard and tiring. But in itself work continues to be something which ennobles man and gives him still greater dignity, because it is a participation in the creative power and activity of God, even though *now it is accompanied by hardship and suffering, by fruitlessness and weariness. It is still a gift that God gives us, although it is also a task that has to be accomplished under difficult circumstances and conditions,*

---

[1] *First Reading*, Year I, Gen 2:15
[2] cf Gen 1:27
[3] St. J. Escrivá, *Letter*, 31 May 1954

in just the same way as the world continues to be God's world, although it is a world in which we are unable to perceive clearly God's voice.[4]

Work is a blessing, something good, something that is in keeping with man's dignity and increases it.[5] *The Church finds in the very first pages of the Book of Genesis the source of her conviction that work is a fundamental dimension of human existence on earth.*[6]

With Christ, in his years of hidden life in Nazareth and in the three years of his public ministry, work acquired a redemptive value. With the Redemption, the difficult aspects of work assumed a sanctifying value for the person doing the work and for the whole of mankind. Sweat and toil offered up with love become treasures of holiness, for work done for love of God is the way that men are given the opportunity to share, not only in the work of Creation, but also in the work of the Redemption. All work brings about a certain tiredness and stress that we can offer to God in expiation for our offences and for the offences of other human beings. The humble acceptance of that exertion, which cannot be completely eliminated however well organised our work may be, means that we can play our part in the purification of our intellect, of our will and of our senses.[7] In our prayer today we should examine whether we often complain about our work – in the office, in the workshop, about the house or when we study. We should consider in God's presence whether we offer, for ends that are nobly ambitious, the tiredness brought about by our hard work. We should check whether in those less attractive aspects that belong to any type of work, we

---

[4] M. Schmaus, *Dogmatic Theology*, II
[5] cf St John Paul II, Encyclical, *Laborem exercens*, I, 9
[6] *ibid*, 4
[7] cf Cardinal Wyszynsky, *Work*

discover that opportunity for offering up the Christian mortification that purifies us, and which we can offer up for others.

39.2 Professional prestige. Laziness, the enemy of work.

Work is a talent that man receives in order to make it produce fruit, and it *bears witness to the dignity of man, to his dominion over creation. It provides an opportunity to develop one's personality. It is a bond of solidarity with other men, and is the way to support one's family, a means of contributing to the improvement of the society in which we live and in aiding the progress of all humanity.*[8] For a Christian, work which is done well is the means of our entering into a personal encounter with Jesus Christ as well as being a way of enabling all the realities of this world to be shaped by the spirit of the Gospel.

So that *man can be more a man*[9] through work; so that work may become a means and an opportunity for man to love Christ and bring others to know him, it is necessary that a whole series of human conditions be fulfilled – diligence, constancy, punctuality ... professional prestige and competence. On the other hand, a lack of interest in what one is doing, incompetence, frequent absenteeism from work ... all these are incompatible with the really Christian meaning of life. The worker who is negligent or who lacks interest, whatever his job or position in society, offends first of all against his own dignity, and then against those who receive the product of that badly-done work. He offends against the society in which he lives, because in some way all the evil and all the good done by individuals have repercussions on human society. Work which is done badly or carelessly or is not properly finished is not only a

---

[8] St. J. Escrivá, *Christ is passing by*, 47
[9] cf St John Paul II, *loc cit*

fault or even a sin against the virtue of justice, but also against charity, because of the bad example it gives and because of its consequences.

The great enemy of work is *laziness*, which has many manifestations. The lazy person is not only the one who wastes time by doing nothing, but also the person who does many things but refuses to see his specific task through to completion. He chooses his occupations according to the whim of the moment, puts no effort into them, and abandons the task at the slightest difficulty. The lazy workman is a friend of 'beginning', but he is put off by the sacrifice that constancy and perseverance in work demand of him, and this prevents him from putting *the last stones* in place, from ever completing what he has started.

If we want to imitate Christ, we must make an effort to acquire the right training for our chosen profession or job. We will then follow this up throughout our working lives. The mother who dedicates herself to looking after her children needs to know how to run a home, how to be a good administrator of the money and equipment at her disposal. She should make sure the house is pleasant, arranged with taste rather than luxury, so that the whole family can feel at home. She needs to understand the character of her children and of her husband, and to know, if needed, how to go about getting them to improve in matters relating to their individual behaviour. She needs to be firm and at the same time gentle and uncomplicated. She will need to carry out her task as efficiently and thoroughly as she would have to do if she went out to work. She should keep to a predetermined timetable. She must not waste time in endless conversations. She ought to avoid switching on the television set at any random time ...

If a student wants to be a good Christian, he has to be a good student – one who studies. He needs to attend classes. He must keep up with his assignments, keep his notes in order and learn to allocate his time to his various subjects. The architect, the secretary, the dressmaker and the entrepreneur all have to be equally competent in their own field.

The Second Vatican Council teaches: *The Christian who shirks his temporal duties, shirks his duties towards his neighbour, neglects God himself, and endangers his eternal salvation.*[10] Such a person has mistaken the road he should take in a matter of fundamental importance, and if he does not change, it will be impossible for him to find God.

Let us look at Jesus as he does his work in Joseph's workshop and ask ourselves today whether we are known by the people around us as people who do their work well.

39.3 The virtues involved in doing our work well.

Professional prestige is earned, day after day, by work which is normally silent, finished off down to the last detail and done conscientiously in God's presence without too much concern about whether people notice it or not. This prestige in one's own profession or trade (for students, in their study) has immediate repercussions on one's colleagues and friends: our words with which we try to lead them to God will carry a proportionate weight and authority. The example we give of competent work will help them to improve in their own work. Our profession will become a pedestal for Christ, so that he can be seen, even by those who are far away.

As well as professional prestige, God asks us for other virtues: for a spirit of service, which is both pleasant for others and demanding on ourselves; for simplicity and humility, so that we teach without giving ourselves too much importance; for serenity, so that intense activity does

---

[10] Second Vatican Council, *Gaudium et spes*, 43

not turn into mere activism. We need to know how to leave our work and worries to one side when the time comes to stop in order to pray or to look after the various members of the family. We do not make it an excuse when the time comes to listen to our wife, our husband, our children, our parents, or our friends ...

Work should not take up so much of our day that it occupies the time that should be dedicated to God, to the family, to our friends ... If this should happen it would be a clear sign that we are not sanctifying ourselves through our work, but rather that we are simply seeking self-satisfaction in it. It would be another form of corruption of that *divine gift*. This deformation is perhaps more dangerous in our day because of the false reasons for which many people work. We, ordinary simple Christians in the middle of the world, should never forget that we must find Christ each day in and through our occupation, whatever it may be.

Let us turn to Saint Joseph and ask him to teach us the basic virtues that we must live in the exercise of our profession: *I am sure Joseph knew how to lend a hand in many difficulties, with work well done. His skilled work was carried out in the service of others, to brighten by its perfection the lives of other families in their neighbourhood; and with a smile, a friendly word, an apparently casual remark, he would restore faith and happiness to those in danger of losing them.*[11] Close to Joseph we will find Mary.

---

[11] St. J. Escrivá, *loc cit*, 51

40. HUMILITY AND PERSEVERANCE IN PRAYER

40.1 The curing of the daughter of the Canaanite woman. Conditions for true prayer.

Saint Mark tells us in the Gospel of today's Mass that Jesus and his disciples came to the region of Tyre and Sidon.[1] A gentile woman approached them. She was a Syrophoenician by birth, one of those belonging to the indigenous population of Palestine. She cast herself at his feet and asked him to cure her daughter, who was possessed by the devil. Jesus did not answer. His disciples, exasperated by the woman's insistence, ask him to send her away.[2] Our Lord explains to the woman that the Messiah must first make himself known to the Jews, to the children of Israel. Then, with an expression that is hard to understand unless we hear his tone of voice and see the affectionate gestures that accompany it, he says, *Let the children be fed first, for it is not right to take the children's bread and throw it to the dogs.* The woman is not offended or humiliated. With deep humility she insists, *Yes, Lord; but even the little dogs under the table eat the children's crumbs.* Jesus is moved by her great faith and immediately grants her the miracle she desires. *For this saying,* he tells her, *you may go your way; the demon has left your daughter.* God opposes the proud but gives grace to the humble.[3] That woman obtained what she wanted and touched the Master's heart.

She is a perfect example for those who tire of praying because they think their prayers have not been heard. In her

---

[1] Mark 7:24-30
[2] Matt 15:23
[3] 1 Pet 5:5

prayer we find the conditions required for all successful petition – faith, humility, perseverance and confidence. Her great love for her daughter who was possessed by the devil would have been most pleasing to Our Lord. The apostles may have remembered this woman later when they heard the parable of the importunate widow[4] who also got what she wanted as a result of her stubbornness and persistence.

Saint Thomas teaches that true prayer is infallibly effective. God has decreed that it should be so, and He does not change his mind.[5] Our Lord teaches us not to become discouraged and give up in our requests. He gives us clear and simple examples to help us understand that when we pray with a right intention, He hears us and listens to us. *What father among you, if his son asks for a piece of bread will hand him a stone, or if he asks for a fish, will instead of a fish give him a snake; or if he asks for an egg, will give him a scorpion ... How much more will your heavenly Father give![6] God has never refused anything and will refuse nothing to those who ask his grace in the proper way. Prayer is the great means we have for overcoming sin, for persevering in grace, for turning our hearts to God and drawing down upon us all kinds of blessings, whether for our souls or for our temporal needs.[7]*

When we ask for some gift we should remember that we are God's children. He takes far greater care of us than the best father in the world takes of that child of his who most wants his help.

40.2 Filial confidence and perseverance in our petitions.

God has foreseen from all eternity the help we need.

---

[4] Luke 18:3
[5] cf St Thomas, *Summa Theologiae*, II-II, 83, 2
[6] cf John 2:11
[7] St Jean Vianney, The Curé d'Ars, *Sermon for the Fifth Sunday of Easter*

He has also foreseen the assistance we will require and the graces that will lead us to make our requests. He treats us as children who are free and simply asks us to co-operate. It is as necessary for us to ask in order to obtain God's help, in order to do good and persevere, as it is necessary to sow the seed in order to reap the harvest of grain.[8] Unless the seed is sown the ears of wheat do not grow; if we do not ask, we shall not receive the graces we require. In so far as we intensify our demands, we identify our will with that of God. It is He who truly knows the depths of our need, of our utter poverty. At times He makes us wait so that we might be better disposed, so that we will desire those graces more earnestly and fervently. On other occasions He rectifies our petition and grants us what we *really* need. And yet there are times when He does not grant us what we are asking for, because, perhaps without realising it, we are actually asking for something that is harmful, something that has presented itself to our will under the appearance of some desirable good. A mother does not give her child a sharp knife that shines attractively just because the little child wants it with all his heart. We are like little children to God. When we ask for something that would be bad for us, even if it seems to us to be good, God acts just as a good mother will act with her little ones. He gives us instead other graces which will be good for us, although we might be less clamourously interested in them. Our prayer has to be filled with trust, as when asking something from our father. It has to be confident, since God knows what we need better than we do ourselves.

Trust leads us to ask with constancy, with perseverance. Undaunted, we insist over and over again, certain that we will receive more and better than we are asking for. We must persist in our asking, like the importunate friend who needed

---

[8] cf R. Garrigou-Lagrange, *The Three Ages of the Interior Life*, vol I, p. 500

bread or the helpless widow who besought the unrighteous judge night and day. *Ask, and it will be given you; seek and you will find; knock, and it will be opened to you. For every one who asks receives, and he who seeks finds, and to him who knocks it will be opened.*[9] This very perseverance in prayer leads by itself to an increase of trust and friendship with God. *And this friendship which produces the request opens the way to a more trusting entreaty ... as though having been introduced into the divine intimacy by the first request we are enabled to implore with greater confidence the next time. Thus, when we address a petition to God, constancy and persistence are never inexpedient. Quite the opposite. They are pleasing to God.*[10] We should imitate the Canaanite woman, that outstanding example of constancy, even though Our Lord seemed not to be willing to pay any attention to her. Our Lord sets no limits to the effectiveness of prayer. *Everyone who asks receives,* for God is our Father. Saint Augustine teaches that on occasion our prayer is not answered because we are not good, because we lack purity of heart or rectitude of intention. We ask in the wrong spirit, without faith, perseverance or humility. We ask for things that are bad, things that are not good for us, that could harm us or lead us astray.[11] In short, prayer is ineffective when it is not real prayer. *Pray. In what human venture could you have greater guarantees of success?*[12] *Truly I say to you, if you ask anything of the Father in my name He will give it to you.*[13]

40.3 We should ask for supernatural graces. The Rosary – a powerful weapon.

Deliver us, Lord, we pray, from every evil, graciously

[9] Luke 11:9-10
[10] St Thomas, *Compendium of Theology*, II, 2
[11] cf St Augustine, *On the Sermon on the Mount*, II, 73
[12] St. J. Escrivá, *The Way*, 96
[13] John 16:23

grant peace in our days, that by the help of your mercy, we may be always free from sin and safe from all distress ... [14] is the priest's audible prayer during the Mass. In our prayer of petition we can ask favours for ourselves or for others. First of all we should ask for the goods and graces needed by our souls. However many and however serious the material limitations or privations we undergo, we invariably have greater need of spiritual benefits – such as the grace to serve God and to be faithful, to grow in personal holiness, to receive help to win through in the struggle against our defects, to make a good confession, to prepare for Holy Communion ... We ask for temporal goods insofar as they are useful for our salvation and are rightly considered secondary to the graces and gifts of the spirit that we first and foremost have need of.

Our Lord taught us how to ask for things: *Give us this day our daily bread* ... The first miracle worked by Jesus, the one by which *he manifested himself to his disciples* [15] was of *a material kind. Mary appears in Cana, where, when she tactfully told her Son of a temporal need, she also obtained an effect of grace. The effect was that Jesus, in working the first of his 'signs', confirmed his disciples' faith in him.* [16] If we are living unity of life, all goods of a material nature contribute in some way to the glory of God. The miracle of Cana worked through the intercession of Mary encourages us and invites us to ask for graces of a temporal nature that are necessary or that will be of help to us in our ordinary everyday life. We can ask for help in solving some financial problem that troubles us, for recovery from an illness, to pass a difficult examination that we have studied for ... *In*

---

[14] *Roman Missal, Ordinary of the Mass*
[15] cf John 2:11
[16] St Paul VI, Apostolic Exhortation, *Marialis Cultus*, 2 February 1974, 18

prayer one person asks for a good and suitable wife, another for a roof over his head, a third for something to wear, and another for food. When we are in need of any of these things we should indeed ask Almighty God for them. But we should bear in mind the command of our Redeemer. *Seek first the kingdom of God and his righteousness, and all these things shall be yours as well.*[17] We should not devote the best of our prayer to asking only for the 'extras'.

God is pleased when we ask him for grace and help for others, and also when we ask others to pray for us and for our apostolate. *Pray for me, I said as I always do. And he answered in amazement: But is there something wrong? I had to explain that something is the matter or happens to us all the time; and I added that when prayer is lacking, 'more and more weighty things are the matter'.*[18] Prayer is the answer to all these problems.

Our prayer should be filled with a spirit of abandonment in God and a deep supernatural sense, since, as St John Paul II put it, it is a question of *doing the work of God* and not our own. We have to respond to *his inspiration* and not to our own feelings.[19] Our Lady will rectify for us those intentions of ours which are not completely sound, so that we always obtain what is best. We have in the Holy Rosary a *powerful weapon*[20] for obtaining from God the help we and the people we pray for need each day. *Grant, Lord God, that we your servants, may rejoice in unfailing health of mind and body, and through the glorious intercession of Blessed Mary ever-Virgin, may we be set free from present sorrow and come to enjoy eternal happiness.*[21]

---

[17] St Gregory the Great, *Homilies on the Gospels*, 27

[18] St. J. Escrivá, *Furrow*, 479

[19] cf St John Paul II, *Address to the French Bishops during an 'ad limina' visit*

[20] cf St. J. Escrivá, *The Way*, 558

[21] *Collect*, Mass of the Blessed Virgin Mary, Option 1

41. HE DID ALL THINGS WELL

41.1 Jesus, our Exemplar and Model, carried out his work at Nazareth with human perfection.

The Gospels frequently mention the feelings and words of admiration evoked by Our Lord during the years He spent here on earth: *'the people were struck with amazement, every one of them astonished at the miracles he performed ...' If you consider the many compliments paid to Jesus by those who saw the things he did and heard him speak, you will find one appreciative expression which in a way embraces all of them. I am thinking of the spontaneous exclamation of wonder and enthusiasm which arose from the crowd at the astounding sight of his miracles: 'bene omnia fecit' (Mark 7:37), he has done everything marvellously well – not only the great miracles, but also the little everyday things that didn't dazzle anyone, but which Christ performed with the accomplishment of one who is 'perfectus Deus, perfectus homo' (in the words of the Athanasian Creed), perfect God and perfect man.*[1]

The Gospel of today's Mass[2] invites us to consider the passage in which the people following Our Lord could not but cry out, *He has done all things well*. Christ is our Model in ordinary life. We can ask ourselves if it can be said of us that we too strive to do all things well, the big things as well as the little things that seem unimportant, *because we want to imitate Christ*.

The greater part of Jesus' life was an ordinary existence spent working in an obscure out-of-the way village. And there too, in that same Nazareth, Our Lord did

---

[1] St. J. Escrivá, *Friends of God*, 56
[2] Mark 7:31-37

everything well, perfectly in fact. In Nazareth it would be said of Jesus that he was a good carpenter, the best they had come across.

A good part of the life of any man or woman is conditioned by the reality of work. It would be hard to find a responsible person who of his own volition is without some occupation or job. Many work for noble human objectives: to support their families, to make a future for themselves ... Others will take up a particular activity in order to develop some special skill, some craft or an art for which they have an aptitude, or simply to contribute to the good of society because they are conscious of a duty to do something for others.

Many more will work with less worthy aims – to amass wealth, to gain fame or power, to assert themselves or to get hold of what they need for the gratification of their passions. We all know competent people who conscientiously work long hours for purely human motives. Our Lord wants those who follow him in the midst of the world to be people who work well. They must be known for the quality of their work, which will have the prestige of excellence, and be thoroughly competent in their job or profession. They cannot be slapdash in their approach to their work. They must be people who will stand out, visibly motivated by noble human objectives, because one's work, of whatever kind it be, is where we must practise the human as well as the supernatural virtues ... *we believe by faith that through the homage of work offered to God, man is associated with the redemptive work of Jesus Christ, whose labour with his hands at Nazareth greatly ennobled the dignity of work.*[3]

We tell Our Lord that we want to carry out our every task, and particularly the work that we do for a living, in an

---

[3] Second Vatican Council, *Gaudium et spes*, 67

exemplary way because we truly want it to be a daily
offering to him, and because we are determined to imitate
him in the years of his hidden life at Nazareth.

41.2 Hard work, 'professional competence'.

When Jesus chooses his disciples he finds them among
men who are used to hard work. *Master, we toiled all night
...*[4] he is told by those who will be his first disciples. *All
night,* hard at work, since it is their livelihood; they are
fishermen. We have the example of Saint Paul himself and
of those who accompanied him, *working, as they say, with
our own hands.*[5] And he writes to the first Christians at
Thessalonica: *We did not eat anyone's bread without
paying, but with toil and labour we worked night and day,
that we might not burden any of you.*[6] Saint John
Chrysostom comments that Saint Paul did not take up work
just to keep himself busy or for 'a change', for relaxation.
He put a lot of effort into it so that he could provide for his
own needs and those of others. Here was a man who could
command devils, who taught the whole world and had
nations and races and whole cities entrusted to his loving
care. That man worked day and night.

To work well we must first of all work hard, using our
time well. It is difficult, impossible even, for a person to live
a spirit of sacrifice and remain spiritually alert, practising the
basic human virtues, unless he uses his time well. A life
without work will cause to degenerate and frequently corrupt
whatever it comes into contact with. *Iron which lies idle is
consumed by rust, and becomes brittle and useless. But if it
is used for work it is much more useful and attractive. It is in
no way inferior to silver itself. The field that lies fallow*

---

[4] Luke 5:5
[5] 1 Cor 4:12
[6] 1 Thess 3:8

produces no healthy crop, but only weeds, thistles, thorns and useless plants. The cultivated acres are filled with ripe fruits. In short, every being is diminished by idleness, and is improved by the exercise of the activity proper to it.[7] This is just as true for the housewife and mother who must spend many hours looking after her home and bringing up her children, as it is for the man who is self-employed, or for the student, or for the head of the firm or the worker in the last place on the production line.

God wants from us human work that is well done. This means our working hard, with order, skill, competence and a striving for perfection; it means a completed job with no rough edges, no flaws or blemishes. It means serious work and an end-product that not only looks good, but *is* good. It doesn't matter whether it is manual work or intellectual work, whether we are the ones who plan the work or the ones who carry it out, whether our efforts are being supervised or not. The Christian brings something new to his work. Apart from the features we have mentioned, he does it for God. He presents it to him as a daily offering which will have eternal value. But the qualities it has are those of any honest work – it will be responsible, competent, hard work. A job done in this way dignifies the one who does it and gives glory to his creator. Our natural talents are put to good use and give constant praise to God. Since we want to follow Christ closely and imitate him, we must add a greater perfection to our work, always keeping in mind the Master who *has done everything well*. In our prayer today let us examine the human quality of our work or our study, and together with Our Lord see where it can be improved. We can work harder, sharpen our punctuality, sustain the effort and finish off well those jobs we begin with such enthusiasm; no doubt we can be more orderly,

---

[7] *ibid*

take better care of the implements, tools, instruments, equipment, etc. that we use ...

41.3 Finishing off our work well. The little details that make any job 'professional'.

The Christian discovers new treasures in his work because *all the pathways of the earth can be an occasion for meeting Christ* [8] as St Josemaría Escrivá would say in so many different ways. He spent his life preaching that *holiness is not reserved for the privileged few.*[9] He recalled an experience which he used in order to teach those who came to his apostolate what work done in the presence of God should be like. *I also remember my stay in Burgos around that time ... Our walks would sometimes take us as far as the monastery of Las Huelgas. On other occasions we would find our way to the Cathedral.*

I used to enjoy climbing up the cathedral towers to get a close view of the ornamentation at the top, a veritable lacework of stone that must have been the result of very patient and laborious craftsmanship. As I chatted with the young men who accompanied me I used to point out that none of the beauty of this work could be seen from below. To give them a material lesson in what I had been previously explaining to them, I would say: 'This is God's work, this is working for God! – to finish your personal work perfectly, with all the beauty and exquisite refinement of this tracery stonework.' Seeing it, my companions would understand that all the work we had seen was part of a prayer, a loving dialogue with God. The men who spent their energies up there were quite aware that no one at street level could appreciate their efforts. Their work was for God alone. Now do you see how our professional work can bring us close to

---

[8] St. J. Escrivá, *Letter*, 24 March 1930
[9] *idem*, *Letter*, 19 March 1954

Our Lord? Do your job as those medieval stonemasons did theirs, and your work too will be 'operatio Dei', a human work with a divine substance and finish.[10]

To finish off what we do often means *taking care of minor details*, of the little things. This demands an effort, demands sacrifice, and when we offer it up it is pleasing to God. Taking care of the details for love of God does not diminish the soul. It ennobles it, because it perfects the work we are doing, and when we offer it up for specific intentions we share in the needs of the whole Church. In this way our job takes on a supernatural dimension it previously lacked. In our work, as in other aspects of ordinary life such as in family and social commerce, in periods of rest and leisure ... we always have this choice – carelessness and shoddiness which impoverish the soul, or the little work of art offered up to God as the expression of a soul with interior life.

In this time of prayer perhaps God wants us to identify points in our way of working that require a change of emphasis or rhythm. Do I live the virtue of order, so that I tackle jobs according to their relative importance and not according to my own whims or fancies? Am I unnecessarily slow in finishing off my work because of lack of interest or punctuality? Do I break off the work I am engaged in on any excuse, perhaps causing others to be held up?

Our Lady will help us to finish our prayer with a definite resolution that will help us to do our work with greater perfection and to think of Our Lord more frequently in the course of it. *From there where you are working, let your heart escape to the Lord, right close to the Tabernacle, to tell him, without doing anything odd, 'My Jesus, I love you'.*[11]

---

[10] idem, *Friends of God*, 65
[11] idem, *The Forge*, 746

FIFTH WEEK: SATURDAY

42. MOTHER OF MERCY

42.1 Mary shares to an eminent degree in the divine mercy.

A great crowd was following Jesus. So attracted by his teaching are they that they have left towns and villages behind, and have run out of food. Jesus calls his disciples and tells them, *I have compassion on this crowd, because they have been with me now three days, and have nothing to eat; if I send them away to their homes they will faint with hunger on the way; and some of them have come a long distance.*[1] Once again merciful compassion leads Jesus to perform the extraordinary miracle of the multiplication of the loaves and fishes.

We should have frequent recourse to the divine mercy. Our salvation and safety lie in God's compassion for us. We should also learn to have mercy on others. This is the way to win God's favour more promptly. Our Mother Mary constantly procures for us the compassion of her Son. She teaches us how to respond to the needs of others. *Hail, Holy Queen, Mother of mercy ...* we keep on saying to her. Perhaps, like so many Christians we dedicate a day of the week – like today, Saturday – to her in a special way, singing or reciting this ancient prayer. Mary is *the one who has the deepest knowledge of the mystery of God's mercy. She knows its price, she knows how great it is. In this sense we call her 'Mother of mercy, Virgin most merciful', each one of these titles having a profound theological meaning. Each of them expresses the special preparation of her soul, of her whole personality, so that she would be able to perceive through the complexity of*

---

[1] Mark 8:1-10

*events, first of all directed to Israel, then to every
individual and ultimately to the whole of humanity, the
need for that abounding mercy of hers in which 'from
generation to generation' people become sharers
according to the eternal design of the Most Holy Trinity.*[2]

Saint Augustine teaches that mercy has its birth in the
heart. It has pity on the misery of others, whether their
wretchedness be corporal or spiritual, and is moved and
saddened by it as if the suffering were its own, in such a
way that it seeks the means to remedy it.[3] Mercy is poured
out on others, taking their defects and their sorrows for its
own, and tries to set them free from such grief and pain.
Hence, Scripture tells us that *God ... is rich in mercy;*[4] and
*it is greater for him to draw good from evil than to create
something new out of nothing; the justification of a sinner
by grace is an act greater than the creation of the whole of
the universe, of heaven and earth.*[5]

In Jesus Christ, who is God made man, we find the
fullest expression of the divine mercy, which has been dis-
played in so many ways throughout the history of salvation.
He gave himself up on the Cross in the supreme act of
merciful love. He continues to show this love in Heaven and
in the Tabernacle, where he waits for us to go and tell him of
our needs and of the needs of others. *For we have not a high
priest who is unable to sympathize with our weaknesses ... Let
us then with confidence draw near to the throne of grace, that
we may receive mercy, and find grace to help in time of
need.*[6] What fruits of holiness will be produced in our souls
when we meditate frequently on this divine invitation!

---

[2] St John Paul II, Encyclical, *Dives in misericordia*, 30 November 1980,
8
[3] cf St Augustine, *The City of God*, 9
[4] Eph 2:4
[5] St Thomas, *Summa Theologiae*, I-II, 113, 9
[6] Heb 4:15-16

Mary shares to the highest degree in this divine perfection. In her, mercy is united to the piety of a mother. She always leads us to the *throne of grace*. The title of *Mother of Mercy*, won by her *fiat* in Nazareth and at the foot of the Cross on Calvary, is one of the greatest and most beautiful of the lovely names of Mary. She is our comfort and our safeguard. *By her maternal charity, she cares for the brethren of her Son, who still journey onwards on earth beset by dangers and difficulties, until they are led to their heavenly home. Therefore the Blessed Virgin is invoked throughout the Church under the titles of Advocate, Helper, Benefactress and Mediatrix.*[7] Not a single day goes by without her coming to our assistance and protecting us, and interceding for us in our necessities.

42.2 Health of the sick, Refuge of sinners

The title of *Mother of Mercy finds its traditional expression in the names Health of the sick, Refuge of sinners, Comfort of the afflicted, Help of Christians. The order of the litany is beautiful. It shows how Mary has mercy on those who endure bodily suffering in order to cure their souls. She then comforts them in their sorrow and gives them the strength to bear and overcome all their difficulties.*[8]

Mary is there for us as *Health of the sick*, and will gladly obtain for us the well-being of our bodies, especially when alleviation of our sickness is ordered to the good of our soul. At other times she grants something more important than bodily health – the grace to understand that suffering, including physical pain, is an instrument of God. Permitting it, He wants us to accept it with love, and will transform it into a great good that purifies us and enables us to obtain countless benefits for the whole Church. By

---

[7] Second Vatican Council, *Lumen gentium*, 62
[8] R. Garrigou-Lagrange, *The Mother of the Saviour*, p. 305

means of sickness borne patiently and with a supernatural outlook, we obtain a good part of the treasure that awaits us in Heaven, to say nothing of abundant apostolic rewards: from such humble and courageous acceptance of God's Will come decisions to dedicate oneself to God and the salvation of many souls who without those graces might not find the path and the gateway to heaven. Our Lady also cures the wounds left in our soul by original sin and aggravated by our personal transgressions. She fortifies those who are wavering, raises the fallen, helps to dispel the mists of ignorance and the darkness of error.

The merciful Virgin is the *Refuge of sinners*. In her we find a safe harbour from the storm. After her Son, no one detests sin more than Mary does. She transmits the grace of light and repentance even to those who are far away; if they do not resist, they are led by her from grace to grace and finally to conversion. *Who, then, shall be able to 'comprehend what is the breadth and length and height and depth' (Eph 3:18) of thy mercy, O Virgin most blessed? It reaches forward, extending even as far as the end of time, to succour all that invoke it. Its breadth is as broad as the vast universe, so that of thee too it can be said, 'the whole earth is full of thy mercy'(Ps 32:5).*[9] We go to her today, imploring her to have pity on us. We tell her we are sinners, but that we want to love her Son Jesus Christ more and more. We ask her to have compassion on our weaknesses and to help us overcome them. *Refuge of sinners*, she is therefore our safeguard, the secure haven where we can drop anchor, sheltered from the waves and tempestuous winds. There we can refit, putting right any damage caused by temptation and our human frailty. The mercy she mediates is our protection and our peace: *Holy Mary, Mother of God, pray for us sinners ...*

---

[9] St Bernard, *Homily on the Assumption of the Blessed Virgin Mary*, 4

42.3 Comfort of the afflicted, Help of Christians.

Throughout her life, the Blessed Virgin Our Mother must have been a source of consolation and support to anyone afflicted by a weight too heavy to bear alone. She surely heartened Saint Joseph on that night in Bethlehem when, as he explained their pressing need for lodging at one house after another, he found no door would open to them. One smile from Mary would be enough for him to find the strength to get ready and make the most of what he had found – a stable on the outskirts of the little town. She would have been a tower of strength to him on the flight into Egypt and in helping him set himself up in that country ... Joseph himself was a man of fortitude, but it would have been easier for him to do what he must to fulfil the Will of God when he was sustained by the encouragement of Mary Her neighbours in Nazareth would always find uplift and understanding in the words of Our Lady ... The apostles found refuge in Mary's company when all had turned dark and meaningless after the death of Christ on the Cross. When they returned from placing the Body of Jesus in the sepulchre, at a time when families in Jerusalem were getting ready to celebrate the Paschal feast, the Apostles, who had fled numb with shock and disoriented, turned almost automatically to Mary's house.

From then on she has never ceased to comfort those who are oppressed by sorrow, loneliness or suffering. *She has sheltered innumerable Christians from persecution, freed many souls possessed by the devil or beseiged by temptations, saved countless imperilled supplicants from anxiety. She has strengthened and helped many of the dying by reminding them as they lay on their deathbeds of the infinite merits of her Son.*[10] If ever our life has become for us a misery and we are overwhelmed by apparently

---

[10] R. Garrigou-Lagrange, *op cit*, p. 311

insoluble difficulties, crushed by illness, daunted by seeming failure in our dedication to an apostolic task, if we are threatened by discouragement in the effort to bring up our family and dismayed at the obstacles that just keep on piling up, let us turn to Mary. We shall always find solace, encouragement and the strength to fulfil the lovable Will of her Son. We shall repeat slowly: Hail, Holy Queen, Mother of mercy, hail, our life, our sweetness and our hope ... From her we shall learn to console and hearten others in their struggle. We shall be compassionate to those who are in need of our help, in disasters or in minor worries – a word of encouragement here, of condolence there – a merciful attitude which is so pleasing to the Lord.

Our Lady is Help of Christians because first of all we favour those we love, and nobody has had a greater love than Mary for those who belong to her Son's family. In her we shall find every grace we need to win through in the fight against temptation, in our apostolate and in our work ... In the Rosary we have a *powerful weapon*[11] with which to overcome all the obstacles we shall meet along the way. Following the constant teaching of the Roman Pontiffs, many Christians throughout the world have made the daily rosary a part of their life of piety. They recite it together as a family prayer, or alone in a church, while walking in the street or travelling in any form of transport.

In me is to be found every grace of doctrine and of truth, every hope of life and of virtue (Eccles 24:25). How wise the Church has been to put these words on our Mother's lips so that we Christians do not forget them! She is our safety, the Love that never fails, the refuge ever open to us, the hand ever ready to caress and console.[12]

---

[11] St. J. Escrivá, *Holy Rosary*, Foreword
[12] *idem*, *Friends of God*, 279

SIXTH SUNDAY: YEAR A

43. STEADFAST IN THE FAITH

43.1 The Deposit of Faith. A treasure that each generation receives from the hands of the Church. She keeps it faithfully with the help of the Holy Spirit and expounds it with authority.

Our Lord tells us in the Gospel of today's Mass[1] that He has not come to abolish the Old Law, but *to bring it to fulfilment*. He restores, perfects and raises the precepts of the Old Testament to a higher order. The doctrine of Jesus is of eternal value to the men of all times. It is *the source of all saving truth and moral discipline*.[2] It is a treasure that each generation receives from the hands of the Church. She keeps it faithfully under the guidance of the Holy Spirit, and has authority to give an authentic interpretation of it. *When we accept the Faith which the Church proposes, we communicate directly with the Apostles ... and through them we communicate with Jesus Christ, our first and only Teacher. We go to their school, as it were, and overcome the distance of centuries that separates us from them.*[3] Thanks to this living Magisterium we can say that, in a way, the whole world has received his doctrine and has been transformed into Galilee. The whole of the earth becomes Jericho and Capharnaum. All humanity stands on the shores of Lake Gennesareth.[4]

To keep the truths of faith in their fulness is essential for the salvation of mankind. What truth is there that can save other than the truth of Christ? What *new truth* could

---

[1] Matt 5:17-37
[2] Second Vatican Council, *Dei Verbum*, 7
[3] St Paul VI, *Address*, 1 March 1967
[4] cf P. Rodrigues, *Faith and Life of Faith*, p. 113

be of interest, even if it sprang from the wisest of men, if it led us away from the teaching of the Master? Who would dare to interpret, alter or accommodate the divine Word to suit his own whims? That is why Our Lord warns us today: *Whoever then relaxes as much as one of the least of these commandments and teaches men so, shall be called the least in the kingdom of heaven.*

Saint Paul exhorted Timothy: *Guard what has been entrusted to you. Avoid the godless chatter and contradictions of what is falsely called knowledge, for by professing it some have altogether missed the mark as regards the Faith.*[5] The Church continues to use the expression deposit for the unalterable content of the Faith as transmitted to us through the centuries, to designate the truths she has received from Christ himself and which she is charged to preserve until the end of time.

The truth of faith *does not change with the passage of time. It is not superseded or modified or overtaken by the course of history. It can allow fresh insights or even call for the kind of pedagogical and pastoral restatements appropriate to the characteristics of a living language, and thus follow a line of development, but without deviating from the well-known traditional formula of Saint Vincent of Lerins: 'quod ubique, quod semper, quod ab omnibus': 'what has been believed everywhere, always, by everyone' must be preserved as part of the deposit of faith ... This stability of dogma defends the authentic patrimony, the Apostolic wholeness of the Catholic religion. The Creed does not change. It does not get out of date. It does not disintegrate.*[6] It is a solid supporting pillar, an unshakeable column, and we cannot give way even in little things, although by temperament we might be inclined to

---

[5] 1 Tim 6:20-21
[6] St Paul VI, *General Audience*, 29 September 1976

compromise. *You are afraid of hurting people, of creating divisions and of giving the appearance of being intolerant ... and you are giving in on certain positions and certain points (though you assure me they are not serious ones) which will have fateful consequences for many.*

Forgive my sincerity: through your behaviour, you are falling into nothing less than the stupid and harmful intolerance that you were concerned to avoid: that of not allowing the truth to be proclaimed.[7] Proclaiming the truth is often the greatest good we can do for those who surround us.

43.2 Avoid everything that undermines the virtue of faith.

The Christian, freed from the total tyranny of sin, is encouraged by the New Law of Christ to behave as a child in the presence of his Father, God. Moral norms are then not merely indicators showing the limits of what is allowed or forbidden. They now reveal the pathway that leads to God; they are signs of love.

We ought to know thoroughly the group of truths and precepts that make up what we call *the deposit of faith*, since this is the treasure that God has given to us through the Church in order that we might be saved. This wealth of truths is protected primarily by piety (prayer and the sacraments), by a serious doctrinal formation suited to the needs of each person, and also by exercising *prudence in our reading*.

No one objects if, for example, a professor of physics or biology recommends certain textbooks, advises against others or says that reading a particular work is useless or even harmful for someone who is really interested in acquiring a serious scientific formation. And yet there are people who are astounded that the Church should reaffirm her doctrine on the need to avoid books that are harmful to

---

[7] St. J. Escrivá, *Furrow*, 600

faith or morals, and that she should exercise her right and duty to examine, judge and in extreme cases condemn books which are contrary to religious truth.[8] The root of this astonishment might well be found in a certain warping of the *sense of truth*. Such easily-surprised people will admit an authority only in the scientific sphere, considering that in the realm of religious truths it is a question of opinions only, however well-founded those truths may be.

In our prayer we shall strengthen our fidelity to the deposit of what has been revealed, remembering at the same time that the natural law God has written on our hearts leads us from within to hold in high esteem the gifts of Heaven. As a result, this natural law written on the hearts of all of us – our conscience – *obliges us to avoid as far as possible everything that tends to undermine the virtue of faith,*[9] just as it requires us to preserve our lives, for example. Thus, *to place our faith in danger voluntarily by reading harmful books without sufficient reason would be a sin, although at present no ecclesiastical sanction would be incurred.*[10]

After a long experience of studying authors who were either pagans or without faith, Saint Basil gave this advice: *You should follow the example of the bees. They do not light upon every flower, nor do they endeavour to take everything from the flowers on which they pause in their flight. Once they have taken enough for their purpose they leave the rest alone.*

We too, if we are prudent, will draw from these authors what is appropriate, what is closest to the truth, and leave the rest. Just as we are careful to avoid the thorns when we are pulling a rose, so shall we take care to avoid what can

---

[8] cf *Code of Canon Law*, Canons 822-832
[9] J. Mausbach and G. Ermecke, *Catholic Moral Theology*, vol II, p. 108
[10] cf *ibid*

hurt the soul when we try to get good out of such readings.[11]

Prudence in reading is a manifestation of fidelity to Christ's teaching. The faith is our greatest treasure, and we cannot run the risk of losing it or weakening it for anything in the world. There is nothing that can be compared with the faith. We must be on the watch for ourselves and for others, especially for those whom God has placed in our care in some way – children, pupils, brothers, friends ...

43.3 Prudence in reading.

They are happy whose life is blameless, who follow God's Law! They are happy who do his will, seeking him with all their hearts,[12] says today's Responsorial Psalm, arousing our desire to follow Jesus Christ faithfully.

The Church has always included among those especially dangerous situations which can put the purity of the faith at risk the reading of books that directly or indirectly attack religious truths or morals. History provides more than enough evidence that a Christian can frequently be led astray, even when he is pious and sound in doctrine, by the grain of truth or the appearance of truth that all errors contain.[13]

Teach me the demands of your statutes ... train me to observe your Law, we tell Jesus in the words of the *Responsorial Psalm.*[14] He will help us to form our consciences well, and to be humble. We shall seek good advice and then make a prudent selection in our reading when we have to study areas in science, the humanities, literature, etc., where there is a risk of our attitudes being corrupted. If we remain faithful to Christ, treasuring our

---

[11] St Basil, *How to read pagan literature*, p. 43
[12] Ps 118:1-2
[13] cf Pius XI, *Deus scientiarum Dominus*, 24 May 1931: AAS 23 (1931), pp 243-246
[14] Ps 118:34

faith, we shall be natural, avoiding a complex of any kind, steering clear of the superficial longing to be *up-to-date* in false doctrines. That is how many Christian intellectuals have behaved – professors, teachers, research workers, etc. If we are humble and prudent, if we have *common sense*, we shall not be *like those who take poison mingled with honey*.[15]

We need to be well-formed, faithful to the teaching of the Gospel and the Magisterium of the Church. This will allow us to value everything worthwhile in the different aspects of culture. For the Christian must always be open to whatever is truly positive. At the same time we shall be able to pick out what is contrary to the Christian view of life. Let us ask Our Lady, *Seat of Wisdom*, for this gift of judgement in our study, our reading and the whole area of ideas and culture. Let us also ask her to teach us to esteem and love more and more the treasure that is our faith.

---

[15] St Basil, *loc cit*

44. THE LEPROSY OF SIN

44.1 Our Lord has come to cure our most deep-rooted ills. The healing of a leper.

The healing of a leper narrated in the Gospel of today's Mass[1] must have moved people very much, and it figured frequently in the preaching of the apostles. The fact that it is related in great detail by three of the Evangelists makes this clear. Saint Luke provides the detail that the miracle was performed in a town, and that the disease was in an advanced state. The leper was covered with it: *a man full of leprosy*,[2] Luke says.

At that time leprosy was an incurable condition. The limbs of the leper became gradually affected by the progressive illness, which would produce disfigurement to the face, hands and feet, and great suffering. For fear of contagion lepers were driven away from built-up areas and forbidden to use the highways. As we see in the *First Reading* of the Mass,[3] they were pronounced legally unclean. They had to keep their heads uncovered and wear torn clothes to distinguish themselves, and were obliged to make their presence known when they passed close to any inhabited place. People fled from even members of their own families. Their affliction was generally held to be a punishment from God for their sins. Thus it is strange to find this leper inside a city. Perhaps he has heard of Jesus and has been eagerly looking for a chance to approach him. At last he has found him and breaks the strict precept of the

---

[1] Mark 1:40-45
[2] Luke 5:12
[3] Lev 13:1-2; 44-46

old Mosaic Law in order to speak to him. Christ is his hope, his only hope.

It must have been an extraordinary scene. The leper knelt before Jesus. *If you want to, he said, you can make me clean.* If you want to ... Perhaps he had prepared a longer speech, explaining things ... but in the end this simple blurted-out aspiration, filled with trust, with sincere sensitivity, is enough: *'Si vis, potes me mundare'*, if you will, you can ... These few words, stammered out, are in a fact a powerful prayer. Jesus took pity on him, and the three Evangelists describe the surprising gesture of Our Lord: *He stretched out his hand and touched him.* Until now everyone had recoiled from him in dread and loathing, but Jesus, who could have healed from a distance as He had done on other occasions, not only did not draw away from him, but even touched his leprosy. It is not hard to imagine Christ's affection and the gratitude of the leper when he saw Our Lord's gesture and heard his words: *I will; be clean.*

Our Lord always wants to heal us of our weaknesses and our sins. And there is no need for us to wait months or days for him to pass through our city or our town ... Every day we can find the same Jesus of Nazareth who healed the leper. He is there in the nearest tabernacle, in the heart of a soul in grace, in the sacrament of Penance. *He is our Physician, and He cures our selfishness if we but let his grace penetrate into the depths of our soul. Jesus has taught us that the worst sickness is hypocrisy, the pride that leads us to conceal our own sins. We have to be totally sincere with him. We have to tell the whole truth, and then we have to say: 'Domine, si vis, potes me mundare'* (Matt 8:2), *Lord, if you will – and you are always willing – you can heal me of my sickness. You know my weaknesses; I feel these symptoms; these failings make me feel wretched. We show him the wound, with simplicity, and if the wound is festering, we show the pus too;*[4] all the wretchedness of our life.

Today we should remember that our very failings and weaknesses can be the opportunity for us to approach Christ as the leper did. From that moment on he would have been an unconditional disciple of his Lord. Do we go to confession with these dispositions of faith and trust? Do we have a real desire for purity of soul? Do we make sure we go to confession regularly?

44.2 Leprosy, an image of sin. Priests forgive sins *in persona Christi*.

Because of its repulsive ugliness and loathsomeness, the separation from others it entailed, the Fathers of the Church saw in leprosy an image of sin ...[5] All in all, sin, even venial sin, is far uglier and far more loathsome than leprosy, and it has far more tragic consequences in this life and in the world to come. *If we had faith and were to see a soul in the state of mortal sin, we would die of horror.*[6] We are all sinners, although by divine mercy we may be free from mortal sin. That is a reality we should not forget; and Jesus is the only one who can cure us; He alone.

Our Lord has come to heal the sick, and only He can judge and measure the offence of sin in all its gravity. So we are moved when He approaches the sinner. He who is Holiness itself is not filled with anger, but is genuinely concerned and respectful. *This is Jesus' way. He came to fulfil, not to destroy.*

When he heals, when he cures us of leprosy, Our Lord performs great miracles. These miracles reveal God's

---

[4] St. J. Escrivá, *Christ is passing by*, 93
[5] cf St John Chrysostom, *Homilies on St Matthew*, 25:2
[6] St Jean Vianney, The Curé d'Ars, quoted by St John XXIII in the letter, *Sacerdotii nostri primordia*

power over the sicknesses of the soul – over sin. The same reflection is developed in today's Responsorial Psalm, which exactly describes and proclaims what joy there is at the forgiveness of sins: 'Happy the man whose offence is forgiven' ... (Ps 31:1). Jesus cures the physical illness, and at the same time frees from sin. In this way He shows himself to be the Messiah whose coming had been foretold by the Prophets, who 'has borne our infirmities' and 'taken our sins upon himself' (cf Is 53:3-12) in order to set us free from all that subverts our spiritual and material health ... For this reason a central theme of today's liturgy is purification from sin, which is 'the leprosy of the soul.'[7]

Jesus tells us that this is why he has come – to forgive, to redeem, to set us free from sin, the leprosy of the soul. And his forgiveness is a sign of omnipotence, a sign of a power that belongs to God alone.[8] Every Confession expresses in its absolution the power and the mercy of God. The priest exercises this power not in his own name, but in the name of Christ. He acts *in persona Christi* – as an instrument in his hands. *Jesus identifies us with himself to such an extent in the exercise of the power He has conferred on us,* said St John Paul II to priests, *that our personality, as it were, disappears in the presence of his. He it is who acts through us ... It is Jesus himself who in the Sacrament of Penance pronounces the authoritative paternal words: Your sins are forgiven.*[9] In the voice of the priest we hear Christ speak.

In Confession we approach Christ himself with veneration and thanksgiving. In the priest we must see Jesus, the only one who can heal our illnesses. *'Domine!'* – Lord – *'si vis, potes me mundare'* – if thou wilt, thou canst

---

[7] St John Paul II, *Homily*, 17 February 1985
[8] cf Matt 9:2 ss
[9] St John Paul II, *Homily*, Rio de Janeiro, 2 July 1980

make me clean.

What a beautiful prayer for you to say often, with the faith of the poor leper, when there happens to you what God and you and I know! You will not have to wait long to hear the Master's reply: 'Volo, mundare' I will: be thou made clean![10] Jesus treats us with the deepest affection and love when we are most in need because of our failings and our sins.

44.3 Apostolate of Confession.

We must learn from this leper. He goes before Our Lord sincerely and *kneeling*,[11] admits his disease, humbly asking to be cured. Our Lord said to the leper: *'I will; be clean.' And immediately the leprosy left him, and he was made clean.* We can imagine the huge joy of the cured leper. So great was his happiness that in spite of Our Lord's warning he began to tell everybody what had happened and spread the news of the great good that had been done to him. Such blessings were too great for him to keep to himself; he had to share his good fortune with others.

We must have the same attitude towards Confession. Through it we too are cleansed of our illnesses, however great they may be. Not only is sin washed away, but the soul receives a new grace, a restored youthfulness, the renewal of the life of Christ in us. We are united to God in a special and distinct way. We must enable everyone, particularly those we love, to share in the new life and new joy we experience in each confession. It is not enough for us to have found the Master ourselves. By means of personal apostolate we must spread the news to many who do not know they are ill, or who imagine that their illnesses

---

[10] St. J. Escrivá, *The Way*, 142
[11] Mark 1:40

are incurable. Take many people to Confession. That is one of the great responsibilities Christ lays upon us in these times when great hordes of people have turned their backs on what they need most of all: the forgiveness of their sins.

In some cases we shall have to begin with an elementary catechesis, advising them to read some simple books, and explaining the basic points of faith and morals in words they can understand. We can help them to see that the empty sadness they notice has its roots in the absence of God from their lives. With great understanding we will help them to make a deep examination of conscience, and encourage them to go to a priest, perhaps the one we normally make our own confession to. We should show them how to be simple and humble and tell everything that is holding them back from God. He is waiting for them. We shall pray for them, offer up hours of work and some mortification for them, and make sure we are regular in our own confessions. In this way we shall obtain new and effective graces from God for those people we want to go to the Sacrament, to Christ himself.

It must have been an unforgettable day for the leper. Every meeting of ours with Christ is equally unforgettable. Our friends, those we have helped along the pathway to God, will never forget the peace and joy of their encounter with the Master. They in turn will become apostles who spread the Good News, what it is to know the joy of a good confession. If we turn to Mary, our Mother will inspire us with joy and a spirit of urgency as we tell people of the great benefits God – the Father of Mercies – has left us in this Sacrament.

45. PERSONAL HUMILITY AND TRUST IN GOD

45.1 Only the humble can truly trust in God.

Be my protector, O God, a mighty stronghold to save me ... we pray in the Entrance Antiphon of today's Mass.[1] He is our refuge, our bulwark in the midst of all the weakness we find in ourselves and in the decay that is all around us. He is our firm support at all times, at any age and in any situation. *Blessed is the man who trusts in the Lord and puts all his confidence in him,* says the prophet Jeremiah in the *First Reading. He is like a tree planted by the water's edge, that sends out its roots to the stream and does not fear when summer's heat comes, for its foliage remains green; nor has it any anxiety in the year of drought, for it does not cease to bear fruit.*[2] By contrast, cursed is *he who puts his trust in man and relies on the strength of his arm, whose heart turns away from the Lord.* His life will be sterile, *like a thistle in a dry place.*

Lord, be my rock of safety: personal humility and trust in God go always hand in hand. Only humility seeks happiness and strength in God. One of the reasons the proud go after praise so avidly, and have an exalted opinion of themselves and resent anything that can bring them down in their own estimation or in the eyes of others, is the lack of inner solidity. They have no point of support, no hope for happiness outside themselves. As a result, they are often ultra-sensitive to the slightest criticism, and insist on getting their own way. They want to be well-known and

---

[1] *Entrance Antiphon*, Ps 30:3
[2] Jer 17:7-8

be given special treatment. They put their trust in themselves just as the drowning man clutches hold of the fragile spar that cannot hold him up. And whatever they might have achieved in life, the proud are always insecure, unsatisfied, without peace. That kind of man, without humility, unable to trust in his Father God who constantly stretches out his arms to him, *shall dwell in the parched places of the wilderness, in an uninhabited salt land*, as the liturgy of today's Mass tells us. The proud man will have nothing to show for his life; he is unsatisfied, knowing nothing of real peace and happiness.

The Christian has his hope in God. He knows and accepts his own weakness and so does not depend inordinately on his own resources. He knows that in any undertaking he must use all the human means open to him, but that above all he must rely on prayer. He knows and accepts joyfully that everything he has he receives from God. Humility is not a matter of despising ourselves, because God does not despise us, since we are the work of His hands. It consists in forgetting ourselves and sincerely thinking about others. Interior simplicity leads us to be aware that we are children of God.[3] *At the very moment when everything seems to be collapsing before our eyes, we realise that quite the opposite is the case, 'for you, Lord, are my strength' (Ps 42:2). If God is dwelling in our soul, everything else, no matter how important it may seem, is accidental and transitory, whereas we, in God, stand permanent and firm.*[4] In the midst of our frailty, in whatever form our weakness presents itself, we take our stand together with God in an indestructible firmness.

---

[3] cf E. Boylan, *This Tremendous Lover*
[4] St. J. Escrivá, *Friends of God*, 92

45.2 The great obstacle is pride. Signs of pride.

The greatest obstacles to the soul's trying to follow Christ and to help others have their origin in a disordered love of self. At times this leads us to overestimate our strength. At other times it brings discouragement and despondency as a result of our own weaknesses and our errors. Pride often reveals itself in an interior monologue, in which we exaggerate the importance of our own interests and get them out of proportion. We end up praising ourselves. In any conversation pride leads us to talk about ourselves and our affairs, and to want people to have a good opinion of us at any price. Some people stick to their own opinion, whether it be right or wrong. They seize any chance to point out another's mistakes, and make it hard to maintain a friendly atmosphere. The most reprehensible way of emphasizing our own worth is by doing down someone else. The proud do not like to hear praise for another person and are always ready to reveal the defects of anyone who stands out from the crowd. A characteristic note of pride is an impatient dislike of being contradicted or corrected.[5]

The man who is filled with pride doesn't seem to have much need of God in his work and undertakings, or even in his ascetical struggle to be better. He exaggerates his personal qualities, closes his eyes to his defects, and ends up thinking that what is a lack of good spirit is really an admirable quality. He is convinced, for example, that he has a generous and bold spirit because he neglects as insignificant the small duties of each day. He forgets that to be faithful in the big things, we have to be faithful in the small ones. So he believes himself to be better than others, and dismisses the good qualities of people who are more

---

[5] cf E. Boylan, *loc cit*

virtuous than himself.[6]

Saint Bernard sets out the various progressive indications in the growth of pride:[7] first, curiosity – wanting to know everything about everybody; then superficiality because of a lack of depth in prayer and in deeds; again, a shrill, misplaced cheerfulness which thrives on the defects of others and lapses into ridicule; there follows boasting, the desire to be in the foreground, to be conspicuous, to stand out; arrogance; presumption; refusing to admit our own faults, even when they are obvious; and, a short step thereafter, a covering up of our faults in Confession ...

The proud man has little interest in knowing the truth about himself. In our prayer today let us ask ourselves if we value humility sufficiently, and ask God for it over and over again. We can examine ourselves as to whether we constantly ask God Our Father to help us, in big things as in little. *O God,* we say with the Psalmist, *thou art my God, I seek thee; my soul thirsts for thee; my flesh faints for thee, as in a dry and weary land where no water is.*[8] We could usefully repeat this prayer throughout the day.

45.3 Practising the virtue of humility.

Forgetting about ourselves is an essential condition for holiness. It enables us to see God as our absolute Good, and to think about others. Together with prayer, which is the first means we must always use, we must also practise the virtue of humility, in our work, in family life, when we are alone ... always. We must make an effort not to be too preoccupied with our own concerns: our health, our rest, whether people think well of us and take us sufficiently

---

[6] cf R. Garrigou-Lagrange, *The Three Ages of the Interior Life*, vol 1, p 442
[7] St Bernard, *On the degrees of humility,* 10
[8] Ps 63:2

into account ... We should try to speak as little as possible about ourselves and our affairs, of whatever can possibly put us in a good light. We should avoid curiosity, the desire to know everything and to let everyone know that we know it. Patiently, with good humour, we will accept difficulties and offer them up joyfully as sacrifices to God. We shall not insist on our own point of view unless the truth or justice demand it, and even then we shall be moderate while remaining firm. We shall overlook the mistakes of others; we shall find excuses for them and in all charity assist them to overcome their failings. We will accept corrections even if these seem unfair, and give way on appropriate occasions to other people's opinions when charity or duty is not at stake. We will avoid making a display of our good qualities, of our material possessions, of our knowledge ... It will matter nothing if we are despised, overlooked or not consulted in a field in which we think we have particular competence or have greater knowledge or experience. We will not crave to be held in high esteem or to be admired, and will rectify our intentions when we are praised. We certainly should seek greater professional prestige, but for God's glory, not out of pride or the desire to be outstanding.

We shall grow in this virtue especially when we are humiliated and accept the humiliation joyfully for Christ,[9] cheerfully put up with being despised, patiently bear with our own defects and make the effort to glory in our weaknesses in front of the Tabernacle. We shall go there to ask Our Lord to give us his grace and not abandon us. We will tell him once again there is nothing good in us that does not come from him. Our personal failings are the only obstacles that prevent the Holy Spirit from filling us with his gifts. In an intimate conversation with Jesus and Mary

---

[9] cf St. J. Escrivá, *The Way*, 594

we shall learn to be humble. Frequent meditation on the Passion will lead us to contemplate the figure of Christ, humiliated and abused for our sake. Our love will be set ablaze and give rise to a sincere desire to imitate him.

The example of our Mother Mary, *Ancilla Domini*, the Handmaid of the Lord, will move us to practise the virtue of humility. As we finish our prayer, we turn to her, since *she is Mother of both mercy and tenderness, and no one has ever gone to her in vain. Cast yourself with confidence into her maternal embrace; ask her to obtain for you this virtue she esteemed so highly. Don't have any fears about not being listened to. Mary will put forward your request to that God who lifts up the humble and casts down the proud, and since Mary is omnipotent in her requests to her Son, she will certainly be heard.*[10]

---

[10] J. Pecci, (Pope Leo XIII), *The Practice of Humility*, 85-86

46. THE SACRIFICE OF ABEL

46.1 The best of our life is for God: our love, our time, our worldly goods ...

The book of *Genesis*[1] tells us that Abel offered to God the first fruits of his endeavour and the finest of his cattle. His offering was pleasing to God, in contrast with his brother's. Cain did not offer the best of his harvest.

Abel was *just*, that is to say, holy and pious. It is not the inherent objective quality of Abel's offering that makes it better. It is his dedication and generosity – his intention. So God looked favourably on the victims Abel sacrificed, and according to an ancient Jewish tradition perhaps sent down fire to consume them as a sign of his acceptance.[2]

In our lives too we have to offer the best we have to God. We have to present the offering of Abel, not that of Cain. We are to give God the best of our time, our goods, our life. We cannot give him the worst, what is surplus to our requirements, what makes no real demand on us or what is left over and we don't need. The whole of our life is for God, and that includes the best years of it. Everything we have is for God, but when we want to make an offering let us use the most precious things, just as we would do in making a gift to a fellow-creature we hold in great esteem. Man is not just a body or merely a soul. He is composed of both, matter and spirit, and needs to show his faith and his love of God in external, visible acts. How pitiful are those who seem to have time for everything except for God – for talking to him in prayer, or for a visit to the Blessed Sacrament that takes no more than a few minutes ... Pitiful

---

[1] *First Reading*, Year 1, cf Gen 4:-5,25
[2] *The Navarre Bible*, note to Heb 11:4

too are those who have money enough for so many things but are so parsimonious when it comes to expenditure on God or on other people. Giving always dignifies the heart of the giver and ennobles it. Meanness becomes ingrained and leads to an envious soul, like that of Cain: he could not bear the generosity of Abel.

We should offer the Lord the sacrifice of Abel. Let it be a sacrifice of young, unblemished flesh, the best of the flock; of a healthy and holy flesh; a sacrifice of hearts that have one love alone – you, my God. Let it be a sacrifice of minds that have been shaped through deep study and will surrender to your Wisdom; of childlike souls who will think only of pleasing you.

Lord, receive even now this sweet and fragrant sacrifice.[3] For you, Lord, the best of my life, of my work, of my talents, of my possessions ... even of those I might have had. For you, my God, everything you have given me in life, totally, unconditionally ... Teach me to deny you nothing, to offer you always the best I have.

We ask God that we may know how to give him the best we have in all situations and circumstances. Let us pray that there may be many sacrifices like those of Abel, the generous offerings of men and women who give themselves to God from their youth, and of hearts that at any age give what is asked of them, without haggling, without counting the cost ... Receive, Lord, this loving, cheerful sacrifice ...

46.2 Generosity with regard to the objects used in worship. They should be dignified, appropriate and worthy.

It is pleasing to think that the first testimony of faith in God was given by a son of Adam and Eve by means of sacrifice. So it is easy to understand why the Fathers of the

---

[3] St. J. Escrivá, *The Forge*, 43

Church saw in Abel a type or figure of Christ: he was a
shepherd, he offered a sacrifice pleasing to God, he shed
his blood and was a 'martyr for the faith.'

The Liturgy in renewing the Sacrifice of Christ asks
God to look with favour on the offerings of Our Lord just
as He accepted the gifts of his servant Abel (cf Roman
Missal, Eucharistic Prayer 1).[4] We should be generous and
love everything related to the worship of God. Everything
we do for him will always be little and insufficient
compared to what God's infinite goodness and excellence
deserve. We Christians must be be very careful to avoid
stingy calculation and a lack of consideration in this field.
The Holy Spirit warns us: *you shall not offer anything that*
has a blemish, for it will not be acceptable.[5]

The best for God: a worship replete with generosity –
generosity in the sacred elements that are used as well as in
the giving of our time, and here it should be no more than
the time required, without hurrying or shortening the
ceremonies or our private thanksgiving after Mass, for
example. The dignity, quality and beauty of the liturgical
vestments and the sacred vessels will show that the best we
have is for God. They are signs of the splendour of the
liturgy that the Church triumphant offers to the Trinity in
Heaven, and a powerful help towards our recognizing God's
presence among us. Lukewarmness, a feeble, cold-hearted
faith, would mean that we were not treating holy things in
a holy way. We would be losing sight of the glory, honour
and majesty that correspond to the Blessed Trinity.

Do you remember the scene from the Old Testament
when David wanted to build a house for the Ark of the
Covenant, which had until that time been kept in a tent? In
that tent Yahweh had made his presence known in a

---

[4] *The Navarre Bible, loc cit*
[5] Lev 22:20

*mysterious way, by means of a cloud and other extraordinary
phenomena. And all this was no more than a figure, a shadow.
On the other hand, God is really present in the tabernacles
where the Blessed Eucharist is reserved. We have Jesus Christ
here – how I love to make an explicit act of faith! – with his
Body, his Blood, his Soul and Divinity. In the Tabernacle
Jesus presides over us, loves us, waits for us.*[6]

The question of money used for the things of God is
raised and dealt with in that scene in the house of Simon
the Pharisee, where Jesus noted the absence of the
attentions normally shown to guests. While Our Lord is
pleased by the signs of repentance given by the woman
who was there, Judas objects and calculates the cost – a
waste, according to him – of what has been used. That
same evening he makes up his mind to betray Jesus. He
sells him for approximately the same sum as the perfume
had cost: thirty pieces of silver, about three hundred
denarii. *That woman in the house of Simon the leper in
Bethany, who anoints the Master's head with precious
ointment, reminds us of our duty to be munificent in the
worship of God. All the beauty, splendour and majesty
seem little enough to me. And against those who attack the
sumptuousness of sacred vessels, of vestments and altars,
stands out the praise given by Jesus: 'opus enim bonum
operata est in me: she has acted well towards me'.*[7]

Our Lord should also be able to say of the dedication
of our lives to him, and of the generosity we can show in
hundreds of ways (in time and in goods): *'he has acted
well towards me'* he has shown his love in deeds.

46.3 Love for Jesus in the Tabernacle.

At his birth Jesus lacks even the cradle of a poor child.

---

[6] Bl. A. del Portillo, *Homily*, 20 July 1986
[7] St. J. Escrivá, *The Way*, 527

At times with his disciples he has nowhere to lay his head. He will die in absolute poverty, with his very clothing stripped from him. But when his dead body is taken down from the Cross and handed over to those who remain close to him, to those who care for him, it is treated with veneration, respect and love. Joseph of Arimathea will buy a fine new linen shroud to wrap the Body in, and Nicodemus the spices they need. St John, perhaps surprised, tells us of the lavish quantity of these spices – about a hundred pounds' weight. They did not bury him in the common graveyard, but in a garden, in a new tomb, probably the one Joseph had had made for himself. *And the women saw the tomb and saw where He was laid.* When they return to the city they prepare more spices ... When the Body of Jesus is in the hands of those who love Him, they rival one another in showing the greatness of their love for him.

Jesus is alive in our Tabernacles, just as He was in Bethlehem or on Calvary. He surrenders himself to our love to be cared for, to be looked after with the very best we can offer, at the cost of our time, our money, our effort, in fact, of our love.

Reverence and love will be shown in generosity towards everything that refers to worship. We cannot fall short in charity for God even under the pretext of charity for our neighbour. Generosity to the poor, who are images of God, is not worthy of praise if it is at the expense of decorum in the worship of God himself. Even more so will this be the case if it is unaccompanied by any personal sacrifice. If we love God, our love for our neighbour will grow in deeds and in truth. It is not a question of putting a price on things. Simple mathematical calculations do not enter into the matter. It is not a question of justifying extravagance, but rather a question of our love of God, of what is fitting, and this love should be expressed in a material way.[8] Does it make sense to spend money on places for leisure and recreation, using good or even luxurious building materials, and yet for divine worship to provide only not just poor but miserable buildings that are cold and shoddily constructed? If so, the poet would be right when he says that the starkness of some churches is *an exterior sign of our sins and defects – of our weakness, our destitution, our lack of faith and feelings, of our dryness of heart and our distaste for the supernatural ...*[9]

The Church is ever vigilant for the honour of God, and she does not reject solutions which differ from those of other eras. She blesses a poverty which is clean and welcoming. How many wonderful churches there are, simple but fitting, in villages with very few economic resources but with a lot of faith! What the Church cannot connive at is neglect, bad taste, or that lack of love of God which dedicates to the divine worship sites or structures which if it could possibly be avoided would scarcely be considered fit for a man and his family to live in.

It is right for the ordinary faithful to contribute in hundreds of different ways to looking after and diligently preserving everything connected with the public worship of God. Liturgical symbols are largely visual ones, and much that is related to the liturgy enters through the eyes. After a liturgical ceremony those who have been present should go away strengthened in their faith, filled with joy and encouraged to love God more than ever.

Let us ask Our Lady to teach us to be as generous as she was with God, in big things and little things, in youth and in maturity ... to offer, as Abel did, the very best that is available to us at any given time, and in all the circumstances of our life.

---

[8] cf Second Vatican Council, *Sacrosanctum Concilium*, 124
[9] Paul Claudel, *Absence and Presence*

47. THE REDEMPTIVE MISSION OF THE CHURCH

47.1 Where salvation is to be found – in the Church instituted by Jesus Christ.

Genesis tells us that God saw how man's wickedness went on increasing, and that his ways of thinking were ever perverse. He regretted having created man, and decided to eliminate him from the face of the earth.[1] But once again God's patience manifests itself and He decides to save mankind in the person of Noah. *Go into the ark,* God tells Noah, *you and all your household, for I have seen that you are righteous before me in this generation.* Then came the deluge by which God punished the rest of mankind for their evil ways. The Fathers of the Church saw in Noah a type or figure of Jesus Christ, who would be the beginning of a new creation. In the ark they glimpsed an image of the Church, which floats upon the waters of this world and gives refuge within itself to *all those who wish to be saved.*[2] *In the symbol of the flood,* says Saint Augustine, *from which the righteous were saved in the ark, the future Church is prophesied. She saves from death in this world through Christ and the mystery of the Cross.*[3] Noah's ark was the place of salvation. *And,* Saint Augustine goes on, *those who were saved in the ark represent the mystery of the future Church, which is saved from disaster by the wood of the Cross.*[4] The group of the righteous saved from the flood in

---

[1] *First Reading*, Year I, Gen 6:5-8; 7:1-5,10
[2] Acts 2:40
[3] St Augustine, *De catechizandis rudibus*, 18
[4] *idem*, 27

the ark is a portent of the future community of Christ.[5]

Our Lord himself before his Ascension into Heaven handed on to his Apostles his own powers for the salvation of the world.[6] The Master spoke to them with all the majesty of God: *All authority in Heaven and on earth has been given to me. Go therefore and make disciples of all nations ...;* and the Church forthwith, with divine authority, began to exercise her saving power.

Imitating the life of Christ, who *went about doing good,*[7] comforting, healing, teaching, the Church strives to do good wherever she is. Throughout history there has been a wealth of initiatives by Christians and by the most varied institutions of the Church to remedy the evils that afflict mankind, to give human help to those in need, to the sick, to refugees, etc. This human assistance is and always will be great, but at the same time it is secondary. Because of the mission she has received from Christ *the Church aspires to much more than this* – to give to men the doctrine of Christ and lead them to salvation. *And the Church has come to confirm one essential, definitive fact for all of us – for those who are in any kind of need and for those who think only to enjoy fully the goods of the earth – that our destiny is a supernatural one, and is eternal. We will be eternally saved only in Jesus Christ, and only in him will we in any way obtain true peace and happiness in this life.*[8]

47.2 Prayer for the Church.

Each day we should give pride of place in our prayers to the needs of the Roman Pontiff in his task of service to

---

[5] M. Schmaus, *Dogmatic Theology*, vol. IV
[6] Matt 28:18-20
[7] cf Acts 10:38
[8] St. J. Escrivá, *In Love with the Church*, 10

the Universal Church, and to the help he is given by his most immediate cooperators *Dominum conservet eum, et vivificet eum, et beatum faciat eum in terra, et non tradat eum in animam inimicorum eius,*[9] the liturgy enjoins us to ask. The Vicar of Christ must bear a crushing burden in his paternal concern for us all. It is not hard to see from the press and the other media what opposition there is from the enemies of the Faith. If we really think about it, in the presence of God, and become more aware of the pressures exerted by those who detest the apostolic zeal of Christians and are opposed to the evangelising task which the Pope is constantly encouraging, we shall fervently ask God in our prayers to preserve the Roman Pontiff, *to breathe his divine life into him, to make him holy and fill him with his gifts, and to safeguard him.*

In the Gospel of today's Mass[10] Our Lord warns his disciples to be on the watch, and to be aware of an insidious influence – a 'leaven', He calls it – *that of the Pharisees and Herod.* He is not referring to the good 'leaven' his disciples must be, but to that other leaven which is not less capable of transforming the batch from within, but only to corrupt it. The hypocrisy of the Pharisees and the disordered life of Herod, who was motivated solely by personal ambition, was the bad leaven that would infect the mass of Israel and corrupt it.

We have the agreeable duty of asking every day for all faithful Christians to act as a true leaven in the midst of a world that has turned away from God, but which the Church can save. *This time is a time of trial, and we have to ask God with an unfailing cry (cf Is 58:1) that He should bring the trial to an end. We ask him to look with mercy on his Church, and to grant once more supernatural light to*

---

[9] Enchiridion Indulgentiarum, 1986, *Aliae concessiones*, n.39
[10] Mark 8:14-21

the souls of his shepherds and of all the faithful.[11] We cannot ignore this filial duty towards our Mother the Church, in her mysterious need for help and protection. *She is a Mother ... a mother should be loved.*[12]

The corrupting leaven of adulterated doctrine and bad example propagated and magnified by those with an axe to grind has caused great harm to souls. When we meet up with false doctrines or are confronted with scandalous situations we must ask ourselves: What have I done to spread good doctrine? How do I fulfil my professional duties? What do I do to help my children, my brothers, my friends, to know the teachings of Jesus Christ? What prayer and mortification do I offer up for the Church?

Many people pray each day in the Mass, in the Rosary and in other ways for all the Pastors of the Church of God, together with the Pope and the Bishops. We should do so, too. There is a very ancient prayer that the faithful can use to pray for the Bishop of the diocese they happen to be in: *Stet et pascat in fortitudine tua, Domine, in sublimitate nominis tui.* The Pastors of the Church are always in great need of divine help in order to carry out their mission. We have the responsibility of helping them, so we ask God *to sustain them and help them to tend his flock with divine fortitude and with the gentleness and sublime wisdom that comes from Heaven.*

Every day in the Mass, with these or other words taken from one of the Eucharistic Prayers, the priest prays: *To you, therefore, most merciful Father, we make humble prayer and petition ... that you accept and bless these gifts, these offerings, these holy and unblemished sacrifices, which we offer you firstly for your holy catholic Church. Be pleased to grant her peace, to guard, unite and govern*

---

[11] St. J. Escrivá, *op cit*, 28
[12] St John Paul II, *Homily*, 7 November 1982

her throughout the whole world, together with your servant N. our Pope and N. our Bishop, and all those who, holding to the truth, hand on the catholic and apostolic faith.[13] Thus we remember the intentions of the Pope and the bishops. We pray for priests and religious, and for the whole People of God. We also pray for those most in need in the Mystical Body of Christ, thus living in a natural way the dogma of the Communion of Saints.

47.3 By Baptism we are made into instruments of salvation in our own environments.

In a letter from Saint John Leonardi to Pope Paul V, who had asked him for advice on revitalizing the people of God, the saint wrote: *As regards these remedies, which have to be the same for the whole of the Church ... we must first of all give our attention to those who are in charge of others. In this way the reform will begin at those points from which it can spread to the other parts of the body. A great effort will have to be made to ensure that the cardinals, patriarchs, archbishops, bishops and parish priests, who have been entrusted with the care of souls, are such as to be safely entrusted with the governing of the Lord's flock.*[14] We also should not cease to ask for their holiness each day; that they should have an ever-deeper love for Jesus present in the Blessed Sacrament, and pray to Our Lady with ever-greater piety. We pray that they should be filled with strength and charity; that they should love the sick, and take great care over the teaching of the Catechism. We ask that they give in their lives clear witness of detachment and sobriety ...

But we who are baptized are also the Church. We are all instruments of salvation for others when we strive to

---

[13] *Roman Missal, Ordinary of the Mass*, Roman Canon
[14] St John Leonardi, *Letters to Pope Paul V for the reform of the Church*

remain united to Christ in the faithful fulfilment of our religious duties: Holy Mass, prayer, presence of God throughout the day; when we are united to the Roman Pontiff and the Bishop of the diocese and their intentions; when we carry out our professional, family and civic duties in an exemplary way, and engage in an effective apostolate in the framework of those relationships that make up our life. This apostolate becomes more urgent the more of those deadly weeds, the devil-sown cockle, we find along our way, the more clearly we perceive the effects of that bad leaven of which our Lord speaks.

Let us increase our faith. The People of God, the Second Vatican Council teaches, has to fill the whole world, reuniting all those who are scattered and confused. That is why God sent his Son, constituted universal heir, to be our Teacher, our Priest and King.[15] Today we can recall to mind Psalm II, which proclaims the Kingship of Christ. We can ask God the Father that the souls will be many in which Christ Our Lord will reign. We ask him, too, that many of the world's peoples may welcome the word of salvation proclaimed by the Church, since she too has received in inheritance all nations, as the Constitution *Lumen gentium* reminds us.[16]

---

[15] Second Vatican Council, *Lumen gentium*, 13
[16] cf *ibid*

48. WITH CLEAR SIGHT

48.1 Guarding the sight.

Jesus came to Bethsaida accompanied by his disciples. As soon as he got there a blind man was brought to him *so that He could touch him*. Our Lord took the blind man by the hand and led him out of the village. Using spittle, He made some mud and put it on his eyes. Then He laid hands on him and asked if he could see anything. The blind man looked up and said, *I see men; but they look like trees, walking* ... And He laid hands on him again, and the blind man *looked intently and was restored, and saw everything clearly.*[1]

Our Lord usually cured people instantaneously. In this case, however, He does it in stages, perhaps because the faith of the blind man was at first weak, and Jesus wanted to cure body and soul together.[2] He helped this man, taking him by the hand with such affection, in order to strengthen his faith. To see nothing at all and then see indistinctly was something. But the Master wanted to give him a clear and penetrating gaze that would let him appreciate the wonders of creation. Probably the first thing the blind man saw clearly was the face of Jesus, looking at him with compassionate satisfaction.

What happened to this blind man in the material order can help us to consider the nature of spiritual blindness. We frequently meet many who are spiritually blind and cannot see the essential thing – the face of Christ present in the life of the world. Our Lord often spoke of this sort of

---

[1] cf Mark 8:22-26
[2] cf *The Navarre Bible*, note to Mark 8:22-26

blindness when He told the Pharisees they were blind,[3] or when he referred to those who had eyes but did not see.[4] To see clearly is a great gift of God: to see what is good, to see God in the midst of our ordinary tasks, to see our fellow men as children of God, to see what is really worthwhile ... and even to contemplate, with God and through God, the divine beauty He has left like his signature on all the works of creation. We need, too, to see with unclouded vision if the heart is to be able to love, if it is to remain young, as God wishes it to be.

Many people are not completely blind, but their faith is weak. Their sight is dim, and they can scarcely make out the good that lies on the horizon of their life. These Christians have little awareness of what it means to have the presence of Christ in the Blessed Sacrament, scant appreciation of the immense worth of the Sacrament of Penance, of the infinite value of a single Mass, of the beauty of apostolic celibacy ... They lack purity of heart, and need to be more vigilant in the guarding of their senses – the doors of the soul – particularly the sense of sight.

The soul that begins to have interior life appreciates the treasure it bears within its heart. Each day it will make a greater effort to deny admission into the mind of any image that prevents or hinders the soul's close contact with God. It is not a question of *not seeing* – after all, we need our sight to get along in the world, to see what we are doing in our work, in our social relationships – but rather a question of *not looking* at whatever we ought not to be looking at, a matter of being clean of heart, of living a necessary recollection with absolute naturalness. Such vigilance over our sight is required in the street, in the environments we frequent, in our social relationships. And

---

[3] Matt 15:14
[4] cf Mark 4:12; John 9:39

the desirability of the same clear-sightedness applies not only as regards lust, which blinds us both to supernatural goods and to truly human values, but also as regards other fields that can fall into the category of facilitating this *concupiscence of the eyes*: longing for clothes, for things to possess, for certain kinds of food or drink ... *The eye is the lamp of the body. So if your eye is sound, your whole body will be full of light. But if your eye is not sound, your whole body will be full of darkness.*[5]

How sad it would be if a lack of care in these matters should cause us to see the face of Christ not clearly but only as a blurred and distant image. In our prayer today we can examine the way we live this *custody of the eyes*. It is vitally necessary if we are to have supernatural life, if we are to see God. If we do not have clear sight we can have only a hazy and often misleadingly deformed vision of things.

48.2 In the midst of the world without being worldly.

The Christian has to use the necessary means to protect himself from the huge wave of sensuality and consumerism that seems in our day to be inundating everyone and everything in its path. We are not afraid of the world, for it was in it we received our initial calling to holiness. We cannot run away, because God wants us to be a source of ferment and to have the effect of leaven on our contemporaries. We Christians *are an intravenous injection into the bloodstream of society*.[6] To be in the midst of the world is not, however, to be frivolous and worldly. *I do not pray that thou shouldst take them out of the world*, Jesus said to the Father, *but that thou shouldst*

---

[5] Matt 6:22-23
[6] St. J. Escrivá, *Letter*, 19 March 1934

keep them from the evil one.[7] We have to be on guard, with a real life of prayer. We should remember that small mortifications – and big ones when they come along or God asks for them – will keep us always alert, just as the soldier takes care not to be overcome by sleep because so much depends on his watchfulness.

The Apostles warned the converts to the Faith to live the doctrine and moral teaching of Christ in a pagan atmosphere rather similar to that of our own times.[8] If anyone were to fail to struggle with determination, he would be swept away by our environment's climate of materialism and permissiveness. The widespread toleration of *modern lifestyles* and a popular approval of standards clearly opposed to the moral demands of the Christian Faith *and of the Natural Law* are now commonplace, even in countries with a long and deep-seated Christian tradition.

The propagators of the new paganism have found an effective ally in the entertainments industry. The influence wielded by the mass media on the opinions of the millions they reach is a vast one. In recent years there has been an ever-increasing proliferation of media productions which for all sorts of different reasons – or for no apparent reason at all – encourage a debasement of taste and an escalating concupiscence that leads to many internal and external sins against chastity. A soul living in that kind of sensual atmosphere would find it not only difficult, but impossible to follow Christ closely ... and perhaps even from afar. The indecency and impurity underlying such productions is often accompanied by an attempt to ridicule religion and the holy truths of Christianity. They make a deliberate exhibition of irreligiosity and atheism, thinking nothing of

---

[7] John 17:15
[8] cf Rom 13:12-14

using obscene and blasphemous language and displaying attitudes of contemptuous irreverence to whatever is sacred.

In their preaching the Fathers of the Church used hard words to deter the first Christians from attending immoral entertainments and shows.[9] Those faithful Christians knew how to do without means of recreation that sat ill with their zeal for holiness or could lead their souls into danger. They avoided such things with ease since it was obviously what the new ideals they had found required of them when they met Christ. Not infrequently, as a result, the pagans would become aware of the conversion of a friend, a relative or a neighbour because he had stopped attending those shows that did not conform or were openly opposed to the discriminating conscience of a person who has found his life in Christ.[10]

Does anything similar happen to us? Do we give up entertainments or going into atmospheres that are unbecoming to a Christian? Do we protect the faith and holy purity of our children or younger brothers and sisters when, for example, there is an unsuitable television programme? Let us ask God for a really Christian sensitivity of conscience that will enable us to turn away firmly, unhesitatingly, from anything that would separate us from him, or diminish our zeal to follow him.

48.3 A Christian does not go to places or shows which are incompatible with his state as a disciple of Christ.

Christianity has not changed. Jesus Christ is the same yesterday, today and for ever.[11] He asks of us the same fidelity, the same fortitude and example that he asked of

---

[9] cf St John Chrysostom, *Homilies on St Matthew's Gospel*
[10] cf Tertullian, *On Entertainment*, 24
[11] cf Heb 13:8

his first disciples. Nowadays we too must row against the current on many occasions. It could arise that our friends might not understand at first. But this is often the first step towards drawing them closer to God and helping them to decide to live themselves a deeply Christian life.

Our loyalty to God will lead us to avoid the occasions of danger to our soul. So before watching television at home or going out to a show we have to be sure what we see and hear will not be an occasion of sin. If there is any doubt in our minds, then the only course for us is to keep away from such entertainments, and if we have been badly informed and attend a show that does not match up to our moral standards, as good Christians we will get up and walk out: *if your right eye causes you to sin, pluck it out and throw it away.*[12] The important thing is, not to go in the first place, or to take one's departure without being afraid of *appearing strange* or in any way unnatural. For a follower of Jesus Christ what is unnatural is precisely the opposite.

To live as real Christians we have to ask God for the virtue of fortitude, so that we will not make concessions for ourselves. We want to speak clearly to others, without worrying about *what people will say,* even when we think they are not going to understand. Our words, accompanied by our example and an attitude of certainty and cheerfulness will help them to understand and look for a more soundly-based life, a better formation. If anyone objects that he is immune to the influence of entertainments of this kind, we can point out to him at a suitable time that gradually, imperceptibly, a sort of hard carapace is formed round the soul, hindering its intimacy with God, and gradually making impossible the delicacy and respect that all true human love demands. When

---

[12] Matt 5:29

someone tells us that no harm is done to him by going to such places or watching such programmes, it is perhaps a clear sign that he needs to give them up even more than others. His eyes are possibly already clouded and his soul hardened as regards the good.

Christians should give such entertainments a wide berth. They should avoid contributing a single farthing towards supporting evil, and do what they can to thwart and overcome it. But they should also make a positive contribution towards ensuring the existence of healthy, clean entertainments and wholesome attractions that help people rest from work, give them an opportunity to get to know others, provide pleasant means of intellectual development and so on.

Saint Joseph was faithful to his vocation as guardian and protector of Jesus and Mary. He loved them with the purest of loves. Let us ask him today that we should have the fortitude to go on using the means that will enable us to contemplate God with a clear and penetrating gaze, that we should love our fellow creatures with a deep and clean love according to the particular vocation we have received.

SIXTH WEEK: THURSDAY

49. THE MASS: CENTRE OF THE CHRISTIAN LIFE

49.1 Participation of the faithful in the sacrifice of the Mass.

Jesus was walking with his disciples towards the inhabited districts of Caesarea Philippi. On the way, He put a question to those who were accompanying him. *Who do men say that I am?*[1] In all simplicity the Apostles tell him what people have been saying about him. Some say He is *John the Baptist; others say Elijah, and others again one of the prophets.* There were all sorts of opinions about Jesus. In a frank and affectionate way He then asks his disciples, *But you, who do you say that I am*? He does not ask them for a more or less favourable opinion. He asks them for the firmness of faith. After they have spent so much time with him, they must know who He is, unhesitatingly, with certainty. Peter immediately replies, *You are the Christ.*

Our Lord has the right to ask also of us a clear confession of faith with words and deeds, in a world in which confusion, ignorance and error seem to be the normal thing. We are closely united to Jesus by Baptism, and the bond grows stronger day by day. In this sacrament a deep, intimate union with Christ was established. In it we received his Spirit and were raised to the dignity of sons of God. It is a communion of life much deeper than could possibly exist between any two human beings. Just as the hand joined to the body is filled with the life that flows from the body as a whole, so the Christian is filled with the

---

[1] Mark 8:27-33

life of Christ.[2] Using a beautiful image He himself taught us how we are united to him: *I am the vine, you are the branches* ...[3] If we struggle to be saints we Christians can achieve such a strong union that we will be able to say, *It is no longer I who live, but Christ who lives in me.*[4] This closeness to Christ should fill us with joy. If we are a living part of the Mystical Body of Christ we share in everything that Christ does.

In each Mass Christ offers himself up completely, together with the Church, which is his Mystical Body, made up of all the baptized. By reason of their union with Christ through the Church, the faithful offer the sacrifice together with him. They also offer themselves with him. They take part in the Mass, therefore, as those who offer and are offered. On the altar, Jesus Christ presents to God the Father the redeeming, meritorious sufferings He underwent on the Cross, and those of his brothers. Is a greater intimacy or union with Christ possible? Is a greater dignity possible? If we live the Mass well it can transform our lives. *If we have in our souls the same sentiments and intentions as Christ on the Cross, we will make our whole life an endless act of atonement, an assiduous petition and a permanent sacrifice for the whole of mankind. God will grant you a supernatural instinct to purify all your actions, raising them to the order of grace and converting them into instruments of apostolate.*[5]

And you, *who do you say that I am?* We know Christ well in the Eucharistic Sacrifice. There, our faith is strengthened and we find the courage to confess openly that Jesus Christ is the Messiah, the only-begotten Son of God, who has come to save us all.

---

[2] cf M. Schmaus, *Dogmatic Theology*, vol V
[3] John 15:5
[4] Gal 2:20
[5] St. J. Escrivá, *Letter*, 2 February 1945

49.2 The *priestly soul* of the Christian and the Mass.

The Mass is offered by priests, but also by the faithful, since *by the 'character' that is graven upon their souls ... they share in the priesthood of Christ Himself*,[6] although the faithful's participation is essentially different from that of those who have received the Sacrament of Orders.[7]

Only by the words of the priest representing Him does Christ make himself present on the altar at the moment of consecration. But all the faithful share in the oblation which is offered to God for the good of the whole Church. They offer the sacrifice together with the priest, uniting themselves to his intentions of praise, entreaty, expiation and thanksgiving. Yet what they are doing is uniting themselves to Christ himself, the Eternal Priest, and to the whole Church.[8]

In the Mass each day we can offer up all created things[9] and all our actions: our work, our sorrows, our family life, our fatigue and tiredness, the apostolic initiatives we want to undertake that day ... *The Offertory* is a particularly appropriate moment for us to present our personal offerings for them to be united to the sacrifice of Christ. What do we place each day on the paten? What does God find there? Guided by our *priestly soul* we are moved to identify ourselves more closely with Christ in our ordinary life. We will offer up not only the material realities of our life, but our very selves, in the most intimate oblation of our being.

Pray, brethren, that my sacrifice and yours may be acceptable to God, the almighty Father. May the Lord accept the sacrifice at your hands for the praise and glory

---

[6] Pius XII, *Mediator Dei*, 20 November 1947, 92
[7] cf Second Vatican Council, *Lumen gentium*, 10
[8] cf Pius XII, *loc cit*, 98
[9] cf St Paul VI, *Eucharisticum Mysterium*, 6

of his name, for our good and the good of all his holy Church.[10] We must give this and other prayers of the Mass a personal meaning, make it into a personal prayer. We go to Mass to make its unique Sacrifice of infinite value our own. We appropriate it to ourselves and present ourselves before the Blessed Trinity clothed in the countless merits of Christ, in certain hope aspiring to forgiveness, to greater grace in our soul and to eternal life. We adore with the adoration of Christ. We make satisfaction with the merits of Christ. We ask with his voice, which is ever efficacious. All that is his becomes ours. And all that is ours becomes his – prayer, work, joys, thoughts and desires, all of which acquire a supernatural and eternal dimension. All that we do is worth while insofar as it is offered on the altar with Christ, who is at once Priest and Victim. When we seek that intimacy with Our Lord, *in our own lives the human side intermingles with the divine. All our efforts, even the most insignificant, take on an eternal dimension, because they are united to the sacrifice of Jesus on the Cross.*[11]

Our participation in the Mass culminates in Holy Communion, the fullest identification with Christ that we could ever dream of. Before the institution of the Eucharist, in the years they spent crossing and re-crossing Palestine with Jesus, the Apostles were never able to enjoy such an intimacy with Jesus as we have after having received him in communion. Let us think about our Mass and our communions. Let us consider whether we prepare well for them, promptly rejecting all voluntary distractions; whether we make many acts of faith and love; whether we frequently make our own Saint Peter's cry of faith: *You are the Christ.*

---

[10] *Roman Missal, Ordinary of the Mass*
[11] St. J. Escrivá, *The Way of the Cross*, Tenth Station, 5

49.3 To live the Mass throughout the day. Preparation.

The Mass is the most important and the most fruitful of our personal encounters with God the Father, Son and Holy Spirit. The whole of the Trinity is present in the Eucharistic Sacrifice, which is the best way of corresponding with the divine love, the most pleasing to God. The Mass is *the centre and source of a Christian's spiritual life.*[12] Just as the radii of a circle all converge on its centre, so all our actions, our words and our thoughts have to be centred on the Sacrifice of the Altar. Everything we do obtains its redeeming value there. It helps the Christian life greatly if we renew our morning offering during the Mass. We offer all that we are engaged in throughout the day, uniting it in desire to the Mass of the following day, or to that which is being said near by, or in any part of the world. Thus, in a mysterious but real way, our day forms part of the Mass. In a certain way our day becomes a prolongation of the Sacrifice of the Altar. Our existence and our activity is, as it were, the matter of the Eucharistic Sacrifice to which it is directed and in which it is offered. The Holy Mass orders and centres the entire day with its joys and sorrows. Our very weaknesses are purified insofar as they form part of a life offered up to God.

We will do our work better if we remember that we have placed it on the priest's paten, or if we unite ourselves internally with another Mass at which we are unable to be physically present. The same will happen with the other events of the day – the small sacrifices of family life, weariness, sorrow ... At the same time the happenings of the day are all an excellent preparation for Mass on the following day. This preparation will be intensified as we draw closer to the time of Mass, avoiding any hint of

---

[12] *idem, Christ is passing by*, 87; cf Second Vatican Council, *Presbyterorum ordinis*, 14

routine. *Never get used to celebrating or attending the Holy Sacrifice: in fact, do so with such devotion as you would if it were the only Mass of your life, knowing that Christ, God and Man, Head and Body, is always present, and together, therefore, with Our Lord, the whole of his Church.*[13]

To obtain the fruits God wants to give us in each Mass, we must also take care of the preparation of our soul, and get ourselves ready for our participation in the liturgical rites, conscious of what we are doing, with devotion and full collaboration.[14] So we should be punctual as a first sign of courtesy to God, as well as to the others who will be attending the same Mass. We will take care of our appearance, and of the way we sit or kneel down ... like someone in the presence of a friend who is at the same time our God and Lord. We show him reverence and respect as a sign of our faith and love. We follow the rites of the liturgy and make our own the acclamations, the hymns, the periods of silence (silent prayer) ... calmly, filling the whole Mass with acts of faith and love, particularly the moment of the consecration. We live each of the parts of the Mass, sincerely asking forgiveness when we pray the penitential rite, following the readings attentively.

If we live the Holy Sacrifice with piety, with love, we will go out into the streets afterwards filled with immense joy, firmly disposed to show the vitality of our faith with deeds: *You are the Christ.* Very close to Jesus we will find Mary, who was present at the foot of the Cross. She shared in our Redemption in a full and particular way. She will show us the feelings and dispositions with which we should live the Eucharistic Sacrifice in which her Son offers himself.

---

[13] St. J. Escrivá, *Letter*, 28 March 1955
[14] cf Second Vatican Council, *Sacrosanctum Concilium*, 48

SIXTH WEEK: FRIDAY

50. HUMILITY

50.1 Relying on God.

In the Book of Genesis[1] we read how men began the colossal enterprise of building the city of Babel and its great Tower. It was to be both a symbol of human solidarity and a centre of unification for the whole human race; but the work was never brought to completion, and men found themselves alienated from each other as never before. They could no longer understand each other's speech and were incapable of reaching any sort of agreement. *Why did the ambitious project fail? Why did 'the builders labour in vain'? They failed because they had set up as a sign and guarantee of the unity they desired a work that was to be of their own hands alone, and had forgotten the action of the Lord.*[2] In commenting on this text from Scripture St John Paul II links the sin of those men who tried to be *powerful and capable without God, while not being precisely hostile to him,* with the sin of our first parents, who were deceived and seduced by the promise that they would become like God.[3] This is the sin of pride, which is at the root of *all* sin and shows itself in many different ways. *In the story of the Tower of Babel, the exclusion of God from human affairs is presented not so much under the aspect of opposition to him as of simply leaving him out of account, of indifference towards him, as if God were of no relevance in the sphere of man's co-*

---

[1] Gen 11:1-9
[2] St John Paul II, Apostolic Exhortation, *Reconciliatio et poenitentia*, 13
[3] cf Gen 3:5

operative undertakings. But in both cases, that of our first parents and that of the constructors of the Tower, the relationship to God is severed with violence.[4]

We should always remember to bring God into whatever we eagerly plan, or are working to achieve, because the tendency to let ourselves be led astray by pride lurks in the heart of every man and woman, and does not leave us right up to the very last moment of life. This pride urges us to *be like God*, even if only in the limited area of our own concerns, and to cut ourselves off from him as though He were not our Creator and Saviour and the one we depend on for our very life and existence. As we see from the story of the Tower of Babel, one of the first results of pride is disintegration – a lack of unity primarily in the family itself, and then in those more extensive relationships with other people, with friends, with colleagues and with our neighbours.

Proud people, like the builders of Babel, tend to rely on their own strength and are incapable of looking beyond their own abilities and the successes they seem to achieve; as a result, their structures are insecurely based, and never in any real sense get off the ground.

Indeed, the proud man shuts God out as not being worth his consideration; he never asks for his help, and never thinks of being grateful to him. Such a man never feels any need to seek support and advice through spiritual direction, though it is by this means that God so often gives strength and light to a soul. The proud man does not see himself as ineffectual and helpless, but as strong in his self-reliance and capable of great things. Because of this he is rashly imprudent and fails to avoid occasions of sin that put his eternal salvation at risk. Saint James the Apostle points out that *God flouts the scornful and gives the*

---

[4] St John Paul II, *op cit*, 14

humble man his grace.[5] We are told repeatedly that pride is the great enemy of holiness because it gives rise to very many sins and deprives the soul of countless graces and merits in the sight of God.[6] It is also the great enemy of friendship, of fortitude and of true happiness.

We can never, without inviting disaster, leave God out of any of our projects. *He is the foundation, and we are what is built on that foundation; He is the vine and we the branches ... He is the life and we live through him ... the light that drives away our darkness.*[7] Our life makes no sense without Christ; we cannot build it on any other foundation. Unless we have constant recourse to him, what faces us is nothing but discord and ruin.

50.2 Pride and selfishness.

Humility is found at the root of every virtue, and provides the support needed for living a Christian life. This is the virtue that opposes pride and the inevitable selfishness that goes with it. The self-centred man evaluates everything by the effect it will have on him personally, and this hardens into the mental attitude Saint Augustine identifies as the origin of all moral deviation – *self-love in contempt of God.*[8] Egocentric people simply do not know how to love. They are always out for what they can get because the only love they understand is self-love. They have no capacity for generosity or gratitude, and when they do give, it is because they calculate the giving is likely to benefit themselves in the long run. Self-interest lies behind their apparently generous action. They cannot comprehend the sort of giving that looks for nothing in

---

[5] Jas 4:6
[6] cf R. Garrigou-Lagrange, *The Three Ages of the Interior Life*, Vol 1, pp 445-6
[7] St John Chrysostom, *Homilies on the First Epistle to the Corinthians*, 8
[8] St Augustine, *The City of God*, book 14, chap 28

return. Basically, the egotist despises everyone else. Pride is the real cause of egoism and selfishness. All wickedness has its origins in this particular vice,[9] but self-love is one of its first products. Selfishness consists in looking at everything from the point of view of personal advantage. Pride generates an inflated idea of one's own abilities and qualities, and is invariably accompanied by an inordinate desire to be the centre of attention. They are two vices that often run in tandem, and between them they provide the ground for that radical disorder from which all sins spring, because *of all sin pride is the root*,[10] and *pride's beginning is man's revolt from God*.[11]

How often our personal experience validates the words of Saint Catherine of Siena. She tells us it is impossible for the soul to live without love, and that if it will not love God it will necessarily love itself in the wrong way. Such love will be a graceless love, *a cloud that blots out the light of reason ... taking for its object only passing things ... and drawing from them nothing but pride and impatience*.[12]

With the help of God's grace we must be always on the alert and ready to attack pride in all its different forms. We have to watch out for signs of vanity and boastfulness, and for those useless fantasies we are prone to weave where we are at the centre of everything and in command of every situation. We need to guard against being scornful of others, to avoid all scoffing and sarcasm and any tendency to judge other people adversely. We cannot be numbered among those who are forever butting into conversations, who always know best and who simply have to have the last word. Proud people are very apt to be

---

[9] St Thomas, *Summa Theologiae*, I-II, 177, 4c
[10] Sir 10:12
[11] *idem*, 10:13
[12] St Catherine of Siena, *Dialogue*, 51

discontented. They can talk about nothing but themselves and their own doings, because there is nothing else that really interests them.

We should beg God not to let us fall into this temptation. Pride is the worst sin of all, and the most absurd. If, with its multiple delusions, it manages to get a hold, the unfortunate victim begins to build up a façade, to fill himself with emptiness, and becomes conceited like the toad in the fable, which, in order to show off, puffed itself up until it burst. Pride is unpleasant, even from a human point of view. The person who rates himself better than everyone and everything is constantly studying himself and looking down on other people, who in turn react by ridiculing his foolish vanity.[13]

Never allow me, Lord, to get into that disgraceful state of mind where I see neither your loving face nor the many virtues and good qualities of the people around me.

50.3 How to grow in humility.

If we want to build up our Christian life we must have a great desire of developing in ourselves the virtue of humility, pleading with Our Lord for it and facing up to our subterfuges and failings in this area while trying by our actions to root out self-love. Humility produces countless fruits and is linked with all the other virtues. It is associated in a special way with cheerfulness, fortitude, chastity, sincerity, simplicity, affability and magnanimity. A humble person has a special gift for friendship and, because of this, for being apostolic. Without humility there is no chance of living a life full of charity, the theological virtue prerequisite for being an apostle and a friend.

To become more humble, we have to be ready to accept the humiliation of finding victory elusive in our

---

[13] St. J. Escrivá, *Friends of God*, 100

struggle to conquer our defects, and of being reminded of our weaknesses day by day. Often when we examine our conscience, especially on those occasions when we can do it more thoroughly, we can ask questions like these: *Have I managed to offer Our Lord in expiation the very sorrow I feel for having offended him so many times? Have I offered him the shame of all my inner embarrassment and humiliation at seeing how little progress I make along the path of virtue?*[14] Then there are the humiliations inflicted on us by others – the ones we were not expecting or the ones that seem unfair or downright unjust. Do we bear these well for Our Lord's sake?[15]

If we are searching for the firm rock of Our Lord's own humility in order to build on it, we are bound to find countless opportunities every day. We can try talking about ourselves only when it is really necessary – and not so much even then. We can be grateful for the little good turns people do for us. Keeping in mind that we deserve nothing, we can thank God for the countless benefits we receive. We can decide to make the world a more pleasant place for those who come in contact with us throughout the day. And what about those useless thoughts that revolve around ourselves? They can be cut off at the start. We should not miss any chance of lending a hand at home with the family, or at work, or anywhere else we may be. Instead of trying to be too independent we can allow ourselves to be helped, or we can ask for advice. If we are very sincere with ourselves we shall ask Our Lord to stop us finding excuses to explain away our sins and failings, those things that humiliate us and for which we sometimes have to ask other people's forgiveness. All of this is done with God's help and with the help of spiritual direction,

---

[14] *idem, The Forge*, 153
[15] cf *idem, The Way*, 594

which is only another way of coming into contact with
him.

Fixing our gaze on Christ, we can have enough
humility to admit our mistakes and set about putting them
right. There are also those blunders we make because of
lack of information, or because things change, or simply
because we fail to appreciate the seriousness of the
problem.

We learn all about this virtue by studying the life of
Our Lady. God has done great things for her *'quia respexit
humilitatem ancillae suae'* – *because he has looked
graciously upon the lowliness of his handmaid ... I am
more convinced every day that authentic humility is the
supernatural basis for all virtues! Talk to Our Lady, so that
she may train us to walk along that path.*[16]

---

[16] *idem, Furrow,* 289

SIXTH WEEK: SATURDAY

51. RESOLUTIONS FROM THE PRAYER

51.1 Jesus speaks to us in prayer.

Jesus went up to Tabor with three of the disciples who were closest to him, Peter, James and John, who were later to accompany him in Gethsemane.[1] There they heard the ineffable voice of the Father: *This is my beloved Son; listen to him. And suddenly looking around they no longer saw anyone with them but Jesus only.*

In Christ we find the fulness of revelation. In his word and life all that God willed to say to mankind and to each person is contained. In Jesus we find all we should know about our own existence, in him we understand the meaning of our daily life. In Christ everything has been said to us; it is for us to listen to him and follow the counsel of Mary: *Do whatever He tells you.*[2] That is our life: to hear what Jesus says to us in the intimacy of prayer, in the advice of spiritual direction and through the happenings and events which He sends or permits, and to carry out whatever He wants of us. *For this reason*, adds Saint John of the Cross, *he who may now wish for some vision or revelation, not only would be wishing something foolish, but would offend God by not turning his eyes totally on Christ, wanting no novelty or any other thing, because God could answer him in this fashion, saying: 'If I have already spoken to you of these things in my Word, who is my Son, and I have no other, what more can I answer or reveal to you? Fix your eyes on him alone, for in him I have said and revealed it all to you, and in him you*

---

[1] Mark 9:1-2
[2] John 2:5

*will find still more of what you are asking for and are
seeking ...; hear him, because I have no more faith to
reveal nor any more things to make known.*[3]

We must go to our prayer to speak with God, but also
to listen to his counsel, his inspirations and Will
concerning our work, our family and friends, whom we
should try to bring closer to him. This is so because in
prayer we speak with God, and because He speaks to us
through those impulses that bring us to improve in the
fulfilment of our daily duties, to be bolder in the
apostolate, and gives us light to resolve, in accordance with
his Will, questions which arise in all these areas.

Our Mother, Mary, whom we should honour today
with particular affection since it is Saturday, teaches us to
listen to her Son and to ponder things in our heart, just as
she did, as we learn from what the Gospels relate in two
different places.[4] *It was the consideration of things in her
heart which – with the passage of time – made the Virgin
Mary keep on growing in the understanding of this
mystery, in sanctity and in union with God. Our Lady,
contrary to the opinion often held by many people, did not
find everything made easy for her on the road to God,
since she was asked to make many efforts and was
subjected to trials which no one born of woman – except
her Son – would have been able to bear.*[5] In her intimacy
with God she knew what He wanted of her; it was there
that she penetrated deeper and deeper into the mystery of
the Redemption, and in her prayer made sense of the events
of her life, of the immense and incomparable joy of her
vocation, of the mission of Joseph, of the poverty of
Bethlehem, of the arrival of the Magi, of the upheaval of

---

[3] St John of the Cross, *The Ascent of Mount Carmel*, 2, 22, 5
[4] Luke 2:19; 2:51
[5] F. Suarez, *Mary of Nazareth*

the hurried flight to Egypt, of the sorrowful search for and joyous finding of Jesus when he was twelve years old, of the normalcy of the days of Nazareth ... The Virgin prayed and understood. The same will happen to us if we learn to enter into dialogue intimately with Jesus.

51.2 We should not get discouraged if it sometimes seems that Our Lord does not hear us ... He is always attentive and fills the soul with fruit.

This is my beloved Son; listen to him. There are many times when we should hear him and ask about what we do not understand, about what surprises us, or about decisions we must make. We ask him: Lord, in this matter, what do you want me to do? What will be most pleasing to you? How can I live my work better? What do you expect from this friend of mine? How can I help him? ... And if we know how to stay attentive we will hear in reply those words of Jesus who is inviting us to a greater generosity, words that will enlighten us in order that we may act according to the will of God. Truly, we can say to Jesus in today's prayer: *Every word of God proves true; he is a shield to those who take refuge in him.*[6] Without his word we would stumble, without any indicated path or direction. Guide me, Lord, in my ways, and do not leave me in the midst of such darkness.

The ears of the Lord are always attentive[7] to a sincere request, made with a right intention, a simple one, like that of a child who speaks with his father, as a friend speaks with a friend. Our heavenly Father always hears us, even if at times we may have the impression that he does not. Just as when Bartimaeus cried out to Jesus as he was leaving Jericho and moving on without paying attention to the cries

---

[6] Prov 30:5
[7] St Peter of Alcantara, *Treatise on Prayer and Meditation*, I, 4

of the blind man,[8] or as on that other occasion when the
disciples asked Our Lord to pay heed to the Syrophoenician woman who followed them and persistently continued
asking a favour for her sick daughter.[9] Jesus knew well the
heartfelt desires of these people and the faith that, with
such perseverance in prayer, becomes stronger and more
sincere. He is attentive to what we say, interested in our
affairs; He receives the praise, the thanksgiving which we
offer him, the acts of love, the petitions, and he speaks to
us, opens up new pathways for us, suggests resolutions ...
On occasion prayer will be a conversation without words,
as at times happens with friends who truly esteem and
know one another. But even without words, as we know,
we can say so many things!

Frequently it will help us in our prayer to consider that
we are the Lord's most intimate friends who, like the
Apostles, find ourselves called upon to serve him from our
place of work, and have occasion to talk to him about
many different matters, just like those others who followed
him. *Our Lord sent out his disciples to preach, and when
they came back he gathered them together and invited them
to go with him to a desert place where they could rest.
What marvellous things Jesus would ask them and tell
them! Well, the Gospel is always relevant to the present
day.*[10] And we, also, should pay attention to Jesus, who
speaks to us in the intimacy of prayer.

Our Lord leaves abundant fruit in the soul, even if at
times we don't realize it; he speaks in an almost impercept-
ible way, but always gives us his light and his help, without
which there can be no possibility of advance. Let us try to
reject any voluntary distraction, let us see what we need to

---

[8] cf Mark 10:46 ff
[9] cf Matt 15:21 ff
[10] St. J. Escrivá, *Furrow*, 470

look after in order to improve that time of conversation with Our Lord (such as custody of our senses, mortification in the regular things of each day, putting more care and attention into the preparatory prayer, asking for more help ...) and follow the example of the saints, who persevered in their prayer in spite of difficulties. *And very often*, recalls Saint Teresa, *over a period of several years, I was more occupied in wishing my hour of prayer were over, and in listening whenever the clock struck, than in thinking of things that were good. Again and again I would rather have done any severe penance that might have been given me than practice recollection as a preliminary to prayer.*[11] Let us never abandon our prayer, even if at times it seems arid, boring and difficult.

It is also of benefit, states Saint Peter of Alcantara, *to consider that we have our Guardian Angel beside us, and in prayer more effectively than at any other time, because he is there to help us and to bear our prayers to heaven and defend us from the enemy.*[12]

This is my beloved Son; listen to him. Jesus speaks to us in prayer. And the Blessed Virgin, our Mother, shows us how to go about it: *Do whatever he tells you,* she advises us, as she did the servants at Cana, because to do what Jesus says to us each day in our personal prayer and through spiritual direction is to find the key that enables us to open the doors of the Kingdom of Heaven, to place ourselves in the way of doing God's will concerning our own existence. And when we are docile to those promptings and counsels we find that our lives become fruitful; we will be like those servants at Cana who, through their obedience to the words of our holy Mother Mary, found the stone jars full of splendid wine.

---

[11] St Teresa, *Life*, 8,3
[12] St Peter of Alcantara, *op cit*, II, 4, note 5

Let us go to her and ask her to teach us to speak to Jesus, and to know how to listen to him. Let us renew our firm resolution to put more effort each day into our prayer. Let us examine ourselves on whether or not we are attentive to whatever he wishes to say to us in that dialogue.

51.3 Concrete, well-thought-out resolutions.

Do whatever he tells you. These words of the Virgin Mary are a permanent invitation to carry out the resolutions that Our Lord suggests to us each day in our personal prayer.

These resolutions should be well thought out in order to be effective, so that they become realities or, at least, become the effort to achieve them: *Make definite plans, not for the whole week but for the day ahead, for this moment and the next.*[13]

Often such resolutions will refer to little things that will help us to improve in our work, in our dealings with others, in trying to develop our awareness of the presence of God that day, while we make our way through the streets or find ourselves in the midst of our family ...

At other times Our Lord speaks to us through the advice received in spiritual direction, which will ordinarily be concerned with the principal area for improvement and provide a frequent topic for prayer. And thus each day, each week, almost without realizing it, the divine influence will cause us to adjust our direction just as the compass needle indicates for the voyager the course he needs to follow to reach his proper landfall. The end of our journey is God; we want to put ourselves on a sure course towards him, without drift or delays, with our whole will. Our first mission is to learn to listen, to recognize the divine voice that makes itself heard in our lives. Our daily resolutions and those carefully chosen points of struggle – the

---

[13] cf St. J. Escrivá, *op cit*, 222

particular examination – will lead us to sanctity, if we do not give up our honest battle.

Today we can go to Our Lord through Our Lady, perhaps by saying more aspirations, by saying the Rosary better, by taking the time to contemplate each mystery briefly, but with more love. *The scene of the Annunciation is a very lovely one. How often we have meditated on this. Mary is recollected in prayer. She is using all her faculties to speak to God. It is in prayer that she comes to know the divine Will. And with prayer she makes it the life of her life. Do not forget the example of the Virgin Mary.*[14] Today we pray her to grant us an attentive ear to listen to the voice of her Son, who makes himself known to us at specific times. *This is my beloved Son; listen to him.* We also ask her for a greater dedication in putting into practice the resolutions drawn from prayer and the advice received in spiritual direction.

[14] *ibid*, 481

52. TREAT EVERYONE WELL

52.1 We must live charity at all times and in all circumstances.

You have heard that it was said, 'An eye for an eye and 'a tooth for a tooth.' But I say to you ... if anyone would go to law with you and take your tunic, let him take your cloak as well; and whoever forces you to go one mile, go with him two...[1] These words of Jesus in the Gospel of today's Mass are an invitation to live charity beyond the criteria of men.

We should not be naive when dealing with people, but rather exercise prudence and justice (which might include demanding our rights). But neither should we regard any renunciation and sacrifice offered for the good of others as a mere excess of zeal, for it is by such actions that we become like Christ, who by his death on the cross gave us the example of a love that knew no human measure.

There is nothing in man more divine, more Christlike, than his meekness and patience in doing good.[2] *Of all the virtues leading to salvation,* Saint John Chrysostom suggests, *let us seek mainly those that benefit our neighbour ... In the things of this world no one lives for himself; the craftsman, the soldier, the farmer, the merchant, all without exception contribute to the common good and to the good of their neighbour. This happens even more fully in the spiritual life, which is the true life. He who lives only for himself and despises his neighbour is useless, is not a man, does not belong to our lineage.*[3]

Our Lord's repeated calls for us to be charitable at all

---

[1] Matt 5:38-48
[2] cf St Gregory Nazianzen, *Prayer*, 17:9
[3] St John Chrysostom, *Homilies on St Matthew's Gospel*, 77:6

times, and especially in his *New Commandment*,[4] must stimulate us to follow His lead by finding concrete ways of being of help to others, such as by making those at our side happy, realizing that we can never be too extravagant in the practice of this virtue. Most of the time the practice of charity will consist in little details, something as simple as a smile, a word of encouragement, a kind gesture ... In the eyes of God all of this is very pleasing and draws us closer to Him. In our prayer today we should also consider areas where we can easily lack charity if we are not careful: rash judgements, negative criticism, neglect of others due to self-centredness, forgetfulness ... The Christian way of conduct is not the way of *an eye for an eye and a tooth for a tooth,* but to do good always, even though occasionally such an attitude will not result in any human gain in this world – but at least we will have enriched our hearts.

Charity makes us understanding, ready to forgive, fit to live alongside everyone, *so that those who think and act differently from us in social, political and even in religious matters will also have a claim on our respect and charity ... Love and courtesy of this kind should not, of course, make us indifferent to truth and goodness. Love, in fact, impels the followers of Christ to proclaim to all men the truth that saves. But we must distinguish between the error – which must always be rejected – and the one who is in error, for he never loses his dignity as a person even though he flounders amid false or inadequate religious ideas.*[5] *A disciple of Christ will never treat anyone badly. Error he will call error, but he will correct the person in error with kindliness. Otherwise he will not be able to help him, to sanctify him.*[6] And that is the greatest manifestation of love.

---

[4] John 13:34-35
[5] Second Vatican Council, *Gaudium et spes*, 28
[6] St. J. Escrivá, *Friends of God*, 9

52.2 Charity towards all – including those who do not like us. Our prayer for them.

The commandment of charity not only applies to those who show us love and kindness, but to everyone without exception. You have heard that it was said, 'You shall love your neighbour, and shall hate your enemy.' But I say to you, love your enemies, do good to those who hate you, and pray for those who persecute and calumniate you.

Should we ever need to, we must also practice charity with those who ill-treat us, those who spread falsehoods about us and injure our reputation, and those who actively seek to cause us harm. Our Lord gave us example on the Cross,[7] and the route of the Master was travelled by his disciples.[8] Jesus taught us to regard sin as the only true evil and to avoid considering anyone as our personal enemy, and the saints of all times have given heroic witness to these teachings. The various manifestations of charity do not conflict with the exercise of prudence in the just defence of one's legitimate interests or those of others, or of the rights of the Church, or in the proclamation of the truth in the face of lies, or with a firm defence of the good. But a Christian should always have a big heart and show respect for all, even for those who act as enemies, *not because they are brothers,* as Saint Augustine points out, *but because brothers they must become; one must show fraternal love towards him who is already a brother, and towards the one who acts as an enemy, so that he may become a brother.*[9]

This way of acting presupposes a deep life of prayer and sets us clearly apart from pagans and from those who in fact do not want to live as Christ's disciples. *For if you*

---

[7] cf Luke 23:34

[8] cf Acts 7:60

[9] St Augustine, *Commentary on the First Epistle of St John,* 4, 10, 7

love those that love you, what reward shall you have? Do not even the Publicans do that? And if you salute your brethren only, what are you doing more than others? Do not even the Gentiles do that? Our Christian Faith does not call for a merely correct human behaviour, but for heroic virtues manifested in ordinary living.

Assisted by grace, we will also show charity towards those who do not behave as children of God but rather offend Him, because, in the words of Saint Augustine, *no sinner, as a sinner, is worthy of love; but every man, as a man, is lovable by God.*[10] They all continue to be children of God, capable of conversion and of reaching eternal life. Trusting in everyone's capacity to rectify his errors, charity will impel us to devote ourselves to prayer, to give good example and to do apostolate and practise fraternal correction. If at some time we suffer through particularly painful offences, injustices or calumnies, we should ask for Our Lady's help. Very often we have contemplated her at the foot of the Cross, enduring the infamous things done to her Son; and many of those offences – let us not forget – came from us. We should be sorry, rather, because injustices offend Our Lord and may harm other people; our reaction shall be to offer atonement to Our Lord and to make reparation if possible.

52.3 Charity gives friendship a deep Christian sense.

A Christian must have a great heart. But since charity must be ordered, the Christian should practise this virtue primarily with those that God has placed close to him; nevertheless our respect and affection for others should be in no way exclusive or focused on only a small circle of friends. Our Lord does not want an apostolate with limited horizons.

That union with God which we try to make fruitful in

---

[10] *idem, On Christian Doctrine,* 1:27

our daily life, with the help of his grace, must bring us to recognize the attractively human dimension of our apostolate. A Christian's dealings with his fellow men should mean a generous outpouring of supernatural affection and human *politesse*, overcoming his tendency to egotism and absorption in his own projects.

In our personal prayer we ask Our Lord that He enlarge our hearts; that He help us to offer our sincere friendship to a wider circle of people; that He may move us to do apostolate with each one of them, regardless of their response, even if we have often to submerge our own ego, or put aside our personal ideas or preferences. It is part and parcel of a loyal friendship to make a positive effort, which we will maintain by means of our constant dealing with Jesus Christ, *to understand the convictions of our friends, even though we may never come to share them or accept them*[11] if they are irreconcilable with our Christian convictions.

Our Lord never fails to forgive our offences as long as we return to Him led by his grace. He has infinite patience with our miseries and errors. That is why He asks us to be patient in turn when circumstances render it difficult for our acquaintances or friends to get closer to God. Jesus himself taught us this doctrine explicitly in the *Our Father*. When others lack formation, are ignorant in doctrinal matters, display character defects, or even seem indifferent to such things, we should not let ourselves be put off. On the contrary, we should regard these failings as urgent calls, signal lights that reveal a greater need of spiritual help, which should be for us an invitation to intensify our concern for these others, rather than leave them alone.

Let us resolve to get close to those relatives, friends and acquaintances that are most in need, and let us ask Our Lady for the necessary graces to make this approach.

---

[11] St. J. Escrivá, *Furrow*, 746

53. HELPING TO DO GOOD

53.1 Helping the spiritual and material good of others.

Mankind has never been so eager to be free, to throw far away all forms of oppression and slavery. Christ appears in today's Gospel as the only true liberator.[1] Four friends bring a paralytic whom they are eager to see rid of a disease that keeps him on a stretcher. After strenuous effort to carry him to Jesus, they listen to these words addressed by our Lord to their friend: *My son, your sins are forgiven.* It is unlikely that they expected to hear this kind of address from the Master to the invalid, but Christ lets us see that the worst of all oppressions – the most tragic of all slaveries from which man can suffer – is sin. It is not just one evil among the many other evils that afflict creatures, but the gravest, the only thing that is evil in absolute terms.

The men carrying the paralytic understand that Jesus has given their incapacitated friend the greatest good – freedom from his own sins. And we cannot forget what a great contribution to the common good it is to do everything possible to exile sin from the world. On many occasions the greatest favour, the greatest good we can do to a friend, to a brother, to parents, to children, is to help them see the beauty of divine mercy in the sacrament of penance. It is a good for the family, for the Church, for the whole of humanity, even though here on earth very few know about it.

Christ frees from sin with his divine power: *Who can forgive sins except God? It was for this that He came on*

---

[1] Mark 2:1-12

earth: God, who is rich in mercy, out of the great love with which he loved us, even when we were dead through our trespasses, made us alive together with Christ.[2] After forgiving the paralytic his sins, Jesus also cured his physical infirmity. The man must have understood in that very instant that his great good fortune that day had been the first cure: to have felt his soul pierced through and through by divine mercy, and be able to look at Jesus with a clean heart.

The paralytic was healed body and soul. And his friends are an example for us today of how we should help others – through our friendship mainly, cooperating in apostolic initiatives, and fostering the good of society with all the means at our disposal: working for the common good, for a decent life and culture, offering positive solutions when faced with evil. We should do this in our own professional circumstances as well as in any other environment in which we happen to be involved (neighbourhood, parents' association, parish ...); it is here that we can cooperate in the building up of good and avoid cooperation in anything that is evil.

53.2 Not being mere spectators of social life. Initiative. Not cooperating in evil; some examples. Offering solutions.

Frequently in social life many become mere spectators in the face of serious problems that are affecting them, their children or their social environment. They have the mistaken notion that others should be the ones to take the initiative, to stop evil and do good. They content themselves with sterile complaint. A Christian cannot behave in this passive way, because he knows that he should be leaven within society. In the midst of human

---

[2] Eph 2:4-5

affairs, *what the soul is in the body, Christians are in the world.*[3] *Such is the place assigned by God to them and they cannot desert it.*[4]

The positive obligation of *cooperating in good* should lead every Christian to bring Christ's message to every human activity – professional work included – in the best way he or she can.[5] The true Christian cannot simply avoid doing evil himself, being careless about the influence actions have on the behaviour of others. The friends of the paralytic do not limit themselves to not doing evil. They act. They help the sick man to get closer to Jesus. They help him in his desire to get well by paving the way for our Lord's miracle: *Your sins are forgiven.*

Cooperating in good implies, of course, avoiding any cooperation with evil, not only in important decisions but also in the small ways that easily lie to hand: not wasting money – even only small amounts   on magazines, newspapers, books, shows and entertainment, which because of their sectarian, anti-Christian or immoral character, damage the soul; buying one's newspaper at a particular news-stand (even if it means a longer walk) rather than from one where publications are sold attacking the Church or Christian morals; avoiding a pharmacy selling contraceptives; or not buying a certain product (possibly very good) which is advertised on an immoral or anti-Catholic programme on radio or television. And our action will be even more effective if we suggest a similar line of conduct to our friends. If lukewarm Christians were to stop buying certain magazines and publications, many of these would not survive. It is regrettable that, on many occasions, much of the immense damage caused is being

---

[3] *Letter to Diognetus*, 5
[4] *ibid*
[5] cf Second Vatican Council, *Apostolicam actuositatem*, 16

subsidised by Christians who, besides, are always complaining about society's moral ruin.

The Christian must cooperate in the common good by seeking and offering positive solutions to the perennial problems; he or she cannot limit himself or herself to simply not voting for a party or a programme which attacks Christian family values, or is against freedom in teaching, or favours legislation directed against life from its conception. There must be a constant, deep doctrinal apostolate, free from false prudence, and not afraid of going against the stream in issues which are vital for society itself and upon which there is complete disorientation or else a partial truth that often causes more confusion.

This amicable apostolate of doctrine, showing affection for everyone and spreading the teaching of Christ as widely as possible will make use of every opportunity (friends, trips, clients ...); it is the *leaven* that ferments society.

53.3 Protecting and fostering whatever is good. Spirit of cooperation. Noticing what is positive.

The work of re-Christianization is similar to the one undertaken by our first brethren in the faith, and makes use of the same means – good example in private and public life, prayer, friendship, nobility, personal prestige, sharing other people's concerns, showing an authentic desire for their happiness, along with the conviction that there is no peace for the individual, the family, or society, in abstraction from God.

The first Christians found a social environment very far distant from the doctrine they had so very much at heart. Though they opposed the customs that vitiated even human dignity, they did not waste their best energies in complaining about and denouncing evil. On the contrary, they chose rather to distribute the treasure they possessed by spreading it with a joyful and fraternal testimony, serving society through innumerable initiatives in the areas of culture, social service, education, ransoming captives, etc. They could have spent their lives observing everything that was out of keeping with an upright life; thus they would never have given the true solution to the world at large. The truth is like a *mustard seed* but it contains a marvellous power.

You don't have to be very clever to see evil; but a deep Christian spirit is required to discover the presence of God in all circumstances. Let us keep our eyes open to good, like the true friends in Saint Mark's narrative, and let us see, following Saint Paul's advice, *how to conquer evil with an abundance of good*.[6]

On many occasions the Christian's task will be to point out whatever is positive, since things well done encourage us to be better and bring us closer to God. Let us be quick to notice the virtues of those around us: a friend's generosity, the industriousness of one of our colleagues, our neighbour's readiness to help, our professor's patience ... If at times we cannot praise, let us hold our tongues. Or we will be of assistance with a kind correction and our prayer. Let us foster whatever good is born around us – sometimes with an encouraging word, at others with our help given in time and money. Faced with so much useless or harmful reading, let us spread news about good books being published, about magazines that will not be unworthy of a Christian home. Let us write a brief letter expressing our praise and thanks for a good show, a sound article. This takes little effort and is always fruitful.

God does not want his children to be naive when faced with life's harsh events. But he asks them never to be bitter

---

[6] Rom 12:21

or resentful. God wants us to see whatever is good in people and social events; he does not want us to spend the best years of our lives denouncing or complaining, but rather giving generously from the treasure of our faith. Thus we can help to transform people and society. Let us not forget, either, that good is attractive and that it always engenders much more happiness than lukewarmness does. A large family, for instance, with its many demands and sacrifices, always brings about more happiness than another family which – out of pure selfishness – sought its well-being in a little bit more of material comfort. This joy that other people sense is also a way of cooperating in the good: at times it is the most fruitful one.

Mary the Virgin, who goes *cum festinatione*[7] – in haste – to help her cousin, teaches us always to seek to cooperate in the good, so that Jesus her son, through his grace, may continue to work miracles on earth for the good of all men and women.

---

[7] Luke 1:39

SEVENTH SUNDAY: YEAR C

54. MAGNANIMITY

54.1 The disposition to undertake great things for God and mankind always accompanies a holy life.

The *First Reading* from today's Holy Mass tells us of David's flight from King Saul across the wastelands of Ziph.[1] One night when the king was sleeping in the midst of his men, David crept close to the camp accompanied by Abishai, the most faithful of his friends. They saw *Saul sleeping, within the encampment, with his spear stuck in the ground at his head; and Abner and the army lay around him.* Abishai whispered to David, *God has given your enemy into your hand this day; now therefore let me pin him to the earth with one stroke of the spear, and I will not strike him twice.* There could be no doubt that the death of the king would be the shortest route to freeing David once and for all from all the dangers he faced, and would raise him to the throne. But for the second time David chose the longer path, and preferred to preserve Saul's life.[2] David's behaviour on this and other occasions shows the great soul of the man. His largeness of spirit won for him first the admiration and then the friendship of his bitterest enemy, and also of the people. Above all, it won him the friendship of God.

The Gospel of the Mass[3] also invites us to be magnanimous, to have a big heart, like the heart of Christ. The Gospel exhorts us to bless those who curse us, to pray for those who persecute us. It calls upon us to do the good

---

[1] 1 Sam 26:2; 7-9;12-13;22-23
[2] cf 1 Sam 24:1 ff
[3] Luke 6:27-38

without expecting anything in return, to be merciful *as your heavenly Father is merciful,* to pardon everyone, to be generous without measuring and calculating. Our Lord ends by telling us: *Give, and it will be given to you; good measure, pressed down, shaken together, running over.* And He admonishes us: *for the measure you give will be the measure you get back.*

The virtue of magnanimity, which is closely related to fortitude, consists in the soul's willingness to undertake great things.[4] Saint Thomas calls it *the ornament of all the virtues.*[5] This disposition to take on important matters for God and for other people always accompanies a holy life. The serious effort to struggle for sanctity is in itself a first manifestation of magnanimity. A magnanimous person keeps his mind on high ideals. He is not daunted by obstacles, criticism, or contempt when it is necessary to endure them for a great cause. He is not prepared to let himself be intimidated by human respect or by a hostile environment. Rumour-mongers or back-biting mean little or nothing to him. He is much more interested in truth than in opinions, which are frequently falsehoods or half-truths at best.[6]

The saints have always been great-souled people, *magna anima,* showing their largeness of spirit when they envisioned and initiated apostolic enterprises, then carried them through to completion. Their soul was seen to be great in their human relationships, in their evaluations of and dealings with other people: they looked upon others as children of God, as being capable of great ideals. We in turn should not be *pusillanimous,* short-sighted and small-minded, with a timid spirit. *Magnanimity means greatness*

---

[4] St Thomas, *Summa Theologiae,* II-II, 129, 1

[5] *ibidem,* a4

[6] R. Garrigou-Lagrange, *The Three Ages of the Interior Life,* vol I.

of spirit, a largeness of heart wherein many can find refuge. Magnanimity gives us the energy to break out of ourselves and be ready to undertake generous tasks that will be of benefit to all. Small-mindedness has no home in the magnanimous heart, nor has meanness, nor egoistic calculation, nor self-interested trickery. The magnanimous person devotes all his strength, unstintingly, to what is worthwhile. As a result, he is capable of giving himself. He is not content with merely giving. He gives his very self. He thus comes to understand that the greatest expression of magnanimity consists in giving oneself to God.[7] There is no greater proof of magnanimity than this: total dedication to Christ, a dedication without measure, without conditions.

54.2 Magnanimity shows itself in many ways.

Greatness of soul proves itself also in a willingness to forgive, in matters large and small, whether it be people close to us in our lives or far from us. It is not Christian to go about the world with a list of grievances in one's heart,[8] cherishing rancorous thoughts and memories that shrink the spirit and make us incapable of the human and divine ideals to which our Lord is calling us. In the same way that God is always ready to forgive everyone everything, our capacity to forgive must have no limits. The number of times does not matter. The seriousness of the wrongs done is irrelevant, as is the status of the persons who were supposedly guilty of the offences. *Nothing makes us like unto God so much as being always ready to forgive.*[9] On the Cross, Jesus did what he had taught: *Father, forgive them,* he prayed. And immediately he added the mitigating

---

[7] St. J. Escrivá, *Friends of God*, 80
[8] cf *idem, Furrow*, 738
[9] St John Chrysostom, *Homilies on St Matthew's Gospel*, 19, 7

reason: *for they know not what they do.*[10] Those words show the greatness of soul of Christ's sacred Humanity. And in today's Gospel we read: *Love your enemies ... pray for those who abuse you.*[11] Jesus has always asked that same greatness of soul from those who are his own. The first martyr, Saint Stephen, died asking pardon for those who killed him.[12] Are we then not to pardon the comparatively trivial incidental things that happen to us each day? And if back-biting and serious defamation should be aimed at us, should we let slip that opportunity to offer something more valuable in return? It would be better still if we never reached the point of finding it necessary to forgive, imitating the saints in refusing to take offence in the first place.

Faced with something really worthwhile (noble ideals, apostolic tasks, and God above all), a great soul gives of his own without reserve: money, effort, time. He knows well and understands the words of our Lord: no matter how much he gives, he will receive more. *Give, and it will be given to you; good measure, pressed down, shaken together, running over, will be poured into your lap. For the measure you give will be the measure you get back.*[13] We should ask ourselves if we give what is ours with generosity. What is more, we should ask whether we give *ourselves,* whether we follow the path, the specific vocation our Lord asks of each one of us, with promptness and sure steps.

Furthermore, taking on great endeavours for the good of mankind, or alleviating the needs of many people, or to giving glory to God, can occasionally lead to the

---

[10] Luke 23:34
[11] Luke 6:27-28
[12] Acts 7:60
[13] Luke 6:38

expenditure of large sums of money, and to putting one's material goods at the service of those great works.[14] The magnanimous person does that if he can, without hesitation and misgivings. Living the virtue of prudence, he evaluates all the circumstances, but not with a fearful or shrinking soul. The great cathedrals are an example of ages in which, although there were far fewer human and economic resources than there are now, there was perhaps a livelier faith. From earliest times the Church has always sought the use of the fine arts, so that *all things set apart for use in divine worship should be worthy, becoming, and beautiful.*[15] Good Christians have given whatever they considered of greatest value, for worship, or to honour the Blessed Virgin. They have been generous in their donations and alms for the things of God and to alleviate the hardship of their brothers in greatest need. They have established works of medical and material help, founded and funded cultural and teaching institutions.

In a society which sets no bounds to its conspicuous consumption, we frequently see apostolic works and the people who have dedicated their entire lives to them deprived of the means to continue, often subjected to privations, and re-organizations, and constantly questioned as to whether they should not cease their activities and close down. The greatness of soul our Lord asks of his own will lead us not only to be very generous with our own time and economic means, but also to assist others to feel moved themselves to help, according to their means, for the good of their fellow man. Generosity always leads people closer to God. On countless occasions this is the greatest favour we can do our friends – encourage and foster their generosity. This virtue enlarges their heart and

---

[14] cf St Thomas, *Summa Theologiae*, II-II, q134
[15] Second Vatican Council, *Sacrosanctum Concilium*, 122

rejuvenates them, making them younger, more capable of love.

54.3 Magnanimity is one of the fruits of interior life.

Saint Teresa insisted that we should not *shrink* our desires, for *His Majesty desires and loves courageous souls.* Such souls set themselves great goals, the way the saints have done. The saints would never have reached such a level of sanctity, if they had not first taken the firm resolve to set their sights high, always counting on the help of God. The great Carmelite lamented the case of those good souls who, even if they lead a life of prayer, stay anchored to the ground *like toads* content *with catching little lizards,* instead of *soaring* toward God.[16]

Do not let your soul and spirit shrink, for you may lose many benefits ... Do not let your soul hide in a corner, because then instead of striving for sanctity you will simply come up with other imperfections, and many more of them.[17] Pusillanimity impedes progress in union with God. It *consists in the voluntary incapacity to conceive or desire great things, and stays constricted in a feeble and low life.*[18] Another symptom is the very poor opinion one tends to have of others, of what they can aspire to and one day become with divine aid, even though they may have been great sinners. A pusillanimous person is a man of closed horizons, resigned to just getting along. He has no high ambitions. Until he overcomes that defect, he will never dare to commit himself to God in a plan of life, or make any apostolic endeavours be effective, or dedicate himself. Everything will be too big for him, because he himself is shrunken.

---

[16] St Teresa, *Life,* 13, 2-3
[17] idem, *Way of Perfection,* 72, 1
[18] *Gran Enciclopedia Rialp,* see entry *Fortitude*

Magnanimity is a fruit of one's relationship with Jesus Christ. The disposition to undertake great enterprises, in one's own surroundings for God's sake, always accompanies an inner life filled with love, a nourishing and demanding interior life. This virtue is based on humility. It includes *an unshakeable firmness of hope, an actually challenging assurance, and the perfect peace of a fearless heart* which *does not bow to any man – but to God alone.*[19] An individual of great soul dares to do what is great because he knows that the gift of grace raises a person to undertakings beyond his natural capacities.[20] Then his actions acquire a divine effectiveness, because they depend on God, who *is able from these stones to raise up children to Abraham.*[21] Such a person will be daring in apostolate, because he is aware that although the Holy Spirit makes use of our human words as an instrument, it is the Spirit Himself who actually brings about the results.[22] A person of great soul has self-assurance, because all his effectiveness originates from God *who gives the increase.*[23] That is the source of his confidence.

The Virgin Mary will give us this greatness of soul which she herself has lived in her relationship with God and with us human beings, her children. *Give and it will be given to you ...* Let us not stop short or be withdrawn. Jesus is present to our lives.

---

[19] J. Pieper, *The Fundamental Virtues*

[20] St Thomas, *Summa Theologiae*, II-II, 171, 1

[21] cf Matt 3:9

[22] cf St Thomas, *op cit*, II-II, 177, 1

[23] cf 1 Cor 3:7

55. ASK FOR MORE FAITH

55.1 Faith is a gift of God.

Jesus came to a place where his disciples awaited him. There also He came upon a father with his sick son, a group of scribes and a great crowd of people. Seeing Jesus, they were filled with joy and came out to meet him: *All the crowd were greatly amazed, and ran up to him and greeted him*[1] – the way we should approach him in prayer and in the Tabernacle. Everybody had felt Our Lord's absence. The father of the boy steps out from the crowd that surrounds Our Lord. *Teacher,* he says, *I brought my son to you, for he has a dumb spirit ... I asked your disciples to cast it out, and they were not able.*

The disciples, who had already performed some miracles in the name of the Lord, had tried to cure the boy, but had not been successful. Jesus later explained to them privately what they had been lacking in order to carry out the miracle. The father of the boy had insufficient faith. He possessed some faith, as can be seen in the way he was searching for a cure. Still, he did not have complete faith, that boundless trust for which Jesus asked and continues to ask. And the Lord, as He always does, moves the man to take a step forward. At first, this supplicant comes to Christ with humility, but vacillating, unsure of his ground: *If you can do anything, have pity on us and help us.* And Jesus, *who knows ... what is troubling the man's soul,* helps him, saying: *'If you can, believe: all things are possible to him who believes'*(Mark 9:23).[2] What a good act of faith this is

---

[1] Mark 9:13-28
[2] St. J. Escrivá, *Friends of God*, 204

for us to pray many times!: Jesus, I believe, but grant firmness to my faith! Teach me to back up my faith with deeds, to weep for my sins, and to trust in your power and mercy!

Faith is a gift of God, and only He can increase it in the soul. He is the one who opens the heart of the believer so that it can receive supernatural light, and that is what we should be praying for. But at the same time, certain interior dispositions are necessary: they are dispositions of humility, of purity, of openness ... of love which opens the way to a greater and greater security.

If at some time our faith were to falter in the face of difficulties, in the apostolate ... or, if the faith of our friends, brothers and sisters or children were to waver or weaken, we should imitate this good father in the Gospel account. In the first place, he asks for more faith because this virtue is a gift. But at the same time it depends on us. *To open the heart*, comments Saint John Chrysostom, *is a work proper to God ... but to be attentive is a work proper to man: the act in this case is a work both of God's doing and of man's.*[3] We should strive to imitate this poor father in his humility: he doesn't have any merits of his own to present, and for that reason has recourse to Our Lord's mercy: *Have pity on us and help us.* This is the sure method that every prayer of ours should follow – to have recourse in this way to God's mercy and compassion. For our part, humility, purity of soul and openness of heart towards the truth will enable us to receive those gifts which Jesus never denies to souls who place no obstacles in the way of his granting them. If the seed of grace has not taken root in our soul, it is simply because that seed has not found fertile ground. Lord, increase my faith!, we ask in the intimacy of our prayer. Don't allow my faith in you ever to be shaken!

---

[3] cf St John Chrysostom, *Homilies on the Acts of the Apostles*, 35

55.2 The need for good dispositions in order to believe.

What did those people who met Jesus in the towns and villages of Galilee see in him? They saw what their internal dispositions allowed them to see. Would that they could have seen Jesus through the eyes of his Mother! What greatness would then have confronted them! And what pettiness and narrow-mindedness they would have observed in many of the Pharisees, who were caught up in the intricacies and nuances of the Law ...! They were not even able to discover in the miracles Our Lord worked that the Messiah had come at last. A great number of them remained blind before the Light of the world. Their knowledge of Sacred Scripture did not help them to see in Jesus the fulfilment of all that had been foretold about the Messiah and his promised arrival. Many of his contemporaries refused to believe in Jesus because they did not have an upright heart, because their works were not motivated by the desire to please God, because they didn't love God, or have a right intention in what they did: *My teaching is not mine,* the Lord will say, *but his who sent me; if any man's will is to do His will, he shall know whether the teaching is from God or whether I am speaking on my own authority.*[4] They did not have the necessary dispositions; they were not seeking God's glory, but their own.[5] Not even miracles can supply for lack of the necessary internal dispositions. The real reason behind the rejection of the Messiah, so long expected and so clearly heralded and announced, is to be found in the fact that not only did they not possess God in their hearts as their Father, but worse, they had for their father *the devil,* because neither their works nor their feelings nor their intentions were good.[6]

---

[4] John 7:16-17
[5] cf John 5:41-44
[6] cf John 8:42-44

God lets himself be seen by those who are able to see him because they have the eyes of their soul open. Everyone has eyes, but the eyes of some are blinded as it were in darkness and they cannot see the light of the sun. But the light of the sun does not cease to shine simply because these sightless ones fail to see it; rather is this darkness due to their own inability to see.[7] What care ought we to take of the frequent confession of our faults and sins, if this sacrament cleanses us and disposes us to see the Lord more clearly already here on earth!

In our apostolate, we should be aware that often the great hindrance to many souls accepting the Faith, recognising their vocation or leading a consistent Christian life, is provided by personal sins unrepented of, disordered affections and a lack of correspondence with divine grace. *Man, influenced by his prejudices or stirred up by his passions or bad will, is not only able to deny the evidence of external signs plain to be seen before his very eyes, but can also resist and reject the higher inspirations God infuses into his soul.*[8] If one is without the desire to believe and to do the will of God in everything, whatever the cost, one will simply not accept even what is glaringly evident. Thus, the person who lives shut up in his own egoism, who doesn't seek the good but only his comfort or pleasure, will have a difficult time believing or understanding a noble ideal. And, in the case of a person who has already taken the step of giving himself to God, he will find within himself a growing resistance to the specific demands of his vocation.

A sincere and contrite confession, well prepared, can then be seen as the great means to rediscover the way of faith; it gives one the interior clarity necessary to see what God is asking of us. When a person purifies and cleanses

---

[7] Pius XII, Encyclical, *Humani generis*, 12 August 1950
[8] St Theophilus of Antioch, *Book I*, 2, 7

his heart in this way, he prepares the ground so that the
seed of faith and generosity can take root in his soul and
grow and bear fruit. We do a great good to souls when we
help them approach the sacrament of pardon, and it is a
common experience that many of the problems and doubts
which afflict souls are cleared up with a good confession.
The soul then sees with great clarity its own restored cleanliness, and much better now are its dispositions of will.

55.3 Faith and prayer. Pray with more faith.

We can see that their failure to cure the possessed boy
weighed on the hearts of the disciples, since when they
returned from the recorded incident they asked the Lord
privately: *Why could we not cast it out?* And the Lord gave
them a reply that must be very useful for us in our
apostolate. He said: *This kind of demon cannot be driven
out by anything but prayer and fasting.*

It is only with prayer that we will overcome the stubborn
obstacles that balk our progress, manage to overcome
temptations ourselves and help many of our friends to find
Christ. Commenting on this passage of the gospel, the
Venerable Bede explains that in teaching the apostles how
to expel this particularly wicked demon, Our Lord shows
us all how we should live, and how prayer is the sure way
to overcome even the greatest of temptations. But prayer
does not consist of only the words with which we invoke
God's mercy; it is also what we offer to God in sincere worship, moved by faith.[9] All our work and every deed should
be a pledge to the Lord, and be therefore full of fruit.

We should reinforce our prayer with deeds of virtue,
with work that is well done, with the effort to improve
ourselves, in that very point in which we want our friend to
improve. This attitude towards God also opens the way for

---

[9] cf St Bede, *Commentary on St Mark's Gospel, in loc*

an increased access of faith in the soul. *It is only in prayer, in the intimacy of a face-to-face and personal dialogue with God which opens up the mind and heart (cf Acts 16:14), that the man of faith can deepen his understanding of God's will with respect to his own life,*[10] and to everything related to it.

Let us ask Our Lord frequently to increase our faith: let us ask for it in the apostolate when the fruits seem to be a long time in coming; let us ask for more faith with respect to ourselves and our personal defects, or to the defects of those around us, when it perhaps begins to look as if those defects are insuperable; let us ask for it when we see ourselves as miserably inadequate for doing all that God wants of us ... all these are reasons to cry out: *Lord, increase our faith!* Thus the apostles prayed when, in spite of having seen and heard Christ himself, they felt their confidence shaken. Jesus never refuses his help. Throughout the day that lies ahead and throughout every succeeding day, we will feel the need to say: *Lord, don't leave me alone to rely on my own strength, because left to myself I can't do anything!* The prayer of that good father we hear about inspires us to go to Jesus with our plea for a greater faith: *We too now, after this time of meditation, can speak the same words to him: 'Lord, I do believe! I have been brought up to believe in you. I have decided to follow you closely. Repeatedly during my life I have implored your mercy. And repeatedly too I have thought it impossible that you could perform such marvels in the hearts of your children. Lord, I do believe, but help me to believe more and better!'*

Let us address this same plea to Our Lady, Mother of God and our Mother, and Teacher of faith: 'Blessed is she who believed that there would be a fulfilment of what was spoken to her from the Lord.'[11]

---

[10] Bl. A. del Portillo, *On Priesthood*
[11] St. J. Escrivá, *loc cit*

56. THE LORD, KING OF KINGS

56.1 The Psalm of royalty and triumph of Christ.

For many generations the psalms have been a channel for the soul's requests for God's help, through which to thank him, praise him, and seek his pardon. Our Lord himself chose to use one of the psalms when He turned to his heavenly Father in the last moments of his life here on earth.[1] They were the principal prayers of the Hebrew family, and our Lady and Saint Joseph must certainly have poured forth their immense piety in their familiar and well-remembered words. Jesus learned them by heart from his parents and made them his own, so it is not surprising that the Church makes use of them every day in the Holy Mass and that they constitute the principal part of the prayer – the Liturgy of the Hours – which the priest directs each day to God in the Church's name.

The Fathers of the Church and ecclesiastical writers have commented repeatedly on the fact that Psalm 2 has always been considered among the messianic psalms,[2] and it has continued throughout the ages to nourish the piety of many of the faithful. The first Christians turned to it to seek courage in the midst of adversities. *The Acts of the Apostles* has left us a testimony of their devotion to this prayer. It relates how Peter and John had been brought before the Sanhedrin for having cured *in the name of Jesus* a cripple who was begging for alms at the entrance to the Temple.[3] When the apostles were miraculously freed, they

---

[1] cf Matt 27:46
[2] cf I. Dominguez, *Psalm 2: Lord, King of Kings*, Madrid, 1977
[3] Acts 4:23-31

returned to rejoin the other Christians, and all together they intoned a prayer to the Lord which has at its heart this same psalm that hymns the kingship of Christ. This was their prayer: *Sovereign Lord, who didst make the heaven and the earth and the sea, and everything in them, who by the mouth of our father David, thy servant, didst say by the Holy Spirit, 'Why did the Gentiles rage, and the peoples imagine vain things? The kings of the earth set themselves in array, and the rulers were gathered together, against the Lord and against his Anointed.* [4]

The words the Psalmist directs to God as he contemplates the menacing situation of his own time are prophetic ones which were to be fulfilled in apostolic times, and repeatedly throughout the Church's life as well as in our own day. We too could realistically say: *Why did the Gentiles rage, and the peoples imagine vain things?* Why so much hatred and so much evil? Since the moment of original sin this struggle has never ceased: the powers of this world unite together against God and against all that is of God. It is enough to see how human dignity is trampled upon in so many places, to be aware of the calumnies, the defamation, the baleful influence of the powerful mass media at the service of evil; to know about the abortion of hundreds of thousands of immature human beings who have been denied any option of developing earthly life or of the supernatural life to which God himself had destined them; to witness so many attacks against the Church, against the Pope, and against all who want to be loyal to the faith.

But God is stronger. He is the *Rock.* [5] It was to him that Peter and John and those united with them on that day in Jerusalem turned, and they were able to *preach with full confidence* his saving word. When they had finished their

---

[4] cf Acts 4:23-26
[5] 1 Cor 10:4

prayer, Saint Luke tells us, everyone felt strengthened and
*they were all filled with the Holy Spirit and spoke the word
of God with boldness.*[6] Meditating on this psalm can give
us fortitude when we are faced with the obstacles that can
arise in an environment very far from God. We can find in
it the sense of our divine filiation and the joy of
proclaiming everywhere Christ's kingship.

56.2 The rejection of God in the world.

'Dirumpamus vincula eorum ...' Let us, they said,
burst their bonds asunder, and cast their cords from us.[7] It
seems to repeat a general clamour. *They break the mild
yoke, they throw off their burden,* a wonderful *'burden'* of
holiness and justice, of grace and love and peace. Love
makes them angry; they deride the gentle goodness of a
God who will not call his legions of angels to his help (cf
John 18:36).[8] But *He who sits in the heavens laughs; the
Lord holds them in derision. Then he will speak to them in
his wrath, and terrify them in his fury.*[9] Divine retribution
is not meted out in this life only. In spite of the apparent
triumphs of many who declare themselves to be, or behave,
as enemies of God, their greatest failure, if they do not
repent, consists in never understanding or attaining true
happiness. Their human, or subhuman satisfactions will be
their bitter reward, can be the sad prize for whatever good
they imagine they have managed to do in this world. For
all that, some saints have affirmed that the path to hell is
already a hell. But in spite of everything, our Lord is
always ready to pardon, to grant them true peace and joy.

Saint Augustine commenting on these verses of the

---

[6] cf Acts 4:29-31
[7] Ps 2:3
[8] St. J. Escrivá, *Christ is passing by*, 185
[9] Ps 2:4-5

psalm points out *that the wrath of God* can also be understood as the mental blindness that afflicts those who spurn the divine law in this way.[10] There is no misfortune comparable to ignorance of God, to the tragedy of living with one's back to him, to the empty affirmation of one's own life in error and in evil.

Nevertheless, in spite of so much shame, God is patient. *He desires that all men be saved.*[11] The wrath of God, of which the psalm speaks, *is no mere corrective 'furor'; rather it is the necessary anger of correction, of a father with a son, of a doctor with a patient, of a teacher with a student.*[12] Even so, the time for taking advantage of God's mercy is limited: *for night comes, when no one can work.*[13] With death, the possibility of repentance ends.

St John Paul II has pointed out that the rejection of divine mercy is a conspicuous characteristic of our age. It is a very sad reality which moves us constantly to a conversion of heart, and to implore our Lord and ask him the reason for such widespread rebellion. For all to see there is the spectacle of multitudes who lock themselves away from divine mercy and the remission of their sins. They consider these to be *not essential or not important for one's life.* It is *an impenetrability of conscience, a state of mind that could be described as fixed by reason of a free choice. This is what Sacred Scripture calls 'hardness of heart.' In our own day this attitude of mind and heart is perhaps reflected in the notable loss of the sense of sin.*[14]

Those of us who wish to follow Christ closely have the duty of making reparation for the violent rejection of God

---

[10] cf St Augustine, *Commentaries on the Psalms*, 2:4
[11] 1 Tim 2:4
[12] St Jerome, *Breviarium in Psalmos II*
[13] John 9:4
[14] St John Paul II, Encyclical, *Dominum et Vivificantem*, 18 May 1986, 46-47

by so many of our contemporaries, and we have to beg an abundance of grace and of mercy. Let us ask that this divine clemency be never exhausted, since it is for so many the last life-line, the only thing left for the drowning man to grasp, after having rejected every other aid to salvation.

56.3 Divine filiation.

To the profound questions that human freedom raises concerning the mystery of evil – the rebellion of the creature – Psalm 2 gives the solution, proclaiming the kingship of Christ and his dominion over evil that exists or can exist: *'I have set my King on Zion, my holy hill.' I will tell of the decree of the Lord: He said to me, 'Your are my Son, today I have begotten you.'*[15] *The kindness of God our Father has given us his Son for a king. When He threatens He becomes tender, when He says He is angry He gives us his love. 'You are my Son': this is addressed to Christ – and to you and me if we decide to become 'alter Christus, ipse Christus': another Christ, Christ himself.*

Words cannot go so far as the heart, which is moved by God's goodness. He says to us: 'You are my son'... Not a stranger, not a well-treated servant, not a friend – that would be a lot already. A son![16] This is our refuge: divine filiation. Here we find the necessary courage in the face of adversities – those of an environment which is at times hostile to Christian life, as well as the temptations our Lord may permit in order for us to reaffirm our faith and love.

We always find our Father God very near to us. His presence *is like a pervasive fragrance which never loses the gentle insistence with which it enters everywhere – the same in the interior of the hearts that accept him as in the exterior, in natural objects, in the middle of a crowd, in all*

---

[15] Ps 2:6-7
[16] St. J. Escrivá, *loc cit*

things God is there, waiting for us to discover him, to call to him, to take him into account ... [17]

Ask of me, and I will make the nations your heritage, and the ends of the earth your possession. [18] Each day our Lord says, *Ask of me,* especially in the moments of thanksgiving after communion. *Ask of me,* Jesus invites us, His desire is to give himself to us, and for us to give ourselves to him.

Saint John Chrysostom comments on these words of the Psalm and teaches that what is promised to us is no longer just a land flowing with milk and honey, or a long life, or an abundance of children, or wheat, or wine, or flocks, but heaven and the good things of heaven – divine filiation and brotherhood with his only-begotten Son, a sharing in his inheritance and being glorified together with him and reigning with him for all eternity... [19]

You shall break them with a rod of iron, and dash them in pieces like a potter's vessel. Now therefore, O kings, be wise; be warned, O rulers of the earth. Serve the Lord with fear, with trembling kiss his feet. [20] Christ has triumphed now and forever. With his death on the cross, He has won life for us. According to the testimony of the Fathers of the Church, the iron rod is the Holy Cross, *which is made of wood, but has the strength of iron.* [21] It is the sign of the Christian, with which he will conquer in every battle: the obstacles will be shattered *like an earthen dish.* The Cross in our mind, on our lips, in our heart, in all our works: this is the weapon of conquest – a sober and mortified life lived without fleeing from the lovable sacrifice that unites us with Christ.

---

[17] M. Eguibar, *Why do the gentiles rage? (Psalm 2)*, pp. 27-28
[18] Ps 2:8
[19] cf St John Chrysostom, *Homilies on St Matthew's Gospel*, 16:5
[20] Ps 2:9-11
[21] St Athanasius, *Commentary on the Psalms*, 2:6

The psalm ends with a call for us to remain faithful along the way and confident in our Lord. *Serve the Lord with fear, with trembling kiss his feet, lest he be angry, and you perish in the way; for his wrath is quickly kindled. Blessed are all who take refuge in him.*[22] We have placed all our confidence in God. We ask the holy guardian angels, those faithful servants of God, to help us live our vocation each day with greater fidelity and more love, serving the kingdom of his Son where He has called us.

---

[22] Ps 2:12

57. UNITY AND VARIETY IN THE CHURCH'S APOSTOLATE

57.1 In the life of the Church there are many and very diverse forms of apostolate.

Christ's disciples once came upon a man who was casting out devils in his name. We don't know if this was someone who had already met Jesus; perhaps he had even been cured by our Lord or had witnessed one of his miracles and decided on his own responsibility to be a disciple. Whatever the case, Saint Mark gives us John's reaction: *Teacher, we saw a man casting out demons in your name, and we forbade him, because he was not following us.*

Our Lord took advantage of this opportunity to answer in a way that applies to all of us: *Do not forbid him, he said, for no one who does a mighty work in my name will be able soon after to speak evil of me. For he that is not against us is for us.*[1] This man had demonstrated his deep, living faith in Jesus with deeds. Christ accepts him as his follower and condemns a narrow-minded and exclusive attitude toward apostolate. He teaches us that the apostolic work done in his name can take many different forms.

The apostolate, through which the laity build up the Church, sanctify the world and persuade it to live in Christ, can take on many forms.[2] The one thing necessary is to be with Christ, with his Church – to transmit his teaching and to love him with deeds. Our Christian spirit should lead us to be open to the most varied forms of

---

[1] Mark 9:37-39
[2] Second Vatican Council, *Apostolicam actuositatem*, 16

apostolate, to make an effort to understand them all – no matter how different they may be from our own way of thinking or acting – and to rejoice in their variety. After all, the harvest is great, and the labourers in the Lord's vineyard are few.[3] *Rejoice when you see others working in a good apostolate. And ask God to grant them abundant grace and correspondence to that grace.*

Then, you, on your way. Convince yourself that, for you – yours is the only way.[4]

It would be inconceivable – it would be impossible, in fact – for a Christian who is truly living his faith to develop an exclusivist mentality, as though anyone who did not conform to one's own rules or ways of acting were to be considered as some kind of *rival*. Not everyone has to be involved in the same sort of apostolate. Any person, as long as he acts with a right intention, performs a useful task. We are all needed. There should be many ways in which Christ and his teaching can be made known.

Certainly, there is a unity that must be preserved *in faith and in moral matters, in the sacraments, in obedience to the Hierarchy, in the common means of attaining holiness and in the great norms of discipline. But this precious unity is to be preserved with the well-known principle of Saint Augustine: 'in necessariis unitas, in dubiis libertas, in omnibus caritas' – unity in all that is necessary, freedom in all that is subject to opinion, and charity in everything.*[5] In other words, the unity that is needed is never the kind of uniformity that leads to an impoverishment of souls and of their apostolates. I*n the garden of the Church there has always been, and there will always be, a remarkable*

---

[3] cf Matt 9:37
[4] St. J. Escrivá, *The Way*, 965
[5] John Paul II, *Address to the Spanish Episcopal Conference*, Madrid, 31 October 1982

variety of beautiful flowers, each with its own aroma, its own size, shape and colour.[6] All this rich diversity only serves to enhance the glory of God.

Whenever we are involved in an apostolic task, we must avoid the temptation to waste our time *evaluating* other people's initiatives. Instead of devoting our attention to what others are doing, we should rather look into our own heart and see if we ourselves are truly committed to making the best possible use of the talents God has given *us*. For the sake of the souls that depend on our work, *You, on your way. Convince yourself that, for you – yours is the only way.*

The wonder of Pentecost is the sanctification of every unique path: no one way has a monopoly, no one way is to be encouraged to the exclusion or the detriment of others.

Pentecost is an incalculable variety of tongues, of methods, of ways of meeting God, and not a forced uniformity.[7]

57.2 We need to bring the Church's teaching to everyone.

Christ's teaching should reach out to the whole world; in fact, in our time there are many parts of the world, once Christian, that are in need of a new evangelization. The Church's mission is universal, embracing persons from every conceivable background, of different ages, cultures, ways of living. From the very beginning the Faith was accepted by the old and the young, the wealthy and the poor, the learned and the unlettered. The Apostles and their successors made sure that, in all necessary matters, unity might be maintained. But the Church did not try to impose a straitjacket of uniformity on all its converts. In the same way, the apostolate was carried out through a great variety

---

[6] St. J. Escrivá, *Letter*, 1 January 1935
[7] St. J. Escrivá, *Furrow*, 226

of channels – some fulfilled the important task of defending Christianity with their writings, others preached in public in the market-places, while the majority of the new Christians carried out a personal work of apostolate in their families and among their neighbours, friends and fellow-workers. What they had in common was their mutual charity, their faithfulness to the doctrine they had received, the sacraments, and their obedience to their legitimate shepherds.

We can bring our Lord's teaching to everyone, carefully separating away the thorns that would make the seed fruitless. We Christians, in the task entrusted to us by God, *do not exclude anyone; we do not leave any soul out of our love for Christ. And so,* St Josemaría Escrivá used to advise, *you must develop firm, loyal, sincere friendships – Christian friendships – with all your fellow-workers, and, indeed, with all men, whatever their personal circumstances may be.*[8] A Christian's calling makes him one who is open to others, who is able to reach an understanding with the most diverse kinds of people, regardless of their age, their cultural background, their personality or their character.

Our friendship with Jesus, expressed in our prayer, leads us to have a big heart, with room for those who are close at hand and for people who are far away, without the slightest narrowness in our outlook. An exclusive and restrictive mentality does not reflect the presence and the love of Christ. Let us examine our behaviour in our prayer. Let us see whether we love and respect the different ways of living and acting that we see in the people we meet every day. Let us make sure that we accept, as part of the wealth of the Church's life, the differences we encounter in other people – their different likes and dislikes, their varied

---

[8] *idem, Letter,* 9 January 1951

ways of living or of expressing themselves, their unique ways of reacting or thinking, within the unity of our faith.

57.3 The unity of the Church does not mean uniformity.

The Church is like the human body made up of many members, all different and all closely united to one another.[9] This diversity does not threaten our unity; rather, it is its most fundamental condition.

We must pray to our Lord for the grace to understand this supernatural reality, and to act accordingly in our task of building up the Body of Christ so that there may always be unity in truth and in charity; so too, that at the same time we may acknowledge the variety that exists in the Church – in matters of spirituality, of theological study, of pastoral action, of apostolic initiative. The variety of forms *is a true richness and brings with it a real fulness; it is true catholicity.*[10] This is quite different from a false pluralism which would involve nothing more than *the juxtaposition of radically opposed points of view.*[11]

The Holy Spirit acts where there is unity and true charity. He inspires each person to follow a specific path toward the fulness of his love. Whoever has received a particular supernatural gift, whoever has been called to follow a specific path, will contribute to building up the Church through his faithfulness to that calling, and along the path that God has marked out for him. It is there, and not anywhere else, that God comes out to meet him.

The unity that our Lord wants – *ut omnes unum sint*, that all may be one[12] – does not constrain or inhibit anyone's personality. Rather, it encourages its development.

---

[9] cf 1 Cor 12:13-27
[10] *Extraordinary Synod 1985, Relatio finalis*, II, C. 2
[11] *ibid*
[12] John 17:22

There are many different ways to live one's spiritual life, and many different possibilities of theological thinking in matters that the Church leaves open to discussion. *You were amazed that I should approve the lack of uniformity in the apostolate in which you work. And I said to you: Unity and variety. You all have to be different from one another, as the saints in heaven are different, each having his own personal and very special characteristics. But also you have to be as identical as the saints, who would not be saints if each of them had not identified himself with Christ.*[13]

Our Lord's teaching leads us to respect the legitimate differences in character, taste, and opinion that should exist in temporal matters. We should rejoice in these differences and even encourage them. Anything that is not opposed to our Lord's teaching or to one's own vocation, anything that does not hinder it, should be characterised by complete freedom. Every individual has a right to that freedom with respect to his likes and dislikes, his work and his other occupations, his ideas on science or his views on politics. In our time and in any time in history, we Christians should be firmly united in Christ, in his love and in his teaching, and faithful to the calling that each has received. And we should be very different from each other in everything else – each with his own gifts and his own personality, striving to be salt and light, like burning coals aflame with the love of God – true disciples of Christ.

---

[13] St. J. Escrivá, *The Way*, 947

SEVENTH WEEK: THURSDAY

58. GETTING TO HEAVEN

58.1 The only thing that really matters in life is getting to Heaven.

Among all the achievements of our life only one is really crucial. It is attaining the goal – Heaven – set for us by God. We must be ready to give up everything, if necessary, to achieve this goal. We must also be ready to set aside anything that even gets in the way of our achieving it, no matter how valuable or appealing it may seem. Everything else has to be subjected to that one supreme objective in our life – possessing God. If anything becomes an obstacle rather than an aid to this end, then we must be prepared either to set things straight or to put the obstacle aside completely. Eternal salvation – our own or our neighbour's – comes first. Our Lord tells us so in the Gospel of the Mass:[1] *If thy hand is an occasion of sin to thee, cut it off! ... And if thy foot is an occasion of sin to thee, cut it off! ... And if thine eye is an occasion of sin to thee, pluck it out! ...* It is better to enter into the kingdom of Heaven maimed, lame or lacking an eye, *than being physically sound to be cast into hellfire, where their worm dies not, and the fire is not quenched.* It is better to lose something as necessary as one's hand, one's foot or one's eye than to lose Heaven, which is our supreme good, implying as it does the beatific vision of God for all eternity. How much truer this is, if, as is usually the case, what we need to put aside with no more than a bit of determination on our part is something that would otherwise not result in any significant harm to us.

By employing these very graphic images Our Lord

---

[1] Mark 9:40-49

teaches us that it is our positive duty not even to run the risk of offending him; we have the serious duty of avoiding or setting aside proximate occasions of sin, *for he that loves the danger shall perish in it.*[2] Anything that entices and draws us closer to sin must be energetically excised from our lives. We cannot toy with our own salvation or with the salvation of our neighbour.

Often the obstacles we have to set aside will not be tremendously significant ones. In the life of a Christian who is striving to please God in all things, this will usually be the case. What will have to be set aside and cut out are our minor whims and preferences. We shall take prudent steps to correct small breaches of temperance where Our Lord asks us to mortify our taste or our appetite, to control our temper or our moods, to overcome any excessive concern we may have about our health or comfort... All of these more or less habitual failings need very much to be taken into account, even though they may not be more than venial sins. They slow our pace and can trip us up – or worse: they can gradually lead to or bring about more serious falls.

If our struggle is generous, if our goal in life is clear in our sight, we will be decisive not to say ruthless, in striving to correct these situations so that they cease to be obstacles and are turned into advantages. This is what Our Lord often did with his Apostles. From Peter's hot-headed impetuosity He formed solid rock on which He would build his Church. From the vehement impatience of John and James (whom He dubbed *sons of thunder*) He fashioned the apostolic zeal of untiring preachers. From Thomas's scepticism he moulded a strikingly articulate testimony to his divinity. What has been previously a crippling liability becomes a powerful asset.

---

[2] Sir 3:26

58.2 Hell exists. We must practice a holy fear of God.

A Christian's life ought to be a continual journeying toward Heaven. Everything should strengthen our steps along this path – sorrows and joys, work and rest, successes and failures. In important financial matters or other great practical enterprises we naturally have to be alert, carefully studying even the smallest details, so it makes even more sense to do so in regard to the most significant of all undertakings – our salvation. At the end of our journey on this earth we will face but one choice: either Heaven (passing through Purgatory first if we require to be purified) or hell, that place of unquenchable fire which Our Lord so explicitly spoke about many times.

Christ would not have taken such pains to reveal the existence of hell with such clarity if it were not real, or if it were not really possible for men to end up there. He certainly would not have warned us so frequently, telling us: be watchful! The devil never relents in his attempt to win over any man or woman still journeying in this world towards his or her definitive goal. The devil never relinquishes his claim upon anyone, quite regardless of position or God-given mission.

The reality of eternal punishment for those who do evil and die in mortal sin had already been revealed in the Old Testament.[3] And in the New Testament Jesus Christ spoke of the punishment prepared for the devil and his angels,[4] for those wicked servants who do not fulfil their Lord's will,[5] for the foolish virgins who find themselves without the oil of good works when the Bridegroom arrives,[6] for those who come to the marriage feast without the wedding

---

[3] cf Num 16:30-33; Is 33:14; Eccles 7:18-19; Job 10:20-21; etc.
[4] cf Matt 25:41
[5] cf Matt 24:51
[6] cf Matt 25:1 *et seq*

garment,[7] for those who offend their brothers seriously,[8] or who choose not to help them in their material or spiritual need...[9] The world is compared to a field in which both wheat and weeds are growing until the time when God takes up his sickle and clears his field. The wheat will be stored in his barns while the weeds will be burnt with unquenchable fire.[10]

Hell was not some sort of symbol for use in preaching or in moral exhortation – in past moments of history – to a humanity which had yet to evolve. It is a stark reality revealed to us by Jesus Christ. It is, unfortunately, one so objectively real that Our Lord was moved to give us the spirited command – as we read in the Gospel of the Mass – to put away from us anything, no matter how important it might seem, rather than eventually find ourselves there forever. Hell is a truth of faith constantly affirmed by the Church's Magisterium. The Second Vatican Council refers to it, in repeating the eschatological characteristics of the Church, *we should ... watch constantly so that ... we may ... not, like the wicked and slothful servants (cf Matt 25:26) be ordered to depart into eternal fire (cf Matt 25:41), into the outer darkness where 'men will weep and gnash their teeth' (Matt 22:13 and 25:30).*[11] Hell's existence is a truth of faith, defined by the Magisterium of the Church.[12]

It would be a serious mistake not to meditate upon or to consider this transcendental topic from time to time or to ignore it in preaching, in teaching catechetics or in one's personal apostolate. *Nor can the Church omit, without*

---

[7] cf Matt 22:1-14

[8] cf Matt 5:22

[9] cf Matt 25:41 *et seq*

[10] Luke 3:17

[11] Second Vatican Council, *Lumen gentium*, 48

[12] Benedict XII, Apostolic Constitution, *Benedictus Deus*, 29 January 1336, Dz 531; Council of Florence, Dz 693

serious mutilation of her essential message, as St John Paul II warns, *a constant catechesis on ... the four last things of man: death, judgement (universal and particular), hell and heaven. In a culture which tends to imprison man immanently in the earthly life, which he is more or less successful at getting through, the pastors of the Church are asked to provide a catechesis which will reveal and illustrate with the certainty of faith what comes after the present life beyond the mysterious gates of death, an eternity of joy in communion with God or the punishment of separation from him forever.*[13] Our Lord wants us to be motivated by love, but given our human weakness – the result of original sin and of our own personal sins – He has preferred to show us just where sin leads, so that we would have a further motive to reject sin – the holy fear of God which is the fear of being separated from our Supreme Good, our true Love. The saints have highly esteemed the personal revelations they have received from God regarding hell's existence as well as the magnitude and unending nature of its punishments. ... *This vision was one of the most signal favours the Lord has bestowed upon me*, writes Saint Teresa of Avila. *It has been of the greatest benefit to me, both in taking from me all fear of the tribulations and disappointments of this life and also in strengthening me to put up with them and to give thanks to the Lord, who, as I now believe, has delivered me from such terrible and never-ending torments.*[14]

Let us see in our prayer today if there is anything in our lives, small as it may be, that might be distancing us from our Lord and which we are not struggling against as we ought. Let us examine ourselves to see whether we do in fact flee from all proximate occasions of sin; whether we

---

[13] John Paul II, Apostolic Exhortation, *Reconciliatio et poenitentia*, 26
[14] St Teresa, *Life*, 32, 4

frequently ask the Blessed Virgin to grant us a profound dread of all sin, even venial sin, which causes such harm to the soul and separates us from her Son, our only unqualified Good.

58.3 We are to be instruments in the salvation of many people.

The consideration of our last end should lead us to be faithful in dealing with the little occurrences of each day so as to acquire Heaven through our daily tasks and the things that happen to us, and set aside whatever could present itself as an obstacle along our way. The consideration of our last end should also induce us to carry out an unremitting apostolate, helping those around us to find God so that they may serve him in this world and be happy with him forever in the next. This is the greatest expression of charity and respect for others that we can possibly have.

The first way to help others is to be aware of the consequences of our own actions and omissions in order to avoid becoming an occasion of scandal or an obstacle to them. The Gospel of the Mass also includes these words of Jesus: *It were better for a man if a millstone were hung about his neck and he were thrown into the sea than that he should cause one of these little ones to sin.* Shortly before this, Jesus had said: *It is impossible that scandals should not come; but woe to him through whom they come!*[15] There are few words in the Gospel as strong as these, few sins as serious as those that bring about the ruin of a soul, for scandal destroys God's greatest work – the Redemption, with the resultant loss of souls. Scandal kills our neighbour's soul, robbing him of the life of grace, which is more precious than the life of the body. These *little ones* are for Jesus, primarily children. In them the

---

[15] Luke 17:1

innocence of God is reflected in an exceptional way. The *little ones*, however, are also the immense multitude of simple souls – those less spiritually formed – and, for this very reason, more easily scandalized.

Faced with so many daily causes of scandal in the world, Our Lord asks his followers to make atonement and reparation for so much evil. He wants us to be living examples as followers of his who attract others to become good Christians by appropriately, affectionately and prudently exercising fraternal correction, which helps others to amend their faults. It can also help them to remedy situations which are dangerous for their souls, motivating them to have recourse to the sacrament of Penance in which their straying steps can be redirected. The reality of hell's existing, which faith teaches us, is a call to the apostolate, for us to be instruments in the salvation of many people.

Let us invoke the Blessed Virgin: *Iter para tutum!*,[16] prepare a safe way for us and for all men, a safe way that leads to a destination which is the eternal happiness of Heaven.

---

[16] *Divine Office*, Second Vespers of the Common of Our Lady, Hymn *Ave Maris Stella*

59. DEFENDING THE FAMILY

59.1 Jesus returns the dignity of matrimony to its original purity. The unity and indissolubility of marriage.

The Gospel of today's Mass[1] speaks of Jesus teaching a multitude of people who have come from all the villages round about. They are simple people who receive the word of God with enthusiasm. But among them are some Pharisees with twisted intentions who attempt to challenge Christ by confronting him with the law of Moses. They put the query whether it is lawful for a husband to divorce his wife. Jesus asks them, *What did Moses command you?* They said, *Moses allowed a man to write a certificate of divorce and to put her away.* This was conceded by all, but what was in question was whether it was licit to divorce a wife *for any reason,*[2] for an insignificant reason, or even without any cause at all.

Jesus Christ, the Messiah and Son of God, knew perfectly well the spirit of that Law. Moses had permitted divorce *because of the hardness of heart* of his people, and by means of it had protected the dignity of the woman. Her condition had been so debased and underrated at that time that in many cases she was considered a slave without rights. The law prescribed a document (the *certificate of divorce*) by which the wife who was *put away* could again recover her freedom. This certificate was in fact a social advance for those times characterised by so many barbarous customs.[3]

---

[1] Mark 10:1-2
[2] Matt 19:3
[3] cf *The Navarre Bible*, St Mark, *in loc*

Christ returned the dignity of matrimony to its original purity, as God instituted it at the beginning of Creation. God made them male and female. For this reason a man may leave his father and mother and be joined to his wife, and the two shall become one. So they are no longer two, but one. What therefore God has joined together, let no man put asunder.

This teaching struck his listeners as being extraordinarily demanding, so much so that, according to Saint Matthew, they told him, *If such is the case of a man with his wife, it is not expedient to marry.*[4] The conversation must have continued later because when the day was over they again asked him about it. Jesus declared once and for all, *Whoever divorces his wife and marries another, commits adultery against her; and if she divorces her husband and marries another, she commits adultery.*

Our Lord shows how God in the beginning had established the unity and indissolubility of marriage. Saint John Chrysostom, commenting on this teaching, uses a clear and simple formula in stating that matrimony means one man with one woman for life.[5] The Magisterium of the Church, which is the guardian and interpreter of the natural and divine Law, has constantly taught that matrimony was instituted by God as a perpetual and unbreakable bond. It *was protected, confirmed and elevated not by human laws, but by the very author of nature, God himself, and by the restorer of that nature, Christ Our Lord. This law, therefore, cannot be subject to the variable choice of men, not even by the contrary judgement of the spouses themselves.*[6]

Matrimony is not simply a private contract. It cannot be broken by either party, or by agreement of both parties

---

[4] Matt 19:10
[5] cf St John Chrysostom, *Homilies on St Matthew's Gospel*, 62, 1
[6] Pius XI, Encyclical, *Casti connubii*, 31 December 1930

of the pact. No human reason, no matter how strong it might seem, is able to justify divorce, because that is contrary to divine and natural Law.

St John Paul II has exhorted Christian spouses that they be faithful in living Christ's teaching on the family, even though they may live in countries where the norms of Christian life do not receive due consideration or are actually violently attacked.[7] We should frequently pray for the stability of the family, starting with our own. We must strive always to be instruments of unity in bringing this about through our genuine service to others, our continuous cheerfulness, and an effective apostolate which brings those around us closer to God.

Do we pray each day for the person in our family who most needs it? Do we show more attention to the weakest member or to the one who feels that he or she is most at risk? Do we affectionately care for the one who is ill?

59.2 Apostolate of education on the nature of marriage. The example of spouses. Sanctity of the family.

When Our Lord explained the meaning of marriage He was not swayed by the fact that the attitude existing among the Jewish people at that time was totally contrary to his teachings. Nor can the Christian afford to be deflected in this matter by the difficulties and even by the derision occasioned in our social environment when he or she must uphold the values and the holiness of marriage. To defend the indissolubility of marriage is to do an immense good to all, to the whole of society.

Jesus went against the current of those times with his teaching concerning the institution of marriage. He return- ed it to its original dignity and raised it moreover to the

---

[7] cf John Paul II, *Homily of the Mass for Christian Families*, Madrid, 2 November 198

supernatural order by establishing it as one of the seven sacraments which serves to sanctify spouses and family life.

In our own times the worth and essential properties of marriage are under attack, and even ridiculed by bitter satire in many quarters. It is the duty of Christians to defend this sacrament, as Christ did in his day, and to rebuild the social foundation so that the family, united and solid, becomes again the backbone of society as it is meant to.

The family must be the object of serious attention and support on the part of everyone who has a hand in public life. Educators, writers, politicians and legislators must keep in mind that a great part of social and even personal problems has its roots in the failure or the collapse of family life. To fight against juvenile delinquency or against the prostitution of women and at the same time to favour the discrediting or deterioration of the institution of the family is both senseless and contradictory.

The good of the family in all of its aspects has to be one of the fundamental concerns of the Christian's activity in public life. In all the different areas of social activity, matrimony and the family must be supported and fostered by economic, social, educational, political and cultural means, with all the help that is necessary and urgent if we are to continue developing our society's basic functions (see Familiaris consortio, 45).

It must be understood, however, that the role of families in social and political life cannot be merely passive. They themselves must be 'the first to take steps to see that the laws and institutions of the State do not offend, but support and positively defend the rights and duties of the family.' (ibid, 44). In this way true 'family politics' (ibid) will be promoted.[8]

---

[8] Spanish Episcopal Conference, Pastoral Instruction, *Catholics in Public Life*, 22 April 1986, 160-162

The example and joy of Christian spouses have to pave the way for the apostolate they must do with their children and with the other families they come in contact with through friendship, social relations, joint tasks in the education of their children, and so forth. This cheerfulness, in the middle of the normal difficulties commonly experienced by any family, is born of the serious attempt to live a holy life, and of corresponding with the graces of the matrimonial vocation. Then the children will follow their own vocations and go on to do great good to society in a way that pleases God, themselves in turn using all the means available to them to maintain the atmosphere of a Christian family, an atmosphere in which everyone lives the human and supernatural virtues – cheerfulness, cordiality, sobriety, industriousness, mutual respect, and so on.

59.3 Christian matrimony.

Human love, being raised to the supernatural order, is made deeper and richer because in the Christian sacrament divine love irradiates human love, transforming what is good and making it holy. God is the one who unites with a holy bond and sanctifies man and wife in matrimony. Therefore, *what God has joined together let no man put asunder.* Precisely because God unites a man and a woman with divine links, what were two bodies and two hearts are now *una caro*, one flesh, one sole body and one and the same heart, resembling the union of Christ with his Church.[9]

Matrimony is not merely a social institution, nor is it only a juridical state, civil and canonical. It is also a new life which is sacrificing and overflowing with love; it sanctifies the spouses and makes holy all those who form part of the family.

It is good for us to stop during our prayer with Our

[9] cf Eph 5:22

Lord to examine the different aspects of our daily conduct. Our family life should be warm and affectionate, free from arguments, criticisms or complaints. We should make ourselves available to play our part in taking care of the home and tending to the material needs of our children, our brothers and sisters or our parents. Our weekends and vacation time should be made good use of to avoid laziness and time-wasting pastimes. We should be serene in the face of difficulties, modestly simple in our manner of celebrating, sensible in an entirely Christian way while sanctifying holidays, preparing family excursions or planning vacations. There should be respect for the freedom and opinions of the others, along with appropriate and opportune advice. We have to be interested in our children's (or younger siblings') studies and human development. We should be ready to make sacrifices for those who require more loving attention and understanding.

If parents care for each other with a human and supernatural love they will be examples to whom their children will look for answers to many of the questions that modern life presents them with. Christian ideals and noble human desires will be maintained if the home atmosphere is cheerful and the practice of the natural virtues is given an important place. Then the family will become a privileged place in which is carried out the *constant renewal of the Church*,[10] and the new evangelization of the world to which the present Pope calls us.

Let us ask the Blessed Virgin, Mother of Fair Love, to obtain for us abundant grace from her Son Jesus Christ, for our own family and for all Christian families on earth.

---

[10] John Paul II, *Address*, 21 November 1978

60. WITH THE SIMPLICITY OF CHILDREN

60.1 Spiritual childhood and simplicity.

On various occasions the Gospel relates how children approached Jesus, who welcomed them, blessed them and held them up as an example to his disciples. Today he shows us again the importance of becoming like one of these little ones in order to enter the Kingdom: *Truly, I say to you, whoever does not receive the kingdom of God like a child shall not enter it. And he took them in his arms and blessed them, laying his hands upon them.*[1]

In these children whom Jesus embraces and blesses are represented not only all the world's children, but all men; Our Lord is indicating how all men should 'receive' the Kingdom of God.

Jesus provides a lively illustration of the essential teaching about divine sonship: God is our Father and we his children; our behaviour as Christians is summarized in knowing how to bring to life the relationship that a good child has with a good father. This spirit of divine sonship implies a sense of being utterly dependent on our Heavenly Father and a facility for abandoning ourselves confidently to his loveable Providence, just as a child entrusts everything to its father; the relationship presupposes the humility to acknowledge that we can do nothing by ourselves; and it implies simplicity and sincerity, qualities that prompt us to let ourselves be seen by others as we really are.[2]

---

[1] Mark 10:13-16
[2] cf *The Navarre Bible*, note to Mark 10:13-26

To become childlike while remaining adult can be costly: it requires courage and strength of will, as well as great abandonment to God. *Spiritual childhood is not spiritual immaturity or foolishness or softness; it is a sane and robust way which, due to its 'difficult easiness', the soul must embark upon and then continue, led by the hand of God.*[3] The Christian who has taken the decision to live spiritual childhood practises charity more easily, because *the child is a creature who does not hold grudges, who is ignorant of duplicity or fraud, who dares not deceive. The Christian, like the small child, does not grow angry if he is insulted, does not seek revenge if he is treated badly. More than that, the Lord even requires him to pray for his enemies, to give his shirt and coat to those who would wear them, to present the other cheek to those who strike him (cf Matt 5:40).*[4] A child easily forgets and does not store up grievances. A child has no real sorrows.

Spiritual childhood always preserves the freshness of love in a soul, because its simplicity keeps it from dwelling on adverse experiences. *You have become younger! You notice, in fact, that getting to know God better has made you regain in a short time the simple and happy age of your youth, including the security and joy – without being at all 'childish' – of spiritual childhood ... You look around and you realize that the same thing has happened to others: the years since their first conscious encounter with the Lord have gone by and, having reached maturity, they are strengthened with a permanently youthful happiness. Although they are no longer young, they are young at heart and happy!*

This patent reality of the interior life attracts, confirms and wins over souls. Give thanks for it daily 'ad Deum qui

---

[3] St. J. Escrivá, *The Way*, 855
[4] St Maximus of Turin, *Homily 58*

laetificat iuventutem' – *to God who fills your youth with joy*.[5] Our Lord truly gives joy to our perennial youth, both at the beginning of life and during the years of maturity or old age. God is always our greatest joy in life as long as we live in his presence like children – small children who are always in need.

60.2 Manifestations of piety and Christian naturalness.

This spirit of divine sonship in the Christian soul gives rise to simple devotions, to countless little deeds honouring our Father God, for a soul full of love is unable to remain inactive.[6] Since he has required all his strength to become childlike, the Christian can give small devotions their true meaning. Each of us must have 'the piety of children, but the doctrine of theologians', as St Josemaría Escrivá used to say. A solid grounding in Christian doctrine helps to give meaning to a mere glance we make at a picture of Our Lady, or to a kiss we give a crucifix; it helps us, moreover, to turn such a glance or kiss into an act of love so that we do not remain indifferent, for example, before a scene from the Way of the Cross. This denotes a solid and deep-rooted piety, real love, which has a need to express itself in just such ways. Then God looks upon us benignly, as a father gazes at his child whom he loves more than all the business ventures in the world.

A simple and deep faith always finds expression in particular acts of piety, whether collective or personal, which are valid for human and divine reasons. Some of them have become the pious customs of Christian people, passed on from generation to generation in the intimacy of the home and within the heart of the Church. So, along with the desire to improve our knowledge of Christian

---

[5] St. J. Escrivá, *Furrow*, 79
[6] cf St Thérése of Lisieux, *Autobiography of a Soul*, 10,41

doctrine more and more – as much as our personal circumstances permit – we must also have the determination to
live the simple details of piety which we have discovered
on our own, or which people of various nations for
generations have found useful and natural in their desire to
express their love for God; with such expressions of piety
they pleased God, because they in practising these
devotions had become like children. From the beginning of
the Church it was customary, for example, to adorn altars
and images of the saints with flowers, to kiss the crucifix
or the rosary, to bless oneself with holy water ...

Out of failure to appreciate the love that inspires these
simple, pious customs of the Christian people, in certain
parts of the world they are rejected by some who
mistakenly consider them to be peculiar to a 'childish
Christianity'. Apparently such disapproving critics have
forgotten those words of Our Lord: whoever does not
receive the kingdom of God like a child shall not enter it;
they are unwilling to recognize that, in God's sight, we are
all like little and needy children, and that in human life
love is frequently expressed in small, unimportant ways.
When observed by an outsider with detached and critical
objectivity, but without understanding and love, these
tokens of affection may well seem meaningless.
Nevertheless, how often was our Lord's heart moved by
the prayer of children and of those who became like them!

The *Acts of the Apostles* have left us a clear record of
how the first Christians used many lamps to light up the
rooms where they celebrated the Holy Eucharist,[7] and of
how they liked to leave small oil-lamps burning above the
graves of their martyrs. Saint Jerome eulogizes a good
priest in these words: *He adorned both the basilicas and
the halls of the martyrs with sketches of flowers, foliage*

---

[7] Acts 20:78

*and vine tendrils, so that everything attractive in the
church, whether made so by its position or by its
appearance, bore witness to the labour and zeal of the
presbyter.*[8] These little external manifestations of piety are
fitting, appropriate to the purpose for which they are used,
and come naturally to us as human beings. Our human
nature employs the help of visible things to address God
and adequately express its needs and desires.

At times simplicity will be shown in daring: when we
are recollected in prayer or simply walking down the street
we can tell Our Lord things which, out of embarrassment,
we would not dare say in front of others, since they belong
to the intimacy of our interior life. Nevertheless, it is
necessary that we know how – and be daring enough – to
tell him outright that we love him, even that we want him
to have us love him 'madly', and that we are ready, if he so
desires, to be more fully nailed to the Cross and to offer
him our life once more ... This daring of the life of
childhood should issue in specific resolutions.

60.3 In order to be simple.

Simplicity is one of the principal manifestations of
spiritual childhood. It is the result of having become
defenceless before God, like a vulnerable and trusting child
before its father. Either to disguise or to make a false show
of our defects and mistakes is completely out of place
when we are in front of God. We should also be simple
when opening our soul to receive personal spiritual
guidance, revealing what is good, bad or doubtful in our
life.

We are living the virtue of simplicity when we
maintain an upright intention in our love for Our Lord.
This will lead us in everything we do to seek the glory of

---

[8] St Jerome, *Epistle 60*, 12

God and the good of souls with a strong, decisive will. If a person is truly seeking God he does not become entangled in a confusion of motivations or complicated from within; he does not look for unusual things to accomplish: he simply does what he should, and tries to do it well, facing God. He says what is on his mind clearly: he does not express himself in half-truths or habitually resort to mental reservations. He is not naive, but neither is he suspicious; he is prudent, but not distrustful. To summarize, he lives the teaching of the Master: *be wise as serpents and innocent as doves.*[9]

By following this route, my friend, you will arrive at great intimacy with our Lord; you will learn to call Jesus by his name and will come to love recollection. Frivolity, superficiality and lukewarmness will disappear from your life. You will be a friend of God; and in your recollection, in your intimacy with him, you will love to consider those words of Scripture: 'God went to speak to Moses face to face, as a man speaks to his friend' (Ex 33:11).[10] Our prayer will be expressed throughout the course of the day in acts of love, of reparation and thanksgiving, in aspirations to the Blessed Virgin, to Saint Joseph, to the Guardian Angel ...

Our Lady shows us how to get to know the Son of God, her Son, without resorting to complex formulas. It is easy for us to imagine her preparing a meal, sweeping the house, taking care of the clothes ... and in the midst of these tasks turning to Jesus with immense love and confidence, with delicate respect – knowing well that he was the Son of the Most High! To him she revealed her needs, or those of others – *They have no wine!*, she will tell him at the wedding of those friends or relatives of hers in Cana; she took care of him, doing him the little acts of

---

[9] Matt 10:16
[10] S. Canals, *Jesus as Friend*

service that are expected of a mother by her child in their daily life together; she gazed at him, thought about him ... all this was perfect prayer.

We need to show God our love. Frequently we will express it in the Holy Mass, through the prayers the Church gives us in the Liturgy, through a momentary visit made in the bustle of daily activity, or by lighting a candle or placing some flowers at the foot of a statue of Mary, Mother of God and our Mother. Today let us ask her to give us a heart that is simple and full of love, so that we can converse with her Son – and also learn from children, who go to their parents and the ones they love with such overwhelming confidence.

EIGHTH SUNDAY: YEAR A

61. TODAY'S TASK

61.1 Living the present to the full, without anxiety. Divine filiation. Trust and abandonment in God.

Our Lord counsels us in the Gospel of the Mass: *Do not be anxious about tomorrow, for tomorrow will be anxious for itself. Let the day's own trouble be sufficient for the day.*[1]

Yesterday is over. We do not know whether we will see tomorrow, since no one has been given knowledge of the future.[2] All that remains to us from yesterday's toil are reasons, many reasons, for giving thanks: we thank God for his bountiful outpouring of graces and blessings; we owe gratitude also to our fellow men. We will have added, too, we hope, even if just a little, to our *treasure* in heaven. From the day that is gone we draw motives for contrition and penance for our sins, our errors and omissions. Of yesterday we can say, in the words of the entrance antiphon of today's Mass: *The Lord has been my strength; He has led me into freedom. He saved me because He loves me.*[3]

Tomorrow 'as yet is not.' If it comes, it will be more wonderful than we could ever dream, because our Father God has prepared it to sanctify us: *Deus meus es tu, in manibus tuis sortes meae: My times are in thy hand.*[4] There are no grounds, objectively speaking, for letting worry and concern for tomorrow weigh us down: we will be given the graces we need in order to contend with anything that

---

[1] Matt 6:34
[2] cf St. J. Escrivá, *The Way*, 253
[3] Ps 18:19-20
[4] Ps 31:15

crops up. We will be victorious!

What matters is *today*. Today is the day we need in which to love, to grow in holiness, through those countless little occurrences that go to make up the texture of our life. Some things will be naturally pleasant, others perhaps less gratifying, but each one of them can be made to shine for God and for eternity, a gem which we will have wrought and polished with human perfection and supernatural meaning.

We cannot dally with wishful thinking. Sometimes our fanciful imagination improves upon the reality of past events and enslaves us by idealising a future reassuringly free from effort; or it may, on the contrary, show us a dark horizon, a prospect that makes us apprehensive. *He who observes the wind will not sow; and he who regards the clouds will not reap.*[5] It is an invitation to get on with carrying out the duty of the moment without stopping to see whether a better opportunity may perhaps arise. It is easy also, in our apostolate, for us to postpone a project for a more suitable occasion. What would have become of the Apostles' preaching if they had waited and looked for more favourable circumstances? What would have happened, in any successful work of apostolate, if Christ's followers had stood down in the off-chance of better conditions? *Hic et nunc: here and now* is where I must love God with all my heart... and with deeds.

Humanly and supernaturally, holiness and efficacy consist mainly in *living each day as if it were the only day in our life*: each day is the one we must fill with love for God; every day is one we must finish, leaving it brimful of good works. We cannot let a single chance of doing good slip through our hands. *Today does not come round again, ever*, and God expects us to fill it with love and with little

---

[5] Eccles 11:4

acts of service towards others. Our Guardian Angel should rejoice when he offers our day to our Father God.

61.2 Fruitless worry. We will always be given enough help to remain faithful.

Do not be anxious... Fruitless worry does not cancel out the misfortune we dread, but foolishly goes out to meet it. We shoulder a burden without yet having received the grace God would give to enable us to carry it. Worry magnifies the difficulties and diminishes our ability to fulfil the duty of the present moment. Above all, we fail to trust in the Providence God exercises over every situation in life. In the *First Reading* of today's Mass our Lord asks us in the words of the prophet Isaiah: *Can a woman forget her child at the breast, that she should have no compassion on the son of her womb? Even these may forget, yet I will not forget you.*[6] Today, in all that happens, our Father God will think of us with love.

And Jesus has reminded us so often already! *Take heart,* He says, *it is I; have no fear.*[7] We cannot carry at the same time the cares of today and the worries of tomorrow. We always have sufficient help to be faithful today, to live this particular day with peace and joy. Tomorrow will bring new graces, and its burden will be no heavier than today's has been. Each day has its toil, its cross and its own joy. Every day of our life is watched over by our Father God, who loves us so much. We can live only in the present. Anxieties almost always arise because we fail to put all our effort into the *here and now*, because we fail to repose all our trust in God's Providence; the anxieties vanish when we repeat sincerely: *Volo quidquid vis, volo quia vis, volo quomodo vis, volo quamdiu vis: Lord, I will*

---

[6] Is 49:15
[7] Matt 14:27

whatever you will, I will it because you will it, I will it in the way you will it, I will it as long as you will it.[8] Then comes the *gaudium cum pace*, the joy and peace.[9]

Sometimes we may be tempted to want to control the future, forgetting that our life is in God's hands. Don't let us be like the impatient child who skips through the pages of his book to find out how the story ends. God gives us our days, one after another, for us to fill them with holiness. In the Old Testament, we read of the Jews in the desert: they gathered the manna that God gave them as daily food. Some of them, wanting to lay up some supplies of it for the future, in case of shortage, took more than they needed and stored it. The next day they found it rotten and inedible. They had lacked trust in Yahweh their God, who watched over them with fatherly love. We should certainly provide prudently for the future, but not like those people during the wanderings in the desert who relied on their own efforts alone.

Ours should be a hopeful happiness, as we take up our daily task, concentrating our mind, our heart and all our energies upon it. This trust in God – holy abandonment – does not lessen our responsibility in acting, and in foreseeing what to do in each case. Nor does it mean that we should not bother about being prudent. It is in stark contrast, nonetheless, with a lack of confidence in God and with a pointless concern about things that have not yet taken place.[10] *Therefore do not be anxious about tomorrow*, our Lord repeats to us. Let us make good use of today.

---

[8] *Roman Missal, Prayer of Clement XI after Mass*
[9] *idem, Prayer before Mass*
[10] cf V. Lehodey, *Holy Abandonment*

61.3 Seeing God in our work. Mortifying the imagination in order to live in the present: *hic et nunc*.

God knows what it is we need. Let us seek first the Kingdom of God and his justice, and all the other things will be given us as well.[11] *Let us have a firm and general determination to serve God wholeheartedly, all our life long. Let us not ask to know any more than that there is a tomorrow about which we need not be unduly concerned. Let our concern be, rather, for the good we can do today. 'Tomorrow' will soon become 'today', and then we will give it our attention. We need to gather our provision of manna for today, and no more. We should never doubt that God will send another shower of manna on the following day, and the next one, and the next one, as long as the days of our pilgrimage last.*[12] God will not fail us.

When we live in the present, we give our attention to real things and to people. This means that we mortify our fancy and waste no time on inopportune and fruitless recollections. Imagination can withdraw us into another world, far away from the only world designed to be the scene of our sanctification. Very often our imagination can occasion a squandering of precious time, and make us miss many real opportunities of doing good. Lack of inner mortification, of our imagination and of our curiosity, is one of the great enemies of our sanctification.

If we live in the present, we will succeed in rejecting unreal fears of imagined future dangers which our fantasy enlarges and distorts. At times, too, the conjectured crosses our imagination depicts put us out of touch with reality. Then we suffer uselessly, instead of joyfully accepting the little crosses God offers his children to carry each day, crosses that can fill them with peace and joy.

---

[11] cf Matt 6:32-34
[12] St Francis de Sales, *Letters*, fragments 131, 766

If we live the present moment to the full, for Love, we unfailingly perceive those apparently obscure details in which we can be faithful. *Hic et nunc*: here and now, we should fulfil punctually the timetable we have set ourselves in advance. *Here and now* we need to be generous with God, with a horror of slipping into lukewarmness. *Here and now* God is expecting us to conquer ourselves in this or that minor detail that can prove so hard for us to do or to omit doing. He wants us to advance in those points of struggle which constitute the matter of our *particular examination of conscience.*

Let us ask the Holy Trinity to grant us the grace to live the present moment of each day with a heart full of Love, as if it were the last possible offering of our life upon earth.

EIGHTH SUNDAY: YEAR B

62. GOD'S LOVE FOR MEN

62.1 God loves us with an infinite love, without our meriting his love in any way.

In a multitude of different ways Sacred Scripture tells us of the infinite love God has for every human being. In the *First Reading* of today's Mass[1] the prophet Hosea uses beautiful imagery to express the unlimited bounty of God's love for his children, from whom He requires that they correspond with it. *Thus says the Lord: behold, I will allure her, and bring her into the wilderness, and speak tenderly to her. And there she shall answer as in the days of her youth, as at the time when she came out of the land of Egypt. And I will betroth her to me forever; I will betroth her to me in righteousness and in justice, In steadfast love, and in mercy ...* The continual apostasies of the Chosen People are an image of our own backsliding and falls: and yet God went on winning them back through mercy and love, just as day after day – now also in these moments of prayer – He comes seeking me and you.

Elsewhere He assures us that though a mother should forget the child of her womb He will never forget us, because, He says, *I have graven you on the palms of my hands; your walls are continually before me;*[2] and *he who touches you touches the apple of my eye.*[3] Truly *the God of our faith is not a distant being who contemplates with indifference the fate of men – their desires, their struggles, their sufferings. He is a Father who loves his children*[4]

---

[1] Hos 2:14-15,19-20
[2] Is 49:16
[3] Zac 2:8
[4] St. J. Escrivá, *Christ is passing by*, 84

with a very different love from ours. Our love, even when purified from its dross, *is always attracted by the good, real or apparent, in things ... Divine love, however, is a love that creates and infuses goodness into creatures*[5] with total disinterest. He really loves us.

The love of God is *gratuitous*, since created things can give him nothing which He does not already possess in absolute degree. The reason for his love is his infinite goodness and the desire to share it. God did not merely create us. Such was his love that He raised us to the supernatural order, making us sharers in his own life and happiness, far in excess of the capabilities of created beings. We in no way deserved it: *In this is love, not that we loved God, but that He loved us.*[6] And it was Christ who revealed to us, in all its depth, the love of God for men.

Reminding us of that love, the Holy Spirit moves us to a total and trusting abandonment to God; *Commit your way to the Lord, trust in him and He will act.*[7] And in another place; *Cast your burden upon the Lord and he will sustain you.*[8] Saint Peter exhorts: *Cast all your anxieties on him, for He cares about you.*[9] This is the advice Saint Catherine of Siena heard from our Lord: *Daughter, forget yourself and think of me, as I will think constantly of you.* Do we have such confidence in the love God has for us?

My Lord Jesus, grant that I may experience the gift of grace and cooperate with it in such a way as to empty my heart so that you, my Friend, my Brother, my King, my God, my Love ... may fill it![10]

---

[5] St Thomas, *Summa Theologiae*, I, 20, 2
[6] 1 John 4:10
[7] Ps 37:5
[8] Ps 55:22
[9] 1 Pet 5:7
[10] St. J. Escrivá, *The Forge*, 913

62.2 The great evil of indifference to God's love.

God's kindness towards men is much greater than anything we can imagine. He has made us his children, with a genuine, true filiation, as the Apostle Saint John teaches us: *See what love the Father has given us, that we should be called children of God; and so we are.*[11] This is the greatest proof of God's love for men. He shows us the tenderness and selflessness of a father, and He himself compares himself to a mother who can never forget her child.[12] This child so dearly loved is every man and woman. When we were lost through sin, He sent his Son to save us. His life, sacrificed for us, would redeem us from our fallen state, from sin, and death, and hell. *In this the love of God was made manifest among us, that God sent his only Son into the world, so that we might live through him.*[13] This same love leads him to give himself to us entirely, in an habitual manner. So He dwells in the soul in grace,[14] and speaks to us in our heart.[15]

How sad it is to see in answer to so much love, the cold indifference men show God, and especially to see how busily they fabricate a world where man becomes the measure of all things. Misinterpreting the passage of Sacred Scripture, *he who does not love his brother whom he has seen, cannot love God whom he has not seen,*[16] some people say that only man deserves to be loved. God, in their book, is a stranger, remote and inaccessible. This is a new and blasphemous humanism, masquerading as defender of the dignity of man while seeking to have the Creator supplanted by his creature. Such an untrue

---

[11] 1 John 3:1
[12] Is 49:15
[13] 1 John 4:9
[14] cf John 14:23
[15] cf John 14:26
[16] 1 John 4:20

humanism destroys the very possibility of truly loving God or man. By its giving a finite and limited creature – the human individual – an absolute value, everything comes to be of only a secondary and utilitarian interest ... The exclusion of God – the only Being lovable in himself and for himself – never leads to a greater love for anyone or anything else. And as certain unfortunate consequences denote, it can only lead to hatred, the condition and atmosphere proper to hell itself. Without God, love for creatures dies or is fatally corrupted.

The Responsorial Psalm[17] is man's true response to the love of God, always compassionate and merciful:

My soul, give thanks to the Lord,
All my being, bless his holy name.
My soul, give thanks to the Lord.
And never forget all his blessings.

When we fail to correspond with this deep love, when we are unfaithful, God rightly complains: *It is not an enemy who taunts me: then I could bear it ... but it is you ... my companion, my familiar friend.*[18]

Saint John of the Cross writes: *Lord, you want the fire of our love to burn until we are set alight, until all that we are is consumed in its flame, so that we become transformed into you, our God. You blow upon that flame with the graces which your life has won for us, and you enkindle it with the death you endured for us.*[19] Let us ask ourselves in the intimacy of our prayer: Does my love for God *burn* in that way? Is it shown in my generously corresponding with what God asks of me, with my vocation? Is my whole life an answer to the commitment of love that binds me to God? *Be convinced, my child, that God has a right to ask*

---

[17] Ps 102:1-4,8,10,12,13
[18] Ps 55:12-13
[19] St John of Avila, *Audi filia*, 69

of us: Are you thinking about me? Are you aware of me?
Do you look to me as your support? Do you seek me as the
Light of your life, as your shield ... as your all?[20]

62.3 God loves us with a personal, individual love: He has showered blessings upon us. And Love is repaid by love.

God decided, in his infinite wisdom to make us sharers
in his love and his truth. Although we were capable of
loving him naturally, with our own strength, he knew that
only if He gave us his Love itself would we be able to
attain to intimate union with him. Through the Incarnation
of his only-begotten Son He restored the order that had
been destroyed, uniting the divine with the human. He
raised us to the dignity of being his children and thus
revealed the fulness of his love for us. Finally, *because we*
are sons, God has sent the Spirit of his Son into our
hearts,[21] him who is the Paraclete, the greatest gift He
could grant us.

God loves us with a personal and individual love. He
loves each one of us as a unique person, He has filled us
with blessings. Often He has *spoken to our heart*, and
perhaps has told us clearly, *'meus es tu', you are mine.*[22]
He has never stopped loving us, helping us, protecting us,
talking to us, not even when our response has been
monstrous ingratitude or serious sin. Perhaps we have
received even more attention from God in these
unregenerate times, as we read in the *First Reading* of the
Mass.

Let us consider now how we should *correspond with*
that love. Let us examine our duties, in the fulfilment of

---

[20] St. J. Escrivá, *The Forge*, 506
[21] Gal 4:6
[22] Is 43:1

which He waits for us, as in the loving attention we give to our practices of piety. How goes our apostolate of friendship with our companions? Do we give ourselves generously, even in the smallest details which our vocation to holiness demands...? Do we perhaps allow lukewarmness to infiltrate through the interstices of a superficial examination which limits itself to the mere external and more or less mechanical carrying out of our obligations?

Let us remember that frequently contemplating the extent of God's love for us does great good to the soul. Saint Teresa reminds us that *we should remember with what love He has bestowed all these favours upon us, and how enormous is the love God has revealed to us ... for love begets love. And though we may be only beginners, and very wicked at that, let us strive ever to bear this in mind and awaken our own love.*[23] And we must be truly convinced of this spiritual reality. When we contemplate the love of God, *love is roused* in us and *awakens us* to a greater love. Speaking of the love of Christ, St John Paul II encourages us to correspondence with it in the well-known popular phrase: *love is repaid by love.*[24] If we contemplate the love God has for us, it will also lead us to ask him for more love, as a great mystic wrote daringly:

Reveal thy presence,
And let the vision and thy beauty kill me.
Behold the malady of love is incurable
except in thy presence, and before thy face.[25]

---

[23] St Teresa, *Life*, 22, 14
[24] John Paul II, *Address at Eucharistic Vigil*, Madrid, 31 October 1982
[25] St John of the Cross, *Spiritual Canticle*, 11

EIGHTH SUNDAY: YEAR C

63. TRIUMPH OVER DEATH

63.1 Death, the consequence of sin. On leaving this life we will take with us only the merit of our good actions and the penalty for our sins.

Saint Paul teaches us in the *Second Reading* of the Mass[1] that when the risen and glorious body clothes itself in immortality, death will be finally conquered. Then we will be able to ask: *O death, where is thy victory? O death, where is thy sting? The sting of death is sin* ... It was sin that brought death into the world. When God created man, besides the supernatural gifts of grace He gave him other gifts which perfected nature in its own order. Among them was the gift of bodily immortality, which our first parents were to transmit, along with life, to their descendants. Original sin carried with it the loss of friendship with God and the consequent loss of that gift of immortality. Death, *the wages of sin*,[2] entered a world which had been created as a place for living beings. Revelation teaches us that *God did not make death, and He does not delight in the death of the living*.[3]

Through sin, death came to all: 'The just and the unjust likewise die, the good and the evil, the clean and the unclean, he who offers sacrifices and he who does not. The same end befalls the saint and the sinner; it befalls him who swears and him who refrains from swearing. Men and animals are all likewise reduced to dust and ashes'.[4]

---

[1] 1 Cor 15:54-58
[2] Rom 6:23
[3] Wis 1:13-14
[4] St Jerome, *Epistle 39*, 3

Everything material comes to an end, each thing in its own time. The physical world and all it contains is directed towards a final consummation, as we are too.

At death, man loses everything he possessed in his lifetime. As with the rich man in the parable, God will say to the one who has thought only of himself, of his well-being and his comfort: *Fool! ... the things you have prepared, whose will they be?*[5] Each one will bring with him only the merits of his good works and the weight of his sins. *Blessed are the dead who die in the Lord henceforth. 'Blessed indeed', says the Spirit, 'that they may rest from their labours, for their deeds follow them!'*[6] The opportunity to acquire merit for eternal life ends with death. Of this, our Lord warns: *Night comes, when no one can work.*[7] At death, our will stays fixed forever on good or on evil, remaining in friendship with God or rejecting his mercy for all eternity.

Meditation on our last end can move us, while we are still on earth, to react against lukewarmness, against any reluctance to commit ourselves entirely to God's service, and to develop our relationship with him. It can wean us from attachment to earthly things, which we must soon leave behind us in any case, encourage us to sanctify our work and enable us to understand that this life is a period, a short one, in which we can gain merit in the sight of God.

Let us remember today that our earthly bodies are no more than perishable clay. We know, nevertheless, that we have been created for eternity, that our souls can never die, and that our bodies will one day rise again glorious, if we have died in God's friendship, to be united once more to our souls. And this fills us with joy and peace and moves

---

[5] Luke 12:20-21
[6] Apoc 14:13
[7] John 9:4

us to live as children of God in the world.

63.2 The Christian meaning of death.

With the Resurrection of Christ, death has been finally conquered. Man is no longer a slave to death, but has death now under his dominion, if he so chooses,[8] for we achieve this sovereignty to the extent that we are united to him who holds *the keys of death*.[9] Sin is the true death, the dreadful separation – the soul separated from God – compared with which the other separation, that of soul and body, is of far less importance. And this latter separation is, moreover, provisional. *He who believes in me, though he die, yet shall he live, and whoever lives and believes in me shall never die.*[10] *In Christ, death has lost its power, its sting. Death has been overthrown. This truth of our faith may seem a paradox, when all around us we see man afflicted by the dread of imminent dissolution, the certainty of dying, recoiling in fear from the torment of pain and sorrow. It is true that sorrow and death disconcert the human spirit. They continue to be a baffling enigma for those who do not believe in God. But by faith we know these evils will be overcome, that the victory has been won already in the death and Resurrection of Jesus Christ our Redeemer.*[11]

Materialism, while denying the immortality of the soul, has adopted various arguments throughout history to explain the desire for eternity which God seems to have placed in the human heart. So this false philosophy offers men the consolation of somehow surviving, in the results of the actions of their mortal life and in the memory and affection of those who are still alive. It is undoubtedly a

---

[8] 1 Cor 3:2
[9] Apoc 1:18
[10] John 11:25-26
[11] John Paul II, *Homily*, 16 February 1981

good thing that those who come after us should remember us, but our Lord tells us more: *Do not fear those who kill the body but cannot kill the soul; rather, fear him who can destroy both soul and body in hell.*[12] This is the holy *fear of God*, which can serve so well at times to keep us from sin.

The moment of death is a difficult one for every creature. But ever since the Redemption wrought by Christ that moment has for us a completely different significance. It is no longer simply the harsh price which every man must pay for sin, as a just punishment for his guilt. It is, above all else, the culmination of our abandonment into the hands of our Redeemer, *the departure from this world to the Father,*[13] the passage to a new life of eternal happiness. If we are faithful to Christ, we will be able to say with the Psalmist: *Even though I walk through the valley of the shadow of death, I fear no evil, for thou art with me.*[14] Serenity and optimism at the prospect of death are born of a firm hope in Jesus Christ, who was willing to assume our human nature entirely, with all its weaknesses except sin.[15] He did so in order that *through death He might destroy him who has the power of death, that is, the devil, and deliver all those who through fear of death were subject to lifelong bondage.*[16] And so Saint Augustine teaches that *our inheritance is the death of Christ,*[17] since through it we can attain Life.

Uncertainty as to our last end should lead us to trust in God's mercy and to be very faithful to the vocation we have received from him. We should spend our life in his service and in the service of his Church, wherever we may

---

[12] Matt 10:28
[13] cf John 13:1
[14] Ps 23:4
[15] cf Heb 4:15
[16] Heb 2:14-15
[17] St Augustine, *Epistle 2*, 94

be. We should remember always, and particularly when that last moment comes, that God is a loving Father, full of tenderness towards his children. It is our Father God who will welcome us! It is Christ who says to us: *Come, ye blessed of my Father ...!*

Friendship with Jesus Christ, the Christian meaning of life, the knowledge that we are children of God, will allow us to look at and accept death with serenity. It will be the meeting of a son with his Father whom he has sought to serve throughout his life. *Even though I walk through the valley of the shadow of death I fear no evil, for thou art with me.*

63.3 The fruits of meditating on our last end.

The Church recommends meditation on what it calls the Last Things, because we can derive incalculable benefit from considering them. The knowledge that life is short does not lessen our involvement in the affairs God has entrusted to us: family, work, worthy interests, noble ideals ... Thinking on the inescapable fact of our mortality and its consequences helps us to be detached from earthly things, to give them their due importance and to sanctify all our temporal affairs. It is our path to Heaven. Whenever we suffer the death of a friend, or of someone in our family, or someone we love, it can be a good occasion, among others, to consider the inescapable truths of our last end.

Our Lord will come when least we expect him, *like a thief in the night.*[18] He should find us ready, vigilant, detached from earthly things. The great mistake we could make is to allow ourselves to become enslaved to the things of this world, which we have to leave so soon. We have to have our feet on the ground: we are in the midst of the world, as befits our Christian calling since God has

---

[18] 1 Thess 5:2

placed us here, but we cannot forget that we are travellers whose eyes are fixed on Christ and on his Kingdom which will one day be ours. We should live every day in the knowledge that we are pilgrims who are travelling – very quickly – to our encounter with God. Every morning we take another step towards God, every evening we find ourselves nearer to him. We should live, therefore, as though God were about to summon us at any moment. The fact that God has hidden from us the exact time of our earthly life's termination helps us to live each day as if it were our very last, always prepared for the event and ready to move to *a new dwelling-place*.[19] In any case, that day *cannot be far off*;[20] any day could be our last. This very day thousands of people have died in all sorts of diverse circumstances. Possibly many of them were taken by surprise, never imagining that they would have no more time in which to acquire merit.

Each day of our life is a blank sheet which we can fill in with an account of wonderful things, or with blots and errors. And we do not know how many pages are left before we come to the end of that book which God will one day read in our presence.

Friendship with Jesus, love for our Mother Mary, the Christian meaning we have tried to give our life, will enable us to look forward with serenity to our definitive meeting with God. Saint Joseph, the patron of a happy death, had at his side the welcome and welcoming company of Jesus and Mary when the time came for him to leave this world. He can teach us to prepare, day by day, for this ineffable encounter with our Father God.

Saint Paul takes leave of the first Christians of Corinth with the consoling words with which the *first reading* of

---

[19] cf St. J. Escrivá, *The Way*, 744
[20] St Jerome, *Epistle 60*, 14

today's Mass ends. We ourselves can take them as being directed to each of us individually: *My beloved brethren, be steadfast, immovable, always abounding in the work of the Lord, knowing that in the Lord your labour is not in vain.*[21] O Mother of ours – we finish our prayer addressing the most Blessed Virgin – win for us from your Son the grace of always having in mind the goal of Heaven in all that we do. In this way we will work diligently, our eyes set on eternity. Holy Mary, Mother of God, pray for us sinners now, and at the hour of our death. Amen.

---

[21] 1 Cor 15:58

64. THE RICH YOUNG MAN

64.1 God calls everyone. If we are to follow Christ we must be detached from earthly things.

The Gospel of the Mass[1] tells us that Jesus was leaving one town on his way to another when a young man came running up and stopped in front of him. The three evangelists who mention this incident say that the young man was well-to-do. He fell at the feet of Christ and asked him a question which is of fundamental importance to everybody. *Good Teacher,* he says to him, *what must I do to inherit eternal life?* Jesus is standing, surrounded by his disciples who are watching the scene. The young man is kneeling. It is an open conversation, and our Lord begins by answering in general terms: *You know the commandments*, and proceeds to list them: *Do not kill, do not commit adultery, do not steal* ... The young man replies: *Teacher, all these I have observed from my youth ... What do I still lack?*[2] We have all asked that question at some time or other, on experiencing the strong attraction of those things which, though noble in themselves, are incapable of satisfying the heart. We have seen the years of our life passing without knowing how to quench that hidden thirst which could not be satisfied. For each of us, Christ has a personal reply – for us the only valid one.

Jesus knew there was a fund of generosity, a great capacity for self-giving, in that young man's heart. Therefore He looked lovingly upon him with a special love, and invited him to follow him unconditionally, without any attachments. He stood there looking at him as

---

[1] Mark 10:17-27
[2] Matt 19:20

only Christ can look, gazing into the depths of his soul. *He looks with love upon every human being. The Gospel confirms this at every step. One can also say that this 'loving look' of Christ, contains, as it were, a summary and synthesis of the entire Good News ... Man needs this 'loving look'. He needs to know that he is loved, 'loved eternally', and specially chosen from eternity (cf Eph 1:4). At the same time, this eternal love of divine election accompanies man during life, just as Christ's look of love did here.*[3] God sees us in this way, now and always, with a deep love, a love of predilection.

The Master said to him, with a particular tenderness: *You lack one thing.* Only one! With what expectancy must that young man have waited for the Master's answer! Without a doubt, it was the most important one he was to hear in his whole life. *Go, sell what you have, and give to the poor ... and come, follow me.* It was an invitation to give himself entirely to our Lord. The young man had not expected this. God's plans do not always coincide with ours, with those we forge in our imagination, in our dreams. God's plans, in one way or another, always demand detachment from everything that enchains. If we are to follow Christ, our soul must be free. That young man's wealth constituted the one big hindrance to his accepting Jesus' demand, the greatest demand of his life.

God calls everyone: sick and healthy: people with outstanding talents and those of lesser ability; those who are rich and those who are poor; the young, the old and the middle-aged. Each man, each woman, should be able to discover the particular path to which God calls him or her. And he calls us all to holiness, to generosity, to detachment, to self-giving. To every one of us He speaks in the depth of our heart: *Come, follow me.* We cannot give a lukewarm response to

---

[3] John Paul II, *Letter to young people*, 31 March 1985, 7

Christ's invitation. He has no use for disciples who are 'half-hearted', who place conditions on their discipleship.

This young man sees his vocation all at once: it is a call to total commitment. His meeting with Jesus reveals to him the meaning and the fundamental purpose of his life. And before Jesus too, his true availability stands revealed. He had thought that he was fulfilling God's will because he had been carrying out the precepts of the Law. When Christ invites him to a complete commitment he manifests a too-firm attachment to his possessions and a qualified love for the Will of God. Today, too, this same scene is repeated: *You say of that friend of yours that he frequents the sacraments, that he is clean-living and a good student. But that he won't 'respond'; if you speak to him of sacrifice and apostolate, he becomes sad and goes away.*

Don't worry. It's not a failure of your zeal. It is, to the letter, the scene related by the Evangelist: 'If you wish to be perfect, go and sell what you own and give the money to the poor' (sacrifice), 'and then come, follow me' (apostolate).

The young man also 'abiit tristis', went away sad; he was not willing to respond to grace.[4] He went away sorrowful, because true happiness is possible only when there is generosity and detachment. Then life is full of joy, in an absolute readiness to accept God's will: it shows itself in little things and at very definite moments of our life. Let us ask our Lord today to help us with his grace so that He can always count on us for what He wants us to do. We will set no conditions, serving him freely, the way He wants to be served. 'Lord, I have no other desire in life than to seek you, love you and serve you ... All the other objectives of my life are directed towards that goal. I no longer love anything that separates me from you,' we tell Jesus in our conversation with him.

---

[4] St. J. Escrivá, *The Way*, 807

64.2 The response to vocation.

The sadness of the young man makes us reflect. We could be tempted to think that having many possessions, owning plenty of the goods of this world, can bring happiness. We see instead in the case of the young man in the Gospel that his many possessions had become an obstacle to his accepting the call of Jesus to follow him. He was not ready to say 'yes' to Jesus, and 'no' to self, to say 'yes' to love and 'no' to escapism. Real love is demanding ... For it was Jesus – our Jesus himself – who said: 'You are my friends if you do what I command you' (John 15:14). Love demands effort and a personal commitment to the Will of God. It means discipline and sacrifice, but it also means joy and human fulfilment ... Open your hearts to the Christ of the Gospels – to his love and his truth and his joy. Do not go away sad![5]

God's call to us to follow him closely demands a positive response at all times, because in his many invitations He asks of us a docile and generous life-long correspondence. Therefore we should stand frequently in God's presence – face to face with him, without anonymity – and ask him, as did the young man, *What do I still lack?* What does my Christian vocation require of me today, in my circumstances? What paths do you want me to follow? Let us be honest. Whoever really wants to find them succeeds in knowing clearly the paths that lead to God. *So it is that the Christian discovers, in the things of everyday life, how his vocation should unfold in the undramatic daily texture of divine promptings and inspirations ... of significant moments, of specific 'calls' to carry out, for the sake of God's love, lesser or greater tasks in the world of men. In his ongoing conversation with God a man can hear that divine voice asking him to make definite and radical*

---

[5] John Paul II, *Homily*, Boston Common, 1 October 1979

decisions ... The word of God can reach us in a hurricane or in a gentle breeze (1 Kings 19:22).[6] But in order to follow his word, we should be free from all fetters: only Christ matters. Everything else has to be in him and for him.

64.3 Poverty and detachment in daily life.

The young man in the Gospels stood up, avoiding the Master's look and invitation to a life full of love. And he went away – all could see it – with sadness in his face. *I think our instinct is that the refusal then made was made once for all.*[7] Our Lord watched him go with regret; the Holy Spirit reveals to us the motive for that particular rejection of grace: *He had great possessions* and he was very much attached to them.

After this incident the group continued on its way. But before they did, or perhaps just as they were starting off, Jesus *looked around and said to his disciples, 'How hard it will be for those who have riches to enter the kingdom of God!'* They were amazed at his words. And our Lord repeated what He had said, even more emphatically: *It is easier for a camel to pass through the eye of a needle than for a rich man to enter the Kingdom of God.* We should pay attention to Jesus' teaching and apply it to our own lives. We cannot reconcile a love for God which means following him closely with attachment to material goods. Those two loves cannot be contained in the same heart. Man can direct to God the material things he uses as a means to his final end – which *is* God – for a means is precisely what they are. But he can also, unfortunately, place all his hopes of fulfilment and happiness in material 'riches', in the unbridled desire to hold on to favourite

---

[6] P. Rodríguez, *Faith and Life of faith*
[7] R. A. Knox, *A Retreat for Lay People*, London 1955, p.90

goods, to seek out greater luxury, to enjoy maximum comfort, to foster ambition and give rein to avarice ...

Today can provide a good occasion for examining ourselves courageously in the intimacy of our prayer. What is the true motivation of my actions? What is my heart really set upon? Have I really tried to be detached from earthly goods, or on the contrary, do I suffer and complain when I am short of something I could be doing with? How quick am I to react against the slightest incitement to self-seeking and ease, promoted very often by the advertisements of the consumer society? Am I sparing in my personal needs, do I put curbs on my extravagance, do I avoid frivolous and unnecessary purchases? Sometimes we can create false 'necessities' which we could well forgo if we wanted to, if we were determined to do our best not to give in to the whims and caprices which so easily solicit our greed. Do I really look after the material things of my home and the implements and goods I use? Have I the clear realisation that I am only a steward over these things, and will one day have to give an account of them to their true owner, God our Lord? Do I cheerfully accept whatever inconveniences me and the lack of means at my disposal? Am I generous in giving alms to those who are in much worse circumstances? Do I contribute to the support of good causes, depriving myself of things I would like to have ...? Only in this way will we live with the joy and freedom necessary if we are to be disciples of our Lord in the midst of the world.

Our highest ideal is to follow Christ closely. We don't want to go away as that young man did, his soul filled with sadness because he was unable to renounce some possessions of little worth in exchange for the immense riches of Jesus Christ.

65. GENEROSITY AND DETACHMENT

65.1 Practical detachment from material goods is necessary if we are to follow Christ.

After their meeting with the rich young man which formed the basis of yesterday's meditation, Jesus and his disciples resume their journey towards Jerusalem. The sad departure of that young fellow who was so unbreakably tied to his property is engraved on their minds, as are the Lord's uncompromising words about those who, through a disordered love of earthly goods, are not able (or do not want) to follow him. Now, along the way, probably in order to break the silence caused by what has just happened, Peter says to Jesus: *Lo, we have left everything and followed you.*[1] Saint Matthew clarifies Peter's meaning: *What then shall we have?*[2] What reward will we receive?

Saint Augustine comments on this passage of the Gospel of today's Mass, appealing to us in these words: I ask you, Christian soul: if you were told, as was that rich man, 'You also, go, sell all that you possess and you will have treasure in heaven, and come and follow Christ; would you go away sad as he did?[3]

Like the Apostles, we have left everything our Lord has asked us to leave, each one according to his own vocation. Moreover, we are firmly determined to break any bond that prevents us from hastening to Christ and following him. Today we can renew our resolution to make him the centre of our existence, with a practical detach-

---

[1] Mark 10:28-31
[2] Matt 19:27
[3] St Augustine, *Sermon 301 A*, 5

ment from the things we have and use, so that we can say with Saint Paul: *Indeed, I count everything as loss because of the surpassing worth of knowing Christ Jesus my Lord.*[4] Certainly *he who knows the riches of Christ the Lord will despise all things when they are compared with them; to him, wealth, riches, power, will appear as dross. Nothing can be compared to, or stand in competition with, that inestimable treasure.*[5] Nothing has any value in comparison with the treasure that is Christ.

'*We have left everything.*' *What have you left, Peter? An old boat and a net. He, however, could answer: 'I have left the whole world, since I have kept nothing for myself'* ... *They left everything ... and they followed him who made the world, and they believed his promises,*[6] as we want to do too. We can rightly say we have left everything when nothing gets in the way of our love for Christ. Our Lord demands the virtue of poverty from all his disciples, at all times and in every situation where the circumstances of their lives find them placed. We have considered this repeatedly, for it is an essential part of following him. He also asks us for a real and practical austerity in the possession and use of material goods, and to live thus supposes *great generosity, much sacrifice and unceasing effort,*[7] says St Paul VI. It is essential for us to learn to practise this virtue in the conditions of everyday life. We should eliminate all useless expenditure, avoiding what can be called impulse spending. We will require to use our time well and generously in the affairs of God. We must be generous also in supporting works of charity, taking good care of clothes, furniture, household utensils and so on ...

---

[4] Phil 3:8
[5] *Catechism of the Council of Trent*, IV, 11, 15
[6] St Augustine, *loc cit* 4
[7] St Paul VI, Encyclical, *Populorum progressio*, 47

Some have received a more specific calling to apostolate in the exercise of their profession in the midst of the world. Like the twelve, God may ask them for a total detachment from possessions, riches, leisure time and family, so as to be more fully available in service to the Church and to souls.

65.2 Jesus rewards with unlimited generosity those who follow him.

We have left everything ... How often it has been our experience that with whole-hearted response to the demands of our Christian vocation, every new act of generosity and practical detachment frees us more and more from a great burden. We become like the soldier who rids himself of excess baggage in order to have greater freedom of movement in battle. In this way we enjoy a kind of dominion over the things around us in order to serve God better. We are no longer enslaved by them and we experience joyfully that sense of liberation to which Saint Paul referred: we are in the world *as having nothing, and yet possessing everything.*[8] Charity more easily finds room in the heart of the Christian who has thus stripped himself of the self's impediments and with charity he is indeed as one who possesses all things: *All are yours; and you are Christ's; and Christ is God's.*[9]

Peter reminds Jesus that, unlike the young man they have just met, they have given up everything for him. Simon has no regrets. But he seems to need the Master's reassurance that they have profited by the exchange, that it is worth while being with him, even though they now own nothing. The Apostle shows himself to be very human, but at the same time his question expresses the trust he has in

---

[8] 2 Cor 6:10
[9] 1 Cor 3:22-23

Christ. Jesus was filled with tenderness towards those men who, in spite of their defects, followed him faithfully. *Truly, I say to you, there is no one who has left house or brothers or sisters or mother or father or children or lands, for my sake and for the gospel, who will not receive a hundredfold – now, in this time – houses and brothers and sisters and mothers and children and lands, with persecutions, and in the age to come eternal life ... Try to find on earth anyone who repays so generously.*[10] Jesus is not to be outdone in generosity. Not even a glass of cold water – an alms, a service, any good action – given or done for Christ's sake will go unrewarded.[11] Let us be sincere when we examine the level of our detachment, the scale of our poverty. Can we really affirm, before God, that we have left *everything*?

If we have, Jesus will not fail to confirm us on our path. How can He forget fidelity that has been shown, day after day, only for love, when He takes account of even the least of our actions? He multiplied loaves and fishes for a multitude that followed him for just a few days, perhaps without much rectitude of intention. What will He not do for those who have left everything to follow him always? If those who follow him need special assistance to keep going, how can Jesus ever forget? What can our Father God refuse us if, seeing our lack of means, we ask him for them? *If the return of a son who had betrayed him is enough for him to prepare a banquet, what will He have in store for us, who have tried to remain always at his side?*[12]

The words of Christ reassured those who went with him that day on the road to Jerusalem. And those words re-echo for those who, throughout the centuries, having given

---

[10] cf St. J. Escrivá, *The Way*, 670
[11] cf Matt 10:42
[12] St. J. Escrivá, *Friends of God*, 309

everything to God, seek again in the teaching of our Lord increased firmness of faith and help in self-giving. Christ's promise goes far beyond all the happiness this world can offer. But He wants us to be happy also here on earth. His followers obtain, already in this life, a joy and peace which far outweigh all human consolation and happiness. And to this joy and peace, which is a foretaste of heaven, we must add eternal happiness when this short life is over. Life is a blink. *It lasts only a couple of hours; our reward is boundless, and even if there were no reward at all but to follow the counsels given us by the Lord, to imitate His Majesty in any degree would bring us a recompense immeasurable.*[13]

65.3 It is always worth while to follow Christ: the hundredfold here on earth and eternal life with God in heaven!

'Man and beast thou savest, O Lord,' – says the Psalmist – *'how precious is thy steadfast love, O God' (Ps 36:6-7). If God grants to all such a precious gift as his love, my brothers – to the good and to the wicked, to men and to animals, what will He not reserve for those who are faithful to him?*[14] It is worth while following our Lord, to be faithful to him in every moment, to give up everything for his sake, to set no limit to our generosity where He is concerned. He says to us in the words of Saint John Chrysostom: *The gold that you plan to lend, give it to me, for I will give you better interest and better security. That body that you plan to enlist in someone's militia, enlist it in mine, because I will outbid everybody in pay and reward ... His love is great. If you wish to make him a loan, he is ready to receive it at lavish interest. If you wish to sow, he buys you the seed. If you wish to build, he says: build on*

---

[13] St Teresa, *The Way of perfection*, 2, 7
[14] St Augustine, *Sermon 255*, on the *Alleluia*

my property! Why run after the things of men, who are poor beggars and are worth nothing? Run after God, who in exchange for little things will give you far greater.[15]

We should not forget that, to the reward He promises, our Lord adds *persecutions*. Persecutions also are a reward for the disciples of Christ. It is the disciple's glory to imitate his Master, to *suffer with him in order that he may also be glorified with him.*[16] These trials can come in the most diverse of forms: bloody persecution, slander, prejudice, job discrimination, mockery ... we should, when they come, grasp the fact that we can turn them to good, which is part of our reward, since God allows us to share in his Cross and be more closely united to him.

Christ has promised eternal happiness to those who are faithful to him. They will hear the voice of the Lord whom they served on earth, telling them: *Come, O blessed of my Father, inherit the Kingdom prepared for you from the foundation of the world.*[17] All we renounce in order to follow Christ more closely, or the little we suffer for him, is rewarded on hearing these words of welcome as we enter into eternity. Jesus himself leads us into heaven.

Although we follow Christ for love, a moment may come when everything is suddenly somehow more difficult. Then is the time for us to utter some aspiration that will help us to think of the prize: *It is worth while,* let us remind ourselves; *it is worth while, it is worth while.* So our hope will be strengthened and our way become more assured.

If we truly possess Jesus Christ, nothing else will seem to count. We are told of Saint Thomas Aquinas that one day our Lord said to him: *You have written well of me,*

---

[15] St John Chrysostom, *Homilies on St Matthew's Gospel*, 76, 4
[16] Rom 8:17
[17] cf Matt 25:34

Thomas. What reward do you desire? Lord – the Saint replied – *none other than yourself.* Neither do we want anything else. With Jesus, close to him, we will go through life full of joy.

May our Lady obtain for us, through her powerful intercession, firm dispositions of detachment and generosity. In this way, just as she did, we will create all around us a joyful attitude of love for Christian poverty.

66. LEARNING TO SERVE

66.1 The example of Christ. 'To serve is to rule.'

The Gospel of the Mass[1] records the petition of *the sons of Zebedee* that they might be given the first places in the new Kingdom. When the other disciples discovered this ambition of theirs, they were indignant with the two brothers. It was not, in all likelihood, the unusual character of the request that annoyed them. It was probably rather because they all felt that each one of them had an equal or better claim than James or John to fill such a top position. Jesus knew the ambition of those who were to be the foundation stones of his Church. He tells them that they cannot behave like those princelings who oppress and lord it over their subjects. The authority of the Church will be very different from this: quite the opposite, in fact. *Whoever would be great among you must be your servant, and whoever would be first among you must be slave of all.* This is a new kind of lordship, a new way of 'being great'. And our Lord shows them the grounds for this new dignity, and the reason for it: *for the Son of Man also came not to be served, but to serve, and to give his life as a ransom for many.*

The life of Christ is a constant exemplary help to man, his doctrine a constant invitation to serve others. Christ is the example to be followed by those who wield authority in his Church, and by all Christians. Although he is God, the Judge who is to come to judge the world, he does not impose himself. He serves, for the sake of love, even to the

---

[1] Mark 10:32-42

point of giving his life for all.[2] This is his way of being first. And this is the way the Apostles came to understand it, especially after the coming of the Holy Spirit. Later, Saint Peter will exhort priests to tend the flock of God that is their charge ... not as domineering overlords ... but as living examples.[3] So too does Saint Paul, who writes: *Though I am free from all men, I have made myself a slave to all, that I might win the more.*[4]

But our Lord speaks not only to his Apostles, but to his disciples and to his followers throughout the centuries. He teaches us that there is a special dignity to be found in helping and in offering assistance to man, in imitation of the Master. *This dignity is expressed in our readiness to serve, in keeping with the example of Christ, who 'came not to be served but to serve'. If, in the light of this attitude of Christ's, 'being a king' is truly possible only by 'being a servant', then 'being a servant' also demands so much spiritual maturity that it must really be described as equivalent to 'being a king'. In order to be able to serve others worthily and effectively we must be able to master ourselves, and possess the virtues that make this mastery possible,*[5] virtues like humility of heart, generosity, fortitude, cheerfulness ... which enable us to put our life at the service of God, to make ourselves available for our family, our friends and the whole of society.

66.2 Different services we can render the Church, society, and those around us.

The life of Jesus is an untiring service of men, a service which includes serving them in a material way. He

---

[2] cf John 15:13
[3] 1 Pet 5:1-3
[4] cf 1 Cor 9:19
[5] John Paul II, Encyclical, *Redemptor hominis*, 21

attends to them, teaches them, consoles them ... and finally gives his life for them. Can we who wish to be his disciples, then, fail to develop in ourselves the same disposition of heart which inspires us to give unstintingly to those around us?

On the night before his Passion, Christ wanted to give us a particularly significant example of how in such matters we should behave. As they were celebrating the Paschal supper our Lord rose, *laid aside his outer garment, and girded himself with a towel. Then He poured water into a basin and began to wash the disciples' feet, and to wipe them with the towel with which He was girded.*[6] He carried out the task of a servant. *Once again He preaches by example, by what He did. In the presence of the disciples, who are arguing out of pride and vanity, Jesus bows down and gladly carries on with the task of a servant... This tactfulness of our Lord moves us deeply. He does not say: 'If I do this, how much more ought you to do it?' He puts himself at their level, and in so doing he lovingly chides those men for their lack of generosity.*

As He did with the first twelve, so does He also with us. Our Lord can and does whisper in our ear, time and again, 'exemplum dedi vobis' (John 13:15), I have given you an example of humility. I have become a slave, so that you too may learn to serve all men with a meek and humble heart.[7] We serve God when we try to do our ordinary duties with perfection. We serve him when we try to proclaim the teaching of the Church, with courage and clarity, to a world which is confused, ignorant, and often in error on key points, even, of the natural law. *In such a situation, which is recognisably that of a large part of twentieth-century society, true of a large part of society,*

---

[6] John 13:4-5
[7] St. J. Escrivá, *Friends of God*, 103

the best service we can render the Church and mankind is to give doctrine.[8]

We cannot look upon the practice of our profession simply as a means of earning our living and of developing our personality in an honourable manner. No. It has to be seen as a service to society, a means of contributing to progress and to building a humane, just and reasonable world. Some professions obviously provide a direct service to others and give an immediate opportunity of practising a series of virtues which make the heart more generous and humble. The thought of Christ giving his attention freely to those who approached him, of his washing the feet of the disciples ... must be a powerful spur to the concern which, in the fulfilment of our duty, we show towards those who are entrusted to our service.

Frequent meditation upon our Lord's words, *I have not come to be served, but to serve*, will help us to tackle without reluctance those more unpleasant tasks which are frequently the most necessary. So we will serve the way He did. Family life is an excellent place in which to show this spirit of service, in countless details which may often pass unnoticed; these are details, however, that help us to live in an harmonious fashion where Christ is present. These small services – in which we strive to outdo one another – ensure also a constant practice of charity. Through them we avoid falling back into mediocrity. We grow in a life of union with God when these things are done *for him*. God is calling us through the needs of other people, particularly the sick, the aged, and those who in any way are seriously impoverished. These services are particularly pleasing to God when they are carried out with such humility and human tact that they are scarcely noticed and do not clamour for reward.

---

[8] *idem, Letter*, 9 January 1932

66.3 Serve with joy and be competent in your profession.

We cannot imagine our Lord looking strained or irritated, or reluctant, when the multitudes surge round him or when He washes the feet of his disciples. He serves joyfully, cheerfully, agreeably. And that is how we should carry out those duties that are a service to God, to society and to our neighbour. *Serve the Lord with gladness,*[9] the Holy Spirit tells us through the Psalmist. More than that, the Lord promises joy, and even worldly happiness, to those who serve other people. After he has washed the feet of his disciples, Jesus says: *If you know these things, blessed are you if you do them.*[10] This is, perhaps, the supreme quality of a heart that gives itself to God and which looks for opportunities – at times not very big ones – to give itself to others. When we serve someone with a smile and a pleasant manner it is as if our action has acquired an enhanced value, apart from its being all the more appreciated. And when a chance or the duty arises of offering a service which is likely to be disagreeable or even repugnant, *do it with a special joy and with the humility you would manifest if you were indeed the servant of everyone. You will draw great treasure of virtue and of grace from acting in such circumstances in this way.*[11] Sometimes we can find this kind of thing hard, and then we will pray: *Jesus, keep me smiling!*[12]

We need to be competent in our work, at the tasks we have to perform, if we want to serve properly. Without this competence the greatest good-will would be of little value: *'If you want to be useful, serve'. For, in the first place, in order to do things properly, you must know 'how' to do*

---

[9] Ps 100:2

[10] John 13:17

[11] J. Pecci, (Pope Leo XIII), *The Practice of Humility*, 32

[12] cf St. J. Escrivá, *The Way*, 626

them. I cannot see where is the integrity of a person who does not strive to attain the highest skills of his profession and to carry out properly the tasks entrusted to his care. It's not enough to want to do good; we must know how to do it, and to do it well. And, if our desire is an authentic one, it will show itself in the effort we make to use the right methods, finishing things as well as they can be finished, achieving human perfection.[13]

We have to give others this attention and service without expecting anything in exchange, giving it generously, knowing that all service ennobles and enriches the heart. And, in any case, let us remember that Christ is a 'good paymaster' and that, when we imitate him, He notices even the accompanying gesture, the smile, the smallest piece of service we have rendered. He looks at us with warm approval and we feel ourselves well rewarded.

Let us make certain today, in the presence of God, whether we have the proper disposition of service in the practice of our profession. Do we really serve society in it? In our home? In our workplace? Do we always, everywhere, imitate the Lord *who did not come to be served, but to serve*? This spirit of service should be evident particularly if we have a post of responsibility, a position of authority, a duty of formation. Let us look at ourselves and see whether we manage to avoid, habitually, accepting services from others which do not derive from our position, when we could well be doing those tasks ourselves. Our attitude has to be totally different from the attitude of people who take advantage of their authority or their prestige or their age in order to ask – or worse, to demand – attentions and services which would be intolerable even from a purely human point of view.

We have recourse to Saint Joseph, that *faithful and*

---

[13] *idem, Christ is passing by,* 50

prudent servant who was always ready to protect the Holy Family with countless sacrifices. He gave unstinting, unbounded service to Jesus and Mary. Let us ask him to help us to have that same disposition of soul with regard to our own family, with the people with whom we live, no matter what position in life we hold, with our professional colleagues or our friends ... with those who ask us in passing for some piece of information or a small favour. With the help of the holy Patriarch, we will see Jesus and Mary in them. That way it will be easy for us to serve them.

EIGHTH WEEK: THURSDAY

67. THE FAITH OF BARTIMAEUS

67.1 Bartimaeus' prayer overcomes all obstacles. Difficulties of those who try to draw nearer to Christ when He is passing by.

Saint Mark tells us in the Gospel of today's Mass[1] that as Jesus was leaving Jericho on his way to Jerusalem, He passed near Bartimaeus (that is, the son of Timaeus), a blind beggar, who *was sitting by the roadside.*

Bartimaeus is *a man who dwells in darkness, a man who lives in perpetual night. He cannot, like other sick people, get to Jesus in order to be cured. And he has heard the news that there is a prophet from Nazareth who restores sight to the blind.*[2] We, also, comments Saint Augustine, *have our hearts blindfolded, and Jesus passes so that we may cry out to him.*[3]

The blind man, when he heard the noise of the multitude, asked what the excitement was; surely he was used to distinguishing sounds – the sound of people going to work in the fields, the noise of caravans making their way through on their way to far-off lands. But one day ... he heard that it was Jesus of Nazareth who was passing by. Bartimaeus heard the sound of an approaching crowd at an hour that was perhaps unusual, and he asked – because these were not the sounds he was used to; it was the sound of a different throng – 'What's happening?'[4] And they tell him: *It is Jesus of Nazareth.*

---

[1] Mark 10:46-52
[2] A. G. Dorronsoro, *Time to Believe*, Rialp, Madrid 1972
[3] St Augustine, *Sermon 88*, 9
[4] A. G. Dorronsoro, *loc cit*

When he heard this name, his heart filled with faith. Here was Jesus. It was the chance of a lifetime. And he began to shout as loud as he could: *Jesus, Son of David, have mercy on me!* In his soul, faith had become prayer. *It happened to you, didn't it, when you sensed that Jesus was passing your way. Your heart beat faster and you too began to cry out, prompted by an intimate longing.*[5]

Difficulties soon arise for the man who searches in darkness for Christ, who is passing by. *Many rebuked him, telling him to be silent.* Saint Augustine comments on this phrase of the Gospel, pointing out that when someone decides to cry out to God, or to follow him, he often finds that others are intent on stopping him. *When I begin to do these things, my relations, my neighbours and friends begin to complain. Those who love secrecy confront me. Are you crazy? Don't be so vociferous. Aren't the rest of us Christians? This is ridiculous, it is madness! And many such things do they shout so that we, the blind, do not cry out.*[6] Then your friends, the need to do 'the done thing', the easy life, your surroundings, all conspired to tell you: 'Keep quiet, don't cry out. Who are you to be calling Jesus? Don't bother him.'[7]

Bartimaeus doesn't pay the slightest attention. Jesus is his great hope, and he doesn't know if their paths will ever cross again. And instead of keeping quiet, he cries out all the louder: *Son of David, have mercy on me. Why do you pay attention to the reproaches of the crowd and not walk in the footsteps of Jesus who is passing by? They will insult you, they will attack you, they will push you back, but you, keep on shouting until Jesus hears your cries. If a person is constant in what God commands, not giving any heed to*

---

[5] St. J. Escrivá, *Friends of God*, 195
[6] St Augustine, *op cit*
[7] St. J. Escrivá, *loc cit*

the opinions of the crowd and not paying too much attention to those who follow Christ only in appearance, preferring the sight that Jesus can restore to the noise of those who try to shout him down, no power can hold that person back, and Jesus will stop and heal him.[8]

And indeed, *when we persevere with fervour in our prayer, we detain Jesus who is passing by.*[9] The blind man's prayer is heard. He has achieved his desire, in spite of external difficulties, in spite of the pressure of his surroundings, and despite his own blindness which has prevented him from knowing exactly where Jesus is. For Jesus has remained silent, apparently indifferent to his petition.

Don't you too feel the same urge to cry out? You who also are waiting at the side of the road, at the side of this highway of life that is so short? You who need more light, you who need more grace to make up your mind to seek holiness? Don't you feel an urgent need to cry out, 'Jesus, son of David, have pity on me!' What a beautiful aspiration for you to repeat again and again![10]

67.2 Faith and detachment in order to follow Jesus. Our prayer should be personal, direct, without anonymity, like the prayer of Bartimaeus.

Our Lord, who had heard him right from the beginning, let him persevere in his prayer. He does the same with you. Jesus hears our cries from the very first, but He waits. He wants us to be convinced that we need him. He wants us to beseech him, to persist, like the blind man waiting by the side of the road out of Jericho.[11]

---

[8] St Augustine, *loc cit*
[9] St Gregory the Great, *Homilies on the Gospels*, 2,5
[10] St. J. Escrivá, *loc cit*
[11] *ibid*

The group pauses. Jesus calls Bartimaeus: *'Take heart', they said, 'rise, He is calling you.' And throwing off his mantle he sprang up and came to Jesus.* He threw aside his cloak! I don't know if you have ever lived through a war, but many years ago I had occasion to visit a battlefield shortly after an engagement. There, strewn all over the ground, were greatcoats, water bottles, haversacks stuffed with family souvenirs, letters, photographs of loved ones... which belonged, moreover, not to the vanquished, but to the victors! All these items had become superfluous in the bid to race forward and leap over the enemy defences. And this is what happened to Bartimaeus, as he raced towards Christ.

Never forget that Christ cannot be reached without sacrifice. We have to get rid of everything that gets in the way; greatcoat, haversack, water bottle.[12]

Now Bartimaeus is standing before Jesus. The people gather around to see what will happen. Our Lord asks him: *What do you want me to do for you*? He, who could restore sight – did He really not know what the blind man wanted? Jesus wants us to ask him. He knows our needs before we do, and He wants to remedy them.

The blind man replies immediately, 'Lord, that I may see'. He does not ask the Lord for gold, but for sight. He has little use for anything except to be able to see, because although a blind man can have many other things, without his sight he cannot see what he has got. Let us imitate, therefore, what we have just heard.[13] Let us imitate his great faith, his persevering prayer, his fortitude in not being discouraged by the adverse reaction to his first attempts to get to Christ. *Would that, realizing our blindness, we were seated by the roadside of the Scriptures, and hearing that*

---

[12] *ibid*, 196
[13] St Gregory the Great, *op cit*, 2, 7

Jesus is passing by, that we could make him stop beside us with the force of our prayer ...,[14] which should be like that of Bartimaeus: personal, direct, without anonymity. We call Jesus by his name and we speak to him in a direct and straightforward way.

67.3 Following Christ on the way, also in times of darkness. Public profession of Faith.

The story of Bartimaeus is our own story, since we also are blind in many matters. Jesus passes near us. Perhaps the moment has come for us to leave the ditch by the roadside and accompany him.

The words of Bartimaeus: *Lord, that I may see*, can serve us as a simple aspiration that we can repeat frequently. This is particularly so when we need light in our apostolate, in questions that we cannot solve, but above all in matters related to faith and vocation. *When darkness surrounds us and our soul is blind and restless, we have to go to the Light, like Bartimaeus. Repeat, shout, cry out ever more strongly, 'Domine, ut videam!' – Lord, that I may see. And daylight will dawn upon you, and you will be able to enjoy the brightness He grants you.*[15] In those dark moments, when perhaps our feelings of enthusiasm are beginning to diminish compared with those first days of following Christ, when our prayer is perhaps more arid and our faith seems to weaken, precisely then is when we need prayer most. When we do not see clearly the reason for making a small mortification and our effort in apostolate seems in vain, then prayer is our greatest ally. Instead of cutting short or abandoning our conversation with God because of the greater effort it is going to take, it is the very moment to demonstrate our loyalty, our fidelity, to

---

[14] Origen, *Commentary on St Matthew's Gospel*, 12:20
[15] St. J. Escrivá, *Furrow*, 862

redouble our endeavour to please him.

Jesus said to him: *Go your way; your faith has made you well. And immediately he received his sight.* The first thing that Bartimaeus sees in this world is the face of Christ. He would never forget it. *And he followed him on the way.*

This is all we know about Bartimaeus: that *he followed him on the way.* From Saint Luke we know that he *followed him, glorifying God; and all the people, when they saw it, gave praise to God.*[16] For the rest of his life, Bartimaeus would remember the mercy Jesus showed him. His witness was to bring faith to many people.

We also have received many graces, as great as or greater than that received by the blind man of Jericho. And our Lord is hoping also that our life and our conduct will help many to find Jesus in the world of today.

And he followed him on the way, glorifying God. This is a summary of what our own life may be if we have the living and operative faith of Bartimaeus.

We end our prayer with the words of the hymn *Adoro te devote*:

Jesu, quem velatum nunc aspicio,
oro, fiat illud quod tam sitio;
ut te revelata cernens facie,
visu sim beatus tuae gloriae.

Jesu! whom for the present veiled I see,
What I so thirst for, oh, vouchsafe to me:
That I may see Thy countenance unfolding,
And may be blest Thy glory in beholding. Amen.

---

[16] Luke 18:43

EIGHTH WEEK: FRIDAY

68. LOVE MEANS DEEDS: APOSTOLATE

68.1 Jesus curses the fig tree which sprouted only leaves. Every moment, every circumstance is an opportunity to produce fruits of holiness and apostolate.

Jesus left Bethany on his way to Jerusalem, a few miles away, and *He felt hungry*, Saint Mark tells us in the Gospel of today's Mass.[1] This is one of many occasions when the blessed humanity of Christ can be seen. He wanted to draw near to us and share in the limitations and necessities of our human nature, so that we in turn would learn to sanctify them. The Gospel tells us that Jesus saw a fig tree some distance away and went to see if he could find any fruit on it. But *he found nothing but leaves, for it was not the season for figs*. And he said: *May no one ever eat fruit from you again*. They returned later that day from Jerusalem to Bethany, where Jesus probably spent the night in that hospitable house where he was always welcome – the home of Lazarus, Martha and Mary. And on the following day, as they again journeyed up to the holy city, they all saw *the fig tree withered away to its roots*.

Jesus knew that it was not the season for figs. He knew too that there were none on the fig tree. He wished, however, to teach his disciples, in a way they would never forget, how God had come to the Jewish people, hungry for fruits of holiness and good works. All he had found were mere lifeless observances: worthless leaves. On that occasion too the Apostles learned that every moment presents a good opportunity for giving results. We cannot wait for special circumstances in order to sanctify

---

[1] Mark 11:11-26

ourselves. God comes to us looking for good deeds in moments of sickness, in our ordinary everyday occupations, both when we are overworked and when everything is going well and all is ordered and peaceful. He visits us as much in our tiredness as in our rest, in success and failure, in financial ruin – if God allows it – and in times of prosperity. It is precisely those circumstances which can and should produce fruit – all different, perhaps, but unique and wonderful. We should find God *in all circumstances* because He gives us the graces we need. *You also*, says the Venerable Bede, *ought to guard against becoming a fruitless tree, in order to offer Jesus, who has become poor, the fruit which He needs.*[2] He wants us to love him always with deeds, at every moment, everywhere, in every conceivable situation. Are we doing our best to give fruit now, at the time, at the age and in the circumstances in which we find ourselves? Are we waiting till there arrives a more favourable time for bringing our friends to God?

68.2 *Love means deeds, not sweet words.* Interior life is expressed in deeds.

Jesus here uses strong language: *May no one ever eat fruit from you again!* He says. Jesus curses the fig tree because he finds on it only leaves, no more than the appearance of fertility, mere foliage. It is a striking gesture which will engrave his teaching on the minds of his disciples, as on ours. The interior life of the Christian, if it is genuine, is accompanied by fruits, practical deeds of service to others. *The danger of deeds done without interior life has been emphasised*, St Josemaría Escrivá reminds us, *but we should also underline the danger of an interior life – if such could exist – without deeds.*

---

[2] St Bede, *Commentary on St Mark's Gospel, in loc*

'Love means deeds, not sweet words': I cannot recall without emotion that affectionate reproach – a divine utterance – which God engraved many years ago with burning clarity on the soul of a poor priest as he was distributing Holy Communion to some nuns, while saying silently to Jesus in his heart: 'I love you more than these do'.

We have to get moving, my children; we have to be up and doing – with courage and energy, with the joy of living, because 'perfect love casts out fear' (cf 1 John 4:18). With daring. Without shyness ...

Don't forget that where there's a will there's a way. 'Deus non denegat gratiam': God does not deny his help to the person who does all he can.[3] We need to live by faith and use the means within our reach in every situation. We cannot sit with arms folded waiting for the ideal moment, which perhaps will never come, in order to start doing apostolate. We cannot wait for everything to be just right in order to work for God. We have to show by our present actions the love we have in our heart. We will see how God will multiply and bless our efforts, puny though they may be, in answer to his demands. And we will be filled with gratitude and admiration.

If it is genuine, our interior life – our conversation with God in prayer and the Sacraments – is seen in the practical fulfilment of our resolutions: apostolate with friends and relations; spiritual or material works of mercy, depending on the circumstances: teaching the ignorant (classes of formation or catechism, opportune advice to someone who is hesitant or ill-informed); working to give a Christian outlook to the educational system; visiting the sick and the aged who live in almost total isolation, bringing them the consolation of companionship ...

Always, in all circumstances, in very varied ways,

---

[3] St. J. Escrivá, *Letter*, 6 May 1945, 44

interior life should continually overflow in works of mercy, in deeds of apostolate. Interior life which is not expressed in deeds is a mere wraith; it fades away and dies. As our intimacy with Christ increases, it is logical that our work, our character, our readiness to undergo sacrifice will all improve. So also will our way of dealing with others in daily life, aided by the virtues of social harmony – understanding, cordiality, optimism, order, friendliness ... These are the fruits our Lord hopes to find each day when he comes to inspect our behaviour. Love, if it is to grow, if it is to survive, needs to express itself in deeds.

68.3 Love of God shows itself in an apostolate that is cheerful and enterprising.

Jesus finds only leaves ... Having an interior life means living with God's vision, seeing our apostolic task from his viewpoint. Apostolic fruit cannot be lasting when a Christian falls prey to *activism*, which is the tendency to be 'doing things', to rush around, without the support of a deep prayer life. In the end, the furious activity turns out to be sterile and ineffective, and is often the sign of a lack of rectitude of intention. It is a purely human activity without any supernatural perspective. It is perhaps the consequence of ambition, of a desire to attract attention, which can infect everything we do, even the most sublime of undertakings.. So there is good reason for stressing the danger of *activism* – of multiplying deeds which, though good in themselves, have no interior life to support them. Saint Bernard, and many authors after him, called such works *accursed occupations*.[4]

But the lack of real fruit in our apostolate can arise also from *passivity*, from the absence of deeds of love. And if activism is bad and sterile, passivity is *deadly*, for it can

---

[4] cf J.D. Chautard, *The Soul of the Apostolate*, New York 1933, p.69

lead us to think that we love God because we perform
works of piety: it is true that these pious exercises are
carried out, but not perfectly, since they do not move us to
good actions. Such barren pious practices are like the
useless and sterile foliage on the fig tree, because true
interior life will inevitably lead to a vigorous apostolate: in
every situation it impels us to act with courage, daring and
initiative. It means that we joyfully shed all human respect,
go ahead imbued 'with the joy of living', with the joy that
an ever-youthful love ensures. Today, as we converse with
our Lord in these moments of prayer, we can examine
ourselves as to whether there is fruit in our life, now, this
very moment. Do I have initiative, as an overflow of my
interior life, of my prayer? Or do I think, on the contrary,
that in my surroundings – in my class, in the factory, in the
office – I can do nothing, that it's impossible to do
anything more for God? Do I give my time, do I help
effectively in apostolic tasks ... or do I 'only pray'? Do I
try to justify myself, saying that between my work, my
family and my devotional practices 'I haven't got any
time'? If that were the case, it would also mean that the
circumstances of work and family life had ceased to be an
occasion for apostolate.

Love means deeds ... Genuine love of God is seen in
an apostolate carried out with tenacity. And if our Lord
were to find us passive, content to perform pious practices
without the accompaniment of a cheerful and constant
apostolate, then perhaps he might say to us in our heart:
More deeds, please, and fewer excuses. Any one day
affords many ways to make Christ known, if our love is
true. Interior life without a deep apostolic zeal withers
away and dies: it is no more than a phantom. On the
following morning *as they passed by*, the Evangelist notes,
they saw the fig tree withered away to its roots,
completely. This is a graphic image of those who do not

produce the fruit which God expects, whether through a fondness for comfort or laziness, or a lack of spirit of sacrifice. The life of an apostle, as that of every Christian should be, is the opposite of the dried-up fig tree: it is brimful of life, of cheerful enthusiasm for the apostolic task, of love expressed in action, cheerfulness, an action which may be silent but which is constant ...

Let us examine our life and see whether we can present to God the ripe fruit He is looking for, practical results attained by a willing spirit of sacrifice. He approaches us with a hunger and a thirst for souls. In spiritual direction we learn to distinguish between what could be *activism* (where we need to pray more) and what could be *lack of initiative* (where we have to 'get moving' more). The Blessed Virgin Mary will teach us to react so that our interior life, our desire to love God, will never become a producer of useless and worthless foliage.

EIGHTH WEEK: SATURDAY

69. THE RIGHT AND THE DUTY TO DO APOSTOLATE

69.1 The right and duty of every Christian to be an apostle derives from union with Christ.

The chief priests and the scribes came to Jesus as he was walking in the porches of the Temple. They asked him: *By what authority are you doing these things, or who gave you this authority to do them?*[1] Perhaps because they were not ready to listen, our Lord in the end left their questions unanswered.

But we know that Christ is sovereign Lord of the universe, and that *in him all things were created, in heaven and on earth, visible and invisible ... all things were created through him and for him ... to reconcile to himself all things ... making peace by the blood of his cross.*[2] Nothing in the universe remains outside Christ's sovereignty and peaceful sway. All power has been given to me ... He holds the fulness of power in heaven and on earth, including the power to evangelise and bring salvation to all men and all nations.

He himself has called us to share in his mission, to intervene in the lives of others, so that they learn to be happy on earth and to reach heaven, for which they have been created. We have received the command to extend his kingdom, *a kingdom of truth and life, a kingdom of holiness and grace, a kingdom of justice, love and peace.*[3] *We are Christ who passes near those who live in the*

---

[1] Mark 11:27-33
[2] cf Col 1:17-20
[3] *Roman Missal*, *Preface of Christ the King*

world.[4] From him we must learn how, in the very fabric of society, to serve and help everyone. We need no other title than that of our Christian vocation in order to spend our lives in the service of others. This title we received in Baptism, and it is motive in itself. *The laity derive the right and duty to the apostolate from their union with Christ the head; incorporated into Christ's Mystical Body through Baptism, and strengthened by the power of the Holy Spirit through Confirmation, they are assigned to the apostolate by the Lord himself.*[5] Our charge and mission come from Christ.

We have the right to intervene in the lives of others, because the life of Christ is shared by all. And if one member falls ill, or becomes weak, or perhaps dies, the whole body is affected: Christ suffers, and so also do the healthy members of his mystical body, since *all men are one in Christ*.[6] All of us, so different from one another, are united in Christ, and charity then becomes part of life. The right to influence other people's lives becomes a joyful duty for every Christian without exception, no matter how unusual his personal circumstances. He, Jesus, *doesn't ask our permission to 'complicate' our lives. He just enters them, and that's that!*[7] And we who want to be his disciples should do the same with those who travel along our way. We should make use of the occasions that arise, as well as creating others ourselves, so as to draw those souls to God. We may suggest a good book for them to read, or give them some advice, or talk clearly to them about the need to go to Confession, or perhaps serve them in some way.

---

[4] St. J. Escrivá, *Letter*, 8 December 1941
[5] Second Vatican Council, *Apostolicam actuositatem*, 3
[6] St Augustine, *Commentary on Psalm 39*
[7] cf St. J. Escrivá, *The Forge*, 902

69.2 We should reject the excuses which prevent our 'getting involved' in the lives of others.

At times, people who witness our behaviour may say to us: but what right do you have to interfere in the lives of others? Who gave you permission to talk about Christ, his doctrine, his sweet demands? Or perhaps it is we ourselves who feel tempted to wonder: Who's asking me to get involved here? Then *we would have to reply: 'Christ himself is telling me, is begging me.' 'The harvest is plentiful enough, but the labourers are few. You must ask the Lord to whom the harvest belongs to send labourers out for the harvesting' (Matt 9:37-38). Don't take the easy way out. Don't say, 'I'm no good at this sort of thing; there are others who can do it; it isn't my line'. No, for this sort of thing, there is no one else ... Christ's plea is addressed to each and every Christian. No one can consider himself excused, for whatever reason, whether it be his age, his health, or his occupation. There are no excuses whatsoever. Either we carry out a fruitful apostolate, or our faith will prove barren.*[8] The Church encourages and in fact requires us to make Christ known. No pretexts or excuses will avail us in the joyful task which is ours all life long. *Young people should become the first to carry on the apostolate directly to other young persons, concentrating their apostolic efforts within their own circle ... Children also have their own work to do. According to their ability, they are true living witnesses of Christ among their companions.*[9] Young people, children, the aged, the sick, the unemployed, those who are successful in life ... all of us should be apostles who make Christ known with the testimony of word and example. What good loudspeakers God could have in the world. He tells all of us: *Go into all*

---

[8] *idem, Friends of God*, 272
[9] Second Vatican Council, *loc cit*, 12

the world and preach the gospel.[10] It is God who sends us!

Love for Christ leads us to love those around us. Our vocation impels us to think of others, not to fear sacrifices which require love with deeds, since *there is no sign or mark that more distinguishes the Christian and lover of Christ than concern for one's brethren and zeal for the salvation of souls.*[11] Therefore, the intensity of the desire to make the Master known is the indicator which measures the sincerity of life of the disciple and the degree of his commitment. If at any time we found that we felt no concern for souls, this would be because our charity had grown cold. If their estrangement from God left us unmoved and their spiritual needs did not provoke a reaction in our own soul, we have almost certainly grown cold. The apostolate is not something extra added on to the normal activity of the Christian. It is the Christian life itself, which has, as a natural manifestation of itself, an apostolic concern for our family, our colleagues, our friends ...

69.3 Jesus sends us now, as in the beginning he sent his disciples.

By what authority are you doing these things? the Pharisees ask Jesus. This is not the right moment to reveal the origin of his power. Later, he will reveal it to his disciples: *All authority in heaven and on earth has been given to me.*[12] Jesus' authority was not given him by men. Rather, God the Father appointed him *heir of all things (cf Heb 1:2), that he might be teacher, king and priest of all, the head of the new and universal people of the sons of God.*[13]

The Church and each of her members share in this

---

[10] cf Mark 16:15
[11] St John Chrysostom, *De incomprehensibili Dei natura*, 6, 3
[12] Matt 28:19
[13] Second Vatican Council, *Lumen gentium*, 13

power. It is a task for every Christian to carry out the work of Christ in the world. This applies especially to those who, in addition to the vocation they have received in Baptism, have had a special call from our Lord to follow him more closely. Jesus is urging us on, because *men are called to eternal life: they are called to salvation. Do you realise this? Do you realise ... that all men are called to live with God, and that without him they lose the key to the 'mystery' of themselves?*

This call to salvation comes directly to us from Christ, who has for man the 'words of eternal life' (John 6:8). He directs himself to every individual person living on earth, in particular to those who suffer, in body or soul.[14]

Jesus sends us, as He sent those disciples to the neighbouring village in search of the tethered donkey on which no man had yet ridden. He commanded them to untie it and bring it to him, because it was to be on this donkey that He would make his triumphal entry into Jerusalem. He charged them that if anyone asked them what they were doing, they should say that the Lord had need of it.[15] They act for our Lord and in his name. They don't do what they are doing on their own initiative, nor do they do it in order to obtain any personal benefit for themselves. The two disciples went and found the donkey, just as our Lord had told them. As they untied it, its owners said to them: *'Why are you untying the colt?' And they said, 'The Lord has need of it'.*[16] And those disciples, whose names we do not know, but who must have been faithful friends of the Master, carried out their mission. They did what has to be done in all apostolate: *they*

---

[14] St John Paul II, *Homily*, Lisbon, 14 May 1982
[15] cf Luke 19:29-31
[16] Luke 19:33-34

brought it to Jesus.[17] When Saint Ambrose explains this passage, he stresses three points: the Master's command, the divine power with which it was carried out, and the exemplary life and intimacy with the Master of those who performed it.[18] St Josemaría Escrivá, adds to this commentary the following: *Saint Ambrose has some words that fit the children of God marvellously well. He is speaking of the ass's colt, tethered to its dam, which Jesus needed for his triumph. 'Only an order of the Lord could untie it', he says. 'It was set loose by the hands of the Apostles. To do such a deed, one needs a special way of living and a special grace. You too must be an apostle, to set free those who are captive.'*

Let me comment on this text for you once more. How often, at a word from Jesus, will we have to loosen souls from their bonds, because He needs them for his triumph! May our hands be apostles' hands, and our actions, and our lives also. Then God will give us an apostle's grace, too, to break the fetters of those who are fast bound,[19] of all those who continue in chains and for whom our Lord is waiting.

---

[17] Luke 19:35
[18] cf St Ambrose, *Commentary on St Luke's Gospel, in loc*
[19] St. J. Escrivá, *The Forge*, 672

NINTH SUNDAY: YEAR A

70. BUILT UPON ROCK

70.1 Holiness means carrying out the Will of God, whether in things of importance or in things that may seem trivial.

Our Lord shows a special love for those who put their heart into serving him in everything, every day, thereby expressing in deeds the words and desires of their conversation with God. This is true prayer. For Jesus declares, in the Gospel of today's Mass: *Not every one who says to me, 'Lord, Lord,' shall enter the Kingdom of Heaven, but he who does the Will of my Father.*[1] On that occasion He was speaking to many who had turned prayer into a mere recital of words and formulae totally unrelated to their hypocritical and malicious behaviour. Our conversation with Christ has got to be different. *Your prayer should be that of a child of God, and not that of the Pharisaical hypocrites who will hear from Jesus' lips these words: 'Not every one that says to me, Lord, Lord, shall enter into the Kingdom of Heaven.'*

Your prayer, your clamour of 'Lord, Lord' should be linked with a thousand different ways throughout the day to a desire and an effective effort to fulfil the Will of God.[2]

Even if we could work wonders and miracles, such as prophesying in his name or casting out devils – if it were possible to do such things without his help – it would not be enough if we did not strive to fulfil his lovable Will. The greatest sacrifice would be useless, we would run our race in vain. By contrast, in Sacred Scripture we see how

---

[1] Matt 7:21-27
[2] St. J. Escrivá, *The Forge*, 358

God loves and blesses the man who seeks to be identified in everything he does with the divine Will: *I have found in David the son of Jesse a man after my heart, who will do all my Will.*[3] And Saint John writes: *The world passes away, and the lust of it; but he who does the Will of God abides for ever.*[4] Jesus himself declares that his food is to do the Will of his Father and to accomplish his business.[5] This is what matters; this is what the sanctification of our duties means: *doing his Will, becoming what He wants us to be.*[6] We have to rid ourselves more and more of our self-interested attitudes and our selfishness, being completely at one with what God wants for us.

The path that leads to heaven, and to happiness here on earth, is *obedience to the divine will, and not simply repeating his name.*[7] Prayer must be backed up by deeds, by a firm desire to carry out God's Will, which is revealed to us in so many different ways. *It would be a terrible thing*, says Saint Teresa, *if God were to be telling us plainly to go about his business in a certain way and we would not do it, but instead stood gazing at him because that gave us greater pleasure.*[8] What a pity if God wanted to lead us by one path, and we were to stick stubbornly to our own! To carry out God's Will: here we have a programme for a lifetime.

You might have thought occasionally, with holy envy, about the adolescent Apostle, John, '*quem diligebat Jesus*' – whom Jesus loved.

Wouldn't you like to deserve to be called 'the one who loves the Will of God'? Then take the necessary steps, day

---

[3] cf Acts 13:22
[4] 1 John 2:17
[5] cf John 4:34
[6] cf St Thérése of Lisieux, *Autobiography of a Soul*
[7] St Hilary of Poitiers, *Catena aurea*, vol I, p. 449
[8] St Teresa, *Foundations*, 5,5

after day.[9] These steps normally consist in fulfilling the small duties of the daily round and asking many times a day: Am I doing at this moment what I ought to be doing?[10] They include accepting the difficulties of ordinary life, struggling tenaciously to follow the advice received in spiritual direction, and rectifying our intention as often as is necessary. And such repeated rectification of intention is indeed necessary, because our tendency is to follow our own will, to opt rather for whatever is more desirable, more pleasant and less arduous.

Lord, I want to do only what you want me to do, the way you want me to do it. I don't want to do my own will, following my silly whims, but your divine Will. Lord, I wish that my life were to be just that: the fulfilment of your Will in everything, so that I could say, as you said, in big things and in small: my food, what gives meaning to my life, is to do the will of my Father God.

70.2 We want what God wants. We abandon ourselves to his care.

The firm purpose of giving all glory to God endows us with a special strength in difficulties and troubles: in sickness, in the face of slander, or confronted with financial problems...

In the same Gospel of the Mass Christ speaks to us of two houses, built at the same time, and apparently identical with each other. But the great difference between them became obvious when the testing time arrived: the rains came, and the floods and the gales. One of them stood firm because it had solid foundations: the other fell because it was built upon sand: its ruin was catastrophic and complete. Our Lord calls the man who built the first house,

---

[9] St. J. Escrivá, *op cit*, 422
[10] cf *idem*, *The Way*, 772

the one that stood firm, *a wise man*. The builder of the second house, He tells us, is a fool.

The first house resisted the wintry blasts and the rising flood-waters so well, not because of its architecturally pleasing design, or even because its roof was soundly put together, but thanks to its foundation on bedrock. That house lasted, it gave secure shelter to its owner and was a model of good construction. Just so is the person who builds on the rock of desires put into practice by fulfilling God's Will in the small things of every day, in more important matters, and also in times of real trouble when they come. So we see sick people, weakened in body by their disease, bear their pain joyfully and lovingly, greatly strengthened by seeing in their condition the hand of God's Providence, which always blesses those who love him, although in mysterious and very different ways. So too the person who has to put up with slander and calumny, or who faces financial ruin and sees the inevitable effects on his family, or who suffers the death of a loved one still in the prime of life, or who experiences job discrimination because of religious bigotry... The house – the life of the Christian who follows Christ in his deeds – does not fall, because it is built upon total abandonment to the Will of his Father God. This abandonment does not prevent him from defending himself when justice is at issue. He also demands the rights to which he is entitled as a worker, or to have access to the means to remedy his legitimate grievances. But all this is done with serenity, without anguish of mind and without bitterness or rancour.

In our prayer today we will tell our Lord that we want to abandon ourselves in his arms; there we will be absolutely safe. *Desire nothing for yourself, either good or bad: want only what God wants. When you are with Jesus you will find that what is bitter becomes sweet, and what is rough turns smooth.*

Jesus, I put myself trustingly in your arms, hiding my head on your loving breast, my heart touching yours: I want what you want, in everything.[11]

70.3 Doing and loving God's Will in all aspects of life, in big matters as in small.

If we are to stand firm in difficult moments we need to accept cheerfully the little setbacks that occur even in relatively untroubled times, at work, in family life ... in all the close-woven fabric of daily life. We need to carry out, faithfully and selflessly, our duties of state, whether it be those of study, of care for the family, or of whatever else our state in life involves. So the foundations go down deeper, and the whole building is strengthened. Fidelity in little, hardly noticeable things, enables us to be faithful in the big things,[12] to be strong when it matters most.

If we are faithful in carrying out God's Will in small things we will acquire the habit of seeing his Providence at work in everything that happens to us. Small things may be daily duties or the advice we receive in spiritual guidance, in the acceptance of those almost inescapable difficulties that can crop up on any ordinary day. We will see God's hand in health and in sickness, in moments of dryness and in moments of consolation, in peace and in temptation, in toil and at rest. And this will fill us with peace. We will learn to brush aside human respect with ease, because what matters to us will be doing whatever it is he wants us to do. So we will enjoy great freedom in acting always account-able to God,[13] confidently, boldly, with daring, unafraid to speak openly about Him.

This same fidelity in small things for the love of God,

---

[11] *idem, The Forge*, 529
[12] cf Luke 16:20
[13] cf V. Lehodey, *Holy Abandonment*

seeing in them, not the littleness itself – which is typical of mediocre souls – but the grandeur of God's will, we ought to respect greatly, even in the smallest things.[14]

A broad, solid and unshakeable foundation can act as a basis for other flimsier and less substantial buildings; it is not exclusively a support for its own structure. When our interior life is grounded on prayer and action, it becomes for many a source of refuge where they find the strength they need when their energies begin to flag, because their difficulties and trials may be great and hard to endure.

Let us never lose sight of Jesus, even momentarily. *When you are troubled ... and also in the hour of success, say again and again, 'Lord, don't let go of me, don't leave me; help me as you would a clumsy child; always lead me by the hand!'*[15] And with him, carrying out what He indicates to us is best for us, we shall reach the end of the road, where we will see him face to face. Together with Jesus, we will find his Mother Mary who is also our Mother. We turn to her now, at the end of our prayer, so that our conversation with Jesus may never be idle chatter. May she grant us a single-mindedness of purpose in life: to fulfil the most holy Will of her Son in all that we do. Lord, don't let go of me! Don't leave me! Help me as you would a clumsy child. Always lead me by the hand!

---

[14] J. Tissot, *The Interior Life*
[15] St. J. Escrivá, *The Forge*, 654

NINTH SUNDAY: YEAR B

71. KEEPING SUNDAYS AND HOLYDAYS OF OBLIGATION HOLY

71.1 Christian feastdays.

As we read in the *First Reading* of today's Mass,[1] it was God himself who instituted the feastdays of the Chosen People and who encouraged the observance of them. *Observe the sabbath day; keep it holy as the Lord your God commanded you. Six days you shall labour, and do all your work; but the seventh day is a sabbath to the Lord your God; in it you shall not do any work ...* As well as the Sabbath, the Jews had other principal feastdays – Passover, Pentecost, the Feast of Tabernacles ... – days on which they renewed the *Covenant* and gave thanks for benefits they had received. The *Sabbath* which followed six days of working at their own occupations was the day dedicated to God, the Master of time, in recognition of his sovereignty over all things. The observance of these days was to be one of the features that distinguished the Jewish people from the Gentiles.

In Our Lord's day many abuses of a rigorist nature had crept in, which gave rise to confrontations between Jesus and the Pharisees such as the one we read about in today's Gospel.[2] The disciples were passing through a cornfield on a Sabbath day: *As they made their way his disciples began to pluck ears of grain. And the Pharisees said to him, 'Look, why are they doing what is not lawful on the Sabbath?'* ... Christ reminds them that the prescriptions as to the Sabbath rest did not have an absolute value and that

---

[1] Deut 5:12-15
[2] Mark 2:23; 3:6

He, the Messiah, is *Lord of the Sabbath*.

Jesus Christ had great regard for the Sabbath and the other great Jewish festivals even though He knew that with his coming all those dispensations would be abolished and replaced by the Christian feastdays. Saint Luke, for example, has left it in writing for us that the Holy Family went up every year to Jerusalem for the Passover.[3] Jesus continues to celebrate this anniversary each year with his disciples. We can see too how, with his presence, He sanctifies the happiness of a wedding feast.[4] In his preaching He frequently makes use of examples drawn from domestic festivities – the king who celebrates his son's wedding,[5] the banquet for the son who had left his father's house and who returns home ...[6] The Gospels are imbued with a festive joy, which is a sign that the *bridegroom, the Messiah,* is already amongst his friends.[7]

Our Lord himself wanted us to celebrate important feasts, when, leaving aside our usual occupations, we can turn to him with greater calmness and attention. We can dedicate more time on these days to our families, and give our body and soul the necessary rest.[8] The Holy Mass is the centre of the Christian life.[9] Without the Mass nothing else would have any meaning. Everything would be like a body without a soul – like a corpse. Truly, Sunday is the *day that the Lord has made; let us rejoice and be glad in it.*[10] And it is in the Holy Mass that we always find the Fountain of

---

[3] Luke 2:41
[4] cf John 2:1-11
[5] Matt 22:1-14
[6] cf Luke 15:23
[7] cf Matt 9:15
[8] cf Spanish Episcopal Conference, *The feasts of the Christian calendar,* 13 December 1982, 1
[9] cf Second Vatican Council, *Christus Dominus,* 30 November 1981, 1:3
[10] Ps 117:24

happiness and of never-ending joy and peace.

71.2 *The Lord's Day.*

Our Lord's resurrection took place on *the first day of the week*. This is testified to by all the evangelists. On the same day, in the evening, He appeared to his disciples who had gathered together in the Cenacle, and showed them his hands and his side with the tangible signs of the Passion.[11] And *eight days later*, that is to say on the next *first day of the week*, Jesus appeared again in similar circumstances.[12] It is possible that Our Lord wanted to point out to us that that *first day* was about to become a very special day. At least that is how the first Christians understood it. From the very beginning they began to gather together to celebrate it in such a way that they called it the *Lord's Day, Domenica dies*.[13] The *Acts of the Apostles*[14] and the *Epistles* of Saint Paul[15] show how our first brothers in the Faith gathered together on the Lord's Day to break bread and to pray,[16] and the same has been done up to our own day. A document dating from the first centuries admonished the Christians of the time: *Do not place your temporal affairs above the Word of God but, rather, abandoning everything on the Lord's Day in order to hear the Word of God, hasten diligently to your churches, for in this do you show your praise of God. If not, what excuse before God will those people have who do not gather on the Lord's Day to hear the word of God and to feed on the divine food which remains eternally.*[17]

---

[11] cf John 20:1
[12] cf John 20:26-27
[13] cf Rev 1:10
[14] cf Acts 20:7
[15] cf 1 Cor 16:2
[16] cf Acts 2:42
[17] *Didascalia*, II, 59:2-3

For us, *Sunday* has to be a very special and much-loved feastday, the more so because in many places it seems to be losing the religious meaning it has always had. Saint Jerome wrote as follows: *God made every day. There are days that can belong to the Jews, to heretics or to pagans. But 'the Lord's day', the day of the Resurrection, is the day that belongs to Christians – our day. It is called 'the Lord's day' because after He had risen on the first day of the Jewish week, He went up to the Father and reigns together with him. If the pagans call it the 'Day of the Sun' we will gladly accept this expression. On this day the 'Light of the world' rose, the 'Sun of Justice' shone.*[18]

From the start, this day has been celebrated in a very special way, without any interruption. The Second Vatican Council teaches that, by a tradition handed down from the Apostles, which took its origin from the very day of Christ's Resurrection, the Church celebrates the Paschal Mystery every seventh day, which day is appropriately called the Lord's Day, or Sunday ...

The Lord's Day is the original name of the feastday, and it should be proposed as such to the faithful, and taught to them, so that it may become in fact a day of joy and of freedom from work.[19]

We begin to live this day well, and all the feastdays in fact, when we try to recapture the new-born faith and joy of those men and women who, on the first Sunday in the life of the Church encountered the risen Christ. We will try to imitate Peter and John on their way to the Sepulchre, and Mary Magdalene who recognises Jesus when He calls her by her name. We will try also to imitate the two disciples as they travel to Emmaus ... for it is the Lord himself we are going to meet. Our first brothers in the

---

[18] St Jerome, *Homily for Easter Sunday*
[19] Second Vatican Council, *Sacrosanctum Concilium*, 106

Faith taught us to celebrate this feast and to realise that observing Sunday and attending the Mass with special attention and piety are inseparable, owing to the intimate and profound relationship both have with the Paschal Mystery. This is why from the very beginning the celebration of the Holy Eucharist has constituted the focal centre of this great day. Today we can ask ourselves in our prayer whether every Sunday we try to give more time and care to the fulfilment of our customary norms of piety, whether we reflect more deeply on the meaning of our divine filiation, whether we make a real effort to seek the presence of God.

71.3 Apostolate as to the nature of Holydays of Obligation and Sundays. The sabbath rest.

Faced with the re-evangelization of the world, it is particularly urgent that we carry out an effective apostolate, which can go deep into the way families think about the sanctification of holy days, about the meaning of Sunday and the Christian way of living it. We can see that people become lukewarm in their spiritual lives because they do not know how to focus their weekend leisure. *It is your duty to be concerned about turning Sunday once again into the day of the Lord, and making the holy Mass once again the centre of the Christian life. The Lord's Day must be a day when we rest in God, a day of adoration, of supplication and thanksgiving. It should be a day when we beg God for forgiveness for the sins we have committed during the week just past, and ask him for the graces of spiritual light and strength for the coming week.*[20] We will then resume our work with greater cheerfulness and the desire to do it with perfection.

We shall be able to teach many people to consider this

---

[20] Pius XII, *Address*, 13 March 1943

commandment of the Church *not only as a primary duty, but also as a right, a need, a privilege, a piece of good fortune which a lively and intelligent believer cannot give up except for grave reasons.*[21]

It is not just a matter of a generic consecration of our time to God, as this stipulation is already contained in the first Commandment of the Decalogue. What is proper to this precept is the setting aside of a particular day for the praise and service of the Lord, in the particular way He wishes to be praised and served during it. God can decree *that man put aside a day each week for proper and due worship of the divinity. He should direct his mind to heavenly things, setting aside daily business. He should explore the depths of his conscience in order to know how necessary and inviolable are his relations with God.*[22]

The Sunday rest and that of other feastdays can never become for us simply more 'leisure' time spent in more or less empty idleness, which can perhaps be excused in those who do not know God. *Rest means recuperation: to gain strength, form ideals and make plans. In other words it means a change of occupation, so that you can come back later with a new impetus to your daily job.*[23] It means *rest dedicated to God.*[24] Even though we see a great change in customs, a Christian must always understand that today, as always, *Sunday rest has a moral and religious dimension of giving worship to God.*[25]

Feastdays provide an opportunity for us to give more time to those people God has entrusted to us – our family and friends. We should make use of this increased leisure

---

[21] St Paul VI, *General Audience*, 22 August 1973

[22] St John XXIII, Encyclical, *Mater et Magistra*, 15 May 1961, 249

[23] St. J. Escrivá, *Furrow*, 514

[24] Leo XIII, *Rerum novarum*, 15 May 1881

[25] Spanish Episcopal Conference, *Sunday, the original feast of Christians*, 22

to pay more attention to the people around us; for parents it means the opportunity – which they may not have during the week – of talking to their children, or of carrying out some work of mercy – such as visiting a sick relative, a neighbour, or someone who is alone and friendless.

Every day, but especially on Sundays, we need to know how *to fill the hours of the day usefully, doing everything as well as we can, and living little details of order, punctuality, and good humour.*[26]

The joy that filled Our Lady on Easter Sunday will be ours if we know how to place Our Lord at the centre of our lives, dedicating Sundays and feastdays to him with special generosity.

---

[26] *Conversations with Monsignor Escrivá,* 111

72. DEVOTION TO THE SAINTS

72.1 They are our intercessors before God and our great allies in any difficulty.

The Gospel of today's Mass[1] presents to us the figure of a Centurion who is the model of many virtues – faith, humility, trust in God. The liturgy has preserved his words in the Holy Mass: *Lord I am not worthy to have you come under my roof* ... Jesus was amazed at the attitude of this man, and after granting his request – the healing of one of his servants – *He turned and said to the multitude that followed him, 'I tell you, not even in Israel have I found such faith '*

This centurion is an example for us too of a man who knows how to ask for things. First he sent some elders to intercede for him. When they *came to Jesus, they besought him earnestly, saying, 'He is worthy to have you do this for him, for he loves our nation, and he built us our synagogue.'* Later, he sends more friends to Jesus when He is close to his house to tell him not to take the trouble to go in, because a simple word from him will be sufficient to cure the sick servant. Jesus had been delighted to hear the Jews speak on behalf of this Gentile: *He is worthy to have you do this for him ....*

In Scripture we find many testimonies to this effective intercession. When Yahweh proposed to destroy the cities of Sodom and Gomorrah, Abraham begged him: *Suppose there are fifty righteous within the city; wilt thou then destroy the place and not spare it for the fifty righteous who are in it? ... And the Lord said, 'If I find at Sodom fifty*

---

[1] Luke 7:1-10

righteous in the city, I will spare the whole place for their sake'. But as there were not fifty righteous men, Abraham went on reducing the number: And if there were forty? ... thirty? ... twenty? ... ten? ...[2] God accepts his intercession each time because Abraham was the *friend of God*.[3]

The saints who already enjoy eternal bliss are the special friends of God, because they loved him above all things and they served him with an heroic life. They are our great allies and intercessors – they always heed our prayers and present them to God, guaranteeing their worth by the merits they obtained here on earth, and by their union with the Blessed Trinity. God gives them honour and glory through the miracles wrought through their intercession and the graces they obtain for us for our material and spiritual needs, *for in this life they merited before God that their prayers should be heard after their death.*[4]

Devotion to the saints is part of the Catholic faith and has been a living tradition in the Church from the very beginning. The Second Vatican Council tells us that it is *most fitting, therefore, that we love those friends and co-heirs of Jesus Christ, who are also our brothers and outstanding benefactors, and that we give due thanks to God for them, 'humbly invoking them and having recourse to their prayers, their aid and help in obtaining from God through his Son, Jesus Christ, Our Lord, our only Redeemer and Saviour, the benefits we need.'*[5] We have *friends* in Heaven. Let us turn today – and every day – to their intercession. They will help us to do our everyday work with rectitude of intention, to surmount whatever we find hardest and to do apostolate.

---

[2] cf Gen 18:24-32
[3] cf Jud 8:22
[4] St Thomas, *Summa Theologiae*, Supplement, 72, 3, 4
[5] Second Vatican Council, *Lumen gentium*, 50

72.2 Cult of the saints. The *dies natalis*.

From the very earliest days of the Church veneration grew up for Our Lady, the Mother of God and our Mother, for the guardian angels and for the apostles and martyrs. Countless testimonies have been handed down to us of the devotion the first Christians had to them. Already in the *Acts* of the martyrdom of Saint Polycarp – who was a disciple of Saint John the Apostle – we are told that the Christians piously buried his mortal remains so that they could celebrate his birthday (the day of his martyrdom) each year in that very place. Saint Cyprian recommended the clergy in Carthage to make a note of the day on which the martyrs died so as to be able to celebrate their anniversary. This celebration took place beside the tomb. Each church remembered its martyrs. The compilation of these accounts soon gave way to the first calendars of saints. Many strove for the privilege of being buried close to a martyr; their tombs constituted a local glory; they symbolised protection and were places where many special graces were obtained. They soon became centres of pilgrimage. Later, especially when martyrdom became less frequent, *there were added to these, others who had chosen to imitate more closely the poverty and virginity of Christ, and still others whom the outstanding practice of the Christian virtues and the wonderful graces of God recommended to the pious devotion and imitation of the faithful.*[6] They are the treasure of the Church and a great help in our daily struggle, in the fulfilment of our work, and in our efforts to carry out our resolutions to do better and to make our desires of bringing souls to Christ a reality.

The saints intercede for us in Heaven; they obtain for us graces and favours, for – comments Saint Jerome – if

---

[6] St John Paul II, *Divinus perfectionis magister*, 25 January 1983

when they were on earth *and having had reasons for being concerned about themselves, they had prayed for others, how much more will they do so after receiving their crown, their victory, their triumph!*[7] We venerate their memory and try to honour them on earth. We should not be satisfied with simply invoking them as intercessors on our behalf: the Church wants us to give them the cult they deserve in recognition of their sanctity and of their being eminently favoured members of the Mystical Body of Christ, who possess for ever eternal bliss. In them we praise God: *we honour his servants, so that this honour may redound in favour of the Lord.*[8] Our intimacy with the blessed in Heaven *in no way diminishes the worship of adoration given to God the Father, through Christ, in the Spirit; on the contrary, it greatly enriches it.*[9]

As well as giving them external veneration, we should speak to them in the depths of our hearts, without the use of words, but with the affection born of friendship and trust. We must speak in their ear, as to a friend who helps us at all times but more especially when we have some difficulty. Often we will turn to the saint or the martyr commemorated by the Church that day, and whose feast frequently coincides with the day of his death, his *dies natalis*, and on which he heard those most blessed words of the Lord: *Come, O blessed of my Father ...,*[10] see what I have prepared for you; it is the anniversary of that day when for the first time they contemplated the ineffable glory of God, which they can never lose. There is great benefit to be gained from our having special devotion to those saints who, because of our particular circumstances,

---

[7] St Jerome, *Contra Vigilantium*, 1, 6
[8] *idem, Letter*, 109
[9] Second Vatican Council, *loc cit*, 51
[10] cf Matt 25:34

seem to us to be closer to our lives. We then experience how *our community with the saints joins us to Christ, from whom as from its fountain and head issues all grace and the life of the People of God itself.*[11]

72.3 Veneration and regard for relics. Images. Our Lady, a special intercessor in our needs.

It is a manifestation of piety to have great esteem and veneration for the bodies of the saints and for the objects they used when on earth. They are precious remembrances that we look after with great devotion, just as we do the objects that belonged to people who were very close to us and whom we loved very much. The first Christians preserved the relics of the martyrs as *treasures of inestimable worth.*[12] *In memory of them we must worthily venerate everything they have left to us, and above all their bodies, which were temples and instruments of the Holy Spirit, who dwelt and worked in them, and which will become one with the Body of Christ, after their glorious resurrection. This is why God himself honours these relics in a fitting manner, performing miracles through them.*[13]

We also give honour to their images because in these we venerate the saints they represent, and they move us to love them and imitate their virtues. God has on occasion glorified these images and relics through miracles. He frequently grants special favours and graces to those who piously venerate them. Saint Teresa wrote for us that she was 'a great friend of images'. *How unfortunate are those who through their own fault lose this benefit!*, she said, referring perhaps to those who, influenced by Protestant doctrines at that time, used to attack the images of saints.

---

[11] Second Vatican Council, *loc cit*, 50
[12] *The Martyrdom of St Ignatius*, 6, 5
[13] St Thomas, *op cit*, 3

We must love and seek the intercession of our Mother Mary in a special way. She who is the Mediatrix of all graces, in whom *the angels rejoice, the righteous find grace and sinners receive forgiveness for ever.*[14] She protects us always and helps us at every moment. She has not failed to carry to her Son a single one of our supplications. Her images are a constant reminder to us to be faithful in our daily occupations.

Holding fast to our Lady's hand, let us finish our prayer by invoking God in the words of the liturgy; *Almighty and eternal God, you have willed to give us a supreme proof of your love by the glorification of your saints; grant to us now that we may be helped by their intercession and moved by their example to faithfully imitate your Son Jesus Christ.*[15]

---

[14] St Bernard, *Homily for Whit Sunday*, 2
[15] *Divine Office, Common of holy men. Prayer for many saints.*

73. THE CORNERSTONE

73.1 Jesus Christ is the cornerstone on whom we must build our lives. Our being disciples of Christ influences the whole of our existence.

In the parable of the vinedressers who commit murder,[1] Jesus sums up the whole history of salvation. He compares Israel to a choice vineyard which God surrounds with a hedge and furnishes with a wine press. He builds a watchtower in which He places a guard to protect the vineyard from thieves and wild animals. God did not fail to provide all the means possible for caring for the vineyard of his heart – his people – as had already been prophesied.[2] The vinedressers in the parable are the leaders of the people of Israel; the owner is God, and the vineyard is Israel, the People of God.

The owner sends his servants time and again to collect his due of fruit from the vineyard, but each time they are badly treated. This was the mission of the prophets. Finally he sent his Son, *the Beloved*, thinking that they would respect him. We are shown here the difference between Jesus – the Son – and the prophets, who were servants. The parable refers to Christ's transcendental and unique Sonship, and clearly expresses the divinity of Jesus Christ. The vinedressers *took him and killed him, and cast him out of the vineyard*, an explicit reference to the crucifixion, which took place outside the walls of Jerusalem.[3] Our Lord, who discretely mentions himself in the parable, must

---

[1] Mark 12:1-12
[2] Is 5:1-7
[3] cf *The Navarre Bible*, notes to Mark 12:1-12 and Matt 21:33-46

have spoken with great sorrow, as He sees how He is to be rejected by those very people to whom He has come to bring salvation. They do not want him. Jesus ends with these words of one of the Psalms:[4] *The stone which the builders rejected has become the head of the corner*.

The leaders of Israel understood the clearly Messianic meaning of the parable and realised that it was directed *against them*. So they tried to arrest him, but once again they feared the people.

Saint Peter was to remember Jesus' words when he came before the Sanhedrin, and the prophecy contained in the parable had already been fulfilled: *Be it known to you all, and to all the people of Israel, that by the name of Jesus Christ of Nazareth, whom you crucified ... This is the stone that was rejected by you builders, but which has become the head of the corner.*[5] Jesus Christ makes himself the keystone which is the foundation and support of the whole building. This stone is essential to the Church and to each man: without it the whole building would collapse.

The *cornerstone* affects the whole construction, our whole life – business affairs, interests, loves, time ...; nothing is beyond the scope of what faith demands in the life of a Christian. We are not disciples of Christ for a number of pre-determined hours (when we pray, for example, or when we take part in a religious service), or just on special days ... The profound unity of life that being a Christian demands, causes absolutely everything in our lives to be affected by the fact that we are followers of Christ. At the same time this does not prevent things retaining their own nature. Following Christ influences the very core of our personality. When someone is in love, this fact influences his whole view of things and events,

---

[4] Ps 118:22
[5] Acts 4:10-11

however trivial they may appear. He is influenced by it as he walks along the street, when he is at work, in his attitude towards social relationships – and not only when he is in the company of the person he loves. Being a Christian is the most important characteristic of our existence, and it has to have incomparably more influence on our lives than even human love has on the most ardent of lovers.

Christ is the centre of our lives and of our whole being. *Let us imagine an architect*, comments Cassian, *who wants to construct the vault of an apse. He has to trace the whole circumference beginning with a key point – the centre. Guiding himself by this infallible norm, he then has to calculate the exact circumference and the design of the whole building ... In this way, a single point becomes the fundamental key to an imposing building.*[6] In a similar way, God is the point of reference of our thoughts, our words and our deeds. We should want to build our very existence in relation to him.

73.2 Faith gives us light by which to recognise the true reality of things and of events.

It is Christ who gives meaning to the way his followers think and live. Thus it would not make sense at all if we set aside the supervening and determining fact that we are Christians whenever we have to judge a work of art or a political programme, whenever we have to carry out some business deal or plan our holidays. Although he respects the autonomy of each discipline, the laws proper to each field of action and the broad freedom allowed to him in everything that is a matter of opinion, the faithful follower of Christ does not consider any matter at all in only one of its aspects, whether that aspect be, for example

---

[6] Cassian, *Conferences*, 24

economic, say, or artistic or cinematographic. He does not simply accept that particular undertakings or projects are good without taking a broader view of them. If due subordination to God is not respected in these undertakings, in those programmes or in that work of art, only one definitive overall assessment is possible – a negative one – however good their partial values may appear to be.

When it comes to doing a piece of business or accepting a particular job, a good Christian should not only look at what is financially to his advantage, but he must examine other aspects too. Is it licit as regards the norms of morality? Does it cause good or harm to others? He tries to evaluate the benefits such a business proposition or job will contribute to society. If it is morally wrong or at best does not give good example, any other characteristics it may have – for example, providing a good income – do not turn it into a morally sound and therefore good transaction. However advantageous a business opportunity may appear, if it is not morally right it is a very bad undertaking and one that may not be entered into by any true follower of Christ.

Error is often presented decked out in the noble garments of art, science or freedom ... But faith has to be, indeed is, stronger than error. It is the powerful light that enables us to see, lurking behind what appears to be good, the evil that lies hidden beneath the surface of an otherwise good literary work, of a beauty that conceals ugliness. It is Christ who must be the cornerstone of every building.

Let us ask Our Lord for his grace so that we may live in a way totally compatible and utterly coherent with our Christian faith. In this way we will never think of our faith as a limiting factor – *I can't do this, I can't go there*. Rather it will be a light that enables us to recognise the reality of things and events, without ever forgetting that the devil will try to make an ally of human ignorance, (which cannot see the complete reality contained in this literary work or in that doctrine) and of the pride and concupiscence that all of us drag along behind us. Christ is the crucible that assays the gold there is in all human things. Anything that does not stand up to the testing clarity of his teaching is a lie and deceptive, even though it may be adorned with the appearance of some attractive good or perfection.

If we make use of the criterion that this *unity of life* gives us -that of being and at all times knowing ourselves to be faithful disciples of Our Lord – we will be able to gather together many of the good things that men, who have been guided by right human criteria, have done and thought, and place them at the feet of Christ. Without the light of faith we would, as often as not, fail to detect and see through the rottenness by which we were at first deceived, since many such works do indeed possess some streak of goodness or of beauty.

If we want to have well-formed standards by which to discriminate and judge, while using the means to acquire them, we need to have a right will, which wants above all else to do the Will of God. This explains why very ordinary simple people, plain folk of scant learning and perhaps with few natural talents, but possessed of a deep Christian faith, can have excellent criteria which enable them to form wise assessments of the various things that happen; whereas others, perhaps more highly cultured or even with far greater intellectual capacity, sometimes show a lamentable absence of sound judgement and make serious mistakes in the most elementary matters.

Unity of life, an habitually Christian way of life, enables us to judge with certainty, and to discover the true human value of things. Thus we will sanctify all noble human realities and take them to Christ. Let us ask ourselves: In every situation, do I live in a way that is consistent with my faith and with my vocation? When I make a decision, however large or small, do I keep in mind above all else what it is God wants of me? Let us see in which specific points God is asking us to behave in a more decisively Christian way.

73.3 The Christian has his own scale of values in relation to the world.

A Christian, who will have built his life upon the *cornerstone* who is Christ, has his own personality, his own way of seeing the world and its happenings. He has a scale of values very different from that of the pagan, who does not live by faith and who has a purely worldly conception of things. A weak and lukewarm Christian faith, however, which exerts very little influence on ordinary life, *can provoke in some people that kind of inferiority complex which manifests itself in an immoderate desire to 'humanise' Christianity, to 'popularise' the Church, to make it somehow seem to conform to the value-judgements prevalent in the world at a given time.*[7]

This is why, as well as being immersed in our secular activities, as Christians we need to be *immersed in God*, through prayer, the sacraments and the sanctification of our daily work. We need to be faithful disciples of Jesus in the middle of the world, in our ordinary everyday life, with all the constant effort and hard decisions this entails. In this way we will be able to put into practice the advice Saint Paul gave to the first Christians in Rome when he alerted them to the risks of accommodating themselves to the pagan customs of the day: *Do not be conformed to this world.*[8] Sometimes this refusal to conform will lead us to row against the current and run the risk of being misunderstood by many of our contemporaries. The

---

[7] J. Orlandis, *What is it to be a Catholic?*, Pamplona, 1977
[8] Rom 12:2

Christian must not forget that he is *leaven*[9] hidden in the lump of dough that has to be fermented by him.

God is the light that shines on all created reality and reveals the truth hidden within it. He is the lighthouse whose beacon-beam directs navigators on whichever sea they steer their course. *The Church ... believes that the key, the centre and the purpose of the whole of man's history is to be found in its Lord and Master.*[10]

Jesus of Nazareth continues to be the *cornerstone* of every man's life. Any building constructed without Christ is raised in vain. Let us think today as we finish our prayer, whether the Faith we profess is coming to bear more and more influence on our existence, on the way we view the world and mankind, and on the way we behave. Let us endeavour so to conduct ourselves that through our actions all men will really come to know Christ, to follow his doctrine and to love him.

---

[9] cf Matt 13:33
[10] Second Vatican Council, *Gaudium et spes*, 10

74. BEING EXEMPLARY CITIZENS

74.1 The Christian in public life. The exemplary fulfilment of our duties.

The Gospel of today's Mass[1] tells how some Pharisees came to Jesus and tried to catch him out in his speech, so that they might bring an accusation against him. With this end in view they asked him maliciously whether it is lawful to pay the tribute to Caesar or not. They were referring to the tax that all Jews had to pay to Rome, and which reminded them of their dependence on a foreign power. It was not a very hefty amount, but it presented them with a problem of both a political and a moral nature; the Jews were divided among themselves as to its binding force. And now they wanted to see Jesus taking sides, letting everybody know whether He was in favour of this Roman tax or against it. *Teacher*, they said, *Is it lawful to pay taxes to Caesar or not?* If Our Lord were to say 'yes', they would be able to accuse him of recommending collaboration with the Roman power, a foreign denomination which the Jews hated because it was imposed on them by an invading force. If He answered 'no', they would be able to accuse him of rebelliousness against Pilate, the Roman authority. To come down either in favour of the tax or against it would mean, after all, that He would be telling them whether He approved of or rejected the lawfulness of the politico-social situation in which the Jewish people found themselves. Whatever He said, He would appear either to sympathise and collaborate with the occupying power or to encourage the latent rebelliousness

---

[1] Mark 12:13-17

of the Jews that was never very far from the surface. Later on they were to bring an accusation against him, saying with a falseness that would be only too obvious: *We found this man perverting our nation, and forbidding us to give tribute to Caesar.*[2]

On this occasion, Jesus, who knew the hypocrisy of their question, said to them: *'Bring me a coin, and let me look at it'* ... *'Whose likeness and inscription is this?'* They said to him, *'Caesar's'*. And Jesus amazed them by the simplicity and trenchant profundity of his answer: *'Render to Caesar the things that are Caesar's, and to God the things that are God's'*. Jesus does not evade the question, but by his answer expresses it in its true terms. The State should not elevate itself to the divine level, and the Church should not take sides in temporal affairs which are constantly changing and which are of no more than relative importance. By replying as He did, He showed his opposition as much to the Pharisees' widespread error of the day about a messianic mission that was political, as He did to the error of the Roman State's – or of any State's – interfering in religious matters.[3] By his answer Our Lord clearly established two separate and distinct spheres of competence. *The political community and the Church are autonomous and independent of each other in their own fields. Nevertheless, both are devoted to the personal vocation of man, though under different titles.*[4]

The Church, as such, has not been given the mission of finding specific solutions for temporal matters. In this way she follows Christ, who, by declaring that his *kingship is not from the world*[5] expressly refused to be constituted

---

[2] Luke 23:2
[3] cf J. M. Casciaro, *Jesus and Politics*, Madrid 1973
[4] Second Vatican Council, *Gaudium et spes*, 76
[5] John 19:36

judge in the realm of earthly affairs.[6] As Christians, therefore, we must never fall into the mistake that Christ himself was so careful to avoid: of uniting the gospel message, which is universal, to a particular political system – 'Caesar'. That is to say, we must avoid any situation where those who cannot give wholehearted allegiance to a particular system, or party, or to Caesar, may be obliged to experience understandable difficulties in accepting a message which has as its ultimate end eternal life. The Church's mission, which continues throughout time the redemptive work of Jesus Christ, is one of leading men to their supernatural and eternal destiny. Her just and necessary concern with problems that pertain to human society is derived from her spiritual mission, and must stay within the bounds of that mission.

It is for us as Christians, placed in the very centre of society, with all the rights and duties this brings with it, to find solutions for temporal problems. We must work to form around us a world which becomes ever more human and more Christian. We must do this by being exemplary citizens who demand all their rights and equally know how to fulfil all their duties towards society. Moreover, very often the way Christians must act in public life will not be limited to the mere fulfilment of the legal norms, of what is laid down by law. The difference between the legal order and the moral criteria governing our own conduct will sometimes oblige us to go even further than the law demands or to behave in a way that differs from what is asked for by the law's strictly juridical criteria.[7] Such occasions might arise, for example, in the case of excessively low wages or unjust situations which are not

---

[6] cf Luke 12:13 *et seq*
[7] cf Spanish Episcopal Conference, *Christians in public life*, 24 April 1986, 85

covered by the law; the dedication of a doctor towards his patients who need him for more hours than those strictly demanded by the rules or agreements of the hospital, etc. Are we known at work – whatever our job may be – as people who do far more, for love of God and of men, than they are strictly obliged to do in terms of hours of work, dedication, interest, sincere concern for people and their problems ...?

74.2 Unity of life.

Render to Caesar the things that are Caesar's ... Our Lord made a distinction between those duties that relate to society and those that refer to God, but in no way did He want to impose on his disciples what would amount to a double existence. Man is one, with just one heart and one soul, with his virtues and his defects, all of which have a bearing on his behaviour, and *in public life just as in private life, the Christian must take his inspiration from the doctrine and following of Jesus Christ.*[8] This will inevitably make his behaviour more human and still more noble. The Church has always proclaimed the just autonomy of temporal realities, understood, of course, in the sense that *created things and society itself are endowed with their own laws and values ...* But *if by the terms 'the autonomy of earthly affairs' is meant that material being does not depend on God, and that man can use it as if it had no relation to its creator, then the falsity of such a claim will be obvious to anyone who believes in God. Without a creator there can be no creature.*[9] Then society itself becomes inhuman and difficult to live in, as can be proved.

The Christian chooses his political, social and pro-

---

[8] *ibid*
[9] Second Vatican Council, *loc cit*, 36

fessional options according to his innermost convictions. And what he gives to the society in which he lives is a true vision of man and of society, because only Christian doctrine offers us the complete truth about man, about his dignity and about the eternal destiny for which he was created. Nevertheless there are many who on occasions would like Christians to live a double life – one life in their temporal and public activity, and the other in their life of faith: they even affirm, by means of sectarian or discriminatory words or actions, that there is incompatibility between one's civic duties and the obligations that following Christ brings with it. As Christians, we must proclaim with our words and with the testimony of our coherent lives, that *It is not true that there is opposition between being a good Catholic and serving civil society faithfully. In the same way there is no reason why the Church and the State should clash when they proceed with the lawful exercise of their respective authorities, in fulfilment of the mission God has entrusted to them.*

Those who affirm the contrary are liars, yes, liars! They are the same people who honour a false liberty, and ask us Catholics 'to do them the favour' of going back to the catacombs,[10] of retreating into silence.

Our testimony in the middle of the world has to be manifested by a deep unity of life. Love of God has to lead us to carry out faithfully all our obligations as citizens: to pay our taxes; to vote conscientiously in seeking to bring about the common good, etc. Failure to make one's own opinion felt at whatever level – out of indifference, laziness or false excuses – by means of the ballot box or its equivalent is a fault against justice, because it means neglecting some rights which, owing to the consequences

---

[10] St. J. Escrivá, *Furrow*, 301

their virtual renunciation may have for other people, are also duties. That neglect can be serious if it means that by failing in our duty we have contributed to the success – within a professional body, on the Governing Body of the school our children attend, in the political life of the country – of a candidate whose ideology is at variance with Christian principles.

St John Paul II has exhorted us: *Be sure to live and to infuse into temporal realities the sap of the faith of Christ, aware that this faith does not destroy anything that is truly human, but rather strengthens, purifies and elevates it.*

Bring that spirit to bear in the attention you give to crucial problems. In the sphere of the family by living and defending the indissolubility of marriage and all the other values contained within it, by fostering respect for all human life from the very moment of its conception. Bringing it to bear in the world of culture, of education and of teaching, by choosing for your children a school in which the bread of Christian faith is presented to them.

Be strong, too, and generous when you are called upon to contribute to the irradication of injustice and social and economic discrimination; when you are called upon to participate in the positive task of increasing and justly distributing earthly goods. Bend every effort so that your laws and customs do not turn their back on the transcendent meaning of man or on the moral aspects of life.[11]

74.3 Our union with God. This is necessary if we are to be better Christians.

... And to God the things that are God's Our Lord also stressed this aspect, although they did not expressly ask him concerning it. *Caesar looks for his own likeness, give*

---

[11] St John Paul II, *Homily*, Barcelona, 7 November 1982

*it to him. God looks for his own likeness: give it back to
him. Do not cause Caesar to lose his coin because of you.
Do not cause God to lose his coin among you,*[12] comments
Saint Augustine. The whole of our life is God's; our works,
our concerns, our joys ... Everything of ours is his;
especially those moments – like these moments of prayer –
that we dedicate exclusively to him. Being good Christians
will lead us to want to be good citizens, because our faith
urges us all the time to be good students; to be good
mothers who are capable of denying themselves and whose
faith and love give them the strength to bring up their
family in the best possible way; to be good and fair-minded
business men, etc. Christ's example leads us all to be hard-
working, warm-hearted, cheerful and optimistic. It urges us
to do more than we are strictly obliged to do. It teaches us
to live loyalty towards our spouse if we are married,
towards the firm we work for and towards the party or
group to which we belong. Love of God, if it is true love, is
the guarantee of love for men and shows itself in deeds.

*A decree went out from the Emperor Augustus,
enjoining that all the inhabitants of Israel should be
registered. Mary and Joseph made their way to Bethlehem.
Has it ever occurred to you that the Lord made use of the
prompt acceptance of a law to fulfil his prophecy?*

Love and respect the ways of behaving by which you
may live in amity with other people. Have no doubt, either,
that your loyal submission to duty can be the means for
others to discover Christian integrity, which is the fruit of
divine love, and to find God.[13]

---

[12] St Augustine, *Commentary on Psalm 57*, 11
[13] St. J. Escrivá, *op cit*, 322

75. WE WILL RISE AGAIN WITH OUR OWN BODIES

75.1 A truth of faith expressly taught by Jesus.

Some Sadducees, who did not believe in resurrection, came up to Jesus and tried to catch him out with a trick question. According to the ancient law of Moses,[1] if a man died without leaving any children, his brother had to marry his widow in order to leave descendants to his brother, and he had to give the name of the dead man to the first of his sons. The Sadducees want to make any belief in the resurrection of the dead appear ridiculous. They therefore invent a clever hypothesis.[2] If a woman marries seven times, having been left a widow by seven brothers in succession, whose wife will she be in heaven? Jesus answers them in a way that clearly shows the superficiality of their thinking. By his reply He reaffirms the truth of the resurrection of the dead. He takes a number of passages from the Old Testament, and as He expounds on the properties of risen bodies, He refutes all the objections brought forward by the Sadducees.[3]

Our Lord reproaches them for their ignorance of the Scriptures and for not acknowledging the power of God, for this truth had already been firmly asserted in what was revealed. Isaiah had prophesied: *Thy dead shall live, their bodies shall rise. O dwellers in the dust, awake and sing for joy! For thy dew is a dew of light, and on the land of*

---

[1] Deut 24:5 *et seq*
[2] Mark 12:18-27
[3] cf *The Navarre Bible*, note on Mark 12:18-27

the shades thou wilt let it fall.[4] The mother of the Maccabees encouraged her sons at the moment of their martyrdom, reminding them of the words of Scripture: *The Creator of the world ... will in his mercy give life and breath back to you again, since you now forget yourselves for the sake of his laws.*[5] And for Job this same truth was to be the consolation of his unhappy days: *For I know that my Redeemer lives, and at last He will stand upon the earth ... then from my flesh I shall see God.*[6]

We have to foster the virtue of hope in our souls, and in particular the hope of seeing God. *Those in love try to see each other. People in love have eyes only for their love. That's logical isn't it? The human heart feels this need. I would be lying if I denied my eagerness to contemplate the face of Jesus Christ. 'Vultum tuum, Domine, requiram!' – I will seek your countenance, O Lord.*[7] This desire will be satisfied if we remain faithful, because God's concern for his human creatures has ensured the resurrection of the flesh, a truth which constitutes one of the fundamental articles of the Creed.[8] *But if there is no resurrection of the dead, then Christ has not been raised. If Christ has not been raised, then our preaching is in vain, and your faith is in vain.*[9] *The Church believes in the resurrection of the dead ... and understands that the resurrection refers to the whole man:*[10] – to his body also.

The Magisterium has repeated on numerous occasions

---

[4] Is 26:19

[5] 2 Mac 7:23

[6] Job 19:25-26

[7] St. J. Escrivá, quoted in *Newsletter* No. 1

[8] cf *Symbolum Quicumque*; Dz 40: Benedict XII, Encyclical Letter, *Benedictus Deus*, 29 January 1336

[9] 1 Cor 15:13-14

[10] Congregation for the Doctrine of the Faith, *Letter about some matters referring to eschaatology*, 17 May 1979

that it is a question of the resurrection of the same body as we had during our passage on earth, in this flesh *in which we live, subsist and move.*[11] Because of this *the two formulae 'resurrection of the dead' and 'resurrection of the flesh'* are complementary expressions from one and the same tradition of the early Church,[12] and both modes of expression must continue to be used.

The liturgy repeats this consoling truth on numerous occasions: *In him* [Christ] *the hope of blessed resurrection has dawned, that those saddened by the certainty of dying might be consoled by the promise of immortality to come. Indeed for your faithful, Lord, life is changed not ended, and, when this earthly dwelling turns to dust, an eternal dwelling is made ready for them in heaven.*[13] God awaits us for ever in his glory. What great sadness for those who have counted solely on this world! What great joy to know that it will be ourselves, soul and body, who, with the help of grace, will live eternally with Jesus Christ, with the angels and with the saints, and who will give praise to the most Holy Trinity!

When we are grieved by the death of a loved one, or we are with mourners who have lost a member of their family, we have to manifest, to them as to ourselves, these truths that fill us with hope and consolation; life does not end here below on earth; we are going forward to meet God in eternal life.

75.2 Qualities and endowments of glorified bodies.

After death, each soul awaits the resurrection of its

---

[11] Eleventh Council of Toledo, year 675, Dz 287 (540); cf Fourth Lateran Council, chap. 1, *On the Catholic Faith*, Dz 429 (801) etc.

[12] Congregation for the Doctrine of the Faith, *Declaration about the translation of the article 'carnis resurrectionem' of the Symbolum Apostolicum*, 14 December 1983

[13] *Roman Missal*, Preface for the Dead I

own body, with which, for all eternity, it will be in Heaven, close to God, or in hell, far away from Him. In Heaven our bodies will have different characteristics, but they will continue to be bodies and they will occupy a particular place, in just the same way as the glorious Body of Christ and that of Our Lady do. We do not know where this place is, or what it looks like. Earth as we know it will be transfigured.[14] God's reward will come upon the glorious body making it immortal, for mortality is a sign of sin, and creation was submitted to mortality as a result of the guilt of sin.[15] Everything that threatens or is inimical to life will disappear.[16] Those who rise unto Glory, Saint John affirms in the Apocalypse, *shall hunger no more, neither shall they thirst any more; the sun shall not strike them, nor any scorching heat.*[17] The sufferings listed in the *Apocalypse* were the ones that caused greatest affliction to the people of Israel as they crossed through the desert: the scorching rays of the sun fell on them like darts, they rapidly became exhausted and the dry desert wind consumed their strength.[18] Those very tribulations are a symbol of the sufferings that the new People of God, the Church, will have to undergo for as long as her pilgrimage towards her final home shall last.

Faith and hope in the glorification of our body will cause us to give it the value and respect due to it. Man *is obliged to regard his body as good, and to hold it in honour, since God has created it and will raise it up on the last day.*[19] Nevertheless, how far removed from this just valuation is the cult that we so often see being given to the

---

[14] cf M. Schmaus, *Dogmatic Theology*, vol. VII, *The Last Things*, p. 514
[15] Rom 8:20
[16] cf M. Schmaus, *op cit*, Vol. VII, p. 225 *et seq*
[17] Rev 7:16
[18] cf Sir 43:4; Ps 121:6; Ps 91:5-6
[19] Second Vatican Council, *Gaudium et spes*, 14

body in our day. Certainly we have a duty to look after our body, to use the opportune means of avoiding illness, suffering, hunger... but without forgetting that it *has to rise again on the last day*. What matters is that it should rise in order to go to Heaven, not to hell. Over and above our health there is the loving acceptance of God's will concerning our lives. We should not have a disproportionate concern for our physical well-being. We should know how to put the pains and discomforts we may suffer to supernatural use – at the same time as we serenely use the ordinary means of avoiding them. If we manage to do this we will not lose our peace and our joy as we would if we were to put our hearts into merely relative and transitory things. Things only reach their final fulness in the glory of Heaven.

We should not forget for a moment what it is we are travelling towards. We should not forget the true value of the things that cause us so much concern. Our goal is Heaven. To be with Christ, soul and body, is what God created us for. This is why here on earth *Our last word? It can only be a smile ... a merry song.*[20] On the other side Our Lord is waiting for us, with his hands held out in a welcoming gesture.

75.3 Unity between the body and the soul.

Although there is a great difference between the earthly body and the transfigured body, there is still a close relationship between them. It is a dogma of faith that the risen body is identical in species and number to the earthly body.[21]

Taking as its basis the nature of the soul and several passages of Holy Scripture, Christian doctrine shows the

---

[20] L. Ramoneda Molíns, *Untattered Winds*, Montevideo, 1984
[21] cf Dz 287, 427, 429, 464, 531

fittingness of the resurrection of one's own body and of its new union with the soul. This is so, in the first instance, since the soul is only a part of man, and whilst it is separated from the body it cannot enjoy a happiness as complete and as fulfilled as that which will be possessed by the whole person. Besides, also, as the soul was created to be united to a body, a ultimate separation would violate the way of being proper to it. But a far more important reason is that it is more in conformity with divine wisdom, justice and mercy that souls should be united once more with their bodies so that both together, the whole man – who is not only soul, or only body – may share in the prize or the punishment merited during his passage through this life on earth. (Although it is of faith that the soul *immediately after death* receives its reward or punishment, without waiting for the moment of the resurrection of the body).

In the light of the Church's teaching, we observe in greater depth that the body is not a mere instrument of the soul, although it is from the soul that it receives its capacity to act and through this to contribute to the existence and development of the person. Through his body, man finds himself in contact with earthly reality, which he has to dominate, work upon and sanctify, because God has willed it so.[22] Through his body, man can communicate with others and work with them to build up and develop the social community. We must not forget, either, that through the body man receives the grace of the sacraments: *Do you not know that your bodies are members of Christ?*[23]

Though we are men and women of flesh and blood, grace exercises its influence on the body as well, divinising it in a certain way in anticipation of the glorious

---

[22] Gen 1:28
[23] 1 Cor 6:15

resurrection. It will greatly help us to live with the dignity and bearing of a follower of Christ if we consider frequently that this body of ours, now a temple of the Holy Spirit so long as we are in a state of grace, is destined by God to be glorified. Let us turn today to Saint Joseph and ask him to teach us to live with a wholesome and proper respect for others and for ourselves. Our body, the one that we have during our earthly life, is destined to share for ever in the ineffable glory of God.

76. THE FIRST COMMANDMENT

76.1 We should adore the 'one God'. Modern idolatry.

In the Gospel of today's Mass we hear how a Scribe asks a question. This man who is full of good will, wants to know which of the precepts of the Law is the most important; the essential one.[1] Jesus ratifies what had already been clearly expressed in the Old Testament: *Hear, O Israel: the Lord our God, the Lord is one; and you shall love the Lord your God with all your heart, and with all your soul, and with all your mind, and with all your strength. The second is this, You shall love your neighbour as yourself.* The Scribe identifies himself fully with Jesus' teaching, and immediately repeats the words that he has just heard. Our Lord speaks to him affectionately in words that will help him towards his definitive conversion. *You are not far from the kingdom of God.*

This commandment which is a summary of the whole *law of the Prophets*, begins by affirming the existence of *one God*. It is thus that it has been handed down to us in the Creed: *I believe in one God.* This is a truth that can be known by the natural light of reason, and the chosen people well knew that all pagan gods were false. In spite of this, idols were a constant temptation to them and a frequent cause of their turning away from the true God, *who took them out of the land of Egypt.* The prophets felt compelled to remind them of the falseness of those deities which they learned about as they came into contact with nations whose power and culture, which were very superior to their own, attracted and dazzled them. It was all a question of richer

---

[1] Mark 12:28-34

nations which were materially more advanced, but which were immersed in the darkness of superstition, ignorance and error. There were many occasions on which the chosen people failed to appreciate the incomparable richness of revelation and the treasure of the Faith. They abandoned the only *fountain of living waters* and turned instead towards broken and cracked cisterns which neither contained water nor had the capacity to hold any.[2]

The ancient pagans, men who were highly civilised for the age in which they lived, invented idols for themselves and found different ways of adoring them. Many civilised men of our day – new pagans – raise up idols which are still better constructed and more sophisticated. In our day there seems to be real adoration and idolatry[3] for everything that makes its appearance in the name of *progress* or that provides yet more material well-being, pleasure or comfort ... It seems that man almost completely forgets the fact that he is a spiritual being destined for eternal life. Those words of Saint Paul in his *Letter to the Philippians* are all too topical. *Their God is the belly, and they glory in their shame, with minds set on earthly things.*[4] It is the modern idolatry that tempts Christians who no longer give any thought to the immense treasure of their faith or the great richness of the love of God.

We break the first commandment of the decalogue when we put other things, even good things, before God, because then we love them in a disorderly way. When he does this man distorts the right order of created things and uses them for an end opposed to, or different from, that for which they were created. When the divine order taught by the decalogue is broken, man no longer finds God in

---

[2] cf Jer 2:13
[3] Second Vatican Council, *Apostolicam actuositatem*, 7
[4] Phil 3:19

creation: he then fabricates his own *God*, and radically hides himself within his own selfishness and pride. Still more, man foolishly tries to put himself in God's place, to set himself up as the source of all that is good and of all that is evil. In this way he falls into the temptation with which the devil coaxed our first parents: *You will be like gods* if you do not obey the commands of God.[5] Because of this very real temptation, each man, each woman, needs to often ask themselves – as we will now in our prayer – whether God is truly the first thing in their lives, the most important, the Highest Good, who guides the way they behave and make any decisions. We will be able to see this better if we examine how much effort we put into getting to know him better, for nobody can love what they do not know. Do we keep to the time that we set aside for our doctrinal-religious formation ...? Do we live an effective detachment from the things we possess or use so that they never become our most important good? *...Thou shalt love the lord thy God. Him only shalt thou adore.* The effort we make to follow the path God wants for each of us – each one's personal vocation – is the specific way we have of living that love and that adoration.

76.2 Reasons for loving God. Some faults and sins against the first commandment.

There are many very powerful reasons that move us to love God. He made us out of nothing and He Himself governs us, He facilitates for us the things necessary for life and sustenance ...[6] As well as this, we increased the debt we owe to him by the mere fact of our existence, when we were elevated by him to the order of grace and redeemed by him from the power of sin through the

---

[5] Gen 3:5

[6] *Catechism of the Council of Trent*, III, 2, no 6

Passion and Death of his Only-begotten Son and because of the countless benefits and gifts that we constantly receive from him. We have been given the dignity of being his children and temples of the Holy Spirit ... It would be a tremendous lack of gratitude on our part if we did not thank him for all that He has given us. Rather, Saint Thomas points out, it would be as though we were to make to ourselves another God, as the children of Israel did, when they left Egypt and made an idol for themselves.[7]

True love – human love and, far more eminently, love for God – always ennobles and enriches man, it makes him a little more like his Creator.

The personal history of each man shows how even human dignity and happiness are achieved by following the path of love of God, never by leaving that path. When the ultimate reason for living is placed in anything other than God, it lays the way open to our falling under the domination of our own passions. It has been truly said that *the way to hell is already hell.* The prophet Jeremiah's words to the people who allowed themselves to be dazzled by the idols of neighbouring nations are fulfilled: *you shall serve other gods day and night, for I will show you no favour.*[8]

Ceasing to love God means starting along a path on which one concession leads to another, for whoever offends God, *does not stop at one sin, but, on the contrary, he is driven to consent to others: everyone who commits sin is a slave to sin.* (John 8:34) This is why it is not at all easy to rise out of it, as Saint Gregory said: *the sin which is not wiped out by penance, gives rise to other sins by its own weight.*[9] Love of God leads us to hate sin, to keep

---

[7] cf St Thomas, *On the double precept of charity*, 1
[8] Jer 16:13
[9] St Thomas, *loc cit*

away – with the help of grace, and with our ascetic struggle – from any occasion in which there may be an offence against God, and to do penance for the faults and sins of our past life.

We must frequently make *positive acts* of love and adoration of God. We must fill each genuflection – a sign of adoration – before the tabernacle with meaning. We can repeat the words *Adoro te devote* or the words we say in the *Gloria* during Holy Mass: *We praise you, we bless you, we adore you, we glorify you, we give you thanks.*

We are lacking in love of God when we do not give him due worship, when we do not pray or when we pray badly. In the voluntary doubts we entertain against the faith, in reading books, newspapers or magazines which go against faith or morals by supporting superstitions or doctrines which are both the result of ignorance – however scientifically they are presented – and which are opposed to the faith. When we expose ourselves, our children or those under our care, to influences which are harmful to faith or morals. Whenever we fail to put our trust in God, in his power and in his goodness ... *This is the sign by which the soul can clearly see whether it loves God or not, with a pure love: if a person loves God, his heart will not be centred in on himself, it will not be concerned only with achieving its own likes and comforts. It will give itself to seeking the honour and glory of God and to pleasing Him. The more a heart keeps for itself, the less it has for God.*[10] We want to have our heart placed in God and in the people and the tasks that we do through Him and with Him.

76.3 Manifestations of our love for God.

Love for God should be expressed not only by giving him the worship which is his due, especially in the Holy

---

[10] St John of the Cross, *Spiritual canticle*, 9, 5

Mass, but it should embrace every aspect of a man's life, and it should have many manifestations. We love God through doing our work well, through faithfully fulfilling our duties towards our family, our work and society. With our mind and our heart ... in our external behaviour which should be proper to a child of God ... This commandment demands first of all adoration – that we give glory to God, which is not simply one more activity among many others, but rather the ultimate aim of all our actions, even those which can seem most ordinary: *whether you eat or drink, or whatever you do, do all to the glory of God.*[11] This basic attitude of adoration demands in practice that we should do everything, or at least want to do everything, in order to please God: that is to say, we should act with rectitude of intention.

Love for God and true love for one's neighbour is nourished by prayer and the sacraments, by the constant struggle to overcome our defects, in our effort to keep ourselves in His presence throughout the day. In a special way, the Holy Eucharist must be the source at which our love for God is constantly nourished. Then we will be able to say, with the words of the *Adoro te devote*: *To thee my heart I bow with bended knee.* I adore you, O Lord, ... my heart submits itself completely to you.

What is it that our heart is immersed in during the day? Let us see in our prayer whether we use *human devices* to remind ourselves frequently about God throughout the day, and in this way to love him and adore him.

---

[11] 1 Cor 10:31

77. THE GUARDIAN ANGEL

77.1 The continuous presence of our Guardian Angel.

As well as creating man and the whole of the visible world, God willed to further transmit his goodness by bringing into being angels, who are creatures which are exclusively spiritual and of the greatest perfection.

The angels, who are pure spirits which have no material or corporeal composition, are the most perfect of all the creatures in creation. On the one hand their intelligence proceeds with a simplicity and acuteness that man is incapable of, and their will is more perfect than the human will. On the other hand, as they have already been elevated to the beatific vision, they are glorified creatures who see God face to face. Through this greater excellence, of both nature and of grace, God constitutes the angels as his ordinary ministers. God generally wills to use secondary causes in the government of the world, and He gives them the capacity to influence men and other inferior beings. *The name attributed to them by Holy Scripture suggests that Revelation gives most importance to the truth as to the 'tasks of the angels in relation to men': angel, in fact, means 'messenger'.*[1]

They are mentioned in many places in the New and Old Testament, and their presence is so obvious as to be inseparable from the salvific action of God towards men.[2]

As well as intervening in the extraordinary events of the history of mankind, angels act constantly in the personal lives of men, because *God in his providence has*

---

[1] St John Paul II, *General Audience*, 30 July 1986
[2] cf *idem*, *General Audience*, 9 July 1986

given to the angels the mission of guarding the human race and of coming to the help of each man.[3] Angels are yet another token of God's goodness towards us, and because of this they help, encourage, and strengthen us. They attract us towards all that is good, and encourage us to have trust and serenity. One whole book of the Old Testament is dedicated to recounting the help given by an archangel, Saint Raphael, to Tobias and his family.[4] Without letting him know of his angelic nature, Saint Raphael accompanies young Tobias on a long and difficult journey, he gives him invaluable advice and performs countless services for him. At the end of the narrative, he presents himself: *I am Raphael, one of the seven holy angels who present the prayers of the saints and enter into the presence of the glory of the Holy One.*[5] God knew all about that family's upright behaviour: *When you ... prayed, I brought a reminder of your prayer before the Holy One; and when you buried the dead, I was likewise present with you. When you did not hesitate ... to go and lay out the dead, your good deed was not hidden from me, but I was with you.*[6]

Our life also is a long journey, and at the end of it when, with the help of grace, we reach the house of our Father God, our Guardian angel will be able to say to us: *I was with you*, for the Guardian Angels have the mission of helping each man to reach the supernatural end to which he has been called by God. *I send an angel before you*, God said to Moses, *to guard you on the way and to bring you to the place which I have prepared.*[7]

Let us thank God for having wanted to put us under

---

[3] *Catechism of the Council of Trent*, IV, 9, 4
[4] cf *First Reading of the Mass*, Year I, Tob 11:5-17
[5] Tob 12:15
[6] cf Tob 12:12-14
[7] Ex 23:20

the care of these princes of Heaven who function so intelligently and effectively. Let us frequently tell them of the respect that we have for them.

77.2 Devotion. Help in our everyday life and in the apostolate.

The *Acts of the Apostles* narrate some episodes that teach us about how the angels take care of man: the freeing of the Apostles from prison, particularly that of Peter, when Herod had threatened him with death: the intervention of an angel in the conversion of Cornelius and his family: the angel who leads the deacon Philip up to the minister of Candace, on the way from Jerusalem to Gaza.[8]

St John Paul II cited these events by way of example in his catechism on the angels. He comments: *we can understand how the Church has a conscious conviction as to the ministry entrusted to angels on behalf of men. Through this ministry, the Church professes her faith in the Guardian Angels, and venerates them in the liturgy with a special feastday. She recommends that we should have recourse to their protection by frequently saying a prayer, such as the one invoking the 'Angel of God'. This prayer is like a treasury of the beautiful words of Saint Basil: 'Each member of the faithful has beside him an angel to be his tutor and shepherd, and to lead him to life.'*[9] This prayer to the Angel of God, which so many Christians have learned from their parents' lips is usually translated into English, with some slight variations, as: *Angel of God, my guardian dear, To whom his love commits me here; Ever this day be at my side, To light and guard, to rule and guide. Amen.* It is a short prayer that even young children can say, and which can still help us when a large part of our life has

---

[8] cf Acts 5:18-20; 12:5-10; 10:3-8; 8:26 *et seq*

[9] St John Paul II, *General Audience*, 6 August 1986

already run and we still have the same need for protection and refuge. If we make a resolution to speak to our Guardian Angel more frequently today, we will not fail to be aware of his presence and we will receive much help and grace through his mediation. As well as giving us his spiritual help, he will give us his help and support in the little necessities of everyday life: finding something we have lost; remembering something we have forgotten and need to remember; arriving on time ... For everything that is ordered to the glory of God – and everything which is humanly good can be so ordered and directed – we can count on our Guardian Angel's help.[10]

We can also relate to the Guardian Angels of our friends, particularly where the task of bringing them closer to God and preventing them from turning away from him is concerned. Suggesting an opportune change of conversation. Supporting an initiative they may have to receive the sacrament of Penance or attend some means of ascetical or doctrinal formation ...

From ancient days, Christian piety has held that wherever the Most Holy Eucharist is reserved, angels are present who constantly adore Jesus in the Blessed Sacrament. Christian art, summarising popular piety, has often shown representations of angels surrounding the *monstrances* with their faces covered by their wings, because they consider themselves unworthy to be in his presence. So great is his majesty! Let us ask them to teach us to treat Jesus, really present in the tabernacle, with greater love and, at the same time, to show him the greatest possible reverence.

77.3 Asking his help for the interior life.

In spite of the perfection associated with spiritual

---

[10] cf G. Hubert, *My Angel will go before you*

nature, the angels do not have divine power or wisdom. They cannot read the inside of consciences, because they do not have unlimited knowledge. This is why it is necessary for us to let them know what we need of them at every moment. We do not need to use words, but it is necessary to direct ourselves to them with our mind, because their intelligence has the capacity to know what we explicitly imagine and think. Hence the frequent recommendation to foster a deep friendship with our own Guardian Angel.

In the order of the senses, our conversation with our Guardian Angel is less ascertainable than our conversation with a friend on earth, but its effectiveness is far greater. The advice he gives us comes from God and affects us more deeply than the human voice can: his capacity to hear and understand us is immeasurably greater than that of even one's best friend; not only because he is constantly at our side, but because he penetrates far more deeply into what we need or what we express.

The help he can give us in our interior life is very valuable. He can improve our piety, direct us in our mental and vocal prayer and help us particularly to keep presence of God. Our Guardian Angel will keep a check on our imagination, if we ask him, when it persists in getting in the way of our work or our relationship with God. Somehow he will suggest to us resolutions to improve, or a simple and practical way of specifying some good desire which has remained inoperative up to now. We will always know we can trustingly ask him to pray to God for us, saying those things to him that we are unable to express in our personal prayer, because of our own clumsiness.[11] We can ask him to suggest to us the right words in spiritual direction so that we learn to live complete simplicity and sincerity

---

[11] cf St. J. Escrivá, *The Forge*, 272

once we have made our examination of conscience together with him. In moments of weakness, our contact with our Guardian Angel will make us more serene.

The mission of the Guardian Angel begins on earth, but it will have its fulfilment in Heaven, because his friendship is destined to last forever. Its subject matter is so intimate and personal that the bonds of supernatural friendship which began on earth will remain forever in Heaven. At the moment when we give an account to God of our life, he will be a great ally of ours. *It is he who, at your particular judgement, will remember the kind deeds you performed for Our Lord throughout your life. Furthermore, when you feel lost, before the terrible accusations of the enemy, your Angel will present those intimations of your heart – which perhaps you yourself might have forgotten – those proofs of love which you might have had for God the Father, God the Son, God the Holy Spirit*

That is why you must never forget your Guardian Angel, and that Prince of Heaven will not abandon you now, or at that decisive moment.[12] He will be our best friend here on earth and afterwards for all eternity.

[12] *idem, Furrow*, 693

78. THE VALUE OF LITTLE THINGS

78.1 The alms of the 'poor widow'.

Saint Mark tells us in the Gospel of today's Mass[1] that Jesus sat opposite the Temple treasury and watched people putting money into the receptacle for alms. The scene takes place in one of the porticos, in the so-called *Treasure Chamber* or *Hall of offerings*. The days of the Passion were almost upon him.

Our Lord did not comment at all on the many people who contributed large amounts. But Jesus saw a woman come up who was dressed in the typical garb of widows, and who was obviously poor. She had perhaps waited for the crowd to thin out before depositing two small coins there. These coins had the least value of any in circulation at the time. Saint Mark explains the real value of these particular units of currency for the benefit of his non-Jewish readers, to whom his Gospel is principally addressed. He wants everyone to know how very little they were worth. In men's eyes that anonymous offering had very little value indeed; the two coins were worth *a quarter*, that is to say a quarter of an *as*. This coin in its turn was a tenth of a *denarius* which was the basic monetary unit; a *denarius* was the day's wages of a farm worker. *A quarter* would buy scarcely anything.

If anybody had been keeping a record of the offerings made that day in the Temple, he would probably have thought it was not worth recording this widow's contribution. We see in fact that this was the most valuable contribution of all! It would be so pleasing to God that

---

[1] Mark 12:38-44

Jesus called together his disciples, who were scattered around the place, so that they might be taught the lesson to be learned from this widow. Those tiny pieces of copper could scarcely be heard falling into the treasury box. Jesus however clearly perceived the love of this woman who said nothing but who was giving God all her savings. *Truly I say to you, this poor widow has put in more than all those who are contributing to the treasury. For they all contributed out of their abundance; but she out of her poverty has put in everything she had, her whole living.*[2]

It often happens that what God considers important is very different from what men consider important. His standard of measurement and theirs are not the same! We are generally impressed by the big gesture, by unusual things of the kind that attract everyone's attention. God is moved – the Gospels have left us plenty of examples – by little details filled with love, which are within the radius of action of everyone. He is, of course, also moved by happenings that we consider to be very important, but only when they are carried out with the same spirit of rectitude of intention, of humility and of love. The Apostles, who later were to be the very foundation of the Church, did not forget the lesson they were taught that day. That woman has taught all of us to touch God's heart every day in the only way most of us can: through little things. *Have you noticed how human love consists of little things? Well, divine Love also consists of little things.*[3]

In this passage of the Gospel we also learn the true value of things. We can turn everything that happens, no matter how inconsequential it may seem, into something very pleasing to God. And because it is pleasing to him, it is turned into something of great value. Only those things

---

[2] Mark 12:43-44
[3] St. J. Escrivá, *The Way*, 824

we make pleasing to God have any true and eternal value.

Today in our prayer we can consider the vast number of opportunities that present themselves to us: *Great opportunities to serve God seldom arise, but little ones are frequent. Understand then that he who is faithful over a few things will be placed over many. Do all things in the name of God, and you will do all things well. Provided you know how to fulfil your duties properly, then 'whether you eat or drink', whether you sleep or take recreation or turn the spit, you will profit greatly in God's sight by doing all these things because God wishes you to do them.*[4]

78.2 Lukewarmness and the neglect of little things.

It is the little things that make a job perfect, and worthy therefore of being offered to God. But it is not sufficient that what we are doing is good (work, prayer ...); it also has to be well finished. For there to be virtue, Saint Thomas Aquinas teaches, it is necessary to attend to two things: to what is being done and to the way it is being done.[5] As far as the way it is being done is concerned, the final touches with the chisel or the brush turn that work into a masterpiece. On the other hand, shoddy workmanship, work which is done clumsily or carelessly, is a sign of spiritual languor and of lukewarmness in a Christian who should be sanctifying himself through his daily work. *I know your works; you have the name of being alive, and you are dead ... For I have not found your works perfect in the sight of my God.*[6] The very nature of our Christian vocation demands that we take care of little things. Our aim should be *to imitate Jesus during his years in Nazareth*, those long years of work, of family life, of

---

[4] St Francis de Sales, *Introduction to the Devout Life*, III, 34
[5] cf St Thomas, *Quodlibet*, IV, 19
[6] Rev 3:1-2

friendly relationships with his countrymen. Doing little things with love for God's sake demands attention, sacrifice and generosity. A single isolated little detail may not in itself be very important: *what is small, is small: but he who is faithful in small things is great.*[7]

Love is what gives little things their value.[8] If this love were lacking, our endeavour to look after little things would be pointless; it would become a mania or be merely Pharisaical; we would pay tithes in mint, dill and cumin – as the Pharisees did – and we would run the risk of leaving out the most essential points of the Law – those of justice and of mercy. Although what we have to offer may seem very little – just as the contribution of that poor widow did – it acquires a great value if we place it on the altar and unite it to the offering that the Lord Jesus makes of himself to the Father. Then, *our humble surrender – insignificant in itself, like the oil of the widow of Sarepta, or the poor widow's mite – becomes acceptable in God's eyes through its union with Jesus' oblation.*[9] At other times, details in our work, in our study and in our relationships with other people *are the crowning of something good* which would remain *incomplete* without those details.

One of the most obvious warning signs that we are starting on the path of lukewarmness is that we give little value to the details of our life of piety, to details in our work, and to little specific acts of virtue: if we ignore these symptoms we end up paying little attention to big things as well. *The misfortune is all the more grievous and incurable when we barely notice that we are sliding downwards and only slowly come to realise this ... That if we are in this state we give a mortal blow to the life of the spirit is*

---

[7] St Augustine, *On Christian Doctrine*, 14, 35
[8] cf St. J. Escrivá, *op cit*, 814
[9] St John Paul II, *Homily*, Barcelona, 7 November 1982

something obvious to everyone.[10] Love for God on the other hand is shown by our inventiveness, by our unremitting zeal and our effort to *find in everything* an occasion for showing our love of God and for giving service to others.

78.3 Holiness is 'a cloth woven of little details'.

God is not indifferent to a love that knows how to care for small details. He is not indifferent, for example, as to whether we go to greet him – first of all – when we go into a church or when we happen to be passing by a church. He is not indifferent to the effort we make to arrive on time (better, a few minutes early) for Holy Mass, to the way we genuflect in front of him in the tabernacle or the way we behave or try to be recollected in his presence. Moreover, when we see somebody make a devout genuflection before the tabernacle, it is easy for us to think: that person has faith and loves God. That sign of adoration helps others to have greater faith and greater love. *It may perhaps seem to you that the Liturgy is made up of little things: the position of the body, genuflections, inclinations of the head, the way the thurible, the missal and the cruets are to be moved. It is then that we have to recall Christ's words in the Gospel: 'He who is faithful in a very little is faithful also in much.' Moreover, nothing is small in the Sacred Liturgy, when we think of the greatness of him towards whom it is directed.*[11]

Our spirit of mortification normally consists in specific little sacrifices throughout the day: keeping up a persevering struggle in our particular examination of conscience, sobriety at meals, punctuality, being pleasant to people, getting up on time, not leaving our work for later even though we find it difficult and trying, having order in

---

[10] B. Baur, *Frequent Confession*
[11] St Paul VI, *Address*, 30 May 1967

our work and taking care of the tools or implements and materials we use, being grateful for whatever food is put in front of us, not allowing ourselves whims and fancies.

In order to live charity in a way that becomes ever more refined and heroic, it will be necessary for us to apply this approach right down to the smallest and least important details of daily life. *Your duty to be a brother to all souls will lead you to practise the 'apostolate of little things', without others noticing it. You will want to serve them so that for them their way becomes agreeable.*[12] At times it will mean taking a real interest in what other people are saying; at other times it will be putting aside our own personal concerns so as to give our attention to the people we live with. It will mean not getting annoyed about what are really trivia, not being touchy, making people feel welcome. We will have to help others in a way they may not notice but which lightens their burden, to pray to God for them, for example, when they are in need, to avoid having critical spirit towards them and always to be grateful to them ... All of these things are within the reach and scope of each one of us. And we should do the same where each one of the virtues is concerned.

If we give attention to little things, we will live each day to the full, and will know how to fill each moment with the sense of preparation for eternity. To do this, let us frequently ask Mary for her help: *Holy Mary, Mother of God, pray for us ... now*, in every ordinary little situation of our life.

---

[12] St. J. Escrivá, *Furrow*, 737

Tenth Sunday: Year A

79. THE VIRTUE OF HOPE

79.1 The virtue of the wayfarer. Its foundation.

Christian asceticism pictures man's life on earth as a journey that has its end in God. We are all *homo viator*, the wayfarer longing to turn his steps quickly towards his definitive goal – God. Because of this we must all *'provide ourselves with hope' if we want to walk with a firm and certain step along the hard path in front of us.*[1] If the traveller were to lose hope of reaching his destination he would not continue with his journey. The only thing that keeps him on his way is his trust that he will some day reach his goal. We want to travel very straight and fast towards holiness – to God.

In human life, when a person sets himself an objective, his hope of achieving it is based on his physical resilience, his training and his own experience. When all is said and done it is based on his will power which enables him, if necessary, to draw strength from his very weakness. To reach the supernatural end of our existence, we do not rely on our own strength, but on God, who is all-powerful. He is the faithful friend who does not let us down. His goodness and mercy are not the same as the mercy and goodness of men, which are frequently *like a morning cloud, like the dew that goes early away.*[2]

Thanks to the supernatural virtue of hope, the Christian can be confident that he will reach his definitive objective which has already begun with Baptism in this life and will remain forever in the next. This objective is not

---

[1] St Paul VI, *Address*, 9 December 1975
[2] *First Reading*, Hos 6:1-6

something merely provisional, it is not the point of departure towards a further goal, as is the case with ordinary journeys. Through this virtue, we hope and long for that eternal life promised by God to those who love him, together with the means needed to achieve it and the support of his omnipotent help.[3] *The greater the difficulties* and the weaker we are, the stronger our hope in God has to be, for *the greater his help will be.* His closeness to our lives will be all the more evident. In the *Second Reading* of the Mass,[4] Saint Paul recalls how Abraham *believed in hope, against hope, that he should become the father of many nations; as he had been told.* John Paul I comments: *You will still say, 'How can this happen?' It can happen because it clings tightly to three truths: God is omnipotent, God loves me immensely, God is faithful to his promises. And it is He, the God of mercy, who awakens trust within me; trust which makes me know that I am not alone, or useless or cast aside, but rather that I am part of a salvific destiny which will end one day in Paradise.*[5]

Abraham did not hesitate despite his advanced years and his wife's sterility, but he trusted firmly in the power and mercy of God, *being fully persuaded that God is able to do what He promises.* And we, *Aren't we going to trust Jesus Christ 'who was delivered up for our sins and rose again for our justification'*? How could God leave us alone to deal with the obstacles we encounter which try to prevent us living in accordance with the call we have received from Him? He holds out his hand to us in many different ways: normally in our daily prayer, in our fulfilment of the plan of life we have set ourselves, in the sacraments, and, in a special way, in the advice we receive

---

[3] cf *Catechism of St Pius X*, 893
[4] Rom 4:18-25
[5] John Paul I, *Address*, 20 September 1978

in spiritual direction. Our Lord will never leave us alone on our journey through this world, and on which we frequently experience faintheartedness and weakness. The hope of becoming saints, of faithfully doing what God expects of each of us, depends on our accepting the hand that He holds out to us. This virtue is not based on our own worthiness, on our personal situation in life, or on the absence of difficulties, but on God's will – on his will that we should reach the goal – a will which is always accompanied by all the grace and help that we can need in any possible circumstances.

'Nam, et si ambulavero in medio umbrae mortis, non timebo mala' – though I should walk through the valley of the shadow of death, no evil will I fear. Neither my wretchedness nor the temptations of the enemy will worry me, 'quoniam tu mecum es' – for you Lord are with me.[6]

79.2 Hope in spite of setbacks, obstacles and pain.

The Gospel of today's Mass[7] shows us, once again, how God is closer to those who need him most. He has come to cure, to forgive, to save, and not only to preserve those who are whole. He is the divine Physician, who cures above all the sicknesses of the soul. *Those who are well have no need of a physician, but those who are sick*, He says to those who criticise him for eating with Publicans and sinners. When the things of the soul are not going well, when they have lost their health – and we are never completely well – Jesus is ready to pour out more care, more help. He does not abandon the sick man, and He does not abandon us. He does not give anybody up for lost. He does not leave us alone with our defects, with those things we can and must improve, because He calls us to sanctity

---

[6] St. J. Escrivá, *The Forge*, 194
[7] Matt 9:9-13

and he has the necessary graces ready for us. It is only the sick man who can cause the medicines, and the actions of the Physician who can cure all ills, to be ineffective by refusing to take them. The saving will of Christ for each one of his disciples – for us – is the pledge that we will reach what He himself asks of us.

The virtue of hope enables us to see that the difficulties of this life have a deeper meaning, they do not happen by chance, or by blind destiny, but because God wills them, or at least permits them, in order to bring forth greater good from those situations. They cause us to strengthen our trust in Him, to grow in the awareness of our divine filiation, to foster a greater detachment from our health and from earthly goods, to cleanse our hearts of intentions which are perhaps not altogether good, and to do penance for our sins and for those of all men ...

God tells each one of us that He prefers *mercy to sacrifice*, and if at some moment He allows pain and suffering to overwhelm us, it is because it is good for us, there is a far more lofty reason that we at times do not understand. It is for our own benefit, for that of our family, our friends, the whole Church. God wants a greater good, in just the same way as the mother who gives permission for an operation that will enable her child to become healthy again. It is at such moments that we have to believe with a faith which is strong and to re-awaken our hope, for it is only this virtue that will teach us to regard as a *treasure* what humanly presents itself to us as failure or perhaps as a great misfortune. These are the moments when we have to go close to the tabernacle and say slowly to Our Lord that we want everything that He wants. *This is our great mistake*, writes Saint Teresa, *we do not want to give ourselves absolutely to the disposition of our Lord, who knows best what is for our good.*[8] *Jesus, whatever you 'want', I love.*[9] Whatever You allow, I with your help, will accept as a great good, without laying down any limits or conditions. I will always thank you for everything, if you are close to me.

79.3 We need to frequently call to mind our hope of becoming saints.

In everything God works for good,[10] we will say in the depths of our heart, even though we may be passing through a great physical or moral difficulty. We have to overcome the way we tend towards selfishness, sadness or merely trivial objectives. We are journeying straight towards Heaven, and everything should become an instrument to bring us closer and enable us to arrive sooner. Everything, even our frailty.

In particular we must frequently practise the virtue of hope in all that concerns the state of own interior life, especially when it seems that we are not advancing, that our defects are slow in disappearing, that we constantly make the same mistakes. We may then view sanctity as something very distant from us; perhaps just an illusion. We have to have very much in mind at those moments the teaching of Saint John of the Cross, that the soul *who has the hope of Heaven achieves all that is hoped for.*[11] There are people who do not receive divine goods precisely because they do not have the hope of receiving them, because their outlook is too human, too narrow, and they do not even glimpse the greatness of the goodness of God who gives us his help us even though we do not in the least deserve it. And, this saintly author continues: *To win love's*

---

[8] St Teresa, *Life*, 6, 8
[9] St. J. Escrivá, *The Way*, 773
[10] Rom 8:28
[11] St John of the Cross, *Poems*, VI

chase I took my way, and full of hope began to fly. I soar'd aloft and soar'd so high, that in the end I reach'd my prey.[12] Our hope should be in God alone, it should be all-embracing, childlike as God wants it to be. If we are not miserly in the way we live it, we will obtain everything from Him. When holiness – which is the final aim of our lives – seems far away, we will try not to slacken in our struggle to come closer to God. We will try to have ardent hope and to fulfil out our duties. We will endeavour to put into practice the advice we have received in spiritual direction and the resolutions from our examinations of conscience or our last day of recollection. We will struggle resolutely against discouragement. At a given moment we may only be able to offer Our Lord the pain we feel for our defeats – on battle-fronts of greater or lesser importance – and our renewed desire to begin again. This will then be a humble offering which is very pleasing to God.

Hope encourages us to begin again with cheerfulness and patience and without getting tired. It makes us certain that, with the help of Our Lord and of His Mother, *Spes nostra*, our Hope, we will achieve victory, for He puts within our grasp all the means by which we may conquer.

---

[12] *idem*

80 THE ROOTS OF EVIL

80.1 Human nature in its original state of justice and holiness.

God placed man above the rest of creation, *to have dominion over the fish of the sea, and over the birds of the air, and over the cattle, and over all the earth, and over every creeping thing that creeps upon the earth.*[1] God therefore endowed man with intelligence and will, so that he might freely give to his Creator a glory far more excellent than that offered to him by any other creature. Led by his love for man, God ordained furthermore that He would raise man up so that he should have a share in his own *divine life*[2] and should be able to penetrate in some way his innermost mysteries. This was an endowment far greater than anything that nature could provide. To this end, God freely endowed man with sanctifying grace,[3] and with the supernatural virtues and gifts. He formed him in a state of holiness and justice and gave him the capacity to act supernaturally.[4] Through grace, the soul is transformed in such a way that, without ceasing to be human, man is divinised: the transformation could be compared to that of iron, which becomes incandescent when it is put into fire, and itself becomes like fire. This example is still imperfect, because grace effects a much deeper transformation in the soul than the one produced on iron by fire.

Moreover, God enriched Adam's nature with other

---

[1] Gen 1:26
[2] cf Second Vatican Council, *Lumen gentium*, 2
[3] cf Pius XII, *Humani generis*, 12 August 1950
[4] cf Council of Trent, Session V, can. 1

free gifts – of immunity from death, from concupiscence and from ignorance – which are called *praeternatural gifts*. This integrity of human nature in the state of original justice derived from the perfect and free subjection of man's will to his Creator. Strengthened by these gifts, man could not be deceived in the things he knew and he was immune from all error. Man's body enjoyed immortality, *not by its own power, but because of a supernatural power imprinted on the soul preserving the body from corruption so long as it was united to God.*[5] In Adam God contemplates the whole human race. The gift of original justice and holiness *had been given to man, not as to a single person, but as the general principle of the whole of human nature, in such a way that, after him, it would be transmitted by means of generation to all future men.*[6] We would all have been born in friendship with God and embellished in soul and body with the perfections granted by God. When the moment came, He would have confirmed each one in grace and carried him away from earth without his suffering any pain or having to undergo the moment of death. He would have come in this way to enjoy everlasting happiness in Heaven.

Thus God poured out his goodness on the first man, and this was in accordance with the divine plan. For this plan to be fulfilled, God wanted man to co-operate freely with grace. In a similar way He is asking us now, during this time of prayer, for our correspondence with the many graces we receive. It is here on earth that we have to earn Heaven, for all eternity.

---

[5] St Thomas, *Summa Theologiae*, I, 97, 1
[6] *idem, de malo*, 4, 1

80.2 The fellowship of all men in Adam. The transmission of original sin and its consequences. The struggle against sin.

We know through Revelation that the presence of original justice and of perfection in man, who was created in God's image, did not exclude man, insofar as he was a creature endowed with freedom, from submitting in the beginning to the test of freedom, just like the other spiritual beings.[7] God placed a single condition on man: *of the tree of the knowledge of good and evil you shall not eat, for in the day that you eat of it you shall die.*[8] We know from Holy Scripture about the sad transgression of this commandment, and today we read in the First Reading of the Mass[9] about the state man was left in. The devil himself, under the guise of a serpent, incited the first woman to disobey God's command: *She took of the fruit and ate; and she also gave some to her husband, and he ate.*[10] Immediately his free subjection to the Creator was broken, and the harmony that had existed among his potencies disintegrated; he lost original holiness and justice, he lost the gift of immortality, and *he became subject to 'him who has the power of death' (Heb 2:14), that is to say to the devil. By that sin of prevarication the whole person of Adam was changed for the worse, in all that concerned both body and soul.*[11] He was turned out of paradise, and even though human nature remained integral in what was proper to it, man has ever since encountered serious obstacles to his doing what is good, because there is now in him an inclination towards evil. Original sin, personally committed by our first parents at the beginning

---

[7] St John Paul II, *Address*, 3 September 1986
[8] *First Reading of the Mass*, Gen 2:17
[9] Gen 3:9-15
[10] Gen 3:6
[11] Council of Trent, Session V, can. 1

of history, is transmitted by means of generation to every man who comes into this world. It is a truth of faith which has been declared on several occasions by the Church.[12]

The reality of original sin and the conflict that it creates in the depths of each man's soul is a verifiable truth. Faith explains its origin, and we all experience its consequences. *What Revelation makes known to us is confirmed by our own experience. For when man looks into his own heart he finds that he is drawn towards what is wrong and feels that he is sinking beneath many evils which cannot originate in his holy Creator.*[13] Without grace, the human creature perceives that he is powerless to recover the dignity that is proper to him.

St Paul VI teaches that man is born in sin, with a fallen nature and without the gift of grace with which man was formerly endowed. The natural powers proper to his nature are wounded and subjected to the power of death. Moreover, *original sin is transmitted jointly with human nature, by propagation, not by imitation,* and *it is found in all men as though proper to each one.*[14]

There is a mysterious fellowship of all men in Adam, to such an extent that *all men can consider themselves a single man, in so far as all of them are bound together in the same nature that they have received from their first parent.*[15] The solidarity of the grace that united all men in Adam before the first disobedience, turned into solidarity in sin. *In the same way that original justice would have been transmitted to Adam's descendants, disorder has been transmitted in its place.*[16]

The spectacle presented by evil in the world and in us,

---

[12] cf Council of Orange, can. 2
[13] Second Vatican Council, *Gaudium et spes*, 13
[14] St Paul VI, *Creed of the People of God*, 16
[15] St Thomas, *Summa Theologiae*, I-II, 163, 1
[16] *ibid*, I-II, 81, 2

the tendencies and the instincts of the body which are not subject to reason, convince us of the profound truth contained in Revelation, and make us struggle against sin, which is the only true evil and is the root of all the evils that exist in the world: *So much wretchedness! So many offences! Mine, yours, those of all mankind ...*

'Et in peccatis concepit me mater mea!' (And in sin did my mother conceive me. Psalm 50:5). I, like all men, came into the world stained with the guilt of our first parents. And then ... my own sins: rebellions thought about, desired, committed ...

To purify us of this rottenness, Jesus willed to humble himself and take on the form of a slave (cf Phil 2:7), becoming incarnate in the spotless womb of Our Lady, his Mother, who is also your Mother and mine. He spent thirty years in obscurity, working as any other man, at Joseph's side. He preached. He worked miracles ... and we repaid him with the Cross.

Do you need more motives for contrition?[17]

80.3 Directing all human realities to God once again.

God expelled our first parents from paradise,[18] as a sign that men would come into the world in a state of separation from God. Instead of transmitting supernatural gifts, Adam and Eve transmitted sin. They lost the inheritance they should afterwards have left to their descendents: the consequences of sin were straight away experienced by the first sons of Adam and Eve. Cain killed Abel out of envy. In the same way all evil, be it personal or social, finds its origin in the sin of the first man. Even though Baptism completely forgives the guilt and the punishment of original sin and of the personal sins a man

---

[17] St. J. Escrivá, *The Way of the Cross*, Fourth Station, 2
[18] Gen 3:23

may have committed before receiving it, it does not free him from the effects of sin: man remains subject to error, to concupiscence and to death.

Original sin was a sin of pride.[19] Each one of us falls into the same temptation of pride when we seek to occupy – in society, in our private lives, in everything – the place that belongs to God: *you will be like gods.*[20] These are the very words man hears within the disorder of his senses and potencies. As at the beginning, he seeks now also – on many occasions – the autonomy that makes him the arbiter between good and evil, and forgets his greatest good, which consists of his love for and his submission to his Creator. It is in his Creator that he regains his peace, the harmony of his instincts and of his senses, and all other good things.

Our apostolate in the midst of the world will lead us to give each man with his deeds (legal ordinances, manual work, teaching ...) the place that really corresponds to him in relation to his Creator. When God is present within a nation or a section of society, fellowship becomes more human. There is no solution for the conflicts that devastate the world, or that prevent the achievement of greater social justice, which does not come about through a new closeness to God, through a conversion of heart. The evil is at the root – in the heart of man – and it is there that it has to be cured. The doctrine of original sin, of that poison so very much at work today in man and in society, is a fundamental point of the catechism and of all sound doctrinal formation which should never be missed out.

When we see ourselves confronted with a world that sometimes seems to be profoundly disturbed, we cannot simply fold our arms and shrug like a person overwhelmed

---

[19] cf St Thomas, *op cit*, II-II, 163, 1
[20] Gen 3:5

by a situation about which he can do nothing. We do not have to take part in the making of great decisions, which perhaps are not our concern anyway, but we do have to play our part in those matters that God has put within our reach, so as to give them a Christian orientation.

Our blessed mother, Mary, who was preserved immune from all stain of the guilt of original sin from the first moment of her immaculate conception by a singular grace and privilege[21] of God, will teach us to go to the root of the evil that besets us. Above all she will strengthen us in our friendship with God, whatever the situation in which we find ourselves.

---

[21] Pius IX, *Ineffabilis Deus*, 8 December 1854

TENTH SUNDAY: YEAR C

81. OUR RESPONSE TO SORROW AND NEED

81.1 The raising of the son of the widow of Nain. Jesus always shows compassion towards sorrow and suffering.

The Gospel of today's Mass[1] enables us to contemplate Jesus arriving in a small town called Nain, accompanied by his disciples and followed by a large crowd. It was about six miles south-east of Nazareth and five miles from Capharnaum.

Just inside the gate of the place the crowd accompanying Our Lord crossed the path of a procession of people who were carrying to his burial the only son of a widow. According to Jewish custom, they were carrying the body, which was wrapped in linen, on a bier or stretcher. The procession, led by his mother, was made up of *a large number of people from the city*.

The group coming into Nain stopped in front of the dead man. Jesus went up to the mother, who was weeping for her son, and He took pity on her. *Jesus crosses paths again with a crowd of people. He could have passed by or waited until they called him. But He didn't. He took the initiative, because He was moved by a widow's sorrow. She had just lost all she had, her son.*

The evangelist explains that Jesus was moved. Perhaps He even showed signs of it, as when Lazarus died. Jesus Christ was not, and is not, insensitive to suffering ...

Christ knows He is surrounded by a crowd which will be awed by the miracle and will tell the story all over the countryside. But He does not act artificially, merely to

---

[1] Luke 7:11-17

*make an effect. Quite simply He is touched by that
woman's suffering and cannot keep from consoling her. So
He goes up to her and says, 'Do not weep' (Luke 7:13). It
is like saying, 'I don't want to see your crying; I have come
on earth to bring joy and peace.' And then comes the
miracle, the sign of the power of Christ who is God. But
first came his compassion, an evident sign of the
tenderness of the heart of Christ the man.*[2] He laid his hand
on the young man's body and ordered him to get up. *And
He gave him to his mother.*

The miracle is at the same time a good example of the
concern we should feel for other people's misfortunes. We
must learn from Jesus. In order to have a heart like his we
have to turn in the first place to prayer; *we should ask Our
Lord to give us a good heart, capable of having
compassion for other people's pain. Only with such a heart
can we realize that the true balm for the suffering and
anguish in this world is love, charity. All other
consolations hardly even have a temporary effect and leave
behind them bitterness and despair.*[3]

We should ask ourselves in our prayer today whether
we know how to love everybody who crosses our path in
this life, whether we have a real concern for their
misfortunes, a concern that leads us to act in an effective
way; thus, when we come to our daily examination of
conscience we will find in the course of it that we have
many acts of charity and of mercy we can offer to God.

81.2 Imitating Our Lord. Love with deeds. Order in charity.

Jesus Christ comes *to save the lost*,[4] to take upon

---

[2] St. J. Escrivá, *Christ is passing by*, 166
[3] *ibid*, 167
[4] Luke 19:10

himself our wretchedness in order to relieve us of the burden of it. He comes in order to show his compassion for those who suffer and are in need. He does not pass by. He halts, as we see in today's Gospel. He consoles and He saves. *Jesus makes mercy one of the principal themes of his preaching ... There are many passages in the teaching of Christ that manifest love-mercy under some ever fresh aspect. We need only consider the Good Shepherd who goes in search of the lost sheep or the woman who sweeps the house in search of the lost coin.*[5] And He himself taught us through his constant example how we should behave towards our suffering neighbour.

And just as God's love is not simply an emotion or feeling, but something that leads Our Lord to perform deeds that show it, so our love for our neighbour has to be a love that shows itself in deeds. *Let us not love in word or in speech*, says Saint John, *but in deed and in truth.*[6] And *those deeds of love, in other words, the service it implies, should also maintain a definite order. Just as love leads us to want the best for those we love and to do good to them, so the order of charity should lead us to want, above all, that people should be united to God, and to endeavour to bring this union about. We have to realise that the most sublime good, the definitive good, consists in union with God. Apart from God no other partial good has any meaning.*[7] The opposite to this, namely the seeking of material goods as the most important thing for oneself and for others, is proper only to pagans or to those Christians who have allowed their faith to grow lukewarm, so that, in fact, it has very little influence on their daily lives.

As we consider the primacy of spiritual good over any

---

[5] St John Paul II, *Dives in misericordia*, 30 November 1980, 3
[6] 1 John 3:18
[7] F. Ocáriz, *Love for God, love for men*

material good, we must not forget the commitment that every Christian with a well-formed conscience has; it is to promote a more just social order, because charity also refers, albeit secondarily, to the material well-being of all men.

The importance of charity as regards the attention we should pay to the material needs of our neighbour, a consideration presupposing justice and help in shaping this virtue, is such that Jesus Christ himself when speaking about the last judgement, declared: *Come, O blessed of my Father ... for I was hungry and you gave me food ... I was thirsty and you gave me drink ...* [8] And forthwith Our Lord draws attention to the way in which those who have neglected these deeds will be condemned.[9] Let us ask Our Lord to give us an ever-watchful charity, because if we are to achieve salvation and arrive at our rightful destination, we need to *recognise Christ when He comes out to meet us in our brothers, in the people around us.*[10] Every day we encounter him; in the midst of our family, in our place of work and when we are away from home ...

81.3 In order to love we need to understand. Love for those whose need is greatest.

Through his meeting with that poor woman of Nain, Jesus wants to show us how He immediately understands the sorrow and the feelings of the mother who has lost her only child. Jesus shares in that woman's suffering. In order to love it is necessary to understand and to share. It is the real meaning of sympathy.

We ask Our Lord today to give us a big heart, a heart which is full of understanding, so that we are able to suffer

---

[8] cf Matt 25:31-40
[9] cf Matt 25:41-46
[10] St. J. Escrivá, *op cit*, 111

with those who suffer, and to rejoice with those who rejoice. We must ask him to help us to prevent that suffering whenever we can, and to make us into people who live and spread happiness wherever we happen to be. We should ask for the vision, too, to understand that the true and principal good of others, which bears no comparison with any material or worldly good, consists in their union with God, which will lead them one day to total happiness in Heaven. It is not a question of *superficial comfort* for the disinherited of this world, or for those who undergo suffering or failure, but rather is it the profound hope of the man who knows he is a child of God and co-heir with Christ to eternal life, no matter what his situation in worldly terms may be. Robbing man of that hope, and substituting for it another hope of a purely natural, material happiness, is to deceive man in such a way that, owing to the precariousness of such a Utopia, it will lead him, sooner or later, into the depths of despair.[11]

Our compassionate and merciful attitude, manifested in deeds, has to be shown in the first place towards the people we are normally with, towards those whom God has placed, day in day out, in our company, and towards those of them who are most in need. It is unlikely that compassion for people further away will be pleasing to God if we neglect the many opportunities that present themselves to us each day to practise justice and charity towards the people who belong to our family or who work beside us.

The Church is aware that the truth about the God who saves cannot be separated from the manifestation of his love of preference for the poor and needy.[12] *Works of mercy, as well as the relief they give to those in need, serve to improve our own souls and those of the people who accompany us in*

---

[11] cf F. Ocáriz, *op cit*
[12] cf St John Paul II, *Redemptoris Mater*, 25 March 1987, 37

those activities. We have all experienced that contact with the sick, with the poor, with children and with adults who go hungry, always means for us a meeting with Christ in his weaker or unprotected members, and for that very reason such contact can mean a spiritual enrichment. The Lord enters with greater intensity into the soul of him who approaches his little brothers, moved not by a desire of mere altruism – which is a noble desire but not one that is supernaturally effective – but by the very sentiments of Jesus Christ, the Good Shepherd and the Physician of souls.[13]

Let us turn to the Most Sacred Heart of Jesus and to the heart of Mary, his Mother, and ask that we should never remain passive with regard the demands of charity. In this way we will be able to invoke Our Lady with confidence, in the words of the liturgy: *Recordare, Virgo Mater Dei...* Remember, O Virgin Mother of God, as you stand in his presence, *ut loquaris pro nobis bona*, to speak good things on our behalf and ask for our needs.[14]

---

[13] Bl. A. del Portillo, *Letter*, 31 May 1987, 30
[14] *Roman Missal, Antiphon from the Common Mass of Our Lady*

82. THE DIVINE MERCY

82.1 God's mercy is infinite, eternal and universal.

Saint Paul calls God *the Father of mercies*,[1] thus indicating God's infinite compassion towards mankind, whom He loves dearly. Few other truths, perhaps, are insisted on as repeatedly as this particular truth: God is infinitely merciful; He has infinite compassion on men, particularly on those who have to bear the greatest of all misfortunes – sin. Scripture uses a great variety of terms and images – so that we should really learn the lesson – to teach us that God's mercy is *eternal*, that is to say without limit in time.[2] It is *immense*, without limitation of place or space. It is *universal*, since it is not restricted to one nation or one race, and it is as extensive and wide-ranging as are the needs of man.

That the Son of God, the Word, took flesh is a proof of this divine mercy. He came to forgive, to reconcile men with one another and with their Creator. *Meek and humble of heart*, He offers relief and rest to all who suffer tribulation.[3] The Apostle James calls the Lord *compassionate and merciful*.[4] In the *Epistle to the Hebrews* Christ is the *merciful high priest*,[5] and this attitude of God towards mankind is ever the reason for his salvific action.[6] He never tires of forgiving men, of encouraging them to journey towards their definitive homeland, and to

---

[1] *First Reading of the Mass*, Year I, 2 Cor 1:1-7
[2] Ps 100
[3] Matt 11:28
[4] Jas 5:11
[5] Heb 2:17
[6] Tit 2:11; 1 Pet 1:3

overcome their weaknesses and the pain and deficiencies they may encounter in this life. *The truth, revealed in Christ, about God 'the Father of mercies', enables us 'to see him' as particularly close to man, especially when man is suffering, when he is under threat at the very heart of his existence and dignity.*[7] This is why the unchanging plea the afflicted (the lepers, the blind, the lame ...) make to Jesus is *have mercy on us.*[8]

Jesus' goodness towards men – towards all of us – goes far beyond human reckoning. *That man who fell among robbers who stripped him and beat him and went away leaving him half dead ... It was He who comforted him and bound up his wounds, pouring on oil and wine. He it was who then made him mount on his own horse, and found accommodation for him at that inn, so that he should be cared for. It was He who paid a large amount of money for him, and promised the inn-keeper that, on his return, He would pay him whatever more He should spend.*[9] He has taken the same care of each individual man. Time and again He has lifted us up when we have been badly injured, He has poured balm into our wounds, and has bound them up. Our salvation is in his mercy; in just the same way as the sick, the blind and the crippled have done, we must turn to the Tabernacle and say to him: Jesus have mercy on me ... God pours out his mercy in a special way through the sacrament of Penance. There he cleanses us from our sins, welcomes us, cures us, washes our wounds, gives us respite ... Moreover, in this sacrament He completely heals us and we receive new life.

---

[7] St John Paul II, *Dives in misericordia*, 30 November 1980, 2
[8] Matt 9:27; 14:20; 15:22; 20:30; Mark 10:47; Luke 17:13
[9] St Maximus of Turin, *Letter*, 11

82.2 Mercy presupposes justice, and surpasses the demands made on us by the virtue of justice.

Blessed are the merciful, for they shall obtain mercy,[10] we read in the Gospel of today's Mass. God is particularly anxious that his children should develop this attitude towards their brothers and sisters, and He tells us that the mercy shown towards us will be in proportion to the mercy we ourselves have shown. *The measure you will give will be the measure you get.*[11] It will be a proportionate amount, not the same amount, for God's goodness surpasses all our reckonings. To a grain of wheat will correspond a grain of gold; to our sack of wheat will correspond a sack of gold. For the fifty denarii we forgive, the ten thousand talents (a fortune of incalculable wealth) that we owe to God will be written off. But if we harden our hearts towards the misfortunes and weaknesses of others, the less accessible and narrower will be the gate by which we are to enter Heaven and find God himself. *He who would receive mercy in Heaven must practise it in this world. Because of this, since we all long for mercy, we must act in such a way that mercy becomes our advocate in this world, so that we may afterwards be free in the next. There is mercy in Heaven which is reached by means of showing mercy on earth.*[12]

Occasionally we try to set mercy up against justice, as though the one meant laying aside the demands of the other. This is certainly a mistaken view, for it makes mercy unjust, whilst the truth of the matter is that mercy is the fulness of justice. Saint Thomas teaches[13] that when God acts with mercy – and when we imitate him – He does

---

[10] Matt 5:7
[11] Matt 7:2
[12] St Caesar of Arles, *Sermon*, 25
[13] St Thomas, *Summa Theologiae*, I, 21, 3, 2

something which is above justice, but which presupposes
having previously had and lived this virtue to the full. In
the same way, if someone gives two hundred denarii to a
creditor to whom he owes only one hundred, he does not
act against justice, but – as well as satisfying what is just –
he behaves with liberality and mercy. This attitude towards
our neighbour is the fulness of all justice. Moreover,
without mercy we come in the end to a *system of
oppression of the weakest by the strongest* or to *an arena of
permanent struggle of some against the others*.[14]

With justice alone it is not possible for there to be real
family life, or harmony at work, or concord amidst the
great variety of social activities. It is obvious that if we do
not live justice in the first place, we cannot practise the
mercy that God asks of us. But after giving to each one
what is his, after giving what belongs to him in justice, a
merciful attitude leads us much further: for example, it
leads us to know how to forgive offences promptly (even
though these offences may be just in our imagination or
caused by our own lack of humility); it leads us to help
someone with his work on those occasions when he has
more to do or is feeling tired, to give a word of encouragement to someone who is finding things difficult or is
feeling worried or anxious (maybe a member of his family
is ill, he has failed an examination, or he has lost some
money ...); it leads us to be ready to perform those little
deeds of service that are so necessary to the people around
us, and so much a part of living and working with other
people ...

82.3 Some effects of mercy.

However just relations between men become, it will still
always be necessary to practise mercy each day. This virtue

---

[14] St John Paul II, *op cit*, 14

enriches and perfects the virtue of justice. Our merciful approach to life should encompass and have an eye to the most diverse needs – material needs (food, clothing, health, employment ...); needs of a moral order (helping our friends go to Confession ... waging a fight against the great ignorance there is as to the most elementary truths of the Faith by teaching the *Catechism* and co-operating in the work of formation ...). Mercy (*misericordia*) is, as we see from its etymology, a disposition of the heart that leads us to commiserate with the misfortunes of others that we encounter each day as though they were our own. When we understand this we must first of all try to show understanding for other people's failings and defects. We must try to develop a positive, kindly outlook that will dispose us to think well of people, to forgive easily their faults and their errors, and never to neglect giving them the most appropriate help. Such an attitude should lead us to respect the radical equality of all men – for they are all children of God – and the differences and peculiarities of each individual's personality. Mercy demands true compassion, and an effective sharing in the misfortunes of our brothers and sisters, both material and spiritual.

Our Lord showed that this beatitude was the straight path along which we will achieve happiness in this life as well as in the next. *It is like a little trickle of fresh water that springs from the outpouring mercy of God and that gives us a share in his very happiness. It teaches us, far better than books can, that true happiness does not consist in having and possessing, in judging and in always being right, in imposing justice according to our lights. It consists rather in letting ourselves be taken up and clasped by God, in ourselves submitting to his judgement and to his generous justice, and in learning from him the daily practice of mercy.*[15] It is then we understand that *it is more blessed to give than to receive.*[16] A compassionate and merciful heart is a heart filled with happiness and peace. In this way we too will receive that mercy that we need so badly; and we will owe it to those who have given us the opportunity of doing something for them and for God. Saint Augustine tells us that mercy is the lustre – the glory – of the soul; it enriches it and causes its appearance to be good and beautiful.[17]

As we finish this time of prayer, let us turn to our Mother, Mary, for she is *the woman who knows most deeply the mystery of God's mercy. She knows its price and she knows how deep it is. In this sense we also call her Mother of mercy.*[18]

Although we may already have abundant proof of her motherly love for each one of us, we can say to Our Lady, *Monstra te esse matrem!*[19] Show us that you are our mother, and help us to show that we are good children of yours and brothers of all men.

---

[15] S. Pinckaers, *In search of happiness*, Madrid, 1981
[16] cf Acts 20:35
[17] cf St Augustine, in *Catena Aurea*, vol. I, p. 48
[18] St John Paul II, *op cit*, 9
[19] *Divine Office, Second Vespers of the Common of Our Lady*, Hymn, *Ave maris stella*

83. SALT THAT HAS LOST ITS SAVOUR

83.1 Lukewarmness.

Our Lord tells his disciples that they are *the salt of the earth*;[1] they do to the world exactly what salt does to food, keeping it from going bad and making it agreeable to the palate. But salt can sometimes lose its savour or in itself deteriorate. Then it quite simply becomes useless. This kind of change is, after sin, the saddest thing that can befall a Christian, the point of whose existence has been to give light to many, whereas he has in fact now become darkness. Far from being able to point the people he comes in touch with in the right direction, he now becomes disoriented and aimless himself. Having been placed on earth so as to give strength to others he has nothing left to communicate now but weakness.

Lukewarmness is a disease of the soul that affects both the intellect and the will, and leaves the Christian devoid of the strength to carry out apostolate, at the same time filling him with a deep feeling of sadness and impoverishment. The sickness starts with a weakening of the will, brought about by means of repeated faults and culpable omissions, of frequently doing wrong and, possibly even worse, failing to do what is right. The Christian no longer sees Christ clearly on the horizon of his life. Because he has been consistently careless regarding the little details that are a proof of love, he discovers that Christ now seems far removed from him. His interior life undergoes a profound change; it no longer has Jesus as its focal point. The man who is lukewarm finds that his practices of piety have

---

[1] Matt 5:13

become empty of content; he no longer puts his heart and soul into them. He 'goes through the motions', performing them out of routine or habit, not any longer out of love.

In this state a man loses all spontaneity and joy – recognisable characteristics of a soul in love – in responding to anything that has reference to God. A lukewarm Christian is somehow 'inside out'; his is a soul that has 'grown weary' in its endeavour to improve. Christ has faded from the horizon of his life. The soul descries God, if it sees him at all, as a remote and distant figure, hazy and indistinct, with ill-defined features, and probably indifferent to him. No longer does he perform positive acts of generosity as he formerly did: he is now prepared to settle for much less.[2]

Saint Thomas cites as a feature of this state *a kind of sadness, whereby a man becomes sluggish in spiritual exercises because they weary the body*.[3] All norms of piety and devotion become for us a burden we find increasingly hard to bear, instead of being for us a powerful centre of energy, driving us forward and helping us to overcome any difficulties we may encounter.

There are many Christians who have sunk into lukewarmness. There is in our time a great deal of savourless salt about. Let us consider in our prayer today whether we are going forward with the firmness and confidence that Jesus asks of us, whether we regard our conversation with him as the treasure which enables our interior life to intensify and keep growing, and whether, we properly nourish our love. Let us consider whether, when we become aware of our weakness and our lack of correspondence with grace, we promptly make acts of contrition in order to close the breach the enemy has made and is attempting to widen in

---

[2] cf F. Fernández, *Lukewarmness*, Madrid, 1986
[3] St Thomas, *Summa Theologiae*, I, 63, 2

our defences.

83.2 True piety; feelings; spiritual aridity.

We must not confuse the state of the lukewarm soul with a sensation of dryness sometimes experienced when we perform our acts of piety, a sensation produced on occasions or for long periods by tiredness or illness, or by the temporary loss of physiological keenness and enthusiasm. In such cases, in spite of the feeling of dryness, our will is firmly set on all that is good. Our soul knows that it is travelling directly towards Christ, even though it is at the moment passing over a stony waste where the going is hard and we cannot find a single well or even a spring of cool water. But our soul knows where its destination lies and goes straight towards it in spite of our weariness and thirst and the unfriendly terrain we have to tread.

In the state of what is called *aridity*, even though the soul has no feeling and it seems difficult to pray, to carry on any real conversation with God, true devotion nevertheless remains. Saint Thomas Aquinas has defined this type of devotion as the *will to give oneself readily to things concerning the service of God.*[4] This 'readiness' grows weak if the will falls into a state of lukewarmness: *I have this against you*, says the Lord, *that you have abandoned the love you had at first,*[5] that you have weakened, that you no longer love me as you did formerly. The person who is determined to keep up his prayer even in times of aridity, when all feeling is absent, is perhaps like him who draws water from a well, bucket by bucket: one aspiration after another, an act of sorrow ... It is hard work and it demands effort, but he does draw out water. On the other hand, in a state of lukewarmness our imagination

---

[4] St Thomas, *op cit*, II-II, 82, 1
[5] Rev 2:4

strays and runs wild, we are no longer firmly determined to dispel voluntary distractions and, in practice abandon prayer with the excuse that we are getting no results from it. Genuine conversation with God, on the other hand, even if God allows it to be *arid*, is always fruitful, whatever the circumstances, as long as we have rectitude of intention and are firmly intent on being close to God.

We must remind ourselves here and now, in God's presence, that true piety is not a matter of feelings, although sensitive affections are good and they can be a great help in our prayer and in the whole of our interior life, because they are an important part of human nature as it was created by God. But such affections must not occupy a disproportionately important place in our life of piety; they are not the main part of our relationship with God. Feelings help, but achieve no more than this assistance, because the essence of piety does not consist in feelings, but in the will's being determined to serve God, quite independently of any state of mind – which is always so changeable! – or of any other circumstances. In matters of piety we must take care not to let ourselves be guided by feelings, but rather by our intellect, enlightened and helped, as we pray it will be, by faith. *To allow oneself to be guided by feelings would be like handing over the management of one's house to a servant whilst you as its real owner abdicate responsibility for it. It is not feelings that are bad, but rather the degree of importance we attribute to them ...* [6]

Lukewarmness is sterile; salt without savour *is no longer good for anything except to be thrown out and trodden under foot by men.* [7] On the other hand, *aridity* can be the positive sign that God wants to purify a particular soul.

---

[6] J. Tissot, *The Interior Life*, p. 100
[7] Matt 5:13

83.3 The need to have interior life.

As men we can be a cause of happiness or of sadness, of light or of darkness. We can be the source of peace or of anxiety, either the leaven that enhances or a dead weight that hinders the progress of others. Our passage over this earth can never be a matter of indifference as far as others are concerned. We help others to find Christ or we separate them from him. We enrich others or we impoverish them. And we come across so many of these others – friends, workmates, members of our family, neighbours ... who seem to go after material goods as though they hungered for them, material goods that only serve to lure them away from their true Good who is Jesus Christ. They journey through life like men who are lost. If the guide of the blind is not to become blind himself,[8] it is not enough for him to know the way from hearsay or from coming across mere references to it. If we are to help the people around us, it is not enough for us to have a vague and superficial knowledge of the way. We need to walk along it ourselves and to have first-hand knowledge of the obstacles that lie in our path and have to be surmounted. We need to have interior life, to enter daily into personal conversation with Jesus. We need to know his doctrine ever more deeply; to struggle with still more determination to overcome our own defects. The apostolate is the result of a great love for Christ.

The first Christians were true *salt of the earth*, and they preserved people and institutions – the whole of society – from corruption. What can it be that has happened in so many nations? Why is it that Christians should now be giving the sad impression that they are unable to slow down and halt that wave of corruption that is bursting in on the family, on schools and on institutions

---

[8] cf Matt 15:14

...? The Faith is still the same. And Christ lives among us now just as He did previously. His power is still infinite – divine. *Only the lukewarmness of so many thousands, indeed millions, of Christians, explains how we can offer to the world the spectacle of a Christianity that allows all kinds of heresies and stupidities to be propounded within itself. Lukewarmness destroys the strength and endurance of the Faith, and is the soulmate, in both a personal and a collective way, of compromise and of a spirit of comfort-seeking.*[9] It is difficult to explain many of the things that happen nowadays at a personal and at a public level, if we do not bear in mind that so many people who should be awake, watchful and attentive have allowed their Faith to fall asleep; love has been snuffed out in so very many hearts. In many spheres, the 'normal Christian' now generally means someone who is lukewarm and mediocre. Among the first Christians the 'normal Christian' meant one who lived the *heroism of each day*, and when the occasion presented itself, accepted martyrdom itself: it could and did mean very often the surrender of one's very life in defence of the Faith.

When love grows cold and faith falls asleep, the salt loses its savour and is no longer good for anything. It is just something for throwing away. What a pity if a Christian were to become as useless as this! Lukewarmness is often the cause of apostolic ineffectiveness, because if we are in its grip the little we do becomes a task devoid of human or supernatural attractiveness, and bereft of a spirit of sacrifice. Faith that appears moribund and radiates little love is unable to win anyone over or find the right words with which to attract others to a deep and intimate relationship with Christ.

Let us fervently ask God for the strength to react. We

---

[9] P. Rodríguez, *Faith and Life of faith*

will be the true *salt of the earth* if we keep up our daily conversation with God and if we go with ever-greater faith and love to receive the Holy Eucharist. Love was, and is, the moving force in the life of the saints. It is the whole *raison d'être* of every life dedicated to God. Love gives us wings with which to soar over any personal barriers to our advance, or any obstacles presented to us by our surroundings. Love makes us unyielding when confronted by setbacks. Lukewarmness gives up at the slightest difficulty (a letter we should write, a telephone call we should make , a visit, a conversation, the lack of some material means ...) It makes mountains out of molehills. Love for God, on the other hand, makes a molehill out of a mountain; it transforms the soul, gives it new lights and opens up new horizons for it; it makes the soul capable of achieving its highest desires and gives it capacities it had never as much as dreamed of possessing. Love does not make a fuss about the effort involved, and fills the soul with happiness as it surveys the results of its efforts.

As we finish our meditation, let us turn with confidence to the Blessed Virgin, the perfect model of loving correspondence with the Christian vocation. Let us ask her to remove effectively from our soul any shadow of lukewarmness. Let us ask our Guardian Angels, also, to make us diligent in God's service.

TENTH WEEK: WEDNESDAY

84. ACTUAL GRACES

84.1 We need grace in order to do good.

Through original sin human nature lost the state of sanctity to which it had been raised by God, and as a consequence it was also deprived of the integrity and interior order that it had once possessed. Since the first sin was committed man has lacked the strength of will that would enable him to fulfil all the moral precepts that are known to him. After sin made its appearance on earth, doing good became something difficult. *Man therefore is divided in himself. As a result, the whole life of men, both individual and social, shows itself to be a struggle, and a dramatic one, between good and evil, between light and darkness.*[1]

God's help is absolutely necessary if we are to be able to perform acts which are directed towards the supernatural life. *Not that we are sufficient of ourselves to claim anything as coming from us; our sufficiency is from God.*[2] Moreover, because of original sin, that help becomes still more necessary. *No one is freed from sin by himself or by his own efforts, no one is raised above himself or completely delivered from his own weakness, solitude or slavery.*[3] We all need Christ, who is the model, master, physician, liberator, saviour, and giver of life.[4] Without him we can do nothing. With him we can do all things.

Although human nature is not corrupted by original sin, even after Baptism we experience a tendency towards

---

[1] cf Second Vatican Council, *Gaudium et spes*, 13
[2] *First Reading of the Mass*, Year I, 2 Cor 3:5
[3] St Irenaeus, *Against Heresies*, 3, 25, 3
[4] cf Second Vatican Council, *Ad gentes*, 8

evil, and we find it hard to do good: it is the so-called *fomes peccati* or concupiscence that – without being in itself a sin – proceeds from sin and inclines us towards sin.[5] Freedom itself, although not entirely suppressed, has been weakened.

We can understand then, in the light of this doctrine, that our good works, which are the fruits of sanctity and apostolate, belong in the first place to God. In the second place – very much in the second place – they are the result of our having corresponded, as instruments which are always weak and disproportionate, with grace. God asks us always to bear in mind the abject penury of our condition, so that we may avoid the danger of ever becoming conceited. Often, as Saint Alphonsus Liguori says, *a man dominated by pride is a thief who is even worse than other thieves because he does not steal anything of earthly value but instead steals God's glory ... According to the Apostle, we cannot in fact do any good work of ourselves; we cannot even think a good thought (cf 2 Cor 3:5) ... Because of this, when we manage to do some good, let us address ourselves to Our Lord, saying: for all things come from thee, and of thy own we have given thee*(1 Chron 29:14).[6] Whenever we find we have good results in our hands, we must offer them once more to God, because we know that only what is evil, or is in some way defective, belongs to us. Beauty and goodness belong to God.

84.2 Actual graces.

We can see from the pages of the Gospel that those encounters individual men and women had with Christ were unique and unrepeatable: Nicodemus, Zacchaeus, the woman taken in adultery, the good thief, the Apostles ...

---

[5] Council of Trent, Decree, *On original sin*, 5
[6] St Alphonsus Liguori, *A jungle of predictable matters*, 2, 6

God's action had already been slowly preparing those souls so that they should be open to God when the moment arrived. And so, as a result of that unique and decisive encounter, God's grace would accompany them, seeking opportunities for a new conversion to take place within their souls and helping them to make further progress. Other people we come across in the Gospels did not correspond fully or even in part, with God's light. Our encounters with Christ, too, have been unique and unrepeatable. They have been like those of the people who met him in Galilee, beside the lake of Gennesareth, in Jerusalem or in some little town as he travelled through Samaria. Jesus is just as much present in our lives. God's goodness enables us to receive those divine inspirations that help us to come close to God. He helps us to finish off a piece of work with perfection, to accept or perform a particular mortification or to make an act of faith. He helps us to conquer ourselves, for love of God, in something we find difficult. These are *actual graces*, free and transitory gifts from God that affect each soul in their own particular way. What a lot of actual graces we have received each day! What a lot more we will receive so long as we do not close the door of our soul to that silent and most effective action of the Sanctifier!

Through grace God grants to each man, to each woman, not only the facility to do good, but the very possibility of doing good, because as creatures we are quite unable, with our strength alone, to keep the Commandments, or to do anything at all that is supernaturally good.

Apart from me you can do nothing,[7] said Our Lord categorically. And Saint Paul teaches that salvation *depends not upon man's will or exertion, but upon God's mercy,*[8] on

---

[7] John 15:5
[8] Rom 9:16

a mercy that is constant and infinite. How well we have experienced this!

The Holy Spirit enlightens us so that we can see the truth. He inspires and moves us, preceding, accompanying and perfecting our good deeds. *God is at work in you, both to will and to work for his good pleasure.*[9] Nevertheless, grace does not take away freedom, for it is we ourselves who will, and we ourselves who act.

We must ask God for the practical wisdom of always relying on him and not on ourselves, of seeking our strength in him and not in the keenness of our intellect or in any other resources of our own. We have to listen frequently, when putting our desires into practice, to the loving warning of the Master: *Apart from me you can do nothing.* In the supernatural life we will always be *beginners*, struggling with the docility and attention of a child who needs the assistance of adults for everything it does. Saint Francis de Sales uses this example to illustrate the delicacy of God's love for men: *When a mother is teaching her little child to walk, she helps him and supports him when necessary. She lets him take a few steps on level ground where there is least danger. She takes his hands and holds him up, or she picks him up in her arms and carries him. In the same way Our Lord pays continuous attention to the steps taken by his children.*[10] This is what we are like before God – little children who have not yet learned to walk.

It is up to us to correspond, to show our good will, to begin and begin again. We can do this by being sincere in spiritual direction, by having a very specific *particular examination of conscience*, (that point on which we are currently fighting). Our days will frequently be summed up

---

[9] Phil 2:13
[10] St Francis de Sales, *Treatise on the Love of God*, 3, 4

as *asking for help, corresponding and giving thanks*.

84.3 Our correspondence.

God treats each soul with infinite respect, and because of this, because He does not force our wills, man can prefer to resist grace and make God's wishes sterile. In fact, throughout the day, perhaps in little things, we do say *no* to God. And we have to try many times to say *yes* to what God asks of us, and *no* to our own selfishness, to the impulses of our pride and to laziness.

Our free response to God's grace must occur in our thoughts, in our words and in our deeds.[11] Faith alone is not enough to enable us to co-operate adequately. God asks for our personal effort, for deeds, for initiative, for effective desires ... Although Our Lord through his death on the Cross merited an infinite treasury of grace, those graces are not granted to us all at once, and their greater or lesser abundance depends on how we correspond. When we are prepared to say *yes* to Our Lord in everything, we attract a veritable cascade of gifts.[12] Grace, love for God, inundates us when we are faithful to the small insinuations of grace each day – when we live the *heroic minute* in the morning and try to give our first thought to God; when we prepare well for Holy Mass and struggle to reject those distractions that try to separate us from what is really important; when we offer up our work ...

Nobody who does everything possible for him can say that he has been forgotten or not cared for by God. God gives his help to everyone, even to those who are outside the Church through no fault of their own.[13] Moreover, God, who is infinitely merciful and infinitely patient, has procured time

---

[11] cf Second Vatican Council, *Lumen gentium*, 14
[12] cf Pius XII, *Mystici Corporis*, 29 June 1943
[13] cf Second Vatican Council, *Lumen gentium*, 16

and time again, in a thousand different ways, the return of some prodigal who has made off with his inheritance and now finds himself in a lamentable situation. Each day God goes out towards him and moves his heart so that he may set out once again on the path that leads to his father's house. And when He meets someone who corresponds with the grace given him, God heaps on him grace upon grace, and encourages him to rise higher and higher.

If in our personal prayer we find that it is difficult for us to correspond, let us follow this advice: *Talk with our Lady and say to her trustingly, 'O Mary, in order to live the ideal which God has set in my heart I need to fly very high – ever so high!'*[14] Beside Mary we will always find Joseph, her most faithful spouse, who knew how to carry out especially well and so promptly what God manifested to him by means of an angel. We can turn to him throughout the day, and ask him to help us to hear clearly the voice of the Holy Spirit in the midst of the many details of our workaday life that are sometimes so very small, and ask for the fortitude to put these divine promptings into practice.

---

[14] cf St. J. Escrivá, *The Forge*, 994

85. REASONS FOR PENANCE

85.1 Removing obstacles. Renouncing one's own ego. Co-redemption.

Jesus summoned the crowds and his disciples and said to them: *If any man would come after me, let him deny himself and take up his cross and follow me. For whoever would save his life will lose it; and whoever loses his life for my sake and the gospel's will save it.*[1]

Our Lord had already taught that to be his disciple it was necessary to be detached from material goods.[2] He now asks for a deeper detachment. One must renounce self, one's own ego, and what is most personal. But for a disciple of Christ every act of self-giving includes an affirmation: to cease living for oneself so that *Christ may live in me.*[3] Life in Christ, *for whose sake I have suffered the loss of all things,*[4] as Saint Paul writes to the Philippians, is a real consequence of grace. The whole of Christian living is an affirmation of life, love and friendship. *I have come that they may have life, and have it abundantly.*[5] Christ offers us divine filiation and a sharing in the intimate life of the Most Blessed Trinity. What stands in the way of that wonderful promise is simply attachment to our own ego, our love of comfort, well-being and success. Thus mortification is necessary. It is not something negative, but rather detachment from self in order to allow Jesus to live in us. Hence the paradox: *to*

---

[1] Mark 8:34-35
[2] cf Luke 14:33
[3] Gal 2:20
[4] Phil 3:8
[5] John 10:10

Live we must die.[6] We must die to ourselves in order to live a supernatural life. *If you live according to the flesh you will die, but if by the Spirit you put to death the deeds of the body, you will live.*[7]

If any man would come after me ... To respond to the invitation of Jesus, who passes alongside us, we need to go forward step by step, continually making progress. We need to die a little each day, to deny ourselves, to *put off our old nature which belongs to our former manner of life,*[8] to reject those works which separate us from God or make friendship with him difficult. To achieve the holiness we are called to by God, we must bring under control our inclination to evil and our passions because, after original sin and also as a result of personal sins, they are no longer rightly subject to our will. To follow Christ we must be master of ourselves and be able to guide our steps in a definite direction. As has been rightly said: *we are like a man with a donkey; either the man leads the donkey or it leads him; either we control our passions or they control us.*[9] When there is no mortification, *it seems as if your spirit were growing smaller, shrinking to a little point. And your body seems to grow and become gigantic, until it gains control. It was for you that Saint Paul wrote: 'I buffet my own body, and make it my slave; or I, who have preached to others, may myself be rejected as worthless'.*[10]

Saint Paul points out another reason for penance: *Now I rejoice in my sufferings for your sake, and in my flesh I complete what is lacking in Christ's afflictions for the sake of his body, that is, the Church.*[11] *Was Christ's Passion not*

---

[6] cf St. J. Escrivá, *The Way*, 187
[7] Rom 8:13
[8] Eph 4:22
[9] E. Boylan, *This Tremendous Lover*
[10] St. J. Escrivá, *Furrow*, 841
[11] Col 1:24

sufficient in itself to save? asks Saint Alphonsus Liguori. Nothing was lacking in the value of his Passion; it was more than sufficient for the salvation of all men. And yet, to have the merits of Christ's Passion applied to us, we need to co-operate, suffering patiently the toils and tribulations God may wish to send us, so as to liken us more closely to his Son Jesus.[12]

When we are generous in practising mortification we are the first to benefit from this sharing in the sufferings of Christ.[13] Besides, the supernatural efficacy of penitence reaches our own family. It touches in a special way those most in need, our friends and workmates, those people whom we wish to bring closer to God and, indeed, the entire Church and the whole world.

85.2 The Church's invitation to penance. Penance and prayer. Friday, a day of penance.

Therefore the Church – while it reaffirms the primacy of the religious and supernatural values of penitence (values extremely suitable for restoring to the world today a sense of the presence of God and of his sovereignty over man, together with a sense of Christ and his salvation) – invites everyone to accompany the inner conversion of the spirit with the voluntary exercise of external acts of penitence.[14] When offered to God in a spirit of penance, a person's physical or moral suffering ceases to be something useless or harmful and acquires a redeeming value *for the salvation of his brothers and sisters. Therefore he is carrying out an irreplaceable service. In the Body of Christ, which is ceaselessly born of the Cross*

---

[12] cf St Alphonsus Liguori, *Meditations on Christ's Passion*, 10

[13] St Paul VI, Apostolic Constitution, *Paenitemini*, II, 17 February 1966

[14] *ibid*

of the Redeemer, it is precisely suffering permeated by the spirit of Christ's sacrifice that is the irreplaceable mediator and author of the good things which are indispensable for the world's salvation.[15]

The Church reminds us frequently of the need for mortification. *If any man would come after me...* In particular she has set aside one day in the week, Friday, as a day on which we are to consider the need and efficacy of denying ourselves and practising some special mortification: abstaining from flesh meat, or doing something we find rather difficult (like finishing our work more perfectly or making life more pleasant for others), or performing some pious act: doing some spiritual reading, saying the Rosary, paying a visit to the Blessed Sacrament or doing the Stations of the Cross. We might also perform one of the corporal works of mercy: visiting the sick, spending some time with a person in need, or giving alms. However, we ought not to be content with just a weekly penitential act as a reminder of our Lord who suffered and died for us, and taught us the value of sacrifice. Each day God expects us to deny ourselves in little ways, in things which will enliven our soul and make our apostolate fruitful.

85.3 Some practices of penance.

First we ought to be aware of what are called passive mortifications. These can be – when offered with love – what happens to us unexpectedly, or what does not depend on our will: cold, heat, pain, patience at having to wait longer than we expected, not reacting in kind to a brusque answer we might receive. Along with these passive mortifications there are many others which can make our dealings with other people more pleasant – punctuality, for

---

[15] St John Paul II, Apostolic Letter, *Salvifici doloris*, 27, 11 February 1984

example, listening with real interest, speaking when there is an uncomfortable moment of silence, being affable and not allowing circumstances to dictate our moods, being courteous and polite with others, saying thank you and apologising when we have annoyed someone. Working intensely, with order, finishing a job once we have started it, and helping others to do their work can also present us with the chance to mortify ourselves. Mortification can also be lived with regard to our intellect, as in avoiding harsh and uncharitable criticism, not being curious or judging hastily. And there are possible mortifications of the will: struggling decisively against self-love, not speaking always about ourselves and of what we have done or plan to do, or talking excessively about our likes and dislikes.

Active mortification of the senses is another area for self-denial: guarding our sight, for instance; practising sobriety and offering up a mortification at every meal. Interior mortification should not be neglected, getting rid of useless thoughts that hinder our search for holiness, and especially avoiding distractions in prayer during Holy Mass, and in the course of our work.

Let us examine ourselves to see whether we live self-denial cheerfully; whether we control our bodies as we ought; whether we have offered to God, with a desire to co-redeem, the suffering and upsets we meet with along our way; whether we are truly resolved to lose our life, step by step, little by little, for the love of Christ and the sake of the Gospel.

Our mortification and penitence in the middle of the world should possess a series of qualities. Above all, it should be joyful. *That sick person, consumed by a zeal for souls, said: 'Sometimes the body protests and complains, but I ... try to transform 'those moans' into smiles, because then they become very effective'.*[16] Many smiles and pleasant comments are found to be possible, if we are mortified, in the midst of suffering and illness.

Our mortification should be continual. Thus it will make presence of God easy wherever we are; it will help us to work intensely and to finish what we are doing. When we have an apostolic spirit we will be more pleasant and courteous in our dealings with other people.

Our mortification should be discreet and natural. It should be seen by the effect it has on the lives of others rather than by being unusual and strange, or otherwise out of place in one of Christ's faithful.

Finally, mortification should be humble and full of love, because what moves us is the contemplation of Christ on the Cross, to whom we want to be united as fully as possible. We want nothing in our lives that does not lead us to Christ.

In our mortification, as on the hill of Calvary, we find Mary. Let us place in her hands the good resolutions we have formed during this time of prayer. Let us ask her to teach us to appreciate the need for a life of self-denial and mortification.

---

[16] St. J. Escrivá, *Furrow*, 253

TENTH WEEK: FRIDAY

86. PURITY OF HEART

86.1 The ninth commandment and purity of soul.

On many occasions our Lord pointed out how the source of human acts lies in the heart, in the interior of a person, in the depths of his or her spirit. This inner life must be kept clean and pure, undefiled by disordered affections, jealousy or spite. Whatever good is done by anyone has its origin in the heart. There, with God's grace, sincere piety towards God can grow and develop, as can pure love, understanding and respect for our neighbour. Purity of heart increases our capacity for love, whereas 'bourgeois' attitudes, selfishness and spiritual blindness, result from an inner life which is stained. *Out of the heart come evil thoughts, murder, adultery, fornication, theft, false witness, slander.*[1] And we are warned in the Book of Proverbs: *Keep your heart with all vigilance, for from it flow the springs of life.*[2] The heart symbolizes what is most intimate to the human person.

In the Gospel of today's Mass we are told: *You have heard that it was said, 'You shall not commit adultery'. But I say to you that everyone who looks at a woman lustfully has already committed adultery with her in his heart.*[3] Here Jesus lays down the essential meaning of the ninth commandment, which forbids internal acts (thoughts, desires, imaginations) against the virtue of chastity. Every disordered affection, although it may seem pure and disinterested, goes against this precept if it is not in accord

---

[1] Matt 15:19
[2] Prov 4:23
[3] Matt 5:27-32

with the will of God in the light of one's personal circumstances.

To live this commandment in a positive way – this is essential if we are to learn to love – we need, in the first place, a deep friendship with God, so that his love may fill our hearts. Besides, we must avoid what can give rise to temptations against holy purity. These can come when there is a lack of prudence in guarding our senses, when we do not mortify our imagination and rather allow it to entertain dreams and fantasies which withdraw us from reality and the fulfilment of our duties; or they can come when we seek compensations of an affective nature, or give in to vanity, or dwell on useless memories of the past. If we do not reject these internal temptations promptly once we have noticed their presence, if we do not use the means available to rid ourselves of them, we create a confused inner attitude, not responding as we ought to God's grace. A person becomes accustomed to not being generous with God. If we play around with temptation, walking a tightrope between consent and rejection, it is possible that this lack of interior mortification may lead to internal sins against the virtue of chastity. With such an attitude it is difficult, not to say impossible, to make real spiritual progress. On the other hand, when a person is resolved to lead a clean life with the help of God's grace, when he uses the means and especially that of humble and trusting prayer, and puts things right whenever there has been a mistake, then the Holy Spirit, the Sweet Guest of the soul, gives more and more grace. Thus does joy, one of the fruits of the Holy Spirit, take deeper root in the soul of the person who puts the Holy Spirit before all others and renounces silly compensations that leave a sad and bitter mark on the soul.

86.2 Guarding one's heart and fidelity according to one's vocation and state in life.

By the ninth commandment not only does God ask that we avoid unchaste thoughts and desires, but also that we guard our heart, defending it against what makes true love impossible. To keep our soul clean entails guarding our own integrity and affections, being prudent so that we do not squander tenderness where and when we ought not to; it means accepting fully at every moment the consequences of our vocation and state in life.[4] Those who have been called to marriage must guard and give their heart only to their own spouse, as much at the beginning of their married life as at the end. To do so they must constantly control their heart, not letting it become enmeshed in real or imaginary compensations. Married people *mustn't forget that the secret of married happiness lies in everyday things, not in daydreams. It lies in finding the hidden joy of coming home in the evening; in affectionate relations with their children; in everyday work in which the whole family co-operates; in good humour in the face of difficulties that should be met with a sporting spirit; in making the best use of all the advances that civilization offers to help us bring up children; it lies in making the house pleasant and life more simple.*[5]

Those from whom God has asked their whole heart, not wishing it to be shared with any other, have even higher reasons for keeping their soul clean and free of attachments. How awfully deceitful it would be to allow the heart to become entangled in small attachments which would choke, as thorns did the seed sown by the sower, the infinite love of God, who has called us from all eternity. *'Do you think,'* asks St Jerome, *'that you have reached the*

---

[4] cf J. L. Soria, *Loving and Living Chastity*
[5] *Conversations with Monsignor Escrivá*, 91

height of virtue because you have offered a part of the whole? God wants you to be a living host, one pleasing to himself. [6] And God always gives his grace to keep the heart intact, to keep it for him alone and for all souls through him; to keep it without compensations, free of the threads or chains which would prevent it from reaching the heights to which it is called. Courage is needed to cut away what binds a person down or to rectify a misdirected affection.

To guard our heart we must first guard our love, because if we are lacking in human love and are lukewarm in our friendship with God it will be easy for unruly desires and compensations to enter our soul. The heart was made to love and will not be satisfied with what is dry and loathsome.

Let us examine our hearts and see what care we put into those times which are dedicated especially to God: Holy Communion, visits to the Blessed Sacrament, moments set aside for prayer during the day and before bedtime. Let us see if our relationship with Jesus is a really personal one, such as it should be between friends. Let us be sure to avoid routine and half-heartedness in this friendship. Let us direct the affections of our heart in accord with the wishes of God, rejecting promptly any thoughts which might cloud or twist our relationship with God.

86.3 Guarding our eyes, affections and internal senses.

Custody of our heart often begins with the guarding of our eyes. Common sense and supernatural sense are like filters placed in front of our eyes to enable us not to fix our gaze on what we ought not to look at. We should do this with naturalness and simplicity, without having to do anything unusual, but we must do so with fortitude, in the

---

[6] St Jerome, *Epistle 118*, 5

street just as in the workplace and when socialising.

To get to know and love other people we must have contact with them. But to prevent our heart becoming wrongly attached to people to whom it might easily become attached and to whom God does not want it attached we must be prudent in keeping our distance. This means a moral, affective and spiritual distance. It means avoiding the unwarranted placing of confidences in other people, speaking to them unnecessarily of our sorrows and sufferings. At times prudence will dictate that we even keep physically distant. If we are upright in our conscience, an attentive and sincere examination of our motives will enable us to measure our behaviour, judging correctly between what we seem to be seeking and what we are actually seeking in our social and professional relationships.

To prevent our affections from spilling over unduly we do not need to suppress them, which in any case is impossible, but to guide and control them according to God's will. Our heart needs to be strengthened by a clean love which will protect it against affections which are not pleasing to God.

Custody of the heart is connected with control of our memory, with rejecting images and interior dialogues which might inflame an attachment or sidetrack our heart. Taking refuge in a hyperactive imagination and opening the door to foolish dreams prevents us from being open to everyday reality. When we give in to this kind of temptation, and we can do so easily in moments of tiredness or interior dryness as a way of seeking compensation for the ordinary faults and failings of normal life, there arises a lack of unity of life. In parallel there exists an inner world where our vanity is always on top, and another hard, real world where we must achieve our personal sanctification, doing the good that God expects of each of us, man or woman. Those who are unhappy with their situation and are prone to escape into that unreal and imaginary inner world will find it very difficult to face up generously and realistically to what they must do at any given moment if they are to grow in virtue. How is it possible to live in a dream world and still do one's duty? How can we struggle against a particular defect if instead of facing up to it we withdraw into our imagination and overcome it there? How can we be joyful in the face of sacrifice when we are accustomed to hide ourselves in a make-believe world of hallucinatory happiness?

Our heart could even become attached to persons we might have seen in a film, or come across in a novel or even in real life, although they are people with whom we have no real contact. A heart thus tied down, and perhaps stained, cannot find its way to God.

Today we can examine ourselves and see where our heart is during the day: what do we think about? Who occupies the foremost place in our thoughts? Let us ask Our Lady that Jesus may be the real centre of our life; that the clean and noble love, one ready for sacrifice, which He wishes each and every man and woman to live, may be lived, with him, in accord with our own vocation.

May I give you some advice for you to put into practice daily? When your heart makes you feel those low cravings, say slowly to the Immaculate Virgin: 'Look on me with compassion. Don't abandon me, my Mother.' And recommend this prayer to others.[7] Don't abandon me, don't abandon anyone, my Mother!

---

[7] St. J. Escrivá, *Furrow*, 849

87. KEEPING ONE'S WORD

87.1 Jesus praises those who keep their word. No need for oath-taking: our word of honour is sufficient guarantee.

In Jesus' time the practice of oath-taking had fallen into disrepute due to the frequency and lack of seriousness with which oaths were taken. Casuistry had legitimized the non-fulfilment of oaths. Jesus opposed this custom, and with the formula *But I say to you* which he frequently used to show the divine origin of what he was saying, he forbade calling on God to witness not only to a lie but also to those matters where a person's word ought to have been enough. The Gospel of today's Mass, from Saint Matthew, reminds us of Jesus' words: *Let what you say be simply 'Yes' or 'No'*.[1]

To take an oath, that is to say, to call upon God to witness to the truth of what we are saying, or as a guarantor of a promise, is lawful and at times even necessary when circumstances warrant it. It is then an act of the virtue of religion and redounds to the honour and glory of God. The prophet Jeremiah tells us that swearing *in truth, in justice and in uprightness*[2] is pleasing to God. What we state must be true, spoken prudently and not lightly or rashly, and must refer to something just and good.

When there is no pressing need, our word as Christians and as honourable men and women should be sufficient, because of our being known as people who seek the truth and keep our pledges and promises. We wish to be loyal

---

[1] Matt 5:37
[2] Jer 4:2

and faithful to Christ, to whatever commitments we have freely taken on, to our family and friends, and to those who employ us.

In most situations in life to give our word will be an adequate guarantee of our truthfulness and fidelity. But for this to be so we must be truthful in little things, willing to correct our mistakes and fulfil our commitments. Do the members of our family, our friends and workmates know us to be loyal and faithful? Do they know that we never tell a lie, even in a jocular way, to achieve some good or avoid an evil?

87.2 Love for the truth always and in every circumstance.

Hypocrisy and falsehood are two vices forcefully attacked by Christ.[3] Truthfulness is one of the virtues most praised. He said of Nathaniel: *Behold an Israelite indeed, in whom is no guile.*[4] Jesus is himself *the Truth*,[5] while the devil, on the other hand, is *a liar and the father of lies.*[6] Those who follow the Master must be honourable and sincere in their doings, must avoid deceitful behaviour and be truthful in their dealings with both God and man.

Truth is taught by word and example. Jesus is a witness of his Father;[7] the Apostles,[8] the first Christians, and now we are witnesses of Christ to a world that needs living testimony. But how will our friends and workmates believe the truths we wish to pass on to them unless our own lives are based on a real love for the truth? We Christians ought to be able to say, with Christ, that we have

---

[3] cf Matt 23:13-32
[4] John 1:47
[5] John 14:6
[6] John 8:44
[7] cf John 3:11
[8] cf Acts 1:8

come into the world *to bear witness to the truth*[9] at a time when many use lies and deceit to achieve promotion or a greater degree of material well-being, to avoid commitment and sacrifice, or simply through cowardice and a lack of human virtue. Jesus taught us that love for the truth is a necessary quality for being his follower. Such love brings peace because *the truth will make you free.*[10]

We must be exemplary in this matter, being ready to live our lives, build up our material wealth and do our job with a great love for the truth. We must love the truth and put effort into finding it. At times blinded by sin, passion, pride and materialism, we will not find it unless we love it. It is so easy to fall in with a lie when it comes, disguised or openly, as a means to achieve prestige or get ahead in our job. When faced with temptation, no matter how it presents itself, we must recall the clear, unambiguous teaching of Christ: *Let what you say be simply 'Yes' or 'No'.*[11]

We are obliged in justice to be truthful, and also out of love and respect for our neighbour. This same respect for those listening to us will bring us sometimes not to express our own ideas and opinions indiscreetly, but to take into account their age and the degree of their formation. Love for the truth which someone has confided to us will bring us to be morally upright in cases of professional secrecy or discretion, or with a person's right to privacy. If need be, we should ask for advice about how to behave when confronted with someone who wants information to which he has no right.

87.3 Loyalty and fidelity to commitments.

When we give our word, in a certain sense we give

---

[9] John 14:6
[10] John 8:32
[11] Matt 5:37

ourselves. We put 'on the line' what is most intimate to ourselves. In spite of his personal failings, a true disciple and follower of Christ will be honest and loyal, a man of his word. In the Church, we Christians are called 'the faithful'. This term underlines the state acquired by the members of the People of God through Baptism.[12] But a person who inspires confidence, whom we can trust, can also be called faithful. People like this live up to the confidence placed in them, to the demands of love, friendship or duty. This kind of person keeps his word. In Holy Scripture the term 'faithful' is applied to God himself because no one is more worthy of trust than He. God is always faithful to his promises; he never fails to keep his word. In Saint Paul's words: *God is faithful, and he will not let you be tempted beyond your strength.*[13]

Whoever keeps his word is faithful. The person who fulfils his commitments to God and to others is loyal. However, our society often falls into doubt and relativism. Many people, irrespective of their age, seem to be ignorant of the noble obligation to keep their word, to fulfil the commitments they once assumed with complete freedom, or to behave in accordance with the decisions they have made before God or man, in civil or religious life. Difficulties may arise, but the faith and teaching of the Church and the example of the saints show us that it is possible to live these virtues. God does not deny his grace to those who do what they can.

We must be firmly convinced and help others have the same conviction, namely, that it is possible to live all the virtues with all the demands they make. There is an idea in vogue that virtues and commitments are 'ideals' or 'goals' to aim at, but without much hope of attaining them. Let us

---

[12] cf Bl. A. del Portillo, *Faithful and Laity in the Church,* pp.15 ff
[13] 1 Cor 10:13

ask God never to allow us to fall into that error.

A Christian who is loyal will not cave in when upright moral behaviour imposes or seems to impose serious difficulties. We should ask God for an upright conscience. One who gives in may desire in theory to practise a particular virtue, may wish not to sin, but in practice considers that when temptation is great or the difficulties serious he is more or less justified in giving in. This can happen in one's work situation, or when faced with the obligation to react energetically when sensuality threatens to supervene, or when a serious effort has to be made to finance the children's education, or to be faithful to one's spouse, or one's vocation. Let us call to mind today, in our prayer, these words of Jesus: *The rain fell, and the floods came, and the winds blew and beat upon that house, but it did not fall, because it had been founded on rock.*[14]

Faithful to Christ. This is the greatest praise we can receive. That Christ can rely on us no matter what present or future circumstances may bring; that our friends can know we will not let them down; that society can trust us, knowing that we will keep our word and fulfil our obligations freely and responsibly. *When making a night journey by train have you never thought how the lives of hundreds of persons are in the hands of the driver and the signalmen, who in spite of hunger and thirst must stay at their posts? The life of a whole country, the life of the world, depends on the fidelity of men in fulfilling their duties at work and in society, in their adhering to their contracts and being faithful to their word.*[15] And all this without having to call upon God as a witness, but simply as upright and loyal persons.

Let what you say be simply 'Yes' or 'No', honourable

---

[14] Matt 7:25
[15] G. Chevrot, *But I say to you*, Madrid 1981

people, loyal in fulfilling small daily duties, without recourse to lies or deceit at work, being simple and prudent, fleeing all murkiness, open and plain in what we say or do. If we are loyal to our fellow men, then with God's grace we will be loyal to Christ and this is what really counts. *He who is faithful in a very little is faithful also in much.*[16] We will not be upright and faithful to Christ unless we are loyal in our everyday human dealings.

How pleasant it is when a friend comes to us in the midst of some difficulty and says: *You can count on me!* So too, in our prayer today, with simplicity and an awareness of our weakness, we approach God and say: *Lord, you can count on me!* We can use the same words as an aspiration right through the day.

Let us ask the Blessed Virgin Mary, who is also 'Virgin most faithful', to help us to be loyal and faithful, each and every day, in fulfilling our obligations and duties.

---

[16] Luke 16:20

Eleventh Sunday: Year A

88. THE MOST EFFECTIVE WAY

88.1 Urgency in the apostolate: the harvest is great and the labourers few.

The Gospel of today's Mass[1] speaks of something that must have happened frequently as Jesus went about towns and villages preaching the coming of the kingdom of God. On seeing the crowds he had pity on them; he was moved by their plight, seeing them *harassed and helpless, like sheep without a shepherd*, not knowing where to turn. Instead of guiding and caring for them, their shepherds had neglected them and behaved more like wolves than like shepherds. Then Jesus said to his disciples: *The harvest is great, but the labourers are few*. The same is the case today; there are too few labourers for the work to be done. The harvest can be lost because there is no one to go out and reap it. So there is a pressing need for Christians to be joyful, effective, simple, faithful to the Church and conscious of what they have to do. We are all involved because God needs workers and students to bring Christ onto the shop-floor and into the university, with their prestige and apostolate. God needs teachers who are exemplary and teach with a Christian outlook, teachers who give time to their students, teachers who are real masters. God needs men and women who live their faith in every activity. God needs parents who are concerned for the education and faith of their children, and who take an active part in school boards, committees, and local associations.

When we see so many people going wrong, empty of God and filled only with concern for their material

---

[1] Matt 9:36, 10:8

possessions, or by the desire to have them, we cannot remain unmoved. For although they may seem indifferent, deep down in their soul these people are thirsty for God. They want someone to speak to them of God and the truths of salvation. If we Christians do not work with a spirit of sacrifice in this matter then what the prophet Joel foretold will happen: *The fields are laid waste, the ground mourns; because the grain is destroyed, the wine fails, the oil languishes. Be confounded, O tillers of the soil, wail, O vinedressers, for the wheat and the barley; because the harvest of the field has perished.*[2] God expected these fruits to be gathered in and they were lost because of the negligence of the harvesters.

The words of Jesus, *the harvest is great, and the labourers few*, should bring us to examine ourselves each day: what have I done today to make God known? Have I spoken to anyone of Christ? What apostolate have I done? Am I concerned for the salvation of friends and colleagues? Do I realise that many people might come closer to God if I were more daring and gave better example in fulfilling my duties?

88.2 There are no excuses. God calls everyone to be an apostle. Prayer is the most effective and necessary means for winning vocations.

Many excuses can be made for not bringing Christ to others – lack of means, inadequate preparation or time, the fact that we live in a small corner of the world and know few people, or because we would have to travel long distances even within the region where we live. However, God continues reminding all of us, and more especially in these times of so much religious indifference, that *the harvest is great, and the labourers few*. A harvest not

---

[2] Joel 1:10-12

saved in time is lost. The following words of St John Chrysostom may help us see in our prayer whether we are too easily excusing ourselves of the noble call to be an apostle as God wishes. *There is no one colder than a Christian who is uninterested in the salvation of others. You must not use your poverty as an excuse. The widow who gave her mite will accuse you. Peter himself said: 'Gold and silver I have none' (Acts 3:6). And Paul was so poor that often he suffered hunger and was lacking in what he needed to live. You must not use as an excuse your humble background. They too were humble, of modest background. Nor should your lack of knowledge be an excuse. They were unlettered men. Slave or fugitive, you must do what you can. Such was Onesimus, and be mindful of his vocation... Do not use your poor health as an excuse. Timothy was frequently ill... Each of us can be useful to our neighbour if we do all that we can.*[3] We want to be faithful to God. We will be if we do all we can.

The harvest is great, and the labourers few. St Gregory the Great comments: *When we hear this we cannot but feel sad, because we know that there are people who want to listen to the good news, but what is missing are people who might announce these tidings to them.*[4]

For there to be many people working shoulder to shoulder in the world, each one in his own proper place, we have only to follow the way shown us by Jesus himself: *Pray, therefore, the Lord of the harvest that he send labourers into the harvest.* Jesus invites us to pray that God may awaken in many souls the desire to take a greater part in the work of redemption. *Prayer is the most effective means of winning new apostles*[5] and of bringing people to

---

[3] St John Chrysostom, *Homilies on the Acts of the Apostles*, 20
[4] St Gregory the Great, *Homilies on the Gospels*, 17
[5] St. J. Escrivá, *The Way*, 800

discover their vocation. The desire to win new apostles must be shown first of all in prayer of petition: constant, trusting and humble petition. All Christians should pray that God send *labourers into his harvest*. If we ask God for vocations we will ourselves feel more obliged to be daring in our apostolate, thus winning reapers for the harvest.

88.3 Asking God for vocations.

By sending out his disciples Jesus prepared his arrival in various towns and villages. Theirs was a work of preparation only, as all apostolate is. They were to go *into all the towns where He himself was to come.*[6] Every apostolic work aims at preparing someone for the coming of God.

The harvest is great... We must continually ask God to awaken in Christian men and women the vocational meaning of their lives; that they may want not just to be good, but to learn to be workers in God's harvest, responding generously to the Lord's call. Men and women, young and old, dedicated to God in the world; many in apostolic celibacy; ordinary Christians, with the same secular activities as their fellow citizens, who bring Christ into the very heart of society.

Pray to the Lord of the harvest... We must also pray that there be many vocations to the priesthood and religious life, vocations that are faithful, holy and joyful, vocations that are so much needed by the Church.

God, who could do the work of redemption in the world all by himself, has wished to count on disciples who will go before him into towns and villages, into universities and factories, announcing the wonders and demands of the coming kingdom of God. Clearly our Mother the Church needs people who will walk in the path of commitment and holiness. The Roman Pontiffs have not ceased to remind us

---

[6] cf Luke 10:1

of the need for apostolic vocations, for in the hands of such lies in great measure the evangelization of the world.

Help me to cry: Jesus, souls!... Apostolic souls! They are for you, for your glory. You'll see how in the end he will hear us.[7]

What am I doing to win these vocations? These vocations should come from among one's children, brothers and sisters, relatives, friends and acquaintances. Let us not forget that God calls many. Let us ask him for the grace to promote and encourage the call of God, directed perhaps to people we are in contact with every day.

Let us ask Our Lady to help us take seriously Our Lord's words: *The harvest is great*, and be resolved to do all we can, with a sense of urgency and with constancy, and thus to see to it that there be many labourers in God's harvest. Let us ask him for the joy of being an instrument used by Jesus to call others. *"Good news: another 'crazy' fellow for the asylum'... And all is excitement in the 'fisherman's " letter... May God make your nets effective.*[8]

God never forgets the *'fisherman'*.

---

[7] St. J. Escrivá, *The Way*, 804
[8] *ibid*, 808

89. THE MUSTARD SEED

89.1 God makes use of little things to act in souls.

Thus says the Lord God: 'I myself will take a sprig from the lofty top of the cedar, and will set it out; I will break off from the topmost of its young twigs a tender one, and I myself will plant it upon a high and lofty mountain; on the mountain height of Israel will I plant it, that it may bring forth boughs and bear fruit, and become a noble cedar; and under it shall dwell all kinds of beasts'.[1] These beautiful words of the prophet Ezechiel, taken from the First Reading of today's Mass, remind us how God uses what is little to work in the world and in souls. Jesus gives us the same teaching. The kingdom of God *is like a grain of mustard seed, which, when sown upon the ground, is the smallest of all the seeds of the earth; yet when it is sown it grows up and becomes the greatest of all shrubs, and puts forth large branches, so that the birds of the air can make nests in its shade.*[2]

Our Lord chose a few men to begin the work of evangelization. For the most part they were humble fishermen, unlettered men, with evident defects and few material resources. *He chose what is weak in the world to shame the strong.*[3] Looking at things from a purely human point of view, it is impossible to explain how these men could have spread the teaching of Christ to the whole known world in so short a time, with so many obstacles and so much opposition to overcome. In the parable of the

---

[1] Ez 17:22-24
[2] Mark 4:31-32
[3] 1 Cor 1:27

grain of mustard seed, writes St John Chrysostom, Jesus urges his disciples to have faith and to be confident that the preaching of the Gospel will be carried out in spite of everything.[4]

We too are like that grain of mustard seed in the task given us by God in the middle of the world. We ought not to forget the disproportion between the means we have, our talents, and the magnitude of the apostolate we have to do. But neither should we forget that we can always count on God's help. Difficulties will come and we will be more aware of our own nothingness. This should bring us to have more trust in the Master and in the supernatural character of the task we are trying to accomplish. *In the moments of struggle and opposition, when perhaps 'the good' fill your way with obstacles, lift up your apostolic heart: listen to Jesus as he speaks of the grain of mustard-seed and of the leaven. And say to him: edissere nobis parabolam: explain the parable to me'... And you will feel the joy of contemplating the victory to come: the birds of the air will lodge in the branches of your apostolate, now only in its beginnings, and the whole of the meal leavened.*[5]

If we don't lose sight of our littleness and the power of grace we will be always strong and faithful in what God asks of us. If we do not keep our eyes fixed on Jesus we will become discouraged and pessimistic and will soon abandon the task. With God we can do all things.

89.2 Difficulties ought not to discourage us.

The Apostles and first Christians faced a society threatened in its very foundations; a society in which it was well nigh impossible to have ideals. St Paul describes Roman society and the pagan world as places where the

---

[4] St John Chrysostom, *Homilies on St Matthew's Gospel*, 46
[5] St. J. Escrivá, *The Way*, 695

natural light of reason had been darkened in many ways, especially in regard to the dignity of the human person. He goes on to say: *Therefore God gave them up in the lusts of their hearts to impurity, to the dishonouring of their bodies among themselves, because they exchanged the truth about God for a lie and worshipped and served the creature rather than the Creator, who is blessed for ever! Amen.*

For this reason God gave them up to dishonourable passions. Their women exchanged natural relations for unnatural, and the men likewise gave up natural relations with women and were consumed with passion for one another, men committing shameless acts with men and receiving in their own persons the due penalty for their error.

And since they did not see fit to acknowledge God, God gave them up to a base mind and to improper conduct. They were filled with all manner of wickedness, evil, covetousness, malice. Full of envy, murder, strife, deceit, malignity, they were gossips, slanderers, haters of God, insolent, haughty, boastful, inventors of evil, disobedient to parents, foolish, faithless, heartless, ruthless.[6] Working from within society, Christians changed it. There the seed fell, then spread to the whole world. Although it was a small seed it carried a divine power, because the seed was Christ's. The first Christians who came to Rome were no different from ourselves, and with God's help were able to do an effective apostolate, working shoulder to shoulder, in the same jobs as everyone else, facing the same problems, obeying the same laws, unless they were directly contrary to the law of God. Truly the first Christians in Jerusalem, Antioch and Rome were tiny mustard seeds seemingly lost in a huge field.

Although our society seems at times to be like the one

---

[6] Rom 1:24-31

described by St Paul, we ought not to lose heart at meeting obstacles. God counts on us to transform the place where we live and work. Although what we can do may seem small and insignificant, like the grain of mustard seed, let us not neglect to do what we can, because God counts on that contribution. With our prayer and sacrifice He will ensure that there is growth and fruit. That 'little' we can do may be advising a colleague or friend to read a particular book; or being attentive to a client, fellow passenger or workmate; or giving a helping hand when needed; or praying for a sick friend or a neighbour's child, and asking that they pray for us; or helping someone get to Confession. And always living a cheerful, honest life. Everybody should be discreetly, quietly and daringly apostolic. This can be so if we remain united to God, if we reject a comfort-loving existence, if we overcome lukewarmness and discouragement. *The time in which we are called to live demands especially that we feel deeply obliged to be always zealous and enthusiastic. We will be so only if we struggle. Only the person who makes a strenuous effort is suitable for bringing the world peace, the peace of Christ.*[7]

89.3 The need to overcome false human respect.

The spreading of the Gospel, often by friends, colleagues at work or neighbours, brought about in whole families a radical change of life and set them on the road to salvation. For others it was a scandal and for still others foolishness.[8] St Paul tells the Christians at Rome that he is not ashamed of the Gospel because *it is the power of God for salvation to every one who has faith.*[9] St John

---

[7] Bl. A. del Portillo, *Letter*, 8 December 1976, 4
[8] cf 1 Cor 1:23
[9] cf Rom 1:16

Chrysostom comments: *If someone approaches you and asks: 'do you adore somebody who has been crucified?' Do not hang your head in shame or blush. Use that reproach as a chance for glory and let your eyes and the look on your face show that you are not ashamed. If they whisper again in your ear: 'What! do you adore somebody who has been crucified?' reply: 'Yes, I adore him!'...I adore and glory in a crucified God who with his Cross reduced the devils to silence and took away all superstition. For me the Cross is the trophy of God's love and kindness.*[10] That is a fine reply. We can use it ourselves.

From the first Christians we must learn not to be inhibited by human respect, not to be afraid of what others will say. Rather must we be concerned to make Christ known no matter where we find ourselves, very much aware of the treasure we have found,[11] of the precious pearl we have located after much searching.[12] The struggle against human respect never ceases, because not infrequently we come across an adverse environment when we are serious about trying to follow Christ closely and trying to live in accordance with our beliefs. Many who call themselves Christians show little courage when they should be witnessing to their faith. They seem to be more concerned about the opinion of others than about the judgement of Christ. They often allow themselves to be carried along by the current, afraid of saying anything. This attitude betrays superficiality, lack of deep convictions and little love of God. Naturally enough, at times it will be hard to behave in accordance with what we are, Christians who wish to live their faith at every moment and in every

---

[10] St John Chrysostom, *Homilies on the Epistle to the Romans*, 2
[11] cf Matt 13:44
[12] cf Matt 13:45-46

circumstance of life. But these times will also be excellent moments to show Christ our love, forgetting about what others think, and not being swayed by public opinion. *God did not give us a spirit of timidity but a spirit of power and love and self-control. Do not be ashamed then of testifying to our Lord,*[13] St Paul says to Timothy.

This was always the attitude of those who preceded us in the task of evangelization. And even before that, we have the example of Judas Maccabaeus. At a time when *many even from Israel... sacrificed to idols and profaned the sabbath*[14] he and his brothers, following the example of their father Mattathias, rebelled against that iniquity and for the honour of God *fought gladly for Israel.*[15] As Judas himself said: *It is not on the size of the army that victory in battle depends, but on the strength that comes from heaven.*[16] This is the way it has always been in the things of God, from the beginning of the Church to our own day. God uses what is weak to do his work. We will not lack his help. He will turn the little we can do into a great power for good.

From the Cross of Christ comes the power and courage we need. Let us look to Mary. *She did not draw back when the crowd cried out, nor did she leave Our Redeemer alone when each person, anonymous in that crowd, was in his cowardice emboldened to ill-treat Christ.*

Call upon her with all your strength: 'Virgo fidelis!, Virgin most faithful!', and ask her that those of us who call ourselves God's friends may be truly so at all times.[17]

---

[13] 2 Tim 2:7-8
[14] 1 Mac 1:41
[15] 1 Mac 3:2
[16] 1 Mac 3:18-19
[17] St. J. Escrivá, *Furrow*, 51

ELEVENTH SUNDAY: YEAR C

90. CONTRITION FOR SIN

90.1 Contrition makes us forget ourselves and make our way to God. Our falls ought not to discourage us.

We read in today's Gospel[1] that Jesus was invited for a meal by a Pharisee named Simon. We are not told where it was, but in all likelihood it was somewhere in Galilee, perhaps in Capharnaum.

Simon showed no special love for Jesus, for he did not even take the trouble to show him the normal courtesy of the times: a kiss of welcome, perfumed water for washing, ointment... When Jesus was seated at table a woman made her way in and went directly towards him. She was *a woman of the city and a sinner*. She must have known our Lord and perhaps have been struck at some time by his words or gestures of mercy. Today she decided she wanted to meet him personally. And she showed many signs of repentance and contrition. She *brought an alabaster flask of ointment, and standing behind him at his feet, weeping, she began to wet his feet with her tears, and wiped them with the hair of her head, and kissed his feet, and anointed them with the ointment*. We know what was going on in her heart because of what Jesus said afterwards: *She loved much*. She showed how great her respect for Jesus was. She forgot about the others who were present and about herself. She was only interested in Jesus.

Her sins, which are many, are forgiven, for she loved much. That's the reason for so much pardon. The scene ends with our Lord's consoling words: *Your faith has saved you; go in peace*. Begin again your life, with new hope.

---

[1] Luke 7:36, 8:3

Peace always comes when there is deep contrition. *Go in peace*. These are the very words the priest says to us after forgiving us our sins. Faith and humility saved that woman; with contrition she began a new life. As St Gregory the Great says: *That woman represents us when, after having committed a sin, we turn back to God with all our heart and imitate her in our cries of penance.*[2] Contrition makes us forget ourselves and return to God through a deep act of love. Contrition is also a sign of the depth of our love and calls down God's mercy upon us. As the prophet Isaiah says: *This is the man to whom I will look, he that is humble and contrite in spirit.*[3] Our worst defects and failings ought not dishearten us, even if they are many and frequent, provided we are humble and repentant.

Let us ask God to engrave on our hearts this consoling teaching so that we continue our effort to be holy and reach God's love. *In this adventure of love we should not be depressed by our falls, not even by serious falls, if we go to God in the sacrament of penance, contrite and resolved to improve. A Christian is not a neurotic collector of good behaviour reports. Jesus Christ our Lord was moved as much by Peter's repentance after his fall as by John's innocence and faithfulness. Jesus understands our weaknesses and draws us to himself on an inclined plane. He wants us to make an effort to climb a little each day. He seeks us out, just as He did the disciples of Emmaus, whom He went out to meet. He sought Thomas, showed himself to him and made him touch with his fingers the open wounds in his hands and side. Jesus Christ is always waiting for us to return to him; He knows our weaknesses.*[4]

---

[2] St Gregory the Great, *Homilies on the Gospels*, 13, 5
[3] Is 66:2
[4] St. J. Escrivá, *Christ is passing by*, 75

90.2 We cannot ignore our faults and failings. Avoid making excuses.

In silence Simon contemplated the scene and despised the woman. Jesus has forgiven her, but he, setting himself up as judge, condemns her. He thinks also that Christ, whom the people have been speaking about so much, cannot be a true prophet. Perhaps he only invited him in order to get a closer look.

Jesus then shows that he knows not only the inner feelings of the sinful woman but also Simon's thoughts. 'Simon,' he said, 'I have something to say to you'. And he answered, 'What is it, Teacher?' 'A certain creditor had two debtors; one owed five hundred denarii, and the other fifty. When they could not pay, he forgave them both. Now which of them will love him the more?' The reply was clear. The one who had more forgiven him should love the more. And Simon replied correctly. The parable then became a real event. What our Lord did next was to praise the woman who did not even dare to speak. And Jesus looks at her while he speaks to Simon. In fact it is to the woman he is speaking: Then turning towards the woman he said to Simon, 'Do you see this woman? I entered your house, you gave me no water for my feet, but she has wet my feet with her tears and wiped them with her hair. You didn't give me... You don't love me, but she does. She loves me in spite of her many sins, or perhaps, because of them, because her need for pardon is very great.

Simon did not offer our Lord the signs of welcome usually extended to an honoured guest. There was no water to wash his feet, now dirty from the dusty roads. There was no kiss of peace. There was no ointment for his head. Yet the woman more than made up for it. She washed his feet, wiped them with her hair and kissed them. Simon did not even advert to his lack of courtesy. Nor did he realize that if he did not commit more and graver sins himself it was because of God's mercy which kept him from evil. In the words of St Augustine: *He who is forgiven little, loves little. You who say you have committed few sins, why did you not commit them? Without doubt because God was leading you by the hand... There is no sin one man commits that another cannot commit if God, who made man, does not lead him by the hand.*[5]

We cannot forget that our faults are real. We cannot blame them on society, or on difficult circumstances in life, or think them inevitable, excusing ourselves and shirking our responsibility. To do so would be to shut the door on forgiveness and any real meeting with Jesus, as happened in the case of Simon the Pharisee. *'More than the sin itself,'* says St John Chrysostom, *'what displeases and offends God is the sinner's not feeling any sorrow for his sins'.*[6] There will be no sorrow for sin if we make excuses for our weaknesses. On the other hand, we should make a good examination of conscience and not be content with acknowledging that we are sinners in some vague, undefined way. In the words of Cardinal Wojtyla: *'We cannot rest content at the outer level of evil. We must get to its roots, its causes, to the truth in the depths of our consciences'.*[7] Jesus knows our hearts well and wishes to purify and cleanse them.

90.3 Humility and repentance. Confession. Sincerity.

We read in the responsorial psalm today: *I acknowledged my sin to thee, and I did not hide my iniquity; I said, 'I will confess my transgressions to the Lord'; then thou didst forgive the guilt of my sin. Thou art a hiding place for me, thou preservest me from trouble; thou dost encompass*

---

[5] St Augustine, *Sermon 99*, 6
[6] St John Chrysostom, *Homilies on St Matthew's Gospel*, 14, 4
[7] Cardinal K. Wojtyla, *Sign of Contradiction*, Slough 1979

me with deliverance.[8] Sincerity brings salvation, for *the truth will set you free.*[9] On the other hand, deceit, pretence and lies lead to separation from God and the fruits of charity dry up. The same psalm says: *My strength was dried up as by the heat of summer.*[10]

At the root of insincerity lies pride. This vice prevents a person from submitting to God, recognising his dependence on God and doing what God wants. A proud person has difficulty in even recognising that he is doing wrong and needs to correct his behaviour. When this vice takes root in the soul it makes objectivity all but impossible. Not wanting to acknowledge faults and failings, such a person seeks excuses for bad behaviour. The end of this road is spiritual blindness. We need then to be humble, as the sinful woman was, if we are to grow in sincerity and self-knowledge and be able to confess our sins. A great help is to make an examination of conscience, in God's presence, rejecting excuses which might justify our behaviour, being sincere when we come to confess our sins sincerely and frankly in the sacrament of Penance.

Humility allows us to see the great debt we owe God and to be aware of our radical personal insufficiency. Being humble, we will ask God for pardon many times a day for our sins of omission and commission, or at least for what is not going well in our life. Thus our many faults will bring us to love much and to give thanks to God who in his love for us has prevented us from falling even more often. If we live in this way, being completely sincere with ourselves, we will have no reason to set ourselves up as judges of others.

If this man were a prophet, he would have known who

---

[8] Ps 31:5,7
[9] cf John 8:32
[10] Ps 31:4

and what sort of a woman this is who is touching him, for she is a sinner. Charity and humility teach us to see in the failings and sins of others our own weaknesses. Thus we will be more heartfeltly united to the sorrow of every sinner who repents. We would fall into the same or worse faults if God in his mercy did not stand by us.

St Ambrose tells us: *Our Lord wanted love, not ointment; he appreciated faith; he praised humility. You also, if you want his grace, must increase your love. Pour out on the body of Jesus your faith in his resurrection, the sweet fragrance of the Church and the ointment of other people's charity.*[11]

Let us ask the Blessed Virgin Mary, *Refugium peccatorum*, the refuge of sinners, that she win for us from her Son a sincere sorrow for our sins and a deep and effective appreciation of the sacrament of Penance.

---

[11] St Ambrose, *Commentary on St Luke's Gospel, in loc*

ELEVENTH WEEK: MONDAY

91. LIFE OF GRACE

91.1 A new life. Dignity of the Christian.

From the moment sanctifying grace is infused into us at Baptism, as Christians we now have a new supernatural life making us different from other people. What we now have is a special life exclusive to those who believe in Christ, who are *born, not of blood nor of the will of the flesh nor of the will of man, but of God.*[1] In Baptism a Christian begins to live the very life of Christ *or Christ's own life,*[2] for there is set up between him and us a communion of life which is distinct from and stronger and more intimate than the communion which exists between the members of human society. The union with our Lord is so profound that it transforms Christian existence altogether, making it possible for God's life to develop within our souls as something actually belonging to them. Our Lord speaks of the vine and the branches.[3] Saint Paul compares this shared life to the union between the head and the body.[4] The same sap vivifies the vine and its branches, and the same blood courses through the head and the members of the body.

The first consequence of this reality is the incomparable blessing of our being made into God's children. *Divine filiation* is not just a title or a descriptive label. When a man adopts another human being as his son he confers on him his name and his goods; he can offer

---

[1] John 1:13
[2] cf Gal 3:27
[3] John 15:1-6
[4] 1 Cor 12:27

him his affection, but is incapable of communicating anything of either his own nature or his life. Human adoption is necessarily an external thing; it does not change the person into another kind of being, or add any perfections to the one adopted, or any qualities except external ones, like clothes, habitation, extra means to improve culture etc. With divine adoption it is different; here we have a genuinely new birth which produces a wonderful improvement in the actual nature of the one who has been adopted. *Beloved, we are God's children now.*[5] This is not fictional, merely a manner of speaking or simply the conferring of an honorary title, because *it is the Spirit himself bearing witness with our spirit that we are children of God.*[6] It is a reality which is so great and joyous that it makes Saint Paul exclaim: *So then you are no longer strangers and sojourners, but fellow citizens with the saints and members of the household of God.*[7]

How much good it will do our soul to reflect frequently that Christ is the fountain source from which springs forth in abundance this new life which has been given to us! Saint Peter writes: *By him God has granted to us his precious and very great promises, that through these you may ... become partakers of the divine nature.*[8]

On considering such marvellous condescension, our head and our heart are inclined to give constant thanks to Our Lord for endowing us with such riches, and we resolve to live in constant awareness of the precious jewels we have received. The angels gaze at the soul in grace with respect and admiration. And we? How do we view our brother men who have received or are called to receive this

---

[5] 1 John 3:2
[6] Rom 8:16
[7] Eph 2:19
[8] 2 Pet 1:4

inestimable treasure? Do we really appreciate what our soul is now worth? Is our appreciation reflected in our behaviour, in the extreme care we take to avoid anything, no matter how slight, that might be unworthy of our condition as Christians?

91.2 Sanctifying grace giving a share in divine nature.

At the beginning, after the first creation, man was new, perfect, as he came fresh from the hand of God. But sin aged him and created havoc in him. And so God made a new creation:[9] sanctifying grace, a *limited participation* in the divine nature, makes man, without ceasing to be a creature, similar to God and share, really and intimately, in the divine life.

This *sanctifying grace* is an interior reality producing *a kind of splendour and light which cleanses our souls from all stains and makes them most beautiful and brilliant.*[10] This grace is what unites our soul with God in the closest bond of love.[11] How then ought we to protect it, convinced that it is the greatest good we have? Sacred Scripture compares it to a garment God places on the hearts of the faithful,[12] a seed which sends down its roots into the interior of man,[13] a fountain of waters springing up without ceasing unto eternal life.[14]

Sanctifying grace is not a passing, transitory gift, like those impulses and inspirations which we call *actual graces*, to help us to carry out or avoid some particular

---

[9] cf St Thomas, *Commentary on Second Epistle to the Corinthians*, IV, 192
[10] *Catechism of the Council of Trent*, II, 2, 50
[11] cf *ibid* I, 9, 8
[12] cf 2 Cor 5:5
[13] cf 1 John 3:9
[14] John 4:14

action. It is a *permanent principle of supernatural life*,[15] a stable disposition founded in the very essence of the soul. Even though it can be lost through mortal sin, for the reason that it produces a stable and permanent mode of being it is called also *habitual grace*.

Grace does not violate the natural order, but presupposes it, elevates and perfects it, and both the natural and the supernatural orders help each other since both proceed from God.[16] And so the Christian, far from renouncing the mundane duties of his earthly life – work, family, etc. – develops, perfects and coordinates them with the supernatural life to the point of ennobling natural life itself.[17]

With this privilege, and the dignity it confers, we have to live and behave in conformity, in all our actions. We should not forget at any moment of the day these gifts we have been favoured with. Our life will be completely different if in the midst of our daily duties we keep in mind the honour done to us by our Father God, an honour by which, through grace, we are able to call ourselves his children and truly be so in effect.[18]

91.3 Grace leads to identification with Christ: docility, life of prayer, love for the Cross.

Sanctifying grace divinises the Christian and converts him into a son of God and a temple of the most holy Trinity. This likeness in being should be reflected necessarily in our work, in our thoughts, actions and desires, in the measure in which we make progress in the ascetical struggle, so that our purely human life gives way

---

[15] Pius XI, *Casti connubii*, 31 December 1930
[16] cf *ibid*, *Divini illius Magistri*, 31 December 1929
[17] cf *ibid*; cf Second Vatican Council, *Lumen gentium*, 40
[18] cf 1 John 3:1

to the life of Christ. There has to be fulfilled in our souls that interior process which the words of John the Baptist indicate: *He must increase, but I must decrease.*[19] We have to ask Our Lord to make more firm in us the aspiration to have in our hearts the same *mind ... which was in Christ Jesus.*[20] We shall ask him to help us uproot our egoism, to cure us of thinking too much about ourselves and to eliminate from our hearts any kind of lukewarmness. Those who boast, then, of bearing the name of Christian not only have to contemplate the Master as the most perfect Model of all virtues, but have to reproduce in their own behaviour the doctrine and life of Jesus Christ, in such a way that they appear like him,[21] in the way they treat others, in their sympathy with others' sorrows, in their striving for perfection in professional work, thus imitating the thirty years of the hidden life in Nazareth ...

In this way Jesus' life is repeated in the life of the Christian, in a growing likeness with him which is gradually brought about in a marvellous way by the Holy Spirit, and which will have its completion with total identity with Our Lord and union with him in Heaven. But let us consider this serenely in our prayer. To achieve this identification with Christ demands a very clear orientation of the whole of our life, co-operating with Our Lord in the work of our own sanctification, removing obstacles to the action of the Paraclete and trying to do always what pleases God most, in such a way that we can say like Jesus: *My food is to do the will of him who sent me, and to accomplish his work.*[22]

This correspondence with grace, which has to become

---

[19] John 3:30
[20] Phil 2:5
[21] cf Pius XII, *Mystici Corporis*, 29 June 1943
[22] John 4:34

a reality day by day, minute by minute, can be summarised in three main points: it involves, first of all, being *docile* to the inspirations of the Holy Spirit, maintaining a life of prayer in every situation through devotional practices we have determined on in the course of spiritual direction, and the purposeful cultivation of a constant spirit of penance. This docility is required because the Holy Spirit *is the one who presses us to adhere to the doctrine of Christ and to assimilate it in depth, giving us the light to become aware of our personal vocation and the strength to fulfil all that God expects of us.*[23] The same Holy Spirit assists us in our personal interior growth and in the abundant apostolate which we have to carry out among our friends, relations and colleagues. A *life of prayer* is necessary too, *because the self-surrender, obedience and meekness of the Christian are born of love and lead to love. And love leads to genuine concern for others and to mutual dealings, to meaningful conversation and to friendship. The Christian life requires a constant dialogue with God, One and Three, and it is to this intimacy that the Holy Spirit leads us.*[24]

Union with the Cross there must be also, *because in the life of Christ, Calvary preceded the Resurrection and Pentecost and this same process must be reproduced in the life of each Christian.*[25] So we will accept in the first place the contradictions, great and small, which come our way, and offer Our Lord each day many other small mortifications through which we will unite ourselves to the Cross with a sense of co-redemption, purifying our life and preparing ourselves for a profound and intimate dialogue with God.

Let us examine today, as we end our prayer, the

---

[23] St. J. Escrivá, *Christ is passing by*, 135
[24] *ibid*, 136
[25] *ibid*, 137

manner in which we correspond with grace in these three points, because the development of the life of grace in us depends on this correspondence. We tell Our Lord that we do not want to rest content with the standard we have already achieved in prayer, in our sense of the presence of God, in sacrifice ...; that with his grace and the protection of Our Lady we will not rest until we reach the goal which gives meaning to our life – complete identification with Jesus Christ.

92. HOLINESS IN THE WORLD

92.1 The universal call to holiness.

All Sacred Scripture is a calling to holiness, to the fulness of charity, but Jesus makes it quite explicit in the Gospel of today's Mass: *You, therefore, must be perfect, as your heavenly Father is perfect.*[1] And Christ is not addressing his words to the Apostles or to just a few of his followers, but to everyone. Saint Matthew makes the point at the conclusion of these discourses that *the crowds were astonished at his teaching.*[2] Jesus does not demand sanctity of an exclusive coterie of disciples who accompany him everywhere, but of all who approach him: *the multitudes*, among whom were mothers of families, labourers, and skilled craftsmen who would stop to hear him after work, children, tax-collectors, beggars and cripples ... The Lord calls people to follow him without distinction of state, race or condition. Christ speaks to us, to each one in particular, to our neighbours, work-mates or friends in the office or in the Faculty and to those who pass us and each other in the street: *Be perfect* ... he says, and grants us the means and the appropriate graces that will make perfection possible. This is not just advice from the master, but an imperative command. *All in the Church, whether they belong to the Hierarchy or are cared for by it, are called to holiness, according to the Apostle's saying: 'For this is the will of God, your sanctification' (1 Thess 4:3).*[3] *All Christians, in any state or walk of life, are called to the fulness of*

---

[1] Matt 5:4-8
[2] cf Matt 7:28
[3] Second Vatican Council, *Lumen gentium*, 39

Christian life and to the perfection of love.[4] In the doctrine of Christ there is no invitation to mediocrity, but a clear call to heroism, to love and to cheerful sacrifice.

Love is within reach of the child, of the invalid who has been confined to a hospital bed for a lengthy period, of the businessman, of the doctor who hardly has a minute to spare ... because sanctity is a matter of love, and of the effort we make to reach the Master with the help of grace. We have to give a new meaning to life, together with all its joys and exhilarations, its pains and woes. Sanctity requires a fight against conformity, against lukewarmness, against an easy-going worldly attitude. It demands heroism – not in extraordinary situations that we are unlikely to encounter, but in continual fidelity to our task in the unremarkable duties of each day.

The liturgical readings today refer to Saint Cyprian, who exhorted the Christians of the third century: *Beloved brethren, we ought to know and remember that since we call God our Father, we have to behave like his children, so that He will be pleased with us ... Let us behave as befits those who are God's temple ... He has said it: 'Be perfect, because I am perfect.' So we pray, beseeching him that we who were sanctified in Baptism may persevere in that initial sanctification, asking this, moreover, for each day.*[5] Today we implore this of God: Lord, grant us a lively desire for sanctity, that we may be exemplary in our duty of loving you more each day. Help us to spread your doctrine everywhere ...

92.2 Becoming saints wherever we find ourselves.

Our Lord is not happy with a lukewarm life and a half-hearted dedication. *Every branch that does bear fruit he*

---

[4] *ibid*, 40
[5] *Divine Office*, Tuesday of the Eleventh Week, Second Reading

prunes that it may bear more fruit.[6] And so the Master purifies his own, permitting them to experience trials and contradictions. *If the goldsmith hammers the gold repeatedly, it is to take off the impurities in it; if the precious metal is abraded again and again it is to make it shine. 'The heated kiln tries the potter's vessel; man is tested in tribulation.'*[7] All the pain God allows, whether it be of body or of mind, serves to purify the soul so that it may yield more fruit. It is of the mystery of suffering that we have to see it always as a grace from Heaven.

All times are good times for entering into the depths of sanctity; all circumstances are opportune for loving God more, for our interior life feeds, as plants do, on the stuff of the circumstances in which we are immersed. Growth is the work of the Holy Spirit. Plants do not choose the ground in which they are nourished; the sower lets the seeds fall to the earth, where they prosper, converting the useful elements in the soil, with the help of rainwater, into the substance of the maturing grain. And so what is sown ripens and reaches up and grows strong.

With even greater reason will we grow in strength, because it is our Father God who has chosen the terrain and gives us the graces necessary for us to bear fruit. The plot of earth where Our Lord has planted us is the particular family of which we are part, and not any other. We grow up among those who form our initial immediate environment, with all their virtues and failings and idiosyncrasies. The rich mould we are rooted in is our work, which we must love so that it will sanctify not only us, but also our colleagues, our classmates, our neighbours ... The earth from whose nutrients we have to produce fruits of holiness is our country, our own country, our city,

---

[6] John 15:2
[7] St Peter Damian, *Letters*, 8,6

our town, the prevailing social or political system, our own condition of life and no other. It is there, in that environment, in the midst of the world where the Lord says we can and must live all the Christian virtues, developing them with all the demands they make on us and not allowing them to be stunted or to wither. God calls people to holiness in every circumstance: in war and in peace, in sickness and in health, when we think we have triumphed and when we face unexpected defeat, when we have plenty of time and when time is at a premium, so that we seem barely to manage to do what we must. Our Lord wants us to be saints at all times. Those who do not rely on grace, and habitually see things with a completely human outlook, are saying constantly: this, now, is not the right time for sanctity ..., later ... perhaps ...

Let us not think that in another place, in another situation we would be ready to follow Our Lord more closely and carry out a more fruitful apostolate. Let us leave that mystical wishful thinking to one side. The fruits of sanctity Our Lord expects are those produced in and from the environment in which we find ourselves, here and now: tiredness, sickness, family, the job, one's colleagues, one's fellow students ... *Leave behind false idealisms, fantasies, and what I usually call mystical wishful thinking. If only I hadn't married ... If only I hadn't this profession ... If only I were healthier ... If only I were young ... If only I were old ...! Instead, turn seriously to the most material and immediate reality, which is where Our Lord is ...* [8] This is the environment in which our love of God should grow and develop, using *precisely* those opportunities we find at hand. Let us not allow them to slip away, for it is in them that Jesus is waiting for us.

---

[8] *Conversations with Monsignor Escrivá*, 116

92.3 All circumstances are good to help us grow in holiness and carry out a fruitful apostolate.

If we contemplate life in a merely human way, could it not seem that there are any number of moments or situations which are surely less propitious for growth in sanctity or for carrying out a fruitful apostolate? Think of journeys, examinations, times of excessive pressure of work, exhaustion, disheartenment ...; or what about tough environments, delicate professional decisions to be made in a paganised atmosphere, slanderous campaigns ...? None the less, those are familiar moments in every ordinary life: modest successes and occasional setbacks, feelings of well-being and bouts of indifferent health, joys and sorrows and slight to serious worries; years of prosperity and perhaps other times of economic distress ... Our Lord is expecting us to turn all these occasions into opportunities for sanctity and apostolate.

In these moments we will give more attention to and put more effort into personal daily prayer – we can always find time: love is ingenious at finding time if need be – into our visits to Jesus in the Blessed Sacrament, into our relations with Our Lady ... for these very occurrences are the ones in which we need more help. We shall obtain the assistance we need in prayer and in the Sacraments. Then it is that virtues are strengthened and the whole interior life matures.

Nor should we wait for special circumstances in order to get on with our apostolate. Any day, any time is good. If the first Christians had waited for more propitious occasions they would have converted very few to the Faith. This task will always call for audacity and a spirit of sacrifice. *It is the hard-working farmer who ought to have the first share of the crops.*[9] Effort and the exercise of

---

[9] 2 Tim 2:6

human virtues are necessary. Apostolate demands constancy in a special way. The Apostle Saint James says: *Be patient, therefore, brethren, until the coming of the Lord. Behold the farmer waits for the precious fruit of the earth, being patient over it until it receives the early and the late rain. You also be patient. Establish your hearts, for the coming of the Lord is at hand.*[10] And with constancy should go the generosity to sow lavishly, freely, even though we may not ourselves see the results. Someone else may harvest what we have sown.

Let us ask the Blessed Virgin for an effective zeal for sanctity in the circumstances in which we find ourselves *now*. Let us not await that *more opportune* moment; there isn't one. This is the most favourable moment, *the acceptable time* to love God with all our heart, with all our being\ ...

---

[10] James 5:7-8

93. MENTAL PRAYER

93.1 Necessity and fruits of such prayer.

The Gospel of today's Mass[1] is an invitation to personal prayer. And when you pray, Jesus tells us, *you must not be like the hypocrites; for they love to stand and pray in the synagogues and at the street corners, that they may be seen by men ... But when you pray, go into your room and shut the door and pray to your Father who is in secret ...*

Our Lord, who gives us this teaching about prayer, himself practised what He preached throughout his life on earth. The Gospel tells us about the many times Jesus withdrew by himself to pray.[2] The Apostles and the first Christians, and then in the course of time all those who have ever wanted to follow the Master closely have taken up his example. *The path that leads to holiness is the path of prayer; and prayer ought to take root and grow in the soul little by little, like the tiny seed which later develops into a tree with many branches.*[3]

Daily prayer helps us to watch out for the enemy, whose attacks are unceasing; it makes us strong in trials and difficulties, and by its means we learn to serve others. It is a beacon of intense light illuminating our way, enabling us to see clearly the obstacles that obstruct our path. Personal prayer moves us to do our work better and to fulfil our family and social duties, besides being a decisive influence on our relationships with others. But

---

[1] Matt 6:1-6; 16-18
[2] cf Matt 14:23; Mark 1:35; Luke 5:6 etc
[3] St. J. Escrivá, *Friends of God*, 295

above all, it teaches us how to deal with the Master and grow in love. *Don't stop praying!* St John Paul II advises us; *prayer is a duty, but it is also a great joy, because it is a dialogue with God through Jesus Christ!*[4]

In prayer we are *with* Jesus – a marvellous consideration. We go to give ourselves to him, to know him and to learn how to love. The way we do so depends on many circumstances: it depends on where we are and what is going on at the moment, on the good things that have gladdened us, on the setbacks or griefs we have experienced ... all of which are convertible into joy when we are close to Christ. Frequently we will study a passage of the Gospel and contemplate the most holy Humanity of Jesus, thus learning to grow in our love for him, since one does not love what one does not know well. On other occasions we can determine whether we are sanctifying our work and drawing closer to God, or reflect on how we are getting on with those we meet, with our family and our friends. Perhaps we may find it useful to follow some book, such as the one you are reading now, relating what we read to our own personal situation, and articulating in our heart the aspiration our reading suggests; we may go on to develop some particular affection the Holy Spirit may be inspiring in the depths of our soul, and either make some small resolution we can put into practice that same day, or renew, perhaps, one we have previously made.

Mental prayer is a task that is going to demand our utilising, with the help of grace, our intelligence and our will-power, determined, as we shall have to be, to fight against distractions, never to accept voluntary ones, and to put real effort into maintaining a dialogue with Our Lord. Such conversation is the essence of all prayer with him while we are speaking to him in our heart, looking at him,

---

[4] St John Paul II, *Address*, 14 March 1979

and listening to his voice in the intimacy of our soul. We
should always be firm with ourselves in making sure we
dedicate to God all the time we had planned to spend with
him, whether or not we feel dry and are apparently gaining
nothing by it. *It doesn't matter if all we can do is to remain
kneeling during this time and fail completely in our
attempts to fight off distractions: we are not wasting our
time.*[5] Prayer is always fruitful if there is a conscious effort
to carry it out in spite of our flagging concentration and
moments of dryness. Jesus never leaves us without
abundant graces for the whole of that day. He always
shows his gratitude generously for the time we have spent
with him.

93.2 The preparatory prayer. Putting oneself in the presence of God.

It is especially important to place ourselves in the
presence of the One with whom we wish to speak. Very
often the rest of the prayer will depend on those first
minutes in which we mentally strive to be close to him who
cares for us and who, we know, awaits our petitions and
our acts of love. This done, we can go on to consider with
him some matter that perhaps worries us, or we can simply
remain in his presence looking at him and knowing he is
looking at us. If we take special care with these first
moments, lovingly placing ourselves in the presence of
Christ, then without doubt a good part of our dryness and
our difficulties in speaking to him will disappear ...
because they have been quite simply an unwanted
dissipation of our attention and a lack of interior
recollection.

In order to place ourselves in the presence of God at
the beginning of mental prayer, we should make some

---

[5] E. Boylan, *This Tremendous Lover*

reflections so as to remove other concerns from our mind. We can say to Jesus: *My Lord and my God, I firmly believe that you are here, listening to me ...* He is there in the Tabernacle, really present in the sacramental species, with his Body, his Blood, his Soul and Divinity. He is present in our own soul in grace, as the driving-force of our thoughts, affections, desires and supernatural works ... *That you see me, that you hear me!*

We begin immediately, St Josemaría Escrivá tells us, *with a greeting such as we usually employ when we converse with anyone in the world. Since He is God, we greet him in adoration: I adore you with profound reverence! And if we happen to have offended the person we greet, don't we ask his forgiveness? I ask you for pardon for my sins, and grace to make this time of conversation with you fruitful ...* And so we are praying, and already find ourselves in intimate colloquy with God.

But supposing this important person we wanted to speak with had a mother, a mother who loved us as well? Would we not seek her recommendation, ask her to put in a word on our behalf? The Mother of God, who also happens to be our Mother, is ready to be invoked: *My Mother Immaculate!* Besides, we have recourse to Saint Joseph, the foster-father of Jesus, who is also an influential advocate for us in the presence of God: *Saint Joseph, my Father and Lord!* And my Guardian Angel, that prince of Heaven who helps and protects us ... *Intercede for me!*

Once we have made our preparatory prayer, with the introductions which are customary in social intercourse, we can now speak with God! About what? About our joys and our sorrows, about our jobs, our desires and ambitions ... About everything!

We can also say to him simply: *My God, here I am like a fool and I don't know what to say to you ... I would like to speak to you, to pray, and enter into intimacy with your*

Son Jesus. I know I am here next to you, and yet I don't seem to be able to put two words together. If I were with that dearest Lady, my Mother, I would speak about all sorts of things, but with you I can't think of anything ...

This is prayer ...! Remain before the Tabernacle, like a little dog at his master's feet, throughout the time fixed beforehand. Lord, here I am! It's hard! I would run away, but I am going to stay here through love, because I know that you see me and hear me and smile on me.[6]

And near him, even when we do not know what to say to him, we are filled with peace; we recover the strength we need to fulfil our duties, and the cross becomes light because now it is no longer ours alone; Christ helps us to carry it.

93.3 The help of the Communion of Saints.

Close to Christ in the Tabernacle, or wherever we are doing our mental prayer, we will persevere through love, both when we are in good spirits and when it is hard going for us and nothing seems to be of any use. It will help us very often to know that we are united to the *Ecclesia orans*, the Church praying in all parts of the world. Our voice is united to the cry that rises up every moment to God the Father, through the Son, in the Holy Spirit. *During our time of mental prayer and also throughout the day*, St Josemaría Escrivá goes on, *remember that we are never alone, although physically we may find ourselves in isolation. In our life ... we remain always united to the Saints in heaven, the souls undergoing purification in Purgatory and all our brothers and sisters who are still going on with their struggle on earth. Besides, (and this is a great consolation for me since it is an admirable sign of the continuity of Holy Church), you can unite your own*

---

[6] St. J. Escrivá, *Historical Records of the Founder*, 20165, p.1410

prayer to the prayer of all Christians of whatever era: those who have gone before us, those who are living now and those who may live in centuries yet to come. In this way, aware of the marvellous reality of the Communion of Saints, that unending song of praise to God, although you may not feel like praying or are facing difficulties like dryness, you will continue to pray with effort but with more confidence.

Fill yourselves with joy, realising that our prayer is united to the prayer of all those who have ever lived with Jesus Christ, the unceasing prayer of the Church Militant, the Church Suffering and the Church Triumphant; they join all those still to come. Therefore ... when you find yourself dry in prayer, make yourself go on praying, and say to the Lord: My God, I don't want my voice to be missing from that great chorus of permanent praise to You which will never come to an end.[7]

In daily prayer we find the origin of all spiritual progress and a continual source of joy, provided we put the effort into it and are determined to be *alone with the one we know loves us.*[8] We grow in our interior life and make progress in it in proportion as our prayer-life develops, increasingly influencing as it does our actions, our work, our apostolate and our spirit of mortification ...

Let us have frequent recourse to the Blessed Virgin, that she may teach us how to treat her Son, for no one has ever known how to address our Saviour the way his Mother did. And along with her, we can always go to Saint Joseph, who conversed so often with the child, the boy, the young man Jesus while he was working or at rest, travelling on long journeys or going about his business in the streets of Nazareth ... After Mary, Joseph was the one

---

[7] *idem*, 20165, p.1411
[8] St Teresa, *Life*, 8,2

who spent most time close to the Son of God. He will teach us how to talk to the Master and, if we ask him, will help us to make firm resolutions, both concrete and clear, which will help us to improve our work, smooth off the rough edges of our character, make us more ready to serve, and be cheerful throughout all the vicissitudes and contradictions that can possibly befall us ...

Sancte Joseph, 'ora pro eis, ora pro me!' Saint Joseph, pray for them (here we can fix our attention on the particular people for whom we wish especially to pray). *And pray for me.*

94. VOCAL PRAYERS

94.1 The need for such prayer.

In the Gospel of today's Mass Our Lord tells us: *And in praying do not heap up empty phrases as the Gentiles do; for they think that they will be heard for their many words.*[1] He wants to disabuse his disciples of the mistaken view held by many Jews of that time who thought that for God to hear them they had to say long vocal prayers. He teaches them to address God with simplicity, as a son speaks to his father. *Vocal prayer* is very pleasing to God, but it has to be true prayer: the words have to express the feelings of the heart. It is not enough to recite mere formulas, for God is not pleased with a worship that is merely external. He wants us to be in intimate contact with him.[2]

Vocal prayer is an indispensable, simple and efficacious means, adapted to our way of being, of enabling us to keep presence of God during the day, to tell him of our love for him, and about our needs. As we read in the Gospel of the Mass, Our Lord wanted to leave us with the vocal prayer, *par excellence*, the *Our Father* which in a few words comprises all that a man can ask of God.[3] Throughout the centuries this prayer has ascended to God, filling innumerable souls in all kinds of situations with hope and consolation.

Neglecting vocal prayer would mean a great impoverishment of the spiritual life. But on the other hand,

---

[1] Matt 6:7-15
[2] St Cyprian, *Treatise on the 'Our Father'*
[3] cf St Augustine, *Sermon 56*

when these prayers are in frequent use, even when short but full of love of God, the path of contemplation in the midst of the world, or in work, is opened up and made easy. *We start with vocal prayers which many of us have been saying since we were children. They are made up of simple, ardent phrases addressed to God and to his Mother, who is our Mother as well. I still renew, morning and evening, and not just occasionally but habitually, the offering I learned from my parents: 'O my Lady, my Mother! I offer myself entirely to you, and in proof of my filial love, I consecrate to you this day my eyes, my ears, my tongue, my heart ...' Is this not, in some way, a beginning of contemplation, an evident expression of trusting self-abandonment?*

First one brief aspiration, then another, and another ... till our fervour seems insufficient, because words are too poor ...: then this gives way to intimacy with God, looking at God without needing rest or feeling tired.[4] And Saint Teresa, like all the Saints, knew well this accessible way for everyone to reach God: *I know,* she says, *that many persons who say vocal prayers are raised by God to high contemplation without their knowing how.*[5]

Let us think today about what interest and concentration we put into our vocal prayers, how many we say throughout the day, on the necessary pauses so that what we say to Our Lord is not *just words that follow one after the other ...*[6] Let us meditate on the need for that modicum of effort we have to put into them to avoid the routine which would soon mean the death of true devotion and true love. Let us try to make each aspiration, each vocal prayer, an act of love.

---

[4] St. J. Escrivá, *Friends of God*, 296
[5] St Teresa, *The Way of Perfection*, 30, 7
[6] R. Garrigou-Lagrange, *The Three Ages of the Interior Life*

94.2 Vocal Prayers.

The secret of the fruitful lives of good Christians lies in their prayer, in that they pray well and pray often. It is from our prayer, whether mental or vocal, that we derive strength for self-denial and sacrifice and overcome tiredness in work, offering our fatigue to God, and so continue faithful in the small heroic acts of each day. It has been said that prayer is the food and breath of the soul, because it puts us in close contact with God and leads us to know and love him more. Genuine piety is the habitual and unchanging attitude that allows the Christian to evaluate from God's standpoint his daily work. Looking at things in this way, he finds opportunity to exercise the virtues, to offer up the well-finished piece of work, the small mortifications ... Scarcely realising it, we become *immersed in God*, and gradually find we are praying as well through faultless work even though we may not be making express acts of prayer. A glance at a crucifix or at a picture of Our Lady, an aspiration, a short vocal prayer, all help us at this stage to maintain *this stable manner of being of the soul*, and it is then possible for us to *pray constantly*,[7] or *always to pray* as Our Lord asks.[8] There are many times when we ought to be concentrating intently on our work, and at such moments the mind is incapable of thinking directly about God and focusing our attention on what we are doing at the same time. Nevertheless, if we maintain that habitual disposition of the soul, that union with God, or at least retain the intention of doing everything for God, then we are in fact praying without interruption.

Just as the body needs food and the lungs crave fresh air, so the soul requires to turn to the Lord for sustenance,

---

[7] 1 Thess 5:17; Luke 18:1
[8] Luke 18:1

Our heart will find an habitual expression in words, in the vocal prayers taught us by God himself – the Our Father – or by his angels – the Hail Mary. On other occasions, we will use the time-proven words that have expressed the piety of millions of our brothers in the faith: prayers from the liturgy – 'lex orandi'; or others whose source is the love of an ardent heart, like the antiphons to Our Lady: 'Sub tuum praesidium', 'Memorare', 'Salve Regina'...[9] Many favourite prayers to the Blessed Virgin, many profound and beautiful poems to Our Lord such as the *Adoro te devote* of Saint Thomas Aquinas, (often said on Thursdays in honour of Our Lord in the Blessed Sacrament), were composed by men and women sometimes well-known and sometimes not. These traditional prayers have been kept lovingly in the bosom of the Church over the years as precious gems so that we could make use of them. Perhaps for many they have the remembered sweetness of those basic lessons for life they learnt at their mother's knee. They are a very important part of the spiritual equipment we need to face up to every kind of difficulty.

Vocal prayer is superabundance, an overflowing of love, and logically should be frequently employed from the start of the day till we give our last thought to God before rest. And it will rise to our lips, this vocal prayer, perhaps silently, at the most unexpected moments. *Acquire the habit of saying vocal prayers in the morning, while you are dressing, like little children. You will have greater presence of God later during the day.*[10]

94.3 Fighting routine and distractions.

Scripture tells us that the Patriarch Enoch walked with

---

[9] St. J. Escrivá, *Christ is passing by*, 119; *idem, Furrow*, 473
[10] *idem, The Way*, 553

God,[11] that he kept him in mind in his joys and sorrows and in all his undertakings. *If only we were more like that! If only we could walk through the world at God's heels; so close to him, so alive to his presence, that we could share everything with him, refer to him every moment of sunshine, every shadow of uncertainty in our lives; accept everything He sends us with conscious gratitude, obey the least whisper of his call!*[12] But often, unfortunately, the true point of reference for us is not God, but ourselves. Hence the necessity for this continual effort to immerse ourselves in God, to be attentive to his least requirement, avoiding self-centredness in our thoughts, or at least keeping them directed to God by doing some good works specifically for him, or offering them up as sacrifices.

Vocal prayers are an incomparable means for keeping God present in the course of our daily duties. To this end it is going to be necessary for us to pay attention to *what we are saying* in our prayer. Consequently we will sometimes have to struggle in very small but necessary details – pronouncing the words clearly and deliberately, and thereby steering clear of routine. There will also have to be time for reflection, so that what we are making vocal becomes in a certain way *mental* prayer, despite the fact that we may not be able to avoid distractions altogether.

Without some special grace from God it is impossible to maintain continual and perfect attention to *the sense and significant meaning* of the words. Sometimes our attention will be directed towards *the manner of pronouncing the words*; at other times we will give our attention to *the person we are addressing*. But there will be occasions when, through circumstances having to do with other people or with our surroundings, it will not be easy to give

---

[11] cf Gen 5:21
[12] R. A. Knox, *A Retreat for Lay People*, p. 18

prayerful attention in any of these three forms. Then it will
be necessary at least to examine our external attitude, being
careful to reject or eliminate any outside activity which *of
its nature* hinders interior attention. Some manual tasks, for
example, do not prevent the mind from concentrating on
something else; such could be the activity, say, of the
mother of a family, who prays the Rosary while she is
cleaning the house or keeping an eye on the little ones.
While she may be distracted from time to time, she
maintains that interior attention, something she could not
do while she was, say, reading a magazine or watching
television. In any event, we should draw up our plan of life
in such a way that whenever possible we can devote the
requisite time to certain vocal prayers like the *Angelus* or
the *Rosary*, on which we can concentrate properly. On the
other hand, the simple involuntary distractions that
momentarily divert our attention are imperfections which
Our Lord excuses when He sees us putting real effort into
our prayers.

Along with vocal prayers, the soul needs the daily
food of mental prayer. *Thanks to these moments of
meditation and to our vocal prayer and aspirations, we
will be able to turn our whole day into a continuous praise
of God, in a natural way and without any outward display.
Just as people in love are always thinking about each
other, we will be aware of God's presence. And all our
actions, down to the most insignificant, will be filled with
spiritual effectiveness.*[13] The Lord will look on them with
satisfaction and will bless them.

---

[13] St. J. Escrivá, *Christ is passing by*, 119

95. WHERE IS YOUR HEART?

95.1 The family, 'the primary environment' in which to sow the seed of the Gospel.

Our Lord advises us not to pile up treasures on earth, because they do not last long, being fragile and perishable: *moth and rust consume*, or *thieves break in and steal.*[1] However much we manage to accumulate in life, there is little point to it. Nothing on earth is worth putting our heart into in an absolute way. Our heart is made for God, and for the noble things of this earth in him. It is useful for all of us to ask ourselves frequently: What do I give my heart to? Exactly what is my treasure? What do I think about usually? What is the focal point of my most intimate concern? Is it God, present in the Tabernacle, perhaps at a short distance from where I live or from the office where I work? Or, on the contrary, is it my business, my study, or my work that occupies the foremost place ... or could it be unsatisfied selfish dreams or hungry desires to have more? Many men and women, if they were honest, would perhaps find themselves obliged to reply: I think about myself ... yes, only about myself and about people and things to do with my own interests. But we need to keep our heart fixed on God, on the mission we have received from him, and on other persons and things for God's sake. Jesus, with his infinite wisdom tells us: *Lay up for yourselves treasures in heaven, where neither moth nor rust consumes and where thieves do not break in and steal. For where your treasure is, there will your heart be also.* Our heart is placed in the Lord because He is the one real and absolute treasure. Not

---

[1] Matt 6:19-21

health, or prestige, or any feeling of well-being can be our treasure ... only Christ. And for his sake, in an ordered way, our treasure subsumes all the other noble aspirations and duties of an ordinary Christian life, the life of a Christian who, by divine vocation, finds himself situated precisely here in the world. In a special way, Our Lord wishes us to put our heart into serving the persons of the particular human or supernatural family we have, those who, ordinarily, are the ones we have to lead to God in the first place, and who constitute for us the first object we ought to sanctify.

Concern for others helps man to break free from his selfishness, to grow in generosity and in consequence to find true joy. He who knows he has been called by Our Lord to follow him closely no longer regards himself as the centre of the universe, because he has found many to serve in whom he sees Christ in need.[2]

The example of parents or of brothers and sisters in the home, is on many occasions of real value for the other members of the family who, from it, learn to see the world from a Christian viewpoint. The family is of such importance, by the Divine Will, that in it *the evangelising action of the Church has its beginning*.[3] It is *the first appropriate environment for sowing the seed of the Gospel and the one in which parents and children, like living cells, go on assimilating the Christian ideal of serving God and the brethren*.[4] It is a splendid place for apostolate. Let us examine today whether our family is like this, to see if we are like a leaven which day after day goes on transforming, little by little, those who live with us. Let us see whether indeed we are praying constantly as we should to Our Lord

---

[2] cf F. Koenig, *Pastoral Letter about the family*, 23 March 1977
[3] St John Paul II, *Address*, Guadalajara, Mexico, 30 January 1979
[4] idem, *Address to Bishops of Venezuela*, 15 September 1979

for our brothers' and sisters' or our children's vocations, and for the vocations of our parents, that they may move towards a complete dedication to God, for this is the greatest grace the Lord could give them, the real and precious treasure that with your help many of them can find.

95.2 Careful attention towards those God has placed in our charge.

Where our own treasure is, there we have love, self-surrender and the best of sacrifices. For this reason we should value greatly the particular call each one of us has received, and the vocation of those we live with, since they are to be the immediate beneficiaries of this treasure of ours. It is hard, after all, to love what is regarded as having little value. Besides, the Lord would not want a kind of charity that denied priority to those He has placed in our care, whether by a natural or supernatural kinship, because this would not be ordered and true.

The family is the basic and most important unit of society, the one God looks upon as its firmest support. And it is perhaps the part of society most insidiously and ruthlessly attacked from all sides: taxes are levied that ignore the social importance and value of the family; certain ideological and politically motivated trends in education militate against the proper formation of children; materialism and hedonism distort the vision of parents and teachers, and promote for specious demographic and social reasons a campaign against life itself, striking in this way at the very heart of the family; a false sense of freedom and independence is inculcated in young people, and advanced social programmes leave mothers with insufficient time to look after their children. Many have lost sight of the fact that parents have the right to educate their own children and, in the face of excessive state intervention, have ended up renouncing an elementary right which by its very nature cannot be given up. Sometimes – and this is due in part to these inhibitions – there are imposed certain kinds of teaching dominated by a materialistic view of man. In such methods the pedagogical and didactic approaches, textbooks employed, schemes of work, curricular programmes and school materials deliberately set aside the spiritual nature of the human soul.

Parents have to be aware that no earthly power can exempt them from the responsibility God has given them in relation to their children. In different ways we have all been given by Our Lord the care of others: the priest has the souls entrusted to him; the teacher has his pupils, the professor his students. Likewise, many others have the responsibility of giving spiritual formation. No one will respond on our behalf before God when we are asked: *Where are those I entrusted to you?* But each one of us will be able to reply: *Of those whom thou gavest me I lost not one,*[5] because, Lord, we knew how to use, with your grace, both ordinary and extraordinary means so that no one would stray.

All of us ought to be able to say with regard to those who have been entrusted to us: *Cor meum vigilat: My heart is vigilant.* This is the inscription on many images of Our Lady in the city of Rome. Our Lord wants us to have a care for all souls, but in the first place for our own, those He has entrusted to us.

Our Lord asks for an attentive love, a love capable of realising that perhaps someone is neglecting his duties towards God, and of then helping him kindly; or of being aware that another is sad and isolated from his fellows, so that we pay him more attention. With another it might be that we gently help him to go to confession, urging more

---

[5] John 18:9

insistently when the opportune moment comes. *A vigilant heart* is alert to notice when behaviour inappropriate to a Christian home has crept in, that programmes on the television, say, are watched without previous selection, or, too often, that conversations seem rarely to touch on other than banal topics, or that there is little evidence of an atmosphere of hard work, or genuine concern for others. The vigilant heart also is concerned to give good example, without losing patience, with prayer and more details of affection, asking Saint Joseph's intercession that we may live with fortitude and constancy, full of charity and human sympathy. And in the event that someone falls ill, those who are vigilant redouble their compassion because they have learnt that the sick are God's favourites and the one who is suffering now is the treasure of the house; he is enabled to make an offering of his sickness, to say some prayer, and in so doing suffers as little as possible, because affection alleviates or even turns the mind from pain, or at least moderates it to something less intolerable.

95.3 Devoting the necessary time, which takes priority over other interests. Family prayers.

Let us consider today in our prayer whether the family or those in our care do occupy the place in our lives desired by God, and see if our heart is truly watchful over them. Here, along with our vocation, is indeed a *treasure which lasts unto eternal life!* Other treasures which previously seemed important to us may well now fall into perspective and begin to lose their charm. Perhaps we may find that a lack of rectitude of intention has corroded them or that they were counterfeit treasures anyway, fool's gold of little value.

To live family life properly very often means making use of the opportunity to spend time for the benefit of others: to have time to celebrate family occasions or

reunions, time to talk, to listen, to understand, to pray
together ... It is not enough to have a generally benevolent
but invisible affection: we must make it overt and
appreciable, and for this we have to make a conscious
effort and pray, deliberately cultivating and exercising the
requisite human virtues and forgetfulness of self. It is far
from being a waste of time to put to ourselves the question:
for what or for whom do I live? What interests fill my
heart?

Now, when it seems evident that attacks on the family
have multiplied, the best way of defending it is by means
of true human affection, taking into account with open eyes
our own defects and those of others, and making God
present in an agreeable way in the home. This we can do
by saying grace at meals, by joining in with the smallest
children for their night prayers, by reading a few verses of
the Gospel with the older ones and saying a short prayer
for the dead, for the Pope's and the family's intentions.
Nor let us forget the *Holy Rosary*, the prayer which the
Roman Pontiffs have recommended so warmly and so
frequently to be recited in the family, and which draws
down so many graces. From time to time it will be possible
to pray while travelling, or at some moment which fits in
with the family timetable. And this need not always be left
to the initiative of mother or grandmother, because the
father or the older children can make a wonderful
contribution in this pleasant task. Many families have kept
up the healthy habit of going to Mass together on Sundays.

It isn't at all necessary for the practices of piety in the
family to be numerous, or lengthy, but it would be
unnatural if there were none at all in a home where all, or
almost all, were professed believers. Then again, it would
not make much sense if they individually regarded
themselves as faithful followers of Christ and the sincerity
of their belief found no reflection in their family life. It has

been said of parents who pray with their children that it is easier for them to find the way that leads to their hearts. And they never forget the help they have got from their parents – to converse with God, to have recourse to Our Lady in every situation. How many will have reached the gates of Heaven thanks to those prayers they learned from their mother's lips, or their grandmother's or older sister's!

United in this way, with great affection and an unshakable faith, they are better and more effectively able to resist attacks from the external environment. And if at any time sorrow or sickness intervene they are more easily borne with, and become opportunities for an even greater union and a deeper faith.

The Blessed Virgin, our Mother, will teach us the treasure we have in the calling from Our Lord, with all it implies, in one's own home, in one's family circle, in the persons God has wanted to involve us with in our life in so many different ways.

Within the Heart of Jesus we will find *an overflowing measure of grace* from the *fount of heavenly gifts*.[6] Let us try to make our heart like to his.

---

[6] *Roman Missal, Collect for Solemnity of the Sacred Heart of Jesus*

96. EVERYTHING WORKS OUT WELL

96.1 Loving the will of God. God has the best possible plans for each man. Serenity in the face of contradictions.

Everything, even the smallest object in the universe, exists because God keeps it in being. *He covers the heavens with clouds, he prepares rain for the earth, he makes grass grow upon the hills. He gives to the beasts their food, and to the young ravens that cry.*[1] The entire creation is the work of God, and He lovingly takes care of all his creatures, beginning by keeping them all in existence. *This 'maintaining' is, in a certain sense, a continual creation (conservatio est continua creatio).*[2] The same care and providence is extended in a particular way to man, the object of God's predilection.

Jesus Christ makes known to us constantly that God is our Father, and that he wants the best for his children. The very best we could imagine, for ourselves and for those we love best, falls far short of the divine plans. Our Father God knows very well what we need, and his all-seeing gaze takes in both this life and eternity; our sight is short and very defective, our view limited. It is in accord with reason that happiness and sanctity consist essentially in knowing, loving and carrying out the Will of God, which is manifested to us in different ways, but with sufficient clarity, throughout life. In the Gospel of the Mass, the Lord makes us a recommendation so that our days may be filled with peace: ... *do not be anxious about your life, what you*

---

[1] Ps 147:8-9
[2] St John Paul II, *General Audience*, 29 January 1986

shall eat or what you shall drink, nor about your body, what you shall put on. Is not life more than food, and the body more than clothing? Look at the birds of the air; they neither sow nor reap nor gather into barns, and yet your heavenly Father feeds them.[3] Here we have an invitation to live with cheerful hope in the carrying-out of our daily duties. It is logical that we shall meet with setbacks, anxieties and laborious difficulties, but we should bear them as God's children, without useless worry, or any spirit of rebellion or sadness, because we know that Our Lord allows these things to happen – this illness, that apparent disaster – to purify us, to convert us into co-redeemers with him. The sufferings and contradictions should serve to refine us as precious metals are refined, to help us grow in virtue and love God more ... *Have you not heard the Master himself tell you the parable of the vine and the branches? Here you can find consolation. He demands much of you, for you are the branch that bears fruit. And he must prune you 'ut fructum plus afferas': to make you bear more fruit'. Of course: that cutting, that pruning hurts. But, afterwards, what richness in your fruits, what maturity in your actions.*[4] Let us not be disconcerted when we encounter the contretemps of the divine plans; God is well aware of what He is about, and of what He is permitting to happen.

Let us take a good look at ourselves today, to see if we are accepting reverses, disappointments or apparent failures with equanimity; whether we are resentful or, no matter how briefly, giving rein to gloomy thoughts or rebelliousness. Let us see, side by side with Our Lord, whether our physical or moral weaknesses are not truly capable of drawing us towards our Father God, and of

---

[3] Matt 6:25-26
[4] St. J. Escrivá, *The Way*, 701

making us more humble. *Do not be anxious about your life
... Our Lord tells us once more in this time of prayer.*

96.2 Abandonment in God and responsibility.

*Very often we do not know what is good for us; and
what confuses matters more is that we think we do. We
have our own plans for our happiness, and too often we
look upon God as someone who will help us to carry them
out. The true state of affairs is invariably the reverse of
this. God has his own perfect plans for our happiness, and
is waiting for us to help him carry them out. And let it be
clear that we can in no way improve on God's plans.*[5]
Being possessed of a thoroughly practical certainty
concerning these truths, and living them day by day, leads
to serene abandonment even when we are faced with some
seemingly insurmountable obstacle which we cannot
understand and that causes us grief and frustration. Nothing
falls apart, there is no disastrous collapse if we are
supported by our sense of divine filiation: *But if God so
clothes the grass of the field, which today is alive and
tomorrow is thrown into the oven, will he not much more
clothe you ...?*[6]

It sometimes happens, Saint Thomas says, that when
an observer not proficient in medical sciences sees a doctor
prescribe water for one sick man and wine for another, he
thinks in his ignorance that the prescription is as random as
the tossing of a coin. *And so it happens with God. He,
knowing the causes of things and according to his
providence, in his Wisdom disposes whatever it is that men
need: he afflicts some who are perhaps good and allows
others who are bad to live in prosperity.*[7] We can never

---

[5] E. Boylan, *This Tremendous Lover*
[6] Matt 6:30
[7] St Thomas, *About the Creed*

forget that God wants us to be happy here, but He wants us to be still happier forever with him in Heaven.

Sanctity consists in the loving fulfilment of the Will of God, which is manifested in the duties of each day in one's own circumstances. Knowing that his loving attention and his divine providence embraces the minutest detail of our lives, we can abandon ourselves in God with complete trust. But this abandonment has to be active and responsible, with our applying the means that each situation demands: it may be going to the doctor when we are sick; it may be taking all the preliminary steps necessary to obtain that post we need so much and for which we have prayed to God: it may be working hard to make progress in our studies or our chosen profession, putting in the hours necessary to get through that difficult examination or achieve that required qualification ... Abandonment in God has to be closely united with responsibility, which leads us to use the most opportune human means, for on many occasions what is disguised as 'bad luck', adverse circumstances etc., is nothing but hidden mediocrity, indolence or imprudence in not employing the precise means that a situation has called for. When work is done conscientiously, with order, (systematically and methodically), when it is properly finished off, when it has been sanctified like constant apostolate done with a spirit of sacrifice, it gives fruit in due course. And if these fruits take their time in coming, it is a sign that God will give them by means we have not suspected, and that He wants us to sanctify ourselves in precisely these circumstances.

96.3 *Omnia in bonum* – **for those who love, everything works out in the best possible way.**

Our awareness of our divine filiation helps us to discover that all the happenings of our life are directed or permitted for our good by the most lovable Will of God. He who is our Father grants us what is best for us, and expects us to see his paternal love as much in adverse occurrences as in those more favourable events that are to our liking.[8]

As Saint Paul says: *in everything God works for good with those who love him.*[9] He who loves God and shows his love with deeds knows that, come what may, everything is for the best, provided one does not stop loving. And precisely because he loves, *he uses the means*, so that the result will be good, so that the finished work, carried out with rectitude of intention, will bear fruits of sanctity and apostolate. And once he has used the means available to him, he abandons himself in God and rests in his loving providence. *Take note*, Saint Bernard says, *he does not say that things serve for caprice, but work together for good. Not for caprice, but usefulness; not for pleasure, but salvation; not for our desire but for our advantage. In this sense, all things work for our good, even death itself, even sin itself ... For do not sins work towards the good of him who through them becomes more humble, more fervent, more solicitous, more cautious, more prudent?*[10] After using the means within our reach, or in matters over which we have no control, we will say in the intimacy of our heart: *Omnia in bonum*, all is for good.

With this conviction, fruit of divine filiation, we will live full of optimism and hope and so overcome many difficulties. *It looks as if the whole world is coming down on top of you. Whichever way you turn you find no way out. This time, it is impossible to overcome the difficulties. But, have you again forgotten that God is your father? All-*

---

[8] cf *The Navarre Bible*, note to Rom 8:28
[9] Rom 8:28
[10] St Bernard, *On the brevity of life*, 6

powerful, infinitely wise, full of mercy. He would never send you anything that is evil. That thing that is worrying you, it's good for you, even though those earthbound eyes of yours may not be able to see it now. 'Omnia in bonum!' Lord, once again and always, may your most wise Will be done.[11] *Omnia in bonum!* All is for good. We can turn everything into something pleasing to God and for the good of the soul. This expression of Saint Paul can serve as an aspiration or a short prayer which will give us peace in difficult moments.

The most holy Virgin, Our Mother, will teach us how to live trustfully and with confidence in God's omnipotence, if we have recourse to her frequently each day. In the most Sweet Heart of Mary, whose feast we celebrate in this month of June, we never fail to find peace, consolation and joy.

---

[11] St. J. Escrivá, *The Way of the Cross*, Ninth Station, 4

TWELFTH SUNDAY: YEAR A

97. DO NOT BE AFRAID

97.1 Courage in ordinary life.

In the Gospel of the Mass[1] Our Lord tells us not to be afraid, but to live as children of God. At times we come across people who are tormented and overwhelmed by the hardships that life brings with it. The adverse circumstances and the obstacles seem only to grow when one relies on human resources alone in order to overcome them. We also frequently meet Christians who seem to be ashamed of speaking clearly about God, of saying *no* to falsehood and, whenever necessary, of showing themselves to be faithful disciples of Christ. They are afraid of what people will say, of a critical remark, of going against the current or of drawing attention to themselves. Is it possible for a Christian not to draw attention to himself in a pagan environment, where so often economic values are the supreme values?

Jesus tells us not to be concerned about possible slander or criticism. *Do not be afraid of men, for everything that is now covered will be uncovered, and everything now hidden will be made clear.* What a shame if it were to be discovered that we were afraid of proclaiming to the four corners of the world the truth that God has entrusted to us! *What I say to you in the dark, tell it in the daylight; what you hear in whispers, proclaim from the housetops.* At times we will keep silent because that is the best thing to do, for reasons of supernatural prudence, or charity, but never out of fear or cowardice. We Christians are not friends of darkness and hidden corners; we are friends of light, of openness in our lives and in our words.

---

[1] Matt 10:26-33

The times we live in are such that we need to proclaim the truth clearly. Falsehood and confusion are leading many souls astray. It seems absurd, but at times even good doctrine, the moral norms of behaviour, following one's conscience in our work and in the demands of married life, common sense itself, are held in less esteem than some scandalous, erroneous doctrine which is held to be 'advanced' or tinged with a progressive hue ...

We shouldn't be afraid of losing the gloss of a superficial prestige, or of being criticised or even slandered because we go against the current or what happens to be fashionable. *If anyone declares himself for me in the presence of men, I will declare myself for him in the presence of my Father in heaven*, Our Lord says. He rewards us fully for all those times when people do not understand us because we try to live bravely, with holy daring, in a world which is frequently unable to understand anything except purely material values.

I consider, says Saint Paul, *that the sufferings of this present time are not worth comparing with the glory that is to be revealed to us.*[2] Therefore, Saint Cyprian comments, *who would not make the effort to achieve such great glory, to become a friend of God, to possess Christ immediately, to receive the divine rewards after the anguish and torments of the earth? If for the soldiers of this world it is glorious to return home after humbling the enemy, how much more glorious and praiseworthy will it be to return in triumph to heaven once the devil is overcome ...; to bear aloft the signs of victory ...; to be seated at God's side when He comes in judgement, be co-heir with Christ, to rank with the angels, and with the Patriarchs, the Apostles and the Prophets; to rejoice in the possession of the Kingdom of Heaven ...?*[3]

---

[2] Rom 8:18
[3] St Cyprian, *Letter to Fortunatus*, 13

97.2 Our strength is based on an awareness of our divine filiation.

Fearing neither life nor death,[4] facing even serious difficulties joyfully, steadfastly confronting obstacles that demand effort and sacrifice, serenely enduring illness, remaining always calm in the face of an uncertain future ... that is how God wants us to live. It is possible if we remember frequently each day that we are children of God, particularly when we are assailed by worry, anxiety or darkness. *Are not two sparrows sold for a penny? And not one of them will fall to the ground without your Father's will. But even the hairs of your head are all numbered. Fear not, therefore; you are of more value than many sparrows.*

God makes clear the great affection He has for us and the great value He places on mankind. Saint Jerome commenting on this passage from the Gospel of the Mass writes, *If the sparrows are so cheap and yet fall under the providence and care of God, how can you who are eternal by the nature of your souls be afraid that He whom you venerate as your Father will not take special care of you?*[5]

Divine filiation strengthens us when we are surrounded by personal weaknesses and the obstacles that we come up against; by the difficulties we encounter in an environment that is so often hostile to God and at times violently opposed to Christian ideals. *But the Lord is with me as a dread warrior*, the prophet Jeremiah tells us in the *First Reading* of the Mass.[6] This is the Prophet's cry of hope and confidence when he is alone, beset on all sides by his enemies. God my Father is with me as a dread warrior, we can repeat when we see danger close at hand and the storm clouds looming. *Dominus, illuminatio mea et salus mea, quem timebo?* The

---

[4] cf St. J. Escrivá, *Friends of God*, 132
[5] St Jerome, *Commentary on St Matthew's Gospel*, 10:29-31
[6] cf Jer 20:10-13

Lord is my light and my salvation; whom shall I fear?[7]

This is the victory that overcomes the world, our faith,[8] proclaimed the apostle Saint John in the midst of the great difficulties proceeding from the pagan world in which Christians, as ordinary citizens, worked in the most diverse trades and professions and carried out an effective apostolate. And the sure foundation of an unshakeable faith gives rise to a confidence that is not vanity or ingenuousness, but the joyful firmness of the Christian who in spite of his personal wretchedness and limitations knows that Christ has won the victory by his death on the cross and his glorious Resurrection. *God is my light and my salvation; whom shall I fear?* Nobody and nothing, Lord. You are the safeguard of my life!

97.3 Courage and trust in God in the great trials and in the little things of ordinary life.

Jesus encourages us to be afraid of nothing, except sin, which destroys our friendship with God and leads to eternal damnation. When faced by difficulties we must be strong and brave, like true sons of God. Our Lord tells us *Do not fear those who kill the body but cannot destroy the soul; rather fear him who can destroy both soul and body in hell.* This fear of God is a gift of the Holy Spirit. It helps us to struggle with greater determination against sin, against everything that separates us from God. It prompts us to avoid the occasions of sin, not to trust ourselves, remembering always that we have 'feet of clay', that we are fragile and brittle. Bodily evils, even death itself, are as nothing compared to the evils of the soul, to sin.

We should be worried by nothing except the fear of losing God. This fear is a filial concern, a care not to

---

[7] Ps 27:1
[8] 1 John 5:4

offend Him. At certain times in our life we may well undergo great trials. God will give us the grace necessary to endure them and to grow in interior life. *My grace is sufficient for you,*[9] Jesus will tell us.

He who helped Paul will take care of us. At such times we will call upon God, humbly and with faith: *'Lord, put not your trust in me. But I ... I put my trust in you.'* Then as we sense in our hearts the love, the compassion, the tenderness of Christ's gaze upon us – for He never abandons us – we shall come to understand the full meaning of those words of Saint Paul, *'virtus in infirmitate perficitur'* (2 Cor 12:9). If we have faith in Our Lord, in spite of our failings – or, rather, even with our failings – we shall be faithful to Our Father, God: his divine power will shine forth in us, sustaining us in our weakness.[10]

Normally, however, we shall have to be strong and brave in little things: when we politely but firmly turn down an invitation to a place or a show where a good Christian would feel ill at ease, when we have to give our opinion on the direction their teachers are giving to the education of our children; when we have to break off that conversation which is taking a dubious turn, or see an opportunity to invite a friend to some talks on the Faith, or lead up to the chat which results in that tactful, opportune advice about going to Confession. An ambitious apostolate is often held back or stopped by diffidence or cowardice in little things. And it is also courage in little things that make our life fruitful.

In the hour of rejection at the Cross, the Virgin Mary is there by her Son, willing to go through the same fate. Let us lose our fear of behaving like responsible Christians when the environment in which we move is not easy. She will help us.[11]

---

[9] 2 Cor 12:9
[10] St. J. Escrivá, *Friends of God*, 194
[11] St. J. Escrivá, *Furrow*, 977

8. CALMNESS IN THE FACE OF DIFFICULTIES

98.1 The storm on the lake. God will never abandon us.

According to the Gospels, the Apostles, while sailing to the opposite shore as the Lord had told them, were twice caught by a storm on the Lake of Gennesareth. In the Gospel of today's Mass[1] Saint Mark tells us that Jesus was with them in the boat. He used the time to rest after a hard day's preaching. He lay down in the stern, resting his head on a cushion, probably a simple, coarse leather bag stuffed with rags or wool. That was the usual thing the sailors had on these boats. How the angels in Heaven would gaze upon their King and Lord as he recovered his strength, lying upon the hard deck planking! He who governs the Universe is stretched out there exhausted!

Meanwhile his disciples, many of them sailors, begin to feel the first squalls of the gathering storm. It soon falls on them, with tremendous force ... *and the waves beat into the boat, so that the boat was already filling*. They did what they could, but the seas grew higher and rougher and they were about to founder. Then as a last resort they turn to Jesus. They wake him with a cry of distress. *Teacher, do you not care if we perish?*

The skill of those sea-hardened fishermen was not enough. Our Lord had to intervene. *And He awoke and rebuked the wind, and said to the sea, 'Peace! Be still!' And the wind ceased and there was a great calm.* Peace also entered the hearts of those frightened men.

Sometimes the storm arises around us or within us.

---

[1] Mark 4:35-40

And it seems that our frail craft cannot take any more. At times we have the impression that God is heedless of our fate. The waves are breaking over us: personal weaknesses, professional or financial difficulties that are beyond our management, illness, problems with children or parents, the menace of calumny, a hostile environment, slander ... But *if you live in the presence of God, high above the deafening storm, the sun will always be shining on you; and deep below the roaring and destructive waves, peace and calm will reign in your soul.*[2]

God will never abandon us. We must go to him, using all the means we need to employ. At all times, tell Jesus with the confidence of one who has taken him as his Master, and wants to follow him unconditionally, 'Lord, do not leave me!' And together with Him we will face up to those trials and surmount them. They will no longer be bitter, and we will not be dismayed by the storms that blow.

98.2 We must be ready to face up to misunderstandings.

Jesus awoke and rebuked the wind and said to the sea, 'Peace! Be still!' This miracle made an unforgettable impression on the Apostles. It confirmed their faith and prepared them for the harder, more testing battles that lay ahead. The sight of a perfectly calm sea, subject to the voice of Christ, was engraved on their hearts. Years afterwards, these men would pray, and the memory of this scene would bring peace to them as they underwent all the trials Our Lord had forewarned them of.

On another occasion, on the way to Jerusalem, Jesus had told them that what the prophets had foretold about the Son of Man was about to be fulfilled. *For he will be delivered to the Gentiles, and will be mocked and shamefully treated and spat upon; they will scourge him and kill him,*

---

[2] St. J. Escrivá, *The Forge*, 343

and on the third day he will rise.[3] At the same time He warns them that they too will go through terrible times of persecution and slander. *A disciple is not above his teacher, nor a servant above his master. If they have called the master of the house Beelzebub, how much more will they malign those of his household?*[4] Jesus wants to convince those first disciples, and us too, that there is no compromise possible between him and his doctrine on the one hand, and the world as a kingdom of sin on the other.[5] He reminds them not to be surprised to be treated in this way: *If the world hates you, know that it has hated me before it hated you.*[6] Hence, as Saint Gregory explains, *the hostility of the wicked echoes like praise for our way of life, because it shows that insofar as we annoy those who do not love God, there is at least some rectitude in us. Nobody can please God and the enemies of God at the same time.*[7] So if we are faithful there will be winds and storms. But Jesus will say once more to the stormy sea *'Peace! Be still!'*

At the very beginning of the Church the Apostles gathered abundant fruits. But at the same time they would suffer threats, insults, persecution.[8] They were not concerned whether opinion was favourable or hostile towards them. They were concerned to make Christ known to all, to take the fruits of our redemption to the uttermost corner of the earth. They preached the doctrine of Christ, which in purely human terms constituted a scandal for some and seemed sheer madness to others.[9] This doctrine entered all environments, transforming souls and customs.

---

[3] Luke 18:31-33
[4] Matt 10:24
[5] cf *The Navarre Bible*, note to John 15:18-19
[6] John 15:18
[7] St Gregory the Great, *Homilies on Ezekiel*, 9
[8] cf Acts 4:41-42
[9] cf 1 Cor 1:23

Many of the circumstances within which the Apostles had to work have changed, but others remain as they were or have become even worse. Materialism, the excessive love of comfort and well-being, sensuality and ignorance represent once again in many places furious winds and stormy seas. And we can add to this the temptation of many people to adapt the doctrine of Christ to the times, seriously deforming the essential message of the Gospel.

If we want to be apostles in the midst of the world we must realise that some people – at times our husband, our wife, our parents, or an old friend – will not understand us. We will have to take heart, because it is not easy to row against the stream. We will have to work calmly and firmly. We cannot be deterred or allow ourselves to be deflected by the attitude of those who in many ways have compromised or so identified themselves with the customs of the new paganism that they seem unable any longer to understand the transcendent, supernatural meaning of life.

Our intimacy with God will give us calmness and strength, and we will be a firm rock for many. We can never forget that, particularly nowadays, *the Lord needs strong and courageous souls who refuse to come to terms with mediocrity, but will be able to enter all kinds of environments with a sure step ...*[10] In parent-teacher associations, in professional bodies, in the universities, in the trade unions, in informal conversation before or after a meeting ... *As a specific example, the influence of families is particularly important in social and public life. 'They should be the first to take steps to see that the laws ... not only do not transgress against, but actually support and positively defend the rights and duties of the family,' (cf Familiaris consortio, 44) in this way promoting real 'family politics' (ibid). In this field it is essential to foster*

---

[10] St. J. Escrivá, *Furrow*, 416

in a renewed and complete way knowledge of the doctrine of the Church on the family, to awaken the consciences and social and political responsibilities of Christian families, and to establish or strengthen existing associations for the good of the family.[11] We cannot remain inactive while the enemies of God strive to eliminate all trace of the eternal destiny of man.

98.3 Our attitude towards difficulties.

'The three concupiscences (cf 1 John 2:16) are like three gigantic forces which have unleashed a tremendous frenzy of lust, of a created being's conceited pride in his own strength, and of a desire for riches' (St Josemaría Escrivá, Letter, 14 February 1974, 10) ... And without being pessimistic or depressed, we can see that ... these forces have achieved an unprecedented development and a monstrous aggressiveness, to such an extent that 'an entire civilization is tottering, powerless and without moral resources to fall back on' (ibid).[12] We cannot remain inactive in such a situation. For the love of Christ urges us on, says Saint Paul in the *Second Reading*.[13] Charity, and the real need of so many creatures, drives us to carry out an untiring apostolic activity in all environments. Each person has to work in his own environment, in spite of the hostility we will meet and the misunderstandings of people who cannot or do not want to understand.

Walk therefore, 'in nomine Domini', with joy and security in the name of the Lord. No pessimism! If difficulties arise, then the grace of God will come more abundantly as well. If more difficulties appear, more of

---

[11] Spanish Episcopal Conference, Pastoral Instruction, *Catholics in Public Life*, 22 April 1986, 162

[12] Bl. A. del Portillo, *Letter*, 25 December 1985, 4

[13] 2 Cor 5:14-17

God's grace will come down from Heaven. If there are many difficulties, there will be many graces from God. Divine help is always proportionate to the obstacles with which the world and the devil oppose apostolic work. And so I would even dare to affirm that, in a way, it is good that there are difficulties, because then we will obtain more help from God. 'Where sin increased, grace abounded all the more' (Rom 5:20).[14]

We can use this opportunity to purify our intentions, to be more attentive to the Master, to strengthen our faith. Our attitude must always be one of forgiveness and calmness, because God is with each of us. *Christian, Christ is sleeping in your boat,* Saint Augustine reminds us; *Wake him, and he will rebuke the storm and peace will be restored.*[15] Everything is for our good and the good of souls. It is enough to be in his company to feel that we are safe. Worry, fear and cowardice arise when our prayer weakens. He knows well enough everything that is happening to us. And if need be, he will rebuke wind and sea, and a great calm will be established, and his peace will flood into us. And we too will be filled with awe like the apostles.

The Blessed Virgin will not leave us for an instant. *If the winds of temptation arise, fix your eyes on the star, call upon Mary ... With her for a guide you will not go astray; whilst invoking her, you will never lose heart; so long as she is in your mind, you are safe from deception. If she holds your hand, you cannot fall; under her protection you have nothing to fear; if she walks before you, you will not grow weary; if she shows you favour, you will reach the goal.*[16]

---

[14] Bl. A. del Portillo, *Letter*, 31 May 1987, 22
[15] St Augustine, *Sermon 361*, 7
[16] St Bernard, *Homilies on the Blessed Virgin Mary*, 2

TWELFTH SUNDAY: YEAR C

99. THE LOVE AND FEAR OF GOD

99.1 Love of God and submission to his infinite holiness.

O God, thou art my God, I seek thee,
My soul thirsts for thee;
My flesh faints for thee,
as in a dry and weary land where no water is.
My soul thirsts for thee,
O God, my God ...

we pray in the *Responsorial Psalm* of the Mass,[1] making the liturgical prayer our own. To get ever closer to God Our Lord we must depend on two solid rock foundations which are united and complementary: confidence and respectful reverence; closeness and reverential submission; love and fear. *They are the two arms with which we embrace God,*[2] teaches Saint Bernard. We are attracted to God the Father, full of mercy and goodness, the fulness of all true good. In the knowledge that we are less than nothing, we humbly bow down before this same God, absolutely sublime, imposing, exalted. We submit our will to him and fear his just punishments. In today's Mass we also pray: *Sancti nominis tui, Domine, timorem pariter et amorem fac nos habere perpetuum ...* – *Grant, O Lord, that we may always revere and love your holy name, for you never deprive of your guidance those you set firm on the foundation of your love.*[3] Love and a holy filial fear are the two wings that will raise us to him.

---

[1] Ps 62:2
[2] St Bernard, *On consideration*, 5:15
[3] *Collect*

The fear of the Lord is the beginning of wisdom,[4] Holy Scripture teaches us. And this is the basis of all the virtues, for *if a man is not steadfast and zealous in the fear of the Lord, his house will be quickly overthrown.*[5] Christ himself teaches his friends that they should not fear those who can kill the body, because there is nothing more they can do. I will tell you whom to fear, he says to his most faithful followers, to those who have left all things to follow him. *Fear him who, after he has killed, has power to cast into hell; yes, I tell you, fear him!*[6] The Acts of the Apostles tell us how the early Church grew, was built up, *walking in the fear of the Lord and in the comfort of the Holy Spirit.*[7]

We should not forget that the love of God grows stronger the farther we are from mortal sin and the greater the efforts we make to overcome deliberate venial sin. The holy fear of God is a great help to us in carrying on this open struggle against everything that offends him. It is always a filial fear, proper to a son who recoils from inflicting sorrow and sadness on his Father. He knows who his Father is, what sin is, and the infinite separation it imposes on the sinner. This is why Saint Augustine says *Blessed the soul who fears God, since it is strong against the temptations of the devil. 'Blessed is the man who fears the Lord always' (Prov 28:14) and he to whom has been given the remembrance of the fear of the Lord. He who fears God leaves the pathway of evil and adheres to the path of virtue. The fear of God makes a man wary and vigilant to avoid sin. The dissolute life triumphs where there is no fear of God.*[8]

Love of God and filial fear are two aspects of the same

---

[4] Ps 110:10
[5] Sir 27:3-4
[6] Luke 12:4
[7] Acts 9:31
[8] St Augustine, *Sermon on humility and the fear of God*

attitude which enables us to walk in safety. As we consider the infinite goodness of God, who approaches us in the Sacred Humanity of Jesus Christ, we are moved to love him more and more. As we contemplate the majesty and justice of God and our own nothingness, the fear of saddening God is awakened, together with the fear of losing him whom we love so much, because of our personal sins. So *fear and love must go together*, St J. H. Newman advises us. *Continue to fear, continue to love until the last day of your lives*, he tells us.[9] From that moment on, only love will remain. *Perfect love casts out fear.*[10]

99.2 The importance of filial fear for the uprooting of sin.

The holy fear of God is a guarantee and support of true love. It helps us to make a definitive break with mortal sins. It impels us to do penance for the sins we have committed, and preserves us from deliberate faults. *The thought of the punishment we deserve for our sins helps us to face the daily difficulties and deprivations and struggles without which there cannot be any real freedom from sin or any perfect union with God. We always have, indeed, plenty of reason to be penetrated with the fear of God when we consider the many occasions of sin that lie all around us, our own extreme weakness, the strength of our inordinate attachments and habits, our natural inclination to self-indulgence, the pull of our own concupiscence from within and the attractions of the world from without, our many faults and defects and the plain carelessness of which we are guilty every day.*[11] When faced with such personal

---

[9] St J. H. Newman, *Parochial Sermons*, 24

[10] 1 John 4:18

[11] B. Baur, *Frequent Confession*, p158

weakness, is it possible not to fear? Is it possible not to trust in the immense divine goodness?

Filial fear turns our affection from sin and keeps the soul on guard against a false and deceptive complacency. The greatest of dangers is perhaps precisely that lack of concern about the sin that has been committed and a thoughtlessness and superficiality which could lead eventually to a total loss of the sense of sin. This attitude, which can be seen in those who seem to be falling back into paganism, is the result of having lost this holy fear of God. In such deplorable situations the offence against God is ridiculed, passed off as trivial or otherwise made light of. The most serious aberrations are held to be 'only natural', because the relationship has been broken between the creature and its Creator, on whom it depends for its very existence. The most serious deformations of conscience, and therefore of the essential direction of man, frequently have their origin in the loss of this attitude of sacred reverence for him who created all things out of nothing.

Filial fear and love always go together. If we were to reject the filial fear of God, the desire to please him, the concern not to grieve him, we would run the risk of altogether neglecting the ascetical struggle and fall into a presumptuous reliance on the goodness of God. On the other hand, if one is motivated only by fear, one cuts oneself off from the great and merciful love of God our Father, from childlike simplicity and trustful abandonment. These attitudes are essential for a soul aspiring to holiness.

The beginning of the fear of God is an imperfect love. It is based on fear of punishment. But this fear can and must be raised to a filial attitude from which we come to contemplate above all the greatness of God, his infinite majesty and our condition as creatures. *'Timor Domini sanctus' – the fear of God is holy. It is a fear which is the veneration of a son for his Father – never a servile fear, for your Father God is not a tyrant.*[12] It is transformed into the fear of a child who sincerely loves his Father, and this love gives him the strength to avoid everything that might grieve his parent or come between them.

99.3 Confession and the holy fear of God.

When we go to the Sacrament of Penance it will help us very much if we foster the holy fear of God in our souls. To receive the sacrament, attrition (a supernatural but imperfect sorrow, arising from fear of punishment, or revulsion from the ugliness of the sin ...) is sufficient. But we will receive much more grace if we impel our soul to a sense of filial fear for having offended an Almighty God who is also Our Father. It will be much easier to pass from this filial attitude to one of genuine contrition, a repentance springing from love, to an attitude of sorrow based on love. Then confession becomes an immense source of grace, a place where love grows constantly stronger.[13]

Interior life grows in sensitivity and depth if we keep continually before us those truths that reveal to us the foundations of this gift of the Holy Spirit: God's holiness and our wretchedness, our daily failures, the absolute dependence of the creature on his Creator, the enormity of a single venial sin in the sight of the divine holiness, the ingratitude implied by our lack of generosity in living up to the demands of our vocation ...[14] We shall understand better the mystery of sin if above all we develop the habit of considering frequently the Passion of Our Lord. We shall learn to love, and thereby dread committing a single venial sin. When we contemplate the suffering that Christ endured for our sins, the countless sins of all the world, our

---

[12] St. J. Escrivá, *The Way*, 435

[13] cf St John Paul II, *Reconciliatio et poenitentia*, 31

[14] cf B. Baur, *op cit*, p. 160

hope will be strengthened and our contrition intensified, and we shall have a firmer resolve to avoid every deliberate fault.

The holy fear of God joined to love gives a special strength to the Christian's life. With it, nothing can make him tremble, for nothing can then separate him from the love of God.[15] The soul is consolidated in the virtue of hope and set free from a false and careless security by maintaining a watchful love – *cor meum vigilat* – against the treacherous lures of temptation.

Let us ask our Mother Mary, *Refugium peccatorum*, to make us understand just how much we lose every time we step aside from the path that leads to her son Jesus, even if our faults are only slight ones.

---

[15] cf Rom 8:35-39

TWELFTH WEEK: MONDAY

100. THE SPECK IN OUR BROTHER'S EYE

100.1 Pride leads us to exaggerate our neighbour's faults and to underestimate and excuse our own. Avoiding negative judgements on others.

On one occasion Our Lord said to those who were listening to Him, *Why do you see the speck that is in your brother's eye, but do not notice the log that is in your own eye? Or how can you say to your brother, 'Let me take the speck out of your eye,' when there is the log in your own eye? You hypocrite, first take the log out of your own eye, and then you will see clearly to take the speck out of your brother's eye.*[1] Avoiding negative, and often unjust, judgements on others is a sign of humility.

The slightest faults of others are exaggerated by our personal pride, whereas our own perhaps much greater defects are minimised and explained away. Moreover, pride tends to see in others what are really our own imperfections and errors. Hence Saint Augustine gives this wise piece of advice: *Strive to acquire the virtues you think your brothers lack, and then you will no longer see their defects, because you yourselves will not have them.*[2]

Humility on the other hand has a positive influence through a series of virtues which favour a good human and Christian atmosphere in social life. Only the humble man is in a position to forgive, to understand, and help, because he alone realises that he has received everything from God. He is aware of his own wretchedness and how much he himself is in need of the divine mercy. So even when he

---

[1] Matt 7:3-5
[2] St Augustine, *Commentary on Psalm 30*, 2, 7

has to judge, he is understanding towards his neighbour. He finds excuses and forgives whenever necessary. Besides, we have a very limited view of what motivates the actions of others. God alone can penetrate into the most intimate interior of hearts, read minds and grasp the real effect and value of all the circumstances that influence and accompany any action.

We must learn to pass over even the obvious and undeniable defects of the people we are with each day, so that we do not keep our distance from them or lose our respect for them because of their mistakes or bad manners. Let us learn from Our Lord, who *could not entirely excuse the sin of those who crucified him, but extenuated its malice by pleading their ignorance. When we cannot excuse a sin, let us at least make it worthy of compassion by attributing the most favourable cause we can to it, such as ignorance or weakness.*[3]

If we make the effort to discover our neighbour's good points, we shall see that the deficiencies in his character, the defects in his behaviour, are as nothing in comparison with his virtues. This positive, just attitude towards those with whom we are constantly in contact will bring us closer to God. We shall grow in interior mortification, charity and humility. *Let us strive always to look at the virtues and good deeds we see in others,* Saint Teresa tells us, *and cover their defects with the thought of our own great sins. This is a manner of acting that, although we cannot do so with perfection right away, gradually gains for us a great virtue – that of considering all other men as being better than ourselves. In such a way, with the help of God, one begins to acquire this virtue.*[4]

We have to adopt a positive attitude towards the

---

[3] St Francis de Sales, *Introduction to the Devout Life*, III, 28
[4] St Teresa, *Life*, 13, 10

shortcomings of others, even when they are external sins like gossiping or working badly. In the first place we must pray for them, atone for them to God and be patient and strong. We must love and esteem them more, because love and esteem is what they need. We must be loyal and help them with fraternal correction.

100.2 Accepting people as they are, with their defects. Helping them by means of fraternal correction.

Our Lord did not discuss the apostles or look down on them because of their defects, which are evident and clearly reflected in the Gospels. At the beginning of their dedication to God they are at times moved by envy, or anger, and are even ambitious for prominence among themselves. At such times the Master corrects them tactfully and is patient with them and continues loving them. He teaches those of his followers who are to hand on his doctrine something that is essential in family life, in a working environment, in personal relationships, and indeed in the whole of the Church: it is to live charity in deeds.

Loving others despite all their defects is the fulfilment of the Law of Christ. *For the whole law is fulfilled in one word, 'you shall love your neighbour as yourself'.*[5] This commandment of Jesus does not say we must love only those who are without defects, or those who have certain virtues. Because charity is an ordered virtue, Our Lord asks us to esteem first of all those whom God has placed at our side by ties of blood or by reason of family relationships, then those who work beside us and those who are our friends and neighbours ... This charity will have its own particular characteristics according to the bonds which unite us. But we must always have an open, welcoming attitude, and have the desire to help everyone. It is not a

---

[5] Gal 5:14

question of practising this virtue with ideal persons, but with those who actually live and work with us, with those we meet in the street at rush-hour, when the traffic is at its worst and public transport overcrowded. Perhaps at home or at the office we shall come across cross-grained people who are irritable or even in a bad temper, those who are unwell or tired, those who are selfish and envious. It is a question of getting along with these real, specific individuals, of being considerate with them and helping them.

Our neighbour's faults demand the response of a Christian. We must be understanding. We must pray for them and, when appropriate, help them by means of fraternal correction. Our Lord recommended no less,[6] and the Church has always practised it.

This fraternal help is the fruit of charity. It has to be exerised humbly, without wounding. The correction should be given alone, in a friendly, positive way, helping that friend or colleague to realise that the point in question harms his soul, or his work, or is making it difficult for others to get along with him. It could detract from the human regard or prestige he should be able to expect. The Gospel precept goes far beyond the purely human level of social convention and even of friendship, when this is based on purely human criteria. It is a sign of human loyalty, and avoids any criticism or gossiping behind people's backs. Is this the way we behave? Do we really carry out this recommendation that comes to us from Christ himself?

100.3 Positive criticism.

If we make a point of not concentrating our attention on *the speck in our brother's eye*, it will be easy to avoid

---

[6] Matt 18:15-17

speaking badly of anyone. In any given case, if we have the duty of judging a particular action, of looking critically at what someone has done, we shall do so, remembering that we are doing it in the presence of God. We shall pray and purify our intentions. We shall respect the elementary norms of prudence and justice. *I shall not tire of insisting,* St Josemaría Escrivá would repeat, *that the person who has the duty of judging must listen to both sides. 'Does our law judge a man without first giving him a hearing and learning what he does?' that noble, loyal and upright man Nicodemus reminded the priests and Pharisees who sought to condemn Jesus.*[7]

If we must criticise, the criticism should always be constructive and appropriate. We must always respect the doer of the action and his intentions, which we can know only in part. The Christian makes his criticism in a very human way, without wounding. He strives to maintain friendly relations even with those who are opposed to him, because he shows his respect and understanding.

In all honesty, the Christian does not judge where he does not know. When he does judge, he knows he must take into account the time and place, and every other available circumstance, and express himself with care. Otherwise he could easily lapse into detraction or slander. Charity and honesty mean that we will not irrevocably make our minds up on the basis of a first simple impression. We will not pass on pieces of gossip as the truth, or that unconfirmed piece of news – perhaps it never will be confirmed – which damages the good name of someone or of an institution.

Charity helps us to see the defects of others only in the context of their motives and positive qualities. Humility, however, enables us to discover so many errors and defects

---

[7] St. J. Escrivá, *Letter*, 29 September 1957

of our own that, without being pessimistic, we are led to ask God to forgive us. We shall understand that others have their faults, and we shall make an effort to improve by amending our own. To do this we must learn to receive and accept the honest and well-meant criticism of those who know us and care for us. *A sure sign of spiritual greatness is listening to advice, accepting it and being grateful for it.*[8] It is characteristic of people overwhelmed by pride that they will not accept advice. They always have an excuse at hand, or react badly to those who out of charity or friendship want to help them overcome a failing or avoid repeating a bad course of action.

We have many reasons to give thanks to God. Among them we hope to have people at our side who will give us a timely warning about where we are going wrong and advise us as to what we can and should do better. This is friendly, honest criticism, and worth more than its weight in gold.

The Blessed Virgin Mary always had an appropriate word. She never gossiped, and many times kept silent.

---

[8] S. Canals, *Jesus as Friend*

TWELFTH WEEK: TUESDAY

101. THE NARROW PATH

101.1 The road that leads to Heaven is narrow. Temperance and mortification.

On the way to Jerusalem someone asked him, *Lord, will those who are saved be few?*[1] Jesus did not give a direct answer, but replied, *Strive to enter by the narrow gate; for many, I tell you, will seek to enter and will not be able.* In the Gospel of today's Mass, Saint Matthew reports this exclamation of Our Lord: *For the gate is narrow and the way is hard that leads to life, and those who find it are few.*[2]

Life is a road that ends in God. It is a short road. It is important that when we reach our journey's end the door be opened and that we may enter. *We press onwards on our journey towards the consummation of history ... The Lord himself said: Behold, I am coming soon, bringing my recompense, to repay each one for what he has done ...* (Apoc 22:12-13).[3]

Two roads there are, two attitudes to life. One is to look for the most comfortable and agreeable way, to pamper the body and avoid sacrifice and penance; the other to seek the will of God even though it takes an effort to guard the senses and keep the body in check. It is either to live like pilgrims who, since they are only passing through, have what they strictly need and do not attach much importance to material things, or to be chained down by comfort-seeking, by pleasure and material goods which are

---

[1] Luke 13:23
[2] Matt 7:14
[3] Second Vatican Council, *Gaudium et spes*, 45

seen as ends in themselves and not simply as means.

One of these two pathways leads to Heaven, the other *to destruction, and those who go that way are many.* We must frequently ask ourselves which of these paths we are following, and where it is we are heading. Are we pressing on – straight for Heaven, in spite of our defects and weaknesses? Are we following the narrow road? Do we practise temperance and mortification constantly, offering up small but none the less real sacrifices? Where are we heading? What is really the underlying objective of all that we do?

To want something (in theory and in principle) does not, however, mean much. We would learn more by looking at actual facts. A student bent on becoming a doctor would not enrol in the Faculty of Languages ... Were he to enrol in this Faculty, however, he would be showing by the very fact of his choosing it that the attainment of his professional ambitions will depend on the study of linguistics rather than medicine, in spite of whatever he may say to the contrary ... This is because when we want something we have to choose the requisite means to obtain it ... If a soldier were to say that he wished to go to his unit's headquarters, but quite deliberately took the road leading to the enemy lines, he would really be wanting to go where he professedly did not want to go.[4] And if the reason offered is that he has chosen that road because it is more convenient, then what he actually wants is the road itself. He does not care in the least where it leads him.

Many people spend their lives in the pursuit of immediate goals. They do not worry about God, the be-all and end-all of their lives, who should be the reference point for everything else. To gain that perspective *we need to smoothe off the rough edges a little more each day – just as if we were working in stone or wood – and get rid of the*

---

[4] F. Suarez, *The Narrow Gate*

hindering defects in our own lives with a spirit of penance ... And with small mortifications.[5]

101.2 Need for mortification, struggle against comfort-seeking.

We show a preference for the broad road, the least uncomfortable way through life, even though it has little to offer us. We choose the wide door, which does not lead to Heaven. Frequently we are overwhelmed by an unruly, intemperate desire for material possessions.

The path Our Lord points out to us is a joyful one. Yet at the same time it is the path of the cross and sacrifice, of temperance and mortification. *If any man would come after me, let him deny himself, and take up his cross daily, and follow me.*[6] *Unless a grain of wheat fall into the earth and die, it remains alone; but if it dies, it bears much fruit.*[7]

We need to practise the virtue of temperance in this life if we desire to enter into the next life. We Christians must live a spirit of detachment in our attitude to the things we possess and use. We must not be unduly concerned about material goods. We should not seek to acquire or hold on to things that are superfluous to our needs. Where necessary, a sign of our rectitude of intention will be the way we live mortification in this area. We cannot be like those people who *seem to be dominated by economics; almost all of their personal and social lives are permeated by a kind of economic mentality.*[8] Their objective is the possession of material goods, thinking that with them they can fulfil their longing for happiness. They have a frenzied urge to obtain them, and forget all too easily that our life

---

[5] cf St. J. Escrivá, *The Forge*, 403
[6] Luke 9:23
[7] John 12:24
[8] Second Vatican Council, *loc cit*, 63

has to be a road that leads to God. It is nothing more than that – a road leading to God. Our Lord warns us: *Take heed to yourselves,* He tells us, *lest your hearts be weighed down with dissipation and drunkenness and the cares of this life.*[9] *Let your loins be girded and your lamps be kept burning, and be like men who are waiting for their master to come home from the marriage feast.*[10]

Along the broad road of ease, comfort and avoidance of mortification, the graces God gives us shrivel and remain fruitless, like the seed that falls among the thorns. *They are choked by the cares and riches and pleasures of life, and their fruit does not mature.*[11] Sobriety, however, makes it easier for us to approach God. *With a pampered and satiated body the soul is not free to fly high.*[12]

We must press on towards God, and our only concern need be that we are on the right road. Are we really on the good road, that of sacrifice and penance, joy and dedication to the service of others? Do we make a serious effort to overcome the desires for ease and comfort that constantly allure us?

101.3 Some examples of temperance and mortification.

Temperance is a very effective apostolic weapon when dealing with an all-too-frequently materialistic environment. It is one of the most attractive characteristics of Christian life. Wherever we are we must make the effort to give the good example the practice of this virtue promotes. It will be a natural feature of the way we behave. For many people, the good example given by a Christian has been the beginning of their finding God.

---

[9] Luke 21:34
[10] Luke 12:35
[11] Luke 8:14
[12] St Peter of Alcantara, *Treatise on Prayer and Meditation*, 11:3

A temperate life is a life of mortification and joy. We shall often find opportunities to practise mortification in the little things that allow our reason to control our bodies and enable the soul to understand the things relating to God. Interior mortification guides our imagination and memory by keeping away useless or harmful thoughts and memories. It is also practised in the control of the tongue, by means of which we steer clear of useless and frivolous conversations, for example, or of gossip.

To follow along the narrow path of temperance we must also practise mortification of the external senses – sight, hearing, taste ... *One has to give the body a little less than its due. Otherwise it turns traitor.*[13] We allow ourselves a little less than we would like in comfort, in indulging our whims etc. There are frequent opportunities for mortifications in ordinary, everyday life, *in hard, constant, orderly work, knowing that the spirit of sacrifice is best lived in finishing off well the work we have started; in punctuality, filling the day with heroic minutes; in taking care of the things we have or use; in showing our zeal for service by our fulfilling to the last detail the smallest obligations; in the specific points of charity by which we make the path to sanctity attractive for others; at times a smile can be the best sign of a spirit of penance ...*[14]

The narrow path passes through all the activities of a Christian, from our attitude to home comforts to the way we use the material and implements we work with or the way we relax. To rest, it is not necessary to spend a lot of money, or devote an inordinate amount of time to playing games to the detriment of our other duties. A good example of temperance and sobriety can also be shown in the moderation with which we make use of television and

---

[13] St. J. Escrivá, *The Way*, 196
[14] *ibid*, *Letter*, 24 March 1930

other aids to enjoyment or entertainment that technology makes available for us.

The narrow path is safe and attractive. Along it, together with a certain note of sobriety and sacrifice, we also encounter joy, because *the cross is no longer a gallows. It is the throne from which Christ reigns. And at his side, his Mother, our Mother too. The Blessed Virgin will obtain for you the strength that you need to walk resolutely in the footsteps of her Son.*[15]

---

[15] *ibid, Friends of God,* 141

102. YOU WILL KNOW THEM BY THEIR FRUITS

102.1 Good fruit is produced by a sound tree. False teachers and their bad doctrine.

Our Lord repeatedly insists on the danger from false prophets who will lead many to spiritual ruin.[1] In the Old Testament there are references to these bad shepherds who wreak havoc on the People of God. The prophet Jeremiah, for example, denounces the impiety of those who *prophesied by Baal and led my people Israel astray ... they speak visions of their own minds, not from the mouth of the Lord ... lead my people astray with their lies and their recklessness, when I did not send them or charge them; so they do not profit this people at all.*[2] Such unreliable guides soon made their appearance in the bosom of the Church. Saint Paul calls them *false brothers* and *false apostles*,[3] and warns the first Christians to be wary of them. Saint Peter calls them *false doctors*.[4] Nowadays also, there are undoubtedly many teachers of error. They have sown the bad seed abundantly and have been the cause of confusion and ruin for many souls.

Our Lord warns us in the Gospel of today's Mass[5] to *beware of false prophets, who come to you in sheep's clothing but inwardly are ravenous wolves.* They inflict great harm on souls. Those who go to them for light find

---

[1] cf Matt 24:11; Mark 13:22; John 10:12
[2] cf Jer 23:9-40
[3] Gal 2:4; 2 Cor 11:26; 1 Cor 11:13
[4] 2 Pet 2:1
[5] Matt 7:15-20

darkness. They seek strength and instead find doubt and weakness. Our Lord points out that both the true and the false messengers of God will be known by their fruits. This is how you can tell them. The preachers of false reform and doctrine bring nothing but separation from the life-giving vine-stem of the Church, the bewilderment and perdition of souls. Jesus tells us: *You will know them by their fruits. Are grapes gathered from thorns, or figs from thistles? So every sound tree bears good fruit, but the bad tree bears evil fruit. A sound tree cannot bear evil fruit, nor can a bad tree bear good fruit.* In this gospel passage Our Lord warns us to be prudent and on our guard against these lying teachers and their deceitful doctrines. It is not always easy to detect them, for sometimes bad doctrine comes with the appearance of being good.

102.2 Intimacy with God and Christian works.

Sound trees give good fruit. The tree is sound when the good sap flows through it. For the Christian, this is the life of Christ himself, personal holiness, and nothing else can take its place. We should never separate ourselves from him. *He who abides in me, and I in him, he it is that bears much fruit, for apart from me you can do nothing.*[6] When we are close to Jesus we become effective. We learn how to be joyful, to be understanding, and to love. In short, we learn how to be good Christians.

The life of union with Christ necessarily transcends the limited sphere of the individual – and this to the benefit of others. This is the source of apostolic fruitfulness: *the apostolate, of whatever kind it be, must be an overflow of the interior life,*[7] of a life-giving union with Our Lord. *This life of intimate union with Christ in the Church is*

---

[6] John 15:5
[7] St. J. Escrivá, *Friends of God*, 239

maintained by the spiritual helps common to all the faithful, chiefly obtained by active participation in the liturgy. Laymen should make such a use of these helps that, while meeting their human obligations in the ordinary conditions of life, they do not separate their union with Christ from their ordinary lives, but through the very carrying out of their everyday tasks, whose performance is God's will for them, actually promote the growth of their union with him.[8] Contact with Christ in Holy Communion, in the Mass (the true centre of the Christian life), in personal prayer and mortification which permit this contact with God, will show itself in the specific way we set about our daily work, in our dealings with others, whether they are believers or not, and in the way we carry out our civic and social duties. The sap is not seen, but the fruit certainly is. Christ should be seen in us in the way we behave, in our joy and serenity in the presence of sorrow and difficulties, in our readiness to forgive others. He will be seen in the demanding way we fulfil our duties and in our exemplary sobriety in making use of material goods; in our sincere gratitude for the help we are offered in the little things of daily life.

If we neglect this intimate union with God our apostolic effectiveness will be reduced to nothing in the lives of the people we habitually come into contact with. The fruits will become bitter, and unworthy of being laid before God. Saint Pius X declares: *But among those who refuse or neglect 'to consider in their heart' (Jer 12:11), there are some who do not conceal the consequent sterility of their souls, but excuse themselves, offering as a reason that they are given entirely to the cares of ministry, to the manifold advantage of others. They are deceived miserably. For, unaccustomed to speak with God, they lack*

---

[8] Second Vatican Council, *Apostolicam actuositatem*, 4

the divine fire when they speak to men about him, or impart the principles of Christian living, so that the gospel message seems to be lifeless in them.[9] At best then it is not unusual for their advice to be merely common sense, with no supernatural content to it. They give their own doctrines instead of the Gospel doctrine. If we neglect personal piety, real intimacy with God, we shall not perform the deeds God expects from every Christian. For out of the abundance of the heart the mouth speaks.[10] If our heart is not in God how can we hand on the words and the life that come from him? Let us take a look at our prayer. Do we have a set time for it, and are we punctual? Do we really try to overcome distractions? Do we pray in the most suitable place? Do we ask Our Lady, Saint Joseph and our Guardian Angel to help us maintain a lively personal dialogue with God? Do we make at least one small resolution each day?

We can also examine our efforts to preserve presence of God while we are walking along the street, while at work and at home ... and we can be definite about what needs putting right or improving in our daily life. Let us make such a resolution. It does not matter if it is small, but it should be definite.

102.3 The bitter fruit of laicism. The activity of the Christian in the world – to hand all things back to Christ.

Just as the man who excludes God from his life becomes a diseased tree that will yield bad fruit, so a society that wants to exclude God from its customs and laws causes countless evils and inflicts the most serious harm on its citizens. *A State from which religion is banished can*

---

[9] St Pius X, Encyclical, *Haerent animo*, 4 August 1908
[10] cf Luke 6:45

never be well-regulated.[11] In it the phenomenon of laicism appears, with the desire of supplanting the honour due to God. A system of morality based on transcendent principles is replaced by merely human ideals and norms of conduct. These inevitably end up as less than human. God and the Church become purely *internal matters of conscience, and the Church and the Pope are subjected to aggressive attacks, either directly or indirectly, through persons or institutions unfaithful to the Magisterium.*

Not infrequently as a result of laicism the individual citizen, the life of the family, and of the commonwealth as a whole are all removed from the beneficent and wholesome influence of God and of his Church. Then, day by day, the symbols and symptoms of those errors which corrupted the heathens of old, declare themselves more plainly and more lamentably. And all this in parts of the world where the light of Christian civilization has shone for centuries.[12] The signs of this secularization can be seen in many countries. Even in those of long-standing Christian traditions this process of secularization is making inroads: the decline is apparently invariable, the symptoms all too plain – divorce, abortion, an alarming increase in the use of drugs even by children and young people, violence, contempt for public morality ... If God is not accepted as a loving Father, man and society inevitably become dehumanized. His laws were established for the protection and preservation of that human nature by means of which the individual is to find his personal dignity and reach the goal for which he has been created.

With the evidence of these bitter fruits before our eyes, we Christians must respond generously to the call we have received from God to be salt and light wherever we may be,

---

[11] Leo XIII, *Immortale Dei*, 1 November 1885, 32
[12] Pius XII, *Summi Pontificatus*, 20 October 1939

however limited might appear the field of activity in which we live our lives. We must show by our deeds that the world is more human, more cheerful, more honest, cleaner, the closer it is to God. Life is the more worth living the more deeply it is penetrated by the light of Christ.

Jesus constantly urges us not to remain inactive, not to waste the slightest opportunity of giving a more Christian orientation to the people who surround us, to the environment in which we live. As we end our prayer today we can ask ourselves: What can I do in my family, at school, at the university, in the office ... to make God more actively present there? We ask Saint Joseph for fortitude of spirit in order to bring Christ into all these human realities. With faith we see the example of his life, which gives us *a picture of Joseph as a remarkably sound man who was in no way, fearful or diffident about life. On the contrary, he faced up to problems, dealt with difficult situations and showed responsibility and initiative in whatever he was asked to do.*[13]

With God's grace and the intercession of the Holy Patriarch we shall make a constant effort to bear abundant fruit wherever God has placed us.

---

[13] St. J. Escrivá, *Christ is passing by*, 40

TWELFTH WEEK: THURSDAY

103. THE FRUITS OF THE MASS

103.1 The Eucharistic sacrifice and the ordinary life of the Christian.

The Second Vatican Council reminds us that *the sacrifice of the Cross and its sacramental renewal in the Mass are, apart from the difference in the manner of offering, 'one and the same' sacrifice of praise, of thanksgiving, of propitiation and of satisfaction.*[1] The ends which Our Saviour gave to His sacrifice on the Cross are usually summed up in these four.

The four ends of the Mass are achieved in different ways and to a different extent. The ends that refer directly to God, namely, adoration, praise and thanksgiving, are always produced infallibly and with all their infinite value, independently of our collaboration. This is true even when the Mass is celebrated without the presence of a single member of the faithful, or, if there is one, if he assists in a distracted way. God our Lord is praised infinitely every time the Eucharistic Sacrifice is celebrated, and thanksgiving is offered up which satisfies God fully. This oblation, says Saint Thomas, pleases God more than all the sins of the world offend him,[2] since Christ himself is the actual Priest who offers, as well as being the actual victim who is offered in every Mass.

However, the other ends of the Eucharistic Sacrifice (propitiation and petition), which are for the benefit of man and are called the fruits of the Mass, do not in fact always achieve the fulness of which they are capable. These fruits – of reconciliation with God and of obtaining from him what

---

[1] *Roman Missal*, *General Instruction*, Foreword, 2
[2] cf St Thomas, *Summa Theologiae*, III, 8, 2

we ask for from his bounty – could also be of infinite value. They too rest on the merits of Christ. We never receive these fruits to that perfect degree, since they are applied to us according to our personal dispositions. The more ardently and intently we take part in the Holy Sacrifice of the Altar, the greater application of these fruits of propitiation and petition we shall receive. Christ's own prayer multiplies the value of our prayer to the extent that we unite our petitions and atonement to his in the Mass, on the Cross itself.

So that we might receive the fruits of the Mass, the Church invites us to unite ourselves with the Sacrifice of Christ. That is, to take part in Jesus Christ's praise, thanksgiving, propitiation and impetration. The external rite of the Mass (comprising the actions and ceremonies) both signifies the interior sacrifice of Jesus Christ and is a sign of the offering and dedication of all the faithful united to him.[3] This dedication of the whole of our being, of all our daily activities, is yet another reason for us to carry them out perfectly and with a right intention. As the Second Vatican Council puts it: *For all their deeds and actions, prayers and apostolic undertakings, family and married life, daily work, relaxation of mind and body, if they are accomplished in the Spirit, indeed, even the hardships of life if patiently borne, all these become spiritual sacrifices acceptable to God through Jesus Christ (cf 1 Pet 2:5). In the celebration of the Eucharist these may most fittingly be offered to the Father along with the body of the Lord.*[4] All our actions and our very life itself take on a new value when they hinge on the Mass as the centre of our day towards which all our thoughts and deeds are directed. It is the source from which flow all the graces we need to sanctify our stay on earth.

---

[3] cf Pius XII, *Mediator Dei*, 20 November 1947
[4] Second Vatican Council, *Lumen gentium*, 34

103.2 Taking part in the Mass conscious of what we are doing, with devotion and full collaboration. Our participation should be personal prayer, union with Jesus Christ, who is at once the Priest and the Victim.

Our Mother the Church wants to obtain ever more fruits from the Mass. So she desires that when we are present we should not be there as *strangers or silent spectators,* but constantly increasing our understanding of the rites and prayers, taking part in the sacred action in full awareness of what we are doing, with devotion and earnest collaboration. We should foster a right disposition of heart, with soul and voice in unison, and co-operating with divine grace.[5] We shall pay particular attention to the dialogues and acclamations. We shall fill the established periods of silence with acts of faith and charity, particularly at the Consecration and when we receive Our Lord in Communion ... The most important thing is interior participation, our union with Jesus Christ who offers himself. The external elements which also form part of the liturgy will be of great help to us in doing this – bodily postures (kneeling, standing, sitting), reciting or singing of other parts together, such as the *Gloria*, the *Creed*, the *Sanctus*, the *Our Father*, etc.

We will often find it helps to follow the prayers of the celebrant in our missal. The effort to be punctual, arriving a few minutes before Mass begins, will help us to be better prepared. Besides, it is a sign of love for Christ and a courtesy towards the priest who is celebrating Mass as well as to others who are attending. God wants us to be exemplary in this, too. Wouldn't we arrive in good time for an important interview? *There is nothing more important than the Mass.*

Internal participation is mainly a question of practising

---

[5] cf Second Vatican Council, *Sacrosanctum Concilium,* 11; 48

the virtues through acts of faith, hope and charity. At the moment of the Consecration we can say with the words of the Apostle Thomas, words overflowing with faith and love, *My Lord and My God,* ... or 'I firmly believe that You are really present on the altar' ... or whatever form of words appeals to our personal devotion.

Above all, our taking part in the Mass must be personal prayer, the high point of our customary dialogue with the Father, Son and Holy Spirit. This prayer, *to the extent possible to each person, is a requisite for a genuine, conscious liturgical participation. But not that alone, it is also the fruit of such a participation. Now and always, but nowadays more than ever, we need to foster the spirit and practice of personal prayer ... We cannot keep going as Christians without a constant, intimate, personal life of prayer, faith, and charity. Without these we cannot usefully and advantageously take part in the liturgical renewal.*

Without them we cannot be effective witnesses to that Christian authenticity that we hear so much about. Lacking such participation we cannot think, breathe, act, suffer and hope with the living, pilgrim Church ... To all we say, 'Let us pray, brethren': 'Orate Fratres'. Never tire of trying to call up from the depths of your soul that intimate voice which addresses God as 'Thou' ..., the God beyond words, the mysterious Other who watches over you, waits for you, loves you. And you will never be let down, or left alone. You will experience the new joy of an enrapturing response: 'Ecce Adsum,' behold I am with you.[6] God is with us and in us in a very special way in Holy Communion, when our taking part in the Mass reaches its highest point. *The proper effect of this Sacrament,* teaches Saint Thomas Aquinas, *is to change man into Christ, so that he can say with the Apostle, 'I live; no, it is not I who*

---

[6] St Paul VI, *Address*, 14 August 1969

live. It is Christ who lives in me.[7]

103.3 Preparation for Mass. Apostolate and the Eucharistic Sacrifice.

Before Mass we have to prepare our soul to be ready for the most important event that takes place in the world each day. The Mass celebrated by any priest in the most out-of-the-way, the remotest corner of the world, even when no other person is attending, is the greatest thing happening on earth at that moment. It is the most pleasing thing that we men can offer to God. It is the opportunity to thank him for the many benefits we receive; to ask forgiveness for so many sins and such lack of love and for all our spiritual and material needs. *We all have things we need to ask for. Lord, this illness ... Lord, that sorrow ... Lord, that humiliation I can't accept even for love of You ... We desire blessings, happiness and joy for the members of our household. We are saddened by the fate of those who suffer hunger and thirst for bread and justice; of those who undergo the anguish of loneliness; of those who at the end of their lives are facing death without an affectionate look or the help of a friend.*

But it is sin which is the wretchedness that causes suffering, and is the great world-wide malaise we have to remedy. It separates us from God and endangers souls with the prospect of eternal damnation. To bring men to eternal glory in the love of God – that was the essential desire of Christ when He gave up his life on Calvary, and that has to be our desire when we celebrate Mass.[8] Our apostolate is therefore directed towards the Mass and is strengthened by it.

Some minutes of thanksgiving after Mass will round off these most important moments of the day. They will

---

[7] St Thomas, *IV Book of Sentences*, 12, 2, 1
[8] St. J. Escrivá, *In Love with the Church*, 47-48

have a direct influence on our work, on our family life, on the cheerfulness we show to everyone, and in the certainty and confidence with which we face up to the rest of our day. The Mass lived in this way will never be an isolated incident. It will nourish all our actions and give them a special tone, value and significance.

We always find our Mother Mary in the Mass. *How could we take part in the sacrifice without remembering and invoking the Mother of the High Priest and Victim? Our Lady played such an intimate part in the priesthood of her Son during his life on earth that she is eternally united to the exercise of his Priesthood. Just as she was present on Calvary, so is she present in the Mass, which is a prolongation of Calvary. She helped her Son on the Cross by offering him to the Father. In the sacrifice of the altar, the renewal of the sacrifice of Christ, she helps the Church to offer herself in union with her Head. Let us offer ourselves to Jesus through the mediation of Mary.*[9] Let us remember Mary during Mass, and she will help us grow in piety and recollection.

---

[9] P. Bernadot, *Our Lady in my Life*, p. 233

104. THE VIRTUE OF FAITHFULNESS

104.1 Faithfulness – a virtue required by love and faith.

Sacred Scripture often speaks to us about the virtue of *faithfulness*, of the need to keep our promises, to carry out undertakings freely contracted, to make the effort to finish off a mission to which one has committed oneself. The Lord said to Abraham: *Bear yourself blameless in my presence. You shall maintain my Covenant, yourself and your descendants after you, generation after generation.*[1] The strength of the covenant with the Patriarch and his descendants would be a continual source of blessing and happiness. On the other hand, breaches of this pact by Israel would be the cause of its misfortune.

God asks for faithfulness from men, from those whom he looks on with predilection, because He himself is always faithful, despite our weaknesses and shortcomings. Yahweh is the God *of loyalty*,[2] who is *rich in love and fidelity*,[3] *faithful in every word of his*,[4] and *his faithfulness remains forever*.[5] Those who are faithful are most pleasing to him,[6] and He promises them the definitive reward: he who is *faithful unto death* will receive *the crown of life*.[7]

Throughout the Gospel Jesus speaks about this virtue. He offers us the example of the faithful and prudent servant, of the honourable administrator ... The idea of

---

[1] *First Reading*, Year 1, Gen 17:1-9
[2] Deut 3:4
[3] Ex 34:6-7
[4] Ps 144:13
[5] Ps 116:1-2
[6] cf Prov 12:22
[7] cf Rev 2:20

faithfulness penetrates the life of a Christian so deeply that
the term *faithful* is enough to describe the disciples of
Christ.[8] Saint Paul, who had repeatedly exhorted the first
Christian generation to practise this virtue, intones a hymn
to faithfulness which can be taken as summarising his life
as he approaches the end of it: he writes to Timothy: *I have
fought the good fight, I have finished the race, I have kept
the faith. Henceforth there is laid up for me the crown of
righteousness, which the Lord, the righteous Judge, will
award to me on the Day: and not only to me but also to all
who have longed for his coming.*[9]

Faithfulness consists in accomplishing what was promised, in making deeds conform to expressed intentions.[10]
We are faithful if we keep our word, if we hold firm, in
spite of the obstacles and difficulties, to the commitments
we have undertaken. Perseverance is intimately united to
this virtue, and is often identified with it.

Faithfulness applies to many areas: our relationship
with God; between spouses, among friends ... It is an
essential virtue. Without it social intercourse becomes
impossible. As far as the spiritual life is concerned, it is
closely related to love, faith and vocation. *That passage of
the Second Epistle to Timothy makes me shudder, where
the Apostle laments that Demas has fallen in love with this
present world and gone to Thessalonica. For a trifle, and
for fear of persecution, this man, whom Saint Paul had
quoted in other epistles as being among the saints, had
betrayed the divine enterprise.*

*I shudder when I realise how little I am: and it leads
me to demand from myself faithfulness to the Lord even in
events that might seem to be indifferent – for if they do not*

---

[8] Acts 10:45
[9] 2 Tim 4:7
[10] cf St Thomas, *Summa Theologiae*, II-II, 110, 3

help me to be more united to him, I do not want them.[11]
What use are they to us if they do not lead us to Christ?

Bear yourself blameless in my presence. You shall maintain my Covenant, God is continually telling us in the secret depths of our hearts.

104.2 The foundations of faithfulness.

Ours is not an age characterised by a flowering of this virtue of faithfulness. It is perhaps for this reason that Our Lord wants us to appreciate this particular virtue all the more, both in the implementing of a dedication freely undertaken in our relationship with him, and in our human relationships with others. Many will ask: how can man, who is changeable and weak, commit himself forever? He can; because his fidelity is sustained by One who is himself unwavering, who is neither lacking in strength nor subject to mutability – by God himself. *Yahweh is faithful in all of his words.*[12] The Lord supports this disposition in those who wish to remain loyal to their commitments, and especially to their most important one. This is the commitment that relates directly to God – and to other men because of God – as is the case when there is a calling to total dedication, a commitment to sanctity. *Every good endowment and every perfect gift is from above, coming down from the Father of Light with whom there is no variation or shadow due to change.*[13]

Christ needs you, and calls you to help millions of your fellow men to be truly human and to work out their salvation. Live with these noble ideals in your soul ... Open your heart to Christ, to the law of love, without placing conditions on your availability, without fear of receiving

---

[11] St. J. Escrivá, *Furrow*, 343
[12] Ps 144:3
[13] Jas 1:17

noncommittal replies, because love and friendship do not vanish over the horizon.[14] They always maintain their plenitude, for love does not grow old.

Saint Thomas teaches[15] that we love someone when we desire the good of that person. If, on the other hand, we try to take advantage of the one concerned, either because it gives us pleasure or because he is of use to us, then, properly speaking, we don't love that person: whatever we want, it is not his good. When we love, we desire what is the best for the other; our whole person is directed to this love, independently of our likes or dislikes or moods: *the payment and the price of love is to receive more love.*[16]

We have to ask the Lord for the firm conviction that the essence of love is not mere sentiment or feeling, but the will and the right-intentioned deeds it evokes: it demands effort, sacrifice and dedication. Feelings and emotions and moods change; on them something as fundamental as faithfulness cannot be built. The virtue of faithfulness acquires its firmness from love, from genuine love. And so, when love – both human and divine – has gone beyond the realm of mere feelings, what remains is not its least important constituent, but rather its most essential, in fact, that which gives ultimate meaning to everything.

The Lord has a calling, a plan, a vocation for every one, for each one in particular. He has promised that this call will always come, and he will sustain it through temptations and the varied difficulties one encounters in life. And to demonstrate this permanence, he uses an analogy that we well understand: it is the love and care which a mother has for her child. Imagine, he says, a mother, deeply maternal, (and not, if it were possible, an egotistical

---

[14] St John Paul II, *Address in Javier*, 6 November 1982
[15] St Thomas, *op cit*, I-II, 26, 4
[16] St John of the Cross, *Spiritual Canticle*, 9, 7

mother who is selfishly immersed in her own world). How could such a mother forget about her own child?[17] We consider it impossible; but we can imagine the possibility that from time to time she does forget about it, or does not continually have its needs in the forefront of her mind. It is possible. But I, the Lord says, will never forget about you, about your commitments in life, about my loving designs for you, about your vocation. Faithfulness is a loving response to this love of God. Without love, cracks and fissures soon appear in the solidity of every commitment.

104.3 Love and fidelity in little things.

What can I give Yahweh in return for all the good things he has given me?[18] For our part, we can all offer whatever we have, in order to fulfil the task of being faithful. For this, perseverance until the end of one's life, is made possible by faithfulness to the little details of daily living and by constantly and purposefully beginning again, when through weakness one has veered off the path, fidelity is the response to this love of God, ceaselessly allowing oneself to be loved by him, removing the obstacles which prevent his merciful love penetrating to the depths of our soul. On many occasions in life, fidelity to God comes down to perseverance in a life of prayer, to a faithful persistence in those devotions and customs which keep us close to the Lord each day. Our own perseverance and the perseverance of others relies on our union with and our filial love for God. Those who love, persevere – because they feel the strength of their Father God in the apparent monotony of the day to day struggle.[19]

---

[17] cf Is 49:15
[18] Ps 115:12
[19] cf R. Taboada, *Perseverance*, Madrid 1987

Love is *the weight which drags me along,*[20] the lodestone, the direction for our soul to be faithful. For this, a recognition of the love of God, a love from which no man can be excluded, leads to sincerity, a sure support for faithfulness. It will be a sincerity, in the first place, with oneself: one will be able, under its influence, to recognise and identify by name, even before they have taken shape, those desires, thoughts, aspirations and dreams that insistently besiege the soul, but which point in unmistakably wrong directions. Immediately thereafter comes sincerity with God – born of an upright intention and interior cleanliness; then will come sincerity with whoever is chosen to guide the soul spiritually by making manifest the symptoms of an egoism, that in diverse forms attempts to harden the heart. In this way we will always be able to count on powerful help.

The virtues of faithfulness and loyalty ought to be present in every aspect of a Christian life: relationships with God, with the Church, with one's neighbour, at work, as regards duties towards the state or nation ... And this fidelity is practised in the different fields where one is faithful to one's vocation, for in it is contained all the other values which we acquire – through loyalty and faithfulness. If fidelity to God is lacking, everything else begins to disintegrate and break down.

The heart of Jesus, the human Heart of the God-Man, is aflame with the 'living call' of triune Love, which can never be extinguished.[21] It is faithful in its love for men. We have to learn from this faithful love. And again we turn to Mary: '*Virgo fidelis, ora pro nobis, ora pro me.*' *Virgin most faithful, pray for us, pray for me.*

---

[20] St Augustine, *op cit*, 13, 9
[21] St John Paul II, *Sunday Reflection*, 23 June 1986

105. MARY, CO-REDEMPTRIX WITH CHRIST

105.1 Mary present in the sacrifice of the Cross.

Throughout Jesus' earthly life his Mother Holy Mary fulfilled the Divine Will by looking after him with loving care – in Bethlehem, in Egypt, in Nazareth. She looked after him in all his ordinary needs as any mother would do for her child, and also in extraordinary necessities, such as when his life was in danger. The Child grew up with Mary and Joseph in an atmosphere full of sacrifice and cheerful love, secure care and protection and work.

Later on, during his public life, Mary rarely followed him in a physical way, but she knew where he was at each moment, and news of his miracles and his preaching reached her. Sometimes Jesus went to Nazareth and while He was there spent more time with his Mother. The majority of his disciples would have known her since the time of the wedding at Cana of Galilee.[1] Apart from the changing of the water into wine, in which she played such an important part, the Evangelists do not record her presence on the occasion of any other miracle. Nor was she present when the people were full of enthusiasm over her Son. *She is not to be seen amid the palms of Jerusalem, nor at the hour of the great miracles – except at the first one at Cana.*

But she doesn't escape from the contempt at Golgotha; there she stands, 'juxta crucem Jesu', the Mother of Jesus, beside his Cross.[2] She stays as a rule in Nazareth, in

---

[1] cf John 2:1-10
[2] St. J. Escrivá, *The Way*, 507

perfect union with her Son, pondering in her heart all that is happening; but in the hour of sorrow and desertion, Mary is there.

God loved her in a unique and singular manner. Nevertheless, He did not spare her the ordeal of Calvary, making her share in suffering no-one else has ever experienced except her Son. Perhaps she could have stayed quietly at home in the consolingly agreeable company of the women; *after all, there was nothing she could do, and her presence neither avoided nor relieved the sufferings and humiliations of her Son. But she was there, nevertheless. She stayed with Christ for the same reason as any mother stays beside the deathbed of her son, instead of going out to try to distract herself when she sees that she can neither keep him alive nor stop his suffering. No, the Virgin Mary identified herself with her Son; her love made her suffer with Him.*[3] Little by little she kept getting nearer to the Cross; finally, the soldiers must have allowed her to stay very close. She looks at Jesus, and her son looks at her. In the closest union, she offers her Son to God the Father, co-redeeming with Him. In communion with her suffering and agonizing Son, she put up with pain and almost death. *As a Mother, she abdicated her rights over her Son, in order to obtain the salvation of mankind, and to satisfy divine justice in as much as it depended on her. She immolated her Son, in such a way that it can rightly be said that she redeemed the human race with Christ.*[4]

The Virgin Mary not only *accompanied* Jesus but was *actively and intimately united to the sacrifice* which was offered on that *first altar*. Voluntarily she shared in the redemption of the human race, thereby fulfilling the *fiat* she had pronounced years before in Nazareth. And so we

---

[3] F. Suarez, *Mary of Nazareth*
[4] Benedict XV, Letter, *Inter sodalicia*, 22 May 1918

may consider that in each Mass, the very centre and heart of the Church, we find Mary. On many occasions this fact will help us to live the Eucharistic Sacrifice better, by uniting our sacrifice, which also has to be a holocaust, to the sacrifice of Christ, feeling ourselves to be on Calvary, very close to Our Lady.

105.2 Co-redemptrix with Christ.

From the Cross, Jesus entrusted his Mystical Body, the Church, to Mary, in the person of Saint John. He knew that we should need a Mother to protect us all the time; someone to lift us up and intercede for us. From that moment, *she guarded and will guard it (the Church) with the same fidelity and the same effort as that with which she guarded her Firstborn – from the crib at Bethlehem, through Calvary, until the Cenacle of Pentecost, where the birth of the Church took place. Mary is present in all the vicissitudes of the Church ... In a particular way she is united to the Church in the most difficult moments of her history ... Mary appears particularly close to the Church at such times because the Church is always like her Christ – first her Child, then the Crucified and then the Risen Jesus.*[5]

The Virgin Mary intercedes so that God will impress on the souls of Christians the same zeal that He placed in hers, namely, the co-redemptive desire that all men may become once more God's friends. *The faith, hope and ardent charity of the Virgin Mary on the summit of Golgotha, which make her Co-redemptrix in an eminent way, are also an invitation to us to grow, to be strong humanly and supernaturally in external difficulties and to persist, without getting discouraged in our apostolate although it may sometimes appear that there are no results, or that the outlook is darkened by the power of evil.*

---

[5] K. Wojtyla, *Sign of Contradiction*

Let us struggle – you struggle! – against this routine, against this just dragging along monotonously, against this conformism which amounts to inactivity. Look at Christ on the Cross: look at Mary next to the Cross: before her gaze she is confronted with a terrifying outburst of insults, mockery, treachery ...; but Christ, and seconding this redemptive action, Mary, continue strong, persevering, full of peace, with optimism in the suffering, fulfilling the mission entrusted to them by the Trinity. It is a sharp reminder to each one of us to be other Christs, and a reminder that Christ fulfils his mission at the time of suffering, of fatigue, and of the most terrible contradiction ... I want to advise you to turn your eyes towards the Virgin Mary, and to ask her, for yourself and for others, that we may have absolute confidence in the redemptive action of Jesus, and that, like you, Mother, we should want to be Co-redeemers.[6] To share the Redemption, to co-operate in the sanctification of the world, to save souls for eternity: could there be a greater ideal to fill one's life? The Blessed Virgin co-redeems now with her Son on Calvary, but she also did so when she pronounced her fiat on receiving the Angel's message; she did so in Bethlehem, she did so during the time she remained in Egypt and in every day of her ordinary life in Nazareth ... Like her we can be co-redeemers at all hours of the day, if we fill them with prayer, if we work conscientiously, if we live in charity with those we meet in our jobs, in the family ... if we offer up calmly the contradictions each day brings with it.

105.3 Mary and the Mass.

When Jesus saw his mother, and the disciple whom he loved standing near, he said to his mother, 'Woman,

---

[6] Bl. A. del Portillo, *Letter*, 31 May 1987, 19

behold, your son![7] It was Jesus' last gift before his Death; he gave us his Mother as our Mother.

Since then Christ's disciple has something of his own: he has Mary as his Mother. Her place as Mother in the Church will be for always: *And from that hour the disciple took her to his own home.*[8] That is Jesus' hour, when with his redemptive death he inaugurates a new era that will last till the end of time. Since then, *if we want to be Christian we have to be Marian,*[9] to be a good Christian it is necessary to have a great love for Mary. The work of Jesus can be summarised in two marvellous facts: He has given us divine filiation, making us children of God, and He has made us children of Mary.

Origen in the third century points out that Jesus did not say to Mary, 'this is *also* your son', but, *here is your son*; and since Mary did not have any other son but Jesus, his words mean in effect: *from now on, for you this will be Jesus.*[10] The Virgin Mary sees her son Jesus in each Christian. She treats us as if Christ himself were in our place. How then will she forget us when she sees us in need? What will she not obtain for us from her Son? We can never imagine, even remotely, how much Mary loves each one of us.

Let us get used to finding Mary while we celebrate or participate in the Holy Mass. *There, in the Sacrifice of the Altar, the participation of Our Lady evokes the silent reserve with which she walked the roads of Palestine. The Holy Mass is an action of the Trinity; by the Will of the Father, co-operating with the Holy Spirit, the Son offers himself in a redemptive oblation. In this unfathomable mystery, one notices, as if shrouded in veils, the most pure*

---

[7] John 19:26
[8] John 19:27
[9] St Paul VI, *Homily*, 24 April 1970
[10] Origen, *Commentary on the St John's Gospel*, 1, 4, 23

face of Mary, Daughter of God the Father, Mother of God the Son, Spouse of God the Holy Spirit.

Treating with Jesus in the Sacrifice of the Altar necessarily brings with it intimacy with Mary, his Mother. Whoever finds Jesus also finds Mary Immaculate and, as happened to those holy persons, the Three Wise Men, who went to adore Christ: 'and going into the house, they saw the child with Mary his mother (Matt 2:11).[11] With her we can offer our whole life, all our thoughts, desires, works, affections, actions, loves, identifying ourselves with the same sentiments which Christ Jesus had.[12] *Holy Father!* we can say in the intimacy of our heart, and we can repeat this interiorly during the Holy Mass, *through the Immaculate Heart of Mary I offer you, your beloved Son Jesus, and also myself in him, with him and through him, for all his intentions and in the name of all creatures.*[13]

To celebrate or attend the Holy Sacrifice of the Altar properly is the best service we can offer Jesus, his Mystical Body and the whole human race. Next to Mary, in the Holy Mass we are particularly united with the whole Church.

---

[11] St. J. Escrivá, *The Virgin Mary*, *Libro de Aragon*, Saragossa 1976
[12] cf Phil 2:5
[13] P. M. Sulamitis, *Prayer of Offering to the Merciful Love*, Madrid 1931

INDEX TO QUOTATIONS FROM THE FATHERS, POPES AND THE SAINTS

Note: References are to **Volume**/Chapter.Section

Acts of Thanksgiving
  St Augustine, **5**/39.2
  St Bede, **5**/78.1
  St Bernard, **5**/10.1, **5**/39.3
  St Francis de Sales, **4**/84.1
  St John Chrysostom, **2**/71.1
  St Thomas Aquinas, **5**/78.2
Advent
  St Bernard, **1**/1.3
Almsgiving
  St Leo the Great, **5**/67.2
  St Thomas Aquinas, **3**/17.3
Angels
  Origen, **2**/9.3
  St Bernard, **7**/30.3
  St John Chrysostom, **2**/7.1
  St John of the Cross, **2**/7.2
  St Peter of Alcantara, **3**/51.2
  St John Paul II, **2**/7.1, **2**/30.3,
    7/27
Apostolate
  Benedict XV, **2**/85.1
  Bl. Alvaro, **2**/29.1,
  John Paul I, **3**/3.2
  Letter to Diognetus, **2**/70.2
  St Ambrose, **4**/87.1
  St Augustine, **1**/8.3, **2**/59.1,
    4/92.3, **5**/52.1, **5**/87.3
  St Cyril of Alexandria, **5**/62.1
  St Gregory the Great, **3**/88.2,
    4/69.1
  St Ignatius of Antioch, **5**/37.3
  St J. H. Newman, **3**/3.2

St John Chrysostom, **1**/4.3,
  2/85.1, **2**/94.1, **3**/88.2,
  3/89.3, **4**/87.1, **7**/42.2
St John Paul II, **1**/45.3, **2**/11.3,
  3/13.3, **4**/37.3, **4**/69.1,
  4/87.3, **5**/10.2, **5**/20.1,
  5/57.1, **5**/68.3, **6**/57.3, **7**/2.3
St Paul VI, **6**/57.2, **7**/25.3
St Teresa, **5**/68.3
St Thomas Aquinas, **1**/9.2,
  3/5.2, **7**/4.3
St Thomas of Villanueva,
  4/40.3
Tertullian, **2**/70.1, **4**/40.2
Ascetical struggle
  Cassian, **2**/67.2
  St Ambrose, **2**/22.3
  St Augustine, **3**/3.1, **3**/18.2,
    4/25.1, **4**/80.2
  St Bernard, **5**/50.2, **6**/12.2
  St Cyprian, **5**/34.2
  St Francis de Sales, **1**/12.3,
    4/25.1
  St Gregory the Great, **2**/4.2,
    4/25.2
  St Ignatius of Antioch, **4**/96.1
  St John Chrysostom, **1**/12.2,
    2/22.3, **4**/14.1, **4**/59.1,
    5/34.2, **5**/50.2, **5**/61.2
  St John Climacus, **2**/67.2
  St John Paul II, **4**/14.3, **6**/20.1
  St Peter Damian, **3**/92.2
  St Peter of Alcantara, **1**/13.2

St Teresa, 1/1.3, 2/12.2
St Vincent of Lerins, 1/6.3

Aspirations
St Teresa, 2/35.3

Atonement
St Bernard, 6/50.2

Baptism
Origen, 2/70.3
St Augustine, 1/51.1
St Cyril of Alexandria, 1/50.1
St John Chrysostom, 2/5.1
St John Paul II, 5/43.2,
  5/59.2, 6/3.2
St Leo the Great, 1/51.1
St Thomas Aquinas, 6/3.3

Blessed Trinity
St Augustine, 6/40.3
St John of the Cross, 6/40.1
St Teresa, 6/40.2, 6/40.3

Catechism
St John Paul II, 3/13.2, 4/86.2

Character
Cassian, 1/11.1

Charity
St Alphonsus Liguori, 2/22.2
St Augustine, 3/52.2, 5/23.1,
  5/52.1
St Bernard, 4/85.3
St Cyprian, 2/94.2, 5/94.3
St Francis de Sales, 3/100.1
St Jerome, 5/23.1
St John Chrysostom, 4/21.2
St Teresa, 3/100.1
St Thomas Aquinas, 2/44.2,
  4/1.2, 5/15.3
Tertullian, 6/4.3, 6/52.3

Chastity
St Jean Vianney, 1/23.3

St John Chrysostom, 1/23.3,
  4/62.2, 4/62.3
St John Paul II, 1/23.1,
  4/62.2, 4/83.2, 4/83.3,
  5/90.3, 6/22.1
St Leo the Great, 1/16.3

Christ
Origen, 5/31.2
Pius XI, 5/91.1
Pius XII, 5/52.2, 6/49.3, 6/50.1
St Ambrose, 5/91.3
St Augustine, 1/2.2, 1/32.2,
  5/3.2, 5/31.1, 5/56.2
St Bernard, 5/56.1
St Hippolytus, 5/47.1
St John Chrysostom, 5/6.1
St John of the Cross, 5/96.2
St John Paul II, 5/2.3, 5/31.1,
  5/64.1, 6/49.1, 6/50.3
St Leo, 7/12.2
St Paul VI, 5/18.3
St Teresa, 5/61.3, 7/35.2
St Thomas Aquinas, 1/40.1,
  7/12.1

Church
Bl. Alvaro, 6/18.3
Gregory XVI, 4/73.3
Pius XI, 3/10.2, 6/8.2
Pius XII, 4/37.3, 6/8.2
St Ambrose, 4/73.3, 5/5.2
St Augustine, 5/5.2
St Cyprian, 3/10.2, 4/13.3
St Cyril of Jerusalem, 3/10.2
St Gregory the Great, 3/10.2
St John Chrysostom, 5/31.2
St John Paul II, 4/37.2,
  5/28.1, 5/41.2, 7/40.3
St John XXIII, 3/10.2
St Leo the Great, 4/73.2
St Paul VI, 4/18.3, 5/47.2, 6/8.1

Civic Duties
St Ambrose, 4/58.1
St Justin, 2/33.2, 2/70.2, 4/58.2
St John Paul II, 5/21.3
Tertullian, 4/58.2

Communion of saints
St Ambrose, 5/68.1
St John Paul II, 1/10.3, 5/68.1
St Teresa, 2/66.1
St Thomas Aquinas, 5/71.3,
6/8.3

Compassion
St Augustine, 1/4.3
St John Paul II, 1/3.2, 1/10.1,
1/10.2, 5/15.1, 5/31.3
St Paul VI, 5/15.1
St Thomas Aquinas, 4/64.2

Confession
Bl. Alvaro, 3/7.2, 5/27.2
St Ambrose, 2/34.2
St Augustine, 3/7.3, 4/60.2
St Bede, 3/4.1
St Gregory the Great, 2/39.2
St Jean Vianney, 2/55.2
St John Chrysostom, 2/21.1,
2/34.3
St John Paul II, 1/4.2, 2/1.1,
2/18.3, 2/34.1, 2/34.3,
4/46.3, 5/5.3
St Paul VI, 5/27.2
St Thomas Aquinas, 2/8.3,
2/21.1

Conscience
St John Paul II, 2/13.1

Contrition
St Augustine, 2/41.2
St John Chrysostom, 4/60.1
St Teresa, 5/16.2

Conversation
St Augustine, 5/15.3

Conversion
St Gregory of Nyssa, 3/19.2
St John Chrysostom, 5/9.3
St John Paul II, 5/6.2

Conversion
St Augustine, 7/20
St John Paul II, 1/10.1

Cowardice
St Basil, 2/69.3
St John Chrysostom, 3/89.3

Cross
St Athanasius, 3/56.3
St Augustine, 4/82.1
St Gregory the Great, 2/12.1
St Irenaeus, 5/28.3
St John Damascene, 7/23.1
St John Paul II, 4/82.1, 5/22.2
St Thomas Aquinas, 5/19.3

Death
Bl. Alvaro, 5/97.3
Leo X, 5/80.3
St Bede, 4/2.2
St Ignatius Loyola, 5/80.3
St Jerome, 4/2.3
St John Paul II, 4/2.1

Dedication
St Augustine, 5/9.2, 5/12.1
St Jerome, 3/86.2
St John Paul II, 3/104.2

Detachment
St Augustine, 5/21.3
St Francis de Sales, 5/24.2
St John of the Cross, 2/16.1
St John Paul II, 5/21.3, 5/38.3
St Teresa, 2/16.3
St Thomas Aquinas, 7/50.3

Devil
Cassian, 2/6.2
St Irenaeus, 2/6.1
St J. H. Newman, 2/6.2, 4/19.1

St Jean Vianney, 2/6.2
St John of the Cross, 2/6.3
St John Paul II, 2/6.1, 2/6.3,
   5/42.1
Tertullian, 5/42.2

Difficulties
Bl. Alvaro, 4/54.2
John Paul I, 5/44.3
Pius XII, 2/60.2, 5/53.2
St Alphonsus Liguori, 5/69.2
St Athanasius, 4/3.1
St Augustine, 1/32.1, 2/24.3,
   2/64.3, 3/98.3, 4/8.1,
   4/25.1, 5/16.2
St Bernard, 4/96.1, 7/43.2
St Cyprian, 1/36.3
St Francis de Sales, 4/25.1,
   6/30.2
St Gregory Nazianzen, 1/13.1
St Gregory the Great, 3/98.2,
   4/96.3, 5/9.2, 5/85.1
St J. H. Newman, 4/5.3, 4/96.3
St Jean Vianney, 5/61.1
St John Chrysostom, 1/32.1,
   1/43.3, 2/5.1, 2/64.1,
   2/64.2, 2/92.3, 4/50.3
St John of the Cross, 4/25.1
St John Paul II, 2/29.3
St Paul VI, 2/2.1
St Teresa, 1/32.1, 4/25.3
St Theophilus of Antioch,
   5/53.2
St Thomas Aquinas, 2/60.1

Divine filiation
St Athanasius, 5/59.1
St Cyprian, 5/33.1
St Cyril of Jerusalem, 6/3.2
St Hippolytus, 6/3.2
St John Chrysostom, 4/24.3,
   7/5.2

St John Paul II, 1/17.1, 4/32,
   5/59.1, 5/59.2
St Teresa, 5/60.3
St Thomas Aquinas, 1/24.3,
   1/36.2, 1/36.3, 4/32.1,
   4/98.1, 5/33.1, 5/59.1,
   5/59.2, 5/64.2, 5/75.3
Tertullian, 5/33.2

Docility
St John Paul II, 7/5.1

Doctrine
St J. H. Newman, 3/18.2
St Pius X, 7/5.1

Duties
John Paul I, 5/51.2
St Gregory the Great, 2/13.3

Early Christians
St Clement, 6/58.2
St John Chrysostom, 5/79.1,
   6/58.1
St John Paul II, 5/2.1, 5/8.2
St Justin, 2/70.2

Ecumenism
St John Paul II, 6/4.3
St Paul VI, 6/5.2

Eucharist
Bl. Alvaro, 3/46.2
Cassian, 6/47.2
St Alphonsus Liguori, 1/2.1,
   6/44.2, 6/47.1
St Ambrose, 5/40.2, 5/40.3,
   6/46.2
St Augustine, 2/56.2, 4/47,
   6/42.2, 6/45.2, 6/47.1
St Cyril of Jerusalem, 4/47.2,
   4/56.2, 6/43.1
St Fulgentius, 2/65.3
St Gregory the Great, 4/70.3
St Ignatius of Antioch, 2/65.3

St Irenaeus, **4**/65.2

St Jean Vianney, **2**/65.3, **4**/65.3

St John Chrysostom, **1**/2.1,
4/70.1

St John of the Cross, **5**/7.3

St John Paul II, **2**/51.2,
4/46.3, **4**/47.1, **4**/65.3,
4/70.2, **4**/70.3, **6**/41.1,
6/41.2

St Paul VI, **1**/2.2, **1**/2.3,
2/44.1, **2**/49.2, **2**/65.1,
2/65.2, **3**/4.3, **4**/43.2,
4/56.2, **5**/89.3, **6**/5.1,
6/41.3, **6**/43.1, **6**/45.3

St Pius X, **1**/2.3

St Teresa, **6**/45.2

St Thomas Aquinas, **2**/65.3,
3/4.1, **3**/103.2,
4/43.3, **6**/43.2, **6**/46.1
6/46.3, **6**/47.1

Evangelisation

St John Paul II, **2**/32.1, **2**/32.3,
4/87.3, **5**/12.2, **6**/12.3, **6**/18.2

St Paul VI, **5**/20.2, **5**/20.3,
6/9.2, **6**/13.2

Examination of conscience

Bl. Alvaro, **4**/93.1

St Augustine, **1**/19.2

St John Chrysostom, **4**/57.2

St John Climacus, **4**/93.2

St John of the Cross, **4**/93.1

St Teresa, **4**/93.3

Example

St Ambrose, **5**/13.2

St Gregory the Great, **2**/32.2

St Ignatius of Antioch, **5**/1.2

St John Chrysostom, **4**/40.2,
4/72.1, **4**/72.2, **5**/62.2

St John Paul II, **4**/4.3, **4**/73.1

St Teresa, **5**/62.2

Faith

Bl. Alvaro, **6**/18.3

Pius XII, **3**/55.2, **5**/53.2

St Ambrose, **1**/6.1, **4**/13.1,
5/64.2

St Augustine, **2**/54.3, **4**/54.1,
4/55.3, **5**/4.2, **5**/48.3, **5**/51.3

St Gregory Nazianzen, **5**/26.1

St Gregory the Great, **2**/54.2,
2/54.3, **6**/45.1

St Jean Vianney, **3**/44.2

St John Chrysostom, **2**/63.1,
3/55.1, **3**/89.1, **4**/55.3

St John Paul II, **1**/44.3, **2**/67.1,
6/6.2, **6**/13.2, **7**/1.3, **7**/12.2

St Justin, **6**/52.1

St Paul VI, **6**/6.2

St Vincent of Lerins, **6**/6.1

St Teresa, **4**/55.1

Family life

St Augustine, **7**/19.1

St John Chrysostom, **2**/70.3

St John Paul II, **1**/31.2, **2**/14.3,
3/95.1, **4**/91.1, **4**/91.3, **5**/29.3,
7/6.2, **7**/19, **7**/28.2, **7**/54.3

St Thomas Aquinas, **5**/29.3

Fear

St Augustine, **3**/99.1

St J. H. Newman, **3**/99.1

St John Chrysostom, **6**/12.3

St John Paul II, **2**/93.3, **5**/82.2

St Teresa, **2**/93.1, **2**/93.3

Forgiveness

St Ambrose, **3**/5.1

St Augustine, **1**/37.2

St John Chrysostom, **3**/54.2,
4/61.3, **5**/41.3

St John of the Cross, **5**/1.1

St John Paul II, **5**/1.3

St Therese of Lisieux, **5**/3.1

St Thomas Aquinas, **4**/60.2
Fraternity
St Augustine, **3**/52.2
St Cyprian, **5**/41.3
St Francis de Sales, **5**/78.3
St Gregory the Great, **5**/78.2
St John Chrysostom, **5**/79.1,
5/88.3
St John Paul II, **5**/78.3,
St Leo the Great, **4**/10.2
St Paul VI, **5**/20.3
Tertullian, **4**/79.2
Freedom
St John Paul II, **4**/74.2, **4**/74.3
Friendship
St Ambrose, **4**/41.2, **4**/41.3,
4/89.3
St Bernard, **4**/89.1
St Paul VI, **2**/80.2
St Teresa, **1**/36.1
St Thomas Aquinas, **2**/80.2,
3/5.2

Generosity
Pastor of Hermas, **5**/92.2
St Ambrose, **4**/94.1
St Augustine, **5**/67.2, **5**/74.3,
5/92.1
St Gregory the Great, **1**/26.2
St Ignatius of Antioch, **4**/97.1
St John Chrysostom, **5**/74.1
St John Paul II, **1**/18.3, **5**/8.3
St Teresa, **1**/26.3, **5**/74.3
St Thomas Aquinas, **5**/74.2
Good Shepherd
St Ambrose, **2**/4.3
St Augustine, **1**/7.2
St Thomas of Villanueva, **1**/7.2
Grace
St Augustine, **5**/77.2, **6**/12.2

St Bede, **4**/99.2
St Irenaeus, **1**/51.1
St John Chrysostom, **4**/97.2
St Teresa, **6**/12.2
St Thomas Aquinas, **2**/17.3,
4/2.2, **5**/30.1

Heaven
St Augustine, **2**/82.3
St Cyprian, **3**/97.1
St Cyril of Jerusalem, **2**/82.1
St John Chrysostom, **2**/12.2
St John Paul II, **3**/58.2
St Leo the Great, **2**/86.2
Hell
St Teresa, **3**/58.2, **5**/73.2
St Thomas Aquinas, **5**/90.1,
5/97.2, **5**/97.3
Holy Spirit
Leo XIII, **2**/83.1
St Augustine, **2**/95.3
St Cyril of Jerusalem, **2**/95.3,
2/96.2
St Francis de Sales, **2**/96.2
St John Paul II, **5**/45.1
St Paul VI, **2**/87.1
St Thomas Aquinas, **2**/90.3,
3/5.3, **5**/45.1
Hope
John Paul I, **5**/93.3
St Ambrose, **5**/66.3
St Augustine, **1**/4.1, **2**/74.1
St Bernard, **2**/74.3
St John Paul II, **4**/57.1
Human dignity
St John Paul II, **7**/28.3
Humility
John Paul I, **5**/47.3
Leo XIII, **1**/27.1
St Ambrose, **5**/77.1

St Augustine, 1/2.2, 1/27.2,
1/47.3, 5/21.1, 5/39.2,
5/57.2, 5/60.2
St Bede, 3/4.1
St Bernard, 3/45.2
St Cyril of Alexandria, 1/50.1
St Francis de Sales, 1/27.2,
4/84.1, 4/84.3
St Gregory the Great, 1/8.2
St Jean Vianney, 1/27.2
St John Chrysostom, 4/84.1
St John Paul II, 1/27.1, 5/74.2
St Thomas Aquinas, 1/27.2

Ignorance
St John XXIII, 2/32.1
St John Chrysostom, 3/18.2
Incarnation
St Augustine, 3/3.1
Instruments of God
Cassian, 2/20.2
John Paul I, 5/2.1, 5/65.2
Leo XIII, 5/77.1
St Augustine, 5/51.3, 5/54.2
St Gregory the Great, 3/98.2
St John Chrysostom, 2/14.1,
3/88.2, 4/55.3
St Pius X, 5/77.3
St Thomas Aquinas, 2/70.1,
5/12.3
St John Paul II, 5/43.2
Theophylact, 5/54.2
Interior Life
Bl. Alvaro, 4/30.1
St John Paul II, 6/4.3

Joy
St Basil, 4/67.3
St Bede, 2/12.2
St John Chrysostom, 4/26.1

St John Paul II, 1/30.2,
2/77.1, 3/15.3
St Leo the Great, 1/30.3
St Paul VI, 2/26.2, 2/48.3,
5/27.1
St Thomas Aquinas, 2/48.3,
2/94.1, 3/15.3, 7/47.2
St Thomas More, 1/39.2
Judgement
St J. H. Newman, 5/73.1
Justice
St Cyril of Jerusalem, 5/83.2
St John Chrysostom, 4/85.2
St John Paul II, 1/35.3,
2/75.1, 3/19.1, 4/12.2, 4/16.3,
4/77.3
St John XXIII, 4/77.1
St Paul VI, 4/12.3
St Thomas Aquinas, 2/75.1,
4/77.2, 5/17.3, 5/21.2,
5/55.2

Leisure
St Augustine, 4/29.1, 4/29.2
St Gregory Nazianzen, 4/29.1
St Paul VI, 5/17.1
St Teresa, 4/29.2
Lent
St John Paul II, 2/1.1, 2/8.2
Little things
St Augustine, 1/16.2
St Bernard, 5/39.2
St John Chrysostom, 2/22.3
St Francis de Sales, 4/57.2
Love
St Augustine, 3/52.2
St Gregory of Nyssa, 2/93.2
St John Chrysostom, 4/71.2
St John of the Cross, 2/14.3,
4/1.2

St John Paul II, 4/1.2, 5/8.2,
   5/64.2, 5/64.3, 5/88.1
St Teresa, 2/14.3, 5/55.2
St Thomas Aquinas, 4/97.2

Love of God
Clement of Alexandria, 5/3.1
John Paul I, 2/24.3, 5/53.3,
   5/65.1
St Alphonsus Liguori, 4/66.1
St Ambrose, 5/28.2
St Augustine, 2/49.2, 4/1.3,
   4/92.3, 5/65.2
St Bernard, 3/99.1
St Catherine of Siena, 3/50.2
St Francis de Sales, 5/77.2
St John Chrysostom, 2/24.1,
   5/39.2
St John of the Cross, 2/69.2,
   3/104.2, 4/95.2
St John Paul II, 3/104.3,
   4/95.1, 5/5.1, 5/5.3, 5/38.2,
   5/66.2, 5/75.3
St Teresa, 2/4.1, 2/69.1, 2/69.2,
   5/14.1, 5/57.3, 5/92.3, 5/95.3
St Thomas Aquinas, 4/66.2,
   5/65.2

Lukewarmness
St Augustine, 5/3.3
St Gregory the Great, 1/12.2,
   5/55.1
St John Chrysostom, 4/19.3,
   4/54.3
St John of the Cross, 4/19.2,
   5/76.2
St Pius X, 3/102.3
St Teresa, 4/19.2
St Thomas Aquinas, 5/30.1

Marxism
St Paul VI, 2/33.3

Marriage
John Paul I, 5/29.2
St Francis de Sales, 4/62.1
St John Chrysostom, 4/62.2
St John Paul II, 4/62.2, 5/29.1

Mass
Pius XII, 5/52.2, 5/92.2
St Augustine, 2/36.3
St Ephraim, 4/26.2
St Gregory the Great, 2/66.2
St Jean Vianney, 2/30.2,
   4/7.1, 4/7.3
St John Chrysostom, 4/26.2
St John Paul II, 2/30.2, 2/30.3
St Paul VI, 2/30.2

Materialism
Bl. Alvaro, 4/82.2
John Paul I, 5/46.3
St Augustine, 5/58.2
St Gregory the Great, 5/58.2
St John Paul II, 4/82.2,
   5/25.1, 7/2.1
St John XXIII, 2/58.2
St Paul VI, 5/49.1

Mercy
Clement of Alexandria, 5/3.1
St Augustine, 5/15.2, 5/93.2
St Bernard, 5/56.2
St Francis de Sales, 5/93.2
St John Paul II, 4/85.1, 5/1.3,
   5/3.2, 5/5.1, 5/5.2, 5/81.2
St Therese of Lisieux, 5/3.3
St Thomas Aquinas, 3/42.1,
   5/5.1, 5/17.3, 5/41.2,
   5/70.2, 5/81.2

Morning Offering
St Bernard, 2/79.1
Cassian, 2/79.2

Mortification
St Augustine, 4/8.1

St Francis de Sales, 2/1.1
St Jean Vianney, 5/26.1
St John Chrysostom, 2/15.2,
  4/8.2
St John of the Cross, 2/2.1,
  2/19.2
St Leo the Great, 2/19.1
St Paul VI, 2/15.2, 2/19.1
St Peter of Alcantara, 3/101.2
St Teresa, 2/19.2

Obedience
Cassian, 2/20.2
St Augustine, 1/49.1
St Gregory the Great, 1/5.2,
  1/49.2, 5/19.3
St John Chrysostom, 1/5.3,
  1/45.1
St Teresa, 1/49.3, 5/19.1, 5/19.3
St Thomas Aquinas, 4/88.2,
  5/19.2
St John Paul II, 4/94.3, 7/12.2
Optimism
St Teresa, 4/49.1
St Thomas Aquinas, 4/49.2
Our Lady
Benedict XV, 3/105.1, 7/13.2
Bl. Alvaro, 3/28.2
Leo XIII, 2/25.3, 3/45.3,
  5/18.1, 7/26.3, 7/34.1
Origen, 3/105.3
Pius IX, 1/25.1, 7/17.2
Pius XII, 2/95.1, 7/3.1,
  7/14.2, 7/17.2
St Alphonsus Liguori, 1/21.3,
  3/9.1, 4/99.2, 5/81.3, 7/9.2,
  7/9.3, 7/41.3, 7/49.3
St Amadeus of Lausanne,
  7/14.1
St Ambrose, 1/50.3

St Andrew of Crete, 7/22.1
St Augustine, 1/23.1, 1/47.3
St Bernard, 1/18.3, 1/38.3,
  1/40.3, 2/9.3, 2/74.3, 2/79.1,
  3/42.2, 3/98.3, 5/48.2, 5/92.3,
  6/1.1, 6/1.2, 6/15.2, 6/16.1,
  6/31.2, 7/11.3, 7/15.3, 7/43.3
St Bonaventure, 7/22.1
St Catherine of Siena, 6/28.3
St Cyril of Alexandria,
  1/38.1, 7/11.2
St Ephraim, 7/17.1
St Francis de Sales, 5/63.2
St Germanus of Constantinop
  le, 5/18.2
St Ildephonsus of Toledo,
  7/15.2
St J. H. Newman, 7/43.2
St Jean Vianney, 2/30.2, 5/63.1
St John Damascene, 2/46.3,
  7/6.1, 7/14.2
St John Paul II, 1/22.3, 1/31.3,
  1/38.2, 2/47.3, 2/56.3, 2/84.3,
  2/95.1, 3/9.2, 3/38.3, 3/42.1,
  4/90.2, 4/90.3, 4/94.3, 4/99.1,
  4/99.3, 5/14.2, 5/18.1, 5/36.1,
  6/10.1, 6/10.3, 6/28.2, 6/31.1,
  6/51.3, 7/3.2, 7/3.3, 7/6.3,
  7/9.1, 7/11.1, 7/15.2, 7/24.3
St Paul VI, 1/38.3, 2/48.3,
  2/84.1, 2/84.3, 2/95.1,
  2/95.3, 3/40.3, 3/105.3, 7/3.2
St Peter Damian, 4/90.1, 7/22.3
St Teresa, 6/31.3, 7/3.2
St Thomas Aquinas, 1/41.1,
  4/90.1, 4/99.3, 5/18.1, 7/43.2
St Vincent Ferrer, 7/3.2

Passion
St Alphonsus Liguori, 2/37.1

St Augustine, 2/39.2, 2/45.1
St John Chrysostom, 2/37.1
St John Paul II, 5/22.2
St Leo the Great, 2/37.1
St Thomas Aquinas, 2/37.1

Patience
St Augustine, 5/94.1
St Francis de Sales, 5/94.2
St Gregory Nazianzen, 5/54.3
St John Chrysostom, 2/28.1,
  2/28.3
St John of the Cross, 5/5.1
St Thomas Aquinas, 5/94.2

Peace
St Augustine, 2/77.2, 2/94.1,
  3/98.3
St Gregory Nazianzen, 2/56.2
St Irenaeus, 2/56.2
St John Chrysostom, 1/3.2
St John of the Cross, 4/25.1
St John Paul II, 1/3.1, 1/3.3
St Paul VI, 2/33.1, 4/12.3

Penance
St Ambrose, 3/90.3
St Cyril of Jerusalem, 5/75.2
St Gregory the Great, 3/90.1
St John Chrysostom, 3/90.2
St John Paul II, 3/85.2, 5/1.3,
  5/41.1
St Paul VI, 2/3.1

Perseverance
Cassian, 2/39.1
St Augustine, 5/4.3, 5/81.1,
  5/86.3
St Gregory the Great, 7/4.1
St John Chrysostom, 4/80.2
St John Paul II, 5/57.1, 5/86.2
St Teresa, 2/92.2, 5/57.3
St Thomas Aquinas, 2/92.2

Poverty
St Augustine, 5/24.3, 7/31.2
St Gregory the Great, 2/16.2,
  2/16.3
St John Chrysostom, 4/48.2
St Leo the Great, 2/1.2

Prayer
St Alphonsus Liguori, 2/12.3,
  2/81.3, 5/48.1, 5/57.2, 7/9.1
St Augustine, 2/9.3, 4/39.2,
  4/64.1, 4/64.2, 5/48.1,
  5/48.3, 5/56.2, 5/81.1, 5/95.2
St Bernard, 5/48.1
St Cyprian, 3/94.1
St Gregory the Great, 3/40.3
St Jean Vianney, 2/9.1,
  3/40.1, 7/35.1
St John Chrysostom, 2/68.2,
  4/64.3
St John of the Cross, 3/51.1
St John Paul II, 1/29.2,
  3/93.1, 4/39.1, 39.3, 4/91.1,
  4/91.3, 4/95.2, 5/33.1,
  5/57.1, 7/32.1
St Paul VI, 5/14.3
St Peter of Alcantara, 3/51.2,
  5/57.3
St Teresa, 1/29.2, 1/29.3, 2/9.3,
  2/15.1, 2/27.1, 2/27.3, 3/51.2,
  3/94.1, 4/95.2, 5/14.1, 5/34.1,
  5/57.1, 5/57.3, 6/18.2, 7/35.1
St Thomas Aquinas, 3/40.2,
  4/64.2, 4/80.3

Presence of God
St Alphonsus Liguori, 5/61.1
St Augustine, 2/76.1, 2/76.2,
  4/30.1
St Basil, 5/72.2
St Gregory the Great, 2/76.2
St John of the Cross, 2/76.2

St John Paul II, **2**/61.2, **5**/83.1

Pride
Cassian, **2**/14.1, **5**/63.3
St Ambrose, **5**/54.1
St John Chrysostom, **2**/25.2, **2**/63.1, **2**/63.3, **5**/33.3
St Gregory the Great, **2**/63.2
St Thomas Aquinas, **5**/55.1

Priesthood
Bl. Alvaro, **1**/51.3, **5**/11.2
St Ambrose, **7**/10.3
St Catherine of Siena, **4**/20.3
St Ephraim, **5**/71.1
St J. H. Newman, **6**/9,3
St John Paul II, **1**/7.2, **4**/20.1, **5**/57.1, **6**/9.3, **7**/10.1, **7**/10.2

Providence, divine
Cassian, **5**/33.2
St Augustine, **5**/60.2
St Bernard, **3**/96.3
St Jerome, **3**/97.2
St John Paul II, **3**/96.1
St Thomas Aquinas, **3**/96.2

Prudence
St Augustine, **4**/17.1
St John Paul II, **4**/17.1, **4**/17.2
St Teresa, **5**/93.2

Purgatory
St Catherine of Genoa, **7**/39.1
St John Paul II, **7**/39.1
St Teresa, **7**/39.1

Purity
St Ambrose, **5**/90.1
St John Paul II, **3**/8.1, **5**/75.3

Reading of the Gospel
St Augustine, **2**/73.1, **2**/73.3, **4**/86.3, **5**/96.3
St Cyprian, **5**/96.3
St Jerome, **7**/8.3

St John Chrysostom, **5**/96.1
St John Paul II, **4**/86.2

Responsibility
St Augustine, **5**/9.3
St Gregory the Great, **2**/63.2, **5**/68.2
St Ignatius of Antioch, **5**/79.2
St Thomas Aquinas, **5**/51.2

Roman Pontiff
St Ambrose, **6**/7.2
St Augustine, **6**/19.1, **6**/19.3
St Catherine of Siena, **6**/7.2
St Cyprian, **6**/19.1
St John Paul II, **6**/7.3
St Leo the Great, **6**/7.2, **6**/19.2

Rosary
Pius XI, **5**/36.2, **7**/32.3
Pius XII, **2**/81.1
St John Paul II, **2**/81.2, **5**/36.2, **5**/36.3
St John XXIII, **2**/81.1, **7**/33.1
St Paul VI, **2**/81.1, **2**/81.2, **5**/18.3, **5**/36.2

Sacraments
St Augustine, **2**/46.1
St John Chrysostom, **4**/36.1
St Pius X, **4**/46.3

Saints, devotion to
St Catherine of Siena, **6**/32.1
St Jerome, **3**/72.2
St John Paul II, **3**/72.2, **6**/2

St John the Baptist
St Augustine, **1**/8.1
St John Chrysostom, **6**/55.3

St Joseph
Leo XIII, **4**/15.2, **6**/20.1, **6**/26.3
St Ambrose, **1**/22.1
St Augustine, **1**/22.2
St Bernard, **4**/15.3

St Bernardine of Siena,
1/40.3, 6/20.3, 6/25.3
St Francis de Sales, 6/25.2
St John Chrysostom, 6/24.1
St John Paul II, 5/64.3, 5/84.3,
6/20.2, 6/26.3, 6/27.3
St John XXIII, 6/26.3
St Teresa, 1/45.2, 4/15.2,
6/26.1, 6/26.3

St Thomas More
St Thomas More, 6/54.3

Sanctity
Cassian, 5/32.3
St John Paul II, 3/7.3, 4/4.3,
5/58.3, 6/21.3, 7/38.1

Search for God
St Augustine, 5/16.3, 5/37.2,
7/4.2
St Bernard, 5/50.3
St Ignatius of Antioch, 5/32.3
St John of the Cross, 2/10.2
St John Paul II, 5/66.1

Self-giving
St Augustine, 5/3.3
St Gregory the Great, 5/92.1
St John Paul II, 1/26.1, 5/90.3

Service
St Augustine, 5/3.3
St John Chrysostom, 2/24.1
St John Paul II, 2/15.3, 5/47.3

Simplicity
St Jerome, 1/24.3
St John Chrysostom, 1/24.3

Sin
Origen, 5/93.1
St Augustine, 2/17.3, 2/21.3,
5/31.1, 5/45.2, 5/93.1
St Bede, 5/31.1
St Francis de Sales, 2/17.3
St Gregory the Great, 5/9.1

St Jean Vianney, 2/17.1, 3/44.2
St John Chrysostom, 4/85.2
St John of the Cross, 4/2.2,
5/45.3
St John Paul II, 2/17.1, 2/17.3,
2/18.2, 2/29.2, 3/56.3, 4/2.2,
4/34.1, 4/34.2, 5/3.2, 5/41.1,
5/45.1, 5/45.2, 5/70.1, 5/71.2
St Paul VI, 1/51.1

Sincerity
St Augustine, 7/18.2, 7/18.3
St Francis de Sales, 2/23.3
St John Chrysostom, 2/23.1
St Thomas Aquinas, 5/44.2

Society
Bl. Alvaro, 4/12.2
Pius XI, 3/37.1
St John Chrysostom, 3/52.1
St Paul VI, 1/35.1

Spiritual childhood
Cassian, 5/34.1
St Alphonsus Liguori, 5/57.2
St Ambrose, 4/63.3

Spiritual direction
St John Climacus, 1/7.3
St John of the Cross, 4/76.1,
5/85.2
St Teresa, 5/85.2
St Thomas Aquinas, 5/19.3
St Vincent Ferrer, 4/92.3

Spiritual reading
St Augustine, 3/18.2
St Basil, 3/43.2, 3/43.3
St Jerome, 7/36.3
St John Chrysostom, 7/8.2
St John Eudes, 7/8.3
St Peter of Alcantara, 7/8.3

Suffering
St Augustine, 5/69.2
St Bede, 7/20.2

St Francis de Sales, **2**/31.2
St John Chrysostom, **2**/64.3,
  5/31.1
St John Paul II, **2**/31.3,
  5/15.1, **5**/15.2, **5**/22.2,
  5/69.1, **6**/17.3, **6**/22.1
St Teresa, **5**/69.3
St Thomas More, **2**/38.3
Supernatural outlook
Pius XII, **3**/55.2
St Augustine, **5**/34.1, **5**/80.1
St Bede, **4**/69.2
St Gregory the Great, **4**/80.2
St John Chrysostom, **4**/82.1
St John Paul II, **5**/58.3, **5**/97.1
St John XXIII, **5**/89.3
St Paul VI, **5**/83.3
St Teresa, **5**/76.3
St Theophilus, **3**/55.2

Temperance
St John Paul II, **4**/35
St Peter Alcantara, **4**/35.1
Temptations
St Athanasius, **4**/3.1
St Basil, **5**/9.2
St Thomas Aquinas, **5**/42.2,
  6/3.3
Time
St Augustine, **4**/65.3
St Paul VI, **5**/17.1
Trust in God
Tertullian, **5**/42.2
St Augustine, **2**/4.3, **5**/67.2,
  5/93.1
St Cyprian, **5**/35.2
St Francis de Sales, **5**/43.3
St Teresa, **5**/60.3, **5**/65.1
St Thomas Aquinas, **5**/33.2
St Thomas More, **5**/61.3

Truth
St Augustine, **4**/18.3
St John Chrysostom, **4**/28.2
St Thomas Aquinas, **5**/44.2

Understanding
St Augustine, **2**/21.2
St Gregory the Great, **2**/72.2
St Jerome, **2**/72.1, **4**/27.3
St John Paul II, **7**/18.2
St Teresa, **2**/87.2
Unity
Aristides, **2**/56.3
Cassian, **3**/72.2
Pius XI, **5**/87.3, **5**/91.2
St Augustine, **2**/56.3, **2**/78.3,
  4/92.1
St Cyprian, **4**/13.3
St Irenaeus, **2**/56.1, **2**/56.2
St John Chrysostom, **2**/56.1,
  3/50.7
St John Paul II, **2**/56.1,
  2/56.2, **3**/57.1, **5**/32.2,
  5/68.2, **6**/18.1
St Paul VI, **2**/56.2, **6**/5.2
St Thomas Aquinas, **2**/56.2

Virtues
Bl. Alvaro, **2**/22.2, **4**/33.1
Pius XI, **4**/33.1
St Augustine, **3**/19.3, **3**/100.1
St Francis de Sales, **3**/6.2
St Gregory the Great, **4**/25.2
St Jerome, **3**/86.3
St John Chrysostom, **3**/52.1
St Teresa, **3**/54.3, **3**/100.1
St Thomas Aquinas, **3**/6.2
**Visit to the Blessed
  Sacrament**
Pius XII, **2**/51.2

St Alphonsus Liguori, **2**/51.3,
  4/56.3
St John Chrysostom, **2**/51.3
St Paul VI, **4**/56.3
St Teresa, **2**/51.3
Vocation
Bl. Alvaro, **2**/32.1,
John Paul I, **1**/45.1
Pius XI, **4**/22.2
St Bernard, **4**/22.1
St Bernardine of Siena,
  6/20.3
St Gregory the Great, **3**/88.2
St John Chrysostom, **7**/25.1
St John Paul II, **4**/22.3, **5**/38.2,
  5/43.1, **5**/90.2, **7**/29.2, **7**/45.1
St Thomas Aquinas, **6**/20.2,
  7/45.2

Will of God
St John Paul II, **5**/43.1
St Augustine, **5**/35.1
St Teresa, **2**/57.2, **5**/35.3
Worldly Respect
St Bede, **5**/44.2
St Jean Vianney, **2**/62.1
St Thomas Aquinas, **5**/30.1
Work
Bl. Alvaro, **4**/30.3
Didache, **4**/78.1
St John Chrysostom, **1**/43.1,
  3/41.2
St John Paul II, **1**/46.2, **3**/11.2,
  5/13.2, **5**/32.2, **5**/84.3
St John XXIII, **3**/11.2

SUBJECT INDEX

Abandonment
   and responsibility, **3**/96.2,
      7/46.2
   confidence in God's Will,
      3/61.1, **3**/96.1, **5**/35, **5**/53.1,
      5/58.1
   healthy concern for *today*,
      3/61.3
   omnia in bonum, **3**/96.3,
      5/58.3, **5**/60.2
   unnecessary worries, **3**/61.2,
      5/17.3, **5**/82.3

Advent
   expectation of second coming,
      1/20.1
   joy of, **1**/2.1
   meaning of, **1**/1.3
   period of hope, **1**/21.1
   period of joy, **1**/15.1
   preparation for Christmas,
      1/1.1

Affability, **3**/6.1, **3**/6.2, **3**/6.3

Angels, **7**/27, **7**/28, **7**/29, **7**/30

Anger, can be just and virtuous,
   1/11.3

Anointing of the Sick,
   2/31.3, **3**/31

Apostolate
   a duty, **2**/53.1, **2**/85.1, **3**/21.3,
      3/69.1, **4**/40.3, **5**/10.2,
      5/25.1, **5**/51.3, **5**/87.3,
      6/30.3, **7**/2.3

ad fidem, **1**/44.3, **4**/21.1
   and difficulties, **1**/9.2, **1**/41.3,
      2/32.3, **2**/53.2, **2**/62.2,
      3/89.2, **5**/52.1, **6**/52.3,
      6/57.3, **6**/58.2
   and doctrine, **4**/18.1, **5**/46.3
   and example, **2**/32.2, **4**/44.3,
      5/13.1, **5**/51.2, **5**/76.3, **6**/58.1
   and faith, **3**/5.1, **7**/34.3
   and God's help, **1**/9.2, **2**/59.2,
      5/26.1, **5**/52, **6**/34.3
   and humility, **1**/8.2, **5**/57.2
   and joy, **1**/15.3, **3**/68.3, **3**/69.1,
      5/25.3, **5**/27.2, **5**/55.1,
      5/55.3, **7**/4.3
   and meekness, **1**/11.3
   and optimism, **2**/53.3, **3**/21.2
   and patience, **2**/52.2, **2**/52.3,
      3/21.2, **5**/94.3
   and prayer, **3**/3.1, **3**/88.2,
      5/57.1, **7**/46.3
   and prudence, **3**/5.2
   and proselytism, **2**/62.2,
      5/10.2, **7**/46.2
   and worldly respect, **2**/62.3,
      3/89.3, **4**/44, **5**/30.1, **5**/44.2,
      5/62, **5**/72.3
   basis of, **1**/9.1, **3**/3.3, **3**/35.2,
      3/68.1, **5**/10.2
   being instruments, **3**/21.1,
      3/36.3, **5**/51.3, **5**/52
   constancy in, **1**/12.2, **2**/85.2,

4/69.2, 5/20.2, 5/50.2, 5/68.3,
5/94.3, 6/2.3, 7/55.3
fruits of, 2/85.2, 3/21.3,
5/52.2, 5/68.3, 5/91.3
how to do it, 2/52.3, 2/59.3,
needs formation, 2/54.3
of friendship, 1/8.3, 1/9.2,
2/53.3, 5/25.2, 7/42.2
of public opinion, 4/45.2,
4/45.3, 5/44, 6/32.2, 7/2.2
part of the Christian vocation,
1/8.1, 2/53.1, 2/86.3, 3/69.2,
5/72.2
role of women, 2/85.3, 5/8,
7/36.1
universal meaning of, 1/44.3,
5/37.3, 5/43.1, 6/58.3, 7/25.3
upright intention, 2/62.3
virtues required, 3/36.1,
3/36.2, 3/36.3, 4/33.3,
5/20.1, 6/11.2
witnesses to Christ, 1/6.2,
1/8.3, 3/35.2, 4/66.3, 5/66.3,
5/87.3, 6/53, 7/2
Ascetical Struggle
beginning again, 1/12.2,
1/12.3, 1/24.3, 2/28.2,
4/14.3, 5/9.3, 5/50.2,
5/60.2, 5/70.2, 6/30.2,
7/20.2
constancy, 2/28.1, 4/14.1,
5/42.3, 5/48.1, 5/70.2, 5/94
develop a spirit of, 1/13.3,
1/19.1, 1/43.3, 5/34.2, 5/43.2
expect defeats, 1/12.3, 4/14.2,
5/93.3
fortitude in the face of
weaknesses, 1/12.1, 1/45.3,
4/11.2, 5/42.2, 5/61.2,
5/70.2, 5/93

until the last moments, 1/12.1,
5/97.3
Aspirations, 1/29.3, 1/40.2,
1/40.3, 2/35.3
remembering to say, 2/35.2
Atonement, 6/35.3, 49.3, 6/50.2

Baptism
effects of, 1/51.2, 5/43, 5/59,
5/71.2
gratitude for having received
it, 1/51.1
incorporation into the Church,
1/51.3, 4/13.2
institution of, 1/51.1
of children, 1/51.3
Beatitudes, 3/25.1, 3/25.2
Blessed Trinity, 2/76.1, 6/3.1,
6/39, 6/40

Calumny, 3/19.1, 3/19.2, 3/19.3
Celibacy
see Chastity, Virginity
Charity
and forgiveness, 2/21.1,
2/21.2, 2/21.3, 5/1.1
and judgements, 2/72.1, 5/41.3
effectiveness of, 2/72.3,
4/10.1, 5/20.3, 5/68.2, 5/94.3
its essence, 3/27.1, 3/27.2,
5/23.1, 5/31.3, 5/52.1,
5/79.3, 6/50.3
ordered, 1/25.3, 3/81.2, 4/21.3
sins of omission, 4/21.2
understanding, 2/72.1, 2/72.2,
3/52.1, 3/52.2, 3/81.3,
5/11.2, 5/6.1, 5/15.3, 5/67.3,
5/93.2
Chastity
and little things, 1/16.2, 5/90.3

clean of heart shall see God,
1/16.3, 3/8.1, 3/48.1, 5/16.1,
5/53.2, 5/75.3, 5/90

fruits of purity, 1/23.2, 5/63.3,
5/75.3, 5/90

guard of the heart, 1/16.2,
5/90.3

purity of heart, 1/16.1, 1/19.3,
1/23.1, 4/62.3, 5/90

ways of living purity well,
1/23.3, 3/8.2, 3/8.3, 5/90.3

Christians
early, 2/70.1, 5/52.3, 5/62.3,
5/68.3, 5/71.1, 5/74.2, 5/79.1,
5/84.1, 5/86.2

exemplary, 2/29.1, 2/70.2,
3/74, 3/102

Christmas
a call to interior purification,
1/16.1

humility and simplicity in
knowing Christ, 1/30.2

joy at, 1/30.3

receiving Christ, 1/30.1

the *Chair of Bethlehem,* 1/30.2

Church
characteristics of, 3/10.1,
3/57.3, 4/37.1, 5/5.2, 6/8

indefectibility, 2/60.1, 4/37.2,
4/37.3

its institution, 3/47.1, 6/4.1

love for, 2/59.2, 3/10.3,
4/13.1, 4/13.3, 7/16.3

mission of, 4/16.1, 4/16.2,
5/1.3, 5/28.1, 5/31.2, 5/41.1,
5/47.2, 5/48.2, 5/75.3, 5/87.1

prayer for, 3/47.2, 6/4.2,
7/27.3

Civic Duties, 4/58.1, 5/21,
5/51.2, 5/67, 5/74

Commandments of God
first, 3/76.1, 3/76.2, 3/76.3,
5/55.2, 5/65.1

fourth, 3/38.1, 3/38.2, 3/38.3

ninth, 3/86.1, 3/86.2, 3/86.3

second, 5/34

Communion
confession, a preparation for,
1/2.3, 5/7.3

dispositions for, 1/2.1, 1/2.2,
5/7.3

effects of, 2/65.3, 3/29.3,
4/46.2, 4/47.3, 4/56, 4/65.3,
5/40.3, 6/46.3

preparation for, 1/2.3, 4/46.3,
5/7.2, 5/7.3, 5/95.2

spiritual communions, 3/29.1,
3/29.2

Viaticum, 4/56.1

see Eucharist

Communion of the Saints
and optimism, 4/49.3

and penance, 2/10.2

entry into, 1/51.2, 2/66.2

gaining merit for others,
1/10.3, 2/66.1, 5/5/33.3, 5/68

indulgences, 2/66.3, 5/71.3

Compassion, 4/10.2, 4/27.3,
5/7.1, 5/15.1, 5/31, 5/33.1,
5/58.1, 5/62.1, 5/88.1

Concupiscence, 1/1.2, 5/58.2

Confession
a good for the whole church,
1/10.3

and contrition, 1/37.2, 1/47.3,
2/41.2, 2/41.3, 3/90.2, 4/9.2,
5/5.3

and peace, 1/3.1, 5/27.2

and the Good Shepherd, 1/7.2

apostolate of, 1/9.1, 2/34.2,

5/5.3

frequent, 1/10.2, 1/16.2, 3/7.3, 4/9.3, 5/5.3, 5/27.2

fruits of, 2/4.2, 2/8.3, 2/18.3, 5/1.3, 5/27.2

institution of, 4/60.1, 5/3.2, 5/93.2

need for and importance of, 1/10.1, 5/7.3, 5/53.2

penance, 2/34.3, 5/5.3

personal, auricular and complete, 1/10.1

preparation for, 1/9.3, 2/8.2, 2/8.3, 3/7.2, 4/9.3

preparation for Communion, 1/1.2, 5/7.3

respect, gratitude and veneration for, 1/9.3, 4/60.2, 5/39.2

the power of forgiving, 1/9.3, 2/8.2, 2/34.1, 4/60.3, 5/.1, 5/41.2

Confidence in God

and divine filiation, 1/36.2, 2/60.3, 4/5.2, 4/5.3, 5/9.3, 5/33.2, 5/81, 7/7.1

its never too late, 1/36.2, 4/55.3, 5/60, 5/93

Consumerism, 1/6.2, 5/25.1, 5/46.3, 5/49.1, 5/55.2, 5/58.2, 7/31.3

Contrition, 4/9.2, 5/5.3, 5/9.1, 5/16.2, 5/28.2, 5/60.2

Conversion, 1/18.3, 2/1.1, 5/9.3, 5/15.3, 5/54.3, 5/70.2, 7/20.1

Culture, 7/2.1

Death, 3/63.1, 3/63.2, 3/63.3, 5/71, 5/75, 5/80, 5/97.1, 5/97.3, 6/25.1

Dedication, 4/3.1, 4/3.3, 5/9.2, 5/12.1, 5/86, 7/41.2

Detachment

examples, 2/16.2, 3/28.3, 3/64.2, 5/24.2, 5/24.3

its need, 1/28.1, 2/16.1, 3/17.1, 4/19.2, 4/48.3, 5/24.1

our practice, 2/16.3, 3/17.2, 3/17.3, 3/65.2, 4/6.2, 5/21.3, 5/38.3, 5/49.2

Devil, 2/6.1, 2/6.2, 2/6.3, 5/42.1, 5/42.2

Difficulties

and faith, 4/50.2, 5/61.1, 5/85.1, 7/21.3

current forms of, 1/32.2, 5/42.1

Christian reaction to, 1/32.2, 1/36.1, 1/41.3, 4/25.2, 5/56.1, 5/59.2, 5/60.2, 5/61.2, 5/69.2, 5/82.3, 5/93, 7/12.3, 7/16.2

develop hope, 1/32.3, 4/5.3, 4/25.3, 5/85.1, 7/5.2

suffered for Christ, 1/32.1, 1/32.3, 4/25.1, 4/96.2, 5/31.3, 7/12.1, 7/23.2

Dignity, human, 3/11.1, 3/11.2, 3/11.3, 5/3.2, 5/75, 5/76, 7/22.2, 7/28.2

Dispositions, interior

humility, 2/20.1, 2/20.2

need for, 1/18.1, 5/16.1, 5/53.2

Divine filiation

and fraternity, 1/39.2, 4/98.3, 5/33.1, 5/79.3

and petition, 4/39.2, 4/39.3, 5/60.3

consequences of, 1/39.2, 3/2.2, 4/24.2, 4/24.3, 4/63.2,

4/98.2, 5/33.2, 5/46.3,
5/59.3, 5/60.2, 5/72, 5/75.3

everything is for the good,
1/36.3, 3/96.3, 5/22.1,
5/58.3, 5/65.1

foundation for peace and joy,
1/3.3, 1/39.3, 5/27.2, 5/33.1,
5/59.2

God is our Father, 1/24.3,
1/36.3, 3/2.1, 3/56, 4/24.1,
4/39.1, 4/58, 4/98.1, 5/3.2,
5/33.2, 5/59, 5/60.1, 5/64

gratitude for, 1/39.1

truly sons, 1/39.1, 3/62.2,
5/33.1, 5/47.1, 5/59.1

Docility
a virtue, 1/24.3, 1/43.2, 7/5.1
and spiritual guidance, 2/20.3,
5/45.3

Doctrine
and piety, 6/14
giving it, 4/28.2, 4/28.3,
5/46.3, 7/16.1
need for, 7/13.1

Ecumenism, 6/4, 6/5, 6/6, 6/7,
6/8
Education, 7/6.3
Eucharist
Adoro te devote, 2/65.1, 3/4.1,
3/4.2, 5/61.1, 5/95.2, 5/95.3
3/4.3, 4/43.3, 4/97.2
and adoration, 1/44.1, 5/40.3,
5/61, 5/89.3
and faith, 6/45
institution of, 2/44.2, 4/26.1,
4/26.2
pledge of Heaven, 4/65.1,
4/65.2, 5/40.3, 6/48
real presence, 4/43, 5/7.3,

5/16.3, 6/41, 6/42, 6/43,
6/44, 6/46
true food, 4/46, 4/47, 4/65.1,
5/40.2, 5/61
see Communion

Examination of Conscience
a means against evil
inclinations, 1/19.2, 5/41.3
a meeting with God, 1/14.2
and hope, 4/57.2
and self-knowledge, 1/14.1,
5/54.2, 5/73.3
contrition and resolutions,
1/14.3
fruits of, 1/14.1, 5/73.3
how to do it, 1/14.3
particular, 2/67.1, 2/67.2,
2/67.3, 4/19.3, 5/23.3

Example, 3/34, 3/74.1, 4/4.3,
4/10.1, 4/40.2, 4/58.2, 5/1.2,
5/13.2, 55/6.3, 5/62.2, 5/68.3,
5/76.3

Faith
and apostolate, 1/9.2
and charity, 6/52.3
and Christ, 1/43.3, 2/20.1,
3/16.1, 3/67.1, 4/50.1,
4/50.2, 4/55.2, 4/55.3,
5/38.3, 5/56.2, 5/64.2, 6/54,
7/1.1, 7/37.2
and optimism, 4/49.2
docility in spiritual guidance,
1/43.2, 1/43.3, 5/45.3
firmness in, 1/43.1, 3/73.2,
4/54.1, 5/4.3, 5/30.2, 5/48,
5/85.1, 6/52.1, 7/1.3
giving it to others, 1/14.3,
6/6.3, 6/13.3, 6/52.2
need for it, 1/6.1, 5/30.3

of Our Lady, 1/6.3, 3/43.3,
3/55.3, 4/54.3, 5/51.3, 5/64.2
operative, 2/54.2, 2/60.3,
2/62.1, 3/12.3, 3/67.1,
4/54.3, 5/48.3, 5/60.2
ways to conserve and increase
it, 1/6.1, 1/6.2, 1/18.2,
3/55.1, 4/31.1, 4/54.2, 5/4.2,
6/6.1, 6/13

Faithfulness
a virtue, 3/104.1, 3/104.2,
5/86, 7/14.3
in little things, 2/50.2, 3/104.3,
5/91.3

Family
domestic church, 1/31.3,
3/95.1, 5/29.3, 5/55.3, 7/19.1
mission of parents, 1/31.2,
3/95.2, 7/6.2, 7/19.1, 7/28.2,
7/54.2
of Jesus, 4/32, 7/54.1
prayer in the, 3/95.3, 7/6.3,
7/19.2, 7/19.3

Family, Holy
example for all families,
1/31.3, 7/6.1, 7/54.1
love in the, 1/22.2, 1/27.3,
5/64.3
meeting with Simeon, 1/41.1
Redemption rooted here,
1/31.1
simplicity and naturalness,
1/42.2

Fear, 1/36.1, 2/93, 3/99, 5/82.2
Feasts, 2/61.1, 2/61.2, 2/61.3,
3/71.1
and Sundays, 3/71.2, 3/71.3

Formation, doctrinal
and interior life, 3/13.3, 3/18.3
in the truths of the faith,

3/13.1, 3/18.1
need to receive and to give it,
3/13.2, 3/18.2

Fortitude
gift of, 2/92.1
in daily life, 1/45.3, 3/32.2,
3/32.3, 3/97.3, 5/94.2
in difficult moments, 2/64.2,
7/21.1
virtue of, 3/32.1, 3/97.3,
4/44.2, 5/94.1

Fraternal correction, 1/7.2,
3/24.1, 3/24.2, 3/24.3
Freedom, 1/35.1

Friendship
and apostolate, 2/80.3, 4/41.3
qualities of a true friendship,
2/80.2, 5/6.2, 5/78.2
true friendship, 2/80.1, 6/11.1
with God, 4/41, 4/55, 5/4.2,
5/61.3, 5/88.1, 7/7.2, 7/7.3

Generosity
prize for it, 1/26.3
towards God, 3/46.1, 4/67.1,
4/98.1, 5/38.3, 5/55.2,
5/67.2, 5/72.3, 5/74, 5/92
with others, 1/26.2, 5/8.3,
5/66.2, 5/67

God's Love for men
gratuitous, 3/62.1, 5/3.2,
5/65.2
infinite and eternal, 2/24.1,
2/24.2, 3/62.1, 4/66.1, 5/1,
5/74.3
personal and individual,
3/62.3, 5/3.1, 5/38.2, 5/66.2,
5/70.2, 5/88
returning his love, 2/57.1,
3/62.2, 3/62.3, 4/66.2, 5/9.3,

5/37.2, 5/39.3, 5/65.2, 5/87.3
unconditional reply expected,
2/24.3, 5/51.1
Goods of the Earth
supernatural end, 4/68.1, 5/21,
5/24, 5/38.2, 5/38.3, 5/49,
5/55.2
Good Shepherd
and spiritual guidance, 1/7.3,
1/43.2
in the Church, 1/7.2, 2/68.1
Jesus Christ is, 1/1, 2/68.1,
5/66.3, 5/70
role of every Christian, 1/7.2
virtues of, 1/7.2, 5/63.3
Gospel
reading of, 1/48.2, 2/73.1,
5/96, 7/36.3
teaching is current, 1/48.3,
5/96.2
Grace
corresponding to it, 2/40.2,
4/19.3, 5/9.3, 5/51.1, 6/2.1,
7/41.2
its effects and fruits, 3/23.2,
3/23.3, 3/84.1, 3/91.1, 5/77,
7/40.3
its nature, 3/23.2, 3/84.2,
3/91.2, 5/30.1
Guardian Angels
help us, 2/7.2, 3/77.2, 3/77.1,
5/42.3, 5/73.3, 5/77.3, 5/84.3
love and devotion for, 2/7.1,
2/7.3, 3/77.2, 3/77.3

Heaven, 2/82.1, 2/82.2, 2/82.3,
5/21.1, 5/73.2, 5/83.3, 5/90,
5/97
hope of, 2/12.2, 2/82.1, 3/58.3,
4/48.2, 5/37.1, 5/80.1,

5/97.1, 7/12.2, 7/14.2,
7/15.3, 7/52.1
and the Eucharist, 4/65
Holy days of Obligation,
4/29.3
Holy Spirit
and Mary, 2/95.2, 2/95.3,
7/44.1
and supernatural virtues,
2/83.1
devotion to, 2/76.3
fruits, 2/94, 5/23.2, 5/45,
5/52.1
gifts,
counsel, 2/90
fear, 2/93
fortitude, 2/92
knowledge, 2/88
piety, 2/91
understanding, 2/87
wisdom, 2/89
Hope
and discouragement, 1/21.1,
2/4.3, 2/74.2, 3/79.2, 5/23.1,
7/1.2
and heaven, 2/12.2, 5/37.1,
5/80.1, 5/97.1, 7/15.3
and Our Lady, 1/21.1, 2/74.3,
5/36.3, 5/73.3, 6/31.2, 7/14.2
confidence in Christ, 1/23.3,
1/21.3, 2/74.1, 5/49.3,
5/53.3, 5/66.3, 5/83.3, 6/12
in apostolate, 2/4.3
its object, 1/21.2, 3/79.1,
4/57.1, 5/93.3
Humility
and prayer, 1/29.3, 4/51.1,
5/4.1, 5/57.2
and pride, 2/25.1, 2/25.2,
3/45.2, 3/50.1, 4/51.2

and simplicity, **1**/42.1, **1**/47.3,
5/63.2
founded on charity, **1**/27.2,
2/25.3, **5**/63.3, **5**/74.2
fruits of, **1**/27.2, **3**/50.1,
5/21.1, **5**/47.3, **5**/77.1,
5/93.3, **6**/55.3
is truth, **1**/27.1, **5**/39.2, **5**/63.2
needed for the apostolate,
1/8.2, **5**/77.3
ways to achieve it, **1**/27.3,
2/14.3, **2**/25.3, **3**/45.3,
3/50.3, **4**/51.3, **5**/9.2

Illness, **2**/31.1, **2**/31.2, **5**/69.3,
5/94.2

Jesus Christ
and Our Lady, **1**/17.2, **5**/18.3,
7/49.1
and the Cross, **1**/20.1, **2**/30.1,
4/36.1, **4**/53.1, **5**/2.3, **5**/19.3,
5/22, **5**/28.3, **5**/69, **5**/70.1,
7/12.2
divinity, **4**/52.1, **6**/28.1
growth of, **1**/50.1
hidden life, **1**/46.1, **1**/46.2,
1/50.1, **4**/45.1, **5**/84.2
high priest, **6**/38
humanity, **1**/17.3, **1**/50.1,
4/52.2, **5**/16.2, **5**/28.3,
5/31.2, **5**/78.1, **5**/84.3, **5**/88,
6/28, **6**/47.3, **6**/49, **7**/7.2,
7/35.2
humility, **1**/30.2, **5**/47.2,
5/52.2, **5**/63.1
Kingship, **2**/42.3, **5**/34.2,
5/34.3, **5**/83.2, **5**/87, **5**/91
merits of, **4**/4.2
Name of, **1**/40.1, **1**/40.2,

5/34.1
Only-Begotten Son, **1**/17.1,
5/59.1
our knowledge of, **1**/17.3,
1/48.2, **5**/53.3, **5**/96
our Model, **1**/17.3, **1**/49.3,
4/52.3, **5**/2.2, **5**/15.2, **5**/31.2,
5/47.1, **5**/66.2, **5**/78.1, **7**/38.3
our support, **1**/36.1, **3**/73.1,
5/56.1, **5**/61.1, **5**/69.3, **5**/70.1
our Teacher, **1**/48.1, **5**/2.1
search for, **2**/12.3, **2**/49.3,
5/16.3, **5**/32.2, **5**/37.2,
5/38.3, **5**/56.2, **5**/66.1,
5/83.1, **5**/85.1

Joseph, Saint
and work, **6**/33
devotion to, **4**/15.2, **6**/20, **6**/21,
6/22, **6**/23, **6**/24, **6**/25, **6**/26,
6/27
exemplar of virtues, **1**/45.2,
4/15.3, **5**/63.3, **6**/21
his dealings with Jesus and
Mary, **1**/22.2, **1**/22.3, **1**/31.1,
4/15.2, **5**/64.3, **5**/84.3, **6**/22
his intercession, **1**/45.2
his mission, **1**/22.1, **4**/15.1
his obedience and fortitude,
1/6.3, **1**/45.1
honour and veneration, **1**/22.3
invoking his name, **1**/40.3
ite ad, **4**/15.3
patron of the Church, **4**/15.2,
4/15.3

Joy
and apostolate, **3**/15.3, **5**/25.3,
5/55, **5**/76.3, **5**/78.3
and divine filiation, **1**/15.2,
3/15.1, **5**/27.2, **5**/33.1, **5**/59.2
and generosity, **2**/26.3, **4**/67,

5/27.2, 5/38.3, 5/55.2,
5/67.2, 5/74.3
and sadness, 2/48.2, 3/15.2,
4/67.3, 5/55.1, 7/47.3
and suffering 2/26.1, 2/26.2,
3/15.2, 4/96.1, 7/23.3
being close to Jesus, 1/15.1,
3/15.1, 3/25.3, 4/96.1, 7/4.2,
7/47.1
in the family, 3/15.3
its foundation, 1/15.2, 3/15.1,
5/5/27
spreading it, 2/48.3, 5/55.3

Judgement
particular, 1/20.3, 5/73.2
preparation for, 1/20.3, 5/73
universal, 1/20.2, 5/73.3, 5/83

Justice
and charity, 1/35.3
and mercy, 1/35.3, 5/17.3
and the individual, 2/33.1,
2/33.2
consequences of, 1/35.2,
2/75.1
its aim, 2/75.3

Laity
role of, 7/10.2

Leisure
and tiredness, 3/33.1, 3/33.3
learning to sanctify it, 3/33.2,
4/29, 5/17.1

Little things
and ascetical struggle, 1/12.1,
1/19.2, 1/50.2, 3/78.1,
3/78.2, 3/78.3, 4/38, 4/57.3,
5/39.2, 5/50.2, 7/20.3

Love
seeing God in ordinary things,
1/33.3, 5/32.2, 5/50.2

Love of God
above all things, 4/1, 5/35.3,
5/38.1, 5/49.1, 5/55.2,
5/74.2, 7/37.3
and the danger of
lukewarmness, 1/13.1,
5/30.1, 5/50.3
far-sighted, 1/33.3
in daily incidents, 2/24.3, 4/58
leading to abandonment,
2/57.3, 5/55.2, 5/60.3, 5/77.2
with deeds, 2/57.2, 4/66.2,
5/51.2, 5/65.2, 5/72.3,
5/73.1, 5/82.2, 5/84, 7/4.1

Loyalty, 3/87.1, 3/87.2, 3/87.3,
5/21.1, 4/44.2, 5/79.3, 5/86

Lukewarmness
causes of, 1/13.2, 1/15.1,
5/28.2, 5/50.3
consequences of, 1/13.1,
1/47.2, 3/83.1, 5/3.3, 5/16.2,
5/30.1, 5/55.1, 5/76.2
remedy for, 1/13.3, 1/47.3,
3/83.2

Magisterium
God speaks through it, 1/48.3

Magnanimity, 3/54.1, 3/54.2,
3/54.3, 5/1.2, 5/46.2, 5/64.2

Marriage, 3/59.1, 3/59.2,
3/59.3, 5/29, 5/90
dignity of, 4/62.1, 5/64.2, 5/90
see Family life

Mass
attendance at, 4/36.2, 4/36.3
centre of interior life, 4/26.3,
5/52.3
its value, 2/30.2, 2/30.3,
3/49.1, 4/7.1, 5/52.2
fruits of, 3/103, 4/7.2, 4/7.3

our offering, 1/44.2, 3/49.3,
   4/61.2, 5/92.2
Materialism, 7/2.1
Maturity, 1/50.3, 1/51.3
Meekness
   and peace, 1/11.1
   dealings with others, 1/11.1,
      5/1.1
   fruits of, 1/11.3
   is foundation, 1/11.2
   Jesus, model of, 1/11.1, 5/1,
      5/41.3
   need for it, 1/11.3
Mercy
   and justice, 1/35.3, 3/82.2,
      5/17.3
   fruits of, 3/82.3
   works of, 1/4.3, 4/16.3, 4/27.3,
      5/15
Mercy, divine
   an example, 1/4.1, 3/82.1,
      5/5.1, 5/66.3
   turn to it, 1/4.1, 5/3, 5/17.3,
      5/39.1, 5/45.2, 5/81, 5/93
   with men, 1/4.2, 4/27.1,
      4/27.2, 5/1.3, 5/3, 5/41.2,
      5/56.2, 5/70.2, 5/81.1
Merit
   of good works, 4/97
Morning Offering, 2/79
Mortification
   and purity, 1/16.3
   and the Cross, 2/2.1, 2/2.2,
      2/15.2, 2/43.2, 4/53.3, 5/75.3
   fasting, 2/3.1
   interior, 1/19.2, 1/19.3, 1/44.2,
      2/3.2, 2/55.1, 5/26.1
   of imagination, 2/55.2, 2/55.3
   small sacrifices, 2/2.3, 2/3.3,
      4/8, 5/26, 5/28.3

Obedience
   and docility, 1/24.3
   and faith, 1/12.3, 1/45.1
   and freedom, 1/49.3, 5/19.2
   and God's Will, 1/5.2
   and humility, 1/5.2
   because of love, 1/49.3,
      5/11.2, 5/19.1
   fruits of, 1/49.2
   model of, 1/49.1, 5/11.3,
      5/19.3
Optimism, 4/49, 5/61.3, 5/78.3
Our Lady
   and confession, 7/51.1
   and faithfulness, 7/14.3
   and God's Will, 1/25.3,
      4/99.1, 6/29.2, 7/45.3
   and joy, 7/47
   and St John, 1/33.2
   and the Mass, 3/105, 6/48.3
   and the Old Testament, 7/5.1
   and the Trinity, 6/1.2
   birth of, 7/22.1
   co-redemptrix, 1/41.2,
      3/105.2, 5/18, 7/24.2
   devotion, 1/33.2, 1/40.3,
      1/38.3, 2/84.2, 7/3.1, 7/9.1,
      7/11, **734.1**, 7/53.3
   full of grace, 4/99.2, 4/99.3
   generosity, 1/26.1, 7/41.1
   her gifts, 7/44.2, 7/44.3
   her help, 1/38.2, 3/9.1, 5/36.1,
      5/48.2, 5/81.3, 6/16, 7/3.2,
      7/34.2, 7/49.3, 7/52.3
   her vocation, 1/25.1, 5/14.1,
      6/29, 7/6.1, 7/41.3, 7/45.3
   Immaculate Heart of, 6/35.3,
      6/51
   humility, 1/27.1, 5/14.2, 5/63,
      6/27.3

invoke her name, **1**/40.3, **3**/9.1,
  3/42, **5**/81.3, **5**/92.3, **7**/5.3
mediatrix, **7**/9.2, **7**/9.3, **7**/11.3
Mother of God, **1**/17.2, **1**/38.1,
  5/18.3, **5**/81.3, **6**/1, **7**/11.2,
  7/26.3
our guide, **7**/43.2
our Mother, **1**/38.2, **2**/84.1,
  5/36.3, **5**/63.2, **6**/1.3, **7**/3.3,
  7/11.2, **7**/14.1, **7**/15, **7**/49.2
Queen, **7**/17
pilgrimages, **2**/84.3, **6**/31.1,
  6/35
rosary, **2**/38.3, **2**/79.3, **2**/81.1,
  2/81.2, **2**/81.3, **5**/18.3, **5**/27.3,
  5/36.2, **5**/36.3, **7**/13.2, **7**/13.3,
  7/32.3, **7**/33.1, **7**/48.3
service, **1**/26.1
to Jesus through Mary, **6**/37.2,
  7/52.1

Parables of the Gospel
banquet, **5**/37
good Samaritan, **4**/21, **5**/31
grain of wheat, **5**/34.2
leaven in dough, **4**/40
lost sheep, **4**/59. **5**/70.2
mustard seed, **5**/34.2
pearl of great value, **4**/42
Pharisee and tax-collector,
  5/57.2
prodigal son, **5**/3, **5**/41.1
shrewd steward, **5**/12
sowing seed, **4**/19, **5**/9
talents, **5**/51, **5**/82, **5**/87
two sons sent out, **5**/19
unjust judge, **5**/48, **5**/81.1
vineyard, **5**/10.2, **5**/28.1, **5**/54
virgins, **5**/73
wheat and cockle, **4**/28

working in vineyard, **4**/69,
  5/10, **5**/94.3
Patience, **2**/28.2, **2**/28.3, **5**/11.1,
  5/9.3, **5**/54, **5**/94
  see Meekness
Peace
and Christ, **1**/3.1, **2**/77.1
causes, lack of, **1**/3.1, **4**/12.2,
  5/14.3
foundation of, **1**/3.3, **1**/35.3,
  5/59.3
fruits of, **1**/3.2
gift of God, **1**/3.1, **2**/77.2,
  4/12.1
source of, **1**/3.2, **4**/12.3
Penance
and Fridays, **3**/85.2
characteristics of, **3**/85.3,
  5/1.3, **5**/5.3, **5**/26.2, **5**/41,
  5/75.2
Persecution
  see Difficulties
Perseverance, **2**/39.1, **2**/40.3,
  5/4.3, **5**/43.3, **5**/57, **5**/81,
  5/86, **7**/4.1
Piety, **2**/91
Way of the Cross, **2**/3.2
  see Our Lady, rosary
Pope, **2**/68.2, **2**/68.3, **5**/64.1,
  6/7, **6**/19.3, **6**/32.2, **7**/16.3
Poverty
and sobriety, **1**/28.3
evangelical poverty, **1**/28.2
Jesus' example, **1**/28.1
ways of practising it, **1**/28.3,
  4/68.2, **5**/24, **7**/31.1, **7**/31.2,
  7/50.3
Prayer
and humility, **1**/29.3
and St Joseph, **1**/29.3, **3**/93.3,

5/64.3, 5/84.3
and thanksgiving, 7/32
dealings with Jesus, 1/29.2,
3/51.1, 5/56.2, 7/35.2, 7/48.1
fruits of, 4/95.1, 5/33.3,
5/57.3, 5/71.1
how to pray, 1/29.3, 2/27.2,
2/27.3, 2/55.3, 3/40.1, 3/55.3,
3/93.2, 4/64.2, 5/4.2, 5/33,
5/40.1, 5/48, 5/96, 7/48.2
mental prayer, 7/34.3
need for it, 1/29.2, 2/38.2,
3/93.1, 5/9.2, 5/14, 5/48.3,
5/81, 7/9.1, 7/35.1
of petition, 2/9.1, 2/9.2, 2/9.3,
3/9.3, 3/40.3, 4/5.1, 4/39.2,
4/39.3, 4/64.1, 4/64.3, 7/32.3
vocal prayers, 3/94.1, 3/94.2,
3/94.3, 4/95.3, 5/94, 5/34.1,
5/95

Presence of God, 2/12.3,
2/76.2, 5/57.3, 5/61.1, 5/72.2,
5/83.1

Priesthood, 2/44.2
identity and mission, 4/20.1,
4/20.2. 5/48.2, 5/57.1, 5/71.1,
6/9, 6/38, 7/10.1
love for, 7/10.3
prayer for, 4/20.3, 7/10.2

Prudence
essence of, 4/17.1, 5/93.2
false, 4/17.3
seeking advice, 4/17.2

Purgatory, 7/39.1

Purification
interior mortification, 1/19.3,
5/26

Purity
see Chastity

Recollection, interior
union with God, 4/19.1, 5/14
Our Lady's example, 1/29.1,
5/14

Rectitude of intention, 2/63,
5/11.1, 5/57.1, 5/67, 5/72,
5/74.3

Redemption, 2/29.2, 2/36.1,
2/36.2, 2/36.3, 5/52.1, 5/56.3,
5/69.1, 5/75, 5/80.2

Resurrection
of the body, 3/75.2, 3/75.3,
5/75, 5/90.1, 5/97.2

Sacraments, 4/13.2, 4/36.1

Saints
as intercessors, 3/72.1, 7/50.1
cult to, 3/72.2
veneration of relics, 3/72.3

Sanctity
consequences of, 1/35.2, 4/4.1,
5/68.1, 5/87.1
developing talents, 4/68.2,
4/68.3, 5/12.2, 5/51.2, 5/82,
5/84
in ordinary life, 1/46.1,
2/11.2, 2/57.1, 2/69, 3/16.2,
3/16.3, 3/92.2, 4/6.3,
4/40.1, 4/45.3, 5/10.3, 5/32,
5/57.3, 5/72, 6/9.2, 7/38.1,
7/55.2
principal enemies of, 1/1.2,
5/50.2
universal call to, 3/92.1,
5/10.2, 5/37.3, 5/43.1, 6/9.1,
7/38.2

Serenity, 3/98

Service, spirit of
2/14.1, 2/14.3, 3/66.3, 5/3.3,
5/67, 5/87.2, 6/37.1

Simplicity
  and humility, 1/42.1
  and spiritual childhood,
    1/24.3, 1/42.2
  fruits of, 1/42.3
  in dealings with God, 1/42.2,
    5/57.2, 7/18.3
  opposite of, 1/42.3
  rectitude of intention, 1/42.2,
    4/17.1
Sin
  consequences of, 2/10.1,
    2/17.1, 2/18.1, 2/41.1,
    3/80.2, 4/2, 4/34.2, 5/28.2,
    5/31.1, 5/41.1, 5/45, 5/69.1,
    5/71.2, 5/85.1
  forgiveness of, 3/44.2, 5/41.2,
    5/70.3
  reality of, 1/47.2, 3/26.2,
    4/23.1, 4/34.1, 5/3.2, 5/45.3,
    5/93.1
  sorrow for, 4/23.2, 4/23.3,
    5/9.1, 5/28.2
  see Confession
Sin, venial
  deliberate, 2/17.3, 3/26.3,
    4/34.3
  does damage, 1/10.2
Sincerity, 2/23, 3/60, 4/18.2,
    5/44, 7/18.2
Society
  and human solidarity, 3/37.2,
    4/58.3, 5/46.1, 5/68
  obligations to, 3/37.3, 3/53.3,
    4/58.1, 5/39.3, 5/44.3,
    5/46.1, 5/51.2
  service to, 3/53, 4/58.3, 5/67,
    5/74
Spiritual childhood
  and divine filiation, 1/24.2,

    4/63.2, 5/34, 5/59, 5/64
  and humility, 1/27.2, 3/100.1,
    4/63.3, 5/57.2
  consequences of, 1/42.2,
    5/33.2, 5/46.3, 5/59.3,
    5/60.2, 5/72, 5/75.3
  nature, 1/24.1, 5/64
  need for, 1/7.3
  virtues associated with it,
    1/24.3, 3/60.2, 3/100.2
Spiritual guidance
  and joy, 1/15.3
  need for, 1/7.3, 1/43.2, 4/31.3,
    5/19.3, 5/43.1, 5/85
Spiritual reading, 7/8
  advice for, 7/8.3
Suffering
  and consolation, 1/34.3
  and divine filiation, 1/24.2,
    5/59.2, 5/60.2
  cross of each day, 1/34.2,
    4/53.1, 7/23.2, 7/23.3
  fruits of, 2/26.2, 2/64.1,
    4/53.2, 7/5.1
  helping others through,
    1/34.3, 5/15, 5/22.3, 5/31.3,
    5/60.3
  in the world, 1/34.1, 5/22.2,
    5/69.1
  Our Lady's example, 1/41.1,
    1/41.3, 5/69.3, 6/17, 7/24.3
  redeeming and purifying
    value, 1/34.2, 5/69, 5/94
Supernatural life
  and apostolate, 2/78.3
  and ascetical struggle, 1/1.3,
    3/9.2, 3/22, 5/60.2
  and human maturity, 1/50.3
  practice of virtues, 1/50.1,
    5/84, 5/87.3

Supernatural outlook
and God's calling, 1/18.2, 5/87
examining situations with,
1/18.2, 5/12.3, 5/17.1,
5/32.2, 5/53.1, 5/58.3,
5/82.3, 5/84

Temperance, 3/101, 4/35
Temptations
4/3.3, 4/11.1, 4/11.3, 5/9.2,
5/42, 5/69.2, 5/90.3
Thanksgiving, acts of
1/37.2, 1/51.1, 2/71.1, 2/71.3,
5/101.1, 5/39, 5/60.2, 5/78,
5/95
after Communion, 2/71.3,
3/29.3, 5/95.2, 5/95.3
human virtue of gratitude,
2/71.2, 4/61.1, 4/61.3, 5/39,
5/60.2, 5/78.2
Time, good use of
acts of contrition, 1/37.2
acts of thanksgiving, 1/37.2,
5/95
Christian value, 1/37.3, 5/8.2,
5/17.1
our life is short, 1/37.1, 4/48.2,
4/48.3, 5/54.2, 5/82.3, 5/84.1
Trust, 4/5.2
Truth, 2/23.2, 2/23.3
love for, 4/18.1, 4/31.2, 5/44
speaking, 4/18.3, 5/44

Unity, 2/56, 5/32.2, 5/68.1,
5/87.3, 5/91.2, 6/4.3, 6/5, 6/7
Unity of life, 2/29, 3/74.2,
4/16.3, 5/122.2, 5/13.3, 5/32,
5/46.2, 5/72, 5/79, 5/84, 5/87,
6/54.3

Vigilance
against evil inclinations,
1/19.2, 5/42.3, 5/76.2
Come Lord Jesus, 1/19.1,
5/83.1
in waiting for Christ, 1/19.1,
5/49.2, 5/73.2, 5/80, 5/97.3
the means, 1/19.2, 5/43.3
Virginity
apostolic celibacy, matrimony
and, 1/23.1, 4/62.2, 5/63.3,
5/64.2, 5/90
free choice, 1/23.1
of Our Lady, 1/23.1, 5/64.2
Virtues, 1/50.3, 2/22.1, 2/22.3,
3/6.3, 4/3.3, 5/78, 5/79.3
**Visit to the Blessed
Sacrament,** 2/51.2, 2/51.3,
4/43.3, 4/56.3, 5/61.1, 5/88.1
Vocation
and apostolate, 7/25.3, 7/29.3
and freedom, 4/22.1, 5/37.1
and joy, 7/25.2
and parents, 4/22.3
grace for, 6/36.2, 7/45.2
of each person, 4/8.1, 1/33.1,
1/51.3, 5/37.3, 6/36.3
of Our Lady, 1/25.1, 7/41.3
of St Andrew, 7/42.1
of St Bartholomew, 7/18.1
of St John, 1/33.1, 5/23.1
of St John the Baptist, 1/8.1,
5/13.1, 6/55
of St Matthew, 7/25.1
prayer to St Joseph, 6/25.3
responding to it, 1/25.2,
3/14.3, 4/22.2, 4/22.3,
4/42.3, 5/38.2, 5/43, 5/51.1,
7/42.3
signs of, 1/18.2, 1/18.3

special calling, **1**/25.2, **3**/14.1,
  4/22.1, **4**/42.2, **5**/43.1,
  5/90.2, **6**/34.1, **6**/36.1,
  6/56.1, **6**/57, **7**/37.1

Will of God
above earthly plans, **1**/47.3,
  5/10.1
and peace of soul, **1**/5.3
and sanctity, **1**/5.1, **5**/35
embracing it, **1**/5.1, **1**/5.3,
  1/18.3, **2**/15.1, **3**/20.3,
  3/70.3, **5**/35, **5**/94.2, **7**/45.3
its manifestation, **1**/5.1, **3**/20.2

Work
and prayer, **4**/30.3, **5**/84.3
in God's presence, **4**/30,
  5/84.2, **7**/22.3
its dignity, **1**/46.3, **5**/84, **6**/33.1

of Jesus, **1**/46.1, **1**/46.2, **3**/1.1,
  3/30.2, **3**/41.1, **5**/84.1, **5**/88.2
sanctification of, **1**/46.2,
  1/46.3, **3**/1, **3**/30, **3**/39, **3**/41,
  5/13.2, **5**/17.2, **5**/32.2,
  5/51.2, **5**/84, **6**/33, **7**/36.1

Works of mercy
see Mercy

World
justice in the, **1**/35.1, **5**/60.3
re-evangelisation of, **2**/58.2,
  2/58.3 , **5**/12.2, **5**/20, **5**/25,
  5/87, **6**/18

Worship, divine, **3**/46.2, **3**/46.3,
  5/65.3, **5**/89, **5**/92.2